▨ Let's Go writers travel on your budget.

"Guides that penetrate the veneer of the holiday brochures and mine the grit of real life."

—The Economist

"The writers seem to have experienced every rooster-packed bus and lunar-surfaced mattress about which they write."

—The New York Times

"All the dirt, dirt cheap."

—People

▨ Great for independent travelers.

"The guides are aimed not only at young budget travelers but at the independent traveler; a sort of streetwise cookbook for traveling alone."

—The New York Times

"Flush with candor and irreverence, chock full of budget travel advice."

—The Des Moines Register

"An indispensible resource, *Let's Go*'s practical information can be used by every traveler."

—The Chattanooga Free Press

▨ Let's Go is completely revised each year.

"Only *Let's Go* has the zeal to annually update every title on its list."

—The Boston Globe

"Unbeatable: good sight-seeing advice; up-to-date info on restaurants, hotels, and inns; a commitment to money-saving travel; and a wry style that brightens nearly every page."

—The Washington Post

▨ All the important information you need.

"*Let's Go* authors provide a comedic element while still providing concise information and thorough coverage of the country. Anything you need to know about budget traveling is detailed in this book."

—The Chicago Sun-Times

"Value-packed, unbeatable, accurate, and comprehensive."

—Los Angeles Times

Let's Go Publications

Let's Go: Alaska & the Pacific Northwest 2000
Let's Go: Australia 2000
Let's Go: Austria & Switzerland 2000
Let's Go: Britain & Ireland 2000
Let's Go: California 2000
Let's Go: Central America 2000
Let's Go: China 2000 **New Title!**
Let's Go: Eastern Europe 2000
Let's Go: Europe 2000
Let's Go: France 2000
Let's Go: Germany 2000
Let's Go: Greece 2000
Let's Go: India & Nepal 2000
Let's Go: Ireland 2000
Let's Go: Israel 2000 **New Title!**
Let's Go: Italy 2000
Let's Go: Mexico 2000
Let's Go: Middle East 2000 **New Title!**
Let's Go: New York City 2000
Let's Go: New Zealand 2000
Let's Go: Paris 2000
Let's Go: Perú & Ecuador 2000 **New Title!**
Let's Go: Rome 2000
Let's Go: South Africa 2000
Let's Go: Southeast Asia 2000
Let's Go: Spain & Portugal 2000
Let's Go: Turkey 2000
Let's Go: USA 2000
Let's Go: Washington, D.C. 2000

Let's Go *Map Guides*

Amsterdam	New Orleans
Berlin	New York City
Boston	Paris
Chicago	Prague
Florence	Rome
London	San Francisco
Los Angeles	Seattle
Madrid	Washington, D.C.

Coming Soon: *Sydney* and *Hong Kong*

Let's Go

2000 NEW ZEALAND

Nick Grossman
Editor

Laura M. Bacon
Associate Editor

Researcher-Writers:

Sarah Gore   **Douglas Rand**

Brian Milder   **Ann Robinson**

Jonathan Summers Paul

St. Martin's Press ✖ New York

HELPING LET'S GO

If you want to share your discoveries, suggestions, or corrections, please drop us a line. We read every piece of correspondence, whether a postcard, a 10-page email, or a coconut. Please note that mail received after May 2000 may be too late for the 2001 book, but will be kept for future editions. **Address mail to:**

> Let's Go: New Zealand
> 67 Mount Auburn Street
> Cambridge, MA 02138
> USA

Visit Let's Go at **http://www.letsgo.com,** or send email to:

> feedback@letsgo.com
> Subject: "Let's Go: New Zealand"

In addition to the invaluable travel advice our readers share with us, many are kind enough to offer their services as researchers or editors. Unfortunately, our charter enables us to employ only currently enrolled Harvard students.

ABOUT LET'S GO

FORTY YEARS OF WISDOM

As a new millennium arrives, *Let's Go: Europe*, now in its 40th edition and translated into seven languages, reigns as the world's bestselling international travel guide. For four decades, travelers criss-crossing the Continent have relied on *Let's Go* for inside information on the hippest backstreet cafes, the most pristine secluded beaches, and the best routes from border to border. In the last 20 years, our rugged researchers have stretched the frontiers of backpacking and expanded our coverage into Asia, Africa, Australia, and the Americas. We're celebrating our 40th birthday with the release of *Let's Go: China*, blazing the traveler's trail from the Forbidden City to the Tibetan frontier; *Let's Go: Perú & Ecuador*, spanning the lands of the ancient Inca Empire; *Let's Go: Middle East*, with coverage from Istanbul to the Persian Gulf; and the maiden edition of *Let's Go: Israel*.

It all started in 1960 when a handful of well-traveled students at Harvard University handed out a 20-page mimeographed pamphlet offering a collection of their tips on budget travel to passengers on student charter flights to Europe. The following year, in response to the instant popularity of the first volume, students traveling to Europe researched the first full-fledged edition of *Let's Go: Europe*, a pocket-sized book featuring honest, practical advice, witty writing, and a decidedly youthful slant on the world. Throughout the 60s and 70s, our guides reflected the times. In 1969 we taught travelers how to get from Paris to Prague on "no dollars a day" by singing in the street. In the 80s and 90s, we looked beyond Europe and North America and set off to all corners of the earth. Meanwhile, we focused in on the world's most exciting urban areas to produce in-depth, fold-out map guides. Our new guides bring the total number of titles to 48, each infused with the spirit of adventure and voice of opinion that travelers around the world have come to count on. But some things never change: our guides are still researched, written, and produced entirely by students who know first-hand how to see the world on the cheap.

HOW WE DO IT

Each guide is completely revised and thoroughly updated every year by a well-traveled set of over 250 students. Every spring, we recruit over 180 researchers and 70 editors to overhaul every book. After several months of training, researcher-writers hit the road for seven weeks of exploration, from Anchorage to Adelaide, Estonia to El Salvador, Iceland to Indonesia. Hired for their rare combination of budget travel sense, writing ability, stamina, and courage, these adventurous travelers know that train strikes, stolen luggage, food poisoning, and marriage proposals are all part of a day's work. Back at our offices, editors work from spring to fall, massaging copy written on Himalayan bus rides into witty, informative prose. A student staff of typesetters, cartographers, publicists, and managers keeps our lively team together. In September, the collected efforts of the summer are delivered to our printer, which turns them into books in record time, so that you have the most up-to-date information available for your vacation. Even as you read this, work on next year's editions is well underway.

WHY WE DO IT

We don't think of budget travel as the last recourse of the destitute; we believe that it's the only way to travel. Living cheaply and simply brings you closer to the people and places you've been saving up to visit. Our books will ease your anxieties and answer your questions about the basics—so you can get off the beaten track and explore. Once you learn the ropes, we encourage you to put *Let's Go* down now and then to strike out on your own. You know as well as we that the best discoveries are often those you make yourself. When you find something worth sharing, please drop us a line. We're Let's Go Publications, 67 Mount Auburn St., Cambridge, MA 02138, USA (email: feedback@letsgo.com). For more info, visit our website, http://www.letsgo.com.

CONTENTS

VII

MAPS

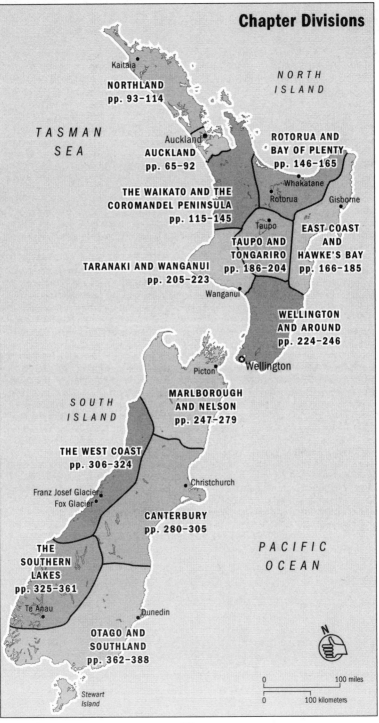

Chapter Divisions

NORTH ISLAND

TASMAN SEA

Kaitaia

NORTHLAND
pp. 93–114

Auckland
AUCKLAND
pp. 65–92

ROTORUA AND
BAY OF PLENTY
pp. 146–165

Whakatane

Rotorua

Gisborne

THE WAIKATO AND THE
COROMANDEL PENINSULA
pp. 115–145

Taupo

TAUPO AND
TONGARIRO
pp. 186–204

EAST COAST
AND
HAWKE'S BAY
pp. 166–185

TARANAKI AND WANGANUI
pp. 205–223

Wanganui

WELLINGTON
AND AROUND
pp. 224–246

Wellington

Picton

SOUTH ISLAND

MARLBOROUGH
AND NELSON
pp. 247–279

THE WEST COAST
pp. 306–324

Christchurch

Franz Josef Glacier
Fox Glacier

CANTERBURY
pp. 280–305

PACIFIC OCEAN

THE
SOUTHERN
LAKES
pp. 325–361

Te Anau

Dunedin

OTAGO AND
SOUTHLAND
pp. 362–388

Stewart Island

N

| 0 | | 100 miles |
| 0 | | 100 kilometers |

RESEARCHER-WRITERS

Sarah Gore   *Rotorua, Bay of Plenty, East Coast, Taupo, Wellington, Coromandel*

Hey hey hey, what can we say? Put simply, Sedona was an unreal RW. Even as she weathered computer meltdowns and lovesick Kiwis, her only demand was peanut-butter cups—we would have bought the Reese's factory to maintain Sarah's pleasant aplomb and sparkling prose. Whether researching Taupo by motorbike or breezing through pool tournaments, Sarah took to Kiwi culture and it took to her—even typists thousands of miles away fell in love. Never once blowing her cover, Sedona was too cool to be forgotten.

Brian Milder   *Christchurch, Canterbury, Southern Lakes, Otago and Southland*

Brian can run a marathon at the drop of a hat—that toughness translated into prodigious research. With a nickname worthy of a Kiwi, Smudge hit his stride in Queenstown, hobnobbing with bungy masters, passing every test of his mettle, and stopping only for mail. Learning that all good things in life are free, he took solo budget travel to its limit, never afraid to share a meal or a bed. Even after his marathon was complete, still ahead of the pack, he returned to Cambridge to secure the future of his stellar work.

Jonathan Summers Paul   *Auckland, Northland, Waikato, Taranaki*

A straight-shooting city slicker, JP redefined the word hard-core. Schlepping through depressed towns and risking life and limb to reach his next phone call, our towering Napoleon found a town worthy of his indisputable authority—Auckland—which he promptly conquered. Bolstered by a critical eye and confident pen, JP's copy revealed an editor's touch and his research perfectly captured the budget mindset.

Douglas Rand   *East Cape, Great Walks, National Parks*

Biologist and editor of *Let's Go: Alaska and the Pacific Northwest 1999*, Doug tramped every Great Walk. Even when he was already off the beaten path, he would explore a new grove of rimu, ambush a pestilent possum, or search for the elusive moa. Like a true tramper, he left no trace save his indelible mark on this guide. Doug's copy was as solid as kauri and it sang like a tui in a kowhai. Only the overwhelming Cascade Saddle could best his impressive vocabulary, and not even a Great Walk through Gondwanaland could match the brilliance of his work.

Ann Robinson   *Kaikoura, West Coast, Marlborough and Nelson*

Powered by pretzels, tongue firmly planted in cheek, Ann returned to her lost love and resourcefully traced the remote coast of the South Island with remarkable diligence. Unflappable and clairvoyant, she accepted a Haka-esque challenge and correctly predicted the fate of the All Blacks in the glow of her Steinie…or was it her Tui? Whether skydiving (twice!), swimming with dolphins, or skiing down slopes, Ann exuded confidence and left us with no worries.

ACKNOWLEDGMENTS

NEW ZEALAND THANKS: Most likely to be the best pod: Lindi, we admire you; Nick W., your wit and enthusiasm blatantly exploded the fun meter; Bede, the man from the land down under, for always helping out; Erica, for taking us pleasantly by surprise; Brendan, our persistent guru—level-headed, diligent, even funny: is there one word for this? Words cannot express. Eds of LGNZ past: Luis, Monica, Jen, Eli, our baby is all grown up—well, almost. And: Kurt, Ben H., Marg, Daniels, Adam, Xian, SAP, Fiore, Klu, Anne, and all the hardworking MEs. RWs, this is your book.

NICK GROSSMAN THANKS: Brendan, my mentor and friend—you lay the tracks and I happily follow. 🖼 Laura, the girl next door, you gave it your heart and soul. Tommy's anytime. I mean it. Weiss, a whirlwind, a wizard, a wit; Lindi, your sense and sensibility awe me; Erica, I never knew phone calls could be so fun; Bede, from Dew one, the embodiment of Kiwi generosity and affability. Jen and Eli, I felt your pain. TJ, Kaya, Wilkie, Xian, and Sonesh, I can't imagine it here without you guys. Speier: the only Red Sox hater worth taking to a game. Pihos, Daniels, Olivia, and the rest of the office—never a dull word. Chuts, the Kitty will collapse. Love always to Mom, Dad, Jonathan, Gill, Adam, and Grandmums for always being there. And the girl who stops me in my tracks and makes me happy, if there was a dedication to this book, it would read: For Tene.

LAURA BACON THANKS: Love always to Mom, Dad, and Jeff. Thanks for everything, always. Nick, for your work, laughs, and understanding—"it's all in here now." Brendan, for guidance and humor. Down Under pod: with lists, super tubes, and meals, you've made every day a Fun Day. Lindi, thanks for your listening and love—can't wait for next year. Nick W., you're my daddy—going nocturnal-styles was fun. Bede, our Kiwi pillar—your humor, tunes, and wisdom are appreciated. Erica, my 24/7 companion—you've always been there and I love it. Roomies...an unforgettable summer. Chris, here's to mac-and-cheese fests. Bryan, Alex: you keep me sane. Jenn, Jen: I miss you lots. Ben, Allon: for long-distance support. Adrienne, surprise visits are always welcome "in my house."

Editor
Nick Grossman
Associate Editor
Laura M. Bacon
Managing Editor
Brendan Gibbon

HOW TO USE THIS BOOK

Kia Ora! Welcome to *Let's Go: New Zealand 2000*. This guide is self-explanatory, but we'd like to call your attention to a few details. It may save you some time down the road.

Essentials (p. 22). This section of the book may seem long and boring...it is. But it's not called Essentials for nothing. It's the one section of the book that could save you thousands of dollars on airfare, keep you out of jail, or help you prevent sandflies from ruining your trip. This is a good section to read before you go. The **Camping and Outdoors** part discusses the amazing outdoor resources New Zealand offers, and provides a description of the country's **Great Walks**.

Prices listed in this book are in New Zealand dollars unless otherwise noted.

Accommodations, Food, and **Nightlife** are listed from best to worst. Why is there a worst? Well, we want to provide a wide range of options, especially in accommodations. Thus you will occasionally find an accommodation that may offer a less than perfect stay, but is included because it is well placed or is the only choice in town. On the flip side, holiday parks and businesses far from town are usually listed last because they are not as popular or accessible to the average traveler.

What's that thumb thingy? In addition to making some recommendations in **Let's Go Picks** (p. xiii) at the beginning of the book, we also identify the researchers' absolute favorite establishments (and travelers) with a ▨. Enter your name here: ▨ _____. Within cities and towns, the most popular sights and outdoor activities are usually listed first, though they are also divided according to type of activity.

Winter hours and rates are noted after the summer hours (e.g., Open 10am-5pm, winter 11am-3pm; $10, winter $5.) In ski towns, summer hours and rates are noted second. Please don't look for regimented, come-hell-or-high-water schedules for transportation or anything else—you're in Kiwi land now. On any night, a restaurant's owners might decide to close early and head home if no customers are in sight. On the other hand, if you come by after closing time and look hungry enough, they just might open up their doors again. In New Zealand, hospitality is a flexible thing.

Great Walks as well as a few other popular and outstanding tramps have their own full coverage (like towns!). You'll find these marked with a ▨. For each tramp, there is an **Essentials** section outlining all you need to know (from length to gear) in order to complete the tramp. This section is followed by **The Track** section, which provides a detailed description of the tramp and all of its huts and campsites.

OTHER FEATURES:

A history and culture chapter at the beginning of the book.

A glossary of **Kiwi-English** and **Maori-English** terms (p. 390).

A **distance chart** and **phone code chart** (on the inside back cover).

Highlights of the Region are at the beginning of every chapter; they contain...well, the highlights of the region. Let's not get too fancy.

A NOTE TO OUR READERS The information for this book was gathered by *Let's Go*'s researchers from May through August. Each listing is derived from the assigned researcher's opinion based upon his or her visit at a particular time. The opinions are expressed in a candid and forthright manner. Those traveling at a different time may have different experiences since prices, dates, hours, and conditions are always subject to change. You are urged to check beforehand to avoid inconvenience and surprises. Travel always involves a certain degree of risk, especially in low-cost areas. When traveling, especially on a budget, always take particular care to ensure your safety.

LET'S GO PICKS

TOWNS OPEN PAST MIDNIGHT: Not every small New Zealand town is a deserted ghost town after the work day. When you mosey on into **Whangarei** (p. 93) late at night, you'll find urban cowboys from Auckland whooping it up to DJ rhythms. In **Queenstown,** The World (p. 331) will keep you turning all night long. In **Ohakune** (p. 201), everyone knows each other by name by day, but forgets them by night.

PASSING THROUGH...WAIT!: There's a good chance you'll plan on passing through these towns. Before you hit the attractions beyond them, though, consider giving them a day or two. Beautiful **Wellington** (p. 224) surprises travelers with its upbeat cafe culture and nightlife. **Nelson** (p. 260) and the small towns of Golden Bay are known for their crafts. **Taupo** (p. 187) may not have as many pure attractions as Rotorua, but it's still an adventure fisher's paradise. **Wanaka's** (p. 338) Puzzling World will a-maze you.

OFF THE *UNBEATEN* PATH: We can't even call these places towns with a straight face. They are magical nowheres barely offering the bare essentials. Each can be visited for a peaceful escape for a day or more. At **Tokomaru Bay** (p. 171) on the East Cape, you can sleep under a lemon tree and let the surf soothe you to sleep. Get the mail truck to drop you off at the House of the Rising Sun. **Opoutere** (p. 144) in the Coromandel Peninsula is a road with a canopy of trees that leads to a lagoon. People? Nope. Except at the Opoutere YHA. Giant bull kelp litters the beach at **Papatowai** (p. 378) in the Catlins. Spend the night at Hilltop Backpackers for a fantastic beach view. Up the coast from Wellington in **Paekakariki** (p. 239) is the shockingly named Paekakariki Backpackers. Who needs an original name when it's twice as nice as any Wellington hostel?

ISLAND GETAWAYS: There aren't even paths to be beaten to these escapes, but that's all the more reason to venture to these time capsules. If New Zealand is the "land of the long white cloud," **White Island** (p. 163) is the land of the short, low-level, gassy cloud. On **Kapiti Island** (p. 238), New Zealand's endangered species come together to piss and moan about their plight. **Poor Knights Island** (p. 97) was a favorite of the late Jacques Cousteau. Don't question Jacques Cousteau. That Jacques Cousteau, he knew his diving. **Rangitoto Island** (p. 87) is where strung-out Aucklanders find peace of mind. On **Great Barrier Island** (p. 90), you can send a pigeongram to Auckland; only the strongest pigeons make it to their winged brethren on Kapiti Island with the message "Only the strongest survive."

WILL MAKE YOU ALL WET: Swimming with the dolphins in **Kaikoura** (p. 256), surfing in **Whangamata** (p. 139), soaking in the hot pools of **Maruia Springs** (p. 260), and learning how to snowboard at **Cardrona** (p. 334).

GOING NOWHERE: Then you may be heading to any of the following towns, but don't despair—they are all worth the trip: **Hokianga** (p. 108), **Okarito** (p. 316), **Russell** (p. 102), and **Takaka** (p. 273).

Best place to make a memento: Carve a bone necklace in **Whitianga** (p. 141).
Best place to dig your own grave and lie in it: **Hot Water Beach** (p. 143).
Best place to spend the day: the Super Loo in **Taupo** (p. 188).
Best place to get smashed: Smash Palace in **Gisborne** (p. 170).
Best place to get up on the bar and dance: Holy Cow in **Taupo** (p. 190).
Best place to catch a rugby match: Eden Park in **Auckland** (p. 81).
Best place for the delicious Maori *hangi*: **Rotorua** (with Tamaki Tours) (p. 153).
Best place to meet the Wizard: Cathedral Square in **Christchurch** (p. 291).
Best place to skydive: **Taupo** (p. 191).
Best drive: **Milford Road** (p. 355).

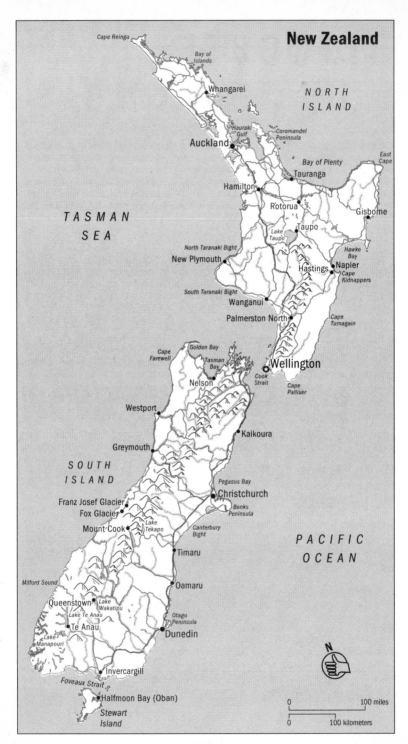

New Zealand

Cape Reinga

Bay of
Islands

Whangarei

*NORTH
ISLAND*

Hauraki
Gulf

Coromandel
Peninsula

Auckland

Bay of Plenty

East
Cape

Tauranga

Hamilton

Rotorua

Gisborne

*TASMAN
SEA*

Lake
Taupo

Taupo

North Taranaki Bight

Hawke
Bay

New Plymouth

Hastings

Napier

Cape
Kidnappers

South Taranaki Bight

Wanganui

Palmerston North

Cape
Turnagain

Cape
Farewell

Golden Bay

Tasman
Bay

Wellington

Cook
Strait

Cape
Palliser

Nelson

Westport

Kaikoura

Greymouth

*SOUTH
ISLAND*

Pegasus Bay

Christchurch

Franz Josef Glacier

Fox Glacier

Banks
Peninsula

Mount Cook

Lake
Tekapo

Canterbury
Bight

*PACIFIC
OCEAN*

Timaru

Milford Sound

Oamaru

Queenstown

Lake
Wakatipu

Lake Te Anau

Otago
Peninsula

Te Anau

Dunedin

Lake
Manapouri

Invercargill

Foveaux Strait

Halfmoon Bay (Oban)

*Stewart
Island*

N

0   100 miles

0   100 kilometers

DISCOVER
NEW ZEALAND

If you spin a globe and stop it with the tip of your finger, your chances of landing on New Zealand will always be next to none. The country's isolation from the rest of the world may evoke images of an exotic land. In fact, New Zealand's startling landscapes are otherworldly: psychedelic lakes perfectly mirror volcanic peaks, black-water caves contain constellations of aqua-blue glow-worms, a 180-million year-old petrified forest dates from the supercontinent Gondwanaland, and twin glaciers creep toward the nearby beach and ocean. The sheer diversity of earthly wonders is matched only by the number of ways to enjoy them. To get to New Zealand, you will cross oceans, even circumnavigate the globe. In return, New Zealanders (who refer to themselves as Kiwis) make the edge of the world both accessible and hospitable. Sustained by its outgoing and infectiously friendly citizens, the country's budget tourism industry is superb. With an abundance of outstanding hostels, an immense network of organized hikes (tramps), and the constant invention of new and challenging modes of travel from bungy jumping to jetboating to skydiving, New Zealand both surprises and inspires travelers. Known also as *Godzone*, the first country to witness the dawn of the millennium awaits your arrival.

FACTS AND FIGURES

- **Capital:** Wellington
- **Human population:** 3,803,900
- **Sheep population:** 45-50 million
- **Major Exports:** wool, lamb, dairy
- **Head of State:** Queen Elizabeth II
- **Drinking age:** 18

THE NEW ZEALAND EXPERIENCE

ADVENTURE

In the adventure capital Queenstown, two bungy jump companies try to outdo each other for the highest bungy jump. One company unveils a gondola suspended by wire cables over a canyon; immediately after, the competing company begins work on its hot-air balloon bungy. New Zealand's drug of choice is natural adrenaline…in high quantities. Travelers who come here thinking skydiving absurd quickly find themselves facing an appointment with death-defiance. Both set on large lakes, **Queenstown** (p. 326) in the South Island and **Taupo** (p. 187) in the North Island offer the most variety of adventure activities. But even some of the smallest towns offer tandem skydiving, and remote rivers once utilized for harnessing the nation's energy are now used for whitewater rafting and pants-wetting jetboating. Not all of New Zealand's adventure activities involve a high degree of irrationality or small measure of insanity: swimming with dolphins in **Kaikoura** (p. 257), hiking the **Franz and Fox Glaciers** (p. 317), contemplating glow-worms in the caves of **Waitomo** (p. 126), and sea-kayaking in the **Marlborough Sounds** (p. 251) are but a few of the hundreds of possibilities.

TRAMPING

Few places in the world combine spectacular scenery with a solid infrastructure for exploring it. With almost one-third of the country protected as wilderness areas and National Parks under the efficient management of the Department of Conservation (DOC), New Zealand leads the field. You do not have to be Sir Edmund Hillary, the first person to conquer Everest—and a Kiwi himself—to participate in what are known as some of the world's best walking tracks. Nine overnight walks in particular, known as Great Walks, are designed to be accessible for people of all abilities. These very popular, sometimes crowded, walks, offering fully maintained campsites and huts along the track for overnight stays, usually take between three and five days to complete. The sheer variety of landscapes these walks encompass is impressive. Many of these walks are located in the far south of the South Island in the enormous **Fiordland National Park** (p. 347). The **Milford Track** (p. 348) is commonly called the world's finest walk. However, comparing it with the nearby **Routeburn** (p. 351) and **Kepler** (p. 353) means simply a choice between superlatives. Other popular walks include the **Abel Tasman Coast Track** (p. 268) at the top of the South Island and the **Tongariro Northern Circuit** (p. 195) in the middle of the North Island. Experiencing the scenery by tramping does not always involve a commitment of more than one day. There are day-hikes leaving from virtually every town covered in this guide.

URBAN BEATS

Though New Zealand is most renowned for its natural beauty, each of its most cosmopolitan cities—Auckland, Wellington, Christchurch, and Dunedin—exemplifies a distinct and captivating aspect of New Zealand culture. Sprawling **Auckland** (p. 65), containing nearly one-third of the nation's entire population, offers big-city diversity and charming, smaller neighborhoods. In **Wellington** (p. 224), the recent opening of Te Papa National Museum has secured the capital city's transformation from a shipping port into the seat of the country's arts and drama. **Christchurch** (p. 281) and **Dunedin** (p. 362) charm visitors with their English and Scottish atmosphere and architecture respectively. Each one of these cities is surrounded by beautiful natural surroundings, contains a lively nightlife, and beats with the strong pulse of Rugby Nation.

OFF THE BEATEN PATH

The best way to stay outside the main veins of tourism is to rent a car and explore more remote coastal regions. Most of these areas are also accesible by bus but involve prior planning. There is no shortage of one-horse towns in New Zealand, many of which have nearby beaches, lagoons, and tramps for casual exploration. The **Marlborough Sounds** (p. 251) is a web of waterways called home by dolphins, seals, and penguins alike. There is an impressive number of outstanding hostels that you can call home, interspersed among the sounds. The **Coromandel Peninsula** (p. 131) has unsealed roads in its northern reaches that extend to hippie outposts and relaxing coastal views. The best budget transport around the rugged **East Cape** (p. 171) is to catch an early-morning ride with a mail truck. **Hokianga** (p. 108) is a sanctuary from the commercialism of the rest of the Bay of Islands. Cows munch on kelp on the sandy beaches of the **Catlins** (p. 375). Besides these areas, there are countless forest parks, National Parks, and beaches that provide relief from the occasionally congested New Zealand.

WINE AND BEER

It would be difficult to determine whether Kiwis take more pride in their wine or their beer. O.K., their beer. Still, New Zealand is known for its quality production of both. Beer drinkers (in New Zealand that's pretty much everyone) are loyal to the beer made in their region. For example, in Dunedin, locals are ever-faithful to

Speights. There are brewery tours in **Dunedin** (p. 370), **Timaru** (p. 300), **Auckland** (p. 65), **Greymouth** (p. 311), among others. New Zealand's vineyards make for a more extensive—if not more happy—daytrip. Most of the vineyards are within short driving distance of major towns and cities. From Auckland, you can take a ferry to **Waiheke Island** (p. 88), where you can sample both sea-salty air and wine. Colorful, Art Deco **Napier** (p. 178) provides a perfect base from which to explore the vineyards of Hawke's Bay. The streets of Martinborough are layed out in the form of the Union Jack, but its wine tastings, not high tea, are the reason to come to the major wine town of the Wairarapa region. Blenheim in the Nelson region is a good base for South Island exploration.

WINTER

New Zealand's ski fields are usually far above the tree line. From the chairlift, it's not uncommon to see clear across to the ocean. Skiing and snowboarding can be difficult—sometimes the views force you to stop in admiration. Asian tourists are particularly enthralled with the New Zealand ski fields. They pack Queenstown and show off their impressive snowboarding skills. While unpredictable conditions and a short season may place New Zealand second tier to American and European slopes, the lack of long lines, specular scenery, and more affordable rates more than compensate. South Island ski fields such as **Mt. Hutt** (p. 293), **Cardrona** (p. 334), and **Coronet Peak** (p. 334) are generally held in higher regard than those of the North Island such as **Whakapapa** (p. 197) and **Turoa** (p. 197).

SUGGESTED ITINERARIES

NORTH ISLAND (2-3 WEEKS) Beginning in **Auckland** (p. 65), the trendy neighborhoods of Ponsonby and Mission Bay, outside the Central Business District, capture the city's vibe. Consider a daytrip to either Great Barrier Island or Waiheke Island. After Auckland, head north for a loop of Northland, through the **Bay of Islands** (p. 98), a hot spot for watersports, and back down past the enormous trees of the **Kauri coast** (p. 111). Next, **Rotorua's** (p. 147) geothermal wonders and Maori hangi will make a camera-happy tourist out of you. Further south, **Taupo** (p. 187), set on New Zealand's largest lake, is the high-adrenaline capital of the North Island. In the Art Deco town of **Napier** (p. 178), you can relax for a day (or two) with a bottle (or two) of wine from your vineyard tour before you catch the train to the the nation's compact cosmopolitan capital **Wellington** (p. 224), with its hopping cafe culture and nightlife. From Wellington, head north with the TranzScenic train to the volcanic moonscapes of Tongariro National Park for the **Tongariro Crossing** (p. 195), one of New Zealand's finest one-day tramps. Then, on to **Waitomo** (p. 126) for spelunking, glow-worms, and black-water rafting. The small town of **Raglan** (p. 123), known for its perfect waves, offers a break from the beaten path, as does the rugged coastline of the **Coromandel Peninsula** (p. 131) that, if you can leave the small towns that dot your path, you can trace back toward Auckland.

SOUTH ISLAND (3 WEEKS) The small gateway town of **Picton** (p. 248) and the nearby **Marlborough Sounds** (p. 251), a stunning sanctuary for seals, penguins, dolphins and laid-back travelers, provide a grand introduction to the South Island. Down the south coast, in the waters of **Kaikoura** (p. 256), spend an afternoon swimming with playful dolphins or whalewatching before moving on to **Christchurch** (p. 281), where New Zealand shows its British colors. Christchurch is a great base for fantastic day trips to **Akaroa** and the **Banks Peninsula** (p. 296). From Christchurch, you can take one of the most scenic train trips in the world to the West Coast via **Arthur's Pass** (p. 298), or continue south to the univeristy pub town of **Dunedin** (p. 362), where rugby, beer, and music represent the Father, Son, and Holy Ghost. From Dunedin, take a day trip through the ecological wonderland of the **Otago Peninsula** (p. 362) and explore the rugged pastures, forests, and beaches of **Catlins** (p. 375) before blitzkrieging **Queenstown** (p. 326), where all of New Zealand's heart-stopping adventure activities converge. In the middle of the Queenstown insanity (plan on 3-4 days), take a daytrip into the heart of the spectacular **Fiordland National Park** through Te Anau to the mystical **Milford Sound** (p. 355). Nearby Wanaka and Glenorchy are also worthwhile stops. As you head north again to the beaches of the west coast, you'll pass the ice palaces of **Franz and Fox Glaciers** (p. 317), several billion cubic meters of moving solid blue ice that you can explore in shorts. Before returning to Picton (or to Christchurch via Arthur's Pass), consider tramping in **Abel Tasman Park** (p. 267), which contains one of New Zealand's most popular Great Walks.

WHIRLWIND NEW ZEALAND (2 WEEKS)

After a day in **Auckland's** (p. 65) flavorful neighborhoods, head immediately south toward **Wellington** (p. 224), stopping at the hot spas and bubbling mud pools of **Rotorua** (p. 147) and for the adventure sports of **Taupo** (p. 187) on the way. After taking in Te Papa, the national museum in the capital city, make the ferry crossing to the South Island and head down the east coast, stopping for the day in **Kaikoura** (p. 256) to swim with the dolphins, an unforgettable experience. After refueling at the cafes of **Christchurch** (p. 281), take the spectaular train ride through **Arthur's Pass** (p. 298) to the rugged **West Coast.** Continue south to the enormous **Franz and Fox Glaciers** (p. 317) where you can navigate a maze of ice. Take a deep breath before jumping into the madness of **Queenstown** (p. 326) where jumping off bridges and from planes is ho-hum. As much as your wallet may hurt at this point, a day trip to the awe-inspiring **Milford Sound** (p. 355) is worth the expense for a grand finale.

TRAMPING NEW ZEALAND (3 WEEKS)

A tramping tour of New Zealand for the serious tramper might start with the **Tongariro Northern Circuit** (4 days) which includes the **Tongariro Crossing** (p. 195). From this central point, day trips to Wellington, Rotorua and Auckland are possible after completing the track. You will ultimately want to hop over to the South Island where the scenery is even more spectacular. The **Abel Tasman Coastal Walk** (3 days; p. 267) is a relatively mellow tramp past the coves and golden beaches of the northern coast. Then make your way down the west coast where the Southern Alps, **Mount Aspiring Park** (p. 343) and **Fiordland National Park** (p. 347) climax New Zealand's scenery. The challenging **Rees-Dart Track** (4-5 days; p. 345) is crowned with glaciers; and the popular **Milford Track** (4 days; p. 348) is heralded as the "finest walk in the world." Finally, it doesn't get more remote than Stewart Island's **Rakiura Track** (2-3 days; p. 387) which winds through lush forest.

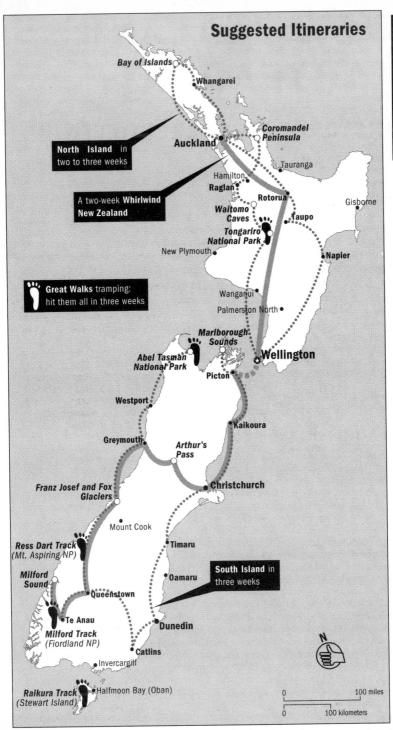

NEW ZEALAND (AOTEAROA)

HISTORY AND CURRENT EVENTS

IMPORTANT EVENTS

AD 900	First settlers arrive from Polynesia
1642	Dutchman Abel Tasman makes European discovery of New Zealand
1769	British explorer Captain James Cook claims country for Britain
1800-20	Whalers, sealers, and missionaries arrive
1820-35	The Musket Wars: Intertribal violence among Maori
1840	Treaty of Waitangi signed by Maori chiefs
1856	Britain declares New Zealand a self-governing colony
1860s	New Zealand Wars between Britain and Maori end in British victory
1867	Four Maori seats established in General Assembly
1893	Women gain suffrage
1907	New Zealand becomes a British dominion
1943	Population reaches 1.5 million
1947	New Zealand declared fully independent
1975	Maori march in protest of land claim treatment
1983	New Zealand signs Closer Economic Trade Relations Agreement with Australia
1984	Labour Party wins election, leading to new free-trade economy
1993	National referendum converts government to proportional representation

MAORI SETTLEMENT

Scholars hold that the first settlers, the ancestors of the modern Maori, came to New Zealand from the eastern Polynesian Islands in the 10th century. Artifacts dredged up from the past provide telling details about the day-to-day life of the earliest New Zealanders. They made their living by hunting the flightless moa bird, fishing, and using stone and carved bone tools developed by their Polynesian predecessors. By the 14th century, they were widely practicing horticulture, mainly in the warmer climes of the North Island. The *kumara* (sweet potato), one of their most common crops, is still grown today. The early Maori were evidently highly territorial. Tribes kept close watch over their hunting, fishing, and burial lands, as attested by the widespread legacy of weapon artifacts and village *pa* (fortified hillsides) they left behind. This fiercely protective attitude toward land was still in full force hundreds of years later, when they encountered the first Europeans.

The most widely told Maori legend tells a different tale. It teaches that Maori forebears had been living happily for many years in **Hawaiki,** the ancestral homeland, when **Kupe** the explorer set out on a scouting expedition to the east. He discovered a lush, mist-covered stretch of land which he named Aotearoa, "the land of the long white cloud." Years later, when intertribal dispute and strife finally forced the ancestors to leave Hawaiki, they remembered Kupe's lavish praise of the paradise to the east. In seven mammoth canoes, each carrying the forebear of a different Maori tribe, the ancestors turned their backs on Hawaiki and set sail, destination Aotearoa.

6

THE EUROPEAN ARRIVAL

The first non-Maori to lay eyes on New Zealand was a Dutchman named **Abel Tasman.** In 1642, Tasman tried to land in what is now Golden Bay in the South Island, but was forced to flee by a hostile Maori tribe that killed several of his men. Several years later, a cartographer used Tasman's account to put the country on the world map for the first time, naming it Nova Zeelandia after a province in the Netherlands.

In 1769, the legendary British explorer **Captain James Cook** cruised in on the *Endeavour.* He established friendly relations with many of the *tangata maori* ("the ordinary people," as they called themselves) that he encountered. In his tour around the coast of New Zealand, Cook also sprinkled place names right and left and claimed the islands for Britain. Much like Kupe's advertisement to the Maori ancestors, Cook's glowing report of New Zealand, published eight years after he returned to England, quickly spread the word in Europe about the largely untouched land of plenty on the other side of the world.

Sealers and **whalers** were the first to respond, arriving in droves in the early 1800s to make short work of New Zealand's resources. The seal colonies were practically wiped clean by the 1820s, followed by the whaling waters. **Missionaries** also made an early appearance, with the first Christian missionary arriving in 1814 from New South Wales. A bevy of earnest reformers followed in their wake, working around the clock to learn Maori so they could teach the precepts of Christianity to the "Indians" and "aborigines," as they were called until "Maori" came into popular usage in the 1830s. Independent **traders** were the next to arrive, seeking flax and novelty items (such as Maori-made trinkets or even preserved heads) in exchange for firearms, metal tools, and other European goods.

In a pattern familiar to colonized peoples the world over, the trading relationship between the Maori and the Europeans had consequences far beyond the economic sphere. Traders brought the fatal gift of European disease, which killed 25% of the Maori population. Western firepower escalated Maori intertribal violence, culminating in the **Musket Wars** of 1820-35. The situation intensified when European armed trade ships began to participate in tribal warfare without governmental authorization. Soon, early settlers began to fear for the peace and stability of their settlements, and appealed to their governments for protection. In 1833, Queen Victoria sent the ineffectual **James Busby** as British Resident to keep law and order. While settlers established their own citizen vigilante associations, Busby began negotiations with Maori chiefs at his house in Waitangi.

THE TREATY OF WAITANGI

In January 1840, dissatisfied with Busby's performance, the British Colonial Office sent **Captain William Hobson** to replace him. Upon royal request, Hobson wrote the **Treaty of Waitangi,** which offered the Maori the rights of British citizens and Her Majesty's protection in exchange for British sovereignty over the land. Captain William Hobson shook each chief's hand, proclaiming, *"He iwi tahi tatou"* ("Now we are one people"). The treaty was then translated into Maori by Henry Williams, an Anglican missionary.

Crucial nuances of meaning were evidently lost in translation, however. In Article One, the English version boldly asked for all "rights and powers of sovereignty over the land," while the Maori understated it as *"kawanatanga"* (government or administration), presumably leaving ultimate sovereignty to Maori chiefs. In Article Two the Maori were merely ensured "exclusive and undisturbed possession of their lands" in the English version, while in the Maori version they were promised *"tino rangatiratanga"*: unrestrained exercise of chiefly authority over lands, villages, and natural treasures.

These discrepancies were not recognized when an assembly of northern Maori chiefs gathered at Busby's house to hear Hobson's presentation of the Treaty of Waitangi on February 6, 1840. Local missionaries certainly made no effort to clarify, as they sought to persuade Maori chiefs that the treaty was an "act of love" on Queen Victoria's part, an effort to ease tribal conflict and to protect them from harsh domination by some other European nation. Their glowing promises must have been at least partially convincing, since 26 of the 34 chiefs who had signed the Declaration of (Maori) Independence signed the treaty on this day, with about 500 more signatures gathered on later treaty-signing campaigns on both the North and the South Islands. Notable refusals took place in the Waikato and the center of the North Island, two areas that later bore the brunt of especially violent conflict.

SETTLEMENT AND LAND WARS

Edward Wakefield's New Zealand Company ushered in a new wave of settlement. Between 1839 and 1843, agents claimed and purchased land for the company, leading to new settlements of immigrants in New Plymouth, Nelson, Wanganui, and Wellington. These settlements were small and fragile, but at the same time, the British government purchased huge parcels of land, especially in the South Island, increasing British investment and making New Zealand a valuable addition to its empire. Around the same time, Governor Hobson shifted the seat of government from the Bay of Islands to Auckland. In November 1840, Britain responded to the burgeoning settlement in New Zealand by declaring the country a separate colony from New South Wales, Australia, in *The Letters Patent*, usually called **The Charter of 1840.** Hobson was named the colony's first governor.

As European settlement increased, the relationship between the Maori and the settlers deteriorated. The support Governor Hobson had won among the Maori quickly disappeared when European settlers began showing increasing disregard for Maori property. Before long, the Maori began to suspect that they had given up more than they had intended and started to rebel against British authority. In 1844, **Hone Heke,** one of the first chiefs to sign the treaty, cut down the British flagpole at Kororareka near Russell, which he saw as a symbol of illegitimate land claims. The government tried to re-erect the pole several times, finally giving up the fourth time Heke and his allies cut it down. The Russell incident marked the beginning of warfare between Heke's army and British-led forces, which lasted until 1846.

In 1852, the **Constitution Act** established a settler government with six provinces and a national parliament with a lower and an upper house. The Constitution Act also gave the vote to men over 25 holding official land titles, a move intended to shut out Maori representation, as Maori land ownership was communal. All hopes of royal intervention on the behalf of the Maori died in 1856, when New Zealand was declared a completely self-governing British colony.

The Maori became increasingly disturbed to see a government that denied them representation taking shape around them. In the mid-1800s, the **King Movement,** based in the King Country region south of Waikato, sought to centralize Maori support, naming Te Wherowhero of Waikato their king in 1858. In a more moderate strain of resistance, they envisioned the Maori king as a local complement to the faraway British monarch, not a usurper of power. Still, the British government refused to recognize the Maori king. When violent conflict erupted once again in Taranaki in 1860, **Governor George Grey** blamed the King Movement and decided to strike at Waikato, the movement's primary stronghold. The **New Zealand Wars** (alternatively known as **The Maori Wars**) exploded across the North Island as a result, with British forces ultimately gaining victory. At the same time, the South Island experienced an influx of settlers with the **gold rushes** at Westland and Otago. By 1860, the non-Maori population of 79,000 had surpassed the Maori population.

LAND ISSUES AND SOCIAL REFORMS

Over the next few decades, non-Maori power and industry were organized and consolidated. Massive public works projects, under the leadership of Julius Vogel, improved New Zealand's infrastructure, and farming exports from butter to wool increased. Land disputes were now settled through the courts. In 1865, the first

Native Lands Act established a court to investigate Maori land ownership and distribute official land titles. While any Maori claimant in a land block could initiate a court investigation, land titles in these disputes usually went to chiefs, making it even harder for individual Maori to hold onto land. In 1873, the second Native Lands Act split up the land title for a land block among its shared owners. Each individual's share had to then be passed on to all natural heirs, whittling down the size of the shares more and more with each generation and making it even harder for a tribe to hold onto communal blocks of land. By the end of the 19th century, an astounding 92% of New Zealand's land was in non-Maori control. In 1882, disillusioned with the colonial government, the Nga Puhi tribe sent the first delegation to England to personally petition Queen Victoria. Although they were never given audience, the Maori continued to send representatives until the 1920s. Ironically, while the Maori were struggling for their rights, the last decades of the 19th century were a period of dramatic **social reforms** for the non-Maori. Factory conditions improved; there were increasing conservation efforts, and, in 1893, New Zealand women were the first women in the world to gain the vote.

WORLD WAR AND PROSPERITY

In the 20th century, New Zealand, still forging its national identity, had to navigate increasingly complicated global relationships, conflicts, and markets. In 1907, New Zealand became a dominion of the British Empire, a status that allowed it to decide its own foreign policy. Courageous performances in two world wars helped pave the way to complete autonomy. In 1915, enlisted to fight in World War I, the **Australia and New Zealand Army Corps (ANZAC)** were chosen to join the infamous Dardanelles campaign. At Gallipoli on April 25, the ANZACs were sent in to attack Turkish forces entrenched in the Dardanelles strait. The battle was a huge military failure, leading to massive casualties for Australia and New Zealand, but winning great respect for the soldiers' bravery. Like most of the western world, New Zealand suffered hard times during the Great Depression of the 1920s. However, the following decades were characterized by increasing prosperity. In 1935, the victory of the liberal Labour Party spurred the creation of the world's first welfare system, resulting in free health care and low-rent public housing, among other things. By the 1940s, New Zealand's main industries were booming and the country maintained one of the highest standards of living in the world.

The early 20th century was also marked by continued negotiations between Maori and non-Maori. In 1909, the third **Native Lands Act** set aside funds specifically for Maori land development in order to aid Maori farmers. In an interesting paradox typical of the era, the same amount was also set aside to buy up Maori land. In 1922, in a landmark case, the government agreed to compensate the Te Arawa tribe for lost fishing and burial rights in the Rotorua lakes. Four years later, another such agreement was made with the Ngati Tuwharetoa tribe concerning Lake Taupo. In 1935, the first **Labour Party** came into government, touting official recognition of the Treaty of Waitangi as part of their platform. They established connections with certain Maori political movements, but never came through on their election promise to incorporate the treaty into official law at last.

POST-WWII

Making a final break from Britain, New Zealand was declared fully independent in 1947. In the second half of the 20th century, New Zealand faced new challenges in maintaining its high standard of prosperity. Reliance on exports, geographical isolation, and the decreasing aid of Britain presented some of the obstacles in New Zealand's struggle to secure its global niche. The **Second World War** demonstrated New Zealand's reliance on the United States for military protection when the U.S. saved New Zealand from possible Japanese hostilities. New Zealand aimed to secure its future by signing the **ANZUS pact** (which secured the mutual defense of Australia, New Zealand and the U.S.) and by independently harnessing its own energy resources. Domestically, the government also attempted to ease tensions with Maori. After World War II, Maori had begun to migrate to cities. By 1972, 65% of the Maori population had moved into urban areas, especially Auckland. Adherence to traditional beliefs among Maori declined dramatically, though the traditional tensions with the Pakeha remained. In 1960, the **Waitangi Day Act** made February 6 a national "day of thanksgiving." It was declared an official public holiday 13 years later. (Today, Waitangi Day is simultaneously a cause for celebration and a day of protest for those speaking out on perceived continued infringement of Maori rights.) By the 1970s, the New Zealand government had emerged as a mediator between its aggrieved Maori citizens and the Crown. The 1975 **Treaty of Waitangi Act** set up the Waitangi Tribunal to hear Maori claims against the Crown. Under the act, the Tribunal had to consider both the Maori and English texts of the treaty in its decisions. In the same year, the **Land March,** a protest against unfair land claim treatment, started at Te Hapua in the Northland and ended at the Parliament building in Wellington.

New Zealand faced some difficult economic times in the late 70s and 80s, culminating in the 1987 stock market crash. The government sought to solve the nation's slow economic growth, caused partially by Britain's entrance into the European Economic Community, by deregulating the economy and opening up to free trade. In 1983, New Zealand and Australia established the **Closer Economic Relations Trade Agreement,** which allowed free and unrestricted trade between the two nations. During the mid-80s, Labour's David Lange and his Finance Minister Roger Douglas cut spending on established national programs, increased privatization, and emphasized free enterprise in a movement known as "Rogernomics." Despite an increase in average income, the inequality between the rich and the poor grew wider. New Zealand continued to nurse its economy back to health in the 1990s by instituting many free-market reforms. Sheep husbandry is believed by some to have driven the recovery. New Zealand is the main global producer of lamb, responsible for a staggering 54% of world export trade.

With its foreign policy, New Zealand continued to retain its independent streak. In 1987, Labour Party Prime Minister David Lange committed New Zealand staunchly to the **antinuclear movement** by barring all nuclear-capable vessels from New Zealand harbors and stepping up pressure on the French government to stop nuclear testing at Moruroa Atoll. His action was the culmination of a movement that was heightened by the 1985 bombing by French agents of the Greenpeace ship, *Rainbow Warrior,* which was to attend a protest of French nuclear testing (see p. 100). Today, the ship's masts are commemorated in the Dargaville Maritime Museum (p. 114), and New Zealand is still a leader in the antinuclear campaign. As recently as 1995, New Zealand tried unsuccessfully to revive a case against French nuclear testing at the International Court of Justice.

RECENT EVENTS

GOVERNMENT

In 1993, the majority of New Zealanders voted to establish a mixed-member proportional representation **(MMP)** system of government, similar to the German system. Under the system, a 120-seat Parliament was established, with a predetermined number of Maori electorate seats, general electorate seats, and party list seats (in which the elected party selects members). The first MMP election took place in October 1996. Although no party won a clear majority, Jim Bolger's **National Party** captured 35% of the vote and 44 seats. Coming in after the National Party were the **Labour** party (the center-left pro-business party), the **Alliance** party (a more left-wing party), and the relatively new party, **New Zealand First,** led by **Winston Peters,** a part-Maori candidate.

New Zealand politics in recent years have been defined by behind-the-scenes maneuvering, fragile power-sharing arrangements, and allegations of corruption. In November 1997, while Bolger was out of the country, National's **Jenny Shipley,** a former schoolteacher and farmer, engineered a "coup" to replace him as their party's leader. Months of secret planning paid off when Bolger resigned in the face of Shipley's leadership bid. She was sworn in as New Zealand's first woman prime minister in December of that year. A primary focus of Shipley's government has been to increase free-market competition and reduce government size. These policies have drawn criticism that she is missing the chance to focus on concerns fundamental to women.

Shipley's term as prime minister was thrown into disarray in August 1998. She inherited a fragile coalition between her own conservative National Party and the more liberal New Zealand First. This coalition dissolved when Peters, the deputy Prime Minister and Treasurer, led his four fellow New Zealand First ministers out of an emergency cabinet meeting in protest of a planned sale of the Wellington airport. New Zealand First characterized the proposed deal as selling New Zealand assets into foreign control, while Shipley argued it was just good business. She sacked Peters for his intransigence, but then faced the difficult task of ruling as a minority leader. Despite dire predictions of Shipley's imminent downfall, she still presides today.

In late 1999, New Zealand elected new members to Parliament. At the time of *Let's Go* printing, the expected outcome was unclear.

MAORI ISSUES

The recognition of **Maori land rights** continues to be an issue of heated governmental debate. Certain tribes in the Wellington area, for example, have made claims on land beneath the Parliament building and the National Museum, touching off a storm of controversy. While many non-Maori New Zealanders feel that they are not responsible for the past and that the country owes no debt to the Maori, the government has generally disagreed. The **Office of Treaty Settlement** is the government organization responsible for mediating between Maori claims and the British crown. In November 1997, the British crown admitted in the **Ngai Tahu Deed of Settlement** that it had acted unfairly and in violation of the 1840 Treaty of Waitangi.

Within New Zealand, the legal definition of Maori was expanded in July 1998, when the **Te Whanau o Waipareira Trust,** an organization of Auckland-area Maori, won recognition as a tribe from the Waitangi Tribunal. Because they are not part of a traditional *iwi* (a common, traceable bloodline), urban Maori were previously unable to access government funds for job training, education, welfare, and health services. Their new status has yet to be approved by New Zealand's High Court and does not accord them rights to land reparations or property, but it is an important step toward remedying the problems that beset urban Maori.

IN THE NEWS

In 1998, a 9½-week **power outage** occurred in Auckland's business district, an event that unfortunately gave New Zealand a rare place in world headlines. Residents were urged to leave town, and a general confusion settled in as pointmen directed traffic, hotels hired extra staff to help guests through darkened corridors, and businesses relocated operations to the suburbs. A report released in August 1998 concluded that the utility company, Mercury Energy, had been negligent in its maintenance of the city's power cables. Losses due to the outage were estimated to be at least $1 million a day.

On July 28, 1999, Parliament amended the Sale of Liquor Act (1989), lowering the New Zealand's **drinking age** from 20 to 18. With a close vote of 59 to 55, the controversial amendment was passed after three hours of discussion. The bill includes the implementation of a photo ID system—issued to those 18 and older, the card must be shown in order to purchase liquor. "Under agers" (those under 18) may not purchase alcohol, but may drink if it is procured by a parent or guardian. Those in favor of changing the law argued that 18-year-old New Zealanders may marry, vote, and fight for their country and, therefore, should be granted the right to drink alcohol. Those opposed worry that the lowered drinking age will increase the rate of underage drinking, drunk-driving accidents, and other alcohol-related injuries and deaths.

In August of 1999, the **New Zealand Tourism Board** embarked on a three-year $90 million campaign promoting tourism in New Zealand. With a mini map of New Zealand in place of the percentage sign, "100 per cent New Zealand" is the slogan for the controversial project. You may even catch this advertisement wave (or flood)—promotions include TV and movie ads worldwide. $30 million taxpayers' dollars a year is a risky price to pay, though, with such an uncertain industry as tourism (New Zealand lost $5 million last year in this area). Many opponents of the campaign feel it is too nature- and adventure-heavy (rather than cultural). It is too soon to tell, though, how successful the venture will be.

THE CULTURE

THE PEOPLE

The total population of New Zealand is about 3.8 million. Two-thirds of the population lives in the North Island (half of which live in Auckland), while the South Island is more sparsely settled. **Caucasians** comprise the majority racial group of New Zealand, but there is still a considerable minority presence. New Zealand **Maori** make up 15% of the population, making them the largest minority ethnic group. Other **Pacific Islanders** are the next largest group at 6% of the population, the result of large-scale immigration movements that began in the 1970s. In fact, a greater concentration of non-Maori Polynesians live in the greater Auckland area than anywhere else in the world. **Asians** are also a fast-growing minority group, comprising 5% of the total population in 1996, an increase of 74% from 1991.

Christianity is the predominant religion; Anglican, Presbyterian, and Catholic denominations are the most commonly practiced. Maori denominations of Christianity, such as the Ratana and Ringatu churches, were first developed during the missionary era of the late 19th and early 20th centuries in an effort to synthesize traditional Maori beliefs with the precepts of Christianity.

LANGUAGE

The cultural mix of Maori and European is reflected in the language; although English is the dominant spoken tongue, the influx of Maori into day-to-day English parlance is immediately striking. The cross-fertilization between English and Maori is evident in phrases from the greeting "Kia ora!" to the farewell "Haere ra!" For every city named Christchurch and river named Avon, there's a town called Tauranga and an estuary named Waikareao. Some places are even bestowed with dual names: Mt. Cook is also known as Aoraki or Aorangi, and Taranaki is a more frequently used alternate for Mt. Egmont and the region surrounding it. A more thorough listing of both Kiwi English and Maori words and phrases can be found in the **Kiwi English and Maori-English Glossary** (p. 389). New Zealanders speak English with a distinctive Kiwi accent and a vocabulary more in sync with British and Australian usage than with American. Regional variation adds an extra twist, such as the slightly rolled "r" characteristic of the Scottish-colonized areas.

After decades of efforts to rekindle Maori culture, the Maori language has revitalized itself as a form of everyday communication rather than being used solely for ceremonial purposes. Maori was established as an official language in New Zealand in 1974, and is spoken by about one-third of the Maori. It is now taught in a number of schools. First captured on paper by missionaries in the early 1800s, Maori uses only fifteen letters (a, e, h, i, k, m, n, ng, o, p, r, t, u, w, wh), gives each syllable equal stress, and ends each with a vowel. The soft Maori "ng" can appear at any point in a Maori word and sounds similar to the ending of "ring." The sound indicated by "wh" is a difficult sound for non-native speakers to attain, one that is closely approximated by a soft, aspirated "f" sound by some tribes (particularly in the north). Though some Maori words may appear at first to be tongue-twisting concoction, most are decipherable with a syllable-by-syllable, phonetic approach.

VISUAL ARTS AND LITERATURE

A number of prominent and critically acclaimed artists have hailed from New Zealand in the last century. **Frances Hodgkins** (1869-1947) and **Colin McCahon** (1919-87) are two of the most famous 20th-century New Zealand painters. Hodgkins left New Zealand in 1913 for the literary and artistic circles of London, eventually becoming a leading figure first in watercolor figurative painting, then in oils. McCahon retained his base in New Zealand and focused the bulk of his work on the landscapes of the South Island. Today he is considered one of the most important influences on modern art in New Zealand.

New Zealand has its share of literary stars as well. **Katherine Mansfield** (1888-1923), short story-writer, was another World War I expatriate to Britain. Her best-known short story collections are *Bliss* (1920), reportedly dismissed by Virginia Woolf as merely "superficial smartness," and *The Garden Party* (1922). Her childhood home in Wellington has been preserved as a museum (see p. 235). **Dame Ngaio Marsh** (1895-1982), most renowned for her mystery series featuring detective Roderick Alleyn, stayed firmly rooted in New Zealand as a member of the leading artistic group in Christchurch in the mid-1900s. Other notable New Zealand writers are poet **James K. Baxter** (1926-1972), renowned for his celebration of the New Zealand wilderness, and novelist **Janet Frame** (b. 1924), best known for *Owls Do Cry* (1957), *A State of Siege* (1966), and her autobiographical trio *An Angel at My Table* (1985), which was also adapted to film by Jane Campion.

Maori writers have surged onto the literary scene as well. For example, **Patricia Grace** (b. 1937), of Ngati Raukawa, Ngati Toa, and Te Ati Awa descent, is known for the bittersweet coming-of-age story *Mutuwhenua the moon sleeps* (1978), about a young Maori girl's love for a Pakeha (non-Maori). **Witi Ihimaera** (b. 1944), of the Te Whanau a Kai tribe, is best-known for *Tangi* (1973), an exploration of father-son relationships. Ihimaera's later works focus on issues of gay identity, in books like *Nights in the Gardens of Spain*. Perhaps the most well-known Maori author is **Keri Hulme** (b. 1947), a South Islander of Scottish, English, and Ngai Tahu descent, whose novel *The Bone People* won the 1985 Booker Prize.

MUSIC

Geographic isolation hasn't disconnected New Zealand from music trends of the past. Kiwis had **punk** in the 1970s too, a phase that continued throughout the decade with the influential Christchurch label **Flying Nun**. In the 1980s, The **Split Enz** and its offshoot **Crowded House** enjoyed worldwide popularity as part of the **New Wave** movement. Today, in the nightclubs, electronic music reigns supreme, in a range of genres from house to drum and bass.

The **Exponents** and **Head like a Hole** are two of the most popular bands playing today, and consistently pack houses wherever they play. The independent label **Kog** is an umbrella for talent in the Auckland area, spearheaded by the grooves of **Chumbwa** and the funkiness of **DJ Amanda**. Check out *The Fix*, a free glossy mag, for info on the Auckland scene. Down in Wellington, **Mu** demonstrates his skills on the vinyl, while **Manuel Bundy** criss-crosses the country with rhythmically centered beats. Perhaps of more interest to Top 40 fans around the world, Maori artists **OTC** (Otara Millionaires Club) have laid claim to the hip-hop and dance music scene. **The Gathering** (http://www.gathering.co.nz) is a multi-day rave in the South Island that celebrates New Year's Eve and draws an international crowd.

New Zealand has a full-time professional orchestra, the New Zealand Symphony Orchestra, whose excellent reputation merits its traveling over 20,000 kilometers a year to perform. Internationally renowned opera star and New Zealand native **Dame Kiri Te Kanawa** also performs for audiences worldwide.

XENA, WARRIOR PRINCESS In a country that worships rugby, beer drinking, and other testosterone-driven activities, there is one exception to the overwhelming culture of machismo: Xena, the star of a popular TV show written, produced, and directed by New Zealanders. Set in the golden age of myth (and filmed near Auckland), the show follows the adventures of Xena as she battles capricious gods and greedy humans in order to free all people from tyranny and injustice. Since its debut a little more than four years ago, the show has enjoyed worldwide popularity. Xena landed on the cover of the American feminist magazine *Ms.* and is all over the Internet. Countless Xenites throng pages and chat rooms devoted to all things Xena. In particular, many female fans are inspired by her unapologetic, sexy, self-determined character. The show's producers and its star Lucy Lawless know that having a female hero puts the show in the position of an underdog, but also opens up possibilities for subversion. The show is witty and self-aware, deliberately manipulating the subtext of the relationship between Xena and her sidekick, Gabrielle. While Xena might be fierce, she's certainly not androgynous, dressing in skimpy outfits even as she battles the forces of evil. But as Lawless explains, "she wears those things because they're better to fight in."

FILM

New Zealand's own film industry was not fully established until the 1970s. One notable figure from the New Zealand film scene was **Len Lye** (1901-80), kinetic sculptor and modern filmmaker of the 60s. Lye pioneered the technique of "direct filmmaking," in which images are etched or painted directly onto the film itself. Born in Christchurch, Lye left New Zealand for London in the early 1900s, joining fellow expatriate Frances Hodgkins (see p. 13) in London's artsy elite of the 20s and 30s, then moving to New York in 1944. Today his work is shown at the Govett-Brewster Art Gallery in New Plymouth (p. 209).

The early 70s saw works mainly by independent filmmakers. A significant event in New Zealand film during this time, as well as a landmark work in Maori representation on the silver screen, was the release of **Tangata Whenua: The People of the Land** (1974), a six-part documentary series by Maori filmmaker Barry Barclay.

In 1978, the government created the New Zealand Film Commission, which encourages and financially supports the film industry. Since then, recent films made in New Zealand have become both popular and critical hits. One-sixth of the country viewed *Goodbye Pork Pie* (1981), directed by Geoff Murphy. A film every Kiwi will tell you to see is *Once Were Warriors* (adapted from Alan Duff's book of 1992), from prominent director Lee Tamahori. The film was critically acclaimed for its stark, honest appraisal of the plight of urban Maori today. Jane Campion's *The Piano* (1994), a dark, haunting love story about turn-of-the-century European settlers, broke box office records and won two Cannes Film Festival awards and a Best Supporting Actress Oscar for teen star **Anna Paquin.** Peter Jackson's *Heavenly Creatures* (1994), based on a true story, depicts two unhappy teenagers' unstable friendship and their escape into a fantasy world.

MAORI ARTS AND CULTURE

Before the European arrival, the Maori sustained a thriving artistic tradition. From performance arts to craftwork, everyday art was vital in maintaining tribal unity, expressing spiritual beliefs, celebrating important occasions, and honoring one's ancestry. Over the course of European settlement, however, many art forms and traditions grew rare or disappeared altogether. A growing movement today seeks to recover these *wahi ngaro* (lost aspects) of Maori tradition and culture. The Maori Arts and Crafts Institute in Rotorua, for example, trains students in the ancient tribal traditions of wood-and-jewelry carving. Annual Maori performing arts festivals encourage modern-day Maori to carry on traditions as well.

DANCE

Maori dance includes more than just fancy footwork; one's entire body, voice, and spirit are incorporated into what may be the Maori's most dramatic art form. The vigorous arm-waving, chanting, foot-stomping **haka** is an all-male dance, once performed by armed warriors before battle as a convocation to the god of war. To see a modern *haka*, head to a *marae* (see below) or just glue your eyes to the **All Blacks** (see p. 17) before the beginning of every rugby match. **Taparahi,** on the other hand, are weaponless dances performed by both genders for a variety of reasons: to greet important guests, to honor the dead, or for sheer entertainment. In the **poi,** a dance now performed by women, balls on strings are twirled in elegant synchronicity. (It was originally designed to increase suppleness and flexibility in the wrists of warriors.)

CARVING

Carving is one early Maori art form still practiced today. The most common materials are bone, wood, and greenstone (also see **A Jaded Perspective,** p. 315). According to traditional Maori beliefs, it is the artist's responsibility to impart certain qualities such as fear, power, and authority to his or her pieces, in order to transform them from mere material objects to *taonga* (highly treasured, even sacred objects). Each object also accumulates its own body of *korero* (stories) with each successive owner. A design particular to a tribe is passed down from generation to generation, distinguishing itself by its repetition of certain stylistic features and motifs, such as *tiki* (human forms), *manaia* (bird men), and *taniwha* (sea spirits). Carvers create items large and small, decorating both towering meeting houses and tiny tiki pendants.

MOKO (FACIAL TATTOOING)

Moko has been one of the most famous Maori art forms since the days when 19th-century Europe was transfixed by portraits and photographs of New Zealand "savages" with full facial tattoos.

While most tribes reserved the practice for males, *moko* sometimes served as a rite of passage for both males and females, as well as a marker of achievements and status. Men's *moko* began with a simple design for youths; more spiral flourishes were added as the wearer won prestige in battle. Thus, only older, highly distinguished warriors could sport full facial tattoos. Women's *moko* were more simple, usually surrounding only the lips and the tip of the nose, although some stout-hearted women elected to have their thighs and breasts tattooed as well.

Traditionally, *moko* was only executed by *tohunga ta moko*, experts trained extensively in using the sharp wooden adze and mallet or birdbone chisel to etch the design into the skin, then using a toothed chisel to fill in the ink dye (a mixture of burned kauri or totara resin and pigeon fat). The tatooing was done in complete silence. The *tohunga ta moko* declared the recipient *tapu* (sacred) while the tattoo was healing. Leaves of the Karaka tree were placed on the carvings for healing purposes. During this time, sexual intimacy was prohibited and no one was permitted to view the *moko*; they believed it would fade if anyone saw it before it healed completely. Today, Maori continue to practice *moko*, often using face paint to replicate this intricate art.

THE MARAE

The *marae* is the sacred grounds around a Maori meeting house. The *whare* (meeting house) symbolizes the body of a Maori ancestor: the spine of the building is the backbone, the front beams are the arms, and the intermediate beams are the ribs. Today, travelers can experience the *marae* throughout the country at open sites. At these open sights, customs and protocol involving the *marae* are reenacted for the benefit of the visitors. Upon arriving at the *marae*, a warrior from the village will greet the group with an elaborate set of prowling steps, body movements, and a tongue-protruding facial gesture (it's exceedingly uncouth to return such a gesture). The *wero* (challenge) ends when a *teka* peace offering is offered and accepted. The entire ritual of arrival and introduction is called the *powhiri* (or formal welcome). The chief of the tribe will welcome your group, and one of your number (your chief) will deliver a brief speech in return. To seal the bond of friendship, both chiefs press noses together in the traditional greeting known as the *hongi*. Shoes are not worn inside the *whare*, and pictures may not be permitted, depending on the tribe. After a *karakia* (prayer) is given, the traditional dinner, *hangi*, is prepared by roasting sweet potatoes, meat, mussels, and other goodies in a pit of heated stones until they reach peak smoky delicacy.

SONG

Traditional Maori song and oratory are particularly important to ceremonial life. *Tau marae* orations are formal, stylized tributes to the dead performed at traditional funeral ceremonies for important chiefs. Another important type of oratory is *karakia* (chants), which were once strictly the property of *tohunga* (priests or specially learned men). *Karakia* imparted *mauri* (spiritual essence) to objects, as in the Maori myth in which Tiki chants a *karakia* in order to bring his clay figurine to life. *Waiata* is the most common type of lyrical song. Two kinds of *waiata* that have survived are the *waiata tangi*, songs of mourning (often composed by women), and the *waiata aroha* (solely composed by women), which often dwell upon unrequited love, obstacles in love, and delinquent lovers. In all of these oral arts, tribes nurtured their own traditions, creating specialized mythology and tribal historical accounts.

FOOD AND DRINK

While New Zealand has some specialties, it does not have a unique cuisine. From the earliest inhabitants' dinners of roast moa and **kumara** (a sweet potato), New Zealanders still maintain a largely meat-and-potatoes diet. While vegetarian and vegan options are becoming increasingly trendy (**kosher** fare is still rare), traditional New Zealand food tends to run on the heavy, meaty side, with lamb, venison (called cervena when farm-raised), and pork dominating the menus of traditional establishments. Fresh **seafood** is another staple; fresh fish, prawns (what Americans call jumbo shrimp), crayfish, shellfish, and more overrun coastal towns. **Ice cream** is also consumed in vast quantities.

In small towns, the tendency toward the basic can be seen today in the Main St. triumvirate of fish 'n' chips dives, cafes, and the ever-present Chinese restaurants, all serving fried and greasy goodies.

PAVLOV'S DOG... ER, DESSERT Sweet and white, creamy and light, **pavlova** is, was, and forever shall be *the* New Zealand dessert. The soft-centered mound of meringue, topped patriotically with whipped cream and slices of kiwifruit, seems an appropriate national specialty for "the Land of the Long White Cloud." It's also considered by some to be a prerequisite to marriage—if one's spouse can't make a decent pav, he or she just isn't fit to bring little Kiwis into the world. The graceful sugary treat draws its name from the famed Russian ballerina Anna Pavlova, who endeared herself to the world down under during a 1929 tour. But controversy continues to reign over who invented and named the dessert. Some poor misguided souls on the West Island (Kiwi jargon for Australia) believe they invented the dessert, after the Esplanade Hotel of Perth got all the press in 1934 for a dish they called pavlova. Research done by the New Zealand National Library, however, shows that the heart and soul belong to New Zealand: the Esplanade's original recipe lacked the crucial vinegar apparent in a "meringue cake" recipe that surfaced in Wellington, New Zealand, in 1927. The name for the dish itself was the idea of another Kiwi cook, as evidenced by a 1929 recipe for "Pavlova Cakes." (For the whimsical Aussie myth of pavlova's origins, see *Let's Go: Australia 2000*.)

In the larger towns and cities, the variety and quality of the takeaways and restaurants has improved tremendously during the past few years. Excellent foreign restaurants, such as Thai, Malaysian and Indian, are no longer few and far between. Middle Eastern **kebab** joints, usually a good value, have proliferated recently. **BYO** (bring-your-own wine) restaurants without a license to sell liquor are widespread; some charge a corking fee. Keep in mind that ordering an **entree** will get you an appetizer or starter in New Zealand; main courses are listed as **mains.** **Tipping** is not expected, and closing hours tend to be flexible; many restaurants, especially in small towns, simply close their doors whenever business seems to have run dry.

With an average of 188 bottles per person annually, New Zealand ranks first in the world in **beer** drinking, consuming even more than their notorious guzzling neighbors, the Aussies. The Kiwis serve up a good brew, with various national lagers and draughts (such as Steinlager), regional beers (such as Speights and Tui), and specialty brews. The **wines** of the Marlborough and Hawke's Bay regions are world-famous, particularly the Sauvignon Blanc, Chardonnay, Riesling, Cabernet Sauvignon, and Pinot Noir varieties. Hard liquor is less popular because import taxes make it more expensive. For non-alcoholic refreshment, try **Lemon and Paeroa (L&P)**, a popular carbonated lemon drink that is "world-famous in New Zealand," as the advertisements tell you with a wink. For a more refined thirst-quencher, you can enjoy a British-style **Devonshire tea.** The late afternoon (around 4pm) snack traditionally plies you with tea, scones with Devonshire cream or jam, crumpets, and other delectables.

SPORTS

New Zealand loves sports like nobody's business. Almost half the population belongs to the New Zealand Sports Assembly, which represents 150 national sporting associations. In addition to the multitude of outdoor sports, including skiing, rafting, swimming, hiking, and jetboating, New Zealanders also hit the grass in organized sports like cricket, golf, tennis, and field hockey. This active country also likes to sit on the sidelines, especially to watch rugby. Kiwi pride swells enormously for the **All Blacks,** the national team whose season runs from April to September (see below). In 1986, the All Blacks won the World Cup. When a crucial match like the **Bledisloe Cup Championships** is being televised (or any Aussie match, for that matter), forget about going out to eat, changing money, or shopping—all the locals will be glued to their TVs, not running businesses. Despite the All Blacks' widespread popularity, however, the team has encountered controversial moments in its history. In 1960, for example, the All Blacks made a vehemently protested national tour of South Africa in which Maori players were excluded. Then, in 1981, the South African Springboks made a tour of New Zealand, prompting many to claim that New Zealand was tacitly supporting apartheid. The **Super 12** tournament is another popular rugby event with the best players from Australia, South Africa, and New Zealand organized into 12 national (and regional) teams. In 1999, the Canterbury Crusaders defeated the Otago Highlanders in an all New Zealand final.

In addition to rugby union, there is also **rugby league,** which features regional teams like the stalwart, ever-popular Auckland Warriors. Another Kiwi favorite is **netball,** a women's sport played in winter. The national team, the **Silver Ferns,** has been steadily gaining in popularity and recognition.

In 1995 the Kiwi sailing team **Black Magic** swiped the America's Cup from the United States, marking only the second time in 144 years that the cup was not won by an American team. The cup's subsequent mauling at the hands and sledgehammer of a Maori activist drew international headlines. Fully restored, the cup has since made several countrywide tours, and plans are well underway for its defense in 2000. The series will be held in Auckland's Hauraki Gulf, with a record 18 challengers already registered (see p. 81).

ALL BLACK ALL OVER From hostel walls to the TV, from the daily paper to bathroom stalls, New Zealand's national rugby team, the All Blacks, are there. Protected with a fierce pride against such abominations as the padded wimpiness of American gridiron, rugby is a source of national unity and honor. Each player must be strong on both offense and defense, quick and powerful, fit enough to last the full grueling 80 minutes, and most of all, tough. In 1986, Buck Shelford gave new meaning to the phrase "he's got balls" when he almost lost his in a test (international match) against France, leaving the game to receive emergency surgery. For opponents, victory over the All Blacks is an unforgettable event—Welsh club team triumphs over the All Blacks in the 1960s are still commemorated with anniversary neckties (supposedly sent to the All Blacks as well). Although they lost to South Africa in the 1995 World Cup final, the team has consistently been one of the world's best. A loss by the All Blacks is so unexpected that tears from devastated fans mix with beer in pubs across the country. The marketing power of the team is so strong that every other national team is spun from their yarn; New Zealand fields the All Whites in soccer, the Tall Blacks in basketball, the Black Sox in softball, and the Black Caps in cricket. While it may take Kiwi blood to fully understand the intricacies and meaning of the game, you don't have to jump in the middle of a scrum to appreciate the athletic prowess of popular star Jonah Lomu, the intensity of the Maori *haka* (war dance) challenge offered to opponents before each game, or the delirious passion of fans at the scoring of a try. Rugby is not merely sport, it is love. The year 2000 for New Zealand will certainly be colored by the All Blacks' performance in the 1999 World Cup.

New Zealand also keeps certain sporting heroes at the center of national pride, including: **Sir Edmund Hillary,** the first to climb Mt. Everest in 1953; **Jack Lovelock,** 1500m gold medalist in the 1936 Berlin Olympics; **Yvette Williams,** long jump champion in the 1952 Helsinki Olympics; and in the 1960 Rome Olympics, **Peter Snell,** 800m gold medalist, and **Murray Halberg,** 5000m gold medalist.

THE LAND AND ENVIRONMENT

BEFORE HUMAN ARRIVAL

The ancient supercontinent of **Gondwana** was a fusion of modern-day South America, Africa, peninsular India, Antarctica, and Australia. When New Zealand split away from this landmass roughly 80 million years ago, it became an isolated biological time capsule.

During the span of time before human arrival, the plants and animals on the island evolved in new and unusual directions as they exploited food and habitat niches. With the absence of predators, New Zealand's birds evolved to occupy the niches that mammals took elsewhere in the world, gaining stronger legs, increasing dramatically in size, and sometimes even losing their wings. Two excellent examples of these unique birds—the **Haast eagle** *(Hapagornis)* and the **moa**—are now extinct. (There are occasional reports of moa-sightings (see p. 299), but it is fairly certain that none exist.) The giant Haast eagle was the top carnivore in New Zealand; the world's largest eagle, it had a wing span of about 3 meters. The moa were the main grazers during this time. Some standing tall enough to look Big Bird in the eye, all 11 species of these flightless wonders were large; the smallest were about the size of turkeys. The **kiwi,** a national emblem for New Zealanders, is another flightless bird that flourished during this time and still exists today.

The flora of New Zealand, like the fauna, took several unusual evolutionary turns since the tectonic exodus from Gondwana. In the absence of large mammalian grazers and browsers, many plants never evolved toxic chemicals, tough leaves, or the spikes, thorns, and other defense mechanisms common in many other parts of the world.

INVASIONS

Since humans began arriving in New Zealand in the 10th century, other species have been coming with them and establishing themselves on New Zealand soil. In addition to losing 43% of the frog fauna and over 40% of the bird fauna since humans first arrived, New Zealand now has over 600 endangered species.

When the first settlers from Polynesia arrived over 1000 years ago with breeds of **dogs** *(kuri)* and **rats** *(kiore)*, the pace of extinction rapidly increased due to the diseases they brought with them. (Interestingly, both the *kuri* and the *kiore* suffered their own twist of fate: the last pure-bred *kuri* disappeared in the mid-1850s, while the *kiore* have held out since the introduction of the European rat only on some small offshore islands.) The Maori also swiftly cleared forests for agriculture and hunted the moa to extinction. Human settlement of New Zealand affected more than one species at a time, too. When the moa went extinct, for example, the Haast giant eagle (see above) also went extinct because its primary food source was moa carrion.

With the arrival of Europeans in the 1800s, more wildlife was depleted. The two main culprits of species decline were wildlife habitat destruction due to industrialization and the introduction of non-native animals. Deer, goats, pigs, rabbits, and possums, brought to provide sporting opportunities, game, and fur, presented a fatal problem to the flightless birds and native animals of New Zealand that had not developed the defense mechanisms necessary for survival. In another example of introductions gone awry, the stoats and weasels brought to the country to serve as predators of rabbits started feeding on hapless native birds when the local rabbit and possum supply diminished. With good reason, the Department of Conservation (DOC) has declared open-season on most exotic bush fauna, happily distributing hunting permits.

Non-native flora, like non-native fauna, disrupts the ecosystem, out-competing endemic flora for sunlight, space, and nutrients. Much flora introduced from harsher climates has a field day in New Zealand with the relatively mild year-round climate, and often ends up reproducing several times per year. With no native predators, and with introduced predators often feeding on indigenous plant life instead, the end result can be calamitous, disrupting the long-term stability of an ecosystem. Of the 20,000 non-native species introduced to the country, the DOC reports that over 200 are now weeds.

FAUNA

Many species that evolved on the supercontinent never came into being in New Zealand; New Zealand has no snakes and no native land mammals apart from bats. One immediately noticeable facet of New Zealand's wildlife, though, is the preponderance of strange and exotic birds. The four different species of **kiwi** display straight, thin, brown, or gray feathers and slender and probing beaks with external nostrils to help in scrounging for food on the forest floor. Solitary, nocturnal, flightless, tailless, and almost wingless, the kiwi is in a class of its own. The **kea**, the world's only alpine parrot, is one of the few birds to make its home in the peaks of the Southern Alps. Any visitor to the ski slopes or national parks of New Zealand will quickly realize that the kea is no ordinary polly, but rather a clever, destructive, and very bold menace (see **To Peck and Destroy,** p. 309). The **kereru** is the native pigeon, and the only bird able to disperse the larger seeds of some native plants. Fanciful names for New Zealand's amazing variety of birds abound: the **morepork** *(ruru,* the only native owl), the **muttonbird** *(titi),* and the **wrybill** *(ngutuparore,* with its slender and twisted beak), among others.

Unfortunately, many of New Zealand's beautiful birds are endangered today. Just 150 turkey-sized, blue-green, and strong-beaked **takahe** remain; the **black stilt** *(kaki)* are down to 70. Only 62 nocturnal **kakapo,** the world's heaviest parrot (males can weigh in at 4kg), are still in existence; the DOC states that the kakapo

POSSUM PROBLEMS

Although New Zealand's reputation of having several times more sheep than people still holds true, the fact is that there are now more possum than sheep. By some estimates, over 70 million of the marsupials are chewing tender leaves and damaging the flowers of New Zealand's native trees, carrying diseases, out-competing native birds for food, and steadily consuming much of the country's remaining native bush. If you visit the rare areas of the country where possums have not struck, such as Great Barrier Island, the damage wreaked by the animals in the rest of the country will become painfully evident. The DOC's response has ranged from poison-trapping to offering head bounties, but in the wake of each subsequent ineffective attempt more and more radical approaches have been tried. The latest is the use of aerial poison bombs. A supposedly natural, biodegradable toxin known as "1080" is being dropped in many of the country's most rugged and intractable forests. DOC insists that studies overwhelmingly attest to 1080's safety, but they do warn surrounding areas before carrying out their aerial missions of eradication.

"is, perhaps, the slowest-breeding bird on earth." Intensive conservation efforts are underway for all three species.

With over 1500 species of **land snails** (some of which are carnivorous), 11 species of the heaviest insect in the world (the ancient, mouse-sized, grasshopper-esque **weta**), teeming crayfish *(koura)*, pesky sandflies *(te namu)*, and the ethereal glow-worms *(titiwai)*, there is no shortage of biological diversity. New Zealand also has the coastal **katipo spider,** a relative of the black widow spider. Another ancient relic found in New Zealand is the **tuatara,** a lizard-like creature old enough to have roamed with the weta and dinosaurs 200 million years ago. An interesting feature of this reptile is its third eye, which helps to regulate its exposure to the sun.

Bats represent the only indigenous land mammals, though there are plenty of marine mammals. Orca, seals, and sea lions can be found in the waters off the South Island. New Zealand also boasts almost half of the world's whale, porpoise, and dolphin population. Species unique to New Zealand include **Hector's dolphin, beaked whales,** the **New Zealand fur seal,** and the **Hooker sea lion.** Today, climate changes and water pollution threaten these marine mammals, whose numbers reached drastic lows from the whaling and sealing trades earlier in the century.

FLORA

Before 1800, 70% of the landscape was covered in forest; today, only 15% of the original lowland forest and only 10% of the original wetlands remain. Ninety percent of the original kauri forests were harvested. Still, there are 2700 plants native to New Zealand (of which DOC reports that 80% are endemic). Among the most notable are the **podocarps,** a broad class of conifers similar to the yew family, which includes totara, rimu, miro, and matai, and **kahikatea.** Podocarps dominate many of New Zealand's forested regions. **Beech forests** are also common; the *Nothofagus* is the most famous genus and can trace its roots to the Nothofagus forests that used to blanket Gondwana. There are 193 different species of fern in New Zealand, 88 of which are endemic. **Mamaku tree ferns** can grow up to 20m in height; the **ponga tree fern,** with its silver-underside fronds, is the national symbol.

The **pohutukawa,** often called "New Zealand's Christmas tree" for the bright crimson flowers that bloom in most varieties during late December, is another distinctive species found in the northern regions. Maori tradition holds that when these gnarled coastal trees bloom early there'll be a long hot summer ahead. The **rata,** similar to the pohutukawa, adds a peachy-orangish cast to the landscape. The North Island rata begins life as a vine, and slowly strangles its host tree to death. Numerous other plant species besides trees are unique to the country as well (such as the world's largest buttercup, the Mt. Cook lily, and New Zealand's only native palm trees, the Nikau palms).

CONSERVATION

New Zealand is hailed worldwide as a leader in conservation efforts, both on land and at sea. About one-third of the country is set aside as protected land, and a massive international whale sanctuary established in 1994 includes more than 11 million square miles. The country is covered with 13 national parks, plus numerous other forest parks, groves, and wildlife reserves. The first national park, **Tongariro National Park,** was created in 1887 as a result of the foresight and efforts of Te Heuheu Tukino IV, the high chief of the Ngati Tuwharetoa Maori tribe. He offered the area as a gift to the New Zealand government on the condition that it be kept *tapu* (sacred).The other national parks see an equal share of visitors, many of whom come to tramp one of New Zealand's nine **Great Walks.** Unique to New Zealand, the Great Walks are designated multi-day hikes equipped with extensive overnight huts and camping facilities (see p. 43 for detailed information).

The **Department of Conservation (DOC)** in New Zealand is involved in many projects to maintain the country's natural beauty (www.doc.govt.nz/cons/cons.htm). In addition to protecting 30% of the land and working with other specialized groups in conservation efforts, the DOC currently oversees 13 marine reserves and regulates the dolphin and whalewatching industries. It plays an active role in habitat protection, predator control programs, relocation of species to safer areas, and conducts surveys and research on the current status of endangered wildlife. A new project involving six "mainland island habitats" (isolated areas on the mainland of New Zealand) allows the DOC to restore endangered species' habitats by managing introduced pests. The DOC strives to protect the endemic and endangered animals of New Zealand in a variety of ways: it regulates the fishing industry, tracks flight patterns, cares for breeding sites of the albatross, rescues beached whales, relocates and cares for kiwi eggs (the kiwibird is now vanishing at an annual rate of almost 6%), creates reserves for and curbs illegal poaching of the keruru, and educates New Zealanders on the importance of wildlife preservation.

NEW ZEALAND

ESSENTIALS

WHEN TO GO

The best time to visit New Zealand depends on the type of activities (warm or cold weather) you are most interested in and your sensitivity to crowds (which increase dramatically during major holidays). If you are traveling to New Zealand from the Northern Hemisphere, be aware that the **seasons are reversed.** Summer arrives in December and lasts roughly until February; winter is from June to August. New Zealand enjoys its **high season** in the warmest months (Nov.-Feb.). Certain areas such as the Tongariro region in the North Island and the ski fields of the South Island draw their biggest crowds in the **winter** (June-Aug.), when the ski season is in full swing. **Major national holidays** add considerable congestion to New Zealand's highways and byways (for dates, see p. 389). During these times, hordes of pleasure-seeking New Zealand families add to the mix of tourists from abroad, and advance reservations for transportation and accommodations become necessary. Christmas through January is particularly busy. You might consider traveling toward the beginning (Oct.-Nov.) or end (Mar.-Apr.) of the summer. If cooler, wetter, and less predictable weather doesn't bother you, you might simply wait until the low season arrives and the crowds disappear. Some areas and activities shut down during low season, however, so you'll want to read on and weigh your options before you decide. Whenever you go to New Zealand, don't worry—you'll never be at a loss for beauty and excitement.

CLIMATE

Year-round, the temperature fluctuation is far from extreme, even from the tip of the North Island to the bottom of the South Island. A prevailing wind blows from the west all year, creating weather systems in mountainous areas which can change instantaneously, so be prepared. Rainfall in most of the North Island and the north end of the South Island is heaviest in the winter (June-Aug.), although the infamous summer rainfall on the West Coast of the South Island can total seven or eight meters annually. The following chart gives the average high and low temperatures during four representative months of the year.

City/Area	January °C	°F	April °C	°F	July °C	°F	October °C	°F
Auckland	16-23	61-73	13-19	55-66	8-13	46-55	11-17	52-63
Bay of Islands	14-25	57-77	11-21	52-70	7-16	45-61	9-19	48-67
Christchurch	12-21	54-70	7-17	45-63	2-10	36-50	7-17	45-63
Dunedin	10-19	50-66	7-15	45-59	3-9	37-48	6-15	43-59
Invercargill	9-18	48-65	6-15	43-59	0-11	34-50	5-15	41-59
Napier	14-24	57-75	10-19	50-66	5-13	41-55	9-19	48-66
Nelson	13-22	55-72	8-18	46-64	3-13	37-55	7-17	45-63
Queenstown	10-22	50-72	6-16	43-61	1-10	34-50	5-16	41-61
Rotorua	12-24	54-75	9-18	48-64	4-13	39-55	7-17	45-63
Wellington	13-21	55-70	11-17	52-63	6-12	43-54	9-16	48-61

DOCUMENTS AND FORMALITIES

ENTRANCE REQUIREMENTS AND RECOMMENDATIONS.
Passport (p. 24): Required for all visitors.
Visa (p. 25): Not usually required unless you are planning to work, study, or seek medical treatment. Contact an embassy or consulate for specific information.
Inoculations: None required.
Work Permit (p. 25): Required for all foreigners planning to work in New Zealand.
Driving Permit (p. 53): Recommended. Required by a few car rental agencies.

NEW ZEALAND'S EMBASSIES & CONSULATES

Australia: High Commission, Commonwealth Ave., **Canberra** ACT 2600 (tel. (02) 6270 4211; fax 6273 3194). Consulate-General, Level 14, Gold Fields Building, 1 Alfred St., Circular Quay (GPO Box 365), **Sydney,** NSW 1041 (tel. (02) 9247 1344; fax 9247 1754). Passports: tel. (02) 9247 7500; fax 9247 1757; www.passports.govt.nz. Immigration information: tel. (02) 9247 1511; fax 9247 1752; info line 190 222 000 96; www.immigration.govt.nz.

Canada: High Commission, Suite 727, 99 Bank St. **Ottawa,** ONT K1P 6G3 (tel. (613) 238-5991; fax 238-5707; www.nzhcottawa.org). All visa queries: tel. (613) 238-6097; fax 238-5707.

Ireland: Consulate General, 46 Upper Mount St., **Dublin** 2 (tel. (01) 676 2464; fax 676 2489).

South Africa: High Commission, Private bag X17, Hatfield, **Pretoria** 0028 (tel. (012) 342 8656; fax 342 8640).

U.K.: High Commission, New Zealand House, The Haymarket, **London** SW1Y 4TQ. Visa queries: tel. (0171) 973 0366; fax 973 0370. Passport queries: tel. (0171) 930 8422; fax 973 0370.

U.S.: Embassy, 37 Observatory Circle NW, **Washington, D.C.,** 20008 (tel. (202) 328-4848; fax 667-5227). Consulate-General, Suite 1150, 12400 Wilshire Blvd., **Los Angeles,** CA 90025 (tel. (310) 207-1605; fax 207-3605).

EMBASSIES & CONSULATES IN NEW ZEALAND

Australia: Consulate General, Union House, 132-138 Quay St. (Private Bag 92023), **Auckland** 1 (tel. (09) 303 2429; fax 377 0798). High Commission, 72-78 Hobson St. (P.O. Box 4036), **Wellington** (tel. (04) 473 6411; fax 498 7118).

Canada: High Commission, 61 Molesworth St. (P.O. Box 12049), **Wellington** (tel. (04) 473 9577; fax 471 2082).

Ireland: Consulate General, Dingwall Building, 2nd fl., 87 Queens St. (P.O. Box 279), **Auckland** (tel. (09) 302 2867; fax 302 2420).

South Africa: Honorary Consul, Consulate of the Republic of South Africa: National Mutual Corporate Superannuation Services Ltd., 80 The Terrace (P.O. Box 1692), **Wellington** (tel. (04) 474 4953; fax 471 0504).

U.K.: Consulate General, 151 Queens St. (Private Bag 92014), **Auckland** (tel. (09) 303 2973; fax 303 1836). High Commission, 44 Hill St. (P.O. Box 1812), **Wellington** (tel. (04) 472 6049; fax 473 4982).

U.S.: Consular services, General Building, 4th fl., 29 Shortland St. (Private Bag 92022), **Auckland** (tel. (09) 303 2724; fax 366 0870).

PASSPORTS

REQUIREMENTS
All visitors need valid passports to enter New Zealand. Passports must be valid for at least three months beyond the time you intend to stay; returning home with an expired passport is illegal, and may result in a fine.

PHOTOCOPIES
It is a good idea to photocopy the page of your passport that contains your photograph, passport number, and other identifying information, along with other important documents such as visas, travel insurance policies, airplane tickets, and traveler's check serial numbers, in case you lose anything. Carry one set of copies in a safe place apart from the originals and leave another set at home. Consulates also recommend that you carry an expired passport or an official copy of your birth certificate in a part of your baggage separate from other documents.

LOST PASSPORTS
If you lose your passport, immediately notify the local police and the nearest embassy or consulate of your home government. To expedite its replacement, you will need to know all information previously recorded and show identification and proof of citizenship. In some cases, a replacement may take weeks to process, and it may be valid only for a limited time. Any visas stamped in your old passport will be irretrievably lost. In an emergency, ask for immediate temporary traveling papers that will permit you to reenter your home country.

NEW PASSPORTS
All applications for new passports or renewals should be filed several weeks or months in advance of your planned departure date. Most passport offices do offer emergency passport services for an extra charge. Citizens residing abroad who need a passport or renewal should contact their nearest embassy or consulate.

Australia: Citizens must apply for a passport in person at a post office, a passport office (found in most major cities), or an Australian diplomatic mission overseas. New adult passports cost AUS$126 (for a 32-page passport) or AUS$188 (64-page), and a child's is AUS$63 (32-page) or AUS$94 (64-page). Adult passports are valid for 10 years and child passports for 5 years. For more info, call toll-free 13 12 32, or visit www.dfat.gov.au/passports.

Canada: Application forms are available at all passport offices, Canadian missions, many travel agencies, and Northern Stores in northern communities. Passports cost CDN$60, plus a CDN$25 consular fee, are valid for 5 years, and are not renewable. For additional info, contact the Canadian Passport Office, Department of Foreign Affairs and International Trade, Ottawa, ON, K1A OG3 (tel. (613) 994-3500; www.dfait-maeci.gc.ca/passport). Travelers may also call 800-567-6868 (24hr.).

Ireland: Citizens can apply for a passport by mail to either the Department of Foreign Affairs, Passport Office, Setanta Centre, Molesworth St., Dublin 2 (tel. (01) 671 1633; fax 671 1092; www.irlgov.ie/iveagh), or the Passport Office, Irish Life Building, 1A South Mall, Cork (tel. (021) 27 25 25). Obtain an application at a local Garda station or post office, or request one from a passport office. Passports cost IR£45 and are valid for 10 years. Citizens under 18 or over 65 can request a 3-year passport that costs IR£10.

South Africa: South African passports are issued only in Pretoria. However, all applications must still be submitted or forwarded to the applicable office of a South African consulate. Tourist passports, valid for 10 years, cost around SAR80. Children under 16 must be issued their own passports, valid for 5 years, which cost around SAR60. Time for the completion of an application is normally 3 months or more from the time of submission. For further information, contact the nearest Department of Home Affairs Office, or check the web at www.southafrica-newyork.net/passport.htm.

United Kingdom: Full passports are valid for 10 years (5 years if under 16). Application forms are available at passport offices, main post offices, and many travel agents. Apply by mail or in person to one of the passport offices, located in London, Liverpool, Newport, Peterborough, Glasgow, or Belfast. The fee is UK£31, UK£11 for children under 16. The process takes about four weeks, but the London office offers a five-day, walk-in rush service; arrive early. The U.K. Passport Agency can be reached by phone at (0870) 521 04 10, and more information is available at www.open.gov.uk/ukpass/ukpass.htm.

United States: Citizens may apply for a passport at any federal or state courthouse or post office authorized to accept passport applications, or at a U.S. Passport Agency, located in most major cities. Refer to the "U.S. Government, State Department" section of the telephone directory or the local post office for addresses. Passports are valid for 10 years (5 years if under 18) and cost US$60 (under 18 US$40). Passports may be renewed by mail or in person for US$40. Processing takes 3-4 weeks. For more info, contact the U.S. Passport Information's 24-hour recorded message (tel. (202) 647-0518) or look on the web at travel.state.gov/passport_services.html.

VISAS AND PERMITS

Citizens of the U.S., Canada, Ireland, South Africa, the U.K., and most European nations do not need a **visa** to enter New Zealand. Australian citizens need neither a visa nor a permit to visit or work in New Zealand. For those travelers who need them, visas are available at most embassies and consulates and are usually valid for three months.

Upon arrival, those travelers not requiring visas are granted **visitor permits.** To qualify for a visitor permit, you must display a valid ticket to a country to which you have the right of entry; you may also need to display sufficient funds to support yourself during your stay (usually NZ$1000). Major credit cards and traveler's checks constitute sufficient funds. The visitor permit allows you to visit New Zealand for three months (six months for citizens of the U.K.); to extend your stay, you must reapply at an immigration office before your current permit expires.

Admission as a visitor does not include the right to work, which is authorized only by a **work permit** or visa. Entering New Zealand to study in a course of three months or less is covered by a visitor permit. For details on longer courses of study or work in new Zealand, see **Alternatives to Tourism** (p. 62).

IDENTIFICATION

When you travel, always carry two or more forms of identification on your person, including at least one photo ID. A passport combined with a driver's license or birth certificate usually serves as adequate proof of your identity and citizenship. Many establishments, especially banks, require several IDs before cashing traveler's checks. Never carry all your forms of ID together, however; you risk being left entirely without ID or funds in case of theft or loss.

STUDENT AND TEACHER IDENTIFICATION

The **International Student Identity Card (ISIC)** is the most widely accepted form of student identification. However, because of the increasing number of forgeries, you should also bring your institution-specific card. Flashing the ISIC can procure you discounts for sights, theaters, museums, accommodations, meals, train, ferry, bus, and airplane transportation, and other services. The international identification cards are preferable to institution-specific cards because the tourism personnel in New Zealand are taught to recognize the former. For U.S. cardholders traveling abroad, the ISIC also provides insurance benefits (see p. 36). In addition, cardholders have access to a toll-free 24hr. ISIC helpline whose multilingual staff can provide assistance in medical, legal, and financial emergencies overseas (tel. 800-626-2427 in the U.S. and Canada; elsewhere call collect 44 181 666 90 25).

Many student travel agencies around the world issue ISICs, including STA Travel in Australia and New Zealand; Travel CUTS in Canada; USIT in Ireland and Northern Ireland; SASTS in South Africa; Campus Travel and STA Travel in the U.K.; Council Travel, STA Travel, and via the web (www.counciltravel.com/idcards/index.htm) in the U.S.; and any other travel agency with a student focus (see p. 49). When you apply for the card, request a copy of the International Student Identity Card Handbook, which lists some of the available discounts by country. You can also write to Council for a copy. The card is valid from September of one year to December of the following year and costs AUS$15, CDN$15, or US$20. Applicants must be at least 12 years old and degree-seeking students of a secondary or post-secondary school. Because of the proliferation of phony ISICs, many airlines and some other services require additional proof of student identity, such as your school ID card. The **International Teacher Identity Card (ITIC)** offers the same insurance coverage, and similar but limited discounts The fee is AUS$13, UK£5, or US$20.

For more information on these cards, contact the **International Student Travel Confederation (ISTC),** Herengracht 479, 1017 BS Amsterdam, Netherlands (from abroad call 31 20 421 28 00; fax 421 28 10; email istcinfo@istc.org; www.istc.org).

YOUTH IDENTIFICATION

The International Student Travel Confederation also issues a discount card to travelers who are 25 years old or younger but not students. Known as the **International Youth Travel Card (IYTC)** (formerly the **GO25 Card**), this one-year card offers many of the same benefits as the ISIC, and most organizations that sell the ISIC also sell the IYTC. A brochure that lists discounts is free when you purchase the card. To apply, you will need either a passport, valid driver's license, or copy of a birth certificate, and a passport-sized photo with your name printed on the back. The fee is US$20.

CUSTOMS

As an island nation, New Zealand is free from many pests and crop blights, and they'd like to keep it that way. Upon **entering** New Zealand, you must declare all food, plant, and animal goods, so look out for the blue declaration of goods forms. Quarantined goods may or may not be confiscated, but they must be declared. Camping equipment must also be declared. Customs officials will likely inspect your equipment and if it is used, they may clean it for you for a charge.

Personal effects and goods up to a total combined value of NZ$700 are admitted free of duty or **Goods and Services Tax (GST)** (see p. 31). Anything beyond the allowance must be declared and is charged a duty in addition to the GST. Visitors over 17 are also allowed to enter with the following concessions duty- and tax-free: 200 cigarettes, 50 cigars, or 250g of tobacco, or a mixture of all three not weighing more than 250g; 4.5L of wine (six 750mL bottles) or 4.5L of beer; and one bottle containing not more than 1125mL of liquor.

Upon **returning home,** you must declare all articles you acquired abroad and pay a **duty** on the value of those articles that exceed the allowance established by your country's customs service. The GST is not refundable upon leaving. Goods and gifts purchased at **duty-free** shops abroad are not exempt from duty or sales tax at your point of return; you must declare these items as well. "Duty-free" merely means no tax in the country of purchase.

Keeping receipts for purchases made abroad will help establish values when you return. It is wise to make a list of any valuables that you carry with you from home; if you register this list with customs before your departure and have an official stamp it, you will avoid import duty charges and ensure an easy passage upon your return. Be especially careful to document items manufactured abroad. Check with the nearest embassy or consulate for more information, or contact the following customs departments in your country.

Australia: Australian Customs National Information Line 1 300 363 263; www.customs.gov.au.

Canada: Canadian Customs, 2265 St. Laurent Blvd., Ottawa, ON K1G 4K3 (tel. (613) 993-0534 or 24hr. automated service 800-461-9999; www.revcan.ca).

Ireland: The Collector of Customs and Excise, The Custom House, Dublin 1 (tel. (01) 679 27 77; fax 671 20 21; email taxes@revenue.iol.ie; www.revenue.ie/customs.htm).

South Africa: Commissioner for Customs and Excise, Private Bag X47, Pretoria 0001 (tel. (012) 314 99 11; fax 328 64 78).

United Kingdom: Her Majesty's Customs and Excise, Custom House, Nettleton Road, Heathrow Airport, Hounslow, Middlesex TW6 2LA (tel. (0181) 910 36 02/35 66; fax 910 37 65; www.hmce.gov.uk).

United States: U.S. Customs Service, Box 7407, Washington D.C. 20044 (tel. (202) 927-6724; www.customs.ustreas.gov).

MONEY

If you stay in hostels, prepare your own food, and stick mostly to the free and low-budget natural attractions, you could probably get by on NZ$40-50 per day. Transportation, dining out, and high-adrenaline adventure activities will dramatically increase this figure. No matter how low your budget, you will need to keep handy a larger amount of cash than usual, especially if you are traveling into more rural areas where credit cards might not be widely accepted.

CURRENCY AND EXCHANGE

New Zealand's unit of currency is the New Zealand dollar. Coins come in denominations of 5, 10, 20, and 50 cents, $1 and $2; notes come in denominations of $5, $10, $20, $50, and $100. Typical bank hours are Monday through Friday 9am to 4:30pm. The currency chart below is based on exchange rates from August 1999. Current exchange rates can be checked at www.bloomberg.com.

US$1 = NZ$1.89	NZ$1 = US$0.53
CDN$1 = NZ$1.23	NZ$1 = CDN$0.78
UK£1 = NZ$3.03	NZ$1 = UK£0.33
IR£1 = NZ$2.52	NZ$1 = IR£0.40
EUR1 = NZ$1.98	NZ$1 = EUR0.50
AUS$1 = NZ$1.23	NZ$1 = AUS$0.82
SAR1= NZ$0.31	NZ$1 = SAR3.24

As a general rule, it's cheaper to convert money in New Zealand. It's good to bring enough foreign currency to last for the first 24-72 hours of a trip to avoid being penniless after banking hours or on a holiday. Travelers living in the U.S. can get foreign currency from the comfort of their home; **Capital Foreign Exchange** (tel. 888-842-0880) or **International Currency Express** (tel. 888-278-6628) will deliver foreign currency or traveler's checks overnight (US$15) or second-day (US$12) at competitive exchange rates.

Watch out for commission rates and check newspapers for the standard rate of exchange. Banks generally have the best rates. A good rule of thumb is only to go to banks or a currency exchange bureau that have at most a 5% margin between their buy and sell prices. Since you lose money with each transaction, convert in large sums (unless the currency is depreciating rapidly). Also, using an **ATM card** or a **credit card** (see p. 29) will often get you the best possible rates.

If you use traveler's checks or bills, carry some in small denominations (US$50 or less), especially for times when you are forced to exchange money at disadvantageous rates. However, it is good to carry a range of denominations, since charges may be levied per check cashed.

Money From Home In Minutes.

If you're stuck for cash on your travels, don't panic. Millions of people trust Western Union to transfer money in minutes to 165 countries and over 50,000 locations worldwide. Our record of safety and reliability is second to none. For more information, call Western Union: USA 1-800-325-6000, Canada 1-800-235-0000. Wherever you are, you're never far from home.

www.westernunion.com

The fastest way to send money worldwide.

ESSENTIALS

TRAVELER'S CHECKS

Traveler's checks are one of the safest and least troublesome means of carrying funds, since they can be refunded if stolen. Several agencies and banks sell them, usually for face value plus a small percentage commission. Buying traveler's checks in New Zealand dollars can be difficult, as many major check companies do not yet offer them.

American Express and **Visa** are the most widely recognized. If you're ordering checks, do so well in advance, especially if you are requesting large sums. Each agency provides refunds if your checks are lost or stolen, and many provide additional services, such as toll-free refund hotlines in the countries you're visiting, emergency message services, and stolen credit card assistance.

In order to collect a **refund for lost or stolen checks,** keep your check receipts separate from your checks and store them in a safe place or with a traveling companion. Record check numbers when you cash them, never countersign your checks until you are ready to cash them, and always bring your passport with you when you plan to use the checks.

American Express: Call 800 251 902 in Australia; in New Zealand 0800 441 068; in the U.K. (0800) 52 13 13; in the U.S. and Canada 800-221-7282. Elsewhere, call U.S. collect 1-801-964-6665. www.americanexpress.com. Travelers checks in New Zealand dollars are not available from American Express, but checks can be purchased for a small fee (1-4%) at American Express Travel Service Offices, banks, and American Automobile Association offices. AAA members (see p. 53) can buy the checks commission-free. American Express offices cash their checks commission-free, but often at slightly worse rates than banks. *Cheques for Two* can be signed by either of two people traveling together.

Citicorp: Call 800-645-6556 in the U.S. and Canada; in Europe, the Middle East, or Africa, call the London office at 44 171 508 7007; from elsewhere, call U.S. collect 1-813-623-1709. Commission 1-2%. Guaranteed hand-delivery of traveler's checks when a refund location is not convenient. Call 24hr.

Thomas Cook MasterCard: From the U.S., Canada, or Caribbean call 800-223-7373; from the U.K. call (0800) 622 101; from elsewhere, call U.K. collect 44 1733 318 950. Commission 2%. Thomas Cook offices cash checks commission-free.

Visa: Call 800-227-6811 in the U.S.; in the U.K. (0800) 895 078; from elsewhere, call U.K. 44 1733 318 949 and reverse the charges. Any of the above numbers can tell you the location of their nearest office.

CREDIT CARDS

Credit cards are generally accepted in all but the smallest businesses in New Zealand. Major credit cards—**MasterCard** and **Visa** are widespread—can be used to extract cash advances in dollars from associated banks and teller machines throughout New Zealand. Credit card companies get the wholesale exchange rate, which is generally 5% better than the retail rate used by banks and other currency exchange establishments. **American Express** cards also work in some ATMs, as well as at AmEx offices and major airports. All such machines require a **Personal Identification Number (PIN).** You must ask your credit card company for a PIN before you leave; without it, you will be unable to withdraw cash with your credit card outside your home country. If you already have a PIN, check with the company to make sure it will work in New Zealand.

Credit cards often offer an array of other services, from insurance to emergency assistance. Check with your company to find out what is covered.

CREDIT CARD COMPANIES

Visa (U.S. tel. 800-336-8472) and **MasterCard** (U.S. tel. 800-307-7309) are issued in cooperation with individual banks and some other organizations. **American Express**

(U.S. tel. 800-843-2273) has an annual fee of up to US$55, depending on the card. Cardholder services include the option of cashing personal checks at AmEx offices, a 24-hour hotline with medical and legal assistance in emergencies (tel. 800-554-2639 in U.S. and Canada; elsewhere call U.S. collect 1-202-554-2639), and the American Express Travel Service. Benefits include assistance in changing airline, hotel, and car rental reservations, baggage loss and flight insurance, sending mailgrams and international cables, and holding your mail at AmEx offices.

ATMS

New Zealand has more ATMs (Automated Teller Machines) per capita than almost any other country in the world. Depending on the system that your home bank uses, you can probably access your own personal bank account whenever you need money. ATMs get the same wholesale exchange rate as credit cards. Despite these perks, do some research before relying too heavily on automation. There is often a limit on the amount of money you can withdraw per day (usually about US$500, depending on the type of card and account), and computer networks sometimes fail. If you're traveling from the U.S. or Canada, memorize your PIN code in numeral form since machines elsewhere often don't have letters on their keys. Also, if your PIN is longer than four digits, ask your bank whether the first four digits will work, or whether you need a new number.

The two most common types of ATMs in New Zealand are those owned by the **national banks (ANZ)** and the **Bank of New Zealand (BNZ).** Both carry the two major international money networks, **Cirrus** and **PLUS.** Cirrus usually charges US$3-5 to withdraw overseas; check with your bank. The back of your ATM card will have the symbol of networks with which it is compatible. To locate ATMs, use www.visa.com/pd/atm or www.mastercard.com/atm.

EFTPOS

Eftpos (Electronic Funds Transfer at Point Of Sale) is an extremely common way for New Zealanders to pay for goods. ATM cards (from New Zealand banks only) swiped at the register work as debit cards, withdrawing money directly from your bank account. This means that people can carry less cash, without worrying about credit card bills. If you'll be in New Zealand for a couple of months or more, the convenience of this service may justify opening a New Zealand bank account. Two forms of identification are required; your home driver's license and your passport are the most sure-fire bets. Be sure to bring along home bank statements from the last three months; although you are allowed to open an account without them, they expedite the process enormously. You can also expect the bank to perform a routine check on your credit history. Accounts can be ready in as little as an hour if you provide bank statements from home.

GETTING MONEY FROM HOME

AMERICAN EXPRESS. Cardholders can withdraw cash from their checking accounts at any of AmEx's major offices and many of its representatives' offices, up to US$1000 every 21 days (no service charge, no interest). AmEx also offers Express Cash at any of their ATMs in New Zealand. Express Cash withdrawals are automatically debited from the Cardmember's checking account or line of credit. Green card holders may withdraw up to US$1000 in a seven day period. There is a 2% transaction fee for each cash withdrawal, with a US$2.50 minimum/$20 maximum. To enroll in Express Cash, Cardmembers may call 800-CASH NOW (227-4669) in the U.S.; outside the U.S. call collect 1-336-668-5041. The AmEx national number in New Zealand is 0800 656 660 (toll-free) or 367 4247 in Auckland.

WESTERN UNION. Travelers from the U.S., Canada, and the U.K. can wire money abroad through Western Union's international money transfer services. In the U.S., call 800-325-6000; in the U.K., call (0800) 833 833; in Canada, call 800-235-0000; in New Zealand, call 0800 270 000. The rates for sending cash are generally US$10-11 cheaper than with a credit card, and the money is usually available at the place you're sending it to within an hour.

U.S. STATE DEPARTMENT (U.S. CITIZENS ONLY). In emergencies, U.S. citizens can have money sent via the State Department. For US$15, they will forward money within hours to the nearest consular office, which will disburse it according to instructions. The office serves only Americans in the direst of straits abroad; non-American travelers should contact their embassies for information on wiring cash. Check with the State Department or the nearest U.S. embassy or consulate for the quickest way to have the money sent. Contact the Overseas Citizens Service, American Citizens Services, Consular Affairs, Room 4811, U.S. Department of State, Washington, D.C. 20520 (tel. (202) 647-5225; nights, Sundays, and holidays 647-4000; fax (on demand only) 647-3000; travel.state.gov).

TAXES AND TIPPING

A **departure tax** is levied at the airport. The prices depend on the airport, but are generally NZ$20-25 for those over 12 (Auckland NZ$20, Christchurch and Wellington NZ$65). Those under 10 are usually charged NZ$10. This fee must be paid in New Zealand dollars. It is sometimes included in your flight price. A 12.5% **Goods and Services Tax (GST)** is applied to all goods and is usually included in the displayed price.

   Tipping is not customary or expected in New Zealand establishments. In restaurants it is always included in the price of the meal. If the service provided is exceptional, you may consider offering a small tip, but it is by no means necessary.

SAFETY AND SECURITY

EMERGENCIES	The emergency number in all of New Zealand is **111.**

PERSONAL SAFETY

With minimal crime, New Zealand enjoys its reputation as a warm and fuzzy tourist haven. As is true anywhere, however, tourists are probably more vulnerable to crime than most—they often carry large amounts of cash and are not as street savvy as locals. To avoid unwanted attention, try to blend in as much as possible. If you are traveling alone, be sure that someone at home knows your itinerary. Because the friendliness of New Zealanders is so infectious, you may be tempted to trust someone quicker than usual, but it is always best to retain a certain measure of caution.

   Nightlife in the cities is rife with tourists and is probably safer than in many other countries. In smaller towns, nightlife may be largely a local affair and may get rough around the edges. If you are concerned, a good **self-defense course** can give you more concrete ways to react to aggression (see **Women Travelers,** p. 58).

FINANCIAL SECURITY

To prevent easy theft, don't keep all your valuables (money, important documents) in one place. **Photocopies** of important documents allow you to recover them in case they are lost or filched. Carry one copy separate from the documents and leave another copy at home. Label every piece of luggage both inside and out. **Don't put a wallet with money in your back pocket.** Secure packs with small combination padlocks which slip through the two zippers. A **money belt** is the best way to carry cash; you can buy one at most camping supply stores. A **neck pouch** is equally safe, although far less accessible. Avoid keeping anything precious in a fanny-pack (even if it's worn on your stomach): your valuables will be highly visible and easy to steal. Keep some money separate from the rest to use in an emergency or in case of theft. In hostel shares, don't tempt your roommates by leaving a wallet or purse unattended.

GETTING AROUND

Some of the more dangerous situations in New Zealand occur on the roads. **Drunk driving** among New Zealanders is a major problem. As a result, police occasionally stops all traffic on certain roads in order to give each driver a quick breath test. The speed limit is 100 kph (63 mph) on major roads. Seatbelts are mandatory. Almost all roads are sealed and in good condition, though they may be more narrow than foreign travelers are accustomed to. For long drives in desolate areas invest in a cellular phone and a roadside assistance program (see p. 53). Be sure to park your vehicle in a garage or well-traveled area, and use a steering wheel locking device in larger cities. **Sleeping in your car** is one of the most dangerous (and often illegal) ways to get your rest. If your car breaks down, wait for the police to assist you. Let's Go does not recommend **hitchhiking,** particularly for women—see p. 51 for more information.

TRAVEL ADVISORIES

The following government offices provide travel information and advisories by telephone or on their websites: the **Australian Department of Foreign Affairs and Trade** (tel. (02) 6261 1111; www.dfat.gov.au); the **Canadian Department of Foreign Affairs and International Trade (DFAIT)** (tel. 800-267-8376 or 944-4000 from Ottawa; www.dfait-maeci.gc.ca); the **United Kingdom Foreign and Commonwealth Office** (tel. (0171) 238 4503; www.fco.gov.uk); and the **United States Department of State** (tel. (202) 647-5225; travel.state.gov).

DRUGS AND ALCOHOL

Remember that you are subject to the laws of the country in which you travel, not to those of your home country, and it is your responsibility to familiarize yourself with these laws before leaving. The legal **drinking age** is 18. First-time drunk-driving offenders can receive three months imprisonment, a $4500 fine, and a six-month suspended license. Illegal drugs are, well, illegal. Possession of marijuana can result in a three-month imprisonment and a $1000 fine, while selling is punishable with a maximum sentence of eight years. Possession of harder drugs can result in a $1000 fine and a six-month imprisonment; selling them can put you in jail for life. If you carry **prescription drugs** while you travel, it is vital to have a copy of the prescriptions themselves and a note from a doctor, both readily accessible at country borders.

HEALTH

In New Zealand, common sense is the simplest prescription for good health. Travelers complain most often about their feet and their gut: drink lots of fluids to prevent dehydration and constipation, wear sturdy, broken-in shoes and clean socks, and use talcum powder to keep your feet dry.

New Zealand offers a high standard of medical facilities, both public and private. However, these are not free; it is important to know that doctors often expect to be paid in cash right away for their services. A foreigner's office visit to most medical treatment centers costs about NZ$35. It may be useful to research various **insurance** options before your trip (see p. 36). With the exception of Medicare, most health insurance plans cover members' medical emergencies during trips abroad; check with your insurance carrier to be sure.

It is common for pharmacies to take turns being the town's **late-night pharmacy;** call the local hospital to get the number.

BEFORE YOU GO

PACKING

For minor health problems, bring a compact **first-aid kit,** including bandages, aspirin or other pain killer, antibiotic cream, a thermometer, a Swiss army knife with tweezers, moleskin, decongestant for colds, motion sickness remedy, medicine for diarrhea or stomach problems, sunscreen, insect repellent, and burn ointment. **Contact lens** wearers should bring an extra pair, a copy of the prescription, a pair of glasses, extra solution, and eyedrops. Those who use heat disinfection might consider switching to chemical cleansers for the duration of the trip.

In your passport, write the names of any people you wish to be contacted in case of a medical emergency, and also list any **allergies** or medical conditions you would want doctors to be aware of. Allergy sufferers might want to obtain a full supply of any necessary medication before the trip. Carry up-to-date, legible prescriptions or a statement from your doctor stating the medication's trade name, manufacturer, chemical name, and dosage. While traveling, be sure to keep all medication with you in your carry-on luggage.

IMMUNIZATIONS

Travel to New Zealand does not require vaccination against infectious diseases. Travelers should be sure that the following vaccines are up to date: MMR (for measles, mumps, and rubella); DTaP or Td (for diptheria, tetanus, and pertussis); OPV (for polio); HbCV (for haemophilus influenza B); and HBV (for hepatitis B).

MEDICAL CONDITIONS

Those with medical conditions (e.g., diabetes, allergies to antibiotics, epilepsy, heart conditions) may want to obtain a stainless-steel **Medic Alert** identification tag (US$35 the first year, and $15 annually thereafter), which identifies the condition and gives a 24-hour collect-call information number. Contact the Medic Alert Foundation, 2323 Colorado Ave., Turlock, CA 95382 (tel. 800-825-3785; www.medicalert.org). Diabetics can contact the **American Diabetes Association,** 1660 Duke St., Alexandria, VA 22314 (tel. 800-232-3472), to receive copies of the article "Travel and Diabetes" and a diabetic ID card, which explains the carrier's diabetic status.

MEDICAL ASSISTANCE

If you are concerned about being able to access medical support while traveling, contact one of the following two services. **Global Emergency Medical Services (GEMS)** has a product called *MedPass* that provides 24-hour international medical assistance and support coordinated through registered nurses who have online access to your medical information, your primary physician, and a worldwide network of screened, credentialed doctors and hospitals. Subscribers also receive a personal medical record that contains vital information in case of emergencies, and GEMS will pay for medical evacuation if necessary. Prices start at about US$35 for a 30-day trip and run up to about $100 for annual services. For more information, contact them at 2001 Westside Dr. #120, Alpharetta, GA 30004 (tel. 800-860-1111; fax (770) 475-0058; www.globalems.com). The **International Association for Medical Assistance to Travelers (IAMAT)** has free membership and offers a directory of doctors who treat members for a set fee. There are chapters in: the **U.S.,** 417 Center St., Lewiston, NY 14092 (tel. (716) 754-4883, 8am-4pm; fax (519) 836-3412; email iamat@sentex.net; www.sentex.net/~iamat); and **Canada,** 40 Regal Road, Guelph, ON, N1K 1B5 (tel. (519) 836-0102) or 1287 St. Clair Avenue West, Toronto, ON M6E 1B8 (tel. (416) 652-0137; fax (519) 836-3412).

ONCE THERE

JET LAG

Many travelers to New Zealand will arrive after a flight of over 12 hours. In such cases, jet lag can be rather severe and take a few days to overcome. To minimize the effects of jet lag, "reset" your body's clock by adopting the time of your destination as soon as you board the plane. While it may be tempting to sleep, some say it is best to force yourself to make it through at least to early evening. If you will be arriving in the morning, one strategy is to stay up all night before your departure and sleep on the plane. On long flights, search for and claim open rows of seats for better sleep. Some travelers also take herbal supplements such as melatonin (or a few glasses of free in-flight wine) to help reset their body clocks.

HOT AND COLD

The most dangerous safety hazards in a country like New Zealand are often the most obvious ones. **Heat exhaustion,** characterized by **dehydration** and salt deficiency, can lead to fatigue, headaches, and wooziness. Avoid heat exhaustion by drinking plenty of clear fluids and eating salty foods, like crackers. Always drink enough liquids to keep your urine clear. Alcoholic beverages are dehydrating, as are coffee, strong tea, and caffeinated sodas. Wear a hat, sunglasses, and a lightweight longsleeve shirt in the hot sun. Continuous heat stress can eventually lead to **heatstroke,** characterized by rising body temperature, severe headache, and cessation of sweating. Heatstroke is rare but serious, and victims must be cooled off with wet towels and taken to a doctor as soon as possible.

Depleted ozone levels and unpolluted air combine to make New Zealand a high risk area for **sunburn.** Even if you're not prone to sunburn, you should apply sunscreen liberally and often. Protect your eyes with good sunglasses, since UV rays can damage the retina of the eye after too much exposure. If you become sunburned, drink more fluids than usual and apply Calamine or an aloe-based lotion.

In some areas of New Zealand during the winter, travelers are at risk of **hypothermia** and **frostbite.** A rapid drop in body temperature is the clearest warning sign of overexposure to cold. Victims may also shiver, feel exhausted, have poor coordination or slurred speech, hallucinate, or suffer amnesia. Seek medical help, and do not let hypothermia victims fall asleep—their body temperature will continue to drop and they may die. To avoid hypothermia, keep dry, wear layers, and stay out of the wind. In wet weather, wool and synthetics such as pile retain heat. Most other fabrics, especially cotton, will make you colder. When the temperature is below freezing, watch for frostbite. If a region of skin turns white, waxy, and cold, do not rub the area. Drink warm beverages, get dry, and slowly warm the area with dry fabric or steady body contact, until a doctor can be found.

PREVENTING DISEASE

New Zealand has few dangerous diseases that travelers should worry about. You can minimize the chances of contracting a disease while traveling by taking a few precautionary measures. When spending time in the outdoors, never drink water from outdoor sources that you have not treated yourself. To purify your own water, bring it to a rolling **boil** (simmering isn't enough) or treat it with iodine drops or tablets.

Parasites (tapeworms, etc.) hide in unsafe water and food. **Giardia,** for example, is a major concern for outdoor enthusiasts, acquired by drinking untreated water. It can stay with you for years. General symptoms of parasitic infections include swollen glands or lymph nodes, fever, rashes or itchiness, digestive problems, eye problems, and anemia. Boil your water, wear shoes, avoid bugs, and eat cooked food. **Amoebic Meningitis,** while rare, is a another serious infection, acquired by putting one's head under the hot, stagnant water in water holes. Symptoms include headaches, a stiff neck, extreme sensitivity to light, and even a coma. Many diseases are transmitted by insects—mainly mosquitoes, fleas, and lice. For information on taking precautions against **mosquitoes,** see **Wilderness Safety,** p. 45.

If you are concerned about disease in New Zealand, or if you will be continuing your travels to other areas of the South Pacific, consult the U.S. **Centers for Disease Control and Prevention (CDC)** (tel. 888-232-3299; www.cdc.gov), an excellent source of information for travelers. It maintains an international fax information service (the same information is available on their website).

ADDITIONAL HEALTH CONCERNS

AIDS, HIV, STDS

New Zealand does not screen incoming travelers for the HIV virus; however, restrictions may apply to those staying longer to work or study (contact your nearest consulate). For more information once in New Zealand, you can contact the **AIDS National Hotline** (tel. (0800) 802 437 or 358 0099 within Auckland), a 24-hour hotline that offers AIDS counseling and information. The hotline is sponsored by the **New Zealand AIDS Foundation,** P.O. Box 6663, Wellesley St., Auckland (tel. (09) 303 3124; fax 309 3149). For more information on AIDS, call the **U.S. Centers for Disease Control's** 24-hour hotline at 800-342-2437. In Europe, contact the **World Health Organization,** Attn: Global Program on AIDS, Avenue Appia 20, 1211 Geneva 27, Switzerland (tel. 44 22 791 21 11; fax 791 31 11), for statistical material on AIDS internationally.

Other **sexually transmitted diseases** (STDs) such as gonorrhea, chlamydia, genital warts, syphilis, and herpes are easier to catch than HIV, and some can be just as deadly. **Hepatitis B** and **C** are also serious diseases that can be transmitted through sexual contact. Warning signs for STDs include: swelling, sores, bumps, or blisters on sex organs, rectum, or mouth; burning and pain during urination and bowel movements; itching around sex organs; swelling or redness in the throat; flu-like symptoms with fever, chills, and aches. If these symptoms develop, see a doctor immediately. When having sex, condoms may protect you from certain STDs, but oral or even tactile contact can lead to transmission.

WOMEN'S HEALTH

Women traveling in unsanitary conditions are vulnerable to **urinary tract** and **bladder infections,** common and severely uncomfortable bacterial diseases that cause a burning sensation and painful and sometimes frequent urination. To avoid these infections, drink plenty of vitamin-C-rich juice and plenty of clean water, and urinate frequently, especially right after intercourse. Untreated, these infections can lead to kidney infections, sterility, and even death. Women are also susceptible to **vaginal yeast infections,** an illness likely to flare up in hot and humid climates. Wearing loosely fitting trousers or a skirt and cotton underwear will help. Bring supplies (such as Monostat or Gynelotrimin) if you are prone to infection. Some travelers opt for a natural alternative such as plain yogurt and lemon juice douche if other remedies are unavailable. Women who need an **abortion** should contact the **International Planned Parenthood Federation** in London (tel. 44 171 487 7900; fax 487 7950) for more information.

For more information, consult the *Handbook for Women Travellers*, by Maggie and Gemma Moss (Piatkus Books, US$15).

CONTRACEPTION

Contraceptive devices are legal and easily accessible in New Zealand; you might want to bring your favorite brand of condoms before you go, as type and quality vary. Women on the pill should bring enough to allow for possible loss or extended stays. Bring a prescription, since forms of the pill vary a good deal.

INSURANCE

Visitors who suffer personal injury by accident in New Zealand are covered by the local **Accident Compensation Co-Operation** (known locally as ACC), which entitles them to a claim, irrespective of fault. Some medical and hospital expenses are included in its benefits, but it does not cover lost wages outside of New Zealand.

Travel insurance generally covers four basic areas: medical/health problems, property loss, trip cancellation/interruption, and emergency evacuation. Although your regular insurance policies may well extend to travel-related accidents, you might consider purchasing travel insurance if the cost of a potential trip cancellation or interruption is greater than you can absorb.

Medical insurance (especially university policies) often covers costs incurred abroad; check with your provider. **Medicare does not cover foreign travel.** Canadians are protected by their home province's health insurance plan for up to 90 days after leaving the country; check with the provincial Ministry of Health or Health Plan Headquarters for details. Australians traveling in New Zealand are entitled to many of the services that they would receive at home as part of the Reciprocal Health Care Agreement. **Homeowners' insurance** (or your family's coverage) often covers theft during travel and loss of travel documents (passport, plane ticket, railpass, etc.) up to US$500.

INSURANCE PROVIDERS

ISIC and **ITIC** (see p. 25) provide basic insurance benefits, including US$100 per day of in-hospital sickness for a maximum of 60 days, US$3000 of accident-related medical reimbursement, and US$25,000 for emergency medical transport. **American Express** (tel. 800-528-4800) grants most cardholders car rental insurance (collision and theft, but not liability) and ground travel accident coverage of US$100,000 on flight purchases made with the card.

Prices for travel insurance purchased separately generally run about US$50 per week for full coverage, while trip cancellation/interruption may be purchased separately at a rate of about US$5.50 per US$100 of coverage. **Council** and **STA** (see p. 49 for complete listings) offer a range of plans that can supplement your basic insurance coverage. Other private insurance providers in the **U.S. and Canada** include: **Access America** (tel. 800-284-8300; fax (804) 673-1491); **Berkely Group/Carefree Travel Insurance** (tel. 800-323-3149 or (516) 294-0220; fax 294-1095; email info@berkely.com; www.berkely.com); **Globalcare Travel Insurance** (tel. 800-821-2488; fax (781) 592-7720; www.globalcare-cocco.com); and **Travel Assistance International** (tel. 800-821-2828 or (202) 828-5894; fax 828-5896; email wassist@aol.com; www.worldwide-assistance.com). Providers in the **U.K.** include **Campus Travel** (tel. (01865) 258 000; fax 792 378) and **Columbus Travel Insurance** (tel. (0171) 375 0011; fax 375 0022). In **Australia** try **CIC Insurance** (tel. (02) 9202 8000; fax 9202 8220).

PACKING

Pack according to the extremes of climate you may experience during your trip and the type of travel you'll be doing. **Pack light:** a good rule is to lay out only what you absolutely need, then take half the clothes and twice the money. The less you have, the less you have to lose (or store, or carry on your back).

Due to New Zealand's unpredictable weather patterns and occasionally fierce winds, a rain jacket and heavy sweater are absolute necessities. Gore-Tex® is a miracle fabric that's both waterproof and breathable. No matter where you are traveling, it's a good idea to bring a warm jacket, sturdy shoes, and thick socks. Remember that wool will keep you warm even when soaked through, whereas wet cotton is colder than wearing nothing at all. You may also want to add one outfit beyond the jeans and t-shirt uniform. **Formal shoes** (not sneakers) are necessary to get into some bars and nightclubs, though the dress code is generally casual.

If you plan to be doing a lot of hiking, see **Camping and the Outdoors**, p. 42.

LUGGAGE

If you plan to cover most of your itinerary by foot, a sturdy **frame backpack** is unbeatable—much more versatile than a suitcase, which is really only useful if you're not moving around a lot. **Internal-frame packs** mold better to your back, keep a lower center of gravity, and can flex adequately on difficult hikes that require a lot of bending and maneuvering. **External-frame packs** are more comfortable for long hikes over even terrain—like city streets—since they keep the weight higher and distribute it more evenly. Look for a pack with a strong, padded hip belt to transfer weight from your shoulders to your hips. Good packs cost anywhere from US$150 to US$500. Before you leave, pack your bag, strap it on, and imagine yourself walking uphill on hot asphalt for three hours; this should give you a sense of how important it is to pack lightly. Organizations that sell packs through mail-order are listed on p. 44.

In addition to your main vessel, a small backpack, rucksack, or courier bag may be useful as a **daypack** for sightseeing expeditions; it doubles as an airplane **carry-on.** An empty, lightweight **duffel bag** packed inside your luggage may also be useful. Once abroad you can fill your luggage with purchases and keep your dirty clothes in the duffel.

SLEEPSACKS

Some youth hostels require that you have your own linen or rent theirs. If you plan to stay in hostels you can avoid linen charges by making the requisite sleepsack yourself: fold a full-size sheet in half the long way, then sew it closed along the open long side and one of the short sides. Sleepsacks can also be bought at any Hostelling International outlet store.

ELECTRIC CURRENT

In New Zealand, electricity is 230/240 volts, 50 hertz—enough to fry any 110V North American appliance. Most hotels and motels provide 110V AC sockets (rated at 20 watts) for electric razors only. (Remember, 230/240V electrical appliances don't like 110V current, either.) Visit a hardware store for an adapter (which changes the shape of the plug) and a converter (which changes the voltage). Don't make the mistake of using only an adapter, unless appliance instructions explicitly state otherwise.

FILM

Film in New Zealand generally costs US$10 for a roll of 12 color exposures. Thus, it makes sense to bring film from home and develop it at home. Despite disclaimers, airport security X-rays *can* fog film, so either buy a lead-lined pouch, sold at camera stores, or ask the security to hand-inspect it. Always pack it in your carry-on luggage, since higher-intensity X-rays are used on checked luggage.

OTHER USEFUL ITEMS

No matter how you're traveling, it's always a good idea to carry a first-aid kit (see **Health,** p. 32). Other useful items include: an umbrella; sealable plastic bags (for damp clothes, soap, food, shampoo, and other spillables); alarm clock; waterproof matches; sun hat; moleskin (for blisters); needle and thread; safety pins; sunglasses; pocketknife; plastic water bottle; compass; string (makeshift clothesline and lashing material); towel; padlock; whistle; rubber bands; flashlight; cold-water soap; earplugs; electrical tape (for patching tears); tweezers; garbage bags; a small calculator for currency conversion; a pair of flip-flops for the shower; a money-belt for carrying valuables; deodorant; razors; tampons; and condoms.

FURTHER READING

The Packing Book, Judith Gilford. Ten Speed Press ($9).

Backpacking One Step at a Time, Harvey Manning. Vintage ($15).

ESSENTIALS

ACCOMMODATIONS

The accommodations and restaurant listings in the book are ranked according to our researchers' assessments. The better accommodations are listed first, and the last hostel entries, while acceptable, may not be the best places to stay a night. Campgrounds, motels, and B&Bs are generally listed last regardless of quality. Unless we state otherwise, you can expect that every establishment has **free hot showers** and **free linen.** When there is a linen charge, it is usually charged once per stay. Most offer **laundry** for a standard fee ($1-3), but do not always have automatic dryers. **Central heating** is not a standard feature in New Zealand and is listed wherever found. In our listings, a **twin** contains two single beds; a **double,** one double bed. **Seasonal fares** are flexible, and some accommodations vary fares at their own discretion. **Booking ahead** is a must in summer and on major holidays.

Budget-conscious bedders may also benefit from the variety of accommodation networks in New Zealand. Those who plan on doing a lot of camping, for example, may choose to join a network like the **Top 10 Holiday Parks** (membership fee $15 for 2 years) to reap consistent discounts.

HOSTELS

A HOSTELER'S BILL OF RIGHTS. There are certain standard features that we do not include in our hostel listings. Unless we state otherwise, you can expect that every hostel has: no lockout, no curfew, a kitchen, free hot showers, secure luggage storage, and no key deposit.

For tight budgets and those lonesome traveling blues, backpackers (the Kiwi term for "hostel") can't be beat. Backpackers are generally dorm-style accommodations, in large, co-ed or single-sex (especially common in YHA backpackers) rooms with bunk beds, although some backpackers do have private rooms for families and couples. They frequently offer bike rentals, shuttle bus connections, and storage areas; most have central kitchens and laundry facilities. Many are also happy to book local activities. Fees range from NZ$14-20 per night for a dorm bed.

Checking in at backpackers in New Zealand can be a remarkably laid-back process; after hours, you may be expected to sign in on a self-check blackboard, or you may be allowed to simply check the listings to see which beds are open and plunk yourself down for the night, making payment in the morning.

Backpackers associated with one of the large hostel associations (HI-YHA, VIP, etc.) often have lower rates for members. If you have Internet access, check out the **Internet Guide to Hostelling** (hostels.com), which includes backpackers in New Zealand and oodles of info about hosteling and backpacking worldwide. The following are the major hostel networks in New Zealand.

Budget Backpacker Hostels: (email bakpak@chch.planet.org; www.backpack.co.nz). Includes over 250 of the nation's independent backpackers. Once a year, BBH surveys guests of all BBH backpackers and then compiles a free guide which lists its members and provides satisfaction ratings. This guide is very helpful and its rankings are reliable. Available at the Auckland and Christchurch airports, Visitor Information Network offices, participating backpackers, or via email. In addition, all BBH establishments that recognize discount cards (YHA, VIP, etc.) give equal discounts to those carrying the BBH guide. Average overnight fee NZ$14-17. Advance reservations recommended, especially in high season. Book directly to the backpackers.

Hostelling International-Youth Hostels Association of New Zealand (HI-YHANZ): National Office, P.O. Box 436, 193 Cashel St., 3rd Floor, Christchurch (tel. (03) 379 9970; fax 365 4476; email info@yha.org.nz; www.iyhf.org); **National Reservations Centre,** P.O. Box 68 149, Auckland (tel. (09) 303 9524; fax 303 9525; email yhaakbg@yha.org.nz; www.yha.org.nz). Because YHANZ is linked to the HI network, your

HI card from home (see below) is recognized at all YHANZ backpackers and at most other establishments that give discounts for YHA membership. Annual membership fee NZ$24. Average overnight fee NZ$14-20. HI-YHA backpackers are inspected annually for quality and service standards; look in the HI-YHANZ Accommodation Guide to see a hostel's quality rating. The privately owned YHA Associate hostels, on the other hand, meet YHA standards, but offer the same rates to all guests. Reservations can be made via the **International Booking Network (IBN)**, a computerized system that allows you to make hostel reservations from overseas (see below). You must book at least 14 days in advance, however, and your reservations are accompanied by a NZ$5 booking fee. HI and YHA cards can be bought at travel agencies (see p. 49), YHA hostels, or HI offices.

VIP Backpackers Resorts: Like HI-YHA cards, a VIP card obtains discounts from VIP backpackers and other establishments. Annual membership fee NZ$30. Average overnight fee NZ$14-20. Book directly to backpackers (have credit card handy). VIP cards can be obtained from many visitor information centers or VIP backpackers. In New Zealand, contact VIP Backpackers Resorts (NZ), P.O. Box 80021, Greenbay, Auckland (tel. (09) 827 6016; fax 827 6016; www.vip.co.nz).

For its various services and lower rates at member hostels, **Hostelling International (HI)** is worth joining if you plan to be staying in backpacker accommodations. HI-YHA hostels are scattered throughout New Zealand, and members of overseas branches receive the same discounts as members in New Zealand. A new **discount database** on HI's website (www.iyah.org) lists hundreds of discounts on accommodations, transportation, tours, and activities in New Zealand. Many YHA hostels accept reservations via the **International Booking Network** for a nominal fee (tel. (02) 9261 1111 from Australia, 800-663-5777 from Canada, (01629) 581 418 from the U.K., (01) 301 766 from Ireland, (09) 379 4224 from New Zealand, 800-909-4776 from U.S.; www.hiayh.org/ushostel/reserva/ibn3.htm). HI's umbrella organization's web page lists the web addresses and phone numbers of all national associations and can be a great place to begin researching hosteling in a specific region (www.iyhf.org). To join HI, contact one of the following organizations in your home country.

Australian Youth Hostels Association (AYHA), 422 Kent St., Sydney NSW 2000 (tel. (02) 9261 1111; fax 9261 1969; email yha@yhansw.org.au; www.yha.org.au). One-year membership AUS$44, under 18 AUS$13.50.

Hostelling International-Canada (HI-C), 400-205 Catherine St., Ottawa, ON K2P 1C3 (tel. 800-663-5777 or (613) 237-7884; fax 237-7868; email info@hostellingintl.ca; www.hostellingintl.ca). One-year membership CDN$25, under 18 CDN$12; 2-year CDN$35.

An Óige (Irish Youth Hostel Association), 61 Mountjoy St., Dublin 7 (tel. (01) 830 4555; fax 830 5808; email anoige@iol.ie; www.irelandyha.org). One-year membership IR£10, under 18 IR£4, families IR£20.

Youth Hostels Association of New Zealand (YHANZ), P.O. Box 436, 173 Cashel St., Christchurch 1 (tel. (03) 379 9970; fax 365 4476; email info@yha.org.nz; www.yha.org.nz). One-year membership NZ$24, ages 15-17 NZ$12, under 15 free.

Hostelling International South Africa, P.O. Box 4402, Cape Town 8000 (tel. (021) 24 2511; fax 24 4119; email info@hisa.org.za; www.hisa.org.za). One-year membership SAR50, under 18 SAR25, lifetime SAR250.

Scottish Youth Hostels Association (SYHA), 7 Glebe Crescent, Stirling FK8 2JA (tel. (01786) 891 400; fax 891 333; email info@syha.org.uk; www.syha.org.uk). Membership UK£6, under 18 UK£2.50.

Youth Hostels Association of England and Wales (YHA), 8 St. Stephen's Hill, St. Albans, Hertfordshire AL1 2DY (tel. (01727) 855 215 or 845 047; fax 844 126; email yhacustomerservices@compuserve.com; www.yha.org.uk). One-year membership UK£11, under 18 UK£5.50, families UK£22.

Hostelling International Northern Ireland (HINI), 22-32 Donegall Rd., Belfast BT12 5JN (tel. (01232) 324 733 or 315 435; fax 439 699; email info@hini.org.uk; www.hini.org.uk). One-year membership UK£7, under 18 UK£3, families UK£14.

Hostelling International-American Youth Hostels (HI-AYH), 733 15th St. NW, Suite 840, Washington, D.C. 20005 (tel. (202) 783-6161 ext. 136; fax 783-6171; email hiayh-serv@hiayh.org; www.hiayh.org). One-year membership US$25, over 54 US$15, under 18 free.

OTHER INEXPENSIVE OPTIONS

MOTOR PARKS AND CAMPS (HOLIDAY PARKS)

Known as holiday parks, these accommodations complexes vary in size from sprawling compounds to grassy plots, all offering a range of options for the budget traveler. Motor parks and camps usually feature tent sites (from $10) and caravan (RV or camper) sites (from $20); powerpoints are what Kiwis call on-site power hook-ups. Some also feature on-site caravans for rent, often with kitchen, sometimes with toilet. Most establishments charge for tent and caravan sites per person. Many also feature cabins or flats with singles (from $20), doubles (from $30), and bunk rooms (from $15) with varying amenities (kitchens, linens, etc.).

Renting a camper will always be more expensive than camping or hosteling, but the costs compare favorably with the price of renting a car and staying in hotels. Rates vary widely by region, season, and type of camper; expect to pay at least $60-80 per day in low season (about $50-70 more in high season), including insurance. In New Zealand, caravan sites cost around $10 per person per night. Check with your local Automobile Association or contact a major international firm, such as Avis, Budget, or Hertz, to arrange camper rentals in New Zealand. Rates vary widely by region, season (summers months are the most expensive), and type of RV. **Auto Europe** (U.S. tel. 800-223-5555; U.K. toll free tel. (0800) 899 893) rents RVs in New Zealand, as does **Maui Rentals** (N.Z. tel. (09) 275 3013; fax 275 9690).

BED AND BREAKFASTS (B&BS)

For a refreshing alternative to impersonal hotel rooms, B&Bs (private homes with rooms available to travelers) can refresh the travel-weary with their homespun hospitality. On the other hand, many B&Bs have steeper prices (doubles from $60) and may not provide phones or private bathrooms. Families may want to look elsewhere, as well, because most B&Bs discourage visits by children under 15.

HOMESTAYS AND FARMSTAYS

An intensely memorable experience, homestays and farmstays in an area are often arranged through the nearest town's tourist office, although some companies also book homestays and farmstays. You stay at a real working farm or orchard, often alone or with a few other guests. The price starts around $100 per person and includes participation in farm activities (more available in winter) and fresh, home-cooked meals. **Rural Tours "Stay in a Country Home" Farmstays** books farmstays throughout New Zealand. Its central booking office is at 92 Victoria St., Cambridge (tel. (07) 827 8055; fax 827 7154; email stay@ruraltours.co.nz). **American International Homestays,** P.O. Box 1754, Nederland, CO 80466 (tel. (303) 642-3088 or (800) 876-2048; fax (303) 642 3365; email ash@igc.apc.org; www.commerce.com/homestays), has lodgings with host families in New Zealand and all over the world.

LONGER STAYS

If you've come in search of employment, go to it—getting a job requires both persistence and savvy. For more info, see p. 63. Once you've got yourself a source of funds, you'll want to open a bank account to store the results in (see **EFTPOS,** p. 30). Housing will be the next pressing concern. Look in the daily paper for rental listings or check out real estate agencies which will arrange rentals or leases for you. You might also try college campus notice boards. Some work programs will help with job placement and housing (see **Volunteering,** p. 63). Obtain a copy of the Residential Tenancies Act 1988 (available from Tenancy Services, the Ministry of Housing) to learn about your tenant rights and obligations in New Zealand. Be sure to check with the nearest New Zealand embassy or consulate to find out about visa, residency, and taxation regulations that could easily thwart your best-laid plans.

Home exchange offers the traveler various types of homes (houses, apartments, condominiums, and villas), plus the opportunity to live like a native and to cut down dramatically on accommodation fees—usually only an administration fee is paid to the matching service. Once you join or contact one of the exchange services listed below, it is then up to you to decide with whom you would like to exchange homes. Most companies have pictures of member's homes and information about the owners. A great site listing many exchange companies can be found at www.aitec.edu.au/~bwechner/Documents/Travel/Lists/Home ExchangeClubs.html. **The Invented City: International Home Exchange,** 41 Sutter St., Suite 1090, San Francisco, CA 94104 (tel. 800-788-2489 in the U.S. or 415-252-1141 elsewhere; fax 252-1171; email invented@aol.com; www.invented_city.com), can arrange home exchanges in New Zealand.

CAMPING AND THE OUTDOORS

TRAMPING IN NEW ZEALAND

Backpacking, trekking, bushwalking: whatever you call it back home, it's called tramping in New Zealand. With all the national parks, forest parks, scenic reserves, and other assorted protected areas in New Zealand, it is no surprise that the opportunities for overnight wilderness excursions are almost limitless. There are hundreds of well-maintained tracks scattered across New Zealand, as well as copious opportunities for route-finding in remote undeveloped wilderness areas. The **Department of Conservation (DOC),** or Te Papa Atawhai, P.O. Box 10420, Wellington (tel. (04) 471 0726; fax 471 1082), is an unparalleled resource with the lowdown on the seasonal availability and safety of hikes, the regulations and practicalities of adventuring in New Zealand, maps, and more. Offices are all over New Zealand and near virtually every protected wilderness areas; staff will know all about current track conditions and weather forecasts and can offer plenty of advice. For most tracks, the DOC produces a $1 brochure with a basic but adequate map and track information. Detailed topographic maps are $11-13.50.

HUTS AND CAMPING

New Zealand's tracks are home to a well-developed **hut system.** Essentially cabins offering overnight indoor accommodation, they can be found on virtually every developed track in New Zealand. Huts provide an excellent opportunity for meeting fellow trampers, provide shelter from extreme weather, and make a tent virtually unnecessary. There are two pricing systems of huts, one for backcountry huts and another for Great Walk huts (see below). Backcountry Hut tickets ($4) are available at all DOC offices and usually from park rangers. Nicer huts cost two tickets ($8), and will have mattresses, water, toilets, and occasionally fireplaces, stoves, or gas cookers. More basic huts are one ticket ($4) and may only have water and toilets. For those planning extensive tramping, an **Annual Hut Pass** can be purchased for $65. Children under age 12 can stay in the huts for free, and ages 12-17 are half-price. However, those who prefer alternate accommodation can **camp** on almost all tracks. There is usually a small charge for camping near huts; where permitted, camping at a distance from the track is free though often difficult because of the heavy foliage.

THE GREAT WALKS

New Zealand's most spectacular and popular tramps are classified as **Great Walks** and are run by the DOC under a separate administration. *Let's Go: New Zealand 2000* has extensive and complete coverage of these eight tramps and one canoe trip. The tracks are well maintained, and camping facilities are a step above those on other backcountry tracks. Huts often have cooking facilities, flush toilets, gas lighting, and a helpful DOC warden on hand. Normal hut tickets do not apply except in the winter; **Great Walks Passes must be purchased** (huts $6-30; campsites $6-9). Camping is not allowed outside of designated sites on Great Walks. The **Milford** and **Routeburn** tracks should be booked well in advance.

The Lake Waikaremoana Track (Te Urewera National Park): 3-5 days, 46km. In the heart of a remote and thickly forested park, this track climbs towering bluffs topped with gnarled beech trees around the lake. Advance reservations required (see p. 175).

Tongariro Northern Circuit (Tongariro National Park): 3-4 days, 41km. Winding around the three great volcanoes, this track passes wild and unique lava formations, desolate moonscapes, and technicolor waterlets. The **Tongariro Crossing**, "the finest one-day walk in New Zealand," is part of the circuit (see p. 198).

Whanganui River Journey (Whanganui National Park): 3-5 days by canoe. The only Great Walk that requires a paddle; canoeists and kayakers battle small rapids beneath the sheer banks and brilliant greenery of the Whanganui River. The chance to stay at two Maori *marae* can make the trip a breathtaking cultural experience as well (see p. 219).

The Abel Tasman Coast Track (Abel Tasman National Park): 3-4 days, 51km. This track may be the most popular of the lot, with golden beaches and turquoise ocean views fringed by fern-filled forest. Advance reservations required (see p. 268).

The Heaphy Track (Kahurangi National Park): 4-5 days, 82km. Sweeping ecological diversity is the name of the game: this track passes through lofty beech forest, wind-swept alpine meadows, lowland podocarp forest, and wild palm-lined beaches (see p. 275).

Routeburn Track (Mt. Aspiring and Fiordland National Parks): 2-3 days, 32 km. This track runs high above the tree line, skirting grand valleys and overlooking great mountain ranges. Advanced reservations required (see p. 351).

The Milford Track (Fiordland National Park): 4 days, 53km. Heralded as "the finest walk in the world," it runs through two green glacier valleys and over a spectacular mountain pass. Sheer rock faces are watered by countless cascades, including Sutherland Falls, the highest in New Zealand. Advanced reservations required (see p. 348).

The Kepler Track (Fiordland National Park): 3-4 days, 67km. The most easily accessible of the Great Walks, this walk runs along awe-inspiring ridgetops high above Lake Te Anau and descends into dense forest alongside Lake Manapouri (see p. 353).

The Rakiura Track (Stewart Island): 2-3 days, 36km. This heavily boardwalked track is far removed from the mainstream, and winds entirely through lush forest (see p. 387).

OTHER RECOMMENDED WALKS

There are plenty of other tramps in New Zealand that rival even the Great Walks for natural splendor and typically have fewer people. These include:

Queen Charlotte Track (Marlborough Sounds): 3-5 days, 67km. This popular, mellow walk winds along the shimmering inlets of the Sounds. Pampered trampers can stay in trackside hostels and have packs transported by boat (see p. 252).

Mt. Taranaki Round-the-Mountain Track (Egmont National Park): 4 days, 55km. This tramp traverses the upper slopes of the volcano, affording excellent views of the surrounding farmland and coast (see p. 210).

Rees-Dart Track (Mt. Aspiring National Park): 4-5 days, 72km. The Rees and Dart River Valleys are crowned with glaciers galore. A one day side trip up to the Cascade Saddle can afford one of the most mind-numbing views in New Zealand (see p. 343).

Greenstone-Caples Tracks (Wakitipu Recreational Hunting Area): 4-5 days, 50km. Cattle graze in paradise, where green mountains overlook the golden meadows of the valley floor (see p. 343).

CAMPING AND HIKING EQUIPMENT

Good camping equipment is both sturdy and light. Camping equipment is generally more expensive in Australia, New Zealand, and the U.K. than in North America. New Zealand customs officials may check and clean used camping equipment when you arrive.

SLEEPING BAGS

Most good sleeping bags are rated by "season," or the lowest outdoor temperature at which they will keep you warm ("summer" means 30-40°F at night and "four-season" or "winter" often means below 0°F). Sleeping bags are made either of down (warmer and lighter, but more expensive, and miserable when wet) or of synthetic material (heavier, more durable, and warmer when wet). Prices vary, but might range from US$80-210 for a summer synthetic to US$250-300 for a good down winter bag. **Sleeping bag pads,** including foam pads (US$10-20) and air mattresses (US$15-50), cushion your back and neck and insulate you from the ground. **Therm-A-Rest** brand self-inflating sleeping pads are part foam and part air-mattress and partially inflate when you unroll them, but are costly at US$45-80. Bring a **"stuff sack"** or plastic bag to store your sleeping bag and keep it dry.

TENTS

The best tents are free-standing, with their own frames and suspension systems; they set up quickly and only require staking in high winds. Low-profile dome tents are the best all-around. When pitched their internal space is almost entirely usable, which means little unnecessary bulk. Tent sizes can be somewhat misleading: two people *can* fit in a two-person tent, but will find life more pleasant in a four-person. If you're traveling by car, go for the bigger tent, but if you're hiking, stick with a smaller tent that weighs no more than five to six pounds (2-3kg). Good two-person tents start at US$90, four-person tents at US$300. Seal the seams of your tent with waterproofer, and make sure it has a rain fly. Other tent accessories include a **battery-operated lantern,** a **plastic groundcloth,** and a **nylon tarp.**

BACKPACKS

If you intend to do a lot of hiking, you should have a frame backpack (see p. 37). Any serious backpacking requires a pack of at least 4000 cubic inches (16,000cc). Allow an additional 500 cubic inches for your sleeping bag in internal-frame packs. This is one area where it doesn't pay to economize—cheaper packs may be less comfortable, and the straps are more likely to fray or rip. Before you buy any pack, try it on and imagine carrying it, full, a few miles up a rocky incline. Better yet, insist on filling it with something heavy and walking around the store to get a sense of how it distributes weight before committing to buy it. A **waterproof backpack cover** will prove invaluable. Otherwise, plan to store all of your belongings in plastic bags inside your backpack.

BOOTS

Be sure to wear hiking boots with good **ankle support.** Your boots should fit snugly and comfortably over one or two wool socks and a thin liner sock. Breaking in boots properly before setting out requires wearing them for several weeks; doing so will spare you from painful and debilitating blisters. You may also want to spray them with a waterproofing agent.

OTHER NECESSITIES

Good raingear may seem expensive, but it is a worthwhile investment. Raingear in two pieces, a top and pants, is far superior to a poncho. **Synthetics,** like polypropylene tops, socks, and long underwear, along with a pile jacket, will keep you warm even when wet. When camping in autumn, winter, or spring, bring along a **"space blanket,"** which helps you to retain your body heat and doubles as a groundcloth (US$5-15). Plastic **canteens** or water bottles keep water cooler than metal ones do, and are virtually shatter- and leak-proof. Large, collapsible **water sacks** will significantly improve your lot in primitive campgrounds and weigh practically nothing when empty, though they are bulky and heavy when full. Bring **water-purification tablets** for when you can't boil water, unless you are willing to shell out money for a portable water-purification system. Though most campgrounds provide campfire sites, you may want to bring a small **metal grate** or **grill** of your own. For those places that forbid fires or the gathering of firewood, you'll need a **camp stove.** The classic Coleman stove starts at about US$40. You will need to purchase a **fuel bottle** and fill it with propane to operate it. A **first aid kit, swiss army knife, powerful insect repellent, calamine lotion, toiletries, toilet paper, moleskin, sunscreen, biodegradable soap, duct tape,** and **waterproof matches** or a **lighter** are other essential camping items.

BUYING EQUIPMENT

The mail-order and online companies listed below offer lower prices than many retail stores, but a visit to a local camping or outdoors store will give you a good sense of items' look and weight.

Campmor, P.O. Box 700, Upper Saddle River, NJ 07458-0700, U.S. (tel. 888-226-7667, outside U.S. call 1-201-825-8300; email customer-service@campmor.com; www.campmor.com).

Discount Camping, 880 Main North Rd., Pooraka, South Australia 5095, Australia (tel. (08) 8262 3399; fax 8260 6240; www.discountcamping.com.au).

Eastern Mountain Sports (EMS), 327 Jaffrey Rd., Peterborough, NH 03458, U.S. (tel. 888-463-6367 or (603) 924-7231; email emsmail@emsonline.com; www.emsonline.com). Call the above number for the branch nearest you.

L.L. Bean, Freeport, ME 04033-0001, U.S. (tel. 800-441-5713; U.K. tel. (0800) 962 954; elsewhere, call U.S. 1-207-552-6878; www.llbean.com). If your purchase doesn't meet your expectations, they'll replace or refund it.

Mountain Designs, P.O. Box 1472, Fortitude Valley, Queensland 4006, Australia (tel. (07) 3252 8894; fax 3252 4569; www.mountaindesign.com.au).

Recreational Equipment, Inc. (REI), Sumner, WA 98352, U.S. (tel. 800-426-4840 or (253) 891-2500; www.rei.com).

YHA Adventure Shop, 14 Southampton St., London, WC2E 7HA, U.K. (tel. (01718) 36 85 41). The main branch of one of Britain's largest outdoor equipment suppliers.

WILDERNESS SAFETY

Stay warm, stay dry, and **stay hydrated.** The vast majority of life-threatening wilderness problems stem from failure to follow this advice. On any hike, however brief, you should fill out enough equipment to keep you alive should disaster befall. Always fill out the **intentions form** at the nearest DOC office before undertaking a hike; also let someone know when and where you are tramping, whether it's a newfound friend, your backpackers, or a local hiking organization. Always get updates on the latest **weather forecasts** from the local DOC. Weather patterns can change instantly, especially in the more volatile mountainous areas. If the weather turns nasty on a day-hike, turn back immediately. Before undertaking overnight or longer hikes, in particular, always check with the nearest DOC office about the hike's weather and safety rating, as well as the availability of huts along the track.

A good guide to outdoor survival is *How to Stay Alive in the Woods,* by Bradford Angier (Macmillan, US$8).

See **Preventing Disease** (p. 34) for info about outdoor ailments such as giardia and insects. **Mosquitoes** are most active in the summer from dusk to dawn; the ever-present and ever-annoying **sandflies** make their home in bushy and grassy areas, and are especially populous in the southern parts of the South Island. To guard against both, wear long pants (tucked into socks) and long sleeves, buy a bed net for camping, and use insect repellent. Soak or spray your gear with permethrin, which is licensed in the U.S. for use on clothing. Natural repellents can also be useful: taking vitamin B-12 pills regularly can eventually make you smelly to insects, as can garlic pills. Still, be sure to supplement your vitamins with repellent. Calamine lotion or topical cortisones (like Cortaid) may stop insect bites from itching, as can a bath with a half-cup of baking soda or oatmeal.

USEFUL PUBLICATIONS AND RESOURCES

Whether novice or expert, you can visit your nearest outdoors equipment store to find publications and general info on camping and adventuring in New Zealand, or contact an outdoors publication company. **Adventurous Traveler Bookstore,** 245 S. Champlain St., Burlington, VT 05401 (tel. 800-282-3963 or (802) 860-6776; fax 860-6667; www.adventuroustraveler.com), sells general adventuring books and specific New Zealand titles, such as *101 Great Tramps in New Zealand,* by Pickering and Smith. For **topographical maps** of New Zealand, contact **Map and Chart Center,** 32 Goodshed Rd. (Private Bag 903), Upper Hutt, New Zealand (tel. (04) 527 7019; fax 527 7246; email mapcentre@terralink.co.nz). Once in New Zealand, you can buy topographical maps from the local DOC office. A variety of publishing companies offer hiking guidebooks to meet the educational needs of novice or expert. For information about camping, hiking, and biking, write or call the publishers listed below to receive a free catalogue:

Family Campers and RVers/National Campers and Hikers Association, Inc., 4804 Transit Rd., Bldg. #2, Depew, NY 14043 (tel./fax (716) 668-6242). Membership fee (US$25) includes their publication *Camping Today.*

Sierra Club Books, 85 Second St., 2nd Fl., San Francisco, CA 94105-3441 (tel. 800-935-1056 or (415) 977-5500; www.sierraclub.org/books). Books on many national parks, including different regions of New Zealand.

The Mountaineers Books, 1001 SW Klickitat Way, #201, Seattle, WA 98134 (tel. 800-553-4453 or (206) 223-6303; email alans@mountaineers.org; www.mountaineers.org). Over 400 titles on hiking (the *100 Hikes* series), biking, mountaineering, natural history, and conservation.

MAIL

TO NEW ZEALAND

Airmail letters under one ounce take seven to 12 days between North America and New Zealand and cost US$1. Allow at least five days from Australia (postage AUS$0.70 for up to 20g) and 10 from Britain (postage £64 for up to 10g). Envelopes should be marked "air mail" or "par avion" to avoid having letters sent by sea.

There are several ways to arrange pickup of letters sent to you by friends and relatives while you are abroad. Mail can be sent via general delivery through **Poste Restante** to almost any city or town in New Zealand with a post office. Address *Poste Restante* letters to: "Brendan Gibbon," Poste Restante, CPO, City, New Zealand. No zip or area code is necessary. The mail will go to a special desk in the central post office, unless you specify a post office by street address or postal code. As a rule, it is best to use the largest post office in the area, and mail may be sent there regardless of what is written on the envelope. When possible, it is usually safer and quicker to send mail express or registered. When picking up your mail, bring a form of photo ID, preferably a passport. There is generally no surcharge. If the clerks insist that there is nothing for you, have them check under your first name as well. *Let's Go* lists post offices in the **Practical Information** section for each city and most towns.

American Express travel offices (U.S. tel. 800-528-4800) will act as a mail service for cardholders if you contact them in advance. Under this free **Client Letter Service,** they will hold mail for up to 30 days and forward upon request. Some offices will offer these services to non-cardholders (especially those who have purchased AmEx Travelers Cheques), but you must call ahead to make sure. Check the **Practical Information** section of the countries you plan to visit; Let's Go lists AmEx office locations for most large cities. A complete list is available free from AmEx.

If regular airmail is too slow, **Federal Express** (U.S. tel. for international operator 800-247-4747) can get a letter from New York to Auckland in two days for a whopping US$29.50; rates among non-U.S. locations are prohibitively expensive (London to Auckland for example, costs upwards of US$47). By **U.S. Express Mail, a** letter from New York would arrive within four days and would cost US$19.

Surface mail is by far the cheapest and slowest way to send mail. It takes one to three months to cross the Atlantic and two to four to cross the Pacific— appropriate for sending large quantities of items you won't need to see for a while. When ordering books and materials from abroad, always include one or two **International Reply Coupons (IRCs)**—a way of providing the postage to cover delivery. IRCs should be available from your local post office and those abroad (US$1.05).

FROM NEW ZEALAND

Aerogrammes, printed sheets that fold into envelopes and travel via airmail, are available at post offices. They cost NZ$1 to send anywhere in the world. It helps to mark "airmail" if possible, though "par avion" is universally understood. Airmail from New Zealand averages 7 to 12 days, although times are more unpredictable from smaller towns. To send a postcard to an international destination costs NZ$1.

TELEPHONES

TIME DIFFERENCES

New Zealand Standard Time is 12 hours ahead of Greenwich Mean Time. For example, when it is noon in New Zealand, it is midnight in London, 5pm the previous day in Los Angeles, and 8pm the previous day in New York. New Zealand observes Daylight Savings Time, which puts the clock ahead one hour from the first Sunday in October to the last Sunday in March.

CALLING NEW ZEALAND FROM HOME

To call New Zealand direct from home, dial:

1. The **international access code** of your home country. International access codes include: Australia 0011; Ireland 00; New Zealand 00; South Africa 09; U.K. 00; Canada 011; U.S. 011.
2. **64** (New Zealand's country code).
3. The **area code** (see the city's **Practical Information** section), **dropping the first zero,** and local number.

CALLING HOME FROM NEW ZEALAND

A **calling card** is probably your best and cheapest bet. Calls are billed either collect or to your account. To obtain a calling card from your national telecommunications service before you leave home, contact one of the following companies: in the U.S., **AT&T** (tel. 888-288-4685), **Sprint** (tel. 800-877-4646), or **MCI** (tel. 800-444-4141); in **Canada,** Bell Canada **Canada Direct** (tel. 800-565-4708); in the **U.K.,** British Telecom **BT Direct** (tel. (0800) 34 51 44); in **Ireland,** Telecom Éireann **Ireland Direct** (tel. 800 250 250); in **Australia,** Telstra **Australia Direct** (tel. 13 22 00); and in **South Africa, Telkom South Africa** (tel. 09 03).

To call home with a calling card, contact the New Zealand operator for your service provider by dialing:

AT&T: tel. 000 911.

Sprint: tel. 0800 760 877.

MCI WorldPhone Direct: tel. 000 912.

Canada Direct: tel. 000 919.

BT Direct: tel. 000 950.

Telkom South Africa Direct: tel. 000 927.

Wherever possible, use a calling card for international phone calls, as the long-distance rates for national phone services are often exorbitant. You can usually make direct international calls from pay phones, but if you aren't using a calling card you may need to drop your coins as quickly as your words. Where available, prepaid **overseas phone cards** (see below) and occasionally major **credit cards** can be used for direct international calls, but they are still less cost-efficient. Look for pay phones in public areas, especially train stations, as private pay phones are often more expensive. Although incredibly convenient, in-room hotel calls invariably include an arbitrary and sky-high surcharge (as much as US$10).

If you do dial direct, you must first insert the appropriate amount of money or a prepaid card, then dial **00** (the international access code for New Zealand), and then dial the **country code** and number of your home. Country codes include: Australia 61; Ireland 353; New Zealand 64; South Africa 27; U.K. 44; U.S. and Canada 1.

The expensive alternative to dialing direct or using a calling card is using an international operator to place a **collect call.** An operator from your home nation can be reached by dialing the appropriate service provider listed above, and they will typically place a collect call even if you don't possess one of their phone cards.

CALLING WITHIN NEW ZEALAND

National directory assistance: 018.

International operator: 0170.

International directory assistance: 0172.

The **North Island** has several different area codes (see p. 389). The **South Island** has a single area code of **(03).** Phone numbers that begin with **(025)** are cellular phone numbers and cost more than a standard local call. Phone rates tend to be highest in the morning, lower in the evening, and lowest on Sunday and late at night. Calls from private phones are substantially cheaper than those from New Zealand's public phones.

The three kinds of public **pay phones** are color-coded: **card phones** are green, **credit card phones** yellow, and **coin phones** blue. Coin phones are gradually being phased out, however, so don't count on being able to access them everywhere. **Phone cards** can be bought at tourist offices, backpackers' hostels, larger hotels, and convenience shops; just look inside any phone card booth to see a listing of the places nearby that sell phone cards. There are two types of phone cards. One type must be inserted at the green color-coded card pay phones, while the other offers a number which can be dialed at any pay phone (the latter is preferable). **Overseas phone cards,** sold in NZ$5, $10, $20, and $50 denominations, can be used at any kind of phone. Local calls from pay phones start at 20¢ per minute; non-local calls start at 50¢ per minute; international calls start at $3 per minute.

Budget Backpacker Hostels New Zealand (BBHNZ) has a phone card with a **voice message mailbox** that you can access during your visit. Cardholders are assigned a mailbox number that friends and family can call and leave a message; you can access these messages from any phone in New Zealand. Cards can be purchased at BBHNZ hostels (NZ$20). For more information, contact BBHNZ (tel. (07) 377 1568; email bbhcard@backpack.co.nz; www.backpack.co.nz).

EMAIL AND INTERNET

New Zealand is known for embracing new technologies, and the Internet is no exception. Cybercafes and other sources for Internet access are proliferating, though fees can be rather high and connections slow. Sometimes the local **library** becomes the first place in town to offer public Internet access. *Let's Go* lists Internet access in **Practical Information** and **Accommodations** sections of cities and towns; **Cybercafe Guide** (www.cyberiacafe.net/cyberia/guide/ccafe.htm) can also help you find cybercafes in New Zealand.

Free, web-based email providers include **Hotmail** (www.hotmail.com), **Rocket-Mail** (www.rocketmail.com), and **Yahoo! Mail** (www.yahoo.com). Almost every Internet search engine has an affiliated free email service.

GETTING THERE BY PLANE

When it comes to airfare, a little effort can save you a bundle. If your plans are flexible enough to deal with the restrictions, courier fares (p. 50) are the cheapest. Tickets bought from consolidators (p. 51) and stand-by seating are also good deals, but last-minute specials, airfare wars, and charter flights can even beat these fares. The key is to hunt around, to be flexible, and to persistently ask about discounts. Budget travel agencies can help (see below); students, seniors, and those under 26 should never pay full price for a ticket.

Flights between capital cities or regional hubs will offer the most competitive fares. Approximate **airfares** from Los Angeles to Auckland range from **US$900-$1300** depending on the season. Airfares to New Zealand peak from December through February, and holidays are also expensive periods in which to travel. Midweek (M-Th morning), round-trip flights run US$40-50 cheaper than weekend flights; the latter are generally less crowded and more likely to permit frequent-flier upgrades. Return-date flexibility is usually not an option for the budget traveler; traveling with an "open return" ticket can be pricier than fixing a return date when buying the ticket and paying later to change it. **Round-trip** flights are by far the cheapest; **"open-jaw"** (arriving in and departing from different cities) and **round-the-world,** or RTW, flights are pricier but reasonable alternatives. Patching one-way flights together is the least economical way to travel.

BUDGET AND STUDENT TRAVEL AGENCIES

A knowledgeable agent specializing in flights to New Zealand can make your life easy and help you save, too, but agents may not spend the time to find you the lowest possible fare—they get paid on commission. Students and those holding **ISIC and IYTC cards** (see p. 25) qualify for big discounts from student travel agencies. Most flights from budget agencies are on major airlines, but in peak season some may sell seats on less reliable chartered aircraft.

Campus/Usit Youth and Student Travel (www.usitcampus.co.uk). Offices include: 52 Grosvenor Gardens, **London** SW1W 0AG (tel. (0171) 730 34 02); 19-21 Aston Quay, O'Connell Bridge, **Dublin** 2 (tel. (01) 677-8117; fax 679-8833); New York Student Center, 895 Amsterdam Ave., **New York,** NY, 10025 (tel. (212) 663-5435; email usitny@aol.com).

Council Travel (www.counciltravel.com). For U.S. cities not listed, call 800-2-COUNCIL (226-8624). Offices include: 273 Newbury St., **Boston,** MA 02116 (tel. (617) 266-1926); 1160 N. State St., **Chicago,** IL 60610 (tel. (312) 951-0585); 10904 Lindbrook Dr., **Los Angeles,** CA 90024 (tel. (310) 208-3551); 205 E. 42nd St., **New York,** NY 10017 (tel. (212) 822-2700); 28A Poland St. (Oxford Circus), **London,** W1V 3DB (tel. (0171) 287 3337).

CTS Travel, 44 Goodge St., London W1 (tel. (0171) 636 00 31; fax 637 53 28; email ctsinfo@ctstravel.com.uk).

STA Travel (www.sta-travel.com). A student and youth travel organization with over 150 offices worldwide. Ticket booking, travel insurance, railpasses, and more. Offices include: 297 Newbury Street, **Boston,** MA 02115 (tel. (617) 266-6014); 429 S. Dearborn St., **Chicago,** IL 60605 (tel. (312) 786-9050); 7202 Melrose Ave., **Los Angeles,** CA 90046 (tel. (323) 934-8722); 10 Downing St., **New York,** NY 10014 (tel. (212) 627-3111); 6 Wrights Ln., **London** W8 6TA (tel. (0171) 938 47 11); 10 High St., **Auckland,** New Zealand (tel. (09) 309 04 58); 222 Faraday St., **Melbourne** VIC 3053, Australia (tel. (03) 9349 2411).

Travel CUTS (Canadian Universities Travel Services Limited) (www.travelcuts.com). 40 offices across Canada, including 187 College St., **Toronto,** Ont. M5T 1P7 (tel. (416) 979-2406). Also 295-A Regent St., **London** W1R 7YA, U.K. (tel. (0171) 255 19 44).

Other organizations that specialize in finding cheap fares include:

Cheap Tickets (U.S. tel. 800-377-1000). Fares worldwide to and from the U.S.

Travel Avenue (U.S. tel. 800-333-3335). Rebates commercial fares to or from the U.S. Also offers package deals, which include car rental and hotel reservations.

COMMERCIAL AIRLINES

The commercial airlines' lowest regular offer is the **APEX** (Advance Purchase Excursion) fare, which provides confirmed reservations and allows "open-jaw" tickets. Generally, reservations must be made seven to 21 days in advance, with seven- to 14-day minimum and up to 90-day maximum-stay limits, and hefty cancellation and change penalties (fees rise in summer). Book peak-season APEX fares early.

Although APEX fares are probably not the cheapest possible fares, they will give you a sense of the average commercial price, from which to measure other bargains. Specials advertised in newspapers may be cheaper but have more restrictions and fewer available seats. Popular carriers to New Zealand include: **Air New Zealand, Qantas, Air Pacific,** and **United,** which all have daily nonstop flights from Los Angeles to Auckland. Combining layovers at other destinations such as Fiji or Bangkok with your flight to New Zealand may be quite easy and inexpensive.

OTHER CHEAP ALTERNATIVES

AIR COURIER FLIGHTS

Couriers help transport cargo on international flights by guaranteeing delivery of the baggage claim slips from the company to a representative overseas. Generally, couriers must travel light (carry-ons only) and deal with complex restrictions on their flight. Most flights are round-trip only with short fixed-length stays (usually one week) and a limit of a single ticket per issue. Most of these flights also operate

It's a **big world.**

And we've got the **network** to cover it.

Use **AT&T Direct**® Service
when you're out exploring the world.

only out of the biggest cities, like New York. Generally, you must be over 21 (in some cases 18). Groups such as the **Air Courier Association** (U.S. tel. 800-282-1202; www.aircourier.org) and the **International Association of Air Travel Couriers,** 220 South Dixie Hwy., P.O. Box 1349, Lake Worth, FL 33460 (U.S. tel. 561-582-8320; email iaatc@courier.org; www.courier.org) provide their members with lists of opportunities and courier brokers worldwide for an annual fee.

For more information, consult *Air Courier Bargains*, by Kelly Monaghan (The Intrepid Traveler, US$15) or the *Courier Air Travel Handbook*, by Mark Field (Perpetual Press, US$10).

CHARTER FLIGHTS

Charters are flights a tour operator contracts with an airline to fly extra loads of passengers during peak season. Charters can sometimes be cheaper than flights on scheduled airlines, some operate nonstop, and restrictions on minimum advance-purchase and minimum stay are more lenient. However, charter flights fly less frequently than major airlines, make refunds particularly difficult, and are almost always fully booked. Schedules and itineraries may also change or be cancelled at the last moment (as late as 48 hours before the trip, and without a full refund), and check-in, boarding, and baggage claim are often much slower. As always, pay with a credit card if you can, and consider traveler's insurance against trip interruption.

Discount clubs and **fare brokers** offer members savings on last-minute charter and tour deals. Study their contracts closely; you don't want to end up with an unwanted overnight layover. **Travelers Advantage,** Stamford, CT (tel. 800-548-1116; www.travelersadvantage.com), has a US$60 annual fee that includes discounts, newsletters, and cheap flight directories.

TICKET CONSOLIDATORS

Ticket consolidators, or **"bucket shops,"** buy unsold tickets in bulk from commercial airlines and sell them at discounted rates. The best place to look is in the Sunday travel section of any major newspaper, where many bucket shops place tiny ads. Call quickly, as availability is typically extremely limited. Not all bucket shops are reliable establishments, so insist on a receipt that gives full details of restrictions, refunds, and tickets, and pay by credit card. For more information, check the website **Consolidators FAQ** (www.travel-library.com/air-travel/consolidators.html) or the book *Consolidators: Air Travel's Bargain Basement*, by Kelly Monaghan (Intrepid Traveler, US$8).

FURTHER INFORMATION

The Worldwide Guide to Cheap Airfare, Michael McColl. Insider Publications (US$15).

Discount Airfares: The Insider's Guide, George Hobart. Priceless Publications (US$14).

The Official Airline Guide, an expensive tome available at many libraries, has flight schedules, fares, and reservation numbers.

Travelocity (www.travelocity.com). A searchable online database of published airfares, with online reservations.

TravelHUB (www.travelhub.com). A directory of travel agents that includes a searchable database of fares from over 500 consolidators.

GETTING AROUND

Transportation in New Zealand is remarkably easy for tourists, particularly in high season, when local shuttles and backpacker buses come out in full force to supplement the main bus lines. **Booking ahead** will often get you significant fare reductions as well as a guaranteed seat. Discounts for students and YHA cardholders can be tremendous. Transportation can be booked at tourist offices and travel agencies, as well as at many backpackers.

BY PLANE

The two major domestic airlines, **Air New Zealand** (tel. 0800 737 000) and **Ansett New Zealand** (tel. 0800 267 388), provide connections between major towns and cities. Air New Zealand covers the country comprehensively; a number of smaller companies are also grouped under Air New Zealand Link. "Flightseeing" is another option. Smaller local companies in each area provide beautiful views from the air for rates competitive to boat or ferry prices, starting at around NZ$90. See the **Sights and Activities** listings in each town for more details.

DISCOUNTED FARES

You can buy special **tourist** and **student/YHA air passes,** packages of flight coupons that can be used with a certain degree of flexibility throughout your stay. (For Air New Zealand, you must buy air passes from outside New Zealand in conjunction with an incoming Air New Zealand ticket.) Air New Zealand's **Visit New Zealand Passes** allow travel within New Zealand; **G'day Passes,** in conjunction with Ansett, allow travel within New Zealand and Australia and between the two countries. Inside the country, ask about the special economy fares available. Some Air New Zealand flights feature Thrifty (up to 30% off standard economy fare), Super Thrifty (up to 40%), and Real Deal (up to 50%) fares, while some Ansett New Zealand flights feature Saver Plus (10%), Good Buy (30%), Good Buy Special (40%), and Good Buy Plus (50%) fares (restrictions apply). To get in on these deals, book as far in advance as possible.

BY TRAIN

TranzRail (tel. 0800 802 802, daily 7am-9pm; www.tranzrail.co.nz) runs localized commuter trains as well as the phenomenal **TranzScenic** that runs between major cities and towns, providing its passengers great views on the way. While train fares are generally more expensive than bus fares, TranzRail offers special discounted fares: for children aged four to 14 (40% off); travelers over 60 (30%); YHA members (30%); ISIC cardholders (20%); and those taking day excursions (30%). Minimum fare is $14 (children $9). There are also a limited number of Economy (15%), Saver (30%), and Super Saver (50%) discounted seats on each train. Some trains such as the one from Christchurch to Picton have a "no-frills carriage" for backpackers with less luxurious seating, smaller windows, and cheaper fares. This is a great way to meet your fellow travelers. Economy fares are offered regularly for travel at certain times of day, as well. Reserve all discounted fares well in advance, especially in peak season.

BY BUS

Many budget travelers, especially backpackers, choose the bus (or coach, as the Kiwis say) as their transport of choice, especially in more remote areas. Remember that bus schedules can be somewhat flexible, and many buses will leave if you are not at the stop when they arrive. Always show up 15 minutes early, and do not be alarmed if buses are 20 to 40 minutes late. Visitors centers will have the most up-to-date information about bus schedules and fares, and many offer discounts if fares are booked through them. **InterCity** (tel. 0800), the major bus line, covers both islands extensively. **Newmans** (tel. (09) 913 6200), an InterCity subsidiary, is another large bus company. All buses can be booked in advance by phone, at travel centers, or at most visitors centers. In addition, cyclists will be happy to know that buses carry **bikes** for a nominal fee. **Northliner Express** (tel. (09) 307 5873) runs north of Auckland and offers a 30% discount for YHA, VIP, Nomads, and BBH members.

SHUTTLE BUSES

Local shuttle buses are your best bet for beating the price offered by main bus lines. These services use vans and often travel to small towns not serviced by the main coach lines. Companies include Atomic, Fiordland Travel, and Westcoaster. However, there is a high turnover in shuttle companies and they can be less reliable and comfortable. Local visitors centers will often have current info on prices and schedules and can do bookings. During winter and in more remote locations, make sure to call ahead.

DISCOUNTED FARES

YHA and VIP membership and ISIC cards offer you 20% off fares for InterCity and Newmans. Children over four and under 16 travel for 40% off the full economy adult fare on major bus companies. A limited number of Saver (30%) and Super Saver (50%) fares on each bus are also available by booking early (at least 5 days prior to travel for Saver and 10 days for Super Saver, with tickets purchased no later than 2 days prior to travel). During school holidays and peak season, these discounts sell out fast. All discounts are valid only on fares over NZ$20. In addition, **Travelpass New Zealand,** P.O. Box 26601, Epsom, Auckland (tel. 0800 339 966 or (09) 357 8400; fax 913 6121), offers 3-in-1 passes that combine discounted travel on InterCity, TranzScenic, and the Interislander Ferry. 4-in-1 passes add a domestic flight on Ansett New Zealand. Prices run NZ$390 and up.

BACKPACKER BUSES

In addition to the standard bus companies, a few cater specifically to **backpackers.** These tours have planned itineraries and always stop for the night at pre-arranged destinations. If you come to a place that particularly grabs you, you can separate from the bus and stick around town. As each company has a fairly constant stream of buses running the same routes, you can join up with a new touring group when you're ready to move on again. The trade-off is that you lose the spontaneity that so many backpackers treasure, but in return, you meet a busload of starry-eyed young travelers and benefit from the knowledgeable tour guides. Accommodations are pre-booked by drivers with your input, but are not included in the overall price; food is also at your own cost. Many backpacker buses also offer decent discounts on adventure activities along the route, such as kayak rentals and guided tours. Reservations must be made at least a couple of days ahead of time and confirmed, especially in high season.

    Kiwi Experience (tel. (09) 366 9830; fax 366 1374; open daily 8am-8pm) is the most conspicuous of the backpacker buses, with over 20 green giants rolling through the country. Popular with North Americans and Europeans, especially Brits, Kiwi Experience caters to the party backpacker. Whether you're riding with them or not, you'll notice the significant impact that the Kiwi Experience buses have on the tourism industry, filling up certain backpackers and showing up en masse (occasionally in drag) at a bar. Kiwi Experience is good for travelers in their late teens and early twenties and is well-suited for those with two weeks or less to explore the country. **Magic Travellers Network** (tel. (09) 358 5600; open daily 7am-7pm) provides a more subdued experience. Kiwi Experience and Magic Travellers both offer 5% off fares for HI-YHA members.

BY CAR

INTERNATIONAL DRIVING PERMIT (IDP)

You probably won't need IDP in New Zealand, as long as you have a current license from your own country. A few car rental agencies do require the IDP, however, and it can serve as an additional piece of ID in a tough situation. Your IDP, valid for one year, must be issued in your own country before you depart; AAA affiliates cannot issue IDPs valid in their own country. You must be 18 years old to

receive an IDP. A valid driver's license from your home country must always accompany the IDP. An application usually needs to include one or two photos, a current local license, an additional form of identification, and a fee.

Australia: Contact your local Royal Automobile Club (RAC) or the National Royal Motorist Association (NRMA), if in NSW or the ACT (tel. (08) 9421 4298; www.rac.com.au/travel). Permits AUS$15.

Canada: Contact any Canadian Automobile Association (CAA) branch office in Canada, or write to CAA, 1145 Hunt Club Rd., Suite 200, K1V 0Y3 (tel. (613) 247-0117; fax 247-0118; www.caa.ca/caainternet/travelservices/internationaldocumentation/idptravel. htm). Permits CDN$10.

Ireland: Contact the nearest Automobile Association (AA) office or write to the U.K. address given below. The Irish Automobile Association (tel. (01) 677 9481) is at 23 Suffolk St., Rockhill, Blackrock Co. Dublin. Permits IR£4.

South Africa: Contact your local Automobile Association of South Africa office or the head office at P.O. Box 596, 2000 Johannesburg (tel. (011) 799 1000; fax 799 1010). Permits SAR28.50.

U.K.: Visit your local AA Shop, contact the AA Headquarters (tel. (0990) 448 866), or write to: The Automobile Association, International Documents, Fanum House, Erskine, Renfrewshire PA8 6BW. To find the location nearest you that issues the IDP, call (0990) 500 600. More info available at www.theaa.co.uk/motoring/idp.asp. Permits UK£4.

U.S.: Visit any American Automobile Association (AAA) office or write to AAA Florida, Travel Related Services, 1000 AAA Drive (mail stop 100), Heathrow, FL 32746 (tel. (407) 444-7000; fax 444-7380). You do not have to be a member of AAA to receive an IDP. Permits US$10.

CAR INSURANCE

Most credit cards cover standard insurance. If you rent, lease, or borrow a car, you will need a **green card,** or **International Insurance Certificate,** to prove that you have liability insurance. Obtain it through the car rental agency; most include coverage in their prices. If you lease a car, you can obtain a green card from the dealer. Some travel agents offer the card. Verify whether your auto insurance applies abroad; even if it does, you will still need a green card to certify this to foreign officials. If you have a collision abroad, the accident will show up on your domestic records if you report it to your insurance company.

CAR RENTAL

Avis (tel. (09) 526 2847 or 0800 655 111; www.avis.com/), **Budget** (tel. 0800 652 227; www.budgetrentacar.com/), and **Hertz** (tel. 0800 654 321; www.hertz.com) are the major car rental operators, and offer their services in all main cities and towns. (To find Avis, Budget, and Hertz numbers for your home country, see **RV and Camper Rentals,** p. 41.) Most agencies rent to those age 21 and over, although some agencies require drivers to be 25. Rates vary according to season, as well as duration of rental and condition of car, and generally include automobile insurance and GST. (**American Express** cardholders, please note that American Express does not cover the required Collision and Damage Waiver in New Zealand, as it does automatically in most other countries.) Expect to pay at least NZ$55 a day for a month's rental from one of these companies; for cars of better condition and make, the price may skyrocket to as high as NZ$130 per day. Smaller operators often offer eye-poppingly low fares, but be cautious—look carefully into the reliability and reputation of the company before committing. **Darn Cheap Rentals** (tel. 0800 800 327) operates out of Auckland, Wellington, Christchurch, and Picton (NZ$35 per day), though the cars are often very small. Also **Cheaper Rental Car** (tel. 0800 243 273) rents at NZ$44 per day. **Hardy** and **Ace** operate out of the South Island only (Picton tel. 0800 422 373 and Christchurch tel. 0800 202 029).

BUY-BACKS

Buying a car, then selling it upon departure, may be a smart option for longer stays. Buy-back outlets, such as the **New Zealand Guaranteed Buy-Back Vehicle Associates,** 825 Dominion Rd., Mt. Roskill, Auckland (tel. (09) 620 6587), sell cars specifically for this purpose. Prices range from NZ$3000-7000; you must keep the car for a minimum of a month. At the end of your stay, the buy-back outlet buys back the vehicle minus the depreciation rate.

If you prefer to strike out on your own car-buying spree, Auckland is definitely a hot spot for the best car deals: check out one of its car auctions or the used car section of *The New Zealand Herald* (especially on Wednesdays). The *Trade and Exchange*, another good place to look, comes out Mondays and Thursdays.

A car must have a V.I.C. (vehicle inspection certificate, sometimes called a W.O.F.), which ensures that it is road safe. Make sure that your potential car has received one within the past month. They are good for six months and cost NZ$25. A car must be **registered** (six months NZ$100; one year NZ$200). Whenever there is a change of ownership, a **MR13A form** must be completed by the buyer and seller and turned in at a post shop. The buyer must also complete a **MR13B form** (NZ$9.20). Insurance is not necessary but highly recommended, as is membership in an Automobile Association (see above). The latter will get you emergency breakdown service, free service for simple problems, and free towing.

Before you buy your car, you should have it inspected. Vehicle inspection services can be found in the yellow pages under that heading and will do comprehensive pre-purchase checks for NZ$60-80. You may want to check out **car fairs** in Auckland; some are **Sell Your Own Car,** 676 Great South Rd., Manukau (tel. 0800 735 596; open daily 7am-7pm); **Sell it Yourself,** 50 Wairau Rd., Glenfield (tel. (09) 443 3800; open daily 7am-7pm); **Ellerslie Racecourse** (tel. (09) 810 9212), off the Greenlane roundabout (open Sunday 9am-noon); and **Manukau City Park and Sell** (tel. 358 5000; open Sunday 9am-1pm). **Car auctions** in Auckland are another option. **Turners Car Auctions,** McNab St., Penrose (tel. 525 1920), sells budget cars Wednesday at 11:30am and family cars Thursday at 6pm. **Hammer Auctions,** 830 Great South Rd., Penrose (tel. 579 2344), sells budget cars on Monday, Wednesday, and Friday.

RULES OF THE ROAD

The Road Code of New Zealand (NZ$14.95), available at AA offices and bookstores, tells you all you need to know. Speed limits are strictly enforced; speed cameras are even set up at the traffic lights of many large towns to catch leadfooted offenders. Drunk driving laws are serious business in New Zealand and are strictly enforced. Americans, join your Kiwi companions and drive on the left hand side of the road; many accidents arise from tourists who don't give themselves some extra practice driving time to adjust before heading out. **Petrol** (gas) costs approximately NZ$1 per liter; it can run you an easy NZ$15-20 per day. State highways are abbreviated SH; SH2 is in the process of being renamed the Pacific Coast Highway. Members of worldwide Automobile Associations (see above) can enjoy the reciprocal agreement with the **New Zealand Automobile Association (AA)** (tel. 0800 500 222) to obtain free maps and other services from AA offices in New Zealand. For assistance on the road, The New Zealand AA **hotline** (tel. 0900 332 22) is NZ$1 per minute.

BY THUMB

Some visitors to New Zealand, particularly backpackers, rely on hitchhiking as their primary mode of transportation, and express satisfaction with its safety and convenience. Others, however, report that hitchhiking is not as safe as it used to be, especially for women traveling alone. A man and a woman are a safer combination; two men will have a harder time finding a ride. No matter how safe or friendly New Zealanders may be, you should always think seriously before trusting your life to a stranger, as you risk suffering from an accident, theft, assault, sexual harassment, or worse. Even at the risk of offending the driver, **do not put your backpack in**

ALL THE COOL KIDS ARE DOING IT. *Let's Go* strongly urges you to seriously consider the risks before you choose to hitch. Although we try to report accurately on the availability of hitching opportunities in each area, we do not recommend hitching as a necessarily safe means of transportation, and none of the details presented here or in this book are intended to do so.

the trunk; you might not get it back. Exercise caution when hitchhiking: avoid getting into the back of a two-door car; when waiting for a ride, stand in a well-lit, public place; start early in the day; avoid hitchhiking at night; and avoid hitchhiking alone. Trust your instincts—if you ever feel unsafe or threatened, do not hesitate to firmly but politely ask to be let off.

If you are planning on hitching, it is reported to be easiest just beyond the end of a town's residential area, but before the open highway. It is illegal on freeways. Hitching is not just a matter of luck. You can increase your chances if you choose a spot on the side of the road with ample space for a car to pull over. No one wants to pick up a lazy backpacker sitting on his pack. Walk backwards with the traffic with your thumb out and try to make eye contact with the driver. Sometimes, drivers will pass and then turn around to pick you up. Keep your destination secret until after you've found out where a prospective driver is headed; that way, if the driver looks threatening and you don't want to go with him, you can always bluff and say otherwise. Finally, avoid accepting offers that will leave you in a small town, short of your ultimate destination.

TOURIST INFO AND SERVICES

NEW ZEALAND TOURISM BOARD (NZTB)

The ever-helpful New Zealand Tourism Board (NZTB) offices can provide you with information galore about any region or aspect of the country that captures your attention. Their web page (www.nztb.govt.nz) is easy to use and enormously useful, offering concise travel info and nifty links to other travel pages. NZTB has offices in the following countries:

Australia: Level 8, 35 Pitt St., Sydney NSW 2000, or P.O. Box R1546, Royal Exchange PO 2000, NSW (tel. (02) 9247 5222; fax 9241 1136).

U.K.: New Zealand House, Haymarket, London SW1Y 4TQ (tel. (0171) 930 1662; fax 839 8928; email enquiries@nztb.govt.nz).

U.S.: Suite 300, 501 Santa Monica Blvd, Santa Monica, CA 90401 (tel. 800-388-5494 (headquarters) or (310) 395-7480; fax 395-5453).

VISITORS INFORMATION NETWORK (VIN)

In most towns, all cities, and many airports, you should watch for the green "i" symbol denoting one of the 81 independently owned and operated Visitor's Information Network (VIN) tourist offices throughout New Zealand. Coordinated by the New Zealand Tourism Board, these offices will help plan every aspect of your travel from A to Z, including booking accommodations, transport, and activities. You can also tune into 88.2 FM, the 24-hour tourist radio station.

USEFUL WEBSITES

Akiko: New Zealand on the Web (http://nz.com/guide). News, cultural essays, and travel info. Recent additions include: a virtual tour of New Zealand; "KiwiChat," a bulletin board of New Zealand questions, thoughts, and travel stories; and "ChatTour," a forum where you can talk to fellow Kiwi aficionados.

New Zealand TravelPlanner (http://travelplanner.co.nz/travel) is an extremely helpful site with travel information, maps, articles, pictures, and accommodation listings.

Microsoft Expedia (expedia.msn.com) has everything you'd ever need to make travel plans on the web: compare flight fares, look at maps, or make reservations. Fare-Tracker, a free service, sends you monthly updates about cheap fares.

Shoestring Travel (www.stratpub.com), an alternative to Microsoft's monolithic site, is a budget travel e-zine that features listings of home exchanges, links, and accommodations information.

The New Zealand Herald (www.nzherald.co.nz/dailycom/index.html) is an excellent source of daily news.

New Zealand Government Online (www.govt.nz) provides statistics and vital visitor info. Follow their link to the **New Zealand Immigration Service** (www.immigration.govt.nz) to find out about the restrictions and requirements for staying in New Zealand.

The CIA World Factbook (www.odci.gov/cia/publications/factbook/index.html) has tons of vital statistics on New Zealand's people, government, and economy.

Let's Go (www.letsgo.com) has our newsletter, information about our books, up-to-the-minute links, and more.

FURTHER READING

How to Plan Your Dream Vacation Using the Web. Elizabeth Dempsey. Coriolis Group (US$25).

Nettravel: How Travelers Use the Internet, Michael Shapiro. O'Reilly & Associates (US$25).

Travel Planning Online for Dummies, Noah Vadnai. IDG Books (US$25).

SPECIFIC CONCERNS

WOMEN TRAVELERS

Women exploring on their own inevitably face some additional safety concerns, even in a country as safe as New Zealand. If you are concerned, you might consider staying in hostels which offer single rooms that lock from the inside. Communal showers in some hostels are safer than others; check them before settling in. Stick to centrally located accommodations and avoid solitary late-night treks.

When traveling, always carry extra money for a phone call, bus, or taxi. **Hitching** is never safe for lone women, or even for two women traveling together. Look as if you know where you're going (even when you don't). Watch out for persistent, too-friendly locals, especially when hitting the pub scene. In general, pubs tend to be havens of machismo culture.

A **self-defense course** will not only prepare you for a potential attack, but will also raise your level of awareness of your surroundings as well as your confidence: **Impact, Prepare, and Model Mugging** can refer you to local self-defense courses in the United States (tel. 800-345-5425) and Vancouver, Canada (tel. (604) 878-3838). Workshop (2-3 hours) start at US$50 and full courses run US$350-500. (Both men and women are welcome.) *Let's Go: New Zealand* lists specific emergency numbers and hotlines (such as **rape crisis lines**) in the Practical Information listings of most cities. The **general emergency number** in New Zealand is **111.**

Women also face some specific health concerns when traveling (see **Women's Health,** p. 35).

RESOURCES FOR WOMEN

Wander Women, P.O. Box 68058, Newton, Auckland 3 (tel. (09) 360 7330; fax 360 7332; email enquiries@wanderwomen.co.nz) offers guided sea kayaking and other outdoor trips for both women-only and mixed groups.

A Foxy Old Woman's Guide to Traveling Alone, Jay Ben-Lesser. Crossing Press (US $11). Information, informal advice, and a resource list for solo travelers on a low-to-medium budget.

A Journey of One's Own: Uncommon Advice for the Independent Woman Traveler, Thalia Zepatos. Eighth Mountain Press (US$17). An inspiring collection of essays by women travelers in addition to practical travel information specific to women.

TRAVELING ALONE

There are many benefits to traveling alone, among them greater independence and challenge. Without distraction, you can write a great travel log in the grand tradition of Mark Twain, John Steinbeck, and Charles Kuralt. Traveling alone in New Zealand is neither unwise nor uncommon. Many solo travelers take advantage of backpacker buses like Kiwi Experience or Magic.

On the other hand, any solo traveler is a more vulnerable target of harassment and street theft. Lone travelers need to be well-organized and look confident at all times. If questioned, never admit that you are traveling alone. Maintain regular contact with someone at home who knows your itinerary.

RESOURCES FOR SOLO TRAVELERS
A number of organizations supply information for solo travelers, and others find travel companions for those who don't want to go alone.

Connecting: Solo Traveler Network, P.O. Box 29088, 1996 W. Broadway, Vancouver, BC V6J 5C2, Canada (tel. (604) 737-7791; email info@cstn.org; www.cstn.org). Bi-monthly newsletter features going solo tips, single-friendly tips and travel companion ads. Annual directory lists holiday suppliers that avoid single supplement charges. Advice and lodging exchanges facilitated between members. Membership US$25-35.

Travel Companion Exchange, P.O. Box 833, Amityville, NY 11701 (tel. (516) 454-0880 or 800-392-1256; www.travelalone.com). Publishes the pamphlet *Foiling Pickpockets & Bag Snatchers* (US$4) and *Travel Companions,* a bimonthly newsletter for single travelers seeking a travel partner (subscription US$48).

The Single Traveler Newsletter, P.O. Box 682, Ross, CA 94957 (tel. (415) 389-0227). 6 issues US$29.

Traveling Solo, Eleanor Berman. Globe Pequot (US$17).

OLDER TRAVELERS

Many **senior citizen** discounts in New Zealand, especially transportation passes, only apply to country citizens. As far as activities and accommodations, however, you may be able to finagle a special price if you ask nicely. Agencies for senior group travel are growing in enrollment and popularity. A few organizations and publications are listed below.

ElderTreks, 597 Markham St., Toronto, ON, Canada, M6G 2L7 (tel. 800-741-7956 or (416) 588-5000; fax 588-9839; email passages@inforamp.net; www.eldertreks.com). Has all-inclusive tours to New Zealand.

Walking the World, P.O. Box 1186, Fort Collins, CO 80522 (tel. (970) 498-0500; fax 498-9100; email walktworld@aol.com; www.walkingtheworld.com), sends trips that cover the North and South Island.

Elderhostel, 75 Federal St., Boston, MA 02110-1941 (tel. (617) 426-7788 or (877) 426-8056; email registration@elderhostel.org; www.elderhostel.org). Programs at colleges, universities, and other learning centers in New Zealand on varied subjects lasting 1-4 weeks. Must be 55 or over (spouse can be of any age).

No Problem! Worldwise Tips for Mature Adventurers, Janice Kenyon. Orca Book Publishers (US$16).

A Senior's Guide to Healthy Travel, Donald L. Sullivan. Career Press (US$15).

BISEXUAL, GAY, AND LESBIAN TRAVELERS

Male homosexual acts were banned until 1986, when sexual intercourse was finally made legal for persons over 16 regardless of sexual orientation. In 1993, discrimination of any kind became illegal in New Zealand. Intolerance does not need to be unduly feared in major New Zealand cities, many of which feature an active gay culture with gay-friendly bars, health centers, and bookstores. Auckland has an active, though partially segregated, gay and lesbian culture, while Wellington's gay and lesbian population is more integrated. More rural and remote areas are less accustomed to displays of homosexuality, however. They may be less friendly, but will not likely be openly or unpleasantly disapproving. The following organizations in New Zealand can offer specific tips. Local organizations and particularly gay-friendly venues are listed throughout the book.

WITHIN NEW ZEALAND

New Zealand Gay and Lesbian Tourism Association, P.O. Box 11-582, Wellington 6001 (tel. 0800 GAY TRAVEL; email nzglta@clear.net.nz; http://nz.com/webnz/tpac/gaynz). This professional, nonprofit organization helps arrange both group and individual travel worldwide, addressing everything from hotel reservations to special tours to transportation needs.

Gaylink Reservation Center, P.O. Box 11-462, Wellington 6001 (tel. (04) 384 1865; fax 384 1835; email gts@clear.net.nz; http://nz.com/webnz/tpac/gaynz/Gaylink Travel.html).

Gay Switchboard (tel. (04) 385 0674).

Travel Desk NZ Ltd., 45 Anzac Ave., Auckland (tel. 377 9031; email out@nz.com).

Lesbian Line, P.O. Box 11-882, Wellington (tel. (04) 389 8082; open Tu, Th, and Sa 7:30-10:30pm).

GENERAL INFORMATION

Listed below are contact organizations, mail-order bookstores, publishers, and publications which offer materials addressing some specific concerns.

Gay's the Word, 66 Marchmont St., London WC1N 1AB (tel. (0171) 278 7654; email gays.theword@virgin.net; www.gaystheword.co.uk). The largest gay and lesbian bookshop in the U.K. Mail-order service available. No catalogue of listings, but they will provide a list of titles on a given subject.

Giovanni's Room, 345 S. 12th St., Philadelphia, PA 19107 (tel. (215) 923-2960; fax 923-0813; email giophilp@netaxs.com). An international feminist, lesbian, and gay bookstore with mail-order service that carries the publications listed below.

International Gay and Lesbian Travel Association, 4331 N. Federal Hwy., Suite 304, Fort Lauderdale, FL 33308 (tel. 800-448-8550 or (954) 776-2626; fax 776-3303; email IGLTA@aol.com; www.iglta.com). Organization of over 1350 companies serving gay and lesbian travelers worldwide. Call for lists of travel agents, accommodations, and events.

Spartacus International Gay Guide, by Bruno Gmunder Verlag (US$33).

Ferrari Guides' Gay Travel A to Z, Ferrari Guides' Men's Travel in Your Pocket, and *Ferrari Guides' Women's Travel in Your Pocket.* Ferrari Guides (US$14-16).

The Gay Vacation Guide: The Best Trips and How to Plan Them, Mark Chesnut. Citadel Press (US$15).

TRAVELERS WITH DISABILITIES

New Zealand is overall an accessible and welcoming country for the disabled. Law requires that every new motel and hotel provides a certain number of fully accessible rooms. In addition, a number of **tramps** and **walks** are wheelchair-accessible; always check with the DOC. Main taxi companies in major cities and many towns have a **Total Mobility Taxi Service** offering transportation for those with wheelchairs. With sufficient notice, some major car rental agencies will offer hand-controlled vehicles at select locations. The following organizations provide information or publications that might be of assistance.

RESOURCES WITHIN NEW ZEALAND
Deaf Emergency Telephone Number: 0800 161 616.

Enable Information: tel. 0800 171 981

Disability Resource Center, P.O. Box 24-042, Royal Oak, Auckland 3 (tel. (09) 625 8069; fax 624 1633).

Disabled Persons Assembly (DPA), Level 4, Tower Block, Wellington Trade Center, 175 Victoria St., Wellington (tel. (04) 801 9100).

New Zealand Disability Resource Centre, 60 Bennett St., Palmerston North (tel. (06) 952 0011; fax 952 0022).

The Paraplegic and Physically Disabled Association, 2 Rodney St., Northcote, and P.O. Box 34, 101 Birkenhead (tel. (09) 418 2677).

Taxi Companies for People with Disabilities: Cannons Total Mobility (tel. (09) 836 4386); Co-op Taxis (tel. (09) 300 3000); Independence Mobility (tel. (09) 836 6761); North Harbor Taxis (tel. (09) 443 1777); South Auckland Taxis (tel. (09) 278 5678); Auckland Mobility (tel. (09) 817 9442); United Taxis (tel. (09) 298 1000).

RESOURCES OUTSIDE OF NEW ZEALAND
Society for the Advancement of Travel for the Handicapped (SATH), 347 Fifth Ave., #610, New York, NY 10016 (tel. (212) 447-1928; fax 725-8253; email sath-travel@aol.com; www.sath.org). Advocacy group publishing a quarterly color travel magazine *Open World* (free for members or US$13 for nonmembers). Also publishes a wide range of information sheets on disability travel facilitation and accessible destinations. Annual membership US$45, students and seniors US$30.

Directions Unlimited, 720 N. Bedford Rd., Bedford Hills, NY 10507 (tel. 800-533-5343; in NY (914) 241-1700; fax 241-0243; email cruisesusa@aol.com). Specializes in arranging individual and group vacations, tours, and cruises for the physically disabled. Group tours for blind travelers.

Global Access (www.geocities.com/Paris/1502/disabilitylinks.html) has links for disabled travelers in New Zealand.

MINORITY TRAVELERS

New Zealand's population is mainly Caucasian; the largest minority group is Maori, followed by other Polynesians and Asians (see **The People,** p. 12) Race relations today between Maori and Pakeha (non-Maori peoples) appear to have reached some measure of stability, although tension remains. Debate, protest, and legal reform over the place of Maori culture, history, and land claims in New Zealand continues.

Asian tourism, particularly Japanese and Korean, is becoming common in New Zealand; as a result, prejudice against Asians in some areas is increasing. Visitors of Asian descent may possibly be at risk for theft, due to the stereotype of the wealthy Asian tourist. Other minorities may find that they stand out in a crowd, but are more likely to invite curious looks than harassment or violence.

As always, however, it is difficult to generalize about how minority travelers will be treated in a foreign country. Let's Go asks its researchers to exclude establishments that discriminate for any reason. If the establishment is listed in this guide, please mail a letter to Let's Go stating the details of the incident (see **Helping Let's Go,** at the beginning of the guide).

TRAVELERS WITH CHILDREN

New Zealand may be best known for its extreme adventure activities and hard-core tramping opportunities, but there is plenty to do for families who prefer a little less danger and a little more structure in their travel diet. From scenic flights to sailing tours, glass-blowing museums to glow-worm caves, and petrified forests to penguin colonies, there is plenty here to entertain parents and wear out even the most energetic of kids. The **Sights and Activities** sections of cities and towns offers a wide range of ways to get your thrills without risking life and limb.

Children's discounts abound in New Zealand. Restaurants often have children's menus, and virtually all museums and tourist attractions have a children's rate. Children under two generally fly for 10% of the adult airfare on international flights (this does not necessarily include a seat). International fares are usually discounted 25% for children ages two to eleven.

As in other countries, family vacations in New Zealand often require that you slow your pace, and always require that you plan ahead. When deciding where to stay, call ahead to hostels and other accommodations to make sure they allow children. Be sure that your child carries some sort of ID in case of an emergency or if he or she gets lost. If your child does get lost, help is always nearby; he or she could hardly pick a friendlier and safer country in which to do so.

FURTHER READING

Backpacking with Babies and Small Children, Goldie Silverman. Wilderness Press (US$10).

How to Take Great Trips with Your Kids, Sanford and Jane Portnoy. Harvard Common Press (US $10).

Have Kid, Will Travel: 101 Survival Strategies for Vacationing With Babies and Young Children, Claire and Lucille Tristram. Andrews and McMeel (US$9).

Adventuring with Children: An Inspirational Guide to World Travel and the Outdoors, Nan Jeffrey. Avalon House Publishing ($15).

ALTERNATIVES TO TOURISM

STUDY

A **student visa** is required for those intending to study in New Zealand for more than three months. Exchange programs are available in Auckland, Christchurch, Wellington, Dunedin, and other smaller cities.

American Field Service (AFS), 310 SW 4th Avenue, Suite 630, Portland, OR 97204 (tel. 800-237-4636; fax (503) 241-1653; email afsinfo@afs.org; www.afs.org/usa). AFS offers summer-, semester-, and year-long homestay international exchange programs with New Zealand for high school students and graduating high school seniors. Financial aid available.

Butler University Institute for Study Abroad, 4600 Sunset Ave, Indianapolis, IN 46208 (tel. 800-858-0229; www.butler.edu/www/isa), offers programs at four New Zealand universities.

School for International Training, College Semester Abroad, Admissions, Kipling Rd., P.O. Box 676, Brattleboro, VT 05302 (tel. 800-336-1616 or (802) 258-3267; fax 258-3500; www.worldlearning.org). Runs semester- and year-long programs in Hamilton, New Zealand. Programs cost US$8200-11,000, all expenses included. Financial aid available and U.S. financial aid is transferable. Also runs the **Experiment in International Living,** Summer Programs (tel. 800-345-2929; fax (802) 258-3428; email eil@worldlearning.org). Founded in 1932, it offers cross-cultural educational homestays, community service, and ecological adventure in New Zealand. Programs are 3-5 weeks long and run from US$1800-5000.

FURTHER READING

Academic Year Abroad. Institute of International Education Books (US$45).

Vacation Study Abroad. Institute of International Education Books (US$40).

Peterson's Study Abroad Guide. Peterson's (US$30).

WORK

Officially, you can only hold a job in New Zealand with a **work visa** or **permit.** To obtain these, you need to be sponsored by a New Zealand employer who can demonstrate that you have skills that locals lack—not the easiest of tasks. Call the nearest New Zealand consulate or embassy to get more info.

Many backpackers (hostels) in New Zealand could aptly be termed "working hostels," for they are filled not with vacationers but with travelers and locals who have set up a temporary home near their jobs. In larger cities, travelers help around the hostel in exchange for room and board, and may eventually establish their own residence in New Zealand. In rural areas, many travelers find seasonal employment picking fruit. Such work is usually arranged through hostel owners. Despite popular misconception, you do need a work permit to do this. Australian citizens and residents with a current Australian resident return visa do not need a visa or permit to work in New Zealand.

Citizens of Canada, the Republic of Ireland, Japan, Malaysia, and the U.K. aged 18-30 are eligible to apply for a place in a New Zealand working holiday scheme; contact the nearest New Zealand Immigration Service office for more details (www.immigration.govt.nz). If you are a U.S. citizen and a full-time student at a U.S. university, the simplest way to get a job abroad is through work-permit programs run by the **Council on International Educational Exchange (Council)** and its member organizations. Potential jobs include fruit-picking, hotel staffing, or working at a ski resort in winter, with weekly rages ranging from around US$300-400 a week. Contact the Voluntary Services Dept., 205 E. 42nd St., New York, NY 10017 (tel. 888-COUNCIL (268-6245); fax (212) 822-2699; email info@ciee.org; www.ciee.org).

FURTHER READING

International Jobs: Where they Are, How to Get Them, Eric Koocher. Perseus Books (US$16).

The Alternative Travel Directory, Clayton Hubbs. Transitions Abroad (US$20).

Work Abroad, Clayton Hubbs. Transitions Abroad (US$16).

International Directory of Voluntary Work, Victoria Pybus. Vacation Work Publications (US$16).

Overseas Summer Jobs 1999, Work Your Way Around the World, and *Directory of Jobs and Careers Abroad.* Peterson's (US$17-18 each).

VOLUNTEERING

New Zealand readily provides volunteer jobs. Jobs on organic farms arranged through **WWOOF** are particularly popular.

Willing Workers on Organic Farms (WWOOF), P.O. Box 1172, Nelson, New Zealand (tel./fax (03) 544 9890; email wwoof-nz@xtra.co.nz; www.phdcc.com/sites/wwoof). Distributes a list of names of over 500 farmers who offer room and board in exchange for help on the farm. Membership fee is NZ$20 from within the country; from overseas, AUS$25, CAN$25, UK£10, or US$20. Couples' discounts available.

Volunteers for Peace, 1034 Tiffany Rd., Belmont, VT 05730 (tel. (802) 259-2759; fax 259-2922; email vfp@vfp.org; www.vfp.org). A nonprofit organization that arranges speedy placement in 2- to 3-week work-camps in New Zealand made up of 10-15 people. Most complete and up-to-date listings provided in the annual *International Workcamp Directory* (US$15). Registration fee US$195. Free newsletter.

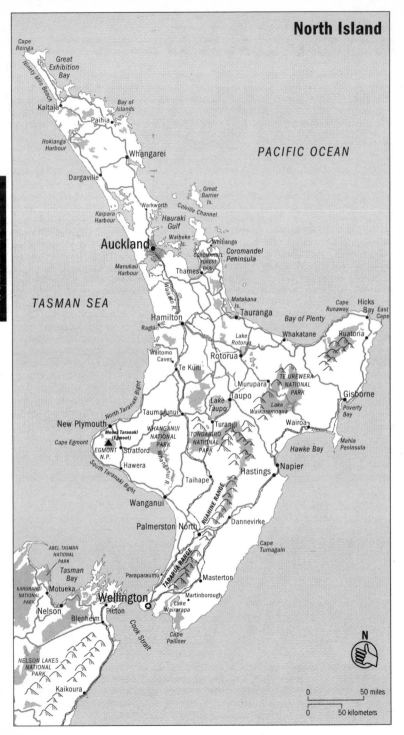

Cape Reinga

Great Exhibition Bay

Ninety Mile Beach

Kaitaia

Paihia

Bay of Islands

Hokianga Harbour

Whangarei

PACIFIC OCEAN

Dargaville

Warkworth

Great Barrier Is.

Colville Channel

Kaipara Harbour

Hauraki Gulf

Auckland

Waiheke Is.

Whitianga

Coromandel Peninsula

COROMANDEL FOREST PARK

Manukau Harbour

Thames

TASMAN SEA

Waikato R.

Matakana Is.

Cape Runaway

Hicks Bay

East Cape

Hamilton

Raglan

Tauranga

Bay of Plenty

Whakatane

Ruatoria

Waitomo Caves

Lake Rotorua

Rotorua

Te Kuiti

Murupara

TE UREWERA NATIONAL PARK

North Taranaki Bight

Taumarunui

Lake Taupo

Taupo

Lake Waikaremoana

Gisborne

Poverty Bay

New Plymouth

Mount Taranaki (Egmont)

WHANGANUI NATIONAL PARK

Turangi

TONGARIRO NATIONAL PARK

Wairoa

Cape Egmont

EGMONT N.P.

Stratford

Whanganui R.

Mahia Peninsula

Hawera

South Taranaki Bight

Taihape

Hastings

Hawke Bay

Napier

Wanganui

RUAHINE RANGE

Palmerston North

Dannevirke

ABEL TASMAN NATIONAL PARK

Tasman Bay

Cape Turnagain

KAHURANGI NATIONAL PARK

Motueka

Paraparaumu

TARARUA RANGE

Masterton

Nelson

Picton

Wellington

Martinborough

Lake Wairarapa

Blenheim

Cook Strait

Cape Palliser

NELSON LAKES NATIONAL PARK

N

Kaikoura

0   50 miles

0   50 kilometers

AUCKLAND

Squeezed onto a narrow isthmus between sparkling Waitemata and Manukau Harbours, the inhabitants of New Zealand's largest and most cosmopolitan city are never far from sea. The brightly colored sails of the windsurfers, yachts, and catamarans of Aucklanders at play form a tapestry that enlivens this most aptly dubbed "City of Sails." Auckland is currently swabbing its decks for the America's Cup competition and hoping for a big economic boom. The bays and strands near the city are perfect for swimming and sunbathing, while the stunning black-sand beaches of Auckland's west coast provide a surfing environment that the drawl of the local's lingo could only praise as "choice!"

Originally settled by Maori from the islands of the Pacific more than 650 years ago, Auckland's numerous extinct volcanoes bear the scars and terracing of previous use as fortified villages. It is from atop any of these hills, such as One Tree Hill, Mt. Wellington, or North Head, that one can obtain the most commanding views of the city and the islands of the gulf. While the massive sleeping form of Rangitoto Island dominates the horizon out to sea, it is the curiously pointless Sky Tower that commands the cityscape.

Auckland's Central Business District throbs with powerwalking suits and overworked cellphones. Like many places on the North Island, the charm and vitality of Auckland lies askance—not at downtown ground-zero but to the sides, in satellite neighborhoods and in the islands of the Waitemata Harbour. By day, the ultrachic and the multi-pierced overflow the High Street cafes, spilling out onto the sidewalks. By night, the hip move to inner-city bars and clubs, while the more alternative migrate to the cafe-culture hubs of Ponsonby and Newmarket.

The combination of its own Maori population and a resplendent community of Pacific Islanders, makes Auckland the world's largest Polynesian city. Add to this 150 years of European and more recent Asian immigration, and you should be prepared for a truly multicultural experience.

❂AUCKLAND HIGHLIGHTS

■ The shops and cafes of **Ponsonby** and **Mt. Eden** possess magnetic charm.
■ **Great Barrier Island** (p. 26) is a time warp to an isolated wilderness while **Waiheke Island** (p. 88) wine tasting is a perfect day in paradise.
■ The party lasts all night at clubs on **Auckland's K Road** and **High Street** (p. 78).

▐ ARRIVAL AND DEPARTURE

BY PLANE

Swank and smartly renovated, the **Auckland International Airport (AKL),** located a 50-minute drive from central Auckland, serves as port of entry for about 80% of New Zealand's overseas visitors. Many vans and shuttles run to and from the airport, but **Airbus** (tel. 275 7685) is most convenient and affordable ($12; children, YHA and VIP $8; seniors $7). Buses run every 20 to 30 minutes and make many stops at the Sheraton Hotel, YHA backpackers, Sky City bus station, Parnell, Newmarket, and other transfer points. Buy tickets from the Airbus driver. **Johnston's Shuttle Link** (tel. 256 0333 or 275 1234) has prearranged pickups, and the **Little Kiwi Airport Shuttle** (tel. 0800 759 994) runs between the airport and the Downtown Airline Terminal at the corner of Albert and Quay St. (every 20min. 7am-7pm, $10). From the airport, **Taxis** are $30 to $40 to downtown.

At the airport, exchange currency at the **Bank of New Zealand (BNZ);** this is also where you'll pay the NZ$20 **departure fee.** Those connecting to domestic flights (with more than 45min. between flights) can check their bags at the airline counters; otherwise, lug them onto the blue airport shuttles.

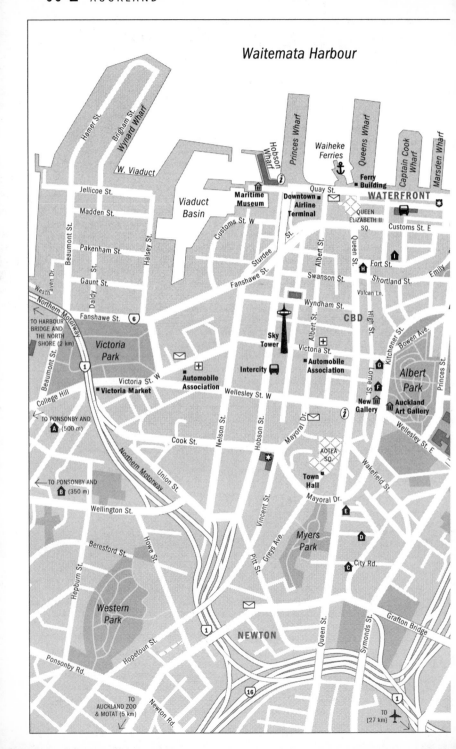

Waitemata Harbour

Hamer St.

Brigham St.

Wynard Wharf

W. Viaduct

Jellicoe St.

Madden St.

Beaumont St.

Daldy St.

Pakenham St.

Gaunt St.

Fanshawe St.

Westh...

Northern Motorway

TO HARBOUR
BRIDGE AND
THE NORTH
SHORE (2 km)

Beaumont St.

College Hill

TO PONSONBY AND
Ⓐ (500 m)

TO PONSONBY AND
Ⓑ (350 m)

Wellington St.

Beresford St.

Hepburn St.

Howe St.

Northern Motorway

Union St.

Ponsonby Rd.

Hopetoun St.

TO
AUCKLAND ZOO
& MOTAT (5 km)

Newton Rd.

*Western
Park*

*Victoria
Park*

Viaduct
Basin

Halsey St.

Customs St. W

Sturdee St.

Fanshawe St.

Hobson
Wharf

Maritime
Museum

Princes Wharf

Waiheke
Ferries

Queens Wharf

Captain Cook Wharf

Marsden Wharf

Quay St.

Ferry
Building

WATERFRONT

Downtown
Airline
Terminal

QUEEN
ELIZABETH II
SQ.

Customs St. E

Albert St.

Queen St.

Fort St.

H

Shortland St.

Emily

Swanson St.

Vulcan Ln.

Wyndham St.

CBD

Sky
Tower

Albert St.

Victoria St.

Intercity

Automobile
Association

High St.

Kitchener St.

Bowen Ave.

*Albert
Park*

Princes St.

Victoria St. W

Automobile
Association

Victoria Market

Lorne St.

G

F

New
Gallery

Auckland
Art Gallery

Wellesley St. W

Cook St.

Nelson St.

Hobson St.

Mayoral Dr.

AOTEA
SQ.

Wakefield St.

Wellesley St. E

Town
Hall

Mayoral Dr.

E

Vincent St.

Greys Ave.

*Myers
Park*

D

Pitt St.

City Rd.

C

Queen St.

Symonds St.

Grafton Bridge

NEWTON

TO
(27 km)

6

1

1

16

1

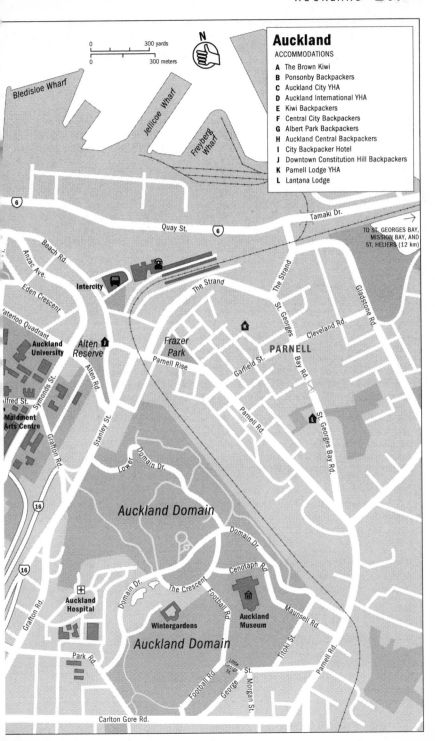

Auckland

ACCOMMODATIONS

A The Brown Kiwi
B Ponsonby Backpackers
C Auckland City YHA
D Auckland International YHA
E Kiwi Backpackers
F Central City Backpackers
G Albert Park Backpackers
H Auckland Central Backpackers
I City Backpacker Hotel
J Downtown Constitution Hill Backpackers
K Parnell Lodge YHA
L Lantana Lodge

While domestic flying is fast, it deprives travelers of spectacular road-level scenery—arguably one of the best and least anticipated parts of traveling New Zealand. **Air New Zealand** (tel. 357 3000) flies direct to: **Wellington** (1hr., every 30min., $290); **Christchurch** (2¼hr., 1-2 per hr., $388); **Rotorua** (45min., 6-11 per day, $200); and **Queenstown** (4hr., 1 per day, $602). **Ansett New Zealand** and **Mt. Cook Airline** fly to the same destinations with similar service and rates. Students and backpackers receive discounts; hefty marked-down prices can also be had by booking ahead or by flying stand-by (see **Getting Around: By Plane,** p. 49, for more details). For international flights, Air New Zealand flies to the Australian cities: **Sydney** (3½hr., 5 per day, $559, return $729); **Brisbane** (3½hr., 2 per day, $559, return $729); and **Melbourne** (4hr., 2 per day, $559, return $729), among other destinations.

BY TRAIN

TranzRail (tel. 0800 802 802; M-Su 7am-9pm) leaves from the **Auckland Railway Station** (tel. 270 5209) which is located just a bit inland, off Beach Rd. (take Custom St. E past Anzac Ave.) between the CBD and the neighborhood of Parnell (open M-F 7:30am-6pm, Sa-Su 7:30am-1pm). Trains head down the main rail line to: **Wellington** (11hr., 2 per day, $135) via **Hamilton** (2hr., $36) and **Palmerston North** (8¾hr., $108); **Tauranga** (3½hr., $54) via **Hamilton;** and **Rotorua** (4hr., $63) via **Hamilton.** Cheaper fares are available (see **Getting Around: By Train,** p. 52).

BY BUS

InterCity (tel. 913 6100; email info@intercitycoach.co.nz; www.intercity-coach.co.nz) arrives at the new travel center of **Sky City,** at Hobson and Victoria St. in downtown Auckland. Service runs north to **Paihia** in the **Bay of Islands** (4hr., 2-3 per day, $42) via **Whangarei** (2¾hr., 2 per day, $30); and **Paihia** (7¾hr., 1 per day, winter less often, $58) via **Dargaville** (3hr., $39). Southbound runs include: **Rotorua** (3½-5hr., 6 per day, $43) via **Hamilton** (2hr., 9 per day, $27); **Tauranga** (3½hr., 2-3 per day, $37); **New Plymouth** (6hr., 2 per day, $69); **Napier** (7hr., 2 per day, $75); **Wellington** (11hr., 2 per day, $94) via **Taupo** (4½-5hr., $49); **Palmerston North** (9-10hr., 2-3 per day, $69); and **Wanganui** (8hr., 1 per day, $68). Special discounts can also be obtained by booking ahead (see **Essentials: By Bus,** p. 52, for more info).

BY CAR

SH1 is the main route into and out of Auckland. Toward the south, it's called the **Auckland-Hamilton Motorway,** with on-ramps at the top of Hobson St., Symonds St., and Khyber Pass Rd. Toward the north, it's called the **Northern Motorway,** with an on-ramp at Beaumont St. by Victoria Park.

BY THUMB

The collective wisdom of Auckland's backpacker community says that the best **hitchhiking** can be found by taking a bus to the outlying suburbs and hitching from there, asking locals for current advice. To head north, hitchers reportedly catch the **Stagecoach** (tel. 366 6400) Hibiscus Coast Bus from the downtown terminal to Orewa ($7.20), a good hitching spot. To head south, hitchers take the Stagecoach bus to Drury ($7.20). It is **illegal** to hitch on the freeway; hitchers recommend thumbing by on-ramps that have room for cars to pull over. See **By Thumb** (p. 56) for more information on hitchhiking in New Zealand.

✺ ORIENTATION

Auckland and the city environs sprawl across a narrow isthmus area that connects Northland to the landmass of the North Island. The **Waitemata Harbour** and the Pacific Ocean lie to the north and east of the city while the **Manukau Harbour** stretches southward with the Tasman Sea in the west. **SH1** (Southern Motorway) pumps traffic up from the south. The road becomes the Northern Motorway north of the city and converges into **SH16,** stretching west to the Waitakeres and north to Ninety Mile Beach. While the greater metropolitan area is low-density suburbia, many of the attractive sights and neighborhoods are fairly centralized and only a walk—or a short bus ride—away from downtown Auckland.

Downtown Auckland is called the **Central Business District (CBD).** This business district teems with modern buildings with mirror-glass facades and corporate logos. Here, banks and pinstripe suits dominate, as do tourist rip-offs and luxury department stores. **Queen St.,** the most central, most commercial strip in Auckland, runs through the heart of the CBD and down toward the water where it greets **Queen Elizabeth II Sq.** (known as **QE II Sq.**) **Victoria St.,** another major street, crosses Queen St. and slices east-west starting from Victoria Park (on the West side of town) and heads to Albert Park (East side). The **Waterfront** sits at the bottom of Queen St., by the Waitemata Harbour. **The New Zealand Cup Village,** the slick marina development for the America's Cup regatta sailing teams, resides in and around **Viaduct Basin,** near Hobson's Wharf along the waterfront. **Quay ("key") Street** keeps close to the waterfront wharfs. The **Ferry Building** (see **Getting Around: By Ferry,** p. 70) is right off Quay St., across from QE II Sq. Inland to the East, in a different corner of town, stands the **Railway Station** (off Beach Rd.; take Custom St. E past Anzac Ave.), between the CBD and Parnell.

The neighborhoods of **Parnell** and **Ponsonby** straddle the CBD. Both areas are accessible—by foot or Link bus—from the CBD. Ponsonby's partner in coolness, **Karangahape Rd.** (universally known as **K Rd.**), sits at the top of Queen St., at the opposite end from the waterfront. K Rd. is the gritty thoroughfare for fashionable clubs, cafes, and some cool bars (and strip clubs too, admittedly). K Rd. leads to Ponsonby and, in the other direction, to the charming suburb of **Mt. Eden,** 2km south of city center. This satellite burb is a major hike from the CBD. Mt. Eden is yet another gem on the outskirts of Auckland proper.

Running East of the CBD, Quay St. turns into **Tamaki Drive,** which then swoops along the stunning coast. Skirting subtropical waters and cream-colored sands, it becomes a prime in-line skating, kayaking, and parading venue in the summer months. Take a look out at **Orakei Basin,** off **Hobson Bay,** home to frequent rainbows and hundreds of pleasure yachts. You'll probably need a car, but hiding around **Bastion Point** from Orakei is **Mission Bay,** a cool, waterfront carousing and sunbathing outpost with an awesome stretch of hip cafes and bars. These coastal spots are a bus or car drive away from the CBD. Definite day trip material.

St. Heliers Bay, a few more minutes east down the shore on Tamaki Dr., has white sand and a tiny shopping district where the *nouveau riche* wage elegant battles with the old money of Paritai.

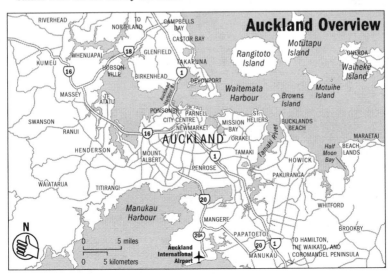

⎧⎫ GETTING AROUND

BY BUS

The **Link bus,** which makes a complete loop through the central city in one-and-a-half hours, is an excellent way to orient yourself ($1). Even better, the buses will take you from the downtown area to the must-see surrounding neighborhoods of Auckland (and back again). The white-and-blue buses make both clockwise and counterclockwise ("anti-clockwise") loops through Queen St., Sky City, Victoria Park, Ponsonby, K Rd., Auckland University, the Auckland Domain, the Auckland Museum, Newmarket, Parnell, the Railway Station, and QE II Sq. Though not technically a tourist bus, you can make it into one by getting on (or off) anywhere along the route at stops marked with the yellow Link logo in a blue oval.

The **Explorer Bus** (tel. 0800 439 756) offers hop-on, hop-off service connecting the Ferry Building, Mission Bay, Kelly Tarlton's, Auckland Museum, Parnell Village, Downtown Airline Terminal, Sky City, and Victoria Park Market. A **satellite bus** operating between October and April goes to Mt. Eden, St. Luke's shopping center, Auckland Zoo, Museum of Technology and Transport, and the Art Gallery. Buses depart on the hour from the Ferry Building (9am-4pm, winter 10am-4pm; $20, children $10; purchase tickets from the driver).

Ordinary city buses run by **Stagecoach** are a bit more challenging to negotiate, so contact **Rideline** (tel. 366 6400, M-Sa 6:30am-9:30pm, Su 8:30am-6:30pm). Fares are calculated by the number of stages traveled, and range from Stage 1 ($1.10, children 60¢) to Stage 8 ($7.20, children $4.30). A pass for a day of unlimited travel is also offered. Most city buses can be caught at the Downtown Bus Centre (not a place to be at night), or across from QE II Sq., both on Customs St., near Queen St.

BY TRAIN

Local commuter train service to Auckland's suburbs is handled by **Tranz Rail.** Call **Rideline** (tel. 366 6400) for assistance with the schedule. Service is generally available between 6am and 6:30pm Monday through Friday. Each journey is broken up into stages; rates range from Stage 1 ($1.10, children 60¢) to Stage 6 ($4.30, children $2.80). Lower priced fares are only valid after 9am. Buy tickets on the train or at the **train station,** located off Beach Rd., between the CBD and Parnell.

BY FERRY

Ferries leave from **Prince's Wharf** behind the Ferry Building, across from QE II Park. The islands of **Rangitoto** (see p. 87) and **Waiheke** (see p. 88) are very accessible, as is the North Shore community of **Devonport** (see p. 85). Contact **Fullers** (tel. 367 9111) for the schedule. The **Pakatoa Cat** (tel. 379 0066; fax 366 3006) leaves from Pier 3 and heads for Coromandel on the **Coromandel Peninsula** (2hr., Tu and F 11:30am, Sa and Su, 9:30am, $31, return $59). The heliport and hydrofoil launching point for the remote beauty of **Great Barrier Island** (see p. 90) is in **Mechanics Bay.**

BY CAR

RESOURCES. The **Automobile Association,** 99 Albert St. (tel. 377 4660), is in the CBD on the corner of Victoria and Albert St. (open M-F 8:30am-5pm). A plethora of maps—free to members of affiliated worldwide AAs with membership card—are moderately priced for nonmembers. Country-wide bookings and travel items like inflatable neck pillows and money belts are available. Get 'em while supplies last! *The Road Code of New Zealand* ($14.95) is a worthwhile investment. The *Driver's Guide* brochure indicates all of the CBD's one-way streets and parking areas. The *Minimap* series is quite comprehensive and available from the Visitor Centre on Wellesley St. Alternatively, **Specialty Maps,** 56 Albert St. (tel. 307 2217), is open M-F 8:30am-4:30pm, Sa 10am-1pm.

RENTALS. Ace Rentals, 39-43 The Strand (tel. 303 3112), in Parnell, rents economy cars from $35 per day for up to 20 days and $25 per day for 20 days or more (includes unlimited km, insurance, 24hr. AA coverage). **Omega Rental Cars,** at the airport (tel. 275 3265), or 75 Beach Rd. (tel. 358 3083 or 0800 525 210), starts its budget cars at $39 (minimum 4 days; includes insurance, AA service, and unlimited km). One-way rentals to joint offices in Wellington, Christchurch, Nelson, Picton, and Queenstown are also offered. **Maui Rentals** (tel. 0800 651 080), also at the airport, rents campers with showers and kitchens from $115 (summer) and $70 (winter) per day. The worldwide chains **Avis** (tel. 526 2847 or 0800 655 111), **Budget** (tel. 0800 652 227), and **Hertz** (tel. 0800 654 321) have offices at the airport.

BUYING AND SELLING. If you'll be in New Zealand for an extended period of time, you may want to consider buying a car. **Car auctions** are one option; **Turners Car Auctions** (tel. 525 1920), on McNab St. in Penrose, sells budget cars at 11:30am on Wednesdays, and family cars at 6pm on Thursdays. **Hammer Auctions,** 830 Great South Rd. (tel. 579 2344), Penrose, sells budget cars on Mondays, Wednesdays, and Fridays. Otherwise, check out the following **car fairs in Auckland** to find a deal when buying or selling a car: **Sell Your Own Car,** 676 Great South Rd., Manukau (tel. 0800 735 596; open daily 7am-7pm); **Sell it Yourself,** 60 Wairau Rd., Glenfield (tel. 443 3800; open daily 7am-7pm); **Ellerslie Racecourse** (tel. 524 4059; open Su 9am-noon), off Greenlane Roundabout; and **Manukau City Park and Sell** (tel. 358 5000; open Su 9am-1pm).

BY TAXI
Alert Taxis (tel. 309 2000), **Auckland Co-op Taxi** (tel. 300 3000), and **Discount Taxis** (tel. 529 1000) are all over the CBD. Large stands can be found at the intersection of Victoria St. E and Queen St., and on K Rd. across from the clubs.

BY BICYCLE AND MOTORCYCLE
Adventure Cycles, 1 Fort Lane (tel. 309 5566 or 0800 335 566), at Quay St., rents mountain bikes from $25 per day and $90 per week. Touring and racing bikes roll from $18 per day and $70 per week. (Open M-Su 7am-7pm.) **New Zealand Motorcycle Rentals,** 31 Beach Road (tel. 377 2005; www.nzbike.com), offers motorcycles and scooters with one-way rentals to Wellington and Christchurch. Rentals from $39 per day, include unlimited km, airport transfers, insurance, and 24hr. support service. (Open M-Sa 9am-5:30pm, Su 10am-3pm.)

⑦ PRACTICAL INFORMATION

TOURIST AND FINANCIAL SERVICES
Visitors Center: Auckland Visitor Centre, 24 Wellesley St. W, CBD (tel. 366 6888, airport branch 256 8646; fax 366 6893). The headquarters of New Zealand's extraordinary Visitor Information Network sits just off Queen St. on Wellesley St. W, up a steep incline and somewhat cached away to the left, inside a walkway. Complete domestic booking network and every existing brochure and map about New Zealand. Operating without company commissions the Visitor Centre remains fairly unbiased. Message boards advertise everything from cars for sale to flatmates wanted. Open M-F 8:30am-5:30pm, Sa-Su and public holidays 9am-5pm. If you arrive by ferry, the most convenient stop for information is the **New Zealand Visitor Centre** (tel. 979 7005; fax 979 7010; email nzvc@aucklandnz.com), on the corner of Quay and Hobson St., in the America's Cup 2000 village area. Open M-Su 9:30am-5:30pm.

Department Of Conservation (DOC): (tel. 379 6476), in the Ferry Building on Quay St. with maps and camping information galore. Open M-W 10am-1pm and 1:30-6pm.

Budget Travel: YHA Travel (tel. 379 4224; fax 366 6275), on the corner of Shortland St. and Jean Batten Pl. Not officially affiliated with the hosteling organization of the same name, but offers some real travel deals. Open M-F 9am-5:30pm, Sa 10am-3pm. **The Ansett New Zealand Travel Shop,** 75 Queen St. (tel. 307 5380), in the CBD, does domestic and international bookings. Open M-F 8:30am-5pm. Otherwise, try the in-house travel centers at **Auckland Central Backpackers (VIP)** (tel. 358 4874), or the

Auckland City YHA (tel. 309 2802)—open to non-guests. The **Flight Centre,** offering consistently low fares has offices at 350 Queen St. (tel. 358 4310), 2 Fort St. (tel. 377 4655) in the CBD, and Broadway Plaza (tel. 529 2400) in Newmarket.

Consulates: Australia, 32-38 Quay St. (tel. 303 2429), in the Union House; **Germany,** 52 Symonds St. (tel. 377 3460); **Ireland,** 87 Queen St. (tel. 302 2867); **Japan** (tel. 303 4106) in ASB Bank, corner of Albert and Wellesley St.; **U.S.** (tel. 303 2724), on the corner of Shortland and O'Connell St. on the fourth floor of the General Building; **U.K.,** 151 Queen St. (tel. 303 2973), in the Fay Richwhite Building.

Currency Exchange: Interforex has the best hours around, with two central locations: 2 Queen St. (tel. 302 3031), in the Endeans Building, and 99 Quay St. (tel. 302 3066), in the Ferry Building. Both branches open daily 8am-8pm. **National Bank,** 205 Queen St. (tel. 359 9828), charges no commission on cashing traveler's checks and foreign currency. Open M-F 9am-4:30pm, Sa 10am-2pm.

American Express: 105 Queen St. (tel. 379 8286 or 0800 801 122). The office changes foreign currency or traveler's checks without commission. Members' mail held for up to one month. Open M-F 9am-5pm, Sa 9:30am-12:30pm.

LOCAL SERVICES

Luggage Storage: National Mini Storage LTD, 68 Cook St. (tel. 356 7020), will store two pieces of luggage for 50¢ per day. For long term storage, **Auckland Central Backpackers,** 9 Fort St. (tel. 358 4877), will store bags for a flat fee of $15 per item.

Bookstores: Whitcoull's (tel. 356 5400), on the corner of Queen and Victoria St., has three glorious floors and a cafe. **The Dead Poets Bookshop,** 238 K Rd. (tel. 303 0555), offers pre-loved books and specializes in collectibles.

Women's Organizations: Auckland Women's Centre, 63 Ponsonby Rd. (tel. 376 3227), is a women-only space offering counseling, a library, and other services. Open M-F 9am-4pm. **Wanderwomen,** 30 Edenvale Crescent, Mt. Eden (tel./fax 630 1108), coordinates weekend adventure trips for women, including kayaking, climbing, and caving. Call for schedules.

Gay-Bi-Lesbian Organizations: Call the **Gay and Lesbian Line** for counseling (tel. 303 3584), or stop by the **The Pride Centre,** 33 Wyndham St., for information, referrals, and a social events calendar. Open M-F 8:30am-5pm.

Ticket Agency: Ticketek (tel. 307 5000) is comprehensive, but a credit card phone booking comes with a $6 surcharge. Book through a music store instead for only $1. Avoid the fees altogether by going in person to the **Countrywide Bank box office** at the **Aotea Centre.** Open daily 9am-5:30pm, later on performance nights.

Weather Conditions: MetPhone (24hr. tel. 0900 999 09; 1.15¢ per min.) or **MetFax** (tel. 0900 779 99).

Publications: The Auckland-based **New Zealand Herald** is the country's most comprehensive daily newspaper. **Metro** magazine keeps its finger on the pulse of Auckland's pop culture and politics, while **Express** is the gay and lesbian local paper of choice. **The Fix** has the dope on Auckland's dance clubs.

EMERGENCY, MEDICAL, AND COMMUNICATIONS

Emergency: Dial **111** throughout New Zealand.

Police: Auckland Central Police Station (tel. 379 4240), on the corner of Cook and Vincent St. The **Downtown Station** (tel. 379 4500) is on the corner of Jean Batten Pl. and Fort St. Other stations include **Airport International Terminal** (tel. 275 9046), the **Karangahape Road Community Constable** (tel. 309 8177), and the **Devonport Community Constable** (tel. 489 4008).

Hotlines: Auckland Central Victim Support (tel. 623 1700). **Lifeline** (tel. 0800 423 743 or 522 2808) has counseling daily 9am-5pm. The **Auckland Help Foundation** (tel. 623 1700) offers aid to victims of sexual assault, as does the **Rape Crisis Centre** (tel. 366 7213). For concerns regarding STDs contact the **AIDS Hotline** (tel. 0800 802 437).

Medical Services: Urgent Pharmacy, 60 Broadway St. (tel. 520 6634), in Newmarket. Open M-F 5:30-11:00pm, Sa-Su and public holidays 8:30am-11pm. On-call bell daily 11pm-7:00am. The **Auckland Hospital** (tel. 379 7440) sits on the edge of the Auckland Domain on Park St. in Grafton. For less dire cases, **Travelcare,** 87 Queen St. (tel. 373 4621) in the CBD, will immunize, vaccinate, heal, and soothe. **Ponsonby Accident and Medical Clinic,** 202 Ponsonby Rd. (tel. 376 9222), has its own **pharmacy.** Open daily 7:30am-10pm.

Post Office: Post shops are scattered throughout the city. **Wellesley Street Post Shop (CPO),** Bledisloe Building, 24 Wellesley St. (tel. 379 6714), has *Poste Restante*. Packages can be forwarded to another post office in the country within 30 days of receipt (from $7). Open M-F 8:30am-5pm, Sa 9am-12:30pm.

Internet Access: Shop around; prices are always changing. **Global Communications,** 137 K Rd. (tel. 309 4412) has bare-bones Internet connection for $6 per hr. Open M-Su 8:30am-10pm. **Net Central Cybercafe,** 5 Lorne St. (tel. 373 5186) costs $12 per hr. Open daily 9:30am-10pm. **Live Wire,** MidCity Complex, 239 Queen St. (tel. 356 0999), is $3 per 15min. Open M-F 9am-10pm, Sa 10am-11pm, Su 10am-10pm.

TELEPHONE CODE | The telephone code for the Greater Auckland area is **09.**

ACCOMMODATIONS

The accommodations of the CBD are, by reputation, impersonal and not very cozy. The hot tip for finding a good landing spot is to think outside of the box and go for a neighborhood—Ponsonby, Mt. Eden and Parnell all have excellent backpackers, not to mention better cafes and more charm than the CBD. For travelers keen on staying in the CBD, keep in mind that some downtown backpackers are geared toward younger crowds—with on-site bars, noise and smoke to prove it. Older travelers or families might look elsewhere. Most CBD accommodations have helpful staff and sometimes travel desks to help journeys begin. Many accommodations welcome your "inspection," so don't be afraid to shop around. **Check-out time** is 10am unless otherwise noted.

CENTRAL BUSINESS DISTRICT (CBD)

Albert Park Backpackers (VIP), 27 Victoria St. E (tel. 309 0336; fax 309 9474; email albertparkbp@yahoo.com). Supercentrally located, this well-worn backpackers is only seconds from Auckland's lovely, green park. Rooms give visitors space to breathe and there's an open-air courtyard (for smoking). Brimming with twentysomethings, the kitchen and lounge area also features a pool table, a view of the city, and premium television. Free bike and luggage storage. Key deposit $10. Reception 7am-11pm. 10- to 12-bunk dorms $17; 4- to 6-bed dorms $18; singles $30; twins and doubles $40.

Auckland City YHA (tel. 309 2802; fax 373 5083; email yhaauck@yha.org.nz; www.yha.org.nz), at the corner of City Rd. and Liverpool St. For travelers in search of a reliable, clean and friendly base camp in central Auckland, put your trust in the professionals here—the Airbus will drop your sorry, jetlagged butt at their doorsteps. In contrast to the Auckland International YHA just down the hill, the Auckland City YHA shows signs of residency and can be a bit chilly in winter. On-site **Tommy's Bistro** (open 7am-10am and 5pm-7pm) is cheap and convenient, though Tommy is a bit cantankerous. Internet. Laundry $4. Key deposit $10. 24hr. reception. Dorms $19; singles $35; twins and doubles $44. Nonmembers $4 extra per night.

Auckland International YHA (tel. 302 8200; email yhaauck@yha.org.nz; www.yha.org.nz) is a brand new facility with a huge kitchen and many fancy, modern accessories; this is the spotless, flagship YHA. 8-bed dorms $17; 4- to 6-bed dorms $19; twins and doubles $44, with bath $66.

City Backpackers Hotel (Nomads), 38 Fort St. (tel. 307 0181 or 0800 220 198; fax 307 0182; www.city-backpacker-hotel.co.nz), at the corner of Gore and Fort St. smack dab in the CBD. This place has no wacky charm but is spotless. Sophisticated apartment-like complexes with telephone (incoming only), living room, television, bathroom, and slick kitchenette for both bunk and double accommodations. A sexy studio apartment for 4 to 6 people is a great group facility ($120). Laundry $4. Luggage storage $2 per day. On-site bar and cafe. Dorms $17; singles $35; twins $40; doubles $45-65.

Downtown Constitution Hill Backpackers (VIP), 6 Constitution Hill (tel. 303 4768 or 0800 366 1444; fax 303 4766), hidden down on a hill on the other side of Albert Park and the Railway Station. The self-proclaimed "smallest hostel in the downtown area" uses almost every inch of their petit, red cottage bordering the Alten Reserve. Come here for a rustic feel—the smell of grass and fresh air are included free of charge. BBQ and open garden space in back. Free luggage storage. Internet. Laundry $4. Key deposit $10. Dorms $14-16; doubles $35, with bath $40. VIP members $1 discount.

Central City Backpackers (VIP), 26 Lorne St. (tel. 358 5685; fax 358 4716). The basement backpackers bar, **Embargo** (tel. 309 1850), which welcomes young travelers from all over the city, is the highlight of the "CCB," as it's affectionately called by the Kiwi and Magic bus kids who tread a well-worn path through this backpackers. Happy Hour daily 7-9pm with $3 beers (bar open M-Su 5pm-3am). The free beer with check-in is the highlight of actually staying here. Internet. Long term storage $5 per item per week. Key deposit $20. 24hr. reception. Credit card necessary to hold a reservation after 4pm. 6- to 10-bed dorms $19; 1- to 4-bed dorms $21; singles $38; twins and doubles $50. Weekly: 6- to 10-bed dorms $100; 1- to 4-bed dorms $115.

Auckland Central Backpackers (VIP), 9 Fort St. (tel. 358 4877; fax 358 4872; email backpackers@acb.co.nz). A decaying 8-story monument to backpacking partying, its 360 beds are more a place to dump your pack before heading up to the 7th floor bar than a place to quietly de-jetlag or unwind. Social lounge and several kitchens (open 6:30am-11pm). Internet and Travel Centre on site. Key deposit $20. 24hr. reception. Bunks $19; dorms (up to 4) $18 per person; singles $33; twins and doubles $45. Rates rise slightly Nov. 1-Apr. 6. Reservations highly recommended (credit card necessary to hold past 4pm).

Kiwi Backpackers, 430 Queen St. (tel./fax 358 3999, guest tel. 358 4501). Underground and with few windows, this museum of kitsch has the cheapest beds in town, if not the country, though the carpet and facility seem to date from several decades past. Laundry $4. Key deposit $20. Parking available. Reception and bar open 8am-midnight. 10- to- 12-bed dorms $10; 6- to- 8-bed dorms $12; doubles and twins $38.

PONSONBY

The Brown Kiwi, 7 Prosford St. (tel./fax 378 0191; email bookings@brownkiwi.co.nz). The Brown Kiwi puts you where you want to be, in trendy Ponsonby, in an accommodation almost too good to be true. This 2-story home is a masterpiece with every detail taken care of—on-site mini-bar, Internet, grownup-scale bunkbeds, elegant garden with tables, BBQ, and two Japanese-style fish ponds. Only minutes, by Link bus, from downtown Auckland—that is, if you ever want to leave the cool, affordable neighborhood. Free storage. Gay friendly. Laundry $3. 8-bed dorms $17; 4-bed dorms $18; doubles $40.

Ponsonby Backpackers, 2 Franklin Rd. (tel. 360 1311 or 0800 476 676; fax 360 1365). This blue-and-white old Victorian house just around the corner from the excellent cafes of Ponsonby Rd. offers easy access and Sky TV. The jumbled lounge is warmed by cushy couches and a big fireplace. Internet. Key deposit $10. Reception 8am-8pm. Check-in as late as 11pm. Dorms $16; singles $25-30; doubles $42; tent sites $12.

PARNELL

Lantana Lodge (VIP), 60 St. George's Bay Rd. (reservation tel. 373 4546; guest tel. 373 4616). This small, simple, but handsome Victorian home on a hill has a gingerbread porch and a flower garden. Every square inch of the place is compulsively clean. It's best to cook in the petit kitchen, considering most Parnell eateries are priced for wealthy tourists. Free storage. Laundry $4. Key deposit $10. Reception 8am-10pm. Dorms $17; twins and doubles from $42, extra person $9. Weekly in winter: dorms $112; doubles or twins $245.

MT. EDEN

Oaklands Lodge, 5a Oaklands Rd. just off Mt. Eden Rd. (tel./fax 638 6545 or 0800 222 725; guest tel. 623 1833; email bookings@oaklands.co.nz.). Call for airport shuttlebus service. For those looking for an Auckland accommodation with a backyard, windchimes, and serenity, come here. Mt. Eden's stretch of cool cafes is just around the corner. The Four Square is a two-minute walk and the CBD is a short bus away ($1.10). Internet. Laundry $4. Key deposit $10. 10-bed dorms $15; 5-bed dorms $16; singles $35, doubles from $42. Prices increase in summer. Family room available.

Bamber House, 22 View Rd. (tel. 638 6545). Recently appropriated and redone by the owners of Oaklands Lodge, this colonial home is a bit smaller than its local "competitor" but strives to create a similarly comfortable environment. Off-street parking. Bunkhouse dorms $13; house dorms $15; twins and doubles from $40.

⊡ FOOD

In the **CBD,** grocery stores and supermarkets are hard to find; instead, head to Newmarket or Ponsonby. Prepared food, however, comes fairly cheap and those-in-the-know can eat well without torturous repetition of standard takeaway fare—kebabs and fish 'n' chips. However, fast food favorites are easy to find, especially in the business district, where McDonalds and ATMs abound. The **Atrium Food Gallery** on Eliot St. has nine takeaway counters (open M-Th 7am-6pm, F 7am-8pm, Sa-Su 10am-5pm). See the **Cafes** section on p. 76 for more dining options.

CENTRAL BUSINESS DISTRICT (CBD)

Cafe Hasan Baba, 466 Queen St. (tel. 358 5308). Those who enter this unassuming but attractive Turkish eatery will discover delectable food at bargain prices. Takeaway kebabs are a bargain at $5, but a sit down meal is more appropriate. The char-grilled chicken dish ($12.50) delights with texture and taste—honey, ginger, garlic and yogurt merge into a sweet sauce which complements everything on the plate. Many vegetarian options. 10% YHA discount. Open M-F 11:30am-11pm, Sa-Su 4:30pm-midnight.

Pizza Pizza, 57 Lorne St. (tel./fax 309 3333), tucked behind Queen St. to the East, on the second floor of an orange building. This funky, laid-back pad is placed on a pizza pedestal by students (who receive 20% discount on smalls and larges). Free toppings and free delivery to Central City. Open M-F 10:30am-10:30pm, Sa-Su 4:30-10:30pm.

Rasoi Vegetarian Restaurant, 211 K Rd. (tel. 377 7780). Here, delicious Indian concoctions put the unimpressive facility to shame. Warm and zesty curries tickle the throat and set tastebuds in motion. The Deluxe Thali platter ($9.50) gives you heaps of food. Savory bags of homemade snack food ($2.50) are perfect for journeys, and mango lassi ($3.50) is a sweet ending. Open M-Sa 11am-9pm.

The Burgerie, 95 K Rd. The flashing "food bar" sign will point you to this sidewalk counter with surprisingly good food. Vegetarian takeaways are their specialty. Try the tempeh burger with peanut sauce and beetroot ($5.40) with kumara chips ($3 more). Everything fried in vegetable oil, except the banana or berry soy shakes ($4.20). Open M-W 11am-1am, Th 11am-3am, F-Sa 11am-5am.

Shochiku, 460 Queen St. (tel. 300 3288). Extremely fresh Japanese food available for takeaway or sit-down. The tables in this cozy restaurant are packed with hungry locals who handle their chopsticks with great dexterity. At lunchtime, food comes cheap. For dinner, prices rise a touch, but tabletop cooking makes for a great show. Dinner mains $8-$13. Open M-F 11am-3pm and 5pm-10pm, Sa 5pm-11pm.

The French Bakehouse, Shop 4 Vulcan Lane, (tel. 377 2836), close to Queen St. This chic boulangerie may look pricey, but bargain sandwiches wait inside. Take your pick from dozens of premade sandwiches with clearly labeled contents. A small ham and mesculin sandwich with dijon mayonnaise ($2) isn't nearly as filling as a large, shredded chicken breast sandwich with lettuce, tomato, carrot and pepper ($3.80). Open M-F 7am-4pm.

Wofem Bros. Bagelry, 54 High St. (tel. 366 7359). Offering a break from cereal, muffins and toast, this sunny cafe caters to bagel lovers for breakfast, lunch, or just a snack. Bagels $1.40 each, $14 per dozen. Open M-F 7am-6pm, Sa 8am-6pm, Su 8am-4pm.

Mexican Cafe Bar & Grill, 67 Victoria St. W. (tel. 373 2311). An inconspicuous street-level entry leads upstairs to inevitable Mexican decor—streamers, piñatas, a cactus-shaped bar tap. Main courses ($15-$20) made with fresh ingredients. Happy Hour (5-7pm) will tempt you with discounted drinks and starters (nachos $5). Open M-F noon-2:30pm and 5pm-late, Sa-Su 5pm-late.

PONSONBY

🗡 **Cafe Cezanne,** 296 Ponsonby Rd. (tel. 376 3338). Students, dilettantes, and starving artists feast at this left bank haunt with an irreverence for art history. A colorful menu of big breakfasts ($2 gigantic muffins), pastas, and salads ($8-10) is complemented by equally colorful murals on the walls. The *pièce de resistance* is hot chocolate ($3), escorted by two chocolate fish. Open Su-Th 8am-midnight, F-Sa 8am-2am.

🗡 **Musical Knives,** 272 Ponsonby Rd. (tel. 376 7354). Chef Peter A. Chaplin's creations from organic materials are so crafty that the Material Girl herself took him along as her personal cuisine artist on 2 world tours. Entrees ($9-13.50) and mains ($22-24) are dear, but near to your heart's content. Open daily from 5pm.

Yuki Sake Bar, 26 Ponsonby Rd. (tel. 360 5050). The sushi and sashimi is served fresh, with a focus on presentation, and is not too expensive. 10-piece combination sushi with salmon and daily catch $12, 5 pieces for $6, or 8 california rolls for $8. Don't bother asking—the lacquered wooden chopsticks cannot be taken home. Open M-Sa 11am-11pm, Su 5pm-11pm.

Open Late Cafe, 134 Ponsonby Rd. (tel. 376 4466). Young party-goers busily devour nacho plates big enough to share (medium bean $7, chicken $10.50) and veggie-friendly dishes (lasagna $14). It may be the classic Ponsonby after-drinking spot, but with BYO and no corking fee, why not bring the party here? **Caro's Wine Merchant's** (123 Ponsonby Rd., tel. 360 0357) has inexpensive vino (open M-Sa 10am-8:30pm). Cafe open Su-W 6:30pm-2am, Th 6:30pm-3am, F-Sa 6:30pm-4am.

MT. EDEN

City Cake Company, 426 Mt. Eden Rd. (tel. 629 0019). An elegant showroom for Auckland's most delicious and modern-looking baked creations. Trendy, thirtysomething financiers mute their cellphones in order to truly appreciate the bliss of chocolate cake ($3), muffins ($2.50) and gourmet pies. Open daily 9am-6pm.

PARNELL AND NEWMARKET

Al & Pete's, 496 Parnell Rd. (tel. 377 5439), at the top of Ayr St. Look for the sign with the dual chef profile. They are pros when it comes to fish 'n' chips ($5). Locals swear by the potato fritter (60¢). Take it away from this nondescript joint to enjoy in your favorite domain. Open M 11am-11pm, Tu-Th 11am-midnight, F-Sa 11am-2am, Su 11am-10pm.

Kebab Kid, 363 Parnell Rd. and 166 Ponsonby (tel. 373 4290). Middle Eastern fast food may seem foreign to most, but the kid has your favorite kebab ($6-7), salad, dips ($5.50-6.50), and baklava ($2) ready to go; take it away into the urban desert, or have them deliver it right to your palace door, or eat it in their clean, modern oasis. Open Su-M noon-10pm, Tu-Th and Sa noon-11pm, F noon-2am.

▣ CAFES

CENTRAL BUSINESS DISTRICT (CBD)

🗡 **Brazil,** 256 K Rd. (tel. 302 2677). Not too far from Queen St., Brazil takes coffee lovers into another dimension of bass and bean bliss. The interior design predicts an apocalyptic future—hardcore, industrial desolation. With a little more floor space this spot would be a nightclub. Electronica music hangs in the air with the distinct java fragrance (bean roasting on premises). Upstairs, resident DJs spin and scratch W-Sa. Internet. Open M-Tu 8am-8pm, W-Th 8am-midnight, F 8am-1am, Sa 9am-1am, Su 9am-8pm.

■ **The Live Poets Cafe,** 238 K Rd., (tel. 359 9936), adjacent to **The Dead Poets Book-shop** (tel. 303 0555). A lively spot has sprung up among shelves of paperbacks. The shop specializes in collectible antiquarian literature and also offers exchanges. Every Friday night, extended hours inspire folk, jazz, and poetry performances in front of a receptive crowd. Open Sa-Th 10am-6:30pm, F 10am-11pm.

Mecca (tel. 309 6300), Upper Vulcan Lane. See and be seen at this trendy spot looking out onto the Vulcan Lane catwalk. Outdoor seating obstructs passing poseurs. Back-packers should change into a pressed shirt and clean pair of underwear before showing up for eggs benedict on a bagel with salmon or ham ($12.50) or smooth mochaccino ($3.50). Lunch meals $8.50-12.50. Open daily 7am-6pm.

The Lost Angel Cafe, 472 K Rd. (tel. 379 3100). Those who muster the courage to wan-der along K Rd. into the porno district (or "accidentally" find themselves there) are rewarded with good coffee and cheap chow. Gutted televisions hang from the ceilings and electronic music infuses this narrow cafe. All coffee drinks $2.50. Open Tu 10am-5pm, W 10am-2am, Th-Sa 10am-4am, Su 10am-midnight.

Manifesto Espresso & Wine Bar, 315 Queen St. (tel. 303 4405). The bright blue store-front reveals a dimly lit interior exuding a reserved, intellectual aura. With the most extensive wine list in Auckland, Manifesto features a different special each month designed to broaden your knowledge of the grape. Large selection of tapas $3-15. Sun-day night jazz session downstairs (8:30pm; cover $10-$15). Open Tu-Su 4pm-1am.

Net Central Cybercafe, 5 Lorne St. (tel. 373 5186). Fast computers, a beautiful, modern interior and coffee bar. For $12 per hr. Open daily 9:30am-10pm.

PONSONBY

Atomic Cafe, 121 Ponsonby Rd. (tel. 376 4954). For simple enjoyment of serious coffee. Heaps of magazines and Dr. Seuss books provide intelligent reading for all ages. Large breakfasts $6-12.50. Open M-W 6am-6pm, Th-F 6am-11pm, Sa 7:30am-5pm, Su 8am-4:30pm; kitchen closes at 2:30pm M-F, 3pm Sa-Su.

PARNELL

The Other Side, 320 Parnell Rd. (tel./fax 366 4426). "The works" breakfast will have you fully functioning with bottomless filter coffee and vegetarian options ($10). Lunch and dinner entrees ($5.50-12.50) and mains ($14.50-19.50). Open M-F 7am-10pm, Sa-Su 8am-10pm.

◪ BARS

English- and Irish-style pubs dominate the scene, but domestic beers are the drink of choice almost everywhere you go. Tap beers like Steinlager, Speight's, Lion Red, DB, and Export Gold are almost invariably higher in quality (and cheaper) than bottled imports. Spirits and cocktails are gaining in popularity, especially with the Ponsonby jet-set. The status drink of the moment is a vodka Redbull (around $10)—a spiked, high-powered, caffeine, "energy" drink. Sweet citrus drinks, such as KGB and Stolchinaya, which have the alcohol content of beer and the tang of lemonade, are also popular. Prices are around $3-4 for a pint of beer, $5 for double spirits and premium spirits. Specialty cocktails and fancy shooters cost as high as $6-7 a shot, and a cocktail shaker will be $20-25. While the **CBD** and the **Waterfront** host mostly pubs and taverns, **Ponsonby** is full of choice places with black-clad yuppies. **Parnell,** while courting students, is also home to the monied European crowd.

■ **Margarita's,** 18 Elliot St. (tel. 302 2764). The Monday, Thursday and Saturday night special of 8 beers for $5 (for the first 100 people) is legendary. Descend from the street to discover a spacious wood-floored watering hole with pool tables and dance floor. $2.50 pints daily between 5-7pm and 9-10pm. Open daily 4pm-3am.

■ **The Dog's Bollix** (tel. 376 4600), at the corner of K and Newton Rd., in Newton, a 15-minute walk from the CBD. Dublin is alive and well in Auckland. A good-natured Guinness crowd gives the pub a feel-good atmosphere, especially when the founders (and namesake band) are playing their brand of traditional Irish music. Live music W-Sa. Sunday is locals' night with Irish dancing and spontaneous eruptions of the best Irish, English, and American folk music in a free-for-all jam session (6:30pm). Handles $4. Open M-Sa 8:30am-midnight, Su noon-midnight.

Bacchus, 5 O'Connell St. (tel. 377 2089), just off Vulcan Lane. When this slick, modern venue isn't hopping with Auckland's trendy set, it's a cool, dark, chill-out spot with premium "Sky" sports programming on the big screen. The mood is perpetually set by far-out dance music which, on Friday and Saturday night, crescendos into full-on house beats courtesy of the resident DJs. Handles $4. Dress code on weekends. Open M-Th 10:30am-10:30pm, F 10:30am-3am, Sa 7pm-3am. Steal off to the **Liquid Lounge** when the downstairs gets too hardcore. Open Tu-Th 5pm-2am, F 5pm-4am, Sa 7pm-3am.

Kiwi Tavern, 3 Britomart Pl. (tel. 307 1717), east of QE II Sq. along Customs St., opposite the Oriental Markets. Tuesday's backpackers night with 6 beers off tap for $6 lures travelers to this multi-level venue in a dark, quiet corner of town. Live music Tuesday. Downstairs, the **Moa Bar** (tel. 307 1110) complements with a more accessible space and creative, rustic aesthetic. Pool table and Happy Hour daily 5-6:30pm (pints, wine $2.50). Open daily 11am-3am.

The Blue Bar, corner of Parnell and Akaroa Rd. (tel. 367 6821), below The New Exchange. A central bar surrounded by sculpted couches breaks up a pale blue interior. The real draw is the adjacent garden BBQ at **The Exchange,** where you choose your own steak and grill it yourself ($14.50). Open M-Tu 4:30-11pm, W-Su 4:30pm-1am.

The Voodoo Lounge (tel. 358 4847), on Vulcan Ln. in the CBD. Head up the stairs under the large, illuminated Steinlager sign which belies the dark and freaky lounge on the second floor. This place drips with all the makings of a devilish evening—from the bats and scorpions embedded in the bar to potent potions like "dragon's blood" (a shooter of sambuca, chartreuse, Wild Turkey, and Jägermeister). Poor bartenders—Halloween all year long must get old, guys. Dance to live music on Thursdays. $2 cover on Fridays. Open Tu-Th 7pm-3am, F 6pm-6am, Sa 9pm-6am.

Eastside, 67 Shortland St., (tel. 373 5434), east of Queen St. This out-of-the way bar reveals attractive, young locals pounding down sexy shooters. The only supervision comes from above—a giant eagle sculpture hangs over the bar creating a funky pulpit from which the DJ preaches his grooves. Martini Madness Mondays deliver $7 'tinis ($5 off suggested retail price). Tequila Tuesday has $7 margaritas. Open M-Sa from 8pm.

◪ NIGHTCLUBS

During the week, the nightlife in Auckland centers around venues with special club events. On weekends, the city busts out all over. The downtown **High Street** clubs are generally more relaxed about dress code and attract a younger crowd. Up on **K Road,** style reigns supreme as everyone dons his or her favorite shade of black and joins the queue. Adding color to the scene are drag queens, who come out at night and stay out until day.

The two magic numbers in Auckland are 5 (the standard cover charge) and 20 (which should be your age, at the least, if you want to get in). Carding is strict, so bring your ID or passport; otherwise, you will be turned away. For the skinny on events, the glossy mag *The Fix* can't be beat, especially since it's free. Pick it up, as well as special events flyers, at **Beat Merchant** on Albert St., **CyberCulture** at 151 K Rd., and the mother of all record stores, **Real Groovy,** at 438 K Rd.

Cause Celebre and **The Box,** 33 High St. (tel. 303 1336), in the CBD. Break into the club scene with a young dancing crowd. Unassuming entrance reveals a sprawling network of bars and dance floors. The two related venues give club kids options. Wednesday night is Retrorama with 80s and other flashback tunes. Thursday is hip hop and house at the Box, while next door, at Cause Celebre, there are live performances. Otherwise, expect sounds along the edge of house and techno. International DJs occasionally jack up the cover price to $20. Open W-Sa 11pm-6am.

Factory, 17 O'Connell St. (tel. 366 1616). Owner and club mastermind Christiaan is building an institution to rival the K Rd. scene. Retro sixties-soul funkiness spiked with an energetic pulse for the new millennium keeps the upstairs shaking, while the second floor's swanky lounge is for low-key lounging. Upstairs open W-Sa 10pm-late. Downstairs open M-Th 7pm-late, F-Su 5pm-late.

The Kiss Club and Bar, 309 K Rd. (tel. 303 2726). This posh club has a seductive red interior and a long, attractive bar which sells $25 drink shakers. To blend in, wear black and drink a vodka Redbull ($10). Split-level club pumps house beats on weekends. Cover $5 F-Sa after midnight. Open W-Th 10pm-3am, F-Sa 10pm-5am, Su 10pm-3am.

Jones, 350 K Rd. (tel. 377 0033). This new, upstairs drink-a-teria is an intimate way to spend an evening in style. Lighting fixtures hang like works of art from the ceiling. French house and uplifting funk keep the place pulsing all the time. Late at night, dance freaks take to the disco floor. DJs Th-Sa from 11pm (cover $5 after midnight F-Sa); triphop jazz Su from 10pm. Open Th 9pm-5am, F 9pm-7am, Sa 9pm-4am, Su 9pm-4am.

☑ GAY AND LESBIAN NIGHTLIFE

Ironically, Queen St. is *not* the center of queer activity in Auckland—rather, Ponsonby takes the cake. Many gay-run bars and brasseries are along Ponsonby Rd., promising numerous opportunities for a fabulous night out. Around the corner, K Rd. clubs also often cater to the gay set. Scope out the *Express* newspaper ($2 at newsstands, or free at Surrender Dorothy or Urge) for the most current listings.

Taking over Auckland for two weeks, the **HERO Gay and Lesbian Festival** (Feb. 4-20, 2000) is a carnivalesque celebration of theater performances, film screenings, and outdoor events culminating in a grand parade and lively all-night dance party on the last night. To find out the schedule of events, check out *Express* or find HERO on the web at www.hero.nz.org.

Surrender Dorothy, 3/175 Ponsonby Rd. (tel. 376 4460), in Ponsonby. At the sign with the hairy legs and ruby slippers, you'll find an unpretentious and fun watering hole. Pairs of glittering pumps and stilettos snake across the ceiling and photos of glamorous drag queens hang from the walls. Mixed but predominantly male couples; lesbian couples and friends of "friends of Dorothy" are more than welcome. Comedy on Wednesdays at 9pm. Open "for joy and fabulousity" daily 5pm-12:30am.

Urge, 490 K Rd. (tel. 307 2155). Touting itself as a space for gay males, only those of that persuasion will probably feel truly comfortable here, which is the point. Push aside a heavy black leather curtain as you enter and step into a small dark environment catering more to denim and leather than satin and cashmere. Promotions and musical guests are advertised in *Express*. DJ party "Grind" on Fridays. Open M-Sa 8pm-late, Su 6pm-late, winter Th-Su from 8pm.

S.P.Q.R., 150 Ponsonby Rd. (tel. 360 1710), in Ponsonby. S.P.Q.R. stands for *Senatus populus que Romanus*, which hearkens back to a Roman republic more tolerant of homosexual activity. This chic cafe and bar, lit by candles and glowing orbs, touts itself as a similar people's forum, attracting a mixed crowd—especially for meals. Pizzas and pastas $15.50-$19.50. Open M-F 11am-2am, Sa-Su 10am-2am.

Sinners, 373 K Rd. (tel./fax 308 9985). Around 4am, the hardcore crowd exudes a hearty gay vibe, with a sizeable contingent of shirtless men dancing to hard uplifting house on the large dance floor. Later, the crowd evolves into a varied mix of hyper-stimulated insomniacs. Amazingly, this is when the club is most crowded, as people come to recover their sanity and melt into the morning. Lesbian night Friday 9pm-1:30am. Open W-Th midnight-7am, F-Sa midnight-noon, Su midnight-7am.

Legends, 335 K Rd. (tel. 377 6062). The large, barred windows might intimidate some from stepping into this famous—yes, legendary—queer spot. The dark, severe space located downstairs from a strip club borrows a similar, erotic aesthetic. For some, Legends may lack coziness and friendliness. Resident drag queens strut their stuff at showtime (11pm Sa and Su). Happy Hour Su with half-price drinks. Open Tu-Su 4pm-3am.

🎵 ENTERTAINMENT

For locals young and old, entertainment in Auckland rarely requires a ticket or opera glasses. Kiwis gather at cafes and bars to sip, guzzle and chat into the wee morning hours. Live music is a regular treat that livens up local joints at the week's end (see the **Bars** p. 77, for live music entertainment).

Temple, 486 Queen St. (tel. 377 4866), close to the YHAs in the CBD. Delivers tunes of all kinds seven nights a week. Mondays offer an open mike jam night, all performers welcome (9pm). Happy Hour 5-8pm (2 spirits or beers $5). Open M-Su 5pm-2am.

Java Jive (tel. 376 5870), corner of Ponsonby Rd. and Pompallier Terr., in Ponsonby. Drop in at this subterranean blues/jazz/rock club with plenty of atmosphere and little attitude. Photos of blues greats gaze down approvingly upon the mixed crowd of all ages. Live bands every night of the week. First note sounds at 8:30pm M-W, 10pm Th-Su. Open M-F 6pm-3am, Sa 11am-3am, Su 11pm-3am.

The Classic Comedy & Bar, 321 Queen St. (tel. 373 4321), near the YHAs in the CBD. The Classic serves up good laughs in their back room theater with a variety of nights ranging from improv (Tuesdays $5) to amateur open mike (Wednesdays $6) to seasoned pros later in the week (cover varies). Bar open from 5pm with the largest selection of flavored vodkas in New Zealand (lap up a Passionfruit martini with a friend). Happy Hour M-F 5-7 with $2.50 tap beers. Shows start at 8pm. Open Tu-Th 4-11pm, F-Sa 4pm-1am.

In the heart of the CBD, coin-operated video arcades appear almost as regularly as kebab takeaway vendors. Somewhat higher brow, the **Auckland International Film Festival** (tel. 377 7420) captures the attention of movie buffs with two weeks of screenings in mid-July (tickets $7 or $11). The rest of the year, standard-issue Hollywood films are shown in the **St. James Theatre,** 312 Queen St. (tel. 377 4241; tickets generally $11, students $9, seniors $6, children $5). Across the road, flashy construction on the **Civic Center** has spawned another multiplex cinema and giant **IMAX** screen (tickets from $10).

At the other end of the theater spectrum stands the **SiLO** (tel. 373 5151), on Lower Greys Ave., behind Town Hall. An underground experimental theater managed and staffed by art students and their friends, SiLO includes free use of Sony Playstation in the funky lobby while you wait for the show to begin or during intermission. (Tickets around $10; reserve by phone, or wait until 1hr. before the show for door sales. Cash or check only.) For a more grass-roots theater experience, consider **Pumanawa,** a recently formed collective of Maori artists whose performances incorporate elements from the stories of their cultural heritage. Contact Taamati Rice (tel. 528 6472) for more information.

The **Ponsonby Snooker Centre,** 106 Ponsonby Rd. (tel. 360 2356), is the classiest pool hall in Auckland, with three full-size snooker tables. Reservations are necessary at night ($10 per hour). For those who prefer games of chance to games of skill, **Sky City** has casinos for all levels of gamblers. Free gaming lessons are available. Across the street is the **Palace,** on Victoria St., the only bar in Auckland that matches the casino by staying open 24 hours.

On those rare occasions when they pass through Auckland, big name bands generally play at the **Powerstation** or the **North Shore Event Centre.** Check at **Real Groovy,** 438 Queen St. (tel. 302 3940), for schedule and ticket info (open Sa-Th 9am-5:30pm, F 9am-9pm). The recently renovated **Auckland Town Hall Concert Chamber** in the town hall, which stands opposite the Aotea Centre, has great acoustics and is home to the **International Chamber Music Festival** (tel. 445 1863) in July. Teenagers may be interested in a recent phenomenon in Auckland, the emergence of **Rib Clubs.** These underage clubs serve up plenty of fun without alcohol and run until late. The music varies, but generally **Beat City** (tel. 373 3551), corner of Hobson and Victoria St. plays mostly R&B and hip-hop (cover $5; open F-Sa from 6pm).

The 2256-seat **ASB Theatre** in Aotea Centre is the majestic home to the **New Zealand Royal Ballet,** the **New Zealand** and **Auckland Philharmonics,** and world-class productions for limited engagements. **Ticketek** (tel. 307 5000) has its box office here; book in person to avoid paying hefty surcharges (open daily 9am-5pm and until show time).

SPECIAL EVENTS

By no small coincidence, several major events are scheduled for 2000 in Auckland. Millenial celebrations, the Olympic games in Sydney (Sept. 2000), and the America's Cup have turbo-charged Auckland-area development; many special services, performances, and events are scheduled to commemorate and cash in on it all.

America's Cup 2000 events begin in October 1999 with the Louis Vuitton Challenger Elimination Series, determining who will challenge the Kiwis for the curvaceous hunk of silver. There are 16 challengers from 10 countries. Four months later, on February 19, 2000, racing for the America's Cup begins with a best-of-nine contest between New Zealand and the recently-determined Challenger. The America's Cup racing takes place on Saturday, Sunday, Tuesday, and Thursday at 1:15pm between February 19 and March 9 in Auckland's Hauraki Gulf. The boats are stored near **Viaduct Harbour** (near the intersection of Quay and Hobson St.) and this is where the massive **American Express New Zealand Cup Village** stands. The free admission "village" is a good place to look at moored boats and mega-yachts, to buy food, take in live performances, and watch the racing on a big screen television. Note: the race course is far out in the Hauraki Gulf. To view the races in person you will need to board a spectator boat. The cheapest seats available are reportedly from **Fullers** whose catamaran boats have a bar and snackfood facility ($48 per person for an LV Elimination Series race; $144 for an America's Cup race; book well in advance). For more info on chartering a boat contact the **New Zealand Visitor Centre** (tel. 979 7005; fax. 979 7010; www.nzvc@aucklandnz.com); with other inquires contact America's Cup 2000 New Zealand (tel. 379 2000; www.amerciascup2000.co.nz).

◉ SIGHTS

VANTAGE POINTS

Volcanic hills rise up around the city and provide keen lookouts; **Mt. Eden** and **One Tree Hill** are two of the more famous vantage points. To reach Mt. Eden and its parks, you can take bus #274 or #275, across from the Downtown Bus Terminal. To get to One Tree Hill, as well as its park and observatory, take bus #30 or #31 from the corner of Victoria and Queen St. At the base of One Tree Hill, **Auckland Observatory** (tel. 624 1246) offers one-hour viewing sessions of the cosmos through the EWB 50cm telescope (W, Th, and Sa 7pm, 8pm, and 9pm; $5). Bookings are essential. The observatory also offers a Stardome Planetarium show where a guide will take you on a tour of the universe (2-6 tours per day; $10, children $5).

Rising above the steel and glass of the CBD is the dominating feature of the city skyline: the new **Sky Tower,** locked by Hobson, Wellesley, Federal, and Victoria St. Its blinking red lights overhead, you'll never lose your sense of direction anywhere in the Auckland area with this behemoth (2m taller than the Eiffel tower) looming. The **observation deck** has a 360° view. The **Sky Deck** is 34m higher and offers essentially the same views, but without all the mayhem of the main deck. You can even step out onto the glass floor in the outer ring. **Orbit** is the upscale rotating restaurant. (Open Su-Th 8:30am-10pm, F 8:30am-11pm, Sa 8:30am-midnight; last elevator up runs 30min. before closing. Admission $15; children $7.50; Sky Deck $3 more.)

THE CENTRAL BUSINESS DISTRICT

Aside from the trendy Vulcan Ln. and High St. spots, visitors may find themselves running for the hills—toward K Rd. or out of the CBD altogether and into a satellite neighborhood that's more charming and affordable and on a manageable scale. Travelers without the time to venture out of the CBD might explore the well-groomed green expanse of **Albert Park,** up Victoria St. E from Queen St.; a tall, free-standing rock and metal arch fronts a wall of green and marks the main entrance. Sitting regally at the southern end of the park on the corner of Wellesley and Kitchener St. is the prim, white **Auckland Art Gallery** (tel. 307 7700). Peruse the standing collection of 19th-century Maori portraiture on the ground floor (free), or head into the rest of the gallery to view one of the traveling shows (admission varies). The sister to this gallery is the **New Gallery** (tel. 307 4540), a block down on the corner of Wellesley and Lorne St. Half the fun is strolling through the steel and glass space, listening to profound comments made by Auckland's art cognoscenti. (Open daily 10am-5pm; admission $4, concessions $2.)

As you traverse Albert Park, it's impossible not to notice the handsome tower of the **Old Arts Building,** 22 Princess St. Built in 1926, the 54m tower was inspired by that of Christ Church College, Oxford (England). The building is now the symbol of **Auckland University,** the largest of New Zealand's seven universities. The university sits on the other side of Albert Park and the modern **Student Union,** which includes a cafeteria, buzzes with students and announcements. The university occupies the better part of four large blocks centered about Symonds St. The main campus **library** stands on the corner of Princess St. (the east edge of Albert Park) and Alfred St. Open to the public, the view from the top floor will distract anyone from Katherine Mansfield's books. Opposite the library is the **Maidment Arts Centre,** 8 Alfred St. (tel. 308 2383), which offers some of the best performances in Auckland (theater performances $16-20; students $12-16).

PONSONBY

No visit to Auckland is complete without a day's jaunt to Ponsonby. This neighborhood has emerged from the slum of Auckland to become the affordable and cool place to live. Visitors should strongly consider staying in Ponsonby rather than city central. Hip young people from Mt. Eden, Newmarket, Parnell, and beyond flood Ponsonby on Sunday afternoon for brunch and some choice people-watching. Populated by students, artists, and a substantial part of the city's gay and lesbian community, Ponsonby Rd. caters to all of their tastes and then some. Both sides of the street are lined with eateries, trendy cafes, and bars, mixed in with little shops peddling second-hand clothes and delicate crafts. When the weather warms, outdoor seating and strolling are prime. Connecting Ponsonby to the top of the city, K Rd. still bears the signs of its adult entertainment industry (which threatens only one's aesthetic sensibility). A walk to Ponsonby can take up to 40 minutes; the Link Bus requires less time and exertion. But if you happen to hike in that direction on a Saturday, you will discover an **open-air market** (Sa 9am-5pm) on the bridge over the motorway which has great bargains on second-hand clothing and funky garments made by aspiring fashion designers.

THE WATERFRONT

Head to the bottom of Queen St. to find **Waitemata Harbour,** whose waters await the high-stakes battle over the America's Cup racing boats. Just west of **QE II Square,** the **American Express New Zealand Cup Village** based in Viaduct Harbour provides lots of America's Cup diversions (see **Special Events,** p. 81). At the base of **Hobson Wharf,** the **New Zealand National Maritime Museum** (tel. 358 3010) has meticulously crafted exhibits on New Zealand's love-affair with the sea, all enhanced by true-to-life settings and sounds. Part of the museum was actually built around the sleek yacht (in dry dock), the fastest ever to race in an America's Cup. Technically, it lost to the American Dennis Connor's *Stars and Stripes* in that race, though the latter had the unfair advantage of being a catamaran (a point of serious contention among Kiwis). The museum has a replica of the America's Cup trophy on display. (Open daily 9am-6pm, winter 9am-5pm. Admission $10, students $5.) The real Cup is on display at the **Royal New Zealand Yacht Squadron** (tel. 378 5200), which is the Kiwi Yacht Club that actually won it (open M-F 10am-2pm). Keep your hands off—the Cup suffered from **violent vandalizing** at the hands and hammer of a Maori activist not too long ago and had to be repaired in London. The museum also administers the **Rangitoto Sailing Centre** (tel. 358 2324) next door. No experience is necessary and everything from a three-hour morning sail to a three-day course can be arranged. (Rates start from $20 per hr.; bookings essential.) **Søren Larsen** (tel. 0800 767 365) offer three-hour sails ($45 per person) as well as voyages to Fiji, Tonga, and New Caledonia. Due to these extended trips, she isn't always in port for daytrips; call ahead.

The beautiful 1912 **Ferry Building** at 99 Quay St. is another important landmark and home of Fullers ferries, which has service to the islands of Waiheke (p. 88), Rangitoto (p. 87), and Great Barrier Island (p. 90), as well as across to the North Shore community of Devonport (p. 85). Fuller's also runs **harbor cruises,** the cheapest being the **Coffee Cruise** (1½hr., 2 per day, $25) for the grand tour, a roll, and coffee or tea. Most of your questions can be answered by the **Harbour Information Office** (tel. 357 6366), a kiosk a bit closer to the water on the right (open daily 9am-3pm).

The Ferry Building is also the start or end point of one of Auckland's most popular activities, the **Coast to Coast Walk** (13km; 4hr.). The walk travels between Waitemata Harbor and Onehunga Beach (Manukau Harbor), the first two European settlements in Auckland.

Strolling west along **Westhaven Drive** on any weekend morning, you'll encounter the **Westhaven Marina,** the largest manmade marina in the Southern Hemisphere. The **Marina Office** (tel. 309 1352), at the end of Westhaven Dr. by the Harbour Bridge, can answer questions and provide information on charter sailings. Down Westhaven Dr. along the arm of the Marina are the uppercrust **yacht clubs,** where crews return from civilized competition to enjoy a civilized drink (or six). The **Royal New Zealand Yacht Squadron,** established in 1859, at the end closest to the city and water, is one of the oldest and fanciest. Continuing back along Westhaven Dr. toward the CBD, **Pier Z** juts out on the left and contains all things boat-related in a series of specialty shops. **Charter services** line the street and loads of boat rental shops lie a bit farther down.

ORAKEI, MISSION BAY, AND ST. HELIERS

Quay St. continues past the wharves and **Mechanics Bay** and turns into pohutukawa-lined **Tamaki Drive.** In December, the white sand beaches are accented by the scarlet carpet of dropped blossoms being trampled underfoot by health-conscious joggers, cyclists, and skaters. Via car, head to **Ian Ferguson's Marine,** 12 Tamaki Dr. (tel./fax 529 2230; open daily 9am-6pm), should you need **in-line skates** (1hr. $10, each additional hr. $5, $25 per day), or **kayaks** (singles $10 per hr., $35 per day; doubles $20 per hr., $70 per day). Fit romantics might enjoy a **moonlight kayak trip** to Rangitoto Island (6-11pm; $50 per person; bookings essential). **St. George's Bay,** inland from Tamaki Dr., is a pretty little pool good for a quick paddle at the base of Parnell. Otherwise try the yacht-filled **Orakei Basin,** sailing grounds of the rich of **Paritai Drive.** Auckland's wealthiest street, it's part of a gated community of million-dollar mansions. Orakei is also home to the **Orakei Marae** (tel. 521 0617) of the Ngati Whatua tribe, just as exclusively located, and up a hill with fantastic views. If you're interested in visiting, call ahead and be aware of *marae* protocol (see p. 15). It was here in 1978, on Bastion Point, that a Maori land claim was made, and tensions eventually escalated into military intervention by the New Zealand government.

Also on Bastion Point is the **Michael Joseph Savage Memorial Gardens,** a poppy-dotted park that pays homage to New Zealand's first Labour Party Prime Minister.

The view of Rangitoto and the Gulf is simply stunning. The golden sands wrap around to a series of small coves, the first of which is **Mission Bay,** named after an 1859 Anglican stone mission (now an upscale French restaurant); the tiny parking lot next door brims in summer with cars of sun-worshippers. The restaurants, bars, and sands of Mission Bay are rivaled only in popularity and accessibility by the next cove, **St. Heliers Bay.** A quiet town throughout the winter, summer brings hordes of people to throng Tamaki Dr. and St. Heliers Bay Rd. Buses #769 and #765 run to both Mission Bay and St. Heliers Bay. The shoreline fun continues to **Music Point,** the site of New Zealand's first international air arrival in 1937.

Deep beneath Tamaki Dr., 6km east of the CBD, lurk the stingrays, eels, and sharks of **Kelly Tarltons Underwater World,** 23 Tamaki Dr. (tel. 528 0603), possibly the most ingenious use ever of converted sewage tanks. A dry-erase board at the entrance serves as a fishy tabloid of who's being fed, who's been born, and who's mating with whom. A moving walkway transports guests into the marine world of rays, sharks, and fish; it only takes a moment to adjust to moving underwater through a plexiglass tube. The newest exhibit is the Antarctic Encounter, which features a colony of live king penguins. (Open Nov.-Mar. 9am-9pm, last entry 8pm; Apr.-Oct. 9am-6pm, last entry 5pm. Admission $20, students and seniors $16, under 13 $10, age 4 $6, under 4 free.)

AUCKLAND DOMAIN

To the east of the CBD lies the vast expanse of grass and trees of the Auckland Domain, best accessed from the Grafton Bridge extending off K Rd. over the motorway. The duck pond is in the center, and a nearby gazebo often hosts jazz bands playing free concerts on summer weekends. East of the pond is the main attraction, the **Auckland Museum** (tel. 306 7076), which holds court to a host of Polynesian, European, and natural history exhibits. The museum's pride and joy are the downstairs galleries that feature Aotearoa's Maori heritage. The center gallery is home to the last completely original war canoe in existence, as well as the **Hotuni whare,** a complete meeting-house on loan from the Tainui tribe of the Thames area. The whare is still considered a sacred space, so guests are asked to remove their shoes before entering. (Museum open daily 10am-5pm. Admission by donation.)

Hotuni is also the venue for the **Pounamu Maori Performance Group** (tel. 306 7080). The blast of a conch shell announces the start of this amazing cultural show of music, dance, and weaponry. (Daily 11am and 1:30pm; $7, concessions $5.) Just across from the Domain are the **Wintergardens** (tel. 373 4229), a collection of glass houses surrounding a Victorian lily pond (open M-Sa 10am-4pm, Su 10am-7pm, winter 10am-5pm; free).

PARNELL AND NEWMARKET

On the far side of the Domain is the flashy, upscale neighborhood of **Parnell,** home to old-money estates, historic buildings, and pricey boutique shopping. To sample Parnell, stroll through the Domain or take the Link Bus. The most notable architecture is a group of Victorian homes-turned-gift-boutiques, along the side of Parnell Rd., known as **Parnell Heritage Village** (look for the fleet of tour buses outside). At the top of the road on the opposite side sits Auckland's Anglican **Cathedral of the Holy Trinity,** which was moved completely intact in all of its 19th-century glory to make room for a larger church. The free and lovely **Parnell Rose Gardens** at the base of the hill burst into bloom from November to March. If the smell of the roses is mingled with hops, that's because they're downwind of the **Lion Breweries,** 5 Kingdon St. Newmarket (tel. 377 8840), the birthplace of what many consider to be New Zealand's best lager, the inimitable Steinie (free tours and tastings Tu-Th 10:30am and 2pm; bookings essential).

Nearby, **Newmarket** is where Auckland residents come to do their shopping, watch movies, and eat out. Take the Link Bus to Newmarket and hike along Broadway St. and then graduate to Parnell. This neighborhood is the bustling "downtown" that the CBD wishes it were.

WESTERN SPRINGS

The mainly residential suburb of Western Springs is home to two of Auckland's big name attractions: the **zoo** and **MOTAT**. To get to Western Springs, take the yellow bus #045 from Point Chevalier, across from QE II Sq. ($3). The **Auckland Zoo** (tel. 360 3800), on Motion Rd., recently added *Rainforest* and *Pridelands* sections. The kiwibird and tuatara exhibits are both worth a look, as are the red panda and the Wallaby Walkabout. (Open daily 9:30am-5:30pm, last entry 4:15. Admission $12, students $9, seniors $8, children $7.) A classic streetcar connects the zoo to its nerdy neighbor, the **Museum of Technology and Transport (MOTAT)**, 805 Gr. North Rd. (tel. 846 7020). Bring your science-bent young ones for the hands-on physics experiments; it's also appropriate for those who live and die for steam engines and antique cars. The admission fee includes **MOTAT II**, a collection of classic aircraft and seaplanes in Sir Keith Park Memorial Airfield, 500m past the zoo on Motions Rd. (Open daily 10am-4:30pm. Admission $10, concessions $5, families $20.)

GREATER AUCKLAND AREA

NORTH SHORE

To the north of Auckland proper lies the North Shore, home to family beaches and suburban shopping centers. Subdivisions in the area took off after the completion of the Harbour Bridge. As the suburbs spread, the bridge soon became so clogged with traffic that the city contracted a Japanese company to come and install extensions on either side of the bridge, expanding the meager four lanes to eight. Today, the North Shore is home to vast numbers of business commuters. When the museums and galleries of Devonport lock up and the sun sets over the beaches, Devonport's theaters and Takapuna's bars are just beginning to wake up.

DEVONPORT

Devonport is a popular weekend destination for Aucklanders. Though only twelve minutes by ferry, the small town with salty sea air feels miles away. Sailors and beach lovers should take an afternoon trip to swim and watch sailboats cruise by and out into the harbor. Multi-colored Victorian rooftops add to the charm of Devonport.

🛈 **PRACTICAL INFORMATION.** The chummy info hive of the **Devonport Visitor Information Centre** (tel. 446 0677) stands in the shade of "Albert" (the Moreton Bay fig tree), on Victoria Rd., only a minute from the ferry, adjacent to the library (open daily 9am-5pm). **Fullers** operates ferry service to Devonport (12min., departs Auckland daily every 30min. 6:15am-7pm, every hr. 7-11pm, $7). **Stagecoach Bus** #813 (tel. 366 6400) runs service between Devonport and Takapuna; limited weekend service leaves on the hour ($2.20, children $1.30). The **Devonport Explorer Bus** (tel. 357 6366 or 0800 868 774) is a hop-on hop-off day tour of Devonport's sights (departs the wharf daily every hr. 10:25am-3:25pm, $22 including ferry return). **North Shore Taxis** (tel. 486 1799) offers more direct transportation to your destination of choice. You can also see Devonport by **TukTuk** (tel. mobile (025) 739 445)—you'll know one when you see it. Or, experience the eight-horsepower thrust of **Town and Country Clydesdales** (tel./fax 238 6675 or (025) 346 400). Cowboy Dan Dufty will take as many as 20 people "up, down, and all around town" to the clippity-clop of his cart ($4), with pickup from the Devonport wharf. Giddy-up. Other services include: **Shorecare Accident and Medical Centres** (tel. 486 7777); **Wigmore's Devonport Pharmacy**, 33 Victoria Rd. (tel. 445 0061; open M-F 8:30am-6pm, Sa-Su 9am-5pm); **Gentronics,** 53a Victoria Rd. (tel. 445 3740) which has **Internet access** ($10 per hr.; open M-F 9am-5:30pm, Sa 10am-2pm); the **post office**, 18 Clarence St. (open M-Tu, and Th-F 9am-5pm, W 9:30am, Sa 9am-1pm); the **police** (tel. 489 4008), in the Visitor Centre. **Telephone Code**: 09.

NORTH ISLAND

🞜🞛🞐 ACCOMMODATIONS, FOOD, AND NIGHTLIFE. Rooms in Devonport are expensive, so budget travelers should strongly consider making just a daytrip. The name of the accommodation game in Devonport is B&Bs, with over 25 to choose from. The Visitor Centre has a complete listing. One exceptional option is the **Esplanade Hotel,** 1 Victoria Rd. (tel. 445 1291; fax 445 1999; email reservations@esplanadehotel.co.nz), which commands a spectacular view of the harbor and city (doubles with private bath $120-195).

Food prices are much more reasonable. **Abide in the Vine Cafe,** 41 Victoria Rd. (tel. 445 0478), has lunch quiches and frittatas that are vegetarian and wallet-friendly ($4-5). The self-proclaimed "best coffee in town" goes well with a $3 slice of cake. (Open daily 6am-4pm.) **Bar 3,** 48-56 Victoria Rd. (tel. 445 4470), is adjacent to the movie theater. An old-fashioned Wurlitzer jukebox cranks out the hits and live bands and Sky sports pick up the slack. Regular pints drop to $4 during Happy Hour 5:30-6:30pm. (Open M-F 11am-1am, Sa-Su 10am-1am.)

🞜🞛 SIGHTS AND ACTIVITIES. To the left of the Devonport Wharf is the base of the **Royal New Zealand Navy,** which supports a fine **Navy Museum** (tel. 445 5186), full of nautical artifacts dating from Cook's 1769 voyage up to the present. (Open daily 10am-4:30pm. Admission by donation). The oral histories on tape are particularly interesting. If the weather is fine, a stroll through the Victorian elegance of downtown Devonport uncovers a host of galleries. The **Devonport Museum** (tel. 445 2661), located just off Vauxhall Rd., is one of the options (open Sa-Su 2-4pm; admission by donation). The museum perches on the side of **Mt. Cambria,** one of three extinct volcanoes in town (lopped off from the 1920s through the 50s as a result of quarrying). Mt. Cambria's taller neighbor to the west, **Mt. Victoria,** offers panoramic 360° views and can be reached by foot or vehicle.

Concrete tunnels snake through the third volcanic cone, **North Head.** Building on the Maori idea to use the peak for a *pa* (a lookout and fort), gun magazines and militia bunkers were installed in the late 1800s during the Russian Scare (they came into play again in WWI). Urban legend holds that the first aircraft built by Boeing is stored deep inside one of the tunnels. The reserve is open daily from 6am to 10pm, but the vehicle gates close at 8pm. The summit of North Head is a possible vantage point for the America's Cup as it affords million-dollar views of the **Hauraki Gulf** and the coastline.

Around the Takapuna Head is **Narrow Neck Beach,** swimmable at all tides. **Devonport beach,** near town, is also swimmable at any tide. **Cheltenham Beach** (a protected area) curves gracefully away just north of North Head, cupping calm waters which are a favorite of beach-going families; it is swimmable 2 hours before and after high tide and is very safe for children. **Torpedo Bay,** on the other side of North Head and closer to town, is also swimmable 2 hours before and after high tide. **The Devonport Food & Wine Festival** is February 19 and 20.

TAKAPUNA TO WHANGAPARAOA

North of Devonport, sprawling suburbs blend slowly into the natural beauty of the coast. To Takapuna, Milford, and beyond, the coast is characterized by curving sandy beaches separated into little bays by outcroppings of basaltic tuft. Some bays are protected areas, and huge fines (up to $5000) for pocketing shellfish are enforced; check the posted signs. Head to the **North Shore Visitor Information Centre,** 49 Hurstmere Rd. (tel. 486 8670), to learn about local highlights (open M-F 9am-5pm, Sa-Su 10am-3pm). **St. Leonard's Beach** slides into **Takapuna Beach,** creating an immense playground for young sun-worshippers, windsurfers, and families in summertime, and joggers and tai-chi practitioners in the grey of winter. The bus from Devonport to Takapuna gives access to the bars, bistros, and breweries of **Hurstmere Road.**

Windsurfing is popular in the volcanic crater of **Lake Pupuke,** a clear blue lake with a reedy shoreline. A coastal walk from Takapuna north through **Thorne Bay** to **Milford Beach** features awesome **volcanic rock formations** and the manmade Algie's Castle (from the 1920s). **Long Bay** is a regional park and marine reserve. Jutting off into the open seas from the top of Long Bay is the lofty **Whangaparaoa Peninsula,** another America's Cup vantage point on land.

THE WAITAKERE RANGES

Gorgeous and undertouristed, the Waitakeres await those who have exhausted Auckland's wild nightspots, harbors, and shops. Occupying a tract of land between the **Manukau Harbour** and the **Tasman Sea,** hundreds of mountainous, bush-covered acres can be explored by way of over 250km of walking and tramping tracks. The **Arataki Visitor Centre** (tel. 813 4941; fax 817 5656) on Scenic Dr. has comprehensive information to help you plan your route (open daily 9am-5pm). Getting there without a car is difficult, though buses from the city go to Titirangi, 6km down the road. Hitchhiking in these parts is also a dim prospect. If you can get a car, the coastline offers some amazing beaches. **Karekare** is perhaps the most scenic and was the setting for the film *The Piano* (see **Film,** p. 14). A great waterfall is accessible by a short walk from the carpark on the approach to the beach. A bit farther north, **Piha** offers excellent surf but is often more crowded. At the southern tip right at the entrance to Manukau Harbor from the ocean is **Whatipu,** which has great fishing and cool caves accessible from the beach. Farther inland along the harbor, **Cornwallis** provides calmer waters well suited for swimming and a beach perfect for picnics. For people without access to cars, **Bush and Beach Ltd.** (tel. 478 2882, bookings 0800 4BEACH) offers guided wilderness tours that take in many highlights of the region, including a rare gannet bird colony at Muriwai Beach, one of two such colonies in the world. Half-day trips run year-round (12:30pm; $60, children $30), while full-day trips run September through April (daily 9:30am; $99, children $50). Free pickup from your accommodation is provided. **Auckland Adventures** (tel. 379 4545 or mobile (025) 855 856) offers trips to Muriwai Beach and Mt. Eden at a relaxed pace. Trekking options include the afternoon adventure (12:45-6pm; $55) or wilderness adventure (9am; $75), while the Mountain Bike Adventure (9am; $75, $20 less if you have a bike) covers more ground. Additional options are the beach barbecue ($10 per person) and group overnight camping on the beach ($15 per person, includes all equipment and breakfast).

HAURAKI GULF

With 57 islands of various terrain and settlement, the Hauraki Gulf has a destination for everyone. A daytrip from Auckland into the Gulf is a must. The islands of Rangitoto, Great Barrier, and Waiheke each contain splendid and remote landscapes. **Fullers Ferries** (tel. 367 9111) is your *uber-host* to the region, running everything from standard transportation to wine tastings and specialty cruises. The Coffee Cruises take in the scenic highlights from the comfort of a sleek catamaran (1¾hr., 3 per day, $20, children $10, families $50), while the **Auckland Super Pass** covers Devonport and Rangitoto as well as land-based activities like Sky Tower and Rainbow's End theme park (valid for 14 days; $69, children $49).

RANGITOTO ISLAND

Te Rangi i totongia a Tamatekapua ("the day the blood of Tamatekapua was shed") is a long name for a little volcano, so the mount is known simply as Rangitoto. Since 1854, when the Crown grudgingly shelled out £15 for what seemed a mere lump of rock, it's been a premier picnic spot for Auckland daytrippers. Most folks head to Rangitoto by ferry. **Fullers** (tel. 367 9111, timetables tel. 367 9102) runs from Auckland's Pier 3 via Devonport (M-F 2-3 per day, Dec. 26-Mar. 1 daily 2-3 per day), returning home from Rangitoto Wharf (45min., return $18, children $9). Of course, the more adventurous could always kayak to the island. In case you miss the boat, at the Rangitoto ferry landing, you'll find a coin phone to call the **resident ranger** (tel. 372 2060), or you can call Fullers.

The area's only **campground** is located at Home Bay. Rudimentary facilities include toilets, running water, and barbecue sites ($5 per night, children $2). Most visitors foot it to the top of the island. Bring solid shoes and a hat if you plan on doing the **Summit Walk** (1hr. one-way), which winds through lunar-like fields of volcanic rock and arboreal glens. During hot summers, walking the track is akin to hiking on charcoal briquettes. Those who don't wish to walk can take Fullers' **Volcanic Explorer** "safari." The narrated 4WD tram ride drops its passengers at the base of the 900m boardwalk leading to the summit. Cruise and volcanic explorer packages are available ($35, students and seniors $17.50). At the top, you can take a peek into the perfectly inverted cone of the **crater.** Green pohutukawa and rewarewa trees flourish where red hot lava once flowed. The **lava caves** are a side trail option (20min. return). Bring a flashlight and wear durable clothes if you plan to explore the jagged passageways formed by hot lava flowing through cooling volcanic rock. The **DOC office** (tel. 379 6476), in the ferry building, has info on local tracks (open M-F 10am-6pm, Sa-Su 10am-3pm). If there's time, the stroll down the mountain to **Islington Bay** yields secluded swimming beaches (arrange for a ferry pickup, or plan for the 1½hr. walk back). The Islington Bay area is also where Rangitoto meets agrarian and pastoral **Motutapu Island** one hour away.

WAIHEKE ISLAND

For its 8000 permanent residents, many of whom have moved away from the city and built their dream home, Waiheke is a haven from the urban grind, yet separated from downtown Auckland by only a 35-minute ferry ride. For the summer inhabitants, who push the population over 30,000, it is an accessible getaway with a laid-back lifestyle and artistic community. Even with summer hordes, Waiheke offers open beaches for soaking up the sun and excellent wine tasting adventures.

■ ARRIVAL AND DEPARTURE

The most common transport is the **Fullers ferry** (tel. 367 9111, timetables tel. 367 9102). The sleek cats depart from Auckland's pier daily (35min., 13 per day, return $23). The **Link** Ferry (tel. 367 9102) travels to Waiheke (M-F 2 per day, Sa-Su 3 per day; return $17). Those with their own vehicles can use **Subritzky Shipping Line Ltd.** (tel. 534 5663), which runs three vehicle ferries departing from Half Moon Bay in Pakuranga on the Auckland waterfront (1hr., every hr. 7am-4pm, $100-120, bookings essential).

■ ORIENTATION AND PRACTICAL INFORMATION

Waiheke lies 24km west of the Coromandel Peninsula and 17km northeast of Auckland, just east of Rangitoto in the Hauraki Gulf. Most of the 134km of coastline folds into secluded rocky coves where waters lap at private shores. The vehicle ferry docks at **Kennedy Point** near the villages of **Surfdale** and **Ostend,** while the Fullers ferry arrives at **Matiatia Bay** nearest to the town of **Oneroa.** The town of **Ostend** has shopping and industry, while **Onetangi** is mostly beach.

The **Waiheke Island Visitor Information Centre** (tel. 372 9999; fax 372 9919; email waiheke@iconz.co.nz), is in the Artworks Centre on Korora Rd. in Oneroa (open daily 9am-5pm, winter 9am-4pm). There are numerous on-island transportation options. The **Waiheke Bus Co.** (tel. 372 8823) meets all ferries and makes a loop around the island (runs M-F 6am-8:15pm, Sa-Su 6:30am-8:15pm, $1-3). Be prepared to wait if you decide to take a bus at any time other than right when you get off the ferry. **Taxis** include **Waiheke Taxi** (tel. 372 8038) and **Dial-a-Cab** (tel. 372 9666). The **WIS Shuttle** (tel. 372 7756) is also available for charters; book ahead. Fullers offers an excellent package deal called the **Island Explorer Tour,** which includes return ferry, a 1½hr. scenic highlights tour of the island (1½), and an all-day bus pass good on any island bus ($34, children $18.50; $11 without ferry ride; bookings essential in summer). Renting a vehicle is the surest way to traverse the island, but locals, especially truck drivers, don't cut visitors much room on the roads. Try **Waiheke Rental Cars** (tel. 372 8635), at the ferry landing in Matiatia ($45 per day, overnight $50, plus 40¢ per km; motorbikes $35 per day, driver's license required). **Waiheke Auto Rentals** (tel. 372 8998) also provides motor vehicles at competitive rates. Bicycles can be hired from **Wharf Rats Bike Hire** in the Matiatia Wharf car park (half-day $15, full day $25). Other services include: **medical centers**, in Ostend (tel. 372 5005), and Oneroa, (tel. 372 8756); an **ATM**, at the corner of Oue St. and Oceanview Rd. in Oneroa; **BNZ** (tel. 372 7171), on Oceanview Rd. on the next block (open M-F 9am-4:30pm); **police** (tel. 372 8777), on Waikare Rd. (available M-F 8:30am-4pm); and **Mail Delivery Service** (tel. 372 7802). **Telephone Code:** 09.

ACCOMMODATIONS

Places to lodge are sprinkled all over the island, though they generally gravitate toward the beaches. To reach your accommodation, take a bus or taxi. **Waiheke Island Youth Hostel (YHA)** is on Seaview Rd. (tel./fax 372 8971; from Auckland tel. 373 7312; email robb.meg@bigfoot.com). A steep staircase up the hill from Onetangi Beach leads to a colorful dolphin mural that beckons guests from all walks of life into this small but cozy hostel. Check yourself in if nobody's there. (50% discount on shuttle from ferry. Key deposit $10. Mountain bikes $20 per day. 2-person bunk room $18 per person; doubles from $38.) The **Palm Beach Backpackers,** 54 Palm Rd. (tel. 372 8662), is near enough to its namesake that you can hear the crashing surf from the sprawling wooden lodge. Relax in the lounge and game room, or in the meditation gazebo tucked among the backyard trees. (Kayak rentals. Key deposit $10. Dorms $16; doubles $40; tent sites Oct.-Apr. $12, May-Sept. $10.) **Onetangi Beach Apartments,** 5 Fourth Ave. (tel. 372 7051; fax 372 5056; email bfw@iconz.co.nz), has self-contained units with bathroom and kitchen plus an indoor spa and outdoor pool. (Free laundry and Internet. 2-person studios Dec.-Apr. $95, May-Nov. $85.) At the other end of the spectrum is the **Waiheke Island Backpackers,** 11 Hekerua Rd. (tel./fax 372 8990), remotely hidden up on a hill. This glorified cabin house advertises a stone swimming pool and hot tub as its main attractions. The large bunk spaces ($17) and double rooms ($34-50) aren't nearly as nice as the more pricey apartments ($65-$75 for 3). (Laundry $5;. Linen $4. Bikes $20 per day. Spa $2 per 30min.; email $10 per hr. Reception closed 11am-3pm.) At **Fossil Bay Lodge (VIP),** 58 Korora Rd. (tel./fax 372 7569), near the beach in Oneroa, guests can work in exchange for food and accommodation as part of WWOOF (see p. 63), or can stay in wood cabins (doubles $40), backpacker rooms ($15), or a spiffy copper A-frame that sleeps five in the top unit ($60 for 1-3, extra person $15) and eight in the lower unit ($80 for 1-6, each extra person $15). **Campers** can trek out to the little-frequented but lovely **Whakanewha Regional Park** on the southeast corner of the island ($5 per person; advance reservation required; call Parksline at tel. 303 1530).

FOOD

Eating establishments are generally concentrated in the towns, ranging from simple cafes to fine wining and dining. **Vino Vino,** 153 Oceanview Rd. (tel. 372-9888), in Oneroa, has spectacular wines and views. Dinner mains are a bit pricey ($20-25) but worth it. (Open M-F noon-9pm, Sa-Su noon-5pm; extended hours in summer.) **Salvage** (tel. 372 2273), on Oceanview Rd. in the Pendragon Mall, Oneroa, commands a nice view of the harbor from covered outdoor seating. Lunch items run $5-7, brunch $4.50-12.50, dinner $12-20 (open Su-Th 7am-11pm, F-Sa 7am-midnight). Ciao down at **Caffe da Stefano** (tel. 372 5309), in Surfdale village. They offer pizzas ($10-17) and stuffed focaccias ($6-7.50), but Italian coffee is their specialty. Open T-Su 6pm-9pm and Sa-Su 9am-3pm; extended hours in summer.

SIGHTS AND ACTIVITIES

Waiheke's prime attraction is its many beaches, especially in the summer, when warm temperatures and high humidity make a dip in the ocean a very alluring activity. **Onetangi Beach** is the largest stretch of sand but is also the most crowded. **Oneroa Beach** has fewer people even though it is closer to town. **Palm Beach** is another lovely spot, and just to the west is the aptly named **Nudie Beach.** To enjoy the coast from another perspective, consider **Waiheke Yacht Charters** (tel. 372 9579 or (025) 764 753), which runs ecotours from their 36-foot craft (half-day $45, full day $65; maximum 10 people). **Waiheke Tours** (tel. 372 7262 or (021) 667 262) does kayaking trips. They provide all equipment and free return taxi from your accommodation or the wharf. For **fishing** charters, try any one of the fleet of fancifully named boats: the **Doolittle** (tel. 372 6163), **Miss Fleur** (tel. (025) 963 918), or **Mermaid Marine** (tel. 372 7185).

Explore the wonderful world of wine at the **Stoneyridge Vineyards,** 80 Onetangi Rd. (tel. 372 8822) which is the only vineyard open to non-tour buses (tours Sa and Su at 11:30am). Fullers also runs a **Vineyard Explorer tour and ferry** (tel. 367 9111), which visits three vineyards in addition to the sights (departs Auckland W-Su noon, winter Sa-Su only; returns by ferry at 5pm; optional return sailings $56).

There are excellent walking tracks on the island, particularly in the lush **Whakanewha Regional Park.** The Visitor Centre has an excellent guide with maps and descriptions. Several cycling loops provide some breathtaking views. Also, the DOC oversees **Stony Batter,** a reserve on the northeast end of the island that was once a WWII gun emplacement. It's a serious hike and you'll need to bring a flashlight and a map if you're going to romp through the tunnels.

Back on dry land, galleries and craft shops are the main attraction. The heart of island creativity is the **Artworks Centre** (tel. 372 6900), in Oneroa on Korora Rd., with two floors to peruse and a community theater that brings the best of Broadway and the West End to the Hauraki Gulf (open daily 10am-4pm). Also in the Artworks Centre resounds the tuneful glory of **Whittakers' Musical Museum** (tel. 372 5573). Every day except Tuesday, Lloyd and Joan Whittaker travel through 500 years of musical history playing their extensive collection of instruments, many of which they have personally restored. (Showtimes from 1-2:30pm; $7, children and seniors $5.)

GREAT BARRIER ISLAND

The largest and most remote of the Hauraki Gulf islands, Great Barrier Island (pop. 1000) maintains very few connections with the mainland or with modern technology. Officially part of Auckland, the island is very much its own isolated world, with its own weather patterns (it can be sunny here while it rains in the city) and no electricity or banks. The island is a naturalist's dream, with lush forests and marshlands covering the terrain, and silky white sand beaches breaking up the rocky coastline.

▰ ARRIVAL AND DEPARTURE

The transport of choice for most visitors is a **ferry.** The swank **Fullers** ferry (tel. 367 9111, timetable tel. 367 9117) is the fastest, departing Auckland's Pier 2 at the ferry building and porting at Tryphena, Whangaparapara, and Port Fitzroy (2hr., 4 per week, winter 2 per week; return $89). **Gulf Trans** (tel. 0800 485 387), operates the **M.V. Tasman** once per week to transport vehicles and passengers (6hr., departs Tu 7am, return $65). One step up in comfort and price is the **M.V. Sealink** (3½hr., departs W-F and Su-M 9am, return $65). **Air travel** to Great Barrier is popular. **Great Barrier Airlines** (tel. 256 6500 or 0800 900 600) is the major carrier, with at least 3-7 flights per day to Claris connecting with Auckland, Whitiangi and Whangarei. All flights are $89 one-way, return $169, except from Paihia ($120, return $240). There is also a fly one-way, ferry the other package in conjunction with Fullers for $115.

▰ ORIENTATION AND PRACTICAL INFORMATION

There are four main settlements on the island: **Tryphena,** where the ferries arrive; **Claris,** where the airport is located; **Whangaparapara;** and **Port Fitzroy.** Visitors to Great Barrier have two major challenges: 1) transportation around the island and

PIGEONGRAM, MA'AM For nearly 500 years, our feathered friends the carrier pigeons were at the forefront of rapid delivery postal service. Today, the species have been driven nearly to extinction by hunting and international courier services; only two pigeon post services remain in use in the world. One is the French Foreign Legion, which keeps a squadron of pigeons ready for important communiques, should more conventional means of communications be severed in time of war. The other is the Great Barrier Pigeongram Service at Port Fitzroy. For $20, your message will be strapped to the bird's leg, wing its way to a loft in Auckland, and from there be forwarded via surface mail anywhere in the world (usually encrusted with bird doo by the time it arrives). Established in 1898, the service sent its most memorable message on Sept. 30, 1900, when a young boy ran from Tryphena to Okupu in order to save his brother's life by pigeongramming an emergency message. Sent in duplicate via the two best birds, one was lost in a storm, but the other, "Velocity," made it through to medical help. You don't have to run to Okupu to send a pigeongram today—just call Pigeon Post (tel. 429 0242) in Claris or the Pigeon Post Outpost in Pa Beach to have your note happily winged away.

2) finding food on the island. To get around, travelers either hitch, drive their own cars, or call **Bob's Taxi** (tel. 429 0988) in Tryphena's Mulberry Grove. Bob rents cars from $60-$80 per day or he'll taxi you around from about $10 per person. His 24-hour service meets all ferries. Regarding **food:** bring groceries, or prepare for very limited food options. Also, there is **no power** on the island; residents generate their own electricity via diesel or gas generators (usually from dusk until 11pm), resulting in conspicuously quiet nights. A **flashlight** is necessary. Roads are graded, **unsealed** in many places, and only one-and-a-half lanes wide. As there are no sidewalks, **pedestrians** should keep to the outside of curves to be seen by approaching vehicles.

The **Great Barrier Island Visitor Centre** (tel. 429 0033; fax 429 0660) is located at the Claris airfield (open M-F 8:30am-6pm, Sa-Su 8:30am-5pm, winter M-F 8:30am-5pm, Sa-Su 9am-4pm). The **Fullers Information Office** (tel. 429 0004; fax 429 0469), next to the Stonewall Store in Pa Beach, keeps more extensive listings of activities on the island and is more convenient for ferry passengers arriving in Tryphena (open daily 8am-5pm, winter 9am-4pm). If you're seeking serious hiking, see the **DOC Field Centre** (tel. 429 0044), at Akapoua Bay in Port Fitzroy. There are **no banks** on the island, and credit-card-friendly shops and services are not common, so bring cash or an Eftpos card. The **Community Health Centre** (tel. 429 0356) is in Claris by the airfield. **Great Barrier Pharmacy** (tel. 429 0006) is just outside of Claris. **Laundry facilities** can be found in the **Stonewall Shopping Centre** in Mulberry Grove by Pa Beach or on the other side of the island, at the **Great Barrier Lodge** (tel. 429 0488) in Whangaparapara. The **post office** (tel. 429 0242) is on Hector Sanderson Rd., Claris. The **police** (tel. 429 0343) are on Kaitoki-Awana Rd., Claris. **Telephone Code:** 09.

■ ACCOMMODATIONS AND FOOD

Lodgings on Great Barrier allow for a broad range of living experiences, from bush camping to a family-style self-contained chalet. While reservations are only essential in the summer, they are advisable year-round, especially since many places will arrange for a free shuttle from the airport or ferry.

The **Stray Possum Lodge (VIP)** (tel. 429 0109 or 0800 767 786), in Tryphena, is the Barrier's most talked-about backpackers, standing in its own exquisite bush-clad valley. Mountain bikes can be rented for $25 per day. Free transport to and from the ferry is offered, as well as free pickup from Claris airfield. The hostel also offers the **Possum Pursuits Activities Pass**, which provides bus transport to the island's sights (daytrip $30, $45 unlimited days). There's an on-site **Possum Trap** bar as well as a pizza cafe. (Dorms $17; twins and doubles $50; self-contained unit $95; tent sites $12. Credit cards and Eftpos.) **The Crossroads Backpackers and Internet**

Cafe in Claris (tel. 429 0889; email pfl@ihug.co.nz) is a brand new backpackers smack-dab in the center of the island. This place has a homey lounge with fireplace. Upstairs there's swanky Internet access to the real world ($10 per hr.). Food and hotsprings are within walking distance. (Dorms $15; singles $30; doubles $50.) Another option is the **Pohutukawa Lodge,** (tel. 429 0211; fax 429 0117), in Tryphena, located in the center of town next to the Fullers Information Office. The adjacent Irish pub, **The Currac,** is the highlight of the facility. This is the only backpackers in town that serves food, with the pub offering burgers and hearty chowders ($4.95-6.50), while rich desserts such as Death by Chocolate ($6.50) offer opportunities to indulge. Every Thursday night is a musical jam session starting at 9pm (pub open daily from 4pm). Check-in and check-out are flexible. (Dorms $17. Rooms with bathrooms $95.) The **Medlands Beach Backpackers,** 9 Mason Rd., (tel. 429 0340), overlooking Medlands Beach, sits in an eden of eucalyptus trees and camellia flowers. Well-worn rooms are a five-minute walk from the white sand beach, and beach equipment is available. (Linen $5. Dorms $20; singles $40; twins $24.)

Couples and groups staying a week or more may find it cheapest to rent a cottage. **DOC** maintains six **campsites** ($6) and one ten-person guest **cottage** convenient to bush walks at Akapoua. ($50 for two people, winter $30; each extra person $10). Rudimentary **huts** that sleep up to 24 people are also maintained at Whangaparapara and Kaiarara ($8 per person, children $4).

▲ ACTIVITIES

The most popular activity on Great Barrier Island is doing absolutely nothing. The east coast beaches of Whangapoua, Haratonga, Kaitoke, and Awana are noted for their surfing. Most accommodations have some boogie boards floating around for guest use. **Medlands Beach,** with its graceful white sand dunes, sapphire water, and blissful breezes, is the island's most popular beach (though, in island lingo, that means 20 people in the height of summer). The west coast is quieter and more popular for yachts. **Tryphena Harbour's beaches** at Puriri Bay, Pa Beach, and Mulberry Grove are good for snorkeling and swimming. **Aotea Kayak Adventures** (tel. 429 0664) runs guided kayak tours ranging from an introductory tour to a twilight paddle ($25-65). Kayak maven and long-time Barrier resident Wayne can also add snorkeling, fishing, and bushwalks (prices negotiable). He may even help you catch a lobster dinner (book through the **Stray Possum Lodge,** tel. 429 0109). **GBI Adventure Horsetreks** (tel. 429 0274) will take you up hill and down dale for $20 per hour. Chartered fishing trips (tel. 429 0110) from $45 can be arranged through Tryphena. **The Great Barrier Island Golf Club** (tel. 429 0420) in Whangapaua hires equipment at a small fee.

Whangaparapara serves as an excellent base for challenging **mountain biking** on the Whangaparapara-Port Fitzroy Rd., accessible by a left-hand turn-off before you reach the Stamping Battery (closed to all non-DOC vehicles). Past the Stamping Battery on the left side of the road is the entrance to the **Hot Springs Walk** (1½hr.). The main pool is formed by a dam at the junction of two rivers, and smaller pools of varying temperatures are farther up the left-hand stream. Just across Whangaparapara Rd. from the mountain bike track is the entrance to the **Te Ahumata Track** (2hr.), also known as the "White Cliffs Walk" for the gorgeous quartz crystals in the stream beds in the lower reaches. The 398m summit offers expansive views of the ocean, Mt. Hobson, and the Coromandel Peninsula. For a more intense rush, try the feisty five-hour **Windy Canyon-Mount Hobson-Kaiarara Stream Track.** Beginning from the main road on the way to Okiwi, the track ascends steeply through untouched subalpine forest to the island's highest point, **Mt. Hobson (Hirakimata).** From the 621m summit, descend to the swimming-hole-friendly Kaiarara Stream and spend the night at the **Fitzroy Hut** (bunks $8). A bit past the hut, the track intersects the forest road that runs north to Port Fitzroy. Ask at the Visitor Centre for information on other tracks.

NORTHLAND

Northland, the narrow landmass that extends up and away from Auckland and the rest of the North Island, offers an enchanting world of verdant valleys, dramatic cliffs, and silky beaches. Home to the first landings of legendary explorers Kupe and Captain Cook, Northland, rich in the cultural history of New Zealand's European and Maori cultures. The sparkling Bay of Islands on the east coast is a collection of small towns admired every summer by tourists and seasonal residents. The west coast shelters the quiet beauty of the Kaipara and Hokianga Harbours. At the very top, the Aupouri Peninsula and Cape Reinga stretch out to the top of the island with hauntingly empty beaches.

Your mode of transportation in Northland will define your experience in the region. If you have the means, rent a car; it gives you the freedom to explore at your own pace. Keep an eye on fuel levels, because petrol pumps are few and far between. If you travel by bus, strongly consider buying a pass that lets you hop on and off at your discretion. **Hitchhikers** on the east coast encounter sparse traffic and consequently long waits once they get past the Bay of Islands. On the west coast, SH12 is the road less traveled, but the locals are said to be more accommodating. **Campers** should note that backcountry hut passes do not apply in Northland; you must book in advance for all huts and lodges.

■ NORTHLAND HIGHLIGHTS

- The **Bay of Islands** (p. 98) is a marine paradise, where visitors can swim with dolphins, sea-kayak among the mangroves, or take a leisurely sail around the isles.
- Scuba diving around the **Poor Knights Islands** (p. 97) is some of the world's best.
- The giant kauri of the **Waipoua Forest Park** (p. 111) tower over the landscape.
- A ferry ride from Paihia to romantic **Russel** (p. 102) reveals an intimate getaway spot. Pack a picnic and enjoy a quiet day on the Bay.

WHANGAREI

A three-hour drive north from Auckland, the journey to Whangarei, whether by bus or car, is a spectacular escape into lush, green, rolling hills. Loosely translated from Maori, Whangarei ("Fahng-a-ray") means "cherished harbor," a name paying homage to the local waters that have brought food, recreation, and profit to the region for centuries. The largest city in Northland (pop. 46,000), Whangarei sits near New Zealand's only oil refinery, and the town reflects an industrial element in its stark warehouse-style architecture. Nevertheless, Whangarei has many activities such as diving, fishing, and caving that attract visitors who, in conjunction with the young locals, maintain Whangarei's surprisingly lively nightlife.

■ ORIENTATION AND PRACTICAL INFORMATION

Whangarei wraps around the **Whangarei Harbour,** 167km north of Auckland up **SH1** on the east coast. The main drag, **Bank St.,** intersects **Cameron St.,** with a pedestrian mall that buzzes during business hours. Locals mill about downtown while tourists gravitate toward the **Town Basin** development along the harbor.

Visitors Center: Whangarei Visitor Bureau, 92 Otaika Rd. (tel. 438 1079; email wre vin@nzhost.co.nz), in Tarewa Park, at the southern entrance to the city. The **DOC Visitor Centre** (tel./fax 430 2007), inside the Visitor Bureau, has info on all of Northland and a fantastic souvenir shop. By request, buses will drop you off. Open M-F 8:30am-5pm, Sa-Su 10am-4pm; Dec. 25-Jan. daily 8:30am-6:30pm.

Buses: Coaches roll into the **bus stop** at **Northland Coach and Travel,** 11 Rose St. Open M-F 8am-5pm. Book tickets at either the Visitor Bureau or the bus station. **Northliner** (tel. 438 3206) and **InterCity** (tel. 438 2653) head to **Auckland** (3hr., 4 per day, $31) and **Kaitaia** (4hr., 2 per day, $38) via **Paihia** (1½hr., $18).

Car Rentals: Whangarei and its surrounding attractions are most easily accessed by car. Rental cars are available in Auckland; prices range, but $30 per day will hire a vehicle with unlimited km, insurance, and roadside service. Drivers under 25 pay more. **Ace Tourist Rentals** (tel. 0800 502 277) and **A 2 B Rentals** (tel. 377 0825) hire out a range of vehicles with one-way options available.

Taxis: For a cab, call **Kiwi Carlton Cabs** (24hr. tel. 438 2299); the company also runs sightseeing tours on the side ($12 return to the falls).

Hitchhiking: Getting to Auckland is considered easiest from the Visitors Bureau in Tarewa Park; those heading to the Bay of Islands often try from SH1 (Western Hills Rd.) before traffic picks up to 70kph.

Police: (tel. 438 7339), on Cameron St.

Medical Services: White Cross Accident & Medical Clinic, 121 Bank St. (tel. 430 0046). Open daily 8am-10pm. **Whangarei Care Chemist** (tel. 438 7767) is in the same building. Open daily 9am-1:30pm and 2:30-9pm.

Post Office: (tel. 430 2761), at Rathbone and Robert St. Open M-F 8:30am-5:30pm, Sa 9am-1pm.

Internet Access: At the **library** on Rust Ave. in front of the carpark. $5 for access card, then $5 per 30min. Open M-F 9am-6pm, Sa 9am-5:30pm.

Telephone Code: 09.

ACCOMMODATIONS

In summer, it's a good idea to reserve a day before you arrive. Whangarei has few backpacker options, and the top spots have limited room even in the winter. In a pinch, local B&B accommodations provide shelter for as little as $35 for a single.

Bunkdown Lodge, 23 Otaika Rd. (tel. 438 8886). This 100-year-old villa has high ceilings, a plush living room, and wood fire. Super-friendly Mr. and Mrs. Dezoete accommodate guests' every interest from diving to caving, with tight budgets in mind. Free pickup. Fancy mountain bikes, Internet (*Let's Go* discount), a telescope, and massages are available for a nominal fee. Dorms $15; twins and doubles $50.

Whangarei YHA Hostel, 52 Punga Grove Ave. (tel./fax 438 8954), off Riverside Dr. Perched above the city, it's a 15-20min. hike up the hill from the bus station. Call for directions and transportation to this quiet residential area. Visitors interested in Maori history should stop in this small, low-key accommodation. Off-street parking. Reception 8-10am and 5-7pm. Dorms $15; singles $34; doubles $34.

Central (Hatea) Hostel, 67 Hatea Dr. (tel. 437 6174; fax 437 6141). Central is not so centrally located, but it's still walkable from downtown Whangarei. A compact home that maximizes every bit of space. The lush garden around back almost provides shelter from the sound of traffic whipping along Hatea Dr. The cabin rooms have individual mini-kitchens and a lovely garden view. Free pickup. Laundry $3. Dorms $15; singles $30; doubles $35; double cabin $40. Cash only.

Whangarei Falls Backpackers (tel. 437 0609), in Tikipungaon, on Ngunguru Rd., on the way to the falls. Call ahead for directions or free pickup. Once called a caravan park, this venue offers lots for tents and trailers. You can sleep in spartan, bunker-like rooms with toilets in a seprate building. The trampoline, jacuzzi, and swimming pool are the sugar that helps this medicine go down. Dorms $14; 6-bed cabins with kitchenettes for 2 $34, extra person $11; caravan and tent sites $9.

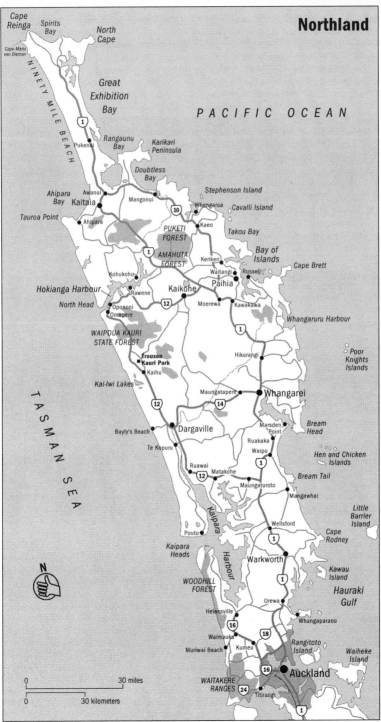

Northland

FOOD

Whangarei food options range from affordable takeaways to high-end seafood dining. Several restaurants and cafes have active bars and, on weekends, they moonlight as dance clubs. The **Pak 'N Save** market (tel. 438 1488), at the Walton St. Plaza across from the town basin, is cheap (open M-F 8:30am-8pm, Sa-Su 8:30am-7pm). All eateries listed below are located in central Whangarei.

Taste Spud, 3 Water St. (tel. 438 1164). This simple hot potato joint hits the spot with cheap stuffed spuds ($5) and burritos ($3.50-5). Chill out with fresh fruit ice cream ($1.50) or a filling frozen yogurt fruit smoothie ($3.50). Open M 8am-7pm, Tu-Th 8am-8pm, F 8am-8:30pm, Sa 11am-8pm, Su 4-8pm.

Bogarts (tel. 438 3088), at Walton and Cameron St. At night, this locals' coffee shop turns into a packed site for dinner. Small Uncle Scrooge gourmet pizza ($9) comes with tomato, cheese, and one topping. Open M-F from 11:30am, Sa 5pm-1am, Su 6-11pm.

Rin Chin Chilla, 6 Vine St. (tel. 438 5882). Loud techno music and ghoulish murals set the mood at this late-night munchie establishment. Share a super nachos for two ($7.50) or wolf down a zesty lamb kebab ($7). Open Tu-Th 11:30am-2:30pm and 5:30-9pm, F 11:30am-2:30pm and 5:30pm-3am.

◤ NIGHTLIFE

One of Whangarei's biggest in-town draws is its nightlife. In addition to the listings below, Whangarei has two large and popular nightclubs—**Powder Hound,** on Vine St., and **Sound Factory**, across the street.

Buzz Bar, 62 Bank St. (tel. 438 6639). The latest and trendiest addition to the vibrant Whangarei dance scene. While most people stumble from club to club into the early morning hours, Buzz Bar hopes to retain hard-core dance freaks. No cover before 2:30am. Open Tu-F 6pm-3am, Sa 8pm-3am. On Fridays, after the club closes, the cool kids head across the street to **The Hive,** a semi-related, underground rave establishment. Open F 3am-6am.

Planet Earth B.C., 27 Bank St. (tel. 430 8000). Clean and comfortable with a contemporary Santa Fe aesthetic, Planet Earth is a good landing spot for couch lounging and some recreational boozing. Gourmet pizzas $6-18 and gourmet burgers $9-13.50. Friday and Saturday nights, this venue turns into a party club, often with live bands. Happy Hour M-F 5-6pm. Open M-Th 11:30am-midnight, F-Sa 11:30am-3am.

Metro Bar, 31 Bank St. (tel. 430 0446). For a late-night snack (fries $3.50) and dancing to rock-and-roll favorites, head to Metro Bar. DJ dancing Friday and Saturday nights 9:30pm-1am. Play pool, or chill out upstairs. Happy Hour M-F 5-6pm. Open M 11:30am-7:30pm, Tu-Th 11:30am-9:30pm, F 11am-1am, Sa 5:30pm-1am.

◉ ⚑ SIGHTS AND ACTIVITIES

Whangarei's primary attraction is the waterfront area. Eccentric museums and pricey cafes connect to each other via paved walkways in this tourist zone called the **Town Basin.** The most compelling of the former is the **Clapham Clock Museum** (tel. 438 3993), identifiable by the gigantic bronze sundial out front and the mural depicting advancements in time-keeping from the early Greeks to the 19th century. The collection began in 1900 with one man's fascination with the gears of a music box, and has since become a 1500-plus piece tribute to time-keeping. (Open daily 9am-5pm. Admission $5.)

For those people looking to connect with the breathtaking surroundings, Whangarei offers numerous **walking tracks** through the hilly landscape that embraces the town. Within walking distance from the center of town and most backpackers, **Mount Parahaki** offers several manageable hikes which reward trekkers with great views of the city and harbor. Automobiles can also make the ascent. No visitor should miss the **Whangarei Falls,** located only a short distance from town (cabs and backpacker hosts are usually willing to shuttle visitors at an affordable price). View the falls from above or take a short but steep 20-minute hike to the breathtaking base of the falls. Maori boys have jumped off the towering cliff for hundreds of years as a rite of passage.

Spend a day on an island in Whangarei's harbor working for a cool conservation program. The **Friends of Matakohe/Limestone Island** (tel. 438 4639) is replanting the little island in the Whangarei Harbour with indigenous flora. They are in search of volunteers to help with replanting and reconstructing walking trails, shelters, and viewing platforms. In return for hard labor, you can camp on the island. Those who want to escape farther should explore the **Whangarei Heads,** where **Ocean Beach** offers great surf and bursts of rocky coastline, and the view from **Mount Manais,** which offers 360° views.

Whangarei has legendary caving opportunities. Those interested in spelunking should contact their hostel host, who can make affordable arrangements (especially at Bunkdown Lodge) to explore the **Abbey Caves.** Or, for a thrilling combo, connect with the folks at **The Bushwacka Experience** (tel. 434 78 39 or mobile 025 578 240) who offer two tours. The "Basic Tour" takes you on bushwalks through rock crevasses, on the "waterfall express," and then to glow-worm caves, with tea, BBQ, and 4WD safari transportation. The "Adventure Seekers" tour adds abseiling and rock climbing. Both tours wind up at the **farm base,** where you can milk cows and shear sheep. (Free pickup from the city. Tours run on demand with a 1-day notice. Basic tour 2hr., $45. Adventure seekers 4hr., $75. Discounts available for large groups.) Whangarei Harbor offers incredible opportunities for **ocean fishing;** ask hostel owners about cheap rental equipment.

NEAR WHANGAREI: POOR KNIGHTS ISLANDS

Eleven million years ago, eruptions off the coast of Northland gave birth to a string of islands, including the Poor Knights Islands. The Ngatiwai tribe called them home for a spell, naming them Tawhiti Rahi and Aorangi Islands. In the early 1800s, however, a string of invasions and deaths earned the islands the distinction of being *tapu* (forbidden). Today, landing on the islands without a permit is also *tapu*, but by decree of the DOC, not the local tribe. Lack of human interference on the islands makes them a haven for all sorts of rare creatures, including tuatara and giant weta.

The big draw is world-class diving; **Jacques Cousteau** has rated the island area one of the ten best diving sites in the world. Special mooring buoys off the coast serve as landing points for the scores of scuba, snorkel, and kayak trips run out of Whangarei and the coastal town of **Tutukaka** (30km east of Whangarei). Sea caves both above and below water make for awesome kayaking and snorkeling among moray eels, stingrays, and subtropical reef fish. Pleasure cruisers and recreational divers are best suited to **The Dive Connection** (tel. 430 0818) out of Whangarei or **Knight Line Cruises** (tel. 0800 288 882) out of Tutukaka. Knight Line's boat *El Tigre* departs the Tutukaka New Marina Complex daily at 8:30am, returning at 4:30pm (snorkeling equipment, kayaks, DOC swim-with-dolphins permit supplied). Guided trips pass through sea caves by boat, kayak, or snorkel, and Knight Line even offers a scuba tour of the "wall of mouths." (Full day $80, children $45; diving with all scuba gear $140. Bookings essential.) The **Dive Shop** (tel. 438 3521), on Water St., will take four or more experienced divers out on their boat ($60 includes scuba gear), and also runs introductory diving sessions for novices ($130-150). Free pickup is available from your accommodation.

BAY OF ISLANDS

A tremendously popular summer destination, the Bay of Islands has long attracted visitors with its temperate climate and beautiful coastline. The most celebrated visitor was Captain Cook, who dropped anchor here in 1769. Cook made friends with Maori and sent word back to England, setting the wheels in motion for the bay's permanent European settlement. He named the region after the 144 islands that today create pockets of tranquility for maritime enthusiasts and delightful exploration for landlubbers. For a taste of the Bay of Islands, take inspiration from Cook—board a boat and discover the spectacular coastline for yourself.

PAIHIA

Any visitor will understand the region's name—Bay of Islands—immediately upon arrival in Paihia, a small town that bears witness to an inlet full of green isles. Paihia is the principal center of commercial activity in the Bay. In the summer, the population of 4000 skyrockets to nearly 20,000. The town is also the transportation hub of the region, with buses arriving and departing from the Maritime Building to various destinations in Northland.

⁊ ORIENTATION AND PRACTICAL INFORMATION

Marsden Rd. runs along the waterfront and is the main artery. **Paihia Wharf** is roughly in the middle of town, opposite the commercial center of **Paihia Mall** and bordered by **Williams Rd.** and **Bayview Rd.**

Visitors Center: Information Bay of Islands (tel. 402 7345; fax 402 7314), in the white octagonal pavilion to the left of Paihia Wharf. Very helpful and knowledgeable staff. Also offers **Internet.** Open daily 8am-8pm, winter 8am-5pm.

Ferries: Fullers Passenger Ferry (tel. 402 7421) departs for Russell daily on the half hour (15min., $3). Buy tickets on board, or at the Fullers desk in the Maritime Building. The **vehicle ferry** departs from Opua (about 10km south of Paihia) for Russell every 10min. (5min. 6:50am-9pm. Cars $7, campervans $12, motorcycles $3.50.)

Buses: Northliner Coaches (tel. 402 7857) and **InterCity** (tel. 357 8400) arrive at the Maritime Building, contract through **Westcoaster,** and run to: **Auckland** (4¼hr., 2 per day, $42) via **Whangarei** (1¼hr., $18); **Auckland** via **Waipoua,** with a stop to see the forest (8hr.; 1 per day, in winter M, W, and F; $58); and **Kaitaia** (2¼hr., 2 per day, $28) via **Kerikeri** (30min., $8).

Taxis: Haruru Cabs (tel. 402 6292) or **Paihia Taxis and Tours** (tel. 402 7506). A more creative transportation option is the rickshaw motorscooter called **Tuk Tuk Shuttle Service** (tel. mobile 025 866 071), which runs to Waitangi ($5) and Haruru Falls ($8).

Car Rentals: Paihia is ideal for renting a car for trips to Cape Reinga. **Budget Rentals** is in the **Paihia Holiday Shop** (tel. 402 7811), at the corner of Williams and Selwyn Rd.

Hitchhiking: Hitchhiking to Kerikeri or points north is best accomplished near the rotary at the end of Marsden Rd. To head south, wait at Paihia Rd. at the edge of town.

Banks: Banks with **ATMs** cluster around the Paihia Mall and are open M-F 9am-4:30pm.

Medical Services: Bay View Medical Centre, 7 Bay View Rd. (tel. 402 7132). Open by appointment M-F 9am-5pm. After-hours, contact on-duty doctor (tel. 404 0328).

Telephone Code: 09.

⌂ ACCOMMODATIONS

The number of beds in Paihia has been steadily increasing for quite some time, with almost every summer bringing the introduction of a new backpackers. In season, reservations are essential. Visitors are well advised to shop around by checking out each of the backpackers sitting no more than 30 seconds away from each other along **Kings Rd.**, only minutes from the bus station.

■ **Mousetrap Backpackers (VIP)**, 11 Kings Rd. (tel. 402 8182). An eclectic mix of maritime bric-a-brac, backpacker art, and the hostess's *joie de vivre* make this landmark a funky and comfy abode. The soul of this hostel is the covered balcony with an ocean view, which has transformed many a well-intentioned active visitor into a "balcony bum." Longer stays encouraged. Outdoor wood BBQ. Bike rentals $10, kayaks $25. Dorms $16; twins and doubles $39. Winter discounts.

Peppertree Lodge (Nomads), 15 Kings Rd. (tel./fax 402 6122; email peppertree.lodge@xtra.co.nz). This backpackers has rooms so sanitary that you would swear you were staying in a motel if there weren't seven snoring Swedes in the same dorm. Internet. 6- to 8-bed dorms $16, winter $15; 4-bed dorms with bath $18, winter $15; twins and doubles $49, extra person $15, winter $40, extra person $10; self-contained studio doubles $75, winter $50.

Pipi Patch Lodge (VIP), 18 Kings Rd. (tel. 402 7111; fax 402 8300). If the giant green bus parked in front with the words "Kiwi Experience" doesn't tip you off, read this: Pipi Patch is party central (especially in the summer). Plant yourself at the **Pipi Patch Bar** (open Su-M 3-11:30pm; Happy Hour 6-7pm) and start making friends, or work your groove in the well-equipped lounge, swimming pool, or free spa. Reception 7:30am-8:30pm, winter 7:30am-7:30pm. Key deposit $20. Internet. Dorms $16; singles, twins, and doubles $45; family units with full kitchen for 2 $45, extra person $20.

Lodge Eleven (tel./fax 402 7487), at the corner of King and MacMurray Rd. Two stories of cheesy, motel-style units are well maintained by a hospitable owner. Each unit has its own bathroom, with an adjacent kitchen. Key deposit $10. Laundry $4. Reception 8am-8pm. Check-out 9:30am. Dorms $16; 4-bed dorms $18; singles $30; twins and doubles $44, winter $44. Popular 6-bed Swedish log cabin in back $90.

◖▣ FOOD AND NIGHTLIFE

Paihia's mall has eating opportunities around every corner. Unfortunately, few nosh options fall between the poles of expensive dining and greasy takeaway grub. The **Four Square market** (tel. 402 8002) is on Williams Rd. (open M-F 8am-8pm, Sa-Su 8am-6pm; winter M-F 8am-6pm, Sa-Su 8am-5pm).

Basrah (tel. 402 8544), toward the Selwyn Ave. side of the Paihia Mall. Tucked away in the corner of the shopping arcade is this Middle Eastern oasis with overflowing pitas stuffed with lamb, beef, chicken, or falafel. Open Su-Th 11am-9pm, F-Sa 11am-10:30pm, winter daily 11am-3pm and Tu-Su 5-9pm.

The Bread Shed, 39 Williams Rd. (tel. 402 8552), in the Four Square Building. A spot-on bakery great for breakfast or snack any time of day. Apple cinnamon muffins ($2) are light and delicious and jammed donuts ($1.30) are so fresh the powdered sugar has barley settled on their surface. Open 24hr., winter 4am-5pm.

Ruffino's, 39 Williams Rd. (tel. 402 7964), hidden above the Four Square building. Some of the area's best pizza is available in this unromantic white room. Generous personal-size pizzas ($7.50-10) and pastas ($10-11) are prepared before your eyes. BYO. Takeaway available. Open daily from 5pm, winter from 5:30pm.

Caffe Over the Bay (tel. 402 8147), on Marsden Rd. across from the wharf. Savory scents entice you to the balcony overlooking the bay. Friendly service, mellow jazz, and cute round tables. Hazelnut pancakes ($10) highlight all-day breakfasts ($7.50-12.50). Lunch pastas and salads $12-14.50. Open daily from 8am, winter 8am-3:30pm.

Blue Marlin Diner (tel. 402 7590), on Marsden Rd. at the mall. Saddle up in the swiveling seats at the blue bar, or sit at booths along the wall while you enjoy diner staple fish and chips ($5). Opt for light snacks or more conventional meals of steak and fish fillets ($12.50-14). Takeaway available. Open daily 7:30am-8:30pm, winter 8:30am-6pm.

The Lighthouse Black Boat Bar (tel. 402 8324), on Marsden Rd. opposite the wharf car-park. On summer nights, Paihia converges on the Lighthouse, the town's primary night spot. This sports bar is also a monument to the multiculturalism of the Bay of Islands. In season, the queue leads out the door, down the stairs, and around the block. DJ daily from 9:30pm. Happy Hour M-F 9-10pm ($2 pints). Open M-Sa noon-2am.

⚡ ACTIVITIES

The Bay of Islands cannot be fully appreciated from an onshore perspective—a water excursion is a must. Luckily, Paihia is the Bay of Islands' hub for water-based activities. The **Maritime Building** by the wharf is the meeting point for many of the tours and trips (open daily 6:30am-9pm, winter 7am-7pm). In summer, expect crowds of fellow tourists; advance booking is key. In winter, many activities require minimum numbers and trips are limited. Always inquire about back-packers' discounts, as they are not always advertised. Many of the trips listed here will also pick you up in Russell.

CRUISES

The focal point of most of the sightseeing cruises is the **Hole in the Rock,** an island at the extreme end of the bay that boats can pass through. Trips offered by differ-ent companies vary significantly; don't let price and duration be the only criteria for your decision. **Fullers** (tel. 402 7421) runs a Cape Brett trip to the Hole (4hr.; $55, children $28). The **Cream Trip** meanders in and out of the smaller bays, deliver-ing the mail. It is one of the few official Royal Mail runs left in New Zealand (5½hr.; $65, children $33). You may also combine the two trips into a **Supercruise** (6½hr.; $85, children $45). None of Fullers' cruises include lunch, so bring your own. **Kings** (tel. 402 8288) offers a cruise route similar to the Supercruise (6hr.; daily Oct.-May.; $75, children $45). It also offers a year-round Hole in the Rock Cruise (3¼hr.; 2 per day; $50, children $25). For a fun evening cruise, contact **Darryl's Mini Cruises** (tel. 402 7848 or 402 7730). Although they don't make it to the Hole in the Rock, dinner is included as part of the cruise (2½hr.; $35).

ADVENTURE CRUISES

For those who want the adrenaline rush of shooting across the waves, several faster cruising options are available. The **Fast Boat Company** (tel. 402 7020) offers "more of the bay in less time," with two exciting possibilities. The Excitor travels at speeds of up to 35 knots, is suitable for all ages, and goes out to the Hole in the Rock (1½hr.; daily every 2hr. 8:30am-9pm, winter 2 per day; $50, children $25). A step up in intensity is the Excitor Extreme, normally used by special armed mili-tary services throughout the world. It is the fastest boat of its type operating in New Zealand. Capable of speeds of over 50 knots, the trip is only suitable for adults in excellent health. (1½hr., $70.) In inclement weather, both of these trips may modify their routes, taking in more territory at slower speeds.

RAINBOW WARRIOR The battered hull of Greenpeace's *Rainbow Warrior* rests offshore in Matauri Bay, the product of a dark series of events. After the French resumed nuclear testing in the South Pacific, Greenpeace dispatched the *Rainbow Warrior* to carry out a mission of protest. The French Secret Service got wind of the highly publicized endeavor and, on July 10, 1985, bombed the ship in Auckland Har-bour. The event became instant international news. A bird reserve near Thames (see p. 131) was established in memory of Fernando Pereira, the on-board photographer who was killed, and the episode remains a sticking point in Kiwi-Franco relations to this day. The hull of the sabotaged ship was moved to the Bay of Islands in 1987 and sunk in Matauri Bay, where the haven for subtropical fish now plays host to world-class divers in an eco-friendly maritime park—an unexpected, but not altogether unfitting, end for the environmentalist vessel.

SWIMMING WITH DOLPHINS

The DOC licenses select companies to go out in search of playful pods; with the right conditions, you can slip into the water and frolic with the slick grey creatures. There is no guarantee of sightings, though some companies will let you try again the next day; check before booking. **Dolphin Discoveries** (tel. 402 8234), in the Maritime Building, has been spotting dolphins since 1991 and has the highest success rate ($85, children $45). The ubiquitous **Fullers** (tel. 402 7421) has a **Dolphin Encounters** trip that includes an underwater microphone to hear all the whistles and clicks (4hr.; $85, children $45). They also have a special safety net that allows passengers not confident in their swimming skills to get in the water. **Kings** (tel. 402 8288) offers a **Bay of Islands Heritage Tour,** a trip to the Hole in the Rock which begins with a *Powhiri*, a traditional Maori welcome ceremony, and continues through the bay with explanation of the Maori connection to the area (6hr.; Oct.-May. 1 per day; $85, children $45). **Carino** (tel. 402 8040 or mobile 025 933 827), a 40- by 30-foot catamaran sailing charter, offers a full day of sailing, sunning, fishing, island beach stops, bushwalks, and swimming with dolphins, all for $60. If you don't find any, console yourself with the $5 BBQ lunch, or drink your marine mammal blues away at the on-board bar.

FISHING AND SAILING

In addition to being the cheapest option for swimming with dolphins, charter boats are a great way to see the islands and get in a little fishing on the side. Naturally, each skipper and boat has a distinct character. The good folks at **Charter Pier** (tel. 402 7127), halfway down the wharf on the left, are familiar with every operator, handle all the bookings, and will match you with a boat and guide. Generally, trips are four hours long, and there are opportunities for big-game fishing. You can also hire self-drive boats. ($45 per person for large boats, $65 for small boats.) For an intimate guided tour of the Bay of Islands aboard a 40-foot sailboat, spend a day with the cool guys of **She's A Lady Charters** (tel. 402 8119 or mobile 025 964 010; 7-8hr. $65, includes lunch). **Fullers** (tel. 402 7421) operates the **R. Tucker Thompson,** a majestic tall ship with a basic bar that endeavors to experience the bay in much the way as Cook and Co. did (7hr.; daily Nov.-May; $75, children $40).

SEA KAYAKING AND RENTALS

Rugged individualists who want to paddle their own way can explore the mangrove forests, Haruru Falls, and the intricacies of the outlying islands via kayak. The trademark logo of a woman drifting serenely through mangroves is highly visible throughout the region, and belongs to **Coastal Kayakers** (tel. 402 8105). They offer independent kayak rentals ($10 per hr., half-day $45, full day $65), guided kayak tours, a mask and snorkel combo (full day $10), package tours, and hardcore **wilderness expeditions** (2-3 days; Nov.-May; from $110). **Bay Beach Hire** (tel. 402 7905), on Marsden Rd. opposite the Edgewater Motel, has both individual and tandem kayaks ($10 per hr., half-day $25, full day $35). They also have catamarans, windsurfers, dinghies, and fishing tackle.

FLYING, FALLING, AND DIVING

Those who would prefer to see the bay from above can take a scenic flight around the islands, Cape Brett, and the Hole in the Rock with **Salt Air** (tel. 402 8338), located in a kiosk just to the south of the Maritime Building. Their 1946 seaplane will take you around for 20 minutes ($85) or 30 minutes ($95). They also run tours to Cape Reinga—take a morning flight to see the Cape before the lunchtime arrival of tour buses (1-2 per day, $239; free pickup from accommodation). **SkyHi Tandem Skydive Ltd.** (tel. 402 6744 or mobile 025 756 758) drops you out, not off. Departing from Watea Airfield, they offer free pickup from your accommodation, and from wherever you land, too. (3000m $185, 4000m $225.) **Dive North** (tel. 401 1777) departs daily for the Rainbow Warrior, one hour away (2 dives $135, including gear). **Paihia Dive** (tel. 402 7551) on Williams Rd., offers a Discover Scuba Course for novices (2 dives, backpacker special $150.) They also offer a two-day dive trip to the **Rainbow Warrior** ($125 including gear).

ON THE GROUND

Although it may be hard to imagine, there are land-based activities in Paihia as well. **Bay Beach Hire** (tel. 402 7905) rents mountain bikes with which you can explore the inland hills ($5 per hr., half-day $15, full day $20). Several walking tracks in these hills lead to scenic views of the waterfront. For a completely unique Paihia experience, visit the **Lily Pond Farm Park** (tel. 402 6099), on Puketona Rd. on the way to Kerikeri. Although it's a bit difficult to reach without a car, those who get there are greeted by black swan salutes, and a chorus of chickens, pheasants, emu, ducks, peacocks, and pigs. Activities include horse and pony rides, feeding the animals, milking the cow at noon, a swimming hole, and a bush walk to a small waterfall. (Open daily from 10am. Admission $5, children $3.) For a more substantial horse ride, **Ginny's Horse Treks** (tel. 405 9999) has a great summer option of five hours of riding, glow-worm caves, and swimming holes (Nov.-Apr.; free pickup in Paihia, 9am at the base of the wharf; $55). They also offer shorter treks in the winter (2hr. $35), but no free pickup. The **Bay of Islands Jazz & Blues Festival,** now in its 16th year, usually takes place over three days in early August and features internationally acclaimed musicians, as well as local talent. The **Bay of Islands Country Rock Festival** in May attracts thousands.

RUSSELL

It's hard to believe that Russell once merited the title "Hell Hole of the Pacific," and was notorious for seedy sailor activity and Maori-European clashes. Today, Russell's small-town charm is a welcome relief from the hubbub of Paihia and only a ferry trip away. While many budget accommodations leave much to be desired, consider Russell if you feel overwhelmed or yearn for a romantic getaway.

🔟 **ORIENTATION AND PRACTICAL INFORMATION.** The **Strand** runs along the water's edge from the **Russell Wharf.** All the shops are within a two block radius of each other, just south of **Long Beach Road.**

Kings runs the **Russell Visitor Centre,** which is in a kiosk on the wharf (open daily in summer 8am-8pm). In the winter, the building is stocked with brochures, but there is no attendant. Direct queries to the **Bay of Islands Maritime & Historic Park Visitor Centre** (tel. 403 7685; fax 403 7649) on the Strand. This is also the main **DOC office** for the Bay of Islands (open daily 9am-5pm, winter 10am-4:30pm). **Fullers Passenger Ferry** (tel. 402 7421) departs for **Paihia** daily on the hour (15min.; 7am-10pm, winter 7am-7pm; $3, children $1.50). Buy tickets on board, or at the Fullers desk in the Maritime Building. The **vehicle ferry** departs from Okiato (about 8km south of Russell) for **Opua** every 10 minutes (Sa-Th 6:40am-8:50pm, F 6:40am-9:50pm; cars $7, campervans $12). Other services include: **BNZ** on York St. (tel. 403 7821; open M-F 10:10am-2pm) and **Westpac Bank** (tel. 403 7809) on Cass St. near the Strand (open M-F 10am-1:45pm); **Russell Medical Services** (tel. 403 7690), in the Traders Mall, between York and Church St. (open M-F 9am-4:30pm); **Russell Pharmacy,** 21 York St. (tel. 403 7835; open M-F 8:30am-5pm, Sa 9am-noon); **post shop,** in the Russell Foodmarket on York St. (open M-F 8:30am-6pm, Sa 9am-1pm); **Internet,** available at **Innovation** (tel. 403 8843), on York St. in the Traders Mall ($5 per 15min.; open M-F 8am-5pm). **Telephone Code:** 09.

🛏 **ACCOMMODATIONS.** Quick! Run to the nearest phone and book one of only six beds at **The End of the Road,** 24 Brind Rd. (tel. 403 7632), at the top of Robertson Rd. and down the hill to the end of Brind. Russell's best budget accommodation has amazing views of Matauwhi Bay, a lemon-tree track to the wharf, and an easy walk to Long Beach. (Dorms $18, winter $16; twins and doubles $40, winter $36.)

Russell Lodge (tel. 403 7640; fax 403 7641), at the corner of Chapel and Beresford St., situated close to the shops, has a communal kitchen, a recreation room, and an outdoor pool shaded by trees. (Laundry $2. Dorms $18; budget rooms for 2 $60; deluxe doubles with TV and kitchenette $75, extra person $10.) Flowering plants and trees abound at **Russell Holiday Park** (tel. 403 7826; fax 403 7221), on Long Beach Rd. This sprawling complex caters to families. (Powered and tent sites $10-12; dorms $14-16 (not available Dec. 20-Jan. 31 and holidays); cabins, flats and motel units also available.)

⚑ FOOD. Waterfront Cafe (tel. 403 7589), on the Strand, has a beautiful beach-front view from the bar seating at the front window and an enclosed outdoor courtyard out back. The selection is standard cafe fare. (Open daily 7:30am-4pm, winter M-Sa 7:30am-4pm.) **York St. Cafe** (tel. 403 7360) in the Traders Mall is a simple place committed to serving fresh food at low prices. Lunch sandwiches like the chicken and avocado sandwich ($4.50) arrive sans frills—a good value. (Open daily 8am-11pm, winter 9am-11pm.) Waterfalls greet diners at the entrance to **Gannets** (tel. 403 7990), on the corner of York and Chapel Streets. This well-presented bistro's specialty is fresh seafood. Meat lasagna ($10-18) is one of a few non-seafood options. (Open Th-Tu from 5pm.)

📷 ⚑ SIGHTS AND ACTIVITIES. The best collection of local historical treasures is at the **Russell Museum** (tel. 403 7701) on York St., which has a functional scaled replica of Cook's *Endeavor*, as well as articles ranging from the ridiculous—cow hairballs and swordfish eye sockets—to the sublime—an excellent video on the turbulent history of the Bay of Islands (open daily 10am-4pm; admission $3). The Anglican **Christ Church,** on the corner of Baker and Robertson Rd., is New Zealand's oldest standing church, built in 1814. Charles Darwin attended services here while the *HMS Beagle* was anchored in the bay; he made a substantial contribution to help fund a church that was later to attack his theory of evolution by natural selection. Not to be outdone by the Protestants, Bishop Pompallier arrived in 1838, and his posse of Catholic missionaries soon followed suit. Although the church is gone, the 1841 **Pompallier House** (tel. 403 7861), on the esplanade at the end of the Strand, is open to the public and displays such artifacts as the mission tannery, printing house, and book bindery—the Bible was even translated into Maori here. (Open daily 10am-5pm; tours 10am-3pm. Admission $5.) The **Russell Film Society** (tel. 403 7048) screens movies every Thursday night, March through September, at 7:30pm in the Russell Town Hall (tickets $6, children $3).

Mirroring Pompallier House on the opposite side of Russell is **Flagstaff Hill.** A short walking track ascends to the site where **Hone Heke,** the man who felled the symbol of British rule (the flagpole) four times in 1844-45, displayed his axe-wielding skills. When the tide is out, the hill can be approached along the beach at the north end of the Strand; otherwise take the signposted route off Flagstaff Rd. Lovely **Long Beach** of Oneroa Bay lies just over the hill at the end of Wellington St. and offers plenty of opportunities to sun and swim. Rent kayaks in the summer outside the **DOC office** by the waterfront.

Trekkers come from all over to walk the **Cape Brett Lighthouse Track,** an eight-hour medium-grade walk in each direction. The old lighthouse keeper's house has been turned into a hut with a gas cooker, running water, and toilets, but no utensils ($8 per person, children $4). You must book ahead at the DOC office in Russell, where you also pay the track fee ($15, children $8). The start of the track is an hour's drive from Russell. Maori guides are available for the track and will introduce you to the history of the region (prices negotiable). A popular option is to be dropped off at the lighthouse by sea, and then hike back, so as to enjoy the coast and save a day. The DOC office has more information. They can also tell you about the **campsite** on the island of **Urupukapuka,** right at the beach with running water and cold showers, but no toilets ($6 per person, children $3).

WAITANGI NATIONAL RESERVE

On February 6, 1840, more than 500 Maori, settlers, traders, dignitaries, and missionaries came ashore on the pebbled beach of Waitangi to witness the signing of the single most important document in New Zealand's history—the **Treaty of Waitangi** (see p. 7). Today, the treaty is the focal point of vigorously debated Maori land rights grievances. Despite the demonstrations and legal battles linked to this place, the **Waitangi National Reserve** (tel. 402 7437) is a remarkably serene and verdant place. About a half-hour walk from Paihia, it promises a day of majestic hikes, good food, and plenty of cultural history too. To reach the reserve from Paihia, follow Marsden Rd. over the Waitangi Bridge, and then head up the rise. Alternatively, you can take the scenic route (if you have a car) and check out **Haruru Falls** on Puketona Rd. The falls can also be reached by way of the **Waitangi National Trust Mangrove Walk,** a beautiful 2½-hour stroll from the Visitor Centre. The grounds include the **Treaty House,** one of the first architectural clues of a British presence in New Zealand. From 1832 to 1844, it was home to the Crown's first watchdog "British Resident," **James Busby** (see p. 7). Today, it is a museum. To the left of the lush lawn that leads to the water is the **Whare Runanga,** a Maori meeting house for all tribes, constructed by a team of master carvers in 1940 for the treaty's centennial celebration. Two spooky 15-minute sound and light presentations illustrate the stories behind the intricate carvings inside (daily on the half hour, 9am-4:30pm). The world's largest war canoe, *Ngatokimatawhaorua,* is on display a short walk away from the Treaty House in the opposite direction. The 35m canoe is hauled out by 80 warriors and paddled around the bay every February 6th to celebrate Waitangi Day. They will also bring out the canoe to celebrate the dawning of the new millennium. See the bits and pieces of ill-fated New Zealand voyages at **Kelly Tarlton's Museum of Shipwrecks** (tel. 402 7018), which floats at the mouth of the Waitangi River by the bridge. The collection of over 1000 artifacts was salvaged from the watery graves of 20 wrecks.

KERIKERI

Kerikeri attracts visitors with its temporary employment in the area's orchards. Sitting to the north and west of Paihia, the small town center is slightly inland of the coast. Craft shops and organic fruit stands line the roads leading into Kerikeri, which has easy access to the water. Visitors reach Kerikeri most easily by car. While Kerikeri has several nice hostels, the budget accommodations are suited best for workers, not travelers.

⚑ ORIENTATION AND PRACTICAL INFORMATION. Kerikeri Rd. is the main street in town, leading from **SH10** through town and to the water. Most of the services are clustered within the triangle it forms with **Hobson Ave.** and **Cobham Rd.** The **Visitor Centre** in Paihia handles most Kerikeri queries, though info can be found in the **library** (tel. 407 9297) on Cobham Rd. Other services include: the **Kerikeri Medical Centre** (tel. 407 7777) on Homestead Rd.; **Kerikeri Pharmacy Ltd.** (tel. 407 1800) on Kerikeri Rd. (open M-F 8:30am-5:30pm, Sa 9am-12:30pm); the **post office** (tel. 407 9721) is Hobson Ave; and **Internet access** at **Kerikeri Computers,** 88 Kerikeri Rd. (tel. 407 7941). **Telephone Code:** 09.

KIWI CARNAGE Man's best friend can be less than a bosom buddy to New Zealand's native fauna, especially when Fido turns out to be a serial killer in disguise. In 1987, one such carnivorous canine went AWOL from his owners in the Waitangi State Forest, in the Bay of Islands. On a systematic rampage, he managed to slaughter as many as 500 kiwi—at least 50% of the area's population—before meeting a bullet-induced death. Keep your dog well-fed and leashed, or you'll bear the guilt of kiwi carnage, and some stiff legal action besides.

⌐ ACCOMMODATIONS. Hostels in Kerikeri are geared toward backpackers who are looking for seasonal work at one of the many orchards and farms in the area. Farms or orchards contact hostels, which then list the job postings. The best times to find work in the area are early June, late March, and late December. Hostels usually offer good weekly rates for dorms and tent sites.

To get to the **Hone Heke Lodge (VIP),** 65 Hone Heke Rd. (tel./fax 407 8120; email honehekelodge@xtra.co.nz), turn off Kerikeri Rd. and then go left up the hill at the sign of the backpacking orange. This low-lying, motel-style structure is a working hostel featuring a TV lounge, recreation room with pool and ping-pong tables, and two small kitchens. (Free pickup from bus stop and shuttle available to orchards. Bike rentals. Dorms $14, twins $34; twins and doubles with bath $40; 3 tent sites $10 each.) The **Hideaway Lodge** (tel. 407 9773), on Wiroa Rd., is a sociable motel village of mostly orchard workers. At the SH10 rotary, go in the opposite direction from Kerikeri and look for the sign. The sprawling hostel attracts many workers by offering free transport to and from the fields. The broken-in lounge has a TV and pool table. (Call for free pickup. Dorms $13; doubles $30; deluxe doubles $35; tent sites $8; powered $8.) The **Kerikeri YHA,** 144 Kerikeri Rd. (tel. 407 9391; fax 407 9328), just past the edge of town toward the water, is a rustic hostel—you won't mind walking in with muddy boots from the orchards. Identical male and female bunkhouses are on either end of the bathroom building. (Dorms $14; twins $34.)

⌐▄ FOOD AND NIGHTLIFE. The **Fishbone Cafe,** 88 Kerikeri Rd. (tel 407 6065), located smack in the center of town, has reasonably priced menu items and an impressive wine list. Breakfasts and lunches are plentiful and affordable ($5.50-12.50); dinner is more expensive (entrees $6.50-12, mains $16-19), and reservations are recommended. (Open M-W 8:30am-4pm, Th-Sa 8:30am-9pm.) Beneath the Fishbone, accessed from Homestead Rd. behind Kerikeri Rd., is **Excess,** a cool, small pub with an outdoor area and a knowledgeable staff (open W-Su from 2pm, winter F-Sa 4:30-11pm). The **Rocket Cafe** (tel. 407 8688), on Kerikeri Rd. between the town and SH10, has glass doors along all four walls. The veggie-friendly menu includes tasty breakfast muffins ($2.50) and other posh nosh. The back doors open onto an expansive lawn with games amid the organic kiwi vines overhead. (Open daily 8am-5pm.) **New World supermarket** (tel. 407 7440) is at the corner of Homestead Rd. and Fairway Dr. (open Sa-Tu 8am-6pm, W-F 8am-8pm).

▨ ◪ SIGHTS AND ACTIVITIES. Kerikeri is rich in Maori and European history. Stroll to the **Kerikeri Basin,** a 20-minute walk down Kerikeri Rd. toward the water, to view a trinity of Anglican missionary power: **St. James Church,** the graceful white **Kemp House** next door (which claims to be the oldest standing European building in the country), and **Stone Store** (constructed in 1832-36 to house supplies for the Church Missionary Society). Cross the footbridge over the **Kerikeri River** and you will find yourself several centuries back in time at **Rewa's Village** (tel. 407 6454). The replica structures of this pre-European Maori fishing village create a worthwhile glimpse into the age of chiefs Hongi Hika and Rewa. (Admission $2.50.) Other activities include swimming in the **Fairy Pools,** magical swimming holes by the Kerikeri River. The pools can be reached via an access road near the YHA. Alternatively, walk along the river away from the ocean or drive along Waipapa Rd. 2.5km east of SH10 to the **Rainbow Falls.**

THE FAR NORTH

KAITAIA

The mostly working-class population of 5,000 has a small, functional town with one central "strip" called Commerce St. The gas stations and warehouse buildings hide the majestic hills and dairy farms of the surrounding landscape. Kaitaia benefits from its proximity to the famous Ninety Mile Beach and other less trafficked sandy nooks that attract beach connoisseurs and surfers to Kaitaia in the summer.

◪ ORIENTATION AND PRACTICAL INFORMATION. For answers to all Cape queries, seek out the **Northland Information Centre** (tel./fax 408 0879; email katvin@nzhost.co.nz), in Jaycee Park on South Rd. (open M-F 8:30am-5pm, Sa-Su 9am-1pm). The **DOC Kaitaia Field Centre,** 127 North Rd. (tel. 408 2100; fax 408 2101), can answer questions about camping on Cape Reinga (open M-F 8am-4:30pm). **InterCity** buses head south daily to **Auckland** (7hr., 10:20am, $62) via **Whangarei** (4hr., $37) and **Paihia** (2hr., $27). Other services include: **banks** and **ATMs** on Commerce St.; **police** (tel. 408 0400) on Rodan Rd.; **Kaitaia Hospital** (tel. 408 0010) on Rodan Rd.; **doctor on call** (tel. 408 3060); **post office,** 101 Commerce St. (tel. 408 3100; open M-F 9am-5pm); and **Internet access,** available at fast connection speeds at **Hackers Internet Cafe,** 84 Commerce St. (tel. 408 4999). **Telephone Code:** 09.

◪◪◪ ACCOMMODATIONS, FOOD, AND NIGHTLIFE. Pak 'N Save (tel. 408 6222), on Commerce St., is a giant warehouse of grocery items (open M-W 8:30am-7pm, Sa-Tu 8:30am-6pm). **Main Street Backpackers,** 235 Commerce St. (tel. 408 1275) is a 10-minute hike from the center of town, but it may be worth your trouble. New Zealand's first Maori-run hostel brings members of the community to teach guests traditional bone carving ($10). Bikes, dune boards, and camping gear are available. (Dorms $13-16; singles $30; twins and doubles $34; tent sites $10.) Host Peter also runs **Tall Tale Travel 'N Tour** (tel. 408 0870), a learning experience about Maori protocol and culture that includes a visit to **Te Rarawa Marae** (2hr., by arrangement, $20). The **Hike and Bike Kaitaia YHA,** 160 Commerce St. (tel. 408 1840), offers neither hikes nor bikes, but does have clean, well-maintained facilities (dorms $15, winter $14; singles $25; twins $32; doubles $36; tent sites $10; non-YHA $4 more). In the center of town, the **Kaitaia Hotel,** 15-33 Commerce St. (tel./fax 408 0360), has a steak restaurant, the **Flame Grill,** and a traditional pub, plus standard hotel rooms at startlingly low prices (singles $38; doubles $52; triples $58). Upstairs, from September to June, **Scandals** nightclub has a DJ spinning eclectic dance music (open F-Sa 9pm-2am). For lighter fare, **Maisey's Main Street Cafe,** 14 Commerce St. (tel. 408 4934), does takeaway specials—fish, chips, fritters—and sinfully good blueberry muffins ($1.50).

◪◪ SIGHTS AND ACTIVITIES. The attractions around Kaitaia are best accessed with a car. Both Kaitaia and its ocean-facing neighbor **Ahipara** offer scenic walkways that serve as windows into the kauri industry of yesteryear, most notably the **Kaitaia Walkway** (45min.) which is expandable into a 9km track suitable for experienced trampers. The Ahipara **Gumfields** spread over most of the peninsula out to **Tauroa Point,** southwest of Kaitaia, and are littered with remnants of 19th-century gum digging (trenches, dams, and an old gum diggers' shack). A mountain bike track goes down to the ocean.

AROUND KAITAIA

For more extensive trails, head to the **Karikari Peninsula,** 20km northeast of Kaitaia between **Rangaunu Harbor** and **Doubtless Bay,** where the **Lake Ohia Gumholes** await. Leave the swimming togs at home—the lake was drained in the early 1900s. Fossilized remains of a kauri forest still poke out of swampland, while rare ferns and orchids flourish on the banks. The **Ancient Kauri Kingdom Ltd.** (tel. 406 7172), on SH1 in Awanui, makes an enterprise of digging up kauri logs that were felled in the swamp 30,000-50,000 years ago, and carving the perfectly preserved wood into high-quality crafts and furniture (open daily). Farther east, along the base of the Karikari peninsula, sits **Coopers Beach,** offering sunbathing and good surfcasting in Doubtless Bay. Farther up the peninsula is a popular DOC campground at **Maitai Bay.** Facilities include cold showers, running water, and toilets. (Tent sites $6, children $3. Reserve through DOC in Kaitaia.) Pushing farther east along SH10, one arrives at **Whangaroa Bay,** a narrow inlet with a snaking coastline. On the eastern shore is the town of **Whangaroa,** which is home to the **Sunseeker Lodge** (tel. 405 0496), on Old Hospital Rd. Call for free pickup from the bus station in Kaeo. A steep hill brings you to this charming accommodation and its brilliant views of the bay. Spacious and clean dorm rooms are $15 (weekly $70), and the private double is small but secluded ($40). With a two-night stay, kayaks and lessons are free. There are also well-appointed motel units for two ($90, winter $65).

AUPOURI PENINSULA AND CAPE REINGA

The Aupouri Peninsula extends up from the northern coast, a narrow finger of rolling land. The Maori believe spirits of the dead travel over this land to the top of New Zealand, to Cape Reinga, and dive into the ocean to return to the mythical homeland of Hawaiki.

🗺 ORIENTATION AND PRACTICAL INFORMATION. The path to the afterlife is gilded on the west by the golden sands of **Ninety Mile Beach,** more poetic a name than "ninety kilometer beach" or "fifty-six mile beach," both of which would be more accurate. Near the top of the beach, the sands are interrupted by the **Te Paki Stream,** which empties into the ocean. This is part of the **Te Paki Reserves,** administered by the **Te Paki DOC Field Centre** (tel. 409 7521), off SH1. With many walking tracks, the reserves offer a meditative serenity punctured in the summer by the screams of thrill-seekers coasting on their boards down the 100m-high sand dunes. Don't venture out to the very tip, which is sacred and protected Maori land. On the opposite side of the peninsula, the boarders boogie in the ocean waters of **Tapotupotu** and **Spirits Bay,** while landlubbers lie on graceful curves of sand. Slightly south along the side of the peninsula is **Great Exhibition Bay,** which, despite the name, entertains more boaters and fisherfolk than nude bathers. The bluff is capped with a lighthouse that perches over the churning waters where the Pacific and the Tasman meet. **Cape Maria van Diemen** to the west and the **North Cape** to the east have just as breathtaking, if less celebrated, scenery.

🏠 ACCOMMODATIONS AND FOOD. The DOC maintains two **campsites** in the area of the Te Paki Reserve. These campsites are beautiful, but only in the summer season—in the winter, conditions are too harsh for camping. One is **Tapotupotu Bay,** just south of the Cape region, which has sheltered golden sands accessible by a posted turnoff 3km before the end of the road to the Cape (camping $6, children $3). The other is at **Kapowairu** (200 sites) along the east coast of Spirits Bay ($5, children $2.50). Both are first-come, first-camped. DOC also maintains a third campsite, approximately in the middle of the Aupouri Peninsula at **Rarawa.** Sites can be found amid pine trees, a stone's throw from the white-sand beaches of Great Exhibition Bay. Follow the signs 1km north of Ngataki on SH1. (Sites $6, children $3; open Labour Day-Easter.) All three sites feature the DOC hallmarks of minimalism: cold showers, running water, and toilets.

Travelers with the blessing of an automobile should steer toward **Pukenui** (pop. 1000), a tiny and charming coastal town with New Zealand's northernmost backpacker accommodations. The **Pukenui Lodge (YHA)** (tel. 409 8837; fax 409 8704; email pukenui@igrin.co.nz), on the corner of SH1 and Wharf Rd., has a mind-blowing view of the water and a cozy backpacker cabin adjacent to their motel accommodation. Enjoy a swim in the pool or a turn in the spa. (Dorms $15.50; singles $35; twins and doubles $40.) A short walk down Lamb Rd., at the **Pukenui Holiday Camp** (tel./fax 409 8803), backpackers install next to trailers. Perks include a bountiful fruit garden in back and trips in an aerochute, a two-seater powered aircraft that hangs from a parachute. (Communal kitchen and bathrooms, and Internet. Great tent sites. Dorms $15; basic cabins for 2 $40; tourist cabins with kitchen for 2 $50; flats with bathroom and kitchen for 2 $55; extra person in cabins and flats $10; winter and extended stay discounts available.) One of Northland's best hostels is 🏠**Northwind Lodge Backpackers** (tel./fax 409 8515), on Otaipango Rd., 9km north of Pukenui in Henderson Bay. This beautiful and remote site offers a convivial cooking space and a cozy sleeping area, great facilities and an affable staff. With 10 beds and a great reputation, you'd better book ahead. (Dorms $15; singles $15; twins $36; doubles $30.)

The **Harbour View Restaurant** (tel. 409 8816), the only licensed restaurant in Pukenui, serves fresh seafood like pan-fried snapper ($18.50) and local vino. Inexpensive takeaways are available from their adjacent annex. (Open M-Su 9am-8pm, later in summer.)

🔲 ⚞ **SIGHTS AND ACTIVITIES.** Most people elect to take a **guided day tour** in a specially designed sand-and-surf-worthy craft out of Paihia or Kaitaia. It makes for a long day, but it's a safer option for navigating the changing sands of an extremely remote region. If you have your own car, don't try to be a hero and impress your friends. You will get stuck. In fact, guided trips pass the rusting automobiles of adventurous yet substantially less-skilled drivers. Rental car companies explicitly forbid such excursions. Choose your tour carefully—many trips are designed with young people in mind and may not be appropriate for less-adventurous travelers.

Though Paihia's tours can sometimes seem more plastic or commercial than those of Kaitaia, they tend to include a stop in the **kauri forest** at Puketi. Out of Paihia, one good bet is **Northern Exposure Tours** (tel. 402 8644 or 0800 573 875), whose "small bus with attitude" stops to hug the kauri in Puketi. Dig for *tua tuas* on Ninety Mile Beach, get sandblasted tobogganing on the dunes at Te Paki, get spiritual at Cape Reinga, and thrash around in the surf of Tapotupotu Bay. (11hr.; $69, lunch included.) The **4x4 Dune Rider** (tel. 402 8681), also of Paihia, runs a similar tour with lunch in a rugged, air-conditioned Mercedes Benz bus with airbrushed cartoons of passengers on the side. (Free pickup daily from Paihia at 7:30am and Kerikeri at 8:15am. $75, children $55; 10% backpackers and AA discount.) **Harrison's cape runner** (tel. 408 1033 or 0800 2273 734 642) offers a similar tour ($40, children $20; lunch included) and a new, rough and wild 4x4 half-day tour of the west coast's Ahipara Kauri Gumfields with sandune surfing (4hr. from Kaitia). For a livelier experience, join the party-hard crowd on board **Kiwi Experience** (tel. 366 9830), which offers a special Cape Reinga trip (departs Paihia 7:30am; $69). **Kings** (tel. 402 8288) offers an "express" trip that stops at the Ancient Kauri Kingdom (9½hr.; departs Paihia 8:15am; $60, children $40). Rounding out the Paihia trips, **Fullers** (tel. 402 7421) runs several comprehensive tours, focusing either on Maori culture or the natural surroundings (11hr., departs Paihia 7:30am; $79, children $40, lunch $10 extra). Fullers and other tours may stop at the **Wagener Museum** (tel. 409 8850), 40km north of Kaitia on SH1 in Houhora; check out the historic homestead ($3) or, better yet, the museum of natural and technological curiosities ($6). Stay a while at their **motorcamp** (tel. 409 8564) and play the 18-hole **golf course** ($15; rental $6).

HOKIANGA

Every summer, refugees from the full-blown commercialism of the Bay of Islands escape to the obscurity of the Hokianga region. In the constellation of tiny towns that sit on the Hokianga Harbor, adventure activities give way to bushwalking, fishing, ocean swimming, and sand dune surfing. Hokianga is hailed as the last spot the great Maori navigator Kupe landed before departing for Hawaiki. Longstanding Maori tradition holds that Kupe (as well as everyone else who pays a visit) will one day return to this area known for its treacherous access to the Tasman Sea.

⚑ PRACTICAL INFORMATION

Limited bus service to and between the Hokianga towns means that either a car or patience with buses is necessary to explore the area.

Visitors Center: Hokianga Visitor Information Centre (tel./fax 405 8869), by Omapere on **SH12**, 450m out of "town" in a shady glen. Watch campy 1950s newsreels about town icon Opo the Dolphin in the "museum" upstairs. Open daily 8:30am-5pm.

Buses: Because the buses are sporadic and relatively expensive, the **Northland Wanderer pass** ($80, available through Intercity) may be the best option. **Northliner** (Auckland tel. 307 5873, Northland tel. 438 3206) and **InterCity** (tel. 0800 401 500) contract out to **Westcoaster** in the region. Service is inconsistent at times, particularly in the winter, and runs on "Hokianga time," which means prior reservations are necessary even if you have a pass. From **Paihia,** buses run daily in the summer, and on Monday, Wednesday, Friday, and Sunday in the winter, departing at 9am for **Kaikohe** (30min., $9) and running through the **Hokianga region** (2hr., about $20), then the **Waipoua Forest** (3¼hr., $35) and eventually on to **Auckland** (8¼hr., $50). Buses from Auckland arrive in **Omapere** by 2:30pm.

Hitchhiking: Hitchers stand on the straightaways or approach drivers at markets and post offices; those heading north or south take the Rawene-Kohukohu ferry and find a ride from the cars on board.

Banks: There are **no banks, ATMs, or cash advances** in the Hokianga, so bring your Eftpos card or cash from Dargaville or the Bay of Islands.

Medical Services: Hokianga Health (tel. 405 7709), located on SH12 just outside of Rawene. Call before coming.

Telephone Code: 09.

KAIKOHE

Pause in this gateway town to relax in the **Ngawha Hot Springs** (tel. 401 0166). They're located 6km north of Kaikohe center, at the end of Ngawha Hot Springs Rd., in the sulfur-smelling **Ngawha Hot Springs Village.** Locals, arthritics, and the occasional travel-weary tourist soak in the separate wood-lined thermal pools, each with its own name, water temperature, and unique mineral content. **Bulldog** and **Kotahitanga,** the two hottest, are touted as cure-alls. **Solomon** reportedly treats bad skin, **Tanemahuta** is good for burns, **Doctor** supposedly cures arthritis, and **Waikato** and **Favorite** are for pure relaxation, and **Baby** changes color. The dark water is not treated at all, and the strong smell will not come out of your clothes even after repeated washings—you may want to hire towels ($1) and togs ($1). (Open daily 7am-9:45pm. Admission $2, children $1.)

RAWENE

Rawene's centrality made it vital to the Kauri shipping industry of yore. Today, ferries rather than ships predominate, carrying passengers and vehicles to **Kohukohu** on the opposite shore. **Ferries** depart every hour on the half-hour (15min.; 7:30am-7:30pm; passenger $1.50, motorcycle $3, car $13, campervans $13). The **Far North District Council** (tel. 405 7829) on upper Parnell Rd., can answer travel queries (open M-F 8am-4:30pm). **The Boat Shed Cafe** (tel. 405 7728) on the water, up a bit from the ferry landing, makes great espresso (open daily 9am-5:30pm). **The Wharf House** (tel. 405 7713), also by the waterfront, makes good burgers (open daily 7am-4:30pm). Just past the service station on the waterfront, are the much-celebrated **musical loos** of Hokianga. The fully automated, self-cleaning toilets play lovely piano music and feature mechanical toilet paper dispensers. Don't get too comfortable, though, as the doors fly open after 10 minutes (luckily there is a one-minute countdown). The **Four Square** at the Waterfront includes a **post center** (open M-F 7:30am-5:30pm, Sa-Su 8:30am-4pm).

KOHUKOHU

Most commonly known as the other end of the Hokianga ferry (departing for Rawene daily at 7:45am, 8:30am, 9am and then every hour on the hour until 8pm, same rates as above), among budget travelers, Kohukohu is distinguished by one of its accommodations. ■**The Tree House** (tel. 405 5855; fax 405 5857) is a sprawling wooden-planked network of decks and rooms situated by a duck pond in a 17-acre forest. Activities include a walking track, mountain biking ($2.50 per hr., half-day

$10, full day $16), and lounging in the TV-free common space. It's hard to predict when you will leave. A small shop at the front desk sells food basics and phone cards. Call from Rawene for free pickup from the ferry landing, or from town if you arrive from points north. Reservations are essential for everything (even tent sites) in the summer; in winter, call ahead for twins and doubles. (Dorms $17; singles $28; twins and doubles $40; tent sites $10.)

To explore farther upstream, you'll need the aid of **The Alma** (tel. 405 7704 or mobile 025 997 450), a 1902 flat-bottomed kauri ship, that swapped its twin masts for twin diesel motors and now runs tours up the harbor in the summer from Rawene, as well as a fishing trip from Opononi (call for departure times). Meals are available for $5 to $15 if you book the day before, including fresh crayfish ($25, children $12.50).

OPONONI

In the 1950s, a friendly dolphin in the nearby waters, nicknamed Opo the Dolphin, captured the affection of the town and the attention of the region. In the four decades since Opo the Dolphin put it on the map, **Opononi** has progressed about four years. It is still a small, fun-in-the-sun resort town with sand, sea, and simple food. **Kupe's monument,** an anchor stone and commemorative plaque, sits at the top of a hill on the harbor side of SH12 between Opononi and Rawene. The grave of **Opo the Dolphin,** who turned belly-up one day, is located in front of the South Hokianga War Memorial. While Kupe may someday return to Hokianga to fulfill the region's myth, Opo isn't going anywhere soon.

Opononi is a scant 3km up from Omapere on **SH12** and 23km from Rawene. Its wharf ties it to the harbor. If you're planning on spending the night, head to the epitome of Hokianga serenity (no TV, no guest phone, no clocks) at the **House of Harmony** (tel./fax 405 8778). A deck overlooking the harbor makes for fine breakfasts and mellow lounging. Each room has a different and curious stylistic theme. There is free pickup from the bus station. First-come, first-harmonized. ($15 bunk and twin; $16 honeymoon double; tent sites $10 per person). For food, stop in at the **Opo Takeaway** (tel. 405 8065) and try dolphin-safe Opo Burger ($4.50), served with chicken breast, cheese, and pineapple. Bread is baked fresh every day. (Open daily 10am-7pm). **The Opononi Resort Hotel** has a genuine local pub with a spacious room featuring three pool tables and an elevated platform for live music (open M-F 11am-11pm, Sa 11am-1am). The **Four Square** (tel. 405 8838; open M-Sa 7:30am-6pm, Su 8am-5:30pm) has a **post shop** inside (open M-F 9am-5pm).

OMAPERE

Keeping watch over the dangerous waters of the mouth of the Hokianga Harbor, Omapere is a breathtaking spot to stop before heading south to Waipoua or eastward to Kaikohe and the Bay of Islands. The dunes across the harbor lure sand surfers keen on sliding down the duneface and into the saltwater. **Hokianga Express** (tel. 405 8872) offers water taxi service across the harbor to the dunes. They loan you boards and pick them up at the end of the day ($15). **CTSH** (tel. 405 8181) offers a scenic tour from the Omapere Tourist Hotel to the Hokianga and Waipoua Forest ($20; call for times). If you choose to stay in Omapere, **Globetrekkers (VIP)** (tel./fax 405 8183), off SH12, makes a good home. The backpackers cottage has a water view, comfortable beds, and a deck with picnic tables and rose bushes. (Dorms $15; singles $20; doubles $35. Free linen, blankets, and pickup from bus at visitors center. Check-out 10:30am.) For a bite to eat, the **The Omopere Restaurant and Takeaway** (tel. 405 8607), on SH12, has simple fare and a super view. It serves fresh bread, a cereal breakfast ($2.50), and toasted $4.50 sandwiches (Open M-F 8am-5:30pm, Sa-Su 9am-4pm). Next door is the **Four Square** (tel. 405 8892; open daily 7:30am-6pm) which has a **post shop** inside (open M-F 9am-5pm).

WAIPOUA FOREST PARK

Waipoua (north of Dargaville on Northland's western coast) is New Zealand's least-logged and best example of primary kauri forest. Remoteness and inaccessibility protected the virgin kauri forests of the Waipoua region from 19th-century axe blades. The 1940s demand for shipbuilding timber stirred up controversy that resulted in Waipoua's being declared a sanctuary by 1952.

Along with the kauri giants, Waipoua is home to the **Waipoua Forest Visitor Centre** (tel. 439 0605; fax 439 5227; open M-F 8:30am-6pm, Sa-Su 9am-4:30pm, winter daily 9am-4:30pm), several walking tracks, and a **campground.** The campground curls up on the banks of the Waipoua River, with tentsites and powered caravan sites ($7 per person, children $3.50). Self-register at the communal kitchen/shower/toilet building, and do your laundry in the tub with your own soap. For the less rugged person, little green two-bunk cabins named for different tree species come with crockery and cutlery ($14 per person, children $7; single bed cabin rooms $8). For groups of people, there are four-bunk cabins that offer sinks and electric stoves ($10 per person, children $5). Obtain cabin keys from the visitors center or, after hours, check in with the caretaker who lives in a little cabin of her own. Open flames of any kind are strictly forbidden. As the kiwi-crossing signs on SH12 attest, this is kiwi country—pets are not welcome.

Almost everyone who comes to the forest is there to see "the big tree" in the northern Waipoua. A brief trek from the carpark off SH12 leads through dense and dripping bush to the 1200-year-old, 52m high, 14m wide **Tane Mahuta.** Nicknamed "Lord of the Forest," it is the world's largest living kauri and New Zealand's biggest tree. The boardwalk keeps admirers at a respectful distance and protects the Lord's delicate, shallow root system. Back at the car park, a caravan sells surprisingly tasty coffee, tea, and sandwiches (open daily 8am-6pm, winter daily 10am-3pm). InterCity buses will stop here long enough for you to snap some photos.

Waipoua's other "big trees" are accessible by walking tracks from the labeled carpark a few kilometers south of Tane Mahuta on SH12 toward the visitor center. A 20-minute walk leads to 30m **Te Matua Ngahere,** "Father of the Forest," the second largest living kauri; a ten-minute walk takes you to close-knit **Four Sisters,** four trees side-by-side; a 30-minute walk goes to the **Yakas Kauri.** Although the Maori began the tradition of naming individual trees, not all bear Maori monikers: witness **Darby** and **Joan,** flanking either side of the bridge on SH12 north of the visitors center. For those with time to explore, the three-hour **Yakas Track** connects the campground and visitors center to Yakas Kauri Carpark, winding through all sorts of trees and fording the Waipoua River. The six-hour **Waiotemarama Walk** begins off Waiotemarama Gorge Rd. near Omapere, reaching a spectacular waterfall within 15 minutes and ending at the base of Mountain Rd. **Okopako Lodge/The Wilderness Farm** which has a panoramic harbor view and farm animals, is at the end of the walk. Halfway through at its steepest point, the walk connects with the **Waima Main Range Route.** This is a serious three-to four-day walk that passes over the highest point in Northland (and often through low-lying clouds); trampers should possess good wilderness skills and be well equipped for foul weather. A less taxing walk along mostly flat beach is the two-to three-day **Waipoua Coastal Walkway,** which links Hokianga Harbour with the **Kai Iwi Lakes.**

NEAR WAIPOUA FOREST PARK: TROUNSON KAURI PARK

Another pocket of kauri stands 17km south of the Waipoua Forest (40km north of Dargaville) at the 450-hectare DOC **Trounson Kauri Park.** Between October and April, a **campground** opens ($7 per person, children $3.50). The **Kauri Coast Holiday Park** (tel./fax 439 0621), on Trounson Park Rd. in Kaihu, has accommodations by a river that include basic cabins ($30 for 2, extra person $14) and tourist cabins with cooking facilities ($45 for 2, extra person $14). They also have tent and powered sites right by the water ($10). It also runs guided night walks through Trounson past glow-worms and calling kiwis (1.5hr., $15, children $9) and scenic horse rides ($22 per hr., $32 for 2hr).

DARGAVILLE

This riverside town is well-suited for stocking up on provisions—gas, food, alkaline batteries. While a handful of amusements, from jet boating to horse trekking, begs travelers to stay awhile, the absence of a seaside location will bump Dargaville down on many tourists' priority lists.

⚡ ORIENTATION AND PRACTICAL INFORMATION

Dargaville borders the **Wairoa River,** 187km north of Auckland on the west coast. **Normanby St.** is the main road by which **SH12** traffic passes through town. One street over toward the river is **Victoria St.,** home to most of the shops.

Visitors Center: Kauri Coast Information Center: (tel./fax 439 8360 or 0800 528 744; www.kauricoast.com), Normanby St. Open M-F 8:30am-5pm, Sa-Su 9am-4pm.

Buses: InterCity (tel. 0800 401 500) contracts out to **Westcoaster,** which runs to **Auckland** (3½hr., M, Th, F, 8:30am, $39) and north to **Paihia** (4¼hr., one per day, winter 3 per week, $32) via the **Waipoua Forest Park** (1¼hr., $15). They also service the **Hokianga** towns of Omapere, Opononi, and Rawene (2½-3hr., $17-25), and Kaikohe (3¾hr., $29).

Hitchhiking: Traffic along the Waipoua Forest Rd. in either direction is fairly regular. Conventional wisdom says to wait at the edge of town.

Currency Exchange: All of the major New Zealand banks can be found on Victoria St., most with **ATMs.** Get plenty of money here, as there are no banks further north in the Hokianga.

Public Toilets: In the park adjacent to the library.

Medical Services: Dargaville Medical Centre (tel. 439 8079), on Hokianga Rd. Open M-F 8am-5pm, Sa 9am-noon. After hours, the phone message will refer you to the doctor on call. **Kaipara Unichem Pharmacy,** 18 Hokianga Rd. Open M-F 8am-6pm, Sa 9am-1pm, Su 9:30am-12:30pm.

Police: (tel. 439 8399) Portland St., across from the YHA.

Post Office: Terartz Stationary Shop, (tel. 439 6051), Victoria St. Open M-F 8am-5pm.

Internet Access: Kauri Computer Company (tel. 439 4315), located in the mall off Victoria St. $10 for up to 1½hr. Open M-F 9am-5:30pm, Sa 9:30am-1pm. Also available at the **Kauri Coast Information Center** for a steep $12 per hr.

Telephone Code: 09.

▚ ACCOMMODATIONS

Just about everyone comes to see the areas that lie *beyond* Dargaville, so there's usually no dire need to book ahead. One exception is the peak of summer (Dec.-Jan.), when the campgrounds teem with those destined for kauri contemplation.

Northern Wairoa Hotel (tel. 439 8923; fax 439 8925), on the corner of Hokianga Rd. and Victoria St. This bargain hotel offers shocking value—an appealing choice for those tired of the backpacking scene. Behind the unappealing facade lie clean, well-kept single rooms. The rollicking pub downstairs features bands and karaoke on Thursday and Friday. Recent restorations accentuate the solid kauri glory of the woodwork and turn-of-the-century velvet luxury. Singles with plush linen and wash basin $15. Singles with private bath $30; doubles with private bath $60; triples with private bath $90.

The Greenhouse (YHA/VIP), 13 Portland St. (tel. 439 6342). Visitors to this spacious backpackers may shy away from the bunk accommodations—two large sleeping hangars, one for each gender, with beds separated by shoulder-high dividers. Communal bathroom facilities may also inspire visions of boarding school asceticism. Free bikes, fishing tackle, and organized fishing trips by arrangement. Polish your own kauri gum pendant ($5-12), play pool, or chill by the TV in the lounge. Dorms $15, weekly $70, 3rd night half-price; singles $25, winter $20; doubles and twins $36; tent sites $8. Laundry $5. Reception 8:15am-9:30pm. Check-out 10am.

Baylys Beach Motor Camp, 22 Seaview Rd. (tel./fax 439 6349). Adorable cabins on a grassy green, edged with pohutukawa trees. Teems with families when the weather warms. Communal kitchen has dishes and pots (7am-10pm). Tent sites and powered sites $9, children $4; basic double cabins $30, extra person $10, children $8; double cabins with bath $45, extra person $12, children $8.

Kai Iwi Lakes Camp (tel. 439 8360), on Kai Iwi Lakes Rd. Divided into two parts, the larger **Pine Beach Camping Ground,** on Lake Taharoa, accommodates up to 500 campers. Rudimentary blocks of showers, toilets, and basins, and coin-op barbecue (50¢ for 6min. of gas). **Promenade Point** is even more basic, with only toilets and basins. Water taps, but no power for caravans. Book through the Information Centre. $8 per person, children $4. Advance reservations essential in summer.

◐ ▣ FOOD AND NIGHTLIFE

Dargaville has a number of smart, new eateries. The aroma of fresh-baked bread wafts from **Woolworths** (tel. 439 3036), the large grocery store on Victoria St. at Gladstone St. Fresh locally grown kumara is the highlight of the wide produce selection (Open Sa-Tu 8am-7pm, W-F 8am-8pm).

Blah Blah Blah Cafe & Bar, 101 Victoria St. (tel. 439 6300). For lunch, fresh baked focaccia ($7.50) and $8.50 meals are the fare. The eclectic cafe dinner menu changes every 6 weeks, though the prices are stable (entrees $6.50, mains $12-18). Kitchen closes by 9-10pm; bar snacks available until close. 10% discount for YHA/VIP members. Open daily 8am-midnight, winter M 8am-5pm, Tu-Th 8am-midnight, F-Sa 8am-1am, Su 4pm-midnight.

UNC Restaurant & Bar, 17 Hokianga Rd. (tel. 439 5777). The premier restaurant in town serves lunch and dinner in a trendy, glass-fronted space. Stuffed potatoes ($5) for lunch can't be beat. Dinner mains range from the mega burger ($9.80) to leg of venison ($22.50), with inventive entrees such as potato pumpkin gnocci ($7.50). The pleasant chef will ably accommodate non-menu requests. Friday and Saturday nights, a dance floor opens up around 9:30pm when the kitchen closes. Open daily 11am-1am.

Belushi's, 102 Victoria St. (tel. 439 8866). Sunny orange-painted bricks liven this daytime cafe serving lighter fare and all things espresso, including smooth shakes ($4). Try toasted sandwiches on bread ($3) or more creative combos on bagels ($3-5). Breakfast available all day. In summer, Monday nights after hours attracts chess players of all abilities (6-9pm). Open M-F 8am-5pm, Sa-Su 9am-3pm.

◉ ▚ SIGHTS AND ACTIVITIES

LAKES AND BEACHES

The **Kai Iwi Lakes** are rimmed with pure white silica sand and are a summertime mecca for water enthusiasts of all sorts. **Lake Taharoa** is the largest of the three and the best bet for swimming. Waterskiing is the sport of choice on **Lake Waikere.** The smallest and most serene is **Lake Kai Iwi** itself, trafficked solely by sails and dinghies and offering excellent fishing. **Buses** make it to the turn-off on Omamari Rd., 24km north of Dargaville on SH12, but you'll need to be resourceful to cover the remaining 11km to the first of the lakes. Closer waters lap the expanse of **Baylys Beach** (also known as Dargaville Ocean Beach or Ripiro Beach), which, at 100km, is New Zealand's longest beach. Astonishing in breadth as well as length, its vanishing point is often obscured by mist, as are the tops of the nearby cliffs. Perhaps more remarkably, the beach is officially a public highway. Road rules apply; it's best to have a 4WD vehicle and a knowledge of conditions.

TREKS AND TOURS

With hopes of jump-starting Kauri Coast tourism, Dargaville has recently welcomed some hot new activities. To explore the beach in full, consider **Taylor Made Tours** (tel. 439 1576 or (025) 361 543), which go to shipwreck relics, visit the 1884 **Kaipara Lighthouse,** and arrange sand tobogganing ($45 per person, lunch included). Although surfing is quite popular here, an equally thrilling ride through the surf is available with **Baylys Beach Horse Treks** (tel. 439 4531); they pick you up and drop you off at the Greenhouse YHA hostel (2½hr., usually 3 per day, $33, Greenhouse guests 10% discount). **Pauto 4x4 Quad Tours** (tel. 439 8360) promises scenic excursions on Ripiro Beach in a brauny 4x4 passenger bus ($25). Trips leave from Pauto Point, accessible only by car. **Kaipara Kapars'** 14-seat jet boat flies up and down the river (every hour on the hour Sa-Su 9am-4pm, $30). **Te Aroha** (tel. 439 8360), a 90-year-old schooner, cruises away from the Dargaville Wharf at 10am and 2pm ($10 per person, children $2).

For an excellent trek, the volcano TokaToka offers panoramic views of the region from its summit, 17km south of Dargaville. A track begins behind the Tokatoka Tavern, a 15-minute drive south along SH12. The 30-minute ascent is steep.

MUSEUMS

The Kauri Museum (tel. 431 7417), on SH12 45km south of Dargaville in Matakohe, has many exhibits about the mighty tree. A shuttle runs between the museum and Dargaville daily, leaving town at 9am and 2pm and returning at 1pm and 4:05pm (return $15). No afternoon shuttle runs on Sunday. (Open daily Nov.-Easter 9am-5:30pm, Easter-Oct. 9am-5pm. Admission $7, children $2.50.) The **Dargaville Maritime Museum** (tel. 439 7555) is just outside of town. Take Victoria St. south to River Rd., and from there to Mt. Wellesley Rd. Follow the signs up to the museum's perch, atop Mt. Wellesley in Harding Park. The museum rounds out the picture of the Kauri industry with a history of the ships that transported both logs and loggers. The museum has an extensive collection of local shipwreck artifacts, culled from the 115 reported shipwrecks along the Kaipara coastline. Outside, draped with strands of flashing lights, stand the masts of the famed **Rainbow Warrior** (see p. 100). (Open daily 9am-4pm. Admission $4.)

THE WAIKATO AND THE COROMANDEL PENINSULA

The Waikato and the Coromandel Peninsula appeal to outsiders not with exotic and unbelievable natural wonders, but with the invocation of a life that much of the developed world has left behind. Neither region offers high profile, photogenic attractions like volcanoes or glaciers; their charms are more subtle. With a rural bent and a pragmatic attitude, the Waikato is one of the primary agricultural centers of New Zealand. Visitors with an appreciation of the farming life or those lucky enough to stumble upon the annual extravaganza of National Fieldays will witness the pride residents take in the region's productive capabilities. Inhabitants of the Coromandel are similarly disinclined toward the rushed frenzy of modern life. Less agrarian and more inclined towards the arts and surf, peninsula dwellers welcome the visitor who feels, as they do, the draw of the sky-blue sea, endless beaches and coves, and kauri forest.

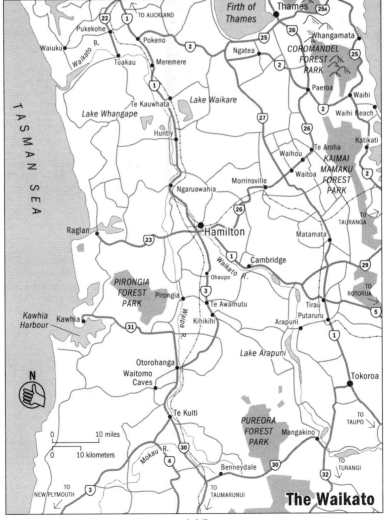

The Waikato

115

■ A scenic drive along the coast of the **Coromandel Peninsula** (p. 131) unveils magnificent coastal vistas and striking natural beauty.
■ Rafting in the **Waitomo Caves** (p. 129) allows curious spelunkers to explore New Zealand's mysterious underworld.
■ **Raglan** (p. 123) promises both an outpost of relaxation by the sea and world-class surfing. This town defines "cruisy" (p. 390).
■ At **Hot Water Beach** (p. 143), those in search of relaxation can dig their own jacuzzi in the sand for the ultimate soothing experience.

THE WAIKATO AND KING COUNTRY

Tranquility settles over the lush and undulating pastureland and lazy streams of the Waikato and King Country today, but life in these parts did not always come so easily. In the 1840s and 50s, the Maori tribes of the Waikato banded together to resist the threat of encroaching European settlement, finally proclaiming Potatau Te Wherowhero the first Maori King in 1859. The king's signature white top hat was passed on to his son, King Tawhiao, who used it during the Waikato War (1863-64) to make a legendary gesture of defiance, casting his "crown" onto a map of the North Island and proclaiming grandly, "There, I rule!" As a result, his people called the region *Rohe Potae*, "the brim of the hat." To the settlers, however, it was simply "King Country," in grudging deference to the Maori dominance that lasted until the 1880s.

Modern times brought a different kind of power to the region. With 12 power stations along its length, the Waikato River churns out 50% of the North Island's electricity. The longest river in New Zealand, it is also the defining geographical feature of the region as it winds through small agricultural communities providing recreation for visitors and locals alike. As it makes its way toward the coast, the river passes through population centers varying from the arboreal charm of Cambridge to the urban bustle of Hamilton, before reaching the end of its journey in Raglan Harbor where it mixes with the salty surf.

HAMILTON

With Waikato University nearby, Hamilton has a reputation as a young person's town, and the extraordinary number of bars are testament to Hamilton's youthful exuberance. More than just a party town, though, Hamilton is a substantial city with tall buildings, movie theaters, and even a handful of Internet connections. It is the largest inland city in New Zealand and the fifth-largest overall. Other than the scenic Waikato River, Hamilton has few astounding geographical features and instead offers a central location. Half of the North Island and its terrestrial wonders are a few hours' drive away, making Hamilton an ideal hub.

⚡ ORIENTATION AND PRACTICAL INFORMATION

Hamilton lies off **SH1** and is bisected by the **Waikato River.** Most commercial activity and nightlife is on the west bank. **Victoria St.** is the main drag, with the stretch between **Ward St.** and **Hood St.** prime for daytime shopping and nighttime carousing. **East Hamilton** is more residential, housing **Waikato University** and many cafes.

> **Visitors Center: Hamilton Visitor's Information Centre** (tel. 839 3580; fax 839 3127; email hlzvin@nzhost.co.nz), in the Transport Centre at the corner of Ward and Anglesea St. Open M-F 9am-5pm, Sa-Su 10am-4pm; winter Sa-Su only until 2pm.

NORTH ISLAND

Trains: TranzScenic heads daily to: **Auckland** (2hr., 4 per day, $36, night $32); **Tauranga** (1½hr., 8:06pm, $29); **Rotorua** (2hr., 10:09am, $40); and **Wellington** (8½hr., 2 per day, $108, night $98) via **Palmerston North** (6½hr., $83, night $74).

Buses: Little Kiwi Bus Co. (tel. 0800 759 999) runs to: **Auckland** (4 per day, $15); the **Auckland airport** (4 per day, $25); and **Rotorua** (2 per day, $16). **InterCity** heads daily to: **Auckland** (2hr., 6 per day, $18); **Gisborne** (7hr., 1 per day, $73); **Wellington** (8½hr., 4 per day, $75); and **Rotorua** (2½hr., 4 per day, $24). **Pavlovich buses** (tel. 856 4579) depart from the Transport Centre for **Raglan** (1hr., M-F 4 per day, $4.70). **Creswell Motors Ltd.** departs from Collingwood St. for **Cambridge** (30min.; M-Th 3 per day, F 5 per day; $5).

Taxis: Red Cabs (tel. 839 0500) and **Hamilton Taxis** (tel. 847 7477) are abundant, especially at the corner of Victoria and Collingwood St.

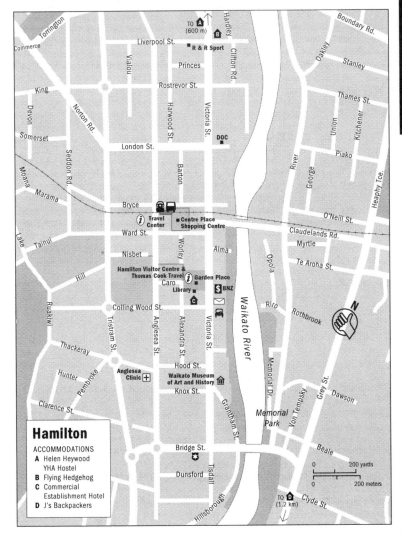

Hamilton

ACCOMMODATIONS
A Helen Heywood
   YHA Hostel
B Flying Hedgehog
C Commercial
   Establishment Hotel
D J's Backpackers

Car Rental: Rent-a-Dent, 383 Anglesea St. (tel. 0800 736 822), rents economy cars with unlimited km for $49 per day. **Waikato Car Rentals** (tel. 856 9908 or mobile 025 990 350), on Brooklyn Rd., rents cars from $25 per day (1 week minimum) and vans from $69 per day. Open M-F 7:30am-5:30pm, Sa 8am-1pm, Su 8:30am-1pm.

Bike Rental: R&R Sports, 943 Victoria St. (tel. 839 3755), at Liverpool St. Rents mountain bikes, canoes, and kayaks (about $25 per day). Also skis, boots, and poles ($20 per day) or snowboard and boots ($40 per day). Open M-Th 9am-5:30pm, F 9am-8pm, Sa 9am-2pm, Su 11am-2pm.

Hitchhiking: Hitching to Raglan is reportedly easiest along SH23. North to Auckland, many try from SH1 past the junction of Te Rapa St. and Avalon Dr., though they say it's best to take a city bus from the outskirts of town and hitch from there.

Currency Exchange: BNZ, across Victoria St. from Garden Pl. **Thomas Cook,** Garden Pl.

Police: (tel. 838 0989), on Bridge St.

Medical Services: Anglesea Clinic (tel. 858 0800), at the corner of Thackeray and Anglesea St. Open 24hr. **Hamilton Pharmacy** (tel. 834 3444). Open daily 8am-10pm. **Waikato Hospital** (tel. 839 8899), on Pembroke St.

Internet Access: The **library** (tel. 838 6826) has Internet for $6 for the first 30min., $4 each additional 30min. Open M-F 9am-8:30pm, Sa 9am-4pm.

Post Office: 346 Victoria St. (tel. 838 2233). Open M-F 9am-5pm.

Telephone Code: 07.

⚑ ACCOMMODATIONS

Accommodations in Hamilton are spread out, so call ahead and arrange a ride. During National Fieldays, prior bookings are absolutely essential. Motels are everywhere, but you can find a nice backpackers with a little persistence.

The Flying Hedgehog, 8 Liverpool St. (tel./fax 839 3906). From the Visitor Centre, turn left onto Victoria St., then turn right on Liverpool St. This house on the edge of Hamilton's main drag has clean and comfortable spaces. The dorm rooms are quite big (sleep more than 10) and the kitchen quite small. Pleasant owners offer helpful advice. Laundry $4. Bike rentals $5. Credit card service charge $1. Reception 8:30am-9:30pm. Dorms $17; twins and doubles $38.

J's Backpackers, 8 Grey St. (tel./fax 856 8934), in residential East Hamilton, with free pickup. J's caters to mellow folks who don't demand close proximity to downtown Hamilton. A petite house with a sunken kitchen/lounge, grassy yard, and impeccable bathrooms. Internet. Linen $2. Laundry $5. Kayaks $35. Ride to town $2. Bikes are free with two-night stay, otherwise $5. Dorms $15; twins $35.

Helen Heywood YHA Hostel, 1190 Victoria St. (tel. 838 0009; fax 838 0837). Head north up Victoria St.; this white and blue cinderblock house will be on your right. Quiet, reserved, and on the outskirts of Hamilton's strip, this 24-bed YHA has a riverside location and a new deck to appreciate it. A simple, utilitarian place to hit the sack. TV lounge. Lockers $2. Laundry $2. Reception 8am-10am and 4pm-8pm. Dorms (sometimes mixed) $15; singles $26; twins and doubles $36. Non-YHA $4 more.

Commercial Establishment Accommodation, 287 Victoria St. (tel. 839 4993; fax 834 2389; email coassess@wave.com.nz). Stay down in the thick of things in a little slice of late 1800s Hamilton. This vintage hotel has private rooms along a long, dim corridor. Pub and restaurant downstairs. Lounge with TV. Laundry $4. Key deposit $10. Reception 7am-11pm. Check-out 10am. Singles $44; twins $78; doubles $55.

◖ FOOD

Multicultural restaurants tempt along Victoria St., mostly between Garden Place and Hood St., and the grass of Garden Place is a great place to eat your takeaway.

East Hamilton also has eats within striking distance of J's Backpackers. **Food Town** (tel. 838 2739), on the corner of Bryce and Tristram St., is the most central market.

Planet Burger, 206 Victoria St. (tel. 839 1444). If McDonald's and the Star Wars cantina joined forces, the result would be this black-lit, sculpted-rock-walled joint serving up burgers that are out of this world. Portions are huge: a basic Comet Burger ($5) and order of fries ($3) can easily feed 2 people, a deal on any planet. Open M-F noon-2pm and 5-10:30pm, F-Sa noon-midnight, Su noon-10:30pm.

Iguana, 203 Victoria St. (tel. 834 2280). One of Hamilton's hippest, happening places. The sprawling floor of tables and the elegantly appointed bar get packed once the sun goes down. Pricey meals aren't so costly if you share the heaping portion with a pal. Sandwiches ($10-14) or salads ($10-16) might arrive with ostrich meat. Open M-F 11am-late, Sa-Su 9:30am-late.

Gourmet Sushi (tel. 838 3500), Marketplace on Hood St. This no-frills sushi shop is well lit and clean. Vegetarian rolls under $1, inventive tofu-wrapped rice pieces $1.50, and fresh salmon Nigiri $1.40. Open M-Sa 10:30am-5:30pm.

Bayon Cambodian Cafe, 783 Victoria St. (tel. 839 0947). Blinking Christmas lights lead you to this simple space with soothing Cambodian music in the background. Picture book menu is helpful in deciding. Spicy mains $7-12. Takeaways available. Open daily 11:30am-2:30pm and 5-9:30pm.

Metropolis Caffe, 211 Victoria St. (tel. 834 2081). Recently voted the best cafe in New Zealand, Metropolis has an art-gallery aesthetic of corrugated steel and high ceilings. A main seating area is supplemented by an upstairs lounge area. Black-clad staff serves mainly wines and coffees, but also items from creative menu such as a plate of hummus, pita, olives, and lemon ($7.25). Open Su-M 10am-6pm, Tu-Sa noon-late.

Rocket Espresso Lounge (tel. 839 6422), on the corner of Victoria and Hood St. Outdoor seating and eclectic bohemian clientele make this an ideal spot to refuel. Potent espresso ($2.50) guaranteed to overcome inertia. Heavenly muffins ($2.50) go fast; panini sandwiches ($4.50) and bleu cheese pizza ($4) complete your mission.

Sahara Tent Cafe and Bar, 254 Victoria St. (tel. 834 0409). Experience an Arabian night of Turkish and Middle Eastern cuisine in a wooden interior that radiates with candles and Middle Eastern melodies. Entrees ($7) and mains ($16-20) include all of the standards prepared with a flourish. Open M-Su 11:30am-2:30pm and 5:30-10:30pm.

ENTERTAINMENT AND NIGHTLIFE

Hamilton boasts numerous theaters, many affiliated with Waikato University. The most dynamic and impressive is the **Meteor,** 1 Victoria St. (tel. 834 2472). Once a roller skating rink, then an indoor wholesale car showroom, it is now a versatile space for performances, raves, and other community events. The **National Street Theater Festival** occurs in December (call 856 4421 or email coprso@ihug.co.nz for exact dates).

With live music bars, university bars, Irish pubs, and two movie theaters to choose from, there's plenty to do at night in Hamilton...on the weekend. When in doubt, tap into the scene with *City Happenings*, published by the City Council and available at the Visitor Centre.

JBC Bar and Cafe, 270 Victoria St. (tel. 839 8522), in the basement. The idea behind this casual, dimly lit jazz blues concept is to provide live entertainment six nights a week and vegan-friendly food. Performers vary from folk to hard-core to you at the open mic. Internet. Monthly art exhibitions. Cover $1-10; discounts available for students, VIP, and seniors. Open M-F 5pm-3am, Sa 8pm-3am, Su sometimes.

Biddy Mulligan's Irish Pub, 742 Victoria St. (tel. 839 0306). Biddy must have done right by St. Patrick somewhere along the way—back in '93, this became the first pub in New Zealand to have Murphy's Irish Stout on tap (pints $5). Guinness on tap, too. DJ on Thursday nights plays hits from the 60 to the 80s. F-Sa nights, an Irish band livens up the scene. Open Tu and Su 11am-11pm, W 11am-midnight, Th-Sa 11am-2am.

Caz Bar (tel. 838 0990), in the Marketplace on Hood St. Located in party central next to the Outback Inn, this slick, airy restaurant and bar gets the young revelers on the weekends and a more mature audience during the week. Live music at 11pm 5 nights a week. Open Tu-Sa 10am-3am, Su-M 10am-midnight.

Liquid Lounge, 21-23 Hood St. (tel. 834 2181). A chill bar with slick, modern decor. The gin and tonic ($5) is one smooth liquid. Antipasto platters ($13-$15) provide substance and house music provides structure. Open Tu-Th from 5pm, F-Sa from 4pm.

The Outback Inn, 141 Victoria St. (tel. 839 6354). Hamilton's largest bar (1000 person capacity) attracts a young crowd that grooves to MTV-style video music in a giant boozing barn. If you dare, order one of their 99 great shooters ($5) with outrageous names like "Ducks Fart," "Passed Out Naked On The Bathroom Floor," and "Monica's Dress." Vegetarians beware: on weekends this place is a meat market. Open Su-M noon-11pm, Tu noon-2:30am, W-Sa noon-3am.

🔘 🔼 SIGHTS AND ACTIVITIES

Not surprisingly, much of the leisure activity in Hamilton is centered around the river. Paths on each side are ideal for joggers and cyclists, while canoes and kayaks are perfect paddling options. Ramps from Victoria St. allow wheelchair access to lovely vantage points of the river. The fully enclosed paddle-wheeler replica **M.V. Waipa Delta** (tel. 854 9415 or 0800 472 3353), with its landing on the eastern bank of the river, just north of Victoria Bridge, offers three trips per day, plus lunch (12:30-2pm, $30), afternoon tea (3-4pm, $20), and dinner with live entertainment (7-10pm, $40; book ahead on weekends). The awe-inspiring hot-air balloon festival, **Balloons Over Waikato,** takes place April 12-16. For info on this and other events in the area call **Events Hamilton** (tel. 838 2736). At the **Waikato Museum of Art and History** (tel. 838 6606), at the corner of Victoria and Grantham St., you can admire towering Maori carved wooden totems, an epic Kauri wood canoe, and rotating exhibits (open daily 10am-4:30pm; admission by donation). More eccentric is the wall of bees behind plexiglass at the **Exscite** (EXplorations in SCIence and TEchnology) **Centre.** The center is full of hands-on displays such as the inertia chair, three-dimensional tic-tac-toe, and a chaotic pendulum. The museum cafe is open for lunch during museum hours, and also for dinner (Tu-Sa 6:30-9pm), with live jazz every Thursday night and periodic wine tastings. (Open daily 10am-4:30pm. Admission $5, students, seniors, and children $3.) Other activities in Hamilton include a trip to the **Hamilton Zoo** (tel. 8383 6720), on Brymer Rd., which has an environmental conservation theme and the largest aviary in New Zealand (open daily 9am-5pm; admission $7, children $3, seniors $5). A walk through the **Hamilton Gardens** (tel. 856 3200) can be a highlight. For a creative outlet, consider a night of art at the **Russel Studio Gallery,** 225 Victoria St. (tel. mobile 025 289 5986). Call ahead, then drop by and create ($10 plus materials). **Vilagrad Winery** (tel. 825 2893) offers tours by appointment. Venturing slightly out of Hamilton to Kihikihi, you'll encounter **Wharepapa South,** some great rock formations for climbing. Rob from J's Backpackers (see **Accommodations,** p. 118) can organized climbing gear.

FIBERGLASS COWS
As anyone who has ever tried to book a room in the greater Hamilton-Cambridge area during the middle of June will attest, the National Fieldays are a huge deal. For four days (June 14-17, 2000), 120,000 people descend on the tiny burg of Mystery Creek (situated between Hamilton and Cambridge) for the Southern Hemisphere's largest A&P (agricultural and pastoral) show. With chainsaw-carving demonstrations, head-to-head tractor pulls, builder competitions, and a fashion show of clothes made from recycled farm materials, there is something for everyone. Any mental paradigm of the simple farmer will be shattered anew with each invention you encounter along the event's 57 hectares. Come get a taste of real, rural Godzone, and pick up some inexpensive wool sweaters, gumboots, and oilskins while you're at it. (Admission $10, children $6. Call 843 4497 for more info.)

CAMBRIDGE

Cambridge is the staid neighbor of Hamilton and Raglan. This town sits in horse country and exudes the refined civility of its English ancestry. Priding itself upon its reputation as the "town of trees," Cambridge roots itself firmly by the banks of the Waikato River, and then branches out into farms that speckle the surrounding volcanic hills.

⚀ ORIENTATION AND PRACTICAL INFORMATION. Cambridge is located 24km east of Hamilton on **SH1. The Waikato River** runs through town, and **Te Kouto Lake** is a short walk from the **village green**. The **Cambridge Information Centre** (tel. 823 3456), on the corner of Victoria and Queen St., has a brand-new facility and lots of space. **InterCity** runs buses daily to: **Auckland** (2½hr., 6 per day, $30) via **Hamilton** (15min., $8); **Rotorua** (1hr., 6 per day, $21); **Wellington** (8½hr., 3 per day, $70); and **Taupo** (2½hr., 4 per day, $25). Bookings can be made at **Cambridge Travel,** 74 Victoria St. (tel. 827 5096). The **bus station** is right around the corner on Alpha St. under a green and tan awning. **Cresswell Motors LTD** (tel. 827 7789) also runs local service to **Hamilton,** stopping at the corner of Victoria and Commerce St. (M-Th 4 per day, F 6 per day; $4.50). **Cambridge Taxis** (tel. 827 5999) operate 24hr. (M-Sa; Su by appointment at least 1 day prior). **Four Seasons Mowers and Cycles,** 42 Victoria St. (tel./fax 827 6763), rents bicycles for $30 per day and also specializes in bike repairs. Many **hitchhikers** headed for Hamilton walk out along Hamilton Rd. (which becomes SH1), and stick their thumbs out before the 50km sign. Other services include: **BNZ,** 51-53 Victoria St. (tel. 827 6122; fax 823 3457; open M-F 9am-4:30pm); **Bubbles Laundrette** (tel. 827 5303), in the Hub Shopping Mall at the corner of Anzac and Alpha St. (open M-F 8:30am-5:30pm, Sa-Su 9am-2pm); **library,** 23 Wilson St. (tel. 827 5403), with **Internet access** ($10 per hr.; open M and Th 9am-5pm, Tu 9:30am-5pm, W and F 9am-8pm, Sa 9:30am-noon); **CES Services** 62D Victoria St (upstairs), with the best service and equipment in town ($12 per hr.; open M-Su 8am-8pm); **police** (tel. 827 5531), on Dick St. across from the town square; **Boyce's Pharmacy** (tel. 827 7358; open M-Th 8:30am-5:30pm, F 8:30am-6pm, Sa 9am-noon); **Citizen's Advice Bureau** (24hr. tel. 827 4855) for info after-hours regarding chemists or doctor on call; **Waikato Hospital** (tel. 839 8899), on Pembroke St; and the **post office,** 43 Victoria St. (tel. 827 5066; open M-F 9am-5pm). **Telephone Code:** 07.

⚀ ACCOMMODATIONS. Cambridge brims with enchanting little B&Bs (many of which come with not-so-enchanting little price tags). To find out about farmstays both locally and nationwide, contact **Rural Tours "Stay in a Country Home" Farmstays,** 92 Victoria St. (tel. 827 8055), in back of the Cambridge Country Store (open M-F 8:30am-5:30pm). For roughly $100 a night, they will organize a short-term stay at a host farm, with all meals included.

You can taste rural life in the midst of a five-acre hobby farm at the **Cambridge Country Lodge,** 20 Peake Rd. (tel. 827 8373), 2km north of Cambridge on SH1. it offers free pickup and dropoff. The low-lying lodge is a series of adjacent units converted from stables into well-appointed rooms with very comfy beds. (Free bikes. Checkout 10am. 2- to 4-bed dorms with sheets $16; self-contained units for 2 with shower, toilet, and kitchen $50, extra person $15.) The **National Hotel** (tel. 827 6731; fax 827 3450), is just around the corner from the bus station, at the corner of Victoria and Alpha St. Licensed since 1865, the present building is in the register of historic places. Pressed tin ceilings and intricate woodwork accent the 14 rooms, all of which come with electric blankets; some have pleasant balconies overlooking Victoria St. It has a sports bar, casino, and genuine old-world New Zealand pub, but very limited cooking facilities. (Singles $30; twins and doubles $60, extra person $10.) The **Karapiro Domain Motor Camp** (tel. 827 4178), at the end of Maungatautari Rd., has a great location by the lake (no linen; large bunkhouse accommodation with nearby facilities $7; tents sites $5.50, powered $6.50).

NORTH ISLAND

🔲🍴 **FOOD AND ENTERTAINMENT.** If the weather's bad, wrap yourself in a cappuccino at one of Cambridge's little cafes. On a sunny day, nothing beats a picnic on the shores of Lake Te Koutu. **Fran's Cafe,** 62C Victoria St. (tel. 827 3946), has antique tea pots and country crafts on display. You might fall in love with Fran's vegetarian lasagna ($4) or the sumptuous desserts ($2-3. Open M-F 7am-5pm, Sa 7am-3pm.) **The Gallery,** 64C Victoria St. (tel. 823 0999; fax 823 0997), has a warm interior with high ceilings, open rafters, and skylights. Lunch items include quiches ($3.50) and other light mains ($7). At dinner, the chefs have the freedom to create truly artful delicacies; presentation is half the experience with delicate entrees ($9-12) and exquisite mains ($20-25), including lamb dishes that have received national recognition. (Open M 9am-5pm, Tu-Sa 9am-11pm.) **Prince Albert English Pub,** 75 Victoria St. (tel. 827 7900), is in the Victoria Plaza. At Cambridge's only real night spot, you can quaff draught beers (handles $3.30, pints $4.50), shoot pool or play air hockey in the arcade hall, or hear live bands or a DJ on Friday and Saturday. Bar meals are available. (Open M-W 11am-midnight, Th-F 11am-3am, Sa 10am-3am, Su 10am-10pm.) **Countdown Foods** (tel. 827 7616), on the corner of Kirkwood and Lake St., is the place to stock up on groceries (open Sa-Tu 8:30am-7pm, W-F 8:30am-8pm). **Pumpkin Planet** (tel. 827 5442), on Victoria St. between Queen St. and Hamilton Rd., has bountiful produce (open M-F 8am-6pm, Sa-Su 8am-5pm).

🔲🏇 **SIGHTS AND ACTIVITIES.** Cambridge is well known for being a stud area. Horny ladies: relax. "Stud area" means it's a district for thoroughbred horse breeding. Add to the horses, antiquing, and craft-working and it's not surprising why this area has a reputation for being on its high horse—these pastimes attract the money-eyed elite of the Waikato and Auckland for weekends of indulgence.

The **Cambridge Country Store,** 92 Victoria St. (tel. 827 8715), has an amazing selection of all things New Zealand housed in its 1898 church frame. The **All Saints Cafe** upstairs offers muffins and scones ($2) and lunch items ($4-5) to be eaten on nice antique wooden furniture. Internet access is available, as well. (Open daily 8:30am-5:30pm, winter 8:30am-5pm.) At the other end of the crafts spectrum, **Tribal Art Collectors & Traders,** 89 Victoria St. (tel. 827 8848), feels like a museum, but you can buy what you like (open M-Sa 10am-5pm). Saturday afternoons from October to May, **cricket matches** transpire on the lawn in the town square.

Cambridge is aptly called "The Town of Trees" for the arboreal splendor that locals have cultivated since the town's inception. The **Cambridge Tree Trust** maintains the many "Tree Trails" around Lake Te Koutu. **Walking tracks** dart back and forth between riverbank and residential road on either side of the water and are accessible from the Victoria St. bridge. Alternatively, climb to the top of nearby **Sanitarium Hill** and observe the green canopy from above. The **Cambridge Museum** (tel. 827 3319), in the Old Court House at the south end of Victoria St., is packed with relics of eras gone by (open Tu-Sa 10am-4pm; admission by donation).

Equine sports lie a bit farther out of town. Throughout the year (apart from July) those 18 and over can slap down $1 or more on the pony of their choice at the renowned **Cambridge Raceway,** 47 Taylor St. (tel. 827 5506), about a six-minute drive. (Races run M-Sa 6:15-10:30pm, Su noon-5pm. Basic stand ticket $4.) **Cambridge Thoroughbred Lodge** (tel. 827 8118), on SH1 6km south of Cambridge, offers special horse shows that encourage audience participation, and involve many breeds of horses. (Open daily 10am-4pm. Show runs Tu-Su at 10:30am. Tickets $12, children $5, families $25.) To ogle the studs working out, head to **Matamata Raceway** (tel. 888 4442), 35 minutes by car outside of Cambridge, New Zealand's largest thoroughbred training center. Eat breakfast while watching jockeys train the horses and amateurs riding before work. A walk or bike ride down **Racecourse Road** in Cambridge will take you past many stud, deer, and other hobby farms.

RAGLAN

The inhabitants of the tiny coastal town of Raglan, or Raglan-by-the-sea, make relaxation mandatory and "no worries" a way of life. The left-handed break at Manu Bay is touted as the world's finest and can be appreciated in full splendor in the 1966 classic surfing movie, *The Endless Summer*. Kick back in Raglan or join the stampede of surfers that cruise here from around the world every summer.

🛈 ORIENTATION AND PRACTICAL INFORMATION

Forty-eight kilometers of mountain road **(SH23)** winding around extinct volcanoes separate Raglan from Hamilton. The town itself sits back in the harbor 6km from the coastline and all the good surfing points. The **Raglan Visitors Information Centre** (tel. 825 0556; fax 825 0557) is on the corner of Bow and Nero St. It also serves as the **AA** and **DOC office.** Call for weather and road conditions, as well as high tide information. (Open M-Su 10am-5pm, winter M-Su 10am-4pm; go next door to the council office if no one is there.) The only public transportation service to Raglan is the **Pavlovich buses** (tel. 856 4579), whose departure schedule is designed primarily for those who live on the coast but work or study in Hamilton. Buses head to Hamilton from West Raglan, pausing right in front of the Visitors Centre about five to 10 minutes later (4 per day, $4.70). There's no weekend service, but a weekend in Raglan might be just what you need if you're *that* concerned about strict schedules. **Hitchhiking** is practiced regularly along SH23, at the edge of town before the traffic picks up to 100kph. The most-used spots are at the top end of Bow St. by the water tower (look for the giant surfing mural) and at the Te Uku outpost dairy. Currency can be exchanged at **WestPac Trust Bank** (tel. 825 8579), at the top end of Bow St., where the palm trees start (open M-Tu and Th-F 9am-4:30pm, W 9:30am-4:30pm). **No ATM** is available. The **Four Square Supermarket** does accept Eftpos cards. The **Raglan Surf Co.,** 3 Wainui Rd. (tel. 825 8988), rents surfboards for $30-35 per day and wetsuits for $20 per day (open daily 9:30am-5pm); for **daily surf conditions,** call **"The Rock" 93 FM** (tel. 838 2693) or Ragland Surf Co. Other services include: the **police** (tel. 825 8200), on Nero St., in a little clapboard house; **Raglan Pharmacy LTD & Lotto** (tel. 825 8164), for medicine or millions of dollars (open M-F 9am-5pm, Sa 9am-7pm); **After Hours Doctors** (tel. 825 0007); **Raglan Medical Centre,** 2 Wallace St. (tel. 825 0402; open M-Tu and F 9am-4:30pm, Th 9am-7pm, W 9am-3pm and 6:30-8pm, Sa 10am-1pm, Su 10am-noon.); **Internet access** for $6 per hr. at the **library,** next door to the Visitor Centre (**Molasses Cafe** (see below) has better equipment); and the **post office,** 39 Bow St. (tel. 825 8007), next to the town hall (open M-F 9am-5pm). **Telephone Code:** 07.

🏠 ACCOMMODATIONS

Raglan's population of 3500 increases by fifty percent during the summer. In the winter, expect to find a number of visitors who came for a weekend and stayed for the season, as the surf is good year-round. For a helpful guide to accommodations, or to call a place, check in with the affable staff at the Visitors Centre.

■ **Raglan Backpackers and Waterfront Lodge,** 6 Nero St. (tel. 825 0515). This prime spot will capture your heart—it has already captured the BBH award for best backpackers in NZ. Smartly appointed rooms open onto an airy inner courtyard complete with hammock, flowers, and surfers lazing in the sun. Some rooms have gorgeous views of the harbor. TV lounge and tidy kitchen round out the premises. Free surfboards, kayaks, bikes. Dropoff to beaches and walking tracks are available. Laundry $4. Mixed dorms $14; twins and doubles $32. Cash only.

Raglan Wagon Cabins, 161 Wainui Rd. (tel. 825 8268), outside of Raglan West. Car drivers should consider pulling in here. This spot is a favorite with surfers who need close access to the raging surf of Manu Bay, only 2km away. Sleep inside a retired railroad car. Large lounge with TV. Bunks start at $15; self-contained cottages $35.

Marcus's Magic Mountain Lodge, Farmstay, and Backpackers, 334 Houchens Rd. (tel. 825 6892 or mobile 025 756 276; fax 825 6896), in nearby Te Mata. "The only place in the world where you can see four volcanoes and three lagoons only two minutes walking from your doorstep." Horse-trekking from $25. Singles $40; doubles $75; group house with 3 doubles and 2 singles $140. Cash only.

The Raglan Holiday Park (tel. 825 8283; fax 825 8284), over the footbridge, on Marine Parade next to the Aerodrome and airstrip. Vast expanse of land can accommodate 1000. Kitchen has no utensils, but the ablution blocks have showers and toilets. Laundry $3. Tent sites $8, winter $7, powered $9/$8; 4-person chalets $10 per person.

FOOD AND ENTERTAINMENT

Petchells Four Square, 16-18 Bow St. (tel. 825 8300), is a market, auto supply, and sundry shop all in one (open M-F 7:30am-5pm, Sa-Su 7:30am-4pm). Raglan has never been the same since **Molasses** (tel. 825 7229) came to town. This new cafe on Bow St., across from the Visitors Centre, has healthy food, good vibes, and a strong focus on well-being. (Read: great food for real cheap.) Dig into a Chicken Burger ($8.50) with bacon, brie, and greens or have a huge hunk of vegetarian lasagna ($4.50). It also has the best coffee in Raglan, acoustic music every few weeks, and Internet access. (Open M-Su 8am-late.) Farmers and surfers chow down at the **Tongue and Groove** (tel. 825 0027), on the corner of Bow St. and Wainui Rd. Local art inspired by the beach and ocean graces the walls. The veggie-friendly menu includes breakfasts served until 2pm ($5-10) and dinner mains beginning at 6pm ($15). In between and during those hours, snacks and sandwiches are available. On weekend nights, the Tongue occasionally grooves to live music or DJs. (Open M, W, and F-Su 10am-late, T-W 10am-4pm.) In 1847, scores of prefab kauri wood cottages were deposited in Raglan in anticipation of a crush of immigrants. The only one remaining was retro-fitted a few years back to become **Vinnie's,** 7 Wainui Rd. (tel. 825 7273), with sparkling stained-glass windows, a deck, and some of Raglan's best grub. Originally a pizza pad (slices $2.50), the menu has grown to cover several blackboards. (Open daily from 11am, winter Tu-Su only.)

SIGHTS AND ACTIVITIES

Whether you're seeking an endless summer on your own or arriving in the dead of winter, Raglan's black-sand beaches are more than worth the trip. Catching a ride to the coast is easy, as beach-bound vehicles abound in town. If you have a car, make sure you lock it while you are at the beach. **Theft** of and from cars has become a problem lately. The most accessible is **Te Kopua Beach,** which can be reached via the footbridge at the base of Bow St. Accessibility has its price, though, as this beach is overrun with families and screaming children in the summer. Te Kopua also occupies a perfect harbor location for windsurfing. Fine swimming and more space can be had at **Ocean Beach (Ngaranui Beach).** Watch out for strong undertows; only the west end of the beach is patrolled by lifeguards. The strong winds also make it ideal for wind surfing.

Hard-core surfers head to **Manu Bay (Waireke).** Farther down the coast is **Whale Bay (Whaanga),** where green surf and rocky shore are accessible by a walking path from the cul-de-sac at the end of Calvert Rd. that goes over volcanic rocks to the black-sand beach. The surfing here is awesome in autumn, and in April and May there are often professional surfing competitions. If you're in search of a holy grail (or a red herring), somewhere between Manu Bay and Ocean Beach the elusive **Tatooed Rocks** can be found. Years ago, an unknown artist chiseled his way to local fame by sculpting two large rocks on the beach. They are only accessible at low tide, and some locals have searched for years without success. Farther down the coast, **Ruapuke Beach** offers rugged coastline and good surfcasting. The less crowded **Cox's Bay** and **Puriri Park (Aro Aro Bay),** to the east of the town center, are ideal for children, picnics, or both. Walk along Wallis St. away from the Visitors Centre to reach them.

Although surfers might lead you to believe otherwise, Raglan does have more to offer than the ocean. If you can't catch a wave, sit on the inactive volcanoes of **Mt. Karioi** and **Mt. Pirongia** in **Pirongia Forest Park.** One glance at Mt. Karioi's curvaceous silhouette and it's no wonder that in Maori legend it is referred to as "the sleeping lady." Mt. Karioi also boasts terrific mountain biking on **Whaanga Road,** which wraps around the mountain's coastal side. Refrain from careening around the curves during the week—the one-lane road carries a considerable amount of traffic, and vehicles seem to be perpetually going over the edge. **Mt. Pirongia** is farther from Raglan, but is larger and has more walking options. Another great view of the ocean can be had from **Te Toto Gorge,** which has recently become infamous as the place where car thieves dump the carcasses of their booty.

Freshwater wonders also await. The locals are mighty proud of **Bridal Veil Falls** and the fact that it is higher than its Niagara counterpart (though not quite as wide). Its thin, delicate spray is best photographed from the lookout, a 20-minute walk from the carpark on Kawhia Rd. You can soak out many of life's aches and pains at the **Waingoro Hot Springs** (tel. 825 4761), north of Raglan on SH22. With the proper DOC permits, you can also hunt wild pigs or go fly-fishing for rainbow trout in the **Kaniwhaniwha Stream.** On a rainy day, contact the secretary of the **Raglan Museum** on Wainui Rd. (tel. 825 8129) to see its photographic chronicle of the town's surfing legacy (open Sa-Su 1-3:30pm or by appointment; free).

OTOROHANGA

While Otorohanga has a reputation for being the little access town to Waitomo, this burg actually trumps its neighbors on accommodations, services, and food. Visitors who want to spend a few days caving in the Waitomo area should strongly considering setting up base camp in Otorohanga. The literal meaning of the town's name, "food for the long journey," originates with the legend of a great Maori king who paused in his journey to multiply his few supplies into enough to sustain his trek. But more than just a spot to resupply, Otorohanga offers quiet rest with tons of nearby amusement all within a few hours drive from Auckland.

⁊ ORIENTATION AND PRACTICAL INFORMATION. Maniapoto St. is the central road in town where most commercial activity takes place. The **Visitor Information Centre,** 87 Maniapoto St. (tel. 873 8951; fax 873 8398; open M-F 9am-5:30pm, Sa-Su 10am-4pm), is located at the intersection with **Wahanui Crescent,** where the **bus** arrives and departs. Keep an eye out for Wiki, the giant kiwi who greets visitors. **InterCity** heads to: **Auckland** (2½hr., 3 per day, $39) via **Hamilton** (1hr., $16); **Wellington** (8hr.; 2 per day, 1 on Sa; $86) via **Wanganui** (5hr., $45); and **Palmerston North** (7hr., $50). The **train station** is at the other end of Wahanui Crescent. Otorohanga was the first stop on the main trunk railway when the King Country was opened to Europeans and their descendants in the 1880s and 90s. Today, **TranzScenic** (tel. 0800 802 802) still stops here, on its way to **Auckland** (2½hr.; 2 per day, 1 on Sa; $37-42) via **Hamilton** (1hr., $18-20) and **Wellington** (7hr.; 2 per day, 1 on Sa; $88-99) via **Palmerston North** (6hr., $64-72). To get to **Waitomo,** take Bill Millar's **Waitomo Shuttle** (tel. 0800 808 279) from the Visitor Centre and learn more about the history of Otorohanga and the King Country in ten minutes than a guidebook could print in 50 pages. The shuttle drops off at accommodations (5 per day, $7; between 8am-8pm additional shuttles by arrangement, $18; during all other hours, $26). Bill also operates **Otorohanga Taxis** (tel. 0800 808 279) for your other local transportation needs (open Su-Th 8am-11pm, F-Sa 8am-1am). **Hitchhiking** opportunities are said to be best from the Visitor Centre, at the end of Maniapoto St. before the bridge, or at the intersection of Waitomo Caves Rd. and SH3. The only **ATM** (servicing Master-Card and Cirrus) is at **WestPac Trust Bank** on Maniapoto St. Card users on other systems should bring cash from Hamilton, Rotorua, or points south. Fill up at one of the three **petrol stations** in town, as there is no petrol station in Waitomo. The **police station** (tel. 873 7175) is located at 4 Ballance St.The **doctor on call** (tel. 873 8399) can be reached all day. **Internet access** is available at the **public library** (tel. 873

8199), in the middle of the main street ($10 per hr.; open M-Th 10am-5pm, F 10am-6pm, Sa 10am-noon). The **post office** is inside King's Paper Plus (tel. 873 8816), on Maniapoto St. (open M-F 8:30am-5pm, Sa 9am-7pm). **Telephone Code:** 07.

■ **ACCOMMODATIONS AND FOOD.** Waitomo visitors will be glad they stayed the night in Otorohanga. By night, the cry of the kiwis from the nearby breeding pens echoes through Otorohanga's best budget accommodations.

At the **Oto-Kiwi Lodge,** 1 Sangro Crescent (tel. 873 6022; fax 873 6066; email oto kiwi@xtra.co.nz), the energetic hosts welcome "backpackers, globetrotters, and musicians" to their compound at the end of the cul-de-sac. Even though the one-story accommodation is a short seven-minute walk from town, free pickup is available. (Internet. Bikes $10 per day. Kayaks $35 per day. Key deposit $10. Laundry $3. Dorms $15; doubles $37; beds in recording studio $12; tent sites $7.50.) For hotel lodgings, try the brown splendor of the **Royal Hotel** (tel. 873 8129; fax 873 8744), at the corner of Turongo and Te Kanawa St., which now offers backpacker rooms. This facility is best known for its bars and discotheque. On weekends, two bouncers keep the party under control. Check in at the bar and pick up some cheap grub. (Dorms $20; singles $35; twins $45; doubles $55.) Adjoining the town's famous Kiwi House is the **Kiwi Town Caravan Park and Motor Camp.** To contact the proprietor, Bill of Waitomo Shuttle (tel. 0800 808 279), use the phone in the communal kitchen. Waitomo Shuttle travels into town at 8:30am or 6:30pm. Simple but clean facilities include a communal kitchen, toilets and showers, and laundry. (On-site caravans for 2 $27; caravan sites for 2 $16, extra person $7.50; tent sites $7.)

Price Cutter (tel. 873 7264), at the south end of Maniapoto St., is the market of choice (open M-Th 8am-6pm, F 8am-7pm, Sa 9am-3pm, Su 10am-2pm). For sublime cafe food, stop at **Tonis,** 13 Maniapoto St. (tel. 873 6611), with tons of tempting homemade goodies, from mood-enhancing chocolate cake ($3) to gourmet sandwiches ($5). (Open M-F 8am-5:30pm, Sa 10am-3pm.) For an inexpensive sit-down meal, consider the **Otorohanga Club Restaurant** (tel. 873 6543), at the south end of Maniapoto St., where steak dinners are $11 and lunches are $4-8. Head to the semi-private club in the back, sign your name in as a guest, and have a beer or shoot some pool. (Open Th-Su 11:30am-3pm and daily from 5pm.)

■ **SIGHTS AND ACTIVITIES.** As Wiki, the overstuffed, moving, grooving and *totally* interactive kiwi bird town mascot (also the welcoming committee), would tell you if he could speak: no stop in Otorohanga would be complete without a pilgrimage to the **Otorohanga Kiwi House and Native Bird Park** (tel. 873 7391), on Alex Telfer Dr. Although the birds spend only four hours of the day awake, a sighting in the "moonlit" kiwi house is guaranteed, as kiwi stay awake in shifts throughout the day. Outside is New Zealand's original walk-through aviary (don't look up), with tuataras, geckos, and cave wetas. (Open daily Sept.-May 9:30am-5pm; June-Aug. 9:30am-4pm. Admission $7.50.)

WAITOMO

Back in 1887, Maori chief Tane Tinorau and European surveyor Fred Mace chose to leave Maori legend behind and explore the depths of the local river cave. Although no gods were found, that day the two spelunkers were treated to an other worldly display of bioluminescent blue, courtesy of thousands of glow-worms. Within a year, Tinorau had opened up the cave to visitors and was guiding them inside to experience the ethereal wonder. One hundred years later, though the glow-worm population has remained stable, the number of tourists has soared to nearly 500,000, putting this minuscule hamlet (pop. 250) squarely on the map. Every day, over 50 tour buses roll into the tiny village of Waitomo. After a few hours—and the observation of several million glow-worms—the buses cruise on out. While most visitors come for the "light show," nearly one-tenth are now attracted by the adventure caving industry, which offers trips of varying degrees of difficulty, consistently low degrees of water temperature, and considerably high degrees of pleasure.

🔢 PRACTICAL INFORMATION

The Museum of Caves Information Centre (tel. 878 7640; fax 878 6184; email waitomomuseum@xtra.co.nz), is just inside the entrance to the Museum of Caves in Waitomo Village. The front desk functions as a base camp for everyone living in, passing through, or even thinking about coming to Waitomo. Aside from booking any cave-related activity you would ever desire, the helpful staff can give detailed first-hand accounts of just how wet you'll get or how many glow-worms you'll see. In **emergencies** consult the front desk. Card **phones** are just outside, as are after-hours **public toilets.** The Info Centre also offers the lowest prices on **groceries** in the village. (Open daily 8:15am-5:30pm, winter 8:15am-5pm, Jan. 8:15am-8pm.)

Nearly 70% of visitors to the caves arrive by coach. **InterCity** runs daytrips from **Auckland** (9am, $45) and **Rotorua** (9am, $37); the bus returning to each departs Waitomo at 2pm. The **Waitomo Wanderer** (tel. 873 7559) offers service between Waitomo (departs 4pm) and **Rotorua** (departs 7:30am). Booking ahead is required, with pickup and dropoff available at all hostels. (Trips 2hr. one-way; $25, return $45, children $15.) The **Waitomo Adventure Shuttle** (tel. 0800 924 866) runs between **Auckland** (departs at 7:30am) and Waitomo (departs at 4pm) for $31. The **Waitomo Shuttle** (tel. 0800 808 279; fax 873 8214) is the best option for those making **InterCity** or **Tranzscenic** connections in **Otorohanga** (10min., 4 per day, $7). Trips after 8pm can be arranged ($18 one-way), and pickups are made from any of the Waitomo hostels. **Hitchhiking** (which Let's Go does not recommend) from Otorohanga is reportedly fairly easy; hitchhikers often hang out at the Information Centre until they find a fellow tourist with a car, or else walk out along Waitomo Caves Rd. Apparently, hitchhiking into Waitomo is best accomplished by standing at the junction of Waitomo Caves Rd. and SH3. Be warned that there are **no banks or ATMs** in Waitomo. For medical help call the **Otorohanga Medical Centre** (tel. 873 8399). The **post office** is located in the Information Centre at the museum. **Telephone Code:** 07.

🏠 ACCOMMODATIONS

Waitomo has limited options in terms of attractive, budget accommodations. Nevertheless, bookings are essential in summer. Check-out is 10am unless noted.

Juno Hall (tel./fax 878 7649), on Waitomo Caves Rd., 1km from the Information Centre and across the road from the Black Water Rafting headquarters. Free pickup and dropoff to village or hitchhiking points. Low-lying brown lodge with a warm interior. Laundry $4. Dorms $17; doubles $42, extra person $9; suites with TV, shower, and toilet $49, extra person $9; tent sites $8 per person. YHA members $1 off.

Dalziel's Waitomo Caves Guest Lodge B&B (tel. 878 7641; fax 878 7466), next door to the general store in the village. Six well-appointed private units, each with bathroom facilities, electric blankets, and TV. Singles $50; doubles $70, extra person $20. "The Cottage" is a slightly smaller twin for $60.

Waitomo Caves Hostel (YHA) (tel. 878 8204; fax 878 8205), behind the Waitomo Caves Hotel in Waitomo Village. Brightly painted rooms with bath and fresh linen make up for spare lounge and kitchen area. Check in at the hotel. Check-out 9:30am. Dorms $17 (non-YHA members $20); twins and triples with bath $20 per person. **Waitomo Caves Hotel** is more upscale, though economy singles without bathrooms are $25.

Cavelands Waitomo Holiday Park (tel./fax 878 7639), across the street from the Museum of Caves. A well-maintained accommodation complex. Laundry $2. Linen $3. Self-contained tourist flats with TV, kitchenette, bathroom $70 for 2, extra adult $10, extra child $5; budget beds $17 (less $1 for VIP); budget cabins for 2 $35; tent sites $5, children $4.50; powered $10, children $5.

FOOD

Beware: Waitomo has very few places to eat. Given the limited selection of over-priced groceries in the village, travelers would be best served stocking up at the markets of Otorohanga, Hamilton, or Rotorua. The best prepared food in town, by far, can be found at the **Black Water Cafe** (tel. 878 7361), in the main Black Water Rafting building 1km east of the village (close to Juno Hall). Recent renovations have created a space for eating somewhat separate from the rafters' waiting area. The kitchen offers large breakfasts ($5-10), and very nice, fresh-made lunch items ($3-5). The pot of soup and basket of bagels by the fireplace are for post-rafting munchies. (Open June-Aug. 8:30am-4pm, Sept.-May 7:30am-8:30pm.) The **Cave-lands Brasserie and Bar and General Store** (tel. 878 7700) is the large building next to the Museum of Caves. For visitors stranded in Waitomo, this may be the only option for breakfast and lunch. Burgers ($8.50-10.50) and fries ($2-3) are standard, while mains ($12.50-17) for dinner in the summer are slightly pricier. The **general store** is overpriced (open daily 8am-9pm, winter 8am-5pm). The **Waitomo Caves Tavern** (tel. 878 8448), located below the Waitomo Caves Hotel, is *the* watering hole for all of Waitomo, and the only place serving dinner in Waitomo during the winter months. Pub grub. Discerning (or sober) eaters will likely balk at the burgers or steaks with fries and salad ($7.50-8.50). (Open for dining daily noon-2:30pm, M-Sa 6-9pm, Su 5:30-8:30pm; winter M-Sa 6-9pm, Su 5:30-8:30pm. Bar open M-Sa 11am-11pm, Su 11am-10pm; winter M-Sa 11am-pm, Su 11am-8pm.)

SIGHTS AND ACTIVITIES

The scores of holes littering the green pastureland around Waitomo are gateways to a mystical world where time and temperature seem to exist—centuries become measured in centimeters rather than years, and the caves remain constantly dark and cool regardless of conditions top-side. New adventure trips are constantly springing up to satisfy growing demand (often offering low introductory prices until they become established), and some only advertise in Waitomo. Given this labyrinthine array of caving possibilities (climbing, canoeing, sightseeing, stroll-ing, and glow-worm watching), the best advice is to book ahead, and to check in with the Information Centre for latest and greatest.

ADVENTURE CAVING

Always go caving with a guide; never cave solo, even if you consider yourself an experienced spelunker. Aside from safety issues, virtually all of the caves in the area are privately owned, and trespassing can be risky business. Before you suit up and head out, you may want to consider testing yourself for claustrophobia. If the company running your tour doesn't already require it, head to the Museum of Caves, explain your situation, and ask to try the cave "crawl-through." Standard protocol for "adventure caving" involves slapping on a full wetsuit and some cov-eralls (or just the coveralls if it's a "dry" trip), a hard hat with a head lamp, and a pair of gumboots. Then it's off to the paddocks where extremely patient guides will walk you through the basics of single-rope technique (SRT), much to your own amusement and that of the sheep and cows around you. Each trip or tour is unique and has its own personality and pace—there is no absolute "best."

   Waitomo Adventures (tel. 878 7788 or 0800 WAITOMO; www.waitomo.co.nz) deals out a great hand of options (office open daily 7:30am-9pm, winter 9am-5pm). All trips depart from the Museum of Caves parking lot. **Haggas Honking Holes,** so-called because the caves are on Farmer Haggas's property, includes three water-fall abseils, plenty of climbing and squeezing, and admirable formations all at an action-packed clip. "The Honk" (4hr.; 2 per day; $125) combines the intensity of boot camp and the camaraderie of summer camp to create the most adrenaline-packed excitement available for first-time cavers. A swimsuit and towel are essen-tial; polypropylene thermals, thick wool socks, and soap are advisable. (Times coincide with the Kiwi Experience and Waitomo Wanderer schedules.) Waitomo

STARRY NIGHT Over the eons, humans have looked heavenward in search of inspiration and answers; standing inside a glow-worm cave, however, the answers might not be what you'd expect. Indeed, few pause to consider the sordid but fascinating details of this little creature's life. The glow-worm (*Arachnocampa luminosa;* in Maori *titiwai*), is actually not a worm at all, but the larva of a fly. After hatching, the baby flies set about the business of excreting sticky threads to make a "hammock" and "fishing lines." On each of the 70 lines (1-50cm long) controlled by each worm is a drop of shiny stuff—the worm's waste product, lit up by the light of the bioluminescent larva itself (with the brightness of one-billionth of a watt). After months of trolling with poo, the glow-worm undergoes metamorphosis and becomes an adult fly. Meanwhile, evolution was so busy figuring out how to make the glow-worm's stool shine that it forgot to develop a digestive tract. After only a day or two of adult life—flying, mating, and laying eggs—the fly dies of starvation (or from being oversexed). The next time you gaze up in awe at the blueish stars in the nighttime sky of a cave's ceiling, remember that the speck of light is a tail-glowing maggot fishing for its lunch with a glob of excrement. Ain't nature grand?

Adventure's other blockbuster trip is the **Lost World,** a 100m freehanging abseil into an ethereal world of mist and miniature ferns not entirely unlike a land of Spielberg dinosaurs. An awestruck reporter from the *King Country Chronicle* in 1906 dubbed it "a fairyland without the fairies." You descend in tandem with your guide; the umbilical-like connection ensures that your guide goes wherever you do. Don't wear jeans. (4hr.; 2 per day; $195. Extra trip at 4:30pm in the summer.) You can combine both the Honk and Lost World into the **Gruesome Twosome** for $295. In addition, Waitomo offers **Tumu Tumu Toobing,** a rafting trip that features more caving and less tubing than comparable trips (4hr.; 2 per day; $65). Waitomo offers a 10% discount to students, as well as to YHA and VIP members.

RAFTING
Black Water Rafting (BWR) (tel. 878 6219 or 0800 CAVING), begun in 1987, is the granddaddy of all adventure caving in Waitomo. To the usual wetsuit, helmet, and boots add some stylish purple "eel pants" and an inner tube, and you're ready to float into the world of the glow-worm. **BWI** is the classic tour and involves a gentle float and the obligatory glow-worms (allow 3hr., mostly for the ritualistic dressing procedure; $65). **BWII** gets flashier with an added abseil, rock climb, and an adventurous escape through a waterfall (lunch and snacks provided; 5hr.; $125). Both BWI and II depart from and return to the Black Water Cafe, where a delicious hot shower (bring soap, towel, and bathing suit), as well as free soup and bagel await.

Waitomo Down Under (WDU) (tel. 878 6577 or 0800 102 604) offers four different tours, frequently guided by direct descendents of Tane Tinorau. **Adventure 1** is a float-through that features formation and worm-spotting (3hr., $65), and runs five times a day. Bring swim gear and towel. **Adventure 2** is a "dry" abseil 50m into an absolutely stunning cave known as the "Baby Grand" (2hr., $65). The adventurous can choose to lock off their ropes and then swing, flip, and dangle in mid-air. Don't wear jeans. Similar dress rules apply for **Adventure 3,** which features all spelunking, all the time (2hr., $50). Guests squeeze, climb, get grubby, and generally have a good time. Bring towel and soap. **Adventure 4** is basically Adventure 2, done under the cover of darkness at 7:30pm (2hr.). Once reaching the free hang, the lights are turned out for a space walk in a galaxy of glow-worms. Again, don't wear jeans. All trips depart from the WDU building next to the museum. Pickup and dropoff are available from area hostels; there is a 10% discount available for students, YHA and VIP members, and groups of six or more.

For a less commercial approach with excellent value and a reputation for the best glow-worming, try an independent operator like Simon Hall's **Waitomo Wilderness Tours** (tel. 878 7640). Smaller groups (max. 6) partake in five different activities. A 27m abseil down a ferny rock slope takes you to the water, where the

NORTH ISLAND

floating options of **cave canoeing** (by canoe) or **Long Tomo rafting** (by inner tube) await. Each trip is tailored to fit the group's interests. (5hr.; 2-4 per day, $65. Bring a towel, t-shirt, swimsuit, socks, and camera.)

GLOW-WORMS AND OTHER CAVE SIGHTS

Any visit to Waitomo should include a visit to the **Museum of Caves** (tel. 878 7640). Learn about how the caves were formed, the wildlife that now resides there, and take in a multimedia spelunking experience in the small theater. **Black Water Rafting** provides a complimentary museum pass as part of their adventure, and **Waitomo Down Under** will provide one on request. (Open daily 8:30am-5pm. Admission $4, children under 18 free.)

If you are curious to see where all of those tour buses are headed, get on down to the **Glow-worm Caves** (tel. 878 8227), 500m around the bend west of Waitomo Village on Waitomo Caves Rd. This is the cave everyone keeps talking about. Stroll along the stage-like boardwalk alongside dramatically lit formations for a truly theatrical experience. "The Cathedral" has served as a performance venue for the likes of Kenny Rogers, the Vienna Boys Choir, and Maori opera diva Dame Kiri Te Kanawa. The Disney-esque boat ride at the end is breathtaking, and probably the only time you'll find silence anywhere in the tourist-filled cave. Hear only the drip of dark water as the boat slips under a mantle of glowing stars. Independent travelers are advised to come at either end of the day. Take a midday tour and you will almost assuredly become an appendage to a large coach tour. (Tours every 30min. 9am-5:30pm and 8pm, winter 9am-5pm. $20, children $10, families $18.)

Aranui Cave holds a treasure trove of formations that you don't even have to get your feet wet to see. (Tours run daily 10am-3pm on the hour, same prices as above. Both caves: $30, children $15. Family pass: 1 cave $50, both caves $65.) The most natural caving expedition also happens to be free; at the museum, you can pick up a guide to the **Waitomo Walkway**, a 2.5km DOC-maintained trek (return 3hr.) that takes you mostly through bush, but at its farthest point leads you into the **Ruakiri Natural Tunnel**. At night, put on some sturdy shoes and grab a flashlight and a friend to find another cache of glow-worms to ogle. Entry points are across the road from the museum, at the rotary intersection of Waitomo Caves and Te Anga Rd., and the car park of the Ruakuri Scenic Reserve on Tumutumu Rd. From this latter point, the tunnel can be experienced in one hour.

WALKS AND OTHER ACTIVITIES

Amazingly enough, there *are* activities in Waitomo that don't involve wetsuits or worms. One of the more interesting topside activities is the bush trek (return 1hr.) to the **Opapaka Maori pa.** As the trail winds through excruciatingly beautiful forest, placards along the way describe local plants, their medicinal uses, and Maori legends. At the crest of the hill, barbed wire separates the trail from the *pa* (or more accurately, where it used to stand—use your imagination); you are allowed to cross over the fence with the makeshift bridge, but mind the livestock. The walk begins from the carpark located just west of Juno Hall on Waitomo Caves Rd.

Farther down along Waitomo Caves Rd. toward Waitomo Village is the turn-off for **Woodlyn Park** (tel. 878 6666). Farmer, historian, and globe-trotting sheep-shearer Barry Woods puts on a thoroughly entertaining and refreshingly authentic **Pioneer Show**, detailing Waitomo's European history with lots of animal antics and audience participation. (Daily in summer 1:30pm; book ahead in winter. $10, children $5, families $30.)

Try your hand at everything from sheep-shearing to jigger-chopping. For an even more hands-on experience, try **Barry's U-Drive Jetboat.** Although those travelers inexperienced at piloting a jetboat might rename this activity "U-Crash," safety equipment abounds and the sloping walls of the water course are lined with tires. (Open daily 9am-5pm, in summer also 6:30-8pm. 8 laps $35. Book ahead.)

At the other end of the spectrum is **Waitomo Horse Trekking** (tel. 878 7659), departing from Juno Hall and led by their multi-talented staff. (Treks $30 per hr.,

$40 per 2hr., half-day $60, full day $100, overnight $200 per day. Meals included. Book in advance.) Hunting outings can also be organized. Lastly, a unique and free experience is **The Shearing Shed** (tel. 878 8371), also on Waitomo Caves Rd., where there is a free daily shearing show at 1pm (show up at 12:45pm) in which the stars of the show are not the usual sheep, but Angora rabbits. Afterwards, browse the gift shop for something soft and fluffy.

THE COROMANDEL PENINSULA

Removed from the standard tourist loop, this charming peninsula of largely untouched natural beauty takes visitors to mythical New Zealand. With lush, sub-tropical forest, rugged hills, and close-knit, friendly communities, the Coromandel crystallizes life before commercialization. The winding, often harrowing coastal road is your time warp. From the transportation gateway of Thames, you can trace the curving edge of the firth to the charming, artisan town of Coromandel. The coastal road continues—with twisting trees bending out over the water—up to the wild Coromandel Walkway, but the main road cuts inland. Occasionally turning to gravel (or metal as Kiwis call it), the rough road passes several tramping trailheads before giving way to Whitianga. At Hot Water Beach, Hahei, and magical Opoutere, life becomes even simpler; in these tiny "towns," Coromandel time seems to stand still. While the peninsula, a favorite Auckland getaway, gets crowded during Kiwi holidays (avoid it altogether in the few weeks after Christmas), in the low seasons and the winter, it's no tour buses, no crowds, and no worries.

▨ COROMANDEL PENINSULA HIGHLIGHTS

■ Way off-the-beaten-path, the **Northern Tip** (p. 138) and its Coromandel Walkway is unmitigated natural beauty.
■ At **Hot Water Beach** (p. 143), you'll gleefully dig a grave and lie in it.
■ **Coromandel town** (p. 137) offers tranquility and local crafts while **Opoutere** (p. 144) is a glowing, magical nowhere.

◰ **GETTING AROUND.** Public transportation on the Coromandel's narrow, winding roads can be a little sparse, especially in winter, when services make limited runs. Check with local visitors centers for current options. If you can't drive it yourself, consider buying a **Coromandel Busplan** from **InterCity** to circuit the peninsula in a clockwise direction from Thames to the town of Coromandel to Whitianga and back to Thames. **The Loop Pass** ($37) allows unlimited segments in the one-way loop, while the **Busplan Pass** ($79) includes the loop plus a starting leg from Auckland and a final leg to Auckland or Rotorua. (Passes valid for 3 months; book each leg the day before. Loop runs daily Oct.-Apr., winter Su-F.)

THAMES

Arriving in this small, sunny town (pop. 6500), you'd never guess that it was briefly the country's largest city in the 1870s, with over 18,000 inhabitants, 100 hotels, and rows of bars pouring whiskey for streams of miners and prospectors. Today, the gold rush is recalled in the pared-down town only by old hotels, a shopping mall called Goldfields, and a surfeit of bright yellow signs marking various bonanza sites and mines. No longer resounding to the pounding of stamper batteries nor carousel by the drunken revelries of miners, Thames now hums only with the sound of passing cars and occasionally buzzes with inebriated students when summer holidays hit. Before passing through, the peninsula-bound should stock up on cash; Thames has one of the last ATMs for a while.

NORTH ISLAND

🔢 ORIENTATION AND PRACTICAL INFORMATION

From Auckland, **SH25** (the new **Pacific Coast Highway**) wraps around the **Firth of Thames** before heading up and around the tip. Thames itself lies on a flat between the Firth and the upsweep of the gold-mine-riddled Coromandel Range. Most of Thames's shops and services stretch out along the 1.6km of **Pollen St.** Parallel and seaward is **Queen St.**, the in-town name of SH25.

Visitors Center: The **Thames Information Centre,** 206 Pollen St. (tel. 868 7284). Open M-F 8:30am-5pm, Sa-Su 9am-5pm, winter M-F 8:30am-5pm, Sa-Su 9am-4pm.

DOC: Kauaeranga Valley Visitors Centre (tel. 868 6381), 13km out of town. Open daily 8am-4pm (see **Coromandel Forest Park,** p. 135).

Airplanes: Air Coromandel (tel. 0800 275 912) flies to **Auckland** (2 per day, $90) from Whitianga, Pauanui, or Matarangi; the company also flies to **Great Barrier Island** from those locations (departs daily 9am, returning at 3pm; $89, return $169).

Buses: InterCity heads from the Visitor Centre to: **Auckland** (2 per day and 3 on Sunday, $16) via **Tauranga** with a transfer (2hr., $20-25); **Coromandel** (1¼hr., 1 per day, winter M-F 3:50pm, $14); and **Whitianga** on a non-loop run (1¾hr.,10:15am, $14). **Turley Murphy** buses go to **Coromandel** (1 per day, winter Su-F 3:55pm, $19-24).

Car Rental: Worth considering, particularly if you want to reach the remote tip or stop at various kauri groves and beaches scattered on and off the road. Roads can be hairy. **Rent-a-Dent,** 503 Queen St. (tel. 868 8838 or 0800 736 822), starts at $40 per day plus 20¢ per km. Discounts after 3 days. Also **Michael Saunders Motors,** 201 Pollen St. (tel. 0800 111 110), rents from $40 per day.

Bike Rental: Bike touring is a popular way to see the Coromandel, if you've got the legs for it—many roads are hilly, unsealed, and winding. **Price and Richards** (with the sign "Sports Cycles Mowers"), 430 Pollen St. (tel. 868 6157), rents 21-speed mountain bikes ($20 per day) with all necessary gear. If you have the desire but not the legs, rent a power cycle (motorized mountain bike) from the Visitors Centre for $40 per day.

Taxis: Thames Gold Cabs (tel. 868 6037). Open M-Th 8am-late, F-Sa 8am-2am.

Hitchhiking: Thumbers report that it's usually no problem catching a ride to Coromandel town, even in winter. Just thumb up the northbound lane on either Pollen or Queen St.

Currency Exchange: BNZ (tel. 868 6020), at the corner of Sealey and Pollen St. Open M-F 9am-4:30pm, Tu-W 9:30am-4:30pm. Get sufficient money in Thames, as there are only four other **ATMs** farther up the peninsula.

Police: (24hr. tel. 868 6040), on Queen St. across from the Mall.

Medical Services: Thames Medical Centre (24hr. tel. 868 9444), on Rolleston St. just down from the hospital's side entrance. A **pharmacy** (tel. 868 9095) is in Goldfields Mall. Open M-Th 8:30am-5:30pm, F 8:30am-8pm, Sa-Su 9am-4pm. The **Thames Hospital** (tel. 868 6550) is on MacKay St., parallel to Pollen St.

Post Office: (tel. 868 7850), on Pollen St. between Mary and Sealey St. Open M-F 8:30am-5pm, Sa 9am-1pm.

Internet: The Information Centre charges $2.50 per 15min. Just a few blocks north on Pollen St., **United Video** (tel. 868 8999) charges $9 per hr.

Telephone Code: 07.

🏠 ACCOMMODATIONS AND FOOD

B&Bs and homestays come out of the native woodwork in the summer when you need to book far, far ahead (ask at the Visitor Centre). Several motor camps lie along the coastal road between Thames and Coromandel, and DOC runs eight **campgrounds** in the Kauaeranga Valley (see **Coromandel Forest Park,** p. 135).

Sunkist Lodge (VIP), 506 Brown St. (tel. 868 8808). Veer onto Brown St. off Queen St. at the Mall, and head up about 4 blocks. This former gold-rush hotel comes with its own

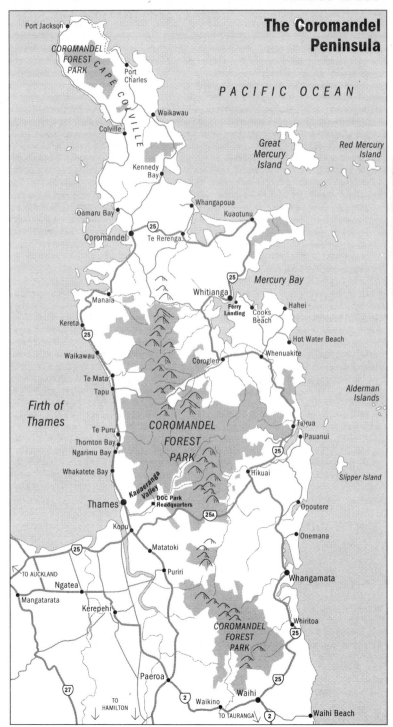

The Coromandel Peninsula

PACIFIC OCEAN

NORTH ISLAND

Port Jackson

COROMANDEL FOREST PARK

Port Charles

CAPE COLVILLE

Waikawau

Colville

Great Mercury Island

Red Mercury Island

Kennedy Bay

Whangapoua

Kuaotunu

Oamaru Bay

25

Coromandel

Te Rerenga

25

Mercury Bay

Whitianga

Manaia

Ferry Landing

Cooks Beach

Hahei

Kereta

25

Hot Water Beach

Waikawau

Coroglen

Whenuakite

Te Mata

Tapu

Firth of Thames

COROMANDEL FOREST PARK

Alderman Islands

Te Puru

Tairua

Thornton Bay

Pauanui

Ngarimu Bay

25

Whakatete Bay

Hikuai

Slipper Island

Kauaeranga Valley

DOC Park Headquarters

Thames

25A

Opoutere

Kopu

Onemana

25

Matatoki

TO AUCKLAND

Puriri

Ngatea

Whangamata

Mangatarata

Kerepehi

Whiritoa

25

COROMANDEL FOREST PARK

Paeroa

27

2

25

TO HAMILTON

Waikino

Waihi

2

TO TAURANGA

Waihi Beach

resident ghost. Sturdy bunks and a sun-kissed second-floor front deck. Internet. Large dorms $14; 4-bed shares $16; twins and doubles $35.

Dickson Holiday Park (YHA) (tel. 868 7308; fax 868 7319), on Victoria St. 3km north of town off SH25. A bit far from town, the beautiful streamside location provides access to great bushwalks, and distance hardly matters with free bikes and free pickup. Game room, solar-heated pool, and both a regular indoor and outdoor "pioneer" kitchen. Metered showers. Mixed dorms, one with triple-decker bunks $15; simple tourist cabins and on-site caravans with kitchenette for 2 $38; tent sites $9 per person.

Adventure Backpackers Coromandel, 476 Pollen St. (tel. 868 6200). Formerly the old Imperial Hotel, this new, centrally located hostel offers a bit of history with an overnight stay. Walk past the old-fashioned cursive labels etched into the bathroom doors, down the old staircase draped with its original rug (ostentatious in its own time, now torn at the crease of each step), and through the dim lobby with two adjoining bars. Dorms $15 (over bar $13); singles $22; doubles $40.

Brookby Motel, 102 Redwood Ln. (tel. 868 6663). From Pollen St., turn on Sealey St. and walk to Rolleston St. (2 streets over). Turn left, veer up Karaka St., and soon Redwood Ln. is on the left. Set next to a stream and backing into bush, this place is well-equipped, extremely clean, and only a few minutes from town. Planned renovation may spruce up uninspired rooms (4 units) with kitchens, TVs, electric blankets, and separate bedrooms. Singles and doubles $65-70, winter $55-60; compact studio room for 2 without kitchen $60.

🗓️ 🍴 FOOD AND NIGHTLIFE

Thame's takeaways and cafes line **Pollen St.** and fill the food court of the Mall. For dinner, many hotel bars have affordable, standard meals. For good food at any time of the day, **Sealey Cafe,** 109 Sealey St. (tel. 868 8641), serves up some class with jazz photos on the mixed brick and plaster wall, and neat wooden tables. Most mains run $9.50-12.50. For breakfast or lunch, the pleasant **Food for Thought,** 574 Pollen St. (tel. 868 6065), stocks a fresh counter full of healthy vegetarian fare every day. The lunch selection includes a kumara bake or a small veggie pizza ($2.80), topped off with bulky muffins ($1.50) and a better-than-average herbal tea and coffee selection. (Open M-F 7:30am-4:30pm.) Whether you eat in or out, flounder, oysters, mussels, and scallops, all of which are locally caught, are worth trying. Save some cash and fill up your trundler at the **Pak 'N Save** (tel. 868 9565), in Goldfields Mall (open M-Tu 8:30am-6pm, W-Th 8:30am-6:30pm, F 8:30am-8pm, Sa-Su 9am-5pm). Bordering Sealey St., **The Udder Bar** is a popular cafe/restaurant, open daily with a sit-down, mellow crowd. More action-packed and open only Thursday through Saturday nights, the **Krazy Cow Bar** encourages rowdy crowds to dance on the tables and write on the walls.

👁️ 🧗 SIGHTS AND ACTIVITIES

One of the most tempting activities in Thames is leaving it, because the winding, narrow, and scenic 55km drive to Coromandel, with rocky inlets and small bays, is so lovely. The views over **Coromandel Harbour** when the road turns inland will undoubtedly pull you over. Notable trees on the way can be found at the **Waiomu Kauri Grove,** one of the peninsula's finest old-growth stands (1hr. walk through farmland and bush from the end of Waiomu Creek Rd., 15km from Thames). About 5km further is the turn-off for the **Tapu-Coroglen Rd.,** which cuts across the peninsula to rejoin SH25. Head up it for a few kilometers and look for the sign marking a steep 10-minute walk through gorgeous native bush to the 2500-year-old "square kauri tree," the 15th largest in the Coromandel. It's worth the quick detour.

Aside from the view offered by nearby tramps, there isn't much in the way of sights here. But Thames's gold-mining history sustains a few attractions. An impressive memorial to the 19th-century industry is the **Gold Mine and Stamper Battery** (tel. 868 7748), on SH25 at the north end of town. (Open for 30min. tours Dec.

THE HARD ROCK BLUES If you've got visions of kiwi-sized chunks of gold plopping into Thames miners' hands, think again—though the hills were rich, it was never an easy process to extract the gold of the Coromandel Peninsula (it's found only in quartz rock). Eking it out of such hard rock required use of massive rods called stampers that weighed as much as 450kg and could hammer down quartz chunks over 60 times per minute. The resulting powder was ejected with water onto a shaking table where the grains of quartz, fool's gold, and the real aurum were separated by weight. The refuse was dumped into the local waters, and built up so much that many houses are now built on the extended coast. Workers who didn't labor in the death-hastening mines could expect to go deaf just manning the stamper batteries (the noise quotient would put even the most vigorous modern rock concert to shame). At its peak, from 1870-71, there were over 800 stampers running 24 hours per day, six days per week in Thames, and rumor has it that none could sleep on Sundays when the mind-numbing clamor ground to a halt.

26-Jan. 31 daily 10am-4pm; Feb.-May daily 11am-3pm; and winter weekends with variable hours. Admission $5, children $2.) The **Thames Historical Museum** (tel. 868 8509), at the corner of Pollen and Cochrane St., provides a less interactive look into the past with a display on the massive mining and kauri logging industries (open daily 1-4pm; admission $2.50). The **WWI Peace Memorial** atop Monument Hill, lit up at night, gives expansive views of both the town and the Firth (up Waiotahi Rd., where Pollen St. meets Queen St. at the north end of town). The **Karaka Bird Hide,** built with compensation funds from the French government for the bombing of the **Rainbow Warrior** (see p. 100), stands just past Goldfields Mall. A short walk through the mangroves takes you to the gazebo to look for shorebirds on the extensive mud flats (donations are requested). The best two hours are on either side of high tide.

Though most people head up the **Kauaeranga Valley** for tramping, several other area walks are worth noting. Best is **Rocky's Goldmine Trail** (3hr. loop), which starts and ends at the Dickson Holiday Park, with great views, green bush, and refreshing streams. The area, however, is riddled with old and dangerous mine shafts. Stay on the path, as some are hidden. The track emerges on Tararu Creek Rd. From there, turn left to go back or right to reach a well-kept secret, the 3m **Black Hole Waterfall** that slides over into the deep pool below (about 2.6km up Tararu Creek Rd. from the entrance to the **Dickson Holiday Park;** ask there for more specific directions). Also at the Holiday Park is a new **Tropical Butterfly Garden** (tel. 868 8080), with 15 different species of the colorful bugs fluttering around a humid greenhouse (open Sept.-July 9am-5pm; admission $8).

COROMANDEL FOREST PARK

The jagged hills of the discontinuous 72,000-hectare Coromandel Forest Park are thick with regenerating bush, tangled with creepers, and sluiced by high waterfalls and small, fern-lined creeks. Hiding deep within the hills that stretch up the peninsula's volcanic backbone are many of the old kauri dams and mine shafts, side by side with the few remaining patches of original forest. Active replanting efforts of native species are underway, as are rigorous pest management techniques (especially in the north, where possums have not fully infiltrated). You'll find plenty of walks in the Kauaeranga Valley east of Thames, as well as some remote walkways in the peninsular fingertip.

🄵 ORIENTATION AND PRACTICAL INFORMATION. The **Kauaeranga Visitors Centre** (tel. 868 6381) lies 13km up Kauaeranga Valley Rd., a winding half-paved job that branches off at the BP station at the south end of Thames (open daily 8am-4pm). Stop in before you head up to clarify your plans or fill out help forms.

There's also a small **DOC office** with irregular hours in the town of Coromandel. Getting to Kauaeranga Valley without your own transportation is a mild pain, especially at non-peak times (though on weekends year-round and in summer it's generally hitchable). Thumbers should arrange a return ride or they run the risk of getting stuck 9km from park headquarters at the end of the road where most trails start. For $15 (return $25), Jason Donald from **Back Country Trekking** (tel. 868 7597) will take you to the trails; and for $40, he'll guide you on a half-day tramp. **The Sunkist Lodge** occasionally runs a shuttle service (return $20). **Thames Gold Cabs** can also take you up for a heady $36 one-way. With your own car it's no problem.

▐ ACCOMMODATIONS. DOC campgrounds are liberally scattered in the park, with eight off the road up Kauaeranga Valley and four at the tip (see p. 135). The **Kauaeranga** sites are basic ($5). The only hut in the park is the **Pinnacles Hut,** a rugged Ritz with views, a year-round warden, wood stove, gas cooking (bring your own utensils), 80 mattresses with fitted sheets, solar lighting, and toilets ($12; book in advance; annual or other hut passes not applicable). It's about a three-hour climb from the road end, including swing bridges and 1080 steps carved into rock. Three other primitive, remote areas for camping are in the vicinity ($6).

▐ ACTIVITIES. Numerous trails criss-cross the Coromandel and signs of human influence (including old mine shafts and deteriorating kauri dams) are everywhere, making much of the park historically as well as naturally attractive. **Kauaeranga Valley** is the most hiked spot, with walks heading off the road. A five-minute hop from the Visitor Centre leads to an old intact kauri dam and the bludgeoned stream bed it helped carve out. A trip from the **Wainora campground** (return 2-3hr.) leads to two of the valley's only surviving large kauri. **The Kauaeranga Kauri Trail** heads up to Pinnacles Hut and the **Pinnacles** themselves, sheer jagged bluffs arcing out of emerald water like fins. It's well worth the 1000-plus stairs through fern-laden regenerating bush, by deep gorges, and over swing bridges. Atop the Pinnacles, an hour from the hut, the views all across the peninsula will take away any breath you have left after scrambling up ladders and a steep rocky trail. Some do it as a day-hike, others as an overnight. The **Kauaeranga River,** running along the road up the valley, sports tons of swimming holes. Find your own, or check out **Hoffman's Pool,** a two-minute walk down the Nature Walk with deep greenish waters and jumping rocks. Rockhounds get a big kick out of the Coromandel: geological hammers (undoubtedly the first thing you packed) are allowed in the park and up to 2kg of surface rock can be removed per day.

FALLEN GIANTS

As stunningly scenic as it may be, the Coromandel is in many ways a case study in human greed—its very name is taken from a Royal Navy vessel that collected massive kauri logs from the peninsula in 1820. The knot-free wood and huge, straight trunks of these noble trees were coveted for ship masts and buildings. By the 1870s, the last of the easily extractable stands disappeared, and logging moved into the area's mountainous ridges, where the insatiable quest for timber led to ever-more-elaborate innovations in tree removal. To get trees off the remote hilltops, logs were dragged, trammed, or rolled into streambeds where they accumulated behind dams. As water built up, loggers tripped the dams, releasing floods of trees that crashed down the valleys in a wasteful process that damaged the logs and gouged out the streambed. Between logging and burning the land for farming, less than 1% of the region's forest survived the short-sighted exploitation. Although today you can see more of the original kauri wood in San Francisco and Auckland buildings than in the forest, much of the irreparably altered (but regenerating) landscape on the peninsula has been set aside as part of the Coromandel Forest Park.

COROMANDEL

The isolated and peaceful town of Coromandel (pop. 1800) unites artisans, individualists, and country bumpkins in their love of location. With the mesmerizingly blue, island-dotted waters of Coromandel Harbour and the deep greens of the hills sweeping above town, there's not much else to do but be visually stimulated by the environs and aesthetically pleased by the plethora of little craft shops.

◪ PRACTICAL INFORMATION. The **Coromandel Information Centre** (tel. 866 8598) lies on Kapanga Rd. just across the creek (open daily 9am-5pm, winter M-F 9am-5pm, Sa-Su 11am-3pm). The small **DOC office,** with irregular hours, is in the same building. Like most of the Peninsula, transport services change rapidly and vary considerably by season—check with the Info Centre for up-to-date schedules. The **InterCity Coromandel Busplan** bus passes through to **Whitianga** (1hr., 11:30am daily, winter Su-F, $16 if not part of Busplan), continuing to **Thames** (3hr., $14). You can go direct to **Thames** with **Turley Murphy** (1hr., Su-F 7:30am, $12), and on to **Hamilton** (3½hr., $34). **Coromandel Bus Service** (run by Rod Carter from Carter Tours) goes to **Whitianga** (M, W, and F 8:30am; $13) and to **Fletcher's Bay** (M, W, and F noon; $17). The **Pakatoa Cat Ferry** runs daily in summer (Th-Su in winter) to **Auckland** (2hr., $31, children $15.50). Purchase tickets from the Info Centre. Rental cars from **Rental Car Centre** (tel. 866 8626 or 0800 736 823) can be delivered to Coromandel from their base in Thames (standard economy vehicles from $59 a day). **Hitchhiking,** which Let's Go does not recommend, is reportedly easy to Thames and only slightly more difficult to Whitianga. The 25A Rd. that turns off just past the fire station on Tiki Rd. is more heavily traveled and considered a better spot than the 309 Rd. Hitching northward in winter is difficult. **Biking** is a good option: Whitianga is a 2½-hour ride; Colville 2½-hour; and Fletcher Bay 5-hour. Other services include: **BNZ** (tel. 866 8876), at the corner of Tiki and Kapanga Rd. (**no ATM;** open M-F 10am-3pm); **police station** (tel. 866 8777), next to the Information Centre; and the **post office,** 190 Kapanga Rd. (tel. 866 8865; open M-F 9am-5pm). **Telephone Code:** 07.

◪ ACCOMMODATIONS. Bring cash; almost none of the hostels (and not many of the motels) have credit card or Eftpos capabilities. Homestays spring up in the holiday season, often in the homes of local artists trying to supplement their incomes. Book ahead in January and February.

About 1km north, at the corner of Rings Rd. and Frederick St., sit the three airy white cottages of **White House Backpackers (VIP)** (tel. 866 8468). Owner Richard organizes driving and fishing trips and group trips anywhere. (Free pickup. Internet. Free bikes. 4-bed dorms $14; 2-bed dorms $16.50; doubles $30.) Up a steep little hill on Alfred St. off Rings Rd., 1km from the town center, sits ▨**Celadon Motel** (tel. 866 8058). You'll never want to leave these lovely, self-contained cottages glowing with shiny wood, original artwork, and unbeatable views. Hospitable and conversational owner Ray Morley even gives pottery lessons. (Cottages $90, winter $70, extra person $10. Private B&B units in main house $79, winter $65; without breakfast $65, winter $50. $5 off with *Let's Go.*) **Tidewater Tourist Park (YHA),** 270 Tiki Rd. (tel. 866 8888), is immaculate. Sauna and mountain bike rentals are available. Try not to track mud into the spacious white tourist flats. Book far in advance from December to March, though there's generally a bit of room on the grass expanse for tents ($9). (Compact shares $15; twins and doubles $34.) To get to **Tui Lodge,** 600 Whangapoua Rd. (tel. 866 8237), from Kapanga/Wharf Rd. turn onto Tiki Rd. by the BNZ, then left on to Whangapoua Rd. The lodge is 500m on the right, down a gravel drive. With sheep grazing in the front pasture and an orchard in back, adjustment to Coromandel time is made easy. (Free laundry and in-season fruit. Sauna $2. Dorms $16; twins and doubles $30; tents $8; private, self-contained camper unit $12.) In peak months you'll be good buddies with the tent next door at **Long Bay Motor Camp** (tel. 866 8720), 3km out on Wharf/Long Bay Rd. But you both will have beautiful views of blue waters, and access to the Kauri-lined 30-minute tramp that passes the secluded back-to-basics **Tucks Bay** campground. (Metered showers. Tent sites $9 per person, powered $11. Tucks Bay tent sites $8.)

◨ FOOD. The Pepper Tree Restaurant and Bar (tel. 866 8211), on Kapanga Rd. in the town center, specializes in fresh seafood and organic beef. You'll have to shell out a bit (the pub menu is less expensive), but the food is memorable. The mussel fritters ($13) are a must. (Open daily from 9am, winter from 11am.) For veggie options or more affordable dinners, head to **The Success Cafe,** 104 Kapanga Rd. (tel. 866 7100). With a specialty of mussel chowder ($6.50), Success also serves up oysters grilled with bacon and spinach ($9). (Outdoor seating. Open F-Su 10am-late, winter W-M from 10am.) If bread is all you need to survive, the **Bakehouse** on Wharf Rd. has a full range of cheap rolls and large loaves as well as hot pies ($2) and tasty pastries (open daily 7:30am-4pm). **Price Cutter** (tel. 866 8669), on Kapanga Rd. just before the bridge, sells ice cream cones on warm days when school lets out (open M-F 7:30am-6pm, Sa 7:30am-6pm, Su 8am-5:30pm). Organic produce is sold at **Myrrh and Cinnamon Health Foods,** 65 Wharf St. (tel. 866 7553).

◨ ⚑ SIGHTS AND ACTIVITIES. With so many artists congregating in this inspiring peninsula, the crafty side of things is unavoidable. Local artists create and display their pottery, weaving, embroidery, sculpture, woodwork, and more in the area's many shops. **Weta Shop** (tel. 866 8823), on Kapanga Rd., is the best of the lot, offering quality over quantity with both local and national art, crafts, and sculpture in the delightful outdoor courtyard. Aside from crafts, Coromandel's biggest attraction, the **Driving Creek Railway** (tel./fax 866 8703), 3km north of town, might bring back childhood memories. Begun as a pet project in 1975 to extract clay and pinewood kiln fuel from his hills, owner and potter Barry Brickell has spent 20 years developing a narrow-gauge railway snaking up through glowingly green forest, through tunnels, around spirals, and over bridges to the views from the terminus. (Admission $10, children $5, families $22.) About a 30-minute walk from town, the **Coromandel Gold Stamper Battery** (tel. 866 7186), on Buffalo Rd. off Rings Rd. north of town, is operational and set in a suitably verdant nook with a short bush walk and New Zealand's largest working water wheel (open daily 10am-5pm; in winter ask at the Visitor Centre before heading up; admission $5).

A short but terrific 25-minute stroll through the **Long Bay Scenic Reserve** to a grove of young kauris starts at the Long Bay campground. It winds back along the rocky waters of the bay, where the walk can stretch into a lazy afternoon of sunning and exploring. For the best and steepest tramp in town, **Castle Rock** is an exposed vertebra of the peninsula's backbone, yielding 360° views of the peninsula to which a camera can't do justice. The trail (return 2hr.) is a bit far from town; driving down 309 Rd. to the trailhead is best, but a rigorous 2-hour bike trip will get you there (much of it uphill). The Castle Rock trail is just one of the attractions along the horrifically narrow and gravel **309 Rd.,** which branches off 4km south of town to cross over to Whitianga. About 8km down from Coromandel, be sure to stop at the **Waiau Kauri Grove.** Walk for ten minutes to join other gape-mouthed visitors in this cathedral of soaring trees that once covered the peninsula, and is now preserved only in such scattered pockets of grandeur. If you have no transport, try **Carter Tours** (tel. 866 8045 or mobile 025 937 259), which runs trips to just about wherever (4hr. trips $30-40). On the other side of town, a short but terrific stroll (25min.) through the **Long Bay Scenic Reserve** to a grove of young kauris starts at the Long Bay campground. It winds back along the rocky waters of the bay, where the walk can stretch into a lazy afternoon of sunning and exploring.

NEAR COROMANDEL: THE NORTHERN TIP

North of Coromandel, travelers are on their own. There are no comfy lodgings, no cafes, no quaint craft shops or gold-stamper batteries. Here, the wealth is of unmitigated natural beauty: jumbled green hills, deserted crescents of bays, and a wild coastline broken up only by sheep placidly gnawing on undulating farmland. The spectacular **Coromandel Walkway,** between Fletcher Bay and Stony Bay, is worth any effort it takes to get there.

GETTING AROUND. The quality of roads in the region is inversely proportional to the "gasp" factor—the harrowing, narrow gravel roads add to the charm, though they have a tendency to flood out in rain. One road winds up the west side to Fletcher Bay at the tip of the Tip; another branches off just past **Colville** (28km north of Coromandel), and finds its way to Stony Bay. Public transport is slim. Before heading out in your own rental car, make sure there's no fine print in your rental agreement about this area. **Coromandel Buses** (tel. 866 8468), in Coromandel, runs a shuttle up to **Fletcher Bay** (M, W, and F; $17). Winter **hitchhiking** in the Northern Tip is all but impossible, though some hitch in summer (once past Colville, thumbers should be sure that their ride is going all the way). Mountain biking is a great but very strenuous way to circuit the tip on the track connecting Fletcher Bay and Stony Bay (5hr. ride to Fletcher Bay).

ACCOMMODATIONS. Fletcher Bay Backpackers (tel. 866 8989) has an enviable location, next to the Coromandel Walkway trailhead. Near the ocean, Fletcher's is a base for tramps into the bush or along the coast as well as prime territory for peaceful meditation. Owned by the DOC, Fletcher's has 16 beds; bookings are essential. (Dorms $13.) The **DOC** (tel. 866 6852) manages five basic campgrounds in the northern region ($7, families $15). Check in with the DOC to book the one at **Waikawau Bay** during the summer holidays. The well-stocked **Colville General Store** (tel. 866 6805) is the last place for groceries and gas on the Tip (open daily 8:30am-5pm, winter M-Th 8:30am-5pm, F 8:30am-6pm, Sa 9am-5pm, Su 9am-4:30pm).

ACTIVITIES. The peninsula's crowning track, the 10.7km **Coromandel Walkway** (3hr. one-way) explores lonely bays and coves, passes turquoise waters along the coast between Fletcher Bay and Stony Bay, and dips into inlets and bushy valleys. Other than a few short, stiff climbs, it's not difficult, though it can be a bit hairy in winter before it's cleared for the summer season (it overgrows quickly, and can get muddy). You can return from the walkway by the same route, on the masochistic 7km mountain bike track, or have someone pick you up at the other end. **Carter Tours** (tel. 866 8045 or mobile 025 937 259) will do dropoffs and pickups in summer ($50, minimum 2 people). If you have to return to a parked car, but don't want to go all the way and back, start from the eastern Stony Bay side, walk for an hour or two and turn around; many regard this half as the best part of the total hike. Another great tramp goes up the peninsula's tallest mountain, 892m **Mt. Moehau.** As the top is Maori land, you're requested to turn back just as you get tantalizingly close. Approachable from several points, the peak is perhaps more easily reached from **Te Hope Stream,** 12km north of Colville (return 5hr.). The more strenuous **Stony Bay** route follows an exposed ridge (taking most of a day).

WHITIANGA

Breaking out of the bush, onto the eastern coast of the peninsula, you'll notice that the mud and rocks of the west have given way to soft sand. Among the dunes, in attractive **Mercury Bay,** Whitianga ("fit-ee-ANG-guh") is the Coromandel's second largest town (pop. 4000) after Thames. A small town born of timber (over 500 million feet of kauri were cut in 60 years), Whitianga is now the Coromandel's main resort town, surviving on tourism. Its population increases tenfold during the summer, when it seems like every angler, boater, and sun worshiper from Auckland descends to plumb the rich, deep-sea fishing waters, explore the nearby marine reserve, or laze on the many beaches.

ORIENTATION AND PRACTICAL INFORMATION. Whitianga sits where **Mercury Bay's** sweep of palm-studded beach meets the calm waters of **Whitianga Harbour.** The route to **Hahei, Hot Water Beach,** and points beyond is a lengthy detour around the harbor, but the pedestrian ferry crossing takes only a minute. **SH25**

runs along the beach as **Buffalo Rd.,** and turns south to become **Albert St.,** the town's main drag.

The **Whitianga Information Centre,** 66 Albert St. (tel. 866 5555; fax 866 2205), is run under the umbrella of the Business Association—be sure to ask the staff about all your accommodation options, because the brochures only list members of the association. Internet access is $3 for 15 minutes. (Open Dec.-Mar. daily 8am-6pm; Apr.-Nov. M-F 9am-5pm, Sa-Su 9am-1pm; closed Su in July and Aug.). Book transportation at the Info Centre or through **Travel Options** (tel. 866 4397), diagonal from the Information Centre (open M-F 9am-5pm, Sa 10am-noon). **Air Coromandel** (tel. 0800 900 600) flies from the airstrip off SH25 south of town to **Auckland** (30min., 2 per day, $89) and **Great Barrier Island** (30min., 3 per week, $89). More flights and destinations may be added during the summer season. The **ferry** (tel. 866 5472) heads across the harbor's neck to **Ferry Landing** (runs 7:30am-11:30pm, winter 7:30am-noon and 1-6:30pm, plus limited evening service; return $2). The **Coromandel Busplan** buses leave from the Information Centre for Dalmeny Corner (2 per day, 7:15am and 1:15pm, winter 3 per week) with a connection to **Thames** via **Hahei** and **Hot Water Beach** (1hr., $24). To get to Whangamata, take the bus to **Hikuai** (1:15pm) to be picked up by InterCity affiliate **Whangamata Tours** (tel. 866 4397; 1½hr., 2:15pm, $29). The **Westpac Trust Bank** (tel. 866 2701), on Albert St. by Monk St., has a **24hr. ATM** (bank open M-Tu and Th-F 9am-4:30pm, W 9:30am-4:30pm). **Mercury Bay Taxis** (tel. 866 5643) will also do a run to **Coromandel** for $50 per van load (van fits 10). **Whitianga Mowers and Cycles,** 15 Coghill St. (tel. 866 5435), a block from the Information Centre, rents mountain bikes. (Half-day $10, full day $20; deposit $25. Open Dec.-Jan. daily; Feb.-Nov. irregular hours roughly M-F 8:30am-5pm, Sa 9am-noon.) Your friendly neighborhood **police** (24hr. tel. 866 4000) are on Campbell St., around the corner from the **post office** (tel./fax 866 4006; open M-F 8:30am-5pm). **Telephone Code:** 07.

▐▝ ACCOMMODATIONS. As a summer resort town, Whitianga has more than its share of motels, motor camps, and other lodgings. There are three good hostel options. The independent traveler's choice, about 1km from downtown, is **Coromandel Backpacker's Lodge,** 46 Buffalo Beach Rd. (tel./fax 866 5380), a sea-green abode with the cheapest ocean views in town year-round. Airy dorms upstairs have window seats; downstairs, twins and doubles offer privacy and separate communal areas, some with their own private bathroom, kitchen, and shower. Enthusiastic owners, a courtesy van, and a miniature visitors center are welcome amenities. Rent a bike or enjoy free use of kayaks, surfboards, fishing rods, and shovels for Hot Water Beach. (Dorms $17; twins and doubles $40.) A javelin toss from the town center, off Albert St., lies **The Cat's Pyjamas Backpackers Lodge (Nomads),** 4 Monk St. (tel./fax 866 4663). Two immense ginger cats sidle around this unassuming hostel with a simple residential house feel. Ask Buster, the affable owner, about scenic flights in his Cessna, and take a peek at the plane he's building out back. (Dorms $16; twins and doubles $36; tent sites $10.) Catering almost exclusively to the busloads of Kiwi Experience bar hoppers, **Buffalo Peaks Lodge,** 12 Albert St. (tel. 866 2933), shows none of the wear and tear you might expect. Bright and clean with an internal courtyard, spa, and lively murals of New Zealand icons, Buffalo Peaks may be worth the reservation it will likely take to arrange a bed. (Dorms $16-17; doubles $40). **The Mercury Bay Motor Camp,** 121 Albert St. (tel. 866 5579), is a half kilometer south of the town center, with standard motor camp facilities. Showers are metered in summer. (Spiffy tourist flat singles $40, for 2 $60 (in peak season $110); compact cabins for 2 $40, extra person $10, children $5, in peak season minimum $60; grassy tent and caravan sites $10.)

◖ FOOD. Dining out is basically a contradiction in terms in Whitianga. There is, fortunately, a diamond in the rough—the little overgrown cottage housing lovely **Cafe Nina** (tel. 866 5440), on Victoria St. at the back side of the park. The savory fruit muffins will melt in your mouth. Lunches ($6-9) have some veggie fare, as well as takeaway sandwiches and cakes. (Open M-Sa 9am-5:30pm, Su 8am-4pm; lunch served noon-2:30pm; later hours in summer.) For dinner, **Smitty's Bar and Grille,** 37 Albert St. (tel. 866 4647), has good greasy, fried fare. Bulky burgers and a double-decker BLT are under $7. (Open M-F 4pm-1am, Sa noon-1am, Su from 5pm). There are also a few standard takeaway and pub options. **Pratty's Takeaways** (tel. 866 5557), on Albert St. by the Esplanade, is the average dive. **Four Square** (tel. 866 5777), on Albert St. by the Information Centre, for groceries (open M-F 7am-8pm, Sa 7am-8pm, winter M-F 7am-6pm, Sa 8am-6pm). Fruits and veggies can be had at **W. Fresh** across the street (open M-F 7:30am-5:30pm, Sa 7:30am-1pm).

SIGHTS AND ACTIVITIES. An excellent option for the painful day after too much sun and too little sunscreen is a chance to do your own bone carving. Maurice of **Bay Carving** (tel. 866 4021), opposite the wharf and beside the museum on the Esplanade, will help you choose from an array of designs or create your own, plunking you down in the studio with a chunk of beef bone, dentist's drills, files, and sandpaper. The end result, from tracing paper to polished pendant in three hours or so, is amazingly satisfying. Designs (and tutelage) cost $25-45. Call ahead to schedule, especially in summer. (Open daily 9am-9pm.)

Head across the river on the ferry to follow the path in the small **Scenic Reserve** just to the right, leading along the water's edge up to the 24m bluff of **Whitianga Rock** (a historic Maori *pa* from which stone for the old ferry landing wharf was taken). The walk from **Ferry Landing** up to the **Shakespeare Lookout** is worth the hour or so it takes (you can also drive). Named for a certain resemblance to the Bard in its rocky profile, it's a jaunt along **Front Beach** to the crescent of **Flaxmill Bay,** and a steep meander up from the sign on the pohutukawa at the far end. The view from the top is expansive and includes, as a bonus, a clear view of **Lonely Bay** below—the only legal nude beach on the Coromandel. Bring your binoculars. Isolated from any unsightly view of buildings and roads, the pristine little cove's golden sands and turquoise surf are accessible only by boat, or by the steep footpath down from Shakespeare Lookout. The next beach over is **Cooks Beach,** a shallow 3km stretch of prime swimming. **Buffalo Beach,** directly on the shores of Whitianga, is named for the HMS Buffalo that wrecked there in 1840 while collecting kauri for England.

The untouched beauty of the peninsula is the perfect setting for a horse trek. **Twin Oaks** (tel. 866 5555), 9km north of town on the road to Kuaotunu, offers two-hour saunters for riders of any skill through farmland and to the top of a ridge with dramatic 360° views of the peninsula. (3 per day; less consistent in winter. Transport possible; call ahead. $30.) **Purangi Winery** (tel. 866 3724) is favorably situated on the main road between Ferry Landing and the Hahei and Hot Water Beach area (Hot Water Beach ConXtions stops here). The rustic, all-organic winery makes 23 varieties of fruit wines, ports, and liquers that you can taste all in succession. Because of the lack of preservatives, people say a little too much of Purangi's offerings won't give you a hangover. The passionfruit liquor and boysenberry port are particularly good. (Open for tastings daily 9am-9pm, winter 10am-5pm.)

It's that blue, blue water and what's in it that draws most people to the Mercury Bay area. With **Cathedral Cove Marine Reserve** nearby, the cluster of the Mercury Bay Islands off the coast, and thriving ocean life, every kind of water activity from snorkelling to banana boating can be found here. Whitianga is one of New Zealand's best bases for big game **fishing** from December to March. Ask around locally for recommended outfitters if you're planning on fishing, kayaking, or seeking Flipper and other marine mammals. There are even glass-bottomed boats. If rough seas turn your sights inland, abseiling and scenic flights are also possibilities. **Air Coromandel** (tel. 0800 900 600) flies all over the peninsula from $30 for a 15-minute hop to hour-long $99 flights up to the Northern Tip.

NEAR WHITIANGA: HAHEI

The name sounds like the sigh of inevitable contentment and the exclamation of finger-pointing glee that you'll likely utter while here: Hah-hey! In reality, it stems from Chief Hei of the Arawa's canoe that docked somewhere off the coast, a contraction of a name that in full means "the outward curve of Hei's nose." A nose by any other name would smell just as sweet in this blissful swath of sand made pink by crushed shells.

⌸ **GETTING AROUND. Hot Water Beach ConXtions** (tel. 866 2478) has great service to these parts, making a circuit between Ferry Landing, Hahei, Hot Water Beach, and Cooks Beach, with narration and short stops for lookouts on the way (summer 2-3 per day 7:30am-5:30pm). If low tide at Hot Water Beach is early, they arrange for a special earlier ferry run. The **Explorer Bus Pass** ($20) lets you on and off all day, or you can travel each segment independently. From the ferry to Hahei, it's $10, return $14. The drivers can help you figure out when to get the bus you want. ConXtions also meets the **InterCity** bus from Whitianga to Thames to bring people into Hahei or Hot Water Beach (return $16 to the bus).

⌸ **ACCOMMODATIONS.** ▨**Tatahi Lodge** (tel. 866 3992; fax 866 3993) is almost reason enough to stay in Hahei instead of Whitianga. Its lovely wood lodge, plush couches, lounge, and numerous windows are perfect for post-beach bliss. Bikes are available for hire. (Dorms $18; twins and doubles $40.) Not quite as spiffy is **Hahei Holiday Resort** and its accompanying **Cathedral Cove Backpackers Lodge (VIP)** (tel. 866 3889; fax 866 3098), at the end of Harsant Ave. off the town's main road. Dorms ($15) lie behind sliding Japanese screens, which are classy but don't quite meet the ceiling, while doubles and twins ($18) are more soundproof. Best of all, it's just over the dune from the beach. (Tent sites $10, powered $11; campervan sites $11, on-site vans $36; double cabins $36.)

⌸ **ACTIVITIES.** Hahei's beach, sheltered by offshore islands, is reportedly great for swimming but bad for surfing—many surfers instead head to **Hot Water Beach.** Once you get tired of tanning, point those feet in either direction and start walking. To the south rises a dramatic bluff, **Hereheretaura Point,** an understandably ideal spot for an old defensive Maori *pa;* cross the creek at the beach's end and follow the path up to the *pa* (30min.) for 360° views. To the north, around a green hill, gaze out at the small islands speckling the ocean and amble down to the Coromandel's ultimate poster: the **Cathedral Cove Marine Reserve (Te Whanganui-a-Hei).** To reach the majestic rock formations over the cove, you can either walk from the beach or turn left past the general store to reach the hour-long track (45min. from the carpark atop the hill) to the cove. The track passes through pastures and hundreds of descending steps, wending along through bush toward the jewels that make the track one of New Zealand's most visited. The white sands and lapping turquoise waters of **Gemstone Bay** and **Stingray Bay** beg a wade or a snorkel in their lucid waters but are themselves merely preludes to their neighbors: **Mare's Leg Cove** (so named by Cook for the now washed-away soaring 10m archway), and **Cathedral Cove** itself. With its pristine beach and arcing rocks, it's an idyllic spot of subtropical water hemmed by high white bluffs, accessible only though a stone archway carved out by the sea (which can fill to the waist at high tide). You can swim out to the warped stone formations, standing like forgotten sculptures in the shallows, or stand under the freshwater falls trickling over the white cliffs.

Nigel and his **Hahei Explorer** (tel. 866 3910) will help those unable to make the trek to Cathedral Cave by foot (Dec.-Feb. $12.50, return $20). At any time of year you can take one of his spectacular scenic trips (1hr., $35) to explore the local islands, hidden caves and archways, and a spectacular 30m blowhole. Though the little rigid-hull inflatable boats fit only seven and bounce in high waves, they can go anywhere, and you'd surely never find all the excitement (or pull 360s) on your own (4 per day, winter usually on demand). He also rents mountain bikes and snorkel gear (both $25 per day).

NEAR WHITIANGA: HOT WATER BEACH

Imagine a beach where you could take a little shovel, dig a little hole, and watch hot water fill in to create your own ocean-side thermal pool. You can stop imagining—it's true. Proving once again that Mother Nature can out-do the resort industry, the 30-50m golden crescent of steaming sands is a free spa, percolating with water as hot as 65°C. Rent a cheap shovel from the beachfront store (open daily 9am-5pm), and for two hours on either side of low tide you can soak in your own dug-out series of pools while watching for dolphins or surfers offshore. Although cyclones in early 1997 removed several meters of sand, letting the tide come in too far to dig pools in the beach, the absolute must-do of the Coromandel is building up again. That said, the pools don't always work; locals say 60-70% of the year, mother nature cooperates, but sometimes, conditions don't allow a soak. While it's unpredictable, your chances are better in summer, when yours probably won't be the only set of legs poking up out of the sand, as 1500 people simultaneously try to create pools in the somewhat limited space. The beach is beautiful, but the rips, reefs, and sandbars that give good surfing breaks also make for treacherous swimming. **Hot Water Beach ConXtions** (tel. 866 2473) runs by several times daily on its circuit ($20 Explorer pass), and also picks up from the holiday park to meet **InterCity** at Dalmeny Corner (1-2 per day, return $15) on its way to Thames. They rent shovels for $2, as well. You can have dibs on the best holes at the beachfront at **Hot Water Beach Holiday Park** (tel. 866 3735), a small and tree-lined park that can cram up to 400 in its tent, caravan, and campervan sites. If it's high tide, there's consolation at the indoor thermal pools. (Caravans and campervan sites $12, winter $8-10; tourist flats (max. 8) are $80-100.)

WHANGAMATA

Whangamata's (Wahn-ga-mah-TAH) four kilometers of white sand sweeping around an island-studded bay are known from here to Raglan as one of the North Island's top surf spots. Outside the summer crunch of surfers and vacationers, small Whangamata remains sleepily residential, carefree, and full of easygoing locals. You're always within a board's length of beach and bush.

⑦ ORIENTATION AND PRACTICAL INFORMATION. Snug against its boomerang of beach at the mouth of the long and narrow **Whangamata Harbour** (for which a controversial and snazzy new marina has been proposed), the town is a maze of residential streets. Any and all action centers on **Port Rd.,** the main street that runs into SH25 at either end. Moored at 616 Port St. is the **Whangamata Information Centre** (tel. 865 8340), a low-key volunteer center (open M-Sa 9am-5pm, Su 10am-1pm). No major bus lines come directly to Whangamata; local shuttles carry passengers out to meet them. Make arrangements with **Whangamata Travel and Services,** 640 Port St. (tel. 865 8776; open M-F 9am-5pm). **Whangamata Tours** (tel. 865 7088) offers a shuttle out to the bump in the road that is **Hikuai** as well as to **Opoutere** ($8, students $6) to meet the **InterCity** bus to Thames (30min., $13) or to **Waihi** (30min., 2 per day, $13) for connections to **Tauranga** and points further afield. To get to **Whitianga,** you must wait three hours at Hikuai for the 4pm bus from Thames—don't try to defy the Coromandel's clockwise transport system. Other services include: **Westpac Trust Bank** (tel. 865 9771; open M-F 9am to 4:30pm, W from 9:30am); **post shop** (tel./fax 865 8230), on Port St. by the bank (open M-F 8:30am-5pm, Sa 9am-noon); and **Internet** at **Bartley Internet & Graphics,** 712 Port Rd. (tel. 865 8832; open M-F 9am-8pm, winter until 5pm). **Telephone Code:** 07.

⚑ ACCOMMODATIONS. Dude, you could imitate the local surfers and hole up in your car, or you could take your pick of Whangamata's lodgings. The pine-green dome at the **Bedshed** (tel. 0800 659 580), on Port St., 500m from the town center, houses the most upscale backpackers lodge you're likely to see, with wall-to-wall carpeting and a surround-sound video theater. (Shares from $23, winter $18; doubles from $55, winter $40; motel units from $80.) By the beach on Beverly Terr., and behind the Pricecutters on Ocean Rd., you'll find the **Whangamata Backpackers Hostel** (tel. 865 8323). You won't be afraid to toss a wetsuit over the mismatched chairs and beds in this tired but comfy house with the ocean a minute away. Low-key owners Barbara and Pauline will agreeably lend sporting gear. (All beds $15.) Park your tent across the fence from chomping sheep at the **Pinefield Holiday Park** (tel./fax 865 8791), 1km or so south on Port St. Standard communal facilities, a swimming pool, and usually a few caravan sites are open for international travelers. (Caravan and tent sites $11; basic cabin shares $15; well-sized cabins for 2 with kitchen $45; terrific chalet doubles start at $65.)

FOOD. Vibes Cafe (tel. 865 7121) spreads good ones with great espresso, cheap vegetarian melts, pitas, and burgers under $5 (open daily 9am-5pm, winter closed Su). Those with very health-conscious tastes will find a friend at **Ginger's Health Foods and Cafe**, 601 Port Rd. (tel. 865 7265), where you can get your vegan wheat- or gluten-free products. They pack lunches ($6-9) and have made-to-order sandwiches from $2.60. (Open daily 7am-5pm, winter closes at 3pm on weekends). Get your groceries at the **Four Square** (tel. 865 9190), at Port and Ocean Rd. (open daily 7am-7pm), or **Quarry Orchards** (tel. 865 8282), next to the post office, with veggies and bulk food (open daily 7am-6pm, winter M-F 7am-5:30pm, Sa until 5pm).

ACTIVITIES. Most come to Whangamata for the beach: to marinate in the sun, take low-tide wades out to the hulk of **Hauturu Island** just offshore, check out shorebirds in the estuary reserve at its south end, or just play in the breakers that draw surfers from all over. Especially good waves are found near the harbor mouth. **Whangamata Surf Shop**, 634 Port St. (tel. 865 8252), is owned by a longtime surfer who makes new rental boards (half-day $18, full day $25), and rents boogie boards and fins, as well as wetsuits ($5; open daily 9am-5pm). Surfcasting and game fishing for offshore tuna and marlin are also good around Whangamata.

Whangamata is surrounded by green hills and close to the good trails and biking opportunities of the 11,500-hectare **Tairua Forest,** north of town. The forest is mostly a pine timber plantation, with roads rugged enough to please any mountain biker for a few hours. Whangamata's premier natural area is the **Wentworth Valley,** on the turn-off 3km south of town on SH25. The river valley's several walks are strewn with mine shafts and relics from turn-of-the-century days. A telegraph line between Auckland and Wellington was diverted here during the Waikato land wars of the 1870s. A one-hour walk leaving from the basic campground ($6 sites) heads up to **Wentworth Falls.** The sea tunnel at **Pokohino Beach** leads at low tide to a rocky little cove where you can relax on isolated white sand. It's reachable via a short but steep walk from a carpark at the end of Pokohino Rd., a forest road that branches off Onemana Rd. 6km north of Whangamata on SH25.

Kiwi Dundee (a.k.a. Doug Johansen; tel. 865 8809 or mobile 025 746 219), earning his title in a country-wide contest to find a Kiwi to match the Aussies' Crocodile, will take you on an above-average ecotour. If Kiwi himself is not available, another one of the trained guides will lead you through lush rainforest, along old miner's trails, and into a cave or two. (Full-day adventure tour $122.)

NEAR WHANGAMATA: OPOUTERE

Come live by the estuarine tides for a day or three and remember the sounds of silence, punctuated only by the shrieks of shorebirds, the chortles of tui and bell-birds, and the wash of surf along kilometers of one of the last utterly undeveloped beaches in the Coromandel. This is Opoutere, a magical nowhere, a 15-minute drive north of Whangamata. The only lights between the YHA and the phone down the road are the constellations of glow-worms in the banks, the shining diamonds in the sky, and the sparkling phosphorescence in the water.

Lying on a harbor estuary at the mouth of the Wharekawa River, Opoutere (oh-POH-tury) isn't a town—it's just a place, home to an idyllic hostel, motorcamp, and little else but 5km of perfect, lonesome beach. **Whangamata Tours** (tel. 865 7088) runs through Opoutere from Whangamata on its connection with the **Inter-City** bus from Whitianga at Hikuai (daily in summer, in winter Su-F).

Capitalizing on this oasis from civilization is the appropriately peaceful ◼**Opoutere YHA Hostel** (tel. 865 9072), 4km in from the Opoutere turn-off from SH25 (follow the light of the glow-worms), north of Whangamata. Housed in a group of older school buildings, it's a communal oasis unto itself. There's no TV to interrupt the night—just a guitar for songs and a big kitchen with solid redwood tables. Try some homemade yogurt ($2 for a big serving), or take a free kayak out on the shallow estuary at high tide. (12-bed dorms $13; smaller shares $15; twins and doubles $18-20; tent sites $10. Non-YHA $4 more.) About 1km down the road is the **Opoutere Park Beach Resort** (tel. 865 9152), at the far end of the estuary (open Sept.-May). Tent and caravan sites ($9.50) are afforded a bit of privacy by pine plantings; tourist flats for three ($48, with 10% discount for 2 or more nights) and chalets ($66, same discount) are set near massive old pohutukawas some 200m from the beach through a pine forest. Although both places have limited stores, you should buy groceries before you come.

The **Wharekawa Harbour Sandspit Wildlife Reserve** here is one of New Zealand's few remaining nesting places for the threatened New Zealand dotterel (30-50 of the remaining 1200-odd individuals make their home here), and for the similarly scarce oystercatcher, a large black bird with shockingly pink extremities. During the nesting season (Oct.-Feb.), the DOC tries to fence off and guard the ridiculously exposed sand where these birds nest (they require close to a 360° view of their environs). You can watch kingfishers dart above herons stalking their prey, digging with the oystercatchers for pockets of clam-like pipis to supplement dinner. Or ponder the waves and the jagged line of the **Alderman Islands** far offshore. Diving into the bush will scare up flighty fantails (small sparrow-like birds that the Maori believed brought death when they entered a home), as well as the other numerous native birds that constantly clamor around Opoutere, en route to the summit of **Maungaruawahine pa.**

NORTH ISLAND

ROTORUA AND BAY OF PLENTY

At the junction of natural wonders, cultural spectacles, and excessive cashflow, the Bay of Plenty is one of the North Island's most popular regions for both international and Kiwi travelers. Land of lakes and hot springs, Rotorua is also the regional heart of Maori culture. Sun-warmed Mt. Maunganui offers relaxed views from white sand beaches, and neighboring Tauranga pulses with nightlife. Further along the coast, Ohope Beach provides gorgeous beach sunsets, while rough-edged Opotiki serves as a gateway to the remote, uncompromising East Cape and its intense natural beauty. From wave-lapping beaches to magical Maori concerts, trace the trail of wide-eyed travelers who in the early 1800s chose this as the first tourism destination in the country.

� ROTORUA AND BAY OF PLENTY HIGHLIGHTS

■ Geysers spray, mud pools gurgle, and ponds glow at **Rotorua's** lively geothermal sights (p. 151).

■ A Maori *hangi* (p. 153) is an incomparable culinary and cultural experience.

■ Enveloped in a perpetual cloud, **White Island** (p. 163) is an other worldly escape from the mainland.

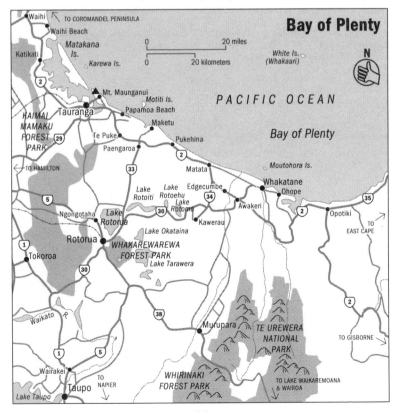

ROTORUA

You'll know when you've hit Rotorua. That boiled-egg smell isn't coming from the exhaust of your car, nor is it the hundreds of tour buses that bring close to a million visitors through the city each year, nor is it your Uncle Gordon snoring beside you. That smell, folks, is the odiferous sulfur stamp of geothermal activity in this gorgeous lake district. Named *Roto-* (lake) *rua* (two), before the Maori discovered that there were actually 15 lakes in the area, the North Island's single most popular destination offers disparate attractions; geothermal wonders, agricultural shows, and enlightening Maori offerings all vie for frames on visiting rolls of film. The plethora of adventure activities in Rotorua rivals the offerings of Christchurch; tourism is an industry here, but you'll undoubtedly find beauty beneath the hype.

🔢 ORIENTATION AND PRACTICAL INFORMATION

The city of Rotorua lies at the southern end of **Lake Rotorua,** but many of the local geothermal and recreational attractions are dispersed on **SH5** and **SH30.** Downtown is a rectangular grid, delineated by **Fenton, Ranolf, Arawa,** and **Amohau Streets,** with the crossroads of **Tutanekai** and **Hinemoa St.** serving as an effective center, home to stores, cafes, and banks.

ARRIVAL AND DEPARTURE

Airplanes: The **Rotorua Airport** is off SH30, around the east side of Lake Rotorua. **Air New Zealand** (tel. 347 9564), at the corner of Hinemoa and Fenton St., and **Ansett,** 113 Fenton St. (tel. 349 0146), both have 2-4 flights per day to: **Auckland** (45min., $97-210); **Wellington** (1hr., $134-230); **Christchurch** (2hr., $207-368); and **Queenstown** (2½hr., $350-625). **Alpha-Xpress** (tel. 346 1606) runs an airport shuttle ($8, $10 for 2).

Trains: **TranzScenic** tracks end a few km from city center off Lake Rd. Trains leave daily for **Auckland** (4hr., 1:30pm, $63) via **Hamilton** (2¼hr., $40). **Rotorua Airport Shuttle** takes you from Tourism Rotorua to the train station (12:45pm, $3).

Buses: All buses come and go from **Tourism Rotorua** (the Visitor Centre). **Newmans, InterCity,** and **Starlighter Express,** all accessible at the bus depot (tel. 349 0590), depart daily for: **Auckland** (4hr., 4-7 per day, $34-43) via **Hamilton** (1½hr., $19-24); **Napier** (4½hr., 3 per day, $50-53); and **Wellington** (7¼hr., 3 per day, $60-75) via **Taupo** (1hr., $16-20). **Waitomo Wanderer** (tel. 873 7559) goes to **Taupo** and **Waitomo** (7:15am and 6:15pm, $25, return $45), with pickup and drop off.

GETTING AROUND

Local Buses: Rotorua City Buses (tel. 349 2994, ext. 2902) are cheap and run M-F 7am-5:15pm. One section $1.60, two $2.20. Most destinations are no more than 2 sections. The main stop is Pukuatua St. between Tutanekai and Amohia St. The green Ngongataha route goes to Rainbow Springs, blue to Whakarewarewa.

Taxis: Fastaxis (tel. 348 2444) or **Rotorua Taxis** (tel. 348 1111). Open 24hr.

Car Rental: All the major companies can be found in Rotorua. **Link Rentals,** 108 Fenton St. (tel. 349 1629), with "super saver" cars at $25 per day and 18¢ per km, and **Rent-A-Dent,** 14 Ti St. (tel. 349 3993), off Fenton St. past Big Fresh, have cheaper rates. Both offer $55 per day rentals, with 100km free.

Bicycle Rentals: Lady Jane's Ice Cream Parlour (tel. 347 9340), at the corner of Tutanekai and Whakaue St., rents city bikes for $15 per day, or dilapidated tandems for $10 per hr. Mountain bikes $12 per hr., $38 per day. **Pin Cycles,** 1275 Fenton St. (tel. 347 1151), also rents used mountain bikes (half-day $35, full-day $45).

Hitchhiking: There's always traffic leaving Rotorua. South toward Taupo, many hitchers start past Amohau St. and work toward Whakarewarewa. Amohau St. is also the branching point for SH5 north and SH30 east; many thumbers head a few blocks away from Pak 'N Save to go east. Catching a ride north is reportedly easier no farther from town than Rainbow Springs, after which traffic speeds up.

TOURIST AND FINANCIAL SERVICES

Visitor Center: Tourism Rotorua, 1167 Fenton St. (tel. 348 5179; fax 348 6044), between Arawa and Haupapa St. Service is excellent in this busy hub. Cafe, **currency exchange,** as well as accommodation, tour, and travel bookings. Open daily 8am-6pm.

DOC: The office is on Pukaki St. (tel. 349 7400; fax 347 9115; open M-F 8am-4:35pm), but most of its services are provided by the **Map and Track Shop** (tel. 349 1845), in the Tourism Rotorua complex. Shop has complete selection of park maps and DOC brochures and sells hut tickets and permits. Open daily 8am-6pm, winter 9am-5:30pm.

Currency Exchange: Banks line Hinemoa St. **Westpac** (tel. 348 1079) is on the corner of Hinemoa and Tutanekai St. Open M-F 9am-4:30pm. **Thomas Cook** (tel. 347 0111), in the **Air New Zealand** office at Hinemoa and Fenton St. Open M-F 8:30am-5pm, Sa 9:30am-12:30pm.

American Express: Galaxy Travel, 1315 Tutanekai St. (tel. 347 9444). Won't cash checks, but will hold mail for members and give advice. Open M-F 8:30am-5pm.

EMERGENCY AND COMMUNICATIONS

Medical Services: Lakes PrimeCare Pharmacy (tel. 348 4385), with the big turquoise sign at Arawa and Tutanekai St. Open daily 9am-9:30pm. **Lakeland Health Centre** (tel. 348 1199) is Rotorua's public hospital on Pukeroa St., off Arawa St., at the northeast corner of the city center. **Lakes PrimeCare** (tel. 348 1000), next to the Lakes Care Pharmacy. Open daily 8am-11pm. Doctor on call 24hr.

Police: Diagonally across Fenton St. from Tourism Rotorua (24hr. tel. 348 0099).

Post Office: 1189 Hinemoa St. (tel. 349 2397), near Tutanekai St. Open M-F 7:30am-5:30pm, Sa 8:30am-4pm, Su 9am-3pm

Internet Access: Vegas Cyber Cafe (tel. 348 5899), above Iconix on the corner of Pukuatua and Tutanekai St. First 15 min. free, $2 per hr. after that. Open daily 9am-11pm, winter 9am-6pm.

Telephone Code: 07.

■ ACCOMMODATIONS

Rotorua has no shortage of beds, though it may feel that way on a summer weekend if you didn't call ahead. **SH5,** both at **Fenton St.** and the northeast side of town, has its share of motels; some relatively budget options line **Ranolf St.** If you're desperate, contact Tourism Rotorua. Overnights with a Maori family or on a *marae* are possible, but are more easily booked for larger groups. Don't be too impressed by "thermal pool" signs—practically every place has one.

Funky Green Voyager, 4 Union St. (tel. 346 1754; fax 347 0078). Walk down Fenton St. to Victoria St. and turn right; Union St. is 2 blocks down. Clean and green, this environmentally conscious hostel is a friendly, fun home away from home. Sunroom, modern kitchen, and creatively decorated toilet seats in the loo. Close to the supermarket. Key deposit $10. Dorms $16; twins and doubles $39. Cash only.

Kiwi Paka YHA, 60 Tarewa Rd. (347 0931), 1km from town center. Walk west on Pukuatua St. past Kuirau Park, turn right on Tarewa St. Swarms with big tour groups that migrate from the cafeteria to the bar to the thermal pool. Quieter lounge shelters bewildered YHA-cardholders. Everything shuts down by midnight, but on weekends, noise continues into the wee hours. Front desk offers discount bookings and shuttle service to bus stop and hitching points. Key deposit $10. Dorms $17; singles $25; twins and doubles $40, with bath $47; tent sites $8.50, powered $10.50.

Rotorua Central Backpackers, 1076 Pukuatua St. (tel./fax 349 3285). From the bus station, turn right down Fenton St. and left on Pukuatua St. Immaculately clean, classic 1936 wood apartment building offers decent rooms and two lounges. Laid-back managers will calm any frayed nerves that withstand the indoor spa. Bike rental. Key deposit $10. Off-street parking. Dorms $15; twins $34-36; doubles $36.

Cactus Jacks (VIP), 1210 Haupapa St. (tel. 348 3121). Wild-Western hostel with goofy murals in the hallways. Courtyard retains the light-hearted spirit. Small, cozy rooms play personalized roles in the mini-town (complete with Madame Fifi's room and a "jail"). Spacious kitchen, TV, video library, pinball machine, bike rental, and thermal pool. Key deposit $10. Dorms $15.50; singles $30; twins $35; doubles $39. Cash only.

Downtown Backpackers (Nomads), 1193 Fenton St. (tel. 346 2831), next to Tourism Rotorua. You could hop (off the bus), skip (twice), and jump into a clean bed at this large hostel. Or, if you're like most guests, you may want to just walk. Attracting a some-what older crowd, this hostel has tidy, organized facilities, and rooms furnished with bedside tables and lamps. Caring owners Graeme and Flick are two of the friendliest people you'll meet in town. Dorms $15; 4-bed dorms $16; twins $36; doubles $38.

Spa Lodge, 1221 Amohau St. (tel. 348 3486). Colorful carpeting that changes from seam to seam makes for a dizzying walk around this winding house with nice, spacious rooms, clean kitchen area, and small, enclosed spa with ivy on the walls. Key deposit $10. Dorms $13-$15; singles $25; twins $14-15; doubles $30, with bath $45.

Motel Monterey, 1204 Whakaue St. (tel. 348 1044; fax 348 2644). Quiet, airy rooms with wicker chairs, couches, TV, and kitchenette. Heated pool overhung with orange trees complements a hidden, greenery-lined spa gazebo. Courtesy pickup and dropoff. Singles $60; doubles $65; family doubles $75, extra person $12. Winter $5-10 less.

Cosy Cottage International Holiday Park, 67 Whittaker Rd. (tel. 348 3793), 2km from town, off Lake Rd. Thermally heated sites, hot stream, and private sand beach make up for the tired feel of communal facilities. Prepare your own *hangi* in a natural steam cooker. Bike rental. Double flats with toilet and kitchenette $46, extra person $11; cabins for 2 with kitch-enettes $40, extra person $10; tourist flats $60; tent sites $10, powered $11, for 2 $20.

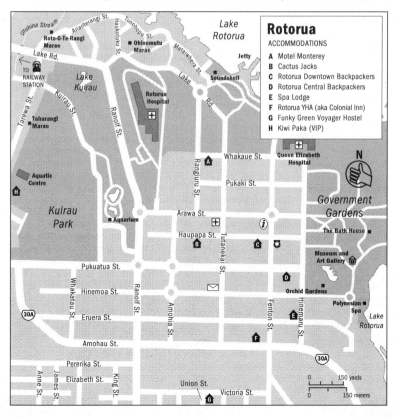

Rotorua
ACCOMMODATIONS
A Motel Monterey
B Cactus Jacks
C Rotorua Downtown Backpackers
D Rotorua Central Backpackers
E Spa Lodge
F Rotorua YHA (aka Colonial Inn)
G Funky Green Voyager Hostel
H Kiwi Paka (VIP)

FOOD

A highly recommended alternative to Rotorua's standard restaurants are Maori *hangis*. Although the meals (which are included in cultural evenings and/or concerts) are hardly inexpensive, they shouldn't be missed (see **A Maori Evening,** p. 153). Rotorua's cafes and several good upscale restaurants line the lake end of **Tutanekai St.,** near **Arawa St.;** except for a few new options, vegetarians may be forced to search and settle. Your market choices are **Pak 'N Save,** at the corner of Fenton and Amohau St. (tel. 347 8440; open M-F 8:30am-9pm, Sa-Su 8:30am-8pm) or fruit and veggie wholesaler **Pumpkin Planet** (tel. 348 1442), down Fenton St. a bit at Ti St. (open daily 7am-6pm).

■ **Tastebuds Mexican Cantina,** 1213 Fenton St. (tel. 349 0591), under a "Mexican Food" sign. Irresistible, with the invitation of the sombrero-wearing stuffed peasant outside and the endless recommendations of locals. Possibly Rotorua's best value, the narrow cantina is always full with patrons bumping elbows to dig into plates of burritos, enchiladas, and tacos (all $4-8). Open M-Sa 10am-8pm or 9pm, Su 11am-8pm.

■ **Zippy Central,** 1153 Pukuatua St. (tel. 348 8288). Great food and good prices at any time of the day. The spinach and basil gnocchi ($9.50) makes lunch a special occasion. For a few bucks more, dinner mains share the small tables with candles. Inviting atmosphere and extremely friendly staff. Open Su-Th 9am-9:30pm, F-Sa 9am-11pm.

Fat Dog Cafe and Bar, 1161 Arawa St. (tel. 347 7586). Doing its roly-poly namesake justice with a playful atmosphere, scrumptious breakfasts, and creative mains. Sandwiches ($5-10) are a tasty prelude to the desserts ($3.50), but the drinks make this place a coffee-lover's best friend. Open daily 9am-late.

Chez Bleu Cafe, 1262 Fenton St. (tel. 348 1828), by Hinemoa St. Mediterranean cafe offers decent burgers (under $7) and luscious desserts ($5-6) outdoors or under indoor umbrellas. Pool table and jukebox. Open Su-W 8:30am-midnight, Th-Sa 8:30am-3am.

Chopsticks, 45 Amohau St. (tel. 347 8011), near the corner of Fenton St. Gurgling pool with bridge in the foyer leads to pagoda in the main dining room. Mains are tasty but pricey at $14.50. Delivery 6-10pm, with $2 charge, if you order 2. Takeaways are a good deal, most under $10. But don't let thriftiness take away from the experience of watching the 7pm Maori cultural performance while dipping your dumplings. Open daily 11:30am-2pm and 5:30pm-late.

⊠ NIGHTLIFE

Rotorua's nightclubs, pubs, and upscale cafes are sustained by tourists determined to have a rowdy night out. Hog a bar stool at the ever-popular **Pig and Whistle City Bar** (tel. 347 3025), at the corner of Tutanekai and Haupapa St. In this former police station and probation office, patrons nowadays are less degenerate, although weekends with live bands can still get rowdy (cover $2). Pub fare under $10 is served until 9:30pm. (Open daily from 11:30am.) At **Monkey Jo's** (tel. 346 1313), on Amohia St. between Eruera and Hiremoa St., the loud and drunk get primitive on the sawdust floor and outdoor patio overlooking the jungle of central Rotorua. There are live bands (W-Th) and long lines, and tidy dress is required. (Open daily from 3pm.) At **Grace O'Malley's Irish Bar,** on Eruera St. by Ranolf St., play a game at the round pool table, or jounce along to rollicking Irish and retro bands on weekends at this local pick. (Happy Hour 5-7pm. No cover. Open 11am-3am.) Those enamored of young foreign drunks slap on cologne and follow the pumping music to **Lava Bar** (tel. 348 8618), at the corner of Ranolf and Arawa St. Dance on the patio or couch with herds of Kiwi Experiencers in this lodge-like mixer. (Happy Hour daily 5-6pm. Open from 4pm.)

SIGHTS

GEOTHERMAL WONDERS

Rotorua's famed thermal activity is caused by a volcanic fault line running from **White Island,** 50km offshore from Whakatane (see p. 163), to Mt. Ruapehu in Tongariro National Park (see p. 195). The tectonic plates have created spectacularly unstable mountains and the bizarre landscape of the region's several major geothermal parks and innumerable small steaming pools, craters, and vents—that's life on the geological edge for you.

Just 30km south of Rotorua on SH5, the amazingly beautiful ⬛**Wai-O-Tapu** (tel. 366 6333) is probably the single finest geothermal spot (though Waimungu is a close contender, with dimmer colors but more activity). Private operators lease the area from the DOC as a "Thermal Wonderland." A self-guided tour weaves among boiling mud pools, an expansive silicate terrace, brilliantly hued pools, craters, and (you're in Rotorua) crowds of tourists. While frustratingly veiled in steam on cold winter days, the stunning ochre and turquoise colors of the bubbling **Champagne Pool** make the celebratory beverage pale in comparison. Erupting up to 21m each day at precisely 10:15am, **Lady Knox Geyser** is another major Wai-O-Tapu attraction. Mother Nature isn't really that regular: the geyser gets an unhealthy dose of soap every morning to disperse the upper level of water and relieve surface tension. Prisoners discovered this handy trick in 1896 when trying to wash clothes. (Open daily 8:30am-5pm. Admission $12, children $4, families $29.)

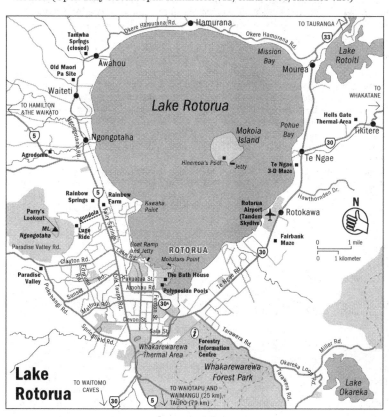

NORTH ISLAND

Whakarewarewa Thermal Reserve & Maori Cultural Centre (tel. 348 9047), on Fenton St., is often referred to as Whaka. The source of a billowing cloud of steam 2km south of town, Whaka has boiling mud pools, a kiwi house, and demonstrations on carving, weaving, and crafts. Along the reserve's walking tour, New Zealand's largest and most famous geyser, **Pohutu**, spurts 30m several times per day. (Open daily 8am-5pm or 6pm. Free guided tours every hr. Daily 30min. cultural performances 12:15pm $13.50. Admission $16.50.)

The **Waimangu Volcanic Valley** (tel. 366 6137), 23km from Rotorua off the Taupo Highway, is the southern end of the rift created by Tarawera's 1886 eruption. Along its trail, the **Echo Crater** is home to the world's largest hot springs, where dancing steam creates fanciful patterns on the gleaming water. The gorgeous, ice-blue, and extremely acidic inferno crater lake is actually a geyser, living on a 38-day cycle. The path also passes the site of **Waimangu**, once the world's largest geyser. The white cross nearby marks the site where four overeager tourists were blown away in 1903. You can also take a one-hour guided cruise to the former sites of the Pink and White Terraces (frozen cascades of silicate awash with hot water above Lake Rotomahana) and steaming cliffs. (Open daily 8:30am-5pm. Admission to valley $14.50, with boat ride $32.50.)

Abandon all hope, ye who enter into the dark underworld of geothermal wonders, also known as **Hell's Gate** (tel. 345 3151), 15km east of Rotorua on SH30. With 10 hectares of seething mud, pools, and rocks, there is basically one true attraction: the largest steaming, hot waterfall in the Southern Hemisphere. Evil-doers never had it so good. Capitalizing on its devilish reputation, it's eerily illuminated on Wednesday nights 6-10pm with a light, sound, and fire performance at 8pm. (Open daily 9am-5pm. Admission $10, children $5.)

TOURS

Because Rotorua's attractions are widely spread out, a sightseeing tour might be your best option. A rented car and a map will get you to the geothermal spots, but the city has a wide variety of shuttle services that make the trip fairly cheap and hassle-free: the **Rotorua Sightseeing Shuttle** (tel. 348 0408) makes daily runs to Wai-O-Tapu and Waimungu from Tourism Rotorua (shuttles run 8:15am-4:40pm; $4, day pass $10). **Carey's Sightseeing Tours,** 18 Haupapa St. (24hr. tel. 347 1197), offers an array of half-, three-quarter-, and full-day tour options including pickup and in-coach commentary (half-day $60, full day $100). A branch of Carey's, **Carey's Capers,** covers all the standard sights, but adds in spicier activities, such as a swim in an isolated hot bush stream, rides up Mt. Tarawera, rafting the Kaituna, and bushwalks ("Get Volcanic" day tour $70). For $120, **Te Kiri Trek** (345 5967 or 0800 835 474) is—as advertised—rough, tough, wet, and wild. After a walk through Wai-O-Tapu and a thermal river swim, four-wheel driver Roger—sporting his daily uniform of gumboots, camouflauge jacket, and buzzcut—takes you to Mt. Tarawera, guiding hikes along the top of the volcano and down through Rotoiti Foresta, with an all-you-can-eat lunch along the way. Pickup is at 8:30am.

OTHER SIGHTS

To gain a greater appreciation for just about everything in Rotorua, give yourself an hour in the outstanding **Rotorua Museum of Art and History/Te Whare Taonga o Te Arawa** (tel. 349 4350), in the stunning neo-Tudor Bath House just to the right of the public Government Gardens at the end of Hinemaru St. A former luxury spa, the building is undergoing an eight-year, multimillion-dollar renovation, but manages to keep its classy exhibitions operational while under construction. The elegant wings house excellent permanent exhibitions on the former spa itself, area geology, the Te Arawa people, and the Mt. Tarawera eruption of 1886. (Open daily 9:30am-5pm. Admission $7.50, backpackers $5, children $1.) The **Whakarewarewa Thermal Village** is separated from the geyser and the cultural center by a criss-crossed wooden barrier erected three years ago. Accessible by Sala St. off Fenton St., this Whaka is a living, steaming thermal village, offering two cultural performances at

PROPHET OF DOOM Strange things had been happening that spring. The flax had not flowered. Streams had been abruptly gushing and drying. But more troubling to the Maori living under Mt. Tarawera were the events of May 31, 1886. Guide Sophia Hinerangi and her boat of tourists returning from a day at the fabled Pink and White Terraces had witnessed a vision: a spectral war canoe, its warrior paddlers wearing ominous symbols on their heads, emerged from a bend in the lake and then disappeared. Consulted for interpretation, the old priest Tuhoto said these natural and supernatural signs foretold something cataclysmic. He had warned his people in Te Wairoa that their departure from the ancestral ways, their gradual adoption of the white man's greed, would lead to punishment sent by his ancestor, the spirit Tamahoi, buried within the mountain. The night of terror came on June 10, 1886, when the three domes on this now flat-topped volcano blew and rent the mountain asunder, ripping a 17km wound of otherworldly red, white, and black scoria-lined craters. The largest eruption in 500 years, it blasted away the bed of Lake Rotomahana, burying Te Wairoa and other nearby villages in mud, rock, and ash. The famed terraces were shattered into splinters, forests burned all around, and as far as Christchurch and Auckland, roars were heard. When the search parties finally uncovered Tuhoto's house, days later, they found the old man still alive. Tamahoi had protected his prophet. The Rotorua Museum of Art and History (see p. 152) screens an excellent dramatized version of this story.

NORTH ISLAND

11:15am and 2pm daily (included in admission price) and a 12:30pm *hangi*. (Open daily 8:30am-5pm. Tours 9am-4pm. Admission $15, children $7.50.)

A visit to **Ohinemutu,** the lakefront Maori village of the Ngati Whakaue tribe, affords a briefer glimpse of Maori culture. Off Lake Rd. (just walk down Tutanekai St.), you'll come to one of the Arawa people's most symbolically important buildings, the **Tamatekapua Meeting House.** Rich, red, and speckled with paua shells, its carvings are a maze of figures tangled into figures. The interior is closed to the public, except for nightly concerts (see **A Maori Evening,** p. 153). Across the way is **St. Faith's Anglican Church,** with a Tudor exterior and a Maori interior. It serves as a potent focus of cultural history and continues to hold services (the original St. Faith's housed Rotorua's first Christian service in 1831). The pulpit is supported by carved figures of five Maori ancestors, while an etched window panel shows Christ clad in the cloak of a Maori chief—from a certain angle, he appears to be walking on Lake Rotorua.

The **Agrodome** (tel. 357 4350), 10km north of town on SH5, gives tourists—particularly family groups—five chances a day to see 19 different breeds of sheep strutting their stuff on stage. Three times a day, they offer tours of a working farm. (Admission $12.) The **Rainbow Farm Show** is on SH5 5km north of town, next to the Skyline Gondola. Combining their farm show with the neighboring nature walk, a $16.50 ticket (children $7) gets you into both. With an indoor/outdoor setup, two "farmers" put on an amusing show shearing sheep, performing a mock auction, leading sheepdog trials, and coaxing the camera-happy crowd to milk cows and pet baby lambs. (5 shows per day. Admission $10, children $5.) Head across the highway to **Rainbow Springs** (tel. 347 9301) to use the other half of your ticket on the 40-minute walk among animal life and beauteous springs.

◤ ACTIVITIES

A MAORI EVENING: THE HANGI
In one of the most accessible places to learn about Maori culture, the classic form of entertainment is participation in a Maori *hangi*, or feast. The many options fall on a wide spectrum: some emphasize learning about Maori history and traditions, while others consist solely of song and dance. Some *hangi* are held on real *marae*, some in specifically built commercial locations, and some in plush motel

restaurants—many evening commercial packages tread a delicate line between education and exoticization. Although the cameras flashing and the sense of "culture on display" can be disconcerting, this may be your best chance to move beyond postcard images of tongue-protruding tattooed Maori warriors to get a glimpse of the beauty, power, and richness of the Maori tradition. The *hangi* is also a damn good meal (see p. 12).

Full evenings offered by the several Maori-owned tour operators usually include an introductory communication protocol, challenge and welcome ceremony, concert, and *hangi*—all with pickup and drop off from any accommodation (book directly or through the Tourism Rotorua). Based at a pre-European village overlooking the **Whakarewarewa Thermal Reserve,** your *hangi* will be prepared by the underground heat of the natural hot water. (6pm, winter 5pm. $60, children $30.) Whakarewarewa also offers concerts during the day. Evenings last three to four hours. **Rotoiti Tours** (tel. 348 8969), of the Ngati Rongamai tribe, does one of the most authentic evenings in the Rakeiao *marae*, on the shores of impossibly scenic Lake Rotoiti, beginning at 6pm. Groups get no larger than 80 to 100 on peak summer nights. Winter groups may be under 20, but are not available every night, so call ahead. (Adults $49, under 12 half-price.) Overnights are also possible, but mainly for groups of more than 10 (bedding, kitchen facilities, breakfast supplied; prices from $60, based on group size). Rotorua's most popular and polished Maori experience is found with ⬛**Tamaki Tours** (tel. 346 2823). From each of the several bus loads of people, a chief is chosen to represent his canoe (tour bus). After the welcoming, groups walk through the impressive, model *pa* built for the purpose of viewing age-old customs performed by well-paid modern Maori. Then there is a fascinating cultural group concert and magnificent *hangi*. (Evening $58, children half-price.) **Mai Ora** (tel. 348 9047) is also highly recommended.

WATER ACTIVITIES

Outdoors on the lakefront is the great cultural melting pot of Rotorua: the ⬛**Polynesian Spa** (tel. 348 1328) at the Government Gardens end of Hinemoa St. Where else can you don your swimsuit, soak in ecstasy, and comfortably chat with travelers from around the globe? The **Radium** and **Priest Springs,** ranging from 33 to 43°C, are famed for their supposed healing powers. Private pools where you can control the temperature are ideal for romantics. (Admission $10, children $4.)

With all its lakes (and purportedly more trout per capita than even Lake Taupo), Rotorua is an angler's paradise. Fly guides begin at $70 per hour; contact Tourism Rotorua for a listing of operators and to get a license ($12 per day). Lakes Rotorua and Okareka are open year-round; other fishable lakes in the district are open October through June. If fishing doesn't interest you but the azure lakes themselves do, **kayaking** is probably your best bet, especially on **Lake Okataina** (the only lake completely surrounded by lush fern and thick native bush, regrown since the 1886 eruption). **Adventure Kayaking** (tel. 348 9451) does full-day guided trips ($75); they also rent kayaks ($35 per day). **Waka Hikoi** (tel. 362 7878) offers guided trips and bushwalks with Maori flavor (half-day $49, full day $79).

ADVENTURE ACTIVITIES

⬛**Skyline Skyrides** (tel. 347 0027), 4-5km from the city center and next to Rainbow Springs on SH5, is an elaborate complex responsible for making Rotorua the semi-official **luge** capital of the country. After ascending in a scenic, if not thrilling, gondola ride ($12), the luge lets you hurl yourself back down part way on a three-wheeled plastic cart (rides 4.50 each or $16 for a 5-ride pass). Other attractions at the top include a sidewinder toboggan, shooting gallery, a ride simulator, and a skyline ride. (Open Su-Th 9am-5pm, F-Sa 9am-7pm.)

It may not be native bush, but the 5667-hectare exotic pine plantation otherwise known as the **Whakarewarewa Forest** draws visitors with awesome mountain biking trails. For walking or riding, get maps and permits from **Fletcher Challenge Forestry Information** (tel. 346 2082) on Long Mile Rd., a short drive or bike from city center off the road to the airport. (Open M-F 8:30am-5pm, Sa-Su 10am-4pm.) **Mountain**

Cats (tel. 0800 871 187) hires out mountain bikes and will drop them at Tourism Rotorua for you (1hr. $15, half-day $35, full day $45).

Newly added onto the Agrodome is the **Agrodome Adventure Center** (tel. 357 2929), with four original attractions immune to the "been there, done that" brag of the bold. **Bungy jump** off of a 43m tower ($80). Or, for $30 each, run the brand-new adrenaline gamut: the **Agrojet,** which zips you around a small rubber-banked pond in a tiny 500 horsepower jetboat; the **Zorb,** a clear sphere in which you can live out a hamster's dream by climbing in and rolling around the field; and the **Swoop,** which drops three people linked in padded sleeping-bag-like-sacs from the bungy tower at stomach-tugging speeds of up to 130kph.

Adrenaline junkies twitching for their next hit will end their search and raft the short but sweet **Kaituna River,** with a 7m high **Okere Falls** drop, spilling out of **Lake Rotoiti** (about $60 for 40min.). Trips to other area rivers, including the Rangitaiki, Wairoa, and Tongariro, are offered by many different companies, but are subject to good weather and safe water levels. The original company, with strong local endorsement, is **Kaituna Cascades** (tel. 357 5032; $55-58).

One of the cheaper options for skydiving in New Zealand, **Tandem Skydiving Rotorua** (tel. 345 7520), offers a 3200m fall and spectacular lake district scenery for $180-195 (book ahead). Getting up Tarawera by foot is possible, but the access point from **Ash Pit Rd.** near Lake Rerewhakaaitu south of town is nearly impossible to reach without your own transport. The land is Maori-owned, so there is a $2 fee, $35 for 4WD. If you don't have one yourself, jounce in the 4WD vehicles of **Mountain Magic** (tel. 348 6399), a Maori-run company (half-day $70, children $30). Other options include full-day bush trips to the **Tarawera Falls,** thermal springs for a swim ($140, children $60), and a rainy day option of cultural and educational tours ($60, children $25). **Mount Tarawera 4WD Tours** (tel. 348 2814; fax 347 8147) also offers trips with commentary on the region (half-day $65, children $35).

Lose yourself in the free **Fairbank Maze,** a large hedge maze right out of *Alice in Wonderland,* located opposite the airport. If you can't get enough, you can head to **Te Ngae Park's 3-D Maze** (tel. 345 5275), a wooden maze located 3km past the airport on SH30 ($4, children $2).

BAY OF PLENTY

TAURANGA

Tauranga's warm weather and commercial conveniences have made it one of New Zealand's fastest-growing cities. This recent growth has resulted in a peculiar mixture of past and present, in which bungy rocketers (see p. 159) enjoy a bouncing 21st-century view of an 1835 Mission. One of the earliest sites of Maori habitation, Tauranga ("resting place for canoes") is still one of the nation's busiest ports, shipping out over 1.6 billion kiwifruit last year alone. While some travelers come for jobs in the winter kiwi industry, most come to Tauranga for its summer nightlife and proximity to Mount Maunganui.

▓ ORIENTATION & PRACTICAL INFORMATION

Downtown Tauranga is located on a narrow northward-pointing peninsula in **Tauranga Harbor.** With the thickest concentration of attractions on **the Strand**—a strip of cafes and clubs along the eastern coast of Waipu Bay—the main commercial area spreads west to **Cameron St.** and south to **Elizabeth St.** Cross-streets south of Elizabeth St. are numbered in a southward ascending order. Fifteenth Ave. is the continuation of SH2.

Visitor Center: Visitor and Information Centre, 91 Willow St. (tel. 578 8103). Open M-F 7am-5:30pm, Sa-Su 8am-4pm.

DOC: 253 Chadwick Rd., West Greerton (tel./fax 578 7677). Somewhat far from town. Staff can answer inquiries about area hikes. Open M-F 8am-4:30pm.

Trains: TranzScenic (tel. 0800 802 802) heads daily to **Auckland** (3½hr., 8am, $54) via **Hamilton** (1hr., $32). Discounts for students and backpackers with ID.

Buses: Station at the **Visitor and Information Centre** on the corner of Wharf and Willow St. **InterCity** and **Newmans** head daily to: **Auckland** (4hr., 4 per day, $37); **Hamilton** (2hr., 1-2 per day, $23); and **Rotorua** (1hr., 11:20am, $20-22; transfer here for points in the East Cape). **Supa Travel** (tel. 571 0583) runs to **Auckland** (3hr., M-F 9am, Su 11am, backpackers $27).

Ferries: (tel. 578 5381), from **Coronation Pier** to Mt. Maunganui (summer 1 per hr., $4).

Hitchhiking: Hitchhikers heading to Auckland or the Coromandel Peninsula suggest trying Waihi Rd. (SH2), just past Jonathon St. about 500m beyond the Otumoetai Rd. roundabout. Thumbers to Whakatane or Rotorua often start on Dive Crescent before the bridge and head east via Mt. Maunganui.

Public Transportation: Newlove's Bus Service (tel. 578 6453) crosses into Mt. Maunganui (M-F every hr., $3) and neighboring suburbs. Departs from Wharf St. by the library. **City Travel** (tel. 544 5494) runs buses along Cameron Rd. into nearby suburbs M-F.

Taxis: Tauranga Taxis (tel. 578 6086), **Bay City Cabs** (tel. 577 0999), and **Coastline Taxis** (tel. 571 8333) are all available 24hr.

Currency Exchange: BNZ (tel. 578 8009), on the corner of Willow and Wharf St., and **National Bank** (tel. 578 2049), at the corner of Spring and Grey St., are both open M-F 9am-4:30pm.

Police: (tel. 578 8199), on the corner of Willow and Monmouth St.

Medical Services: John's Photo Pharmacy (tel. 578 3566), on the corner of Cameron Rd. and 2nd Ave., operates in evenings. Open daily 8am-9pm. For after hours, try **Baycare Medical Services** (tel. 578 8111), on Tenth St. and Edgecumbe Rd. Open 5pm-8am. The **hospital** (tel. 579-8000) is on Cameron Rd. between 17th and 18th Ave.

Post Office: 17 Grey St. (tel. 577 9911). Open M-F 8:30am-5pm, Sa 9am-noon.

Internet: Cybersurf (tel. 579 0140), in the Picadilly Arcade between Devonport Rd. and Grey St. $14 per hr. Open M-F 9am-6pm, Sa 10am-4pm, Su 11am-4pm. **Tauranga Library** (tel. 577 7177), in the Civic Arcade on Willow St. $15 per hr. Open M-Th 9:30am-5:30pm, F 9:30am-4pm, Sa 9:30am-10:30pm.

Telephone Code: 07.

ACCOMMODATIONS

Finding a comfortable bed in Tauranga shouldn't be a problem. While those without vehicles will want to stick close to downtown, more mobile visitors will find an array of motorparks and motels along **Waihi Rd.** (coming from Auckland) or **Turret Rd./15th Ave.** All the hostels in town offer free pickups and dropoffs and coordinate with each other to ensure that all travelers find a place to stay. During the winter, a couple backpackers could aptly be termed "working hostels," for kiwifruit contractors frequently look to hostels to supply labor, and the majority of guests may be working rather than on holiday. The season runs mid-April through May, with packing and pruning lasting into June.

YHA Hostel, 171 Elizabeth St. (tel./fax 578 5064), a convenient 10min. walk from the Strand. The triangular beacon of this cozy complex shines on a cul-de-sac past the Cameron Rd. intersection. New hosts Jane and Patrick welcome guests with a relaxed and friendly attitude that permeates the hostel itself. Discounts for area activities, informed advice, and employment help are offered in addition to a spacious kitchen, a small shop, and rental bikes. Reception 8-10am and 5-10:30pm, winter 5-8:30pm. Ring any time and leave a message. Dorms (mostly single-sex quads) $15; doubles $34; tent sites $8 per person.

Just the Ducks Nuts (VIP), 6 Vale St. (tel. 576 1366), in Otumoetai. Take Chapel St. from Tauranga. A free pickup in the hand-decorated station wagon whisks you to a homey hostel with a great glassed-in conservatory, fireplace, pool table, and graffiti wall. Rental bikes available. Ask for the front twin with superb views of Mt. Maunganui and the harbor. Singles $15; twins or doubles $36; tent sites $8. Weekly: singles $90; tent sites $56. Discount with *Let's Go.*

Bell Lodge, 39 Bell St. (tel. 578 6344; fax 578 6342; email bell.lodge@host.co.nz), near the Otumoetai Rd. roundabout off Waihi Rd. (or SH2). In addition to the free ride to check-in, drivers shuttle guests the several km to town and back at 10am and 5pm every day. Relaxed and secluded in a green residential setting with a view of the surrounding hills, it offers modern rooms with sliding glass doors overlooking a patio and small courtyard. The TV lounge with a mini pool table and large kitchen fosters a mellow communal spirit. Internet. Reception from 8am (just ring the bell). Dorms $16; twins with bath $36; doubles with bath $40, with TV $42; (for each additional person $11); tent sites $9. Suites with double bed and twin beds, personal bath and kitchen $70. Weekly dorms $80. Discount with *Let's Go.*

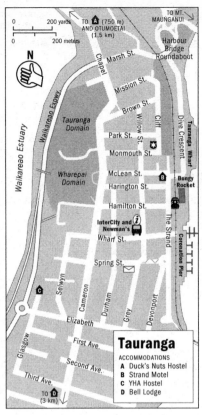

Tauranga

ACCOMMODATIONS
A Duck's Nuts Hostel
B Strand Motel
C YHA Hostel
D Bell Lodge

Strand Motel, 27 the Strand, (tel. 578 5807), is centrally located and typical of the motel offerings, though a bit cheaper. Offers a pretty view from a terrace above ample parking. Check-out 10am. Adequate doubles with shower, bathroom, TV, and microwave $59. Call ahead for availability.

FOOD

Many of Tauranga's better restaurants are clustered along the Strand and the downtown end of Devonport Rd. For **fast food,** Cameron Rd. and its surrounding streets offer major Americana.

Shiraz Cafe, 12 Wharf St. (tel. 577 0059). The cream of Tauranga's cafe crop, offering unbeatable taste for your dollar, from hummus ($5) to kebab ($6.50). Outdoor seating in front and pleasant courtyard in back. Serves lunch and dinner ($15). Open M-Sa 11am-2:30pm and 5-9pm (closing time flexible).

The Sunrise Natural Cafe, 10 Wharf St. (tel. 578 9302). Vegetarian sandwiches, hot dishes, and tantalizing desserts (all around $2-3) offer refuge from the deep-fried delights of Kiwi cuisine. Shares outdoor seating with the Shiraz. Open M-F 8am-3:30pm, Sa 9am-2pm.

The Hobler, 116 Cameron Rd. at corner of Wharf St. (tel. 577 9177). The hokey Hollywood film theme is thankfully overpowered by the rustic, natural decor. The fireplace outshines the James Dean paintings, and delicious, artfully presented dishes upstage their movie-title names. If the show must go on, try the Famous Hollywood Bowl, a salad with marinated chicken and cashews covered in mustard dressing ($13.95). Before the credits roll, any one of the desserts ($8.95) is a guaranteed showstopper. Open daily noon-2pm, plus Sa-Su 5-10pm.

Mongolian Feast, 61a the Strand (tel. 577 6518). When stomach growling exceeds a socially acceptable decibel, an all-you-can-eat Mongolian feast ($20) will appease. Surrounded by battle murals, mounted shields, and hanging swords, watch the chef cook your own concoction of meats, veggies, oils, sauces, and spices—and if you over-eagerly mix garlic powder with soy with sweet and sour, consult the suggested recipes and watch again. For dessert, pancakes ($5) also endure your own creative sauce selection. BYO wine. Karaoke Thursdays. Open daily 6pm-late.

◪ NIGHTLIFE

Oak and Ale, (tel. 577 1305), on the corner of Spring and Grey St. Live music every weekend and table service—shake your booty or leave it pasted to the stool for the entire night. Either way, the $3-5 pints, bar food, or daily Happy Hour (5-7pm) will satisfy. No cover. Tidy dress. Open daily 10:30am-3am.

Straight Shooters, 19 Wharf St. (tel. 571 0839), off the Strand. Pool tables, alcohol, and sawdust combine to create some of Tauranga's rowdiest nightlife. Some stay until they can't shoot, walk, or even see straight. Then they try the zip-wire drinking game. Live music on Friday and sometimes Saturday. Open M-Sa 2pm-3am.

Grumpy Mole Saloon, 41 the Strand (tel. 571 1222). John Wayne never knew this playground version of the Wild West with its separate cigar parlor, sleek pool tables, adjoining courtyard, pulsing music, and giant TV. No fists swinging here, only twentysomethings. The dress code sign is almost as long as the bar (just avoid tennis shoes and biker wear). Pints $3.50. Happy Hour F 4-10pm. Open Sept.-May M-Sa 1pm-3am; Oct.-Apr. M-Sa 4pm-3am.

Flannagan's, 14 Hamilton St. (tel. 578 9222), the Strand. Catering to an older crowd, this popular Irish pub taps into nostalgia for the Emerald Isle, while keeping its patrons busy with constant theme nights and activities. Fight Club W; Karaoke Th; Disco on F and Sa; free Jukebox all day Su. Happy Hour Tu, Th, and Sa 4-6pm ($2 pints). Open Th-Sa 11pm-3am, Su-W 11pm-1am.

The Fat Snapper, 20 Hamilton St. (tel. 578 5499). Sea-salty gumboots track the wooden floor of this spacious pub, as local and visiting fishermen reel in some fun with after-work dinner and drinks. Meals ($6) and sandwiches ($2) fill up those taking a break from pool, poker, and horse-betting on the overhead monitors. No dress code, no credit cards. Open M-W 11am-3am, Th-Sa 9am-3am, Su 11am-7pm.

◉ SIGHTS

While Tauranga has a notable history, don't expect to spend the day marveling at architecture or museums—people come here for what's around Tauranga (read: the beach). If the line at the **Bungee Rocket** (see activities below) is too long, some historical buildings and parks clustered around the north end of town give a deeper cultural context. At the end of the Strand sits **Te Awanui,** an intricately carved replica Maori canoe. The small greenhouse and rose gardens of **Robbins Park** have a view of the harbor and the less-than-picturesque shipping industry. Up Cliff Rd. and left on Mission St. you'll find the beautiful grounds of the **Elms Mission Station** (tel. 578 4011), established in 1835 as Tauranga's first mission. Walk the small path through the quiet and beautiful grounds where ripe kiwifruit and tangerines hang down by the chapel in late fall. A bit farther off the beaten track, is the Mission's cemetery on a mound, just to the right of Dive Crescent's intersection with Marsh St. (Building open "fine" Sunday afternoons from 2-3:30pm, but grounds open anytime.) At the **Mills Reef Winery,** 143 Moffat Rd. (tel. 576 8800), off

Waihi Rd. on the way out of town, makes both kiwifruit and grape wine and tastings flow for free (open daily 10am-5pm; tastings begin at 8:30am).

⚡ ACTIVITIES

Activities and adventure options abound in the burgeoning tourist mecca of Tauranga. Most involve water, but landlubbers can explore the local wineries, a nearby *marae*, and various local hikes.

ADVENTURE

For the more reckless, there is skydiving, gliding, and, in a bizarre manifestation of the Kiwi obsession with all things bungy, the **Bungee Rocket** (tel. 578 3057). Situated on the Strand right on the waterfront, the contraption shoots its hapless passenger 50m into the air at a speed up to 160kph in 1.3 seconds ($30; open daily 10am-10pm, later on weekends). **Papamoa Adventure Park** (tel. 542 0972), in Papamoa off Welcome Bay Rd., provides horse-trekking, 4WD bikes, grass-skiing, paintball, and 160 acres of pastoral land with superb vistas for picnics. If these attractions and the community of farm animals (pigs, roosters, wild turkeys, goats, chickens, and cattle) don't immediately redeem the 15-minute drive from town, the death-defying dirt luge track certainly will.

Tauranga is not far from the **Wairoa River** and its gut-wrenching Grade 5 rapids. The river is only raftable 26 days a year from January to March, however, when the

---

MONEY DOESN'T GROW ON TREES New Zealand's fuzzy unofficial mascot has endeared itself to many a visitor, but don't let such sentimentality lead you to a career as a kiwifruit picker. Although the idea of alternately backpacking and picking one's way across the North Island may be appealing, the job is far from glamorous. Those who work in the orchards do it for the cash, not the love of the fruit. Kiwifruit contractors assemble groups of 9 to 15 pickers, who earn about $12.50 for each bin they pick. Depending on the speed of their team, pickers can earn anywhere from $60-100 a day. Because picking is a group effort, one slacker can ruin both the speed and paycheck of an entire team. Workers must wear gloves, and those working in T-bar kiwi trees must climb into branches after their elusive quarry. The days are a grueling nine hours long, weather-permitting; blessedly, rain means an automatic day off. Although the teamwork and bonding under stress create a distinct culture, the fruits of this labor might not be worth the physical and mental frustration of the job.

---

dam on its upper reaches is opened. **Woodrow Expeditions** (tel. 576 2628 or 577 0817) does one-hour jaunts down the Wairoa ($65 per person). Whether it's deep-sea fishing or reefer-game, most trips are booked at and leave from the **Fishing and Boat Charters office** on Coronation Pier (tel. 577 9100). A full-day excursion with shaggy-bearded Butler and **Gemini Galaxsea Charters** (evening/winter tel. 578 3197 or mobile 025 272 8353) will take you onto the open seas to swim with the dolphins, explore off-shore islands and seal colonies, or simply relax as your grizzled captain booms his opinions across the deck ($80 per person, gear provided). For those with an aversion to water, there are other fish in the proverbial sea of activities. You can act out your death wish in a 2500m fall ($190) with **Tandem Skydiving** (tel. 576 7990). Slightly less precipitous for both body and budget is gliding: the **Tauranga Gliding Club** (tel. 575 6768) offers varying height levels of flights on weekends and Wednesday afternoons ($50-75).

DAYTRIPS AND WALKS

Thirty-five kilometers offshore lies **Mayor Island,** an isolated and undeveloped volcanic region under Maori ownership. Snorkeling and diving areas abound, but the island has no amenities besides a rugged campground, and you must obtain permission to land beforehand. **MV Manutere** makes seasonal runs to the island—more information can be found at **Coronation Pier.** Few people make it out to the 24km of beaches at nearby **Matakana Island.** Stretching across the entrance to Tauranga Harbour and absorbing the blows of the Pacific, the island makes for one of the Bay of Plenty's best surf spots.

If you've run out of money from one too many rocket bungees, head over to the **DOC** and learn about the area's hikes. Otherwise, you'll have to duke it out with the joggers on the boardwalks around the popular **Waikareao Estuary.** The **McLaren Falls Park tracks,** a 15-minute drive down SH29 toward Hamilton, are pleasantly pastoral. For bunkhouse accommodations at the park, call 543 3382; if you get the answering machine also try the Tauranga District Council at 577 7000. For more mobile travelers, the **Kaimai Mamaku Forest Park,** its hills stretching to the west of town, provides 37,140 hectares of forests and rivers laced with trails. It's basically an extension of the **Coromandel Forest Park,** but doesn't get the same crowds.

MT. MAUNGANUI

From the mists of Tauranga Harbour rises Mt. Maunganui, an extinct volcanic cone visible from kilometers away. Attracting tourists from all over New Zealand and abroad, "the Mount" explodes in the summer months. Formerly a Maori residence and stronghold, the mountain now reigns over the seasonal town that bears its name. In mellow Maunganui, tiled sidewalks, palm trees, and turquoise-painted street lamps frame layers of beach, crashing waves, and sky.

⊠ ORIENTATION AND PRACTICAL INFORMATION. When in doubt, head toward anything with the word "Maunganui" in it; the town's main drag is **Maunganui Rd.,** and the center of town is almost directly below the Mount. **Marine Pde./ Ocean Beach Rd.** runs along the ocean and toward the fine sands of **Papamoa Beach Reserve. The Mall** runs on the harborside of downtown.

The **Information Centre** (tel. 575 5099), on Salisbury Ave. is open daily 8:30am-5:30pm, winter M-F 9am-5pm, Sa 9am-4pm. For local **buses, InterCity** (tel. 575 4669) and **Newmans** run daily to **Tauranga** (15min., every hr., $3), with stops at the Hot Pools, the Bayfair Shopping Center 3km from town, and the McDonald's before Prince St. on Maunganui Rd. In the summer, take the **ferry** to **Tauranga** from Salisbury Wharf (every hr. 9am-5pm, $4). Other services include: **Thomas Cook,** 194 Maunganui Rd. (tel. 575 3058; open M-F 8:30am-5pm (Tu 9:15am) and, blessedly, Sa 10am-noon; **police** (tel. 575 3143), next door to the Information Centre (open M-F 8am-4pm); **Post Shop and Copy Centre,** 155 Maunganui Rd. (tel. 575 8180; open M-F 9am-5pm). **Telephone Code:** 07.

⌂ ACCOMMODATIONS. Prices go up and space goes down for most accommodations in summer. Phone well in advance if you want to stay at the **Maunganui Domain Motor Camp** (tel. 575 4471) at the base of the mountain. They have 274 powered tent or caravan sites stretching from the harborside to the beachfront, as well as one tourist cabin with a kitchenette. The location is prime, but your view will most likely be of your neighbor 30m away. (Tent sites from $10; vehicles or caravans from $10 per person, children under 15 $5.) You can't miss **Mount Backpackers,** 87 Maunganui Rd. (tel./fax 575 0860), the sunny yellow hostel in the town center. Space is tight throughout, but the beds are cushy, the hosts are laid-back and helpful, and it's a stone's throw from the beach and the best bars in town. (Free pickups. Dorms Su-Th $15, F-Sa $16; doubles $45; weekly dorms $100). If you're looking for space, bright blue **Pacific Coast Backpackers (Nomads),** 432 Maunganui Rd. (tel. 574 9601 or (08) 066 6622), provides enough room for a large game of hide-and-seek inside its massive kitchen, game room, communal areas, and camouflaging murals. Thick, comfy mattresses and a quiet atmosphere may tempt travelers to make the 15-minute walk from the center of town. (Key deposit $10. Singles $16; twins and doubles $20.)

FOOD. Across the street from Mount Backpackers, **Ship to Shore Takeaways** (tel. 575 5942), provide giant, cheap, fresh meals of the daily catch ($5-6). The proprietors love backpackers and make sure to dole out extra big portions if they know you're on a tight budget. (Open daily 9am-9pm, winter daily 10am-7:30pm.) Totally vegan and totally mellow is the **Zucchini Cafe,** 79 Maunganui Rd. (tel. 574 4149), a coffee house and restaurant serving breakfast, lunch, and dinner, with local artwork and couches begging you to sink into them—totally. The recipes make being vegan seem sinful, with filling veggie samosas ($5.50), falafel ($8.50), and all-you-can-eat Tuesday and Wednesday dinners for $15. (Open daily 9am-11pm, winter Tu-Su 10am-10pm, M 10am-3pm.) **Tail Gators** (tel. 575 TAIL) and **THAIphoon Restaurant** (tel. 572 3545), next door to one another on Pacific Avenue off Mt. Maunganui Rd., offer good sandwiches ($4.50) and Thai food (entrees around $12), respectively. **Price Cutters,** at the corner of Pacific Ave. and Maunganui Rd., has beach snacks (open M-Sa 7:30am-6pm, Su 7:30am-5pm).

ACTIVITIES. It doesn't take a bloodhound to sniff out the attractions in the Mount—they stick out like, well, an **extinct volcano** rising 232m from sea level. Follow Adams Ave. or The Mall out to where they peter out into a paved lot and well-maintained track around the base of the volcano (it's even wheelchair-accessible; ask at the motor camp office for access keys). The track is an easy and dramatic 45-minute walk with fantastically warped rocks and crashing surf on one side, munching sheep and tangled forest on the other. You can start from the other side as well, by following the motor camp road around to the ocean side and going though the marked gate. Routes go up the mountain at several spots off the base track, each offering a strenuous 35-minute ascent and a knee-knocking 20-minute descent. There's also a short jaunt out onto the misnamed peninsular **Moturiki Island** that juts into the main beach, and the nearby **Blow Hole.**

The Mount's other major draw is the **hot saltwater pools,** located at the base of the mountain. Once natural, these pools are now preserved artificially. But your body won't know the difference if you make the $2.50 investment (children $1.50) and splash into the main pool's 39°C welcome. A more tepid lap pool, private pools ($3.50 per 30min., children $2.50), small water slide, storage lockers, massages, and multi-trip passes are all available. (Open M-Sa 6am-10pm, Su 8am-10pm.) The main **beach** with the best surfing is right up against the mountain, but white sand stretches away to the east for kilometers, and there are more sheltered waters just across the peninsula in **Pilot Bay.** In the three weeks following Christmas, the main beach comes alive with concerts, surf championships, and more. The Information Centre has schedule booklets.

WHAKATANE

Whakatane (FAH-ka-taw-nee) struggles to complement the wealth of natural offerings surrounding it. Visitors come mainly for the beaches, the climate (the town enjoys more days of sun than almost anywhere else in New Zealand), and the town's single largest draw, White Island, the ominously smoking volcanic island 50km offshore. As transportation options are limited, it's a good idea to rent a car to reach the surrounding attractions, using Whakatane (pop. 14,400) as a base.

ORIENTATION AND PRACTICAL INFORMATION. Whakatane is situated on drained wetlands between high bluffs and the final bend of the Whakatane River. The main commercial center is pushed up against the bluffs along **the Strand,** with **Boon St.** and **Richardson St.** branching off it. **Landing/Domain Rd.,** the western entrance of SH2, and **Commerce St.** against the bluffs are the main routes in and out of town. **Discover Whakatane** (tel. 308 6058), on Boon St., is the information center (open M-F 9am-5pm, Sa 9am-1pm, Su 10am-2pm; Jan. daily 7am-7pm). **InterCity** (tel. 308 6169) leaves from Pyne St. for **Rotorua** (1hr., 1-2 per day, $24) and **Gisborne** (3hr., 1 per day, $48) via **Opotiki** (45min., $16). For **taxis,** call Dial a Cab (tel. 0800

342 522'). For rental cars, **Hertz,** 105 Commerce St., (tel. 308 6155) is the most accessible from downtown. **Hitchers** often head immediately across the Whakatane River Bridge. The roundabout where Gorge Rd. branches off Commerce St. towards Ohope is considered by many to be the best spot for those going east. Other services include: **WestpacTrust Bank,** on the Strand between Boon and Commerce St. (open M-Tu and Th-F 9am-4:30pm, W 9:30am-4:30pm); **police** (24hr. tel. 308 5255); **hospital** (tel. 307 8999), west on Domain St., left on King St., and right on Stewart St; **post office** (tel./fax 307 1155), on Commerce St. at the Strand (open M-F 8:30am-5pm, Sa 9am-noon). **Telephone Code:** 07.

⌂ ACCOMMODATIONS. While there may not be much to do in town, Whakatane houses backpackers in hotels for hostel prices. Tending toward the old and dark, the motels found along Landing/Domain Rd. are generally cheap. For beachfront views at comparable prices, those with transportation should head over the hill 7km to the campground or motels at Ohope Beach. In town, the **Whakatane Hotel,** (tel. 307 1670) at George St. and the Strand, is the closest thing to a hostel. With long carpeted hallways reminiscent of *The Shining*, the second floor provides backpackers with quality rooms without all that spooky "RED RUM" business. It's clean and centrally located with a kitchen and lounge area. (Dorms beds in doubles or quads $16; singles $30.) You're certainly not paying for the view at the **Camelia Court Motel,** 11 Domain Rd. (tel. 308 6213)—scenic as the KFC may be—but the price is redeemed by soft beds and a relatively central location in a modern and attractive colonial-looking motel. Extras include a trampoline, game room, and free pickup and dropoff at the bus depot or airport. (Singles $65; doubles $73, extra person $10; 4-person family unit with queen-sized bed and 2 singles $100.) Like its straightforward name, the **Whakatane Motor Camp and Caravan Park** (tel. 308 8694) pulls no punches. Follow Beach Rd. to the end of McGarvey Rd., 1km from the town center, to find typical cement-floored campground bathrooms, a kitchen, and a TV lounge with worn chairs. A game room and decently sized swimming pool help to liven things up. (Tent sites, caravans, and vehicles $10 per person; austere cabins $20, extra person $10; tourist cabins with TV, kitchen, and fridge $35, $40 for 2, extra person $10.)

⌂ FOOD. Next door to the Whakatane Hotel, the **Why Not Cafe and Bar** serves a delicate lunch and dinner including crispy calamari rings ($7.50), all-day omelettes ($8), and an assortment of specialty coffees ($6.50). Take your drink into the comfier lounge next door with its large-screen TV, toe-tappin' music, and fireplace (Open from 10am.) If you're in the mood for a quick bite, let the blinking marquee lights guide you to **Neptune's Takeaways,** 64 Boon St. Eat the burgers and toasted sandwiches (under $5) behind beaded curtains while admiring the intricacies of the Little Mermaid-esque ocean mural—just hope it doesn't come alive and exact revenge if you're eating the fish 'n' chips. (Open Su-W 9am-9pm, F 9am-midnight, Sa 10:30-9pm.)

⌂ ACTIVITIES. By far, the two biggest attractions in the area are trips to **White Island** (see below) and swimming with the resident dolphins that congregate in the offshore waters. **Dolphins Down Under** (tel. 308 4636), on the wharf at the end of the Strand, is the main operator. They provide all equipment, instruction, refreshments, and even hot showers for the three- to four-hour trip. Depending on the tides and weather, there can be as many as five trips per day during the summer (direct booking $93; under 12, $50). For a more predatorial interaction with Whatkane Marine life, join **M.V. Charmaine** (tel. 308 6871) on a line fishing trip (8am-4pm; $30). Don't leave Whakatane without taking at least a few of the bush walks in the area. There are three **scenic reserves** in a small area: **Kohi Point,** atop the hill over Whakatane, with its panoramic views; **Ohope Scenic Reserve,** home to one of New Zealand's largest remaining pohutukawa forests; and **Mokorua Bush Scenic Reserve,** a recovering pasture land. The walk around the hill between Whakatane and

NORTH ISLAND

nearby Ohope Beach is especially fantastic. A long walk (over 20km), **Nga Tapuwae o Toi** (the Footprints of Toi), connects all three; it can be done in one day, but many split it into three shorter segments. Also try the one-hour walk to the **Tauwhare Pa,** built several hundred years ago, or the **Mt. Tarawera Crater Walk,** a rather challenging but very rewarding two-hour walk up a dormant volcano. Access may be restricted during the summer, due to the danger of fires. The **Information Centre** on Boon St. has pamphlets with more information and departure points on area walks.

A huge fern-covered rock reposes in its own green park along the Strand at the center of town. That's **Pahaturoa,** a sacred Maori ceremonial site that now bears a plaque to the Maori who died serving in World War I. One quick turn off the Strand, the **Wairere Falls** drop impressively from the bluffs above. If the falls inspire, you may want to stroll down the riverbank to where the river meets the sea. On the large rock on the other side stands a bronze statue of **Wairaka,** the female trailblazer whose bravery gave the town its name. The small **Whakatane District Museum and Gallery** (tel. 307 9805), at Boon St. near Pyne St., is a rainy day activity (open Tu-F 10am-4:30pm, Sa 11am-1:30pm, Su 2-4:30pm).

NEAR WHAKATANE: WHITE ISLAND

Fifty kilometers off the coast of the Bay of Plenty, sheathed in its own cloud of steam and gas, sits Whakaari, "that which can be made visible, uplifted to view." Captain Cook, in his circuit around New Zealand, called it White Island after the steam cloud forever hanging above its volcanic peaks. Actually composed of three distinct cones, two of which are now extinct, White Island is a landscape of lunar dimensions, with its craters and steaming vents, boiling sulfuric acid pools, and sinuous flows of solid rock. Even in such an inhospitable place, ever-resourceful humans attempted to eke out profit with a sulfur mine that operated intermittently throughout the late 1800s and early 1900s. This evidently did not please the gods, as a violent explosion and landslide killed 10 men in 1914. Today, a more successful way of exploiting White Island has been found in the pockets of visitors eager to experience the geologic adrenaline rush of visiting this otherworldly isle. For a price, anyone can brave the noxious sulfur fumes and make their own offering to the volcanic gods. Although the island is a privately owned reserve is and relatively inaccessible (to put it mildly), there are several options for those wanting to visit. The most affordable approach is by boat. **PeeJay Charters** were named "guardians" of White Island (tel. 308 9588; 5-6hr. round-trip; $95 per person, lunch included; weather- and tide-dependent). **Te Kahurangi** (tel. 323 7829) runs daily trips in the summer and weekend trips in the winter ($85, lunch included). Boat landings are occasionally stymied by wind, so don't count your volcanoes before they explode. Another option is a thrilling if slightly more vicarious fly-over. Both **Bell-Air** (tel. 308 6656) and **East Bay Flight Centre** (tel. 308 8446) offer trips over White Island as well as other nearby sights (50min. round-trip, $110 per seat). For a touch-down on the cratered surface *and* a fly-over, **Volcano Helicopters** (tel. 0800 804 354) charges $295 per person. Whichever medium you choose, the Visitors Centre charges a commission for booking, so it's cheaper to book on your own.

NEAR WHAKATANE: OHOPE BEACH

Ohope Beach is just that—11km of spectacular unbroken beach blessed with rolling azure waves and views of the rugged East Cape sweeping away to the northeast. Visitors to this largely residential town come to marinate in sun and sand with the option of taking leisurely tramps around Mokorua, the hill between Ohope and Whakatane. A two-hour journey by sand (or a quick ride on the free bus service running 3 times a day in summer) traverses the length of Ohope's narrow strip of land, taking you from the steep bluffs of Mokorua, where surfers struggle to ride small waves, to the entrance of Ohiwa Harbour, a historically rich shell-fishery for area Maori and modern resting place for wayward golf balls from the Ohope Beach Golf Course.

The main road, branching off at the end of the highway, is West End Rd., which moving east becomes Pohutukawa Rd., which becomes Harbour Rd. The Whakatane Information Centre staffs a beachfront **hut** off West End Rd. from December to February. **Buses** on the way to Opotiki stop across from the Mobil Station on Pohutukawa Ave., about 300m down from the West End turn-off (around 3:45pm daily; book in Whakatane). Thumbers who head to Ohope Beach report that **hitchhiking** prospects are fairly good.

Lovely beachfront lots in Ohope sell for $300,000, but if you already blew the inheritance, the **Ohope Beach Holiday Park** (tel./fax 312 4460), at the far east side of the beach, offers similar views for a slightly less exorbitant price. Mini-golf, a pool with a waterslide, a food shop, and sporting equipment rental are all part of the bargain. There are 200 tent sites, 100 powered sites ($9), and tourist flats or cabins for two (from $36). Right next door on Harbour Rd. is **Surf & Sand Holiday Park** (tel. 312 4884). New facilities (showers, toilet, kitchen, TV room, and laundry) are all available free of charge. (Open Nov.-Feb. Powered sites $13 per person.). Most motels are on West End Rd., and it's the same seasonal story.

The **Ohope Beach Resort,** 5 West End Rd. (tel./fax 312 4692), the sole provider of Ohope's nightlife, is quite a complex with accommodations, bar, restaurant, and hopping nightclub appropriately separated from each other. The rooms have small beds in sunny rooms with beach views and kitchenettes. There's a small pool (though shame on those who swim in a kidney-shaped pool when the Pacific is within spitting distance) and volleyball net. (Backpackers room, with nose-bleed triple-decker bunk beds $14; room with double waterbed and two singles $75, Jan. $120.) The native Kauri timber glows at the **Kauri Kafe and Bar** downstairs, where Kiwi culinary delights like steak or seafood dinners ($20), or less expensive bar snacks satisfy those dancing up an appetite to DJ Ivan's tunes at the packed Saturday nightclub (9:30pm-2am). (Bar and Kafe open daily Nov.-Feb. noon-midnight. Feb.-Nov. bar open 3pm-close, Kafe from 5pm-close.) Upstairs at the polished wooden tables, wrap-around windows, and outdoor balcony of **The Local** (locally called the O.B.R.), you'll find other ways to work up an appetite. Pool tables, a mini-casino, and easy conversation integrate visitors with the folks who give the bar its name. (Open from noon, winter from 3pm.) There aren't any other restaurant options in Ohope, but for a hot breakfast or a quick snack ($3-7), pop into **Beach Haven** (tel. 312 4755), inside a convenience store just a few steps east from the Ohope Beach Resort. Those with wheels can take Wainui Rd. out to **Ohiwa Oyster Farm** (tel. 312 4565) for a $4 cup of fresh oysters.

OPOTIKI

Poorer and more raw than its neighbor Whakatane, Opotiki (o-PO-tah-kee) can seem as if the isolation and wildness of its surroundings have seeped into the town limits—but it's for that wildness and wilderness that most visitors come. As the gateway to the East Coast and the last town of any real size (pop. 4153) before the remote, rugged beauty and the isolated Maori settlements along the spectacular coast, Opotiki straddles the presence of two cultures—and bears the battle scars to show it. From the earliest resistance to missionaries in the 1800s to the series of battles ignited by the 1865 murder of Rev. Karl Volker in the Hiona St. Stephen's Anglican Church, Opotoki has accumulated a fascinating and tumultuous history. Today, surf, isolation, and a couple of well-placed budget accommodations make it a worthwhile stopping point.

◪ ORIENTATION AND PRACTICAL INFORMATION. It's anyone's guess why the original settlement was placed where it was (an evenly spaced grid boxed between the confluence of the **Waioweka** and **Otara** Rivers) when the ocean is so close, but so it went. Ponder the possibilities at the **Information Centre** (tel. 315 8484; fax 315 6102), at the intersection of St. John and Elliott St. (open daily 8:30am-5pm, winter M-F). The **DOC** office is in the same place (open 8am-4:30pm).

Be sure to pick up the super-helpful *Opotiki and the East Cape* brochure. **Inter-City** leaves from the **bus depot**, across the street from the Information Centre, to **Gisborne** (2hr., 1-2 per day, $28) and **Rotorua** (2hr., 1-2 per day, $40, if booked 2 weeks in advance $24) via **Whakatane** (1hr., $16). To book tickets come to the **Holiday Shoppe** (tel. 315 6125) on 109b Church St. The **BNZ** is on the corner of Elliott and Church St. (open M-F 9am-4:30pm). The **post office** is on Church St. (open M-F 8:30am-5pm, Tu from 9:30am, Sa 9:30am-noon).

▛▟ ACCOMMODATIONS AND FOOD. You can almost skip a rock across the surf from the porch of the **Opotiki Beach House Backpackers** (tel. 316 5117), on Appelton Rd. at Waiotohi Beach, 5km west of town on SH2. The toilet is in a separate building and bunk beds in the barn-style loft sport thin mattresses—but oh-baby, what a location! Sit on the deck (an informal cafe in summer) and watch White Island smoke, or borrow a free surf kayak or surfboard and hit the secluded beach. (Free bikes available to get into town. Dorms $13; doubles $30; tent sites $11. Cash only.) Though the outside has seen better days, the inside of **Central Oasis Backpackers,** 30 King St. (tel. 315 5165), endears itself with high ceilings, a homey kitchen, and a comfy lounge. Overlook the wildly overgrown garden from the charming chairs of the veranda. But millennium enthusiasts beware: new owner Lothar is cynical of hype-happy New Year fever. (Dorms $12; doubles $16; twins $14; tent sites $8.) There's an old yesteryear feeling to the **Masonic Hotel** (tel. 315 6115), at the corner of Elliott and Church St., that the baby blue walls and high ceilings can't disguise. Maybe it's the small rooms or the 19th-century reproductions on the walls. Maybe it's downtown Opotiki. Still, with a popular restaurant and bar downstairs, it's central and clean. (Singles $25; twins and doubles $45.)

The quick answer to what the choices are for eating and going out in Opotiki is: not many. Once you've cruised Church St., you've pretty much seen all your options. But even without much competition, the restaurant of **The Opotiki Hotel** (tel. 315 6173), on Church St. opposite the museum, has delicious food. Chef Klaus Horman changes the menu often, but Opotiki diners can always count on a good steak or venison dish with tasty, creative sauce options ($20-21). (Open Tu-Sa noon-2pm and 5:30-8:30pm, winter W-Sa.)

◪ SIGHTS. Most of Opotiki's attraction is its beach (which is currently lined with driftwood accumulated from a four-day flood in Feb.) and wilderness (which can be difficult to access without your own vehicle). Entertain yourself only on a very rainy day at the **Opotiki Heritage and Agricultural Society Museum,** 123 Church St. (open M-Sa 10am-3:30pm, Su 1:30-4pm; admission $2, children 50¢, families $3), or head across the street (ask at the museum for a key) to the **Hiona St. Stephen's Anglican Church.** The Rev. Karl Volkner was brutally murdered here in 1865 during a Maori-Pakeha conflict. One popular attraction 7km from town is **Hukutaia Domain,** an 11-acre park with a great collection of New Zealand's native plant species. It's worth going, if only for the **Taketakerau,** a huge hollow puriri tree that was sacred to the local Whakatorea tribe. Bones of the deceased used to be dug up after a few years and placed in the hollow to keep them safe from enemies. Today, the bones have been moved to another site. Also just outside of Opotiki, 12km down Rt. 2 on the way to Gisborne, **Waioweka Gorge** lures travelers with picnic spots and gorgeous photo ops.

EAST COAST AND HAWKE'S BAY

The East Coast and Hawke's Bay are blessed with the boundless optimism of those first to see the sun. The entire coast is sun-drenched, from the sunbursts of Napier's Art Deco buildings to the home of the world's first dawn, Gisborne's Mt. Hikurangi. (Or does the sun strike first on Hastings's Te Mata Peak? See p. 184.) Ripening the "Fruit Bowl of New Zealand," the sun's rays give rise to orchards and fields overrun with luscious produce and grapes. Wineries and award-winning Chardonnays draw visitors to both easterly Gisborne and cosmopolitan Napier. The stubborn streak of the East Coast's personality appears in the remote East Cape and the dense inland wilds of Te Urewera National Park and the North Island's largest remaining tract of native forest.

▧ EAST COAST AND HAWKE'S BAY HIGHLIGHTS

■ The streets of **Napier** (p. 178) are ripe for exploration of all things Art Deco.
■ The waterfalls and tramps of **East Cape** (p. 171) afford a glimpse of virtually tourist-free New Zealand.
■ The isolation of **Whirinaki Forest Park** (p. 177) contains a wide range of New Zealand's native flora and fauna.

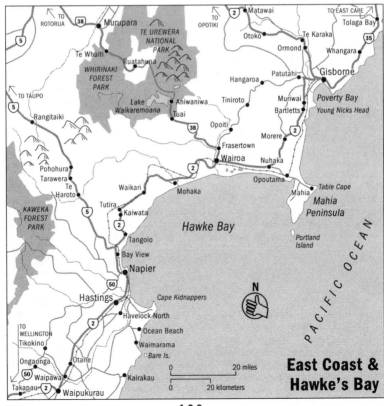

East Coast & Hawke's Bay

EAST COAST

GISBORNE

Greeting the dawn has become something of an industry for Gisborne (pop. 30,000), which markets itself as the first city to see the sun each morning. New Year's festivities have long attracted international enthusiasts, but this year, Gisborne parties like it's 1999, pulling out all the stops to entertain thousands of expected visitors. Overall, it's not a bad place to begin the next 1000 years. The town is small and friendly, with notably strong cultural offerings. A 50% Maori population combined with Polytech art classes make this city New Zealand's largest center for contemporary Maori art. But beauty extends beyond the galleries: stellar beaches offer excellent surfing and swimming, surrounding bluffs give great vistas across the sea, and the relatively mild, sunny climate makes for ideal farmland. The site of Captain Cook's first landing in 1769, the city also has a vast history it won't let you forget, no matter how hard you may endeavour.

■ ORIENTATION AND PRACTICAL INFORMATION

Gisborne is laid out where the **Taruheru** and the **Waimata Rivers** join to form the **Turanganui River** (at 1200m, one of the world's shortest rivers). **Gladstone Rd. (SH35,** which turns into **Wainui Rd.** over the Turanganui Bridge) is the main drag; orient yourself by the **clock tower** at Gladstone and Grey St., alongside the mock-up of the *Endeavour*. The **Esplanade** runs along the Wainui Rd. side of the river, while **Awapuni** and **Salisbury Rd.** run parallel to the main beaches.

Visitors Center: Gisborne Information Centre, 209 Grey St. (tel. 868 6139; fax 868 6138). Headquarters for East Cape tourism. 18-hole mini-golf course out back. Open daily 7:30am-7:30pm, winter 9am-5pm.

DOC: 63 Carnarvon St. (tel. 867 8531; fax 867 8015), between Gladstone and Palmerston St. Open M-F 8am-4:30pm.

Airplanes: The **airport** is west of the city, at the end of Chalmers Rd. off Gladstone Rd. **Air New Zealand Link** (tel. 867 1608) has many daily flights to **Auckland** (1hr., $235) and **Wellington** (1hr., $250). Fare reductions possible. Book direct or use the **ANZ office,** 37 Bright St. (tel. 868 2700; fax 868 2701). Taxis to the airport run around $7.

Buses: Buses (tel. 868 6196) arrive at and depart from the Info Centre. **InterCity** departs daily for: **Auckland** (9hr., 8am, $79); **Rotorua** (summer only, 4hr., 1-2 per day, $59) via **Whakatane** (3hr., $43); and **Napier** (4hr., 9am, $33). **Coachrite Connections** (tel. 868 9969 or mobile 025 469 867) goes to **Napier** (4hr., 3-6 per week, $28) and points further south via **Wairoa** ($18). For transport in the East Cape, see p. 172.

Taxis: Gisborne Taxis (tel. 867 2222), **Sun City Taxis** (tel. 867 6767), and **Eastland Taxis** (tel. 868 1133). All run 24hr.

Car Rental: Scottie's, 265 Grey St. (tel. 867 7947), next to the Information Centre and part of Ray Scragg Motors, offers cheaper rates than the major chains. Standard economy vehicle $35 per day, 19¢ per km, or $55 per day, unlimited distance. Open daily M-F 7am-5pm. For weekend service, use **Budget** (tel. 0800 650 700), based at the airport. Standard economy vehicle $74 per day, unlimited distance. Deposit $250.

Bicycle/Surf Rental: Maintrax Cycle (tel. 867 4571), at the corner of Roebuck and Gladstone St., has bikes ($10 per day, deposit $50). **Sungate,** 55 Salisbury Rd. (tel. 868 1673), rents surfboards ($30 per day), body boards ($20), and kayaks ($35). Hourly and half-day rates also available.

Hitchhiking: To head to the surf beaches at Wainui or Makorori, many hitchhikers start out along Wainui Rd. Hitchers going southwest toward Wairoa or north to Opotiki head to the end of SH35/Gladstone Rd. at Makaraka Rd., where the highway branches off to its respective destinations. Even in the midst of all this, Let's Go does not recommend hitchhiking.

Currency Exchange: Westpac (tel. 867 1359 or 0800 400 600), at the corner of Gladstone Rd. and Peel St. Open M-Tu and Th-F 9am-4:30pm, W 9:30am-4:30pm.

Police: (tel. 867 9059), at the corner of Peel St. and Gladstone Rd.

Medical Services: Kaiti Road Medical Center (tel. 867 7411), at the corner of Turenne and De Lautour Rd., off Wainui Rd. Open M-F 8am-8pm, Sa-Su 9am-6pm. For **urgent care** only, look to the **hospital** (tel. 867 9099) on Ormond Rd. Take Lytton Rd. north from Gladstone Rd. and follow the signs.

Post Office: The Gisborne Post Shop, 166 Gladstone Rd. (tel. 867 8220), inside **Books and More.** Open M-F 8:30am-5:30pm, Sa 9am-4pm, Su 10am-3pm.

Internet Access: Verve Cafe, 121 Gladstone Rd. (tel. 868 9095). $7 per 30min. **Cyberzone,** 83 Gladstone Rd. (tel. 868 7138). $14.50 per hr. Open M-Sa 10am-10pm, Su noon-6pm, winter M-Sa 10am-8pm, Su noon-6pm.

Telephone Code: 06.

 ACCOMMODATIONS

Gisborne's beachfront places often charge $10-20 more than those just across the street. In the off season, hostels attract permanent boarders who rent out rooms for months at a time, creating a very different atmosphere from the summer. Call ahead in summer.

Gisborne Backpackers, 690 Gladstone Rd. (tel. 868 1000; fax 868 4000). 2km from downtown. Free pickup from bus station or airport. Years of exhausted backpackers haven't managed to erase the sterility of this former orphanage and rest home. Small, clean, motel-like rooms with thick-mattress beds overlook the well-kept grounds. Pool table. Sheet and blanket $4. Dorms $16; singles $25; twins $40; doubles $40.

Flying Nun Backpackers, 147 Roebuck St. (tel. 868 0461), off Gladstone Rd. at the corner of Childers and Roebuck Rd. Sleep in Mother Superior's sewing room and kick back in confessional while you wait your turn for the pool table at this convent-turned-backpackers, complete with stained-glass windows and a stone cross steeple. Cheap rates, rowdy summer atmosphere, and an irreverent (if a little creepy) attitude displace vows of poverty, chastity, and obedience here—but patience may be required for an early morning stream of squeals and giggles from nearby children's schools. Key deposit $10. Dorms $15; singles $25; doubles $40; tent sites $10. Cash only.

Gisborne YHA Hostel (tel. 867 3269), on the corner of Wainui Rd. and Harris St. A 5min. walk from downtown, this bright orange YHA attracts young and old alike with a diverse offering of rooms. While the mattresses may make for a hammock-like sleeping experience, the TV lounge and kitchen area entertain and bond its steady stream of guests. Cooking lessons from Wayne, the manager's husband. Dorms $15; singles $20; twins, doubles, and triples $18; self-contained family units $18, children 5-17 $11.

Waikanae Beach Holiday Park (tel. 867 5634; fax 867 9765), end of Grey St. Fronting the beach and central to downtown. Facilities galore. Tent and powered sites granted privacy by rows of Norfolk pines. Cabins $26; tourist flats $52; tent sites for 2 $18, powered $20, extra person $9-10. Prices rise $2-4 in summer.

Beachcomber Motel, 73 Salisbury Rd. (tel. 868 9349; fax 868 6974). You could bounce off one of their trampolines right onto the beach, though you'll need 10min. to walk to the town center. Complimentary newspaper, kitchen facilities, TV, and spa pool. Singles $75; doubles $85.

FOOD

Find respite from the usual artery-clogging budget cuisine at downtown Gisborne's nicer cafes and quality restaurants, most on **Gladstone Rd.** The eatery complex on the wharf is a great waterfront option for food and nightlife. And there's always **Pak 'N Save,** a block up from the clock tower on Gladstone Rd., and **Woolworth's,** on the corner of Gladstone and Carnarvon St. (both open daily 8am-8pm).

■ **Mega Bite** (tel. 867 5787), on Peel St. by Palmerston Rd. Backpackers from across the globe find home-cooking sanctuary here—just read the personal testimonies written on the walls. You'll be writing home to mom after creating your own sandwich masterpiece for only $3 or enjoying a BLT or burger for under $5. Free coffee or espresso with *Let's Go.* Open daily 6:30am-5pm, with longer hours over the summer.

Fettucini Brothers (tel. 868 5700), on Peel St. near Palmerston Rd. Menu descriptions alone will make you salivate. Pastas in a heaping main size ($17.50) or smaller but sufficient entree ($11.50) have a variety of enticing vegetarian or meat sauces. Open daily from 6pm, bar from 5pm.

Dago's Famous Pizzeria and Thai Cuisine, 50 Gladstone Rd. (tel. 868 7666 or 0800 PIZZAS). Nelson Dago and Soon Chia join hands and chopsticks to make some of Gisborne's tastiest and most creative dishes. Read National Geographics while waiting for takeaway sweet-and-sour pizza. Or mix and match your own masterpiece from the ever-changing ingredients of seafoods, veggies, meats, and sauces. Pizzas $6.50-$20 and Thai mains $12-14. Delivery $3. Open Su-W 5-9pm, Th 5-10pm, F-Sa 5pm-2:30am.

Verve Cafe, 121 Gladstone Rd. (tel. 868 9095). Hip without being overbearing, the airy Verve has local artwork on the walls, couches in the back, and Internet access. Decent espresso drinks ($2.50), grilled sandwiches with a choice of meat ($7), and fulfilling fish dishes ($12). Open daily 8:30am-10pm, longer hours around New Year's.

NORTH ISLAND

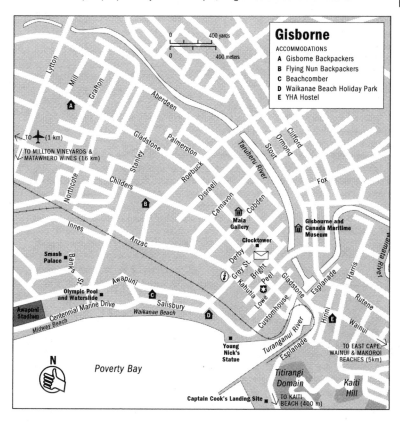

Gisborne

ACCOMMODATIONS
A Gisborne Backpackers
B Flying Nun Backpackers
C Beachcomber
D Waikanae Beach Holiday Park
E YHA Hostel

NIGHTLIFE

Smash Palace Wine and Food Bar, 24 Banks St. (tel. 867 7769). Follow Awapuni Rd. west into the industrial district. A zany event unto itself, the Smash Palace is a must-do. A surreal post-industrial atmosphere and trove of junk decor, from the antique cars suspended in mid-air to the old DC-3 flying into the roof. Consume local brews like Gisborne Gold ($3) or Parker Wines ($3). Occasional free wine tastings. Open noon-late, except Su and W from 3pm.

The Irish Rover (tel. 867 1112), on Peel St. Snag a Guinness ($4.20) in this welcoming and popular barn-style pub. Weeknights are low-key, but weekends often feature live music with a $3 cover. Handles on tap $3; bar snacks and dinner menu. Open M-Sa 11am-3am, Su 11am-8pm (may close earlier).

No. 9, 9 Gladstone Rd. (tel 868 5666). Centrally located, this shagadelic pub is No. 1 with surfers. Collecting residual sand on Friday and Saturday nights, the wooden floorboards resound with live music every weekend. Draft beer $3. Open Th-Sa 8pm-late.

 SIGHTS

Titirangi Domain, also known as **Kaiti Hill,** is a good starting place for seeing Gisborne's sights. Once across the river, follow the signs from Hirini Rd. At the base of the hill sits **Te Poho-o-Rawiri,** the largest traditional *marae* built from modern materials in New Zealand. It is cavernous and stunningly crafted, with painted roof rafters, woven tukutuku reed panels, and intricately carved dark wood panels with iridescent paua shell eyes. Step back and watch the tangle of swirling lines resolve into faces, birds, and bodies unfurling and weaving into one another. The large panels, *pou pou,* stylize a Maori genealogy: each figure represents an ancestor—figures with grotesquely long tongues recall a verbose elder, for example. Be sure to ask permission at the office first and remove your shoes before entering. Nearby sits **Toko Toru Tapu,** a small Maori church nestled on the hillside.

Continue up the hill—it's a steep one, popular with masochistic local joggers— for a series of phenomenal views across the city and Poverty Bay to the white cliffs of **Young Nick's Head,** named after Captain Cook's cabin boy Nicholas Young, who first sighted New Zealand from the Endeavour. Midway up the hill is a statue of Cook. Kaiti Hill can also be tackled via a path winding up from the base of the Cook Landing Site (accessible from the Esplanade along the river). Back across the Turanganui, at the end of Waikanae Beach, sits the dutifully rendered (if not particularly stunning) **Young Nick's Statue,** where the spacey-looking young lad points eternally to his eponymous bluffs.

The **Gisborne Museum of Art and History** (tel. 867 3832), on Stout St., features changing art galleries and several displays on natural and cultural history, with this year's focus on indigenous people's sculpture. Just behind the Art and History museum on the riverbank sits the **Star of Canada Maritime Museum,** the transplanted bridgehouse of a British steamer that grounded on Kaiti Beach in 1912. (Both museums open M-F 10am-4pm, Sa-Su 1:30-4pm. Free.) For contemporary art-in-progress, head to the **Maia Gallery** (tel. 868 8068), on Cobden St., between Gladstone Rd. and Palmerston St. This airy space is both showroom and workshop studio for students in the Toihoukura (Maori Visual Arts) course at the local Tairawhiti Polytechnic. (Open M-F 8am-5pm. Free.)

The **Eastwoodhill Arboretum** (tel. 863 9800) is a popular attraction 35km northwest of the city on the Ngatapa-Rere Rd. Laid out by an obsessive collector, the 64 hectares grow one of the finest assortments of authentic genetic plant material from the Northern Hemisphere (around 500 genera). Even if you don't care about the science involved, it's spectacularly beautiful. A 45-minute walk provides views of both flora and grander scenery. Unfortunately, you must find your own transportation. (Open daily 9am-5pm. Admission $5.)

NORTH ISLAND

◤ ACTIVITIES

For the area's safest and most convenient waters, try **Waikanae Beach,** stretching from the end of Grey St. Sandy and excellent, it gets a bit crowded at peak times. The shore becomes **Midway Beach** a little farther along Poverty Bay, with soft sand and a prime surf spot at its western end. While the bay beaches have their golden wave moments, many surfers with more experience head north of the city to the coastal beaches at **Wainui,** about 6km out on SH35, and **Makorori,** another 4km along. These beaches are pretty safe for swimming as well, but have been known to have riptides. **Kaiti Beach,** at the base of Kaiti Hill, is rocky and unpatroled, but the exposed location provides great gusts for windsurfing.

For more chlorinated, controlled water sports, head one block inland from Waikane Beach to the **Gisborne Olympic Pool Complex** (tel. 867 6220), on Centennial Marine Drive. Twist, turn, and splash down the Super Hydroslide ($3 for unlimited runs), swim olympic-sized laps, or unwind in the $1 spa pool. (Open daily in summer 6am-8pm. Admission $2.50, children $1.50.)

If you want to get out of your bathing suit for a bit, there are land-based leisure options in town. Accounting for one-third of New Zealand's total wine production, Gisborne's many vineyards offer tours in the summer months (by appointment in winter), and most have at least a cellar shop or tastings (contact the Information Centre for more information). You can try the strictly organic **Millton Vineyard** (tel. 862 8680) in Manutuke, on Papatu Rd. off SH2 towards Wairoa. **Matawhero Wines** on Riverpoint Rd. (tel. 868 8366) also has tours. For touring and tasting of a different spirit, clear your palate for the cider, scrumpy, and schnapper of **Bulmer Harvest** (tel. 868 8300), on Customhouse St. right by the water (open daily 9am-5pm, winter closed Sa-Su). **The Sunshine Brewing Co.,** 109 Disraeli St. (tel. 867 7777), off Gladstone St., makes Gisborne Gold, Sundowner, Moonshine, and other naturally brewed beers (open M-Sa 9am-6pm; call ahead for a free tour).

Waimoana Horse Trekking (tel. 868 8218), based on Mysnar St. off Wainui Rd., offers spectacular views and an unforgettable experience. Trek over the sheep-dotted bush and surf-crashing beach; all experience levels welcome. (1hr. $20. 2hr. $30.; $5 off with *Let's Go.*)

If you're around in October, the annual **East Coast Wild Tastes Festival** (Oct. 25, 2000), up the coast in Tolaga Bay, is where you can sample bizarre bush foods. Taste, if you dare, the chocolate-dipped huhu grubs that are the avian kiwis' favorite, or the wild pork burgers. The next day is the **Gisborne Wine and Food Festival,** with buses making the winery circuit.

THE EAST CAPE

New Zealand's final frontier of tourism, the East Cape, with its stunning seascapes and ample outdoor offerings, is drawing more and more travelers in search of the ever-elusive *"real* New Zealand." From Gisborne to Opotiki, the Pacific Coast Highway (SH35) passes scores of sleepy seaside towns on its way around the rugged Raukumara Mountains of the interior. The vast majority of the people living here are Maori, and intricate carvings adorn the many churches and *marae.* The region has suffered a gauntlet of economic setbacks ever

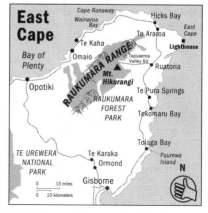

since the 19th century, first with whaling, then meat processing, farming, and, most recently, with the tailspin of the forestry market. Today, this lack of industry may be the East Cape's greatest selling point.

⚡ ORIENTATION AND PRACTICAL INFORMATION

Well-maintained and fully paved, **SH35** runs the perimeter of the cape, 334km between **Opotiki** and **Gisborne.** Most towns have at least one store, takeaway, gas station, and postal service, often all combined into a tiny conglomerate.

Visitors Center: The visitors centers in **Opotiki** and **Gisborne** make fine starting points, with plenty of expertise on the East Cape's northern and southern coasts, respectively. The tiny **Te Puia Springs Service Centre** (tel. (06) 864 6853) is the only official info outlet in between, although most backpackers stock plenty of pamphlets. Open M-F 8am-12:30pm and 1-4:30pm. The comprehensive and free *Opotiki and East Cape* lists most traveling resources, kilometer by kilometer.

Shuttles: **Slim's East Cape Escape** (tel. (07) 345 6645; fax 345 6647) is the only transportation to circumscribe the region. In partnership with Kiwi Experience, the legendary *Slim* departs from **Rotorua** (M, W, and F 7-7:30am), arranges an overnight at the **East Cape Lighthouse** ($17), stops for lunch in **Gisborne,** and returns to Rotorua via SH2 and the Waioweka Gorge. Passengers can get on and off this 2-day circuit as they please ($152, not including meals and accommodations). Book through **Kiwi Experience** (tel. (09) 366 9830; fax 366 1374) at most visitors centers.

Courier Services: These mini-vans deliver parcels and supplies from **Opotiki** and **Gisborne** to the various settlements and farms, allowing passengers to see much that would be missed from the main highway. **Matakaoa Transport** (in Te Araroa tel. (06) 864 4728, in Gisborne tel. (06) 867 7038) runs M-F from the Hicks Bay store to the Gisborne Visitor Centre (3hr., 6:30am) and back again (4hr., 12:30pm), hitting all the towns along the way (one-way $25, students $20). **Cook's Courier Service** (tel. (06) 864 4711 or mobile 025 371 364) departs Hicks Bay M-F at 7:30am and returns from Gisborne at 2pm (one-way $26, backpackers $20). **Fastway Couriers** (tel. (06) 868 9080), at Grey St. and Awapuni Rd. in Gisborne, makes weekend runs up the coast to Hicks Bay (departs Sa 9:30am and Su 7:30am; one-way $27, students $22). Stops in between cost less; just ring up to get on. **Eastland Couriers** (tel. (07) 315 6350 or mobile 025 842 453) is the only such provider for the northern half of the cape, departing Opotiki M, W, and F at 11:30am for **Te Araroa** or **Potaka** (Tu and Th only) plus points between (one-way $25). A cheap overnight homestay in Whanarua Bay can be arranged ($15, meals included).

Hitching: Hitchhikers find friendly rides around the cape in summertime; late afternoon is peak traffic time, as people return from Gisborne or Opotiki. In winter, increased rain and greatly reduced traffic makes hitching a more dubious prospect.

Banks: Westpac (tel. (06) 864 8443), in Ruatoria, is the only bank in East Cape. Open M, Tu, Th, and F 9am-4:30pm, W 9:30am-4:30pm. There are **no ATMs.**

Telephone Codes: 06 from Hicks Bay to Gisborne; 07 from Opotiki up to Hicks Bay.

🏠🍴 ACCOMMODATIONS AND FOOD

The coastline between Gisborne and Hicks Bay contains several designated spots for **freedom camping,** usually recognizable by a morass of caravans: **Turihaua Beach** (14km from Gisborne), **Pouawa Beach** (17km), **Loisel's Beach** at Waihau Bay (50km), **Tolaga Bay** (55km), **Tokomaru Bay** (90km), **Waipiro Bay** (106km), and **Hicks Bay** (180km). Free camping is permitted between Labour Day and Easter in most of these areas; Turihaua Beach is prohibited between December 26 and February 1. The East Cape's northern shore tends to restrict mass tenting, and the Gisborne district might follow suit soon, if campers persist in their slovenly ways. In general, however, there are plenty of private landowners throughout the region who will grant permission to camp for a pittance or less. As for **food,** the East Cape lacks restaurants and supermarkets alike; small groceries and takeaways are the name of the game, and fresh seafood is always handy for the nimble-reeled.

■ **House of the Rising Sun** (tel. (06) 864 5858), on Potae St. in **Tokomaru Bay.** A cozy home, half a block from the beautiful beach. In summer, Japanese owner Miki serves up a deliciously hospitable combination of tea, banter, and fresh plums. Free bicycles and boogie board. Dorms $15; doubles $17; tent sites $9.

Robyn's Place (tel (07) 325 2904), in **Whanarua Bay.** A character-laden house complete with a lounge deck, an ocean view, excellent music, and friendly atmosphere. Free laundry and linens. Dorms $15; one double $35; emergency campsites $10.

Hicks Bay Backpackers Lodge (tel. 864 4731). Next to a good swimming and surfing beach, this lodge has 15 dorm beds ($15), a double room ($45), grassy beachfront tent sites ($9), and a reasonably spacious kitchen. Sunrise tours of the East Cape lighthouse are available for early birds ($25; 2 person minimum).

Te Araroa Holiday Park (tel. (06) 864 4873; fax 864 4473). Situated on 14 acres, garnished with a stream and a deserted beach with pounding surf. Facilities include: kitchen, washer and dryer, small store, and the **world's easternmost cinema,** complete with Dolby surround sound, 70 seats, couches, and popcorn. Bunks $12; cabins $35; flats $50; tent sites $7.50, powered $8.50.

Te Kaha Holiday Park and Motel (tel. (07) 325 2894). A new dormitory, part sprawling tent sites at the end of a flower-lined driveway. Play a round of budget golf at the neighboring nine-hole, par 64 course with ocean views ($10 per round; club hire $5). Dorms $15; tent sites $9, powered $10.

Rendezvous on the Coast Holiday Park (tel. (07) 325 2899), in **Whanarua Bay** next door to Robyn's Place. An expansive, well-kept campground with a full range of leisure equipment. Bike tours, kayak rental, fishing, and scuba trips. Dorms ($11) include fridge and cooking utensils; tent sites $8, powered $9.

◉ ◭ SIGHTS AND ACTIVITIES

The highway that skirts the lush, vegetation-cloaked coast between Opotiki and Hicks Bay presents the Cape's most spectacular views, especially in December when a profusion of **pohutukawa trees** explodes with red flowers. **Whanarua Bay** has some of the most beautiful bits of beach and bush in the region. Back in town, just beneath the holiday park's roadside advertisement, a door marked "Track" leads down to a stunning and undeveloped section of beach, ringed with pohutukawa and full of rocky tidal pools. Farther along the road at the beachfront schoolyard in **Te Araroa** is the **world's largest pohutukawa tree,** a massive tangle of trunks and thick branches. This tiny town is the gateway to the lonely little **East Cape lighthouse,** at the easternmost point in mainland New Zealand. In addition to Hicks Bay Backpackers, **East Cape 4WD Sunrise Tours** (tel. 864 4775) does an early morning run along the 20km part-gravel road to the lighthouse ($25; 2 person minimum).

Tikitiki lies some 27km south of Te Araroa. Its **Anglican Church,** perched on a hill overlooking the highway, is one of the most impressive Maori buildings in the region. The church's Western exterior belies an inner sanctuary filled with ornate carvings and weavings. Visitors are welcome to let themselves in. **Ruatoria,** 19km south of Tikitiki, is the gateway to **Mount Hikurangi** (1752m), sacred guardian of the region. While access to the peak is restricted, permission can be obtained to stay in a hut on the slope ($5); contact outdoor pursuits officer Kerry Johnson (tel. (06) 867 8436) for info and bookings. Ruatoria's *iwi* (tribal) affairs office, **Te Runanga Ngati Porou** (tel. (06) 864 8121), handles inquiries about local Maori events and issues. **Tokomaru Bay,** 37km south of Ruatoria and 91km north of Gisborne, is the home of **Brian's Horse Treks** (tel. (06) 864 5870), one of the most renowned outfitters in the cape. From three-hour jaunts ($30) to four-day journeys ($250 including meals and lodging), Brian blithely leads riders across beaches and over steep bush. Labour Day weekend 2000, Tokomaru Bay will host the annual **Ngati Porou Cultural Festival,** when up to 30 local performing groups come together to Haka; contact Wayne Ngata (tel. (06) 868 0334) for the latest details.

NORTH ISLAND

Tolaga Bay, 36km south of Tokomaru Bay and 52km north of Gisborne, is home to the longest wharf in the southern hemisphere, a deteriorating 600m testament to the days before highways. Nearby is the trailhead for the **Cooks Cove Walkway,** an easy two-and-a-half hour (5.8km) return trip past excellent ocean and cliff views to the site of one of Captain Cook's first landings in Aotearoa (closed Aug.-Oct. for lambing season). The wharf and walkway hide out at the end of Wharf Road, a 1.5km detour off the main highway.

TE UREWERA NATIONAL PARK

The lush and misty mountains of Te Urewera National Park shelter a mesmerizing blend of cultural and natural history. This is the largest national park in the North Island, and the only one in the country to be named after a camping accident ("ure-wera" means "burnt penis," the ailment of a legendary and highly unfortunate Maori chief who rolled onto his fire one night). The region's isolated bush is the historic home of the Tuhoe (TOO-hoi) Maori, the "Children of the Mist" who resisted European intrusion with greater force and success than many other tribes. Today, the floor of Lake Waikaremoana and several adjoining parcels of land remain under Maori ownership. Whether by land or water, by day-hike or Great Walk, Te Urewera delights with its unspoiled diversity.

◪ ORIENTATION AND PRACTICAL INFORMATION

The park is accessible via **SH38,** which runs between **Wairoa** near the East Coast and the junction with SH5 out of Rotorua. From Wairoa, SH38 winds 20km past tiny **Frasertown** to Lake Waikaremoana, passing the **Orepoto Trailhead,** the **DOC motorcamp,** and the **Aniwaniwa Visitor Centre.** The highway then weaves a total of 90km, past the **Hopuruahine trailhead** and the villages of **Ruatahuna** and **Te Whaiti,** on its way to **Murupara.** This stretch of road is largely gravel and full of splendid mountain views. From Murupara, it's about 76km to **Rotorua,** the biggest transportation hub in the region.

Buses: The main bus lines stopped serving SH38 years ago, and local shuttles are in a state of flux. **Tipi Shuttle Service** (tel. (06) 383 7960) runs by Tipi Backpackers Hostel (see below), and between Wairoa (departs 11am) and the park on weekdays, with stops at **Frasertown, Tuai,** the **Orepoto trailhead,** the **motor camp,** and the **Hopurua trailhead.** Return trips from Wairoa cost $45, or $40 if you park at the backpackers (bookings essential; 3-person minimum).

Hitching: Thumbing to and within Te Urewera can be a difficult proposition, since cars are often full of camping gear and vacation toys, but those with patience report success.

Parking: Although the DOC assumes no responsibility for vehicles, the **motor camp lot** (free for 10 days) is safer than the trailheads, where vandalism and theft occur often.

DOC: The **Aniwaniwa Visitor Centre** (tel. (06) 837 3803; fax 837 3722), at Lake Waikaremoana, houses the park headquarters. Open daily 8am-5pm. The **Rangitaiki Area DOC Office** (tel. (07) 366 5641; fax 366 5289), on SH38 at Murupara, provides info and booking services. Open Oct.-Apr. daily 8am-5pm; May-Nov. M-F 8am-5pm.

Banks: Load up on cash in Rotorua or Wairoa; there are **no ATMs** between them.

Emergency: Call the DOC after hours (tel. 837 3803 or 837 3824).

Telephone Code: 06.

▟▟ ACCOMMODATIONS AND FOOD

Beautiful, central, and with all the amenities, the DOC-owned **Waikaremoana Motor Camp** (tel. 837 3826; fax 837 3825), has a gem of a location on the lake shore, with dock facilities and a petrol station. (Dorms $16; 2-person cabins $30; 2-person chalets or motels $55; tent sites $7.50; caravan sites $9. Non-dorm prices go up $5-10 during holidays and Dec.15-Feb.20. Call ahead.) **Tipi Backpackers Hostel** (tel. 838 7960 or mobile 025 231 8590), in Frasertown, makes another excellent base for planning explorations of the park. (Giant teepee on the lawn $11; chipper yellow-walled dorm $14; doubles $34; tent sites $9.) The DOC runs several more primitive campgrounds (toilets, no showers) within the park, including those at **Mokau, Hopuruahine, Aniwaniwa,** and **Rosie Bay** (tent sites $2-3 per person). There is free camping all around the lake, as long as tents are pitched more than 500m from the track and not on private land (clearly marked on most maps).

As for **food,** bring it with you. There's a limited selection at the **Waikaremoana Motor Camp Store** (open daily 8am-6pm., winter 8am-noon and 1-5pm). Tuai and Murupara have general stores, but it's best to shop in advance in Wairoa or Rotorua, where prices aren't as jacked up for desperate trampers.

◪ WALKS

For information on the **Lake Waikaremoana Great Walk,** see below. **Whirinaki** is accessible year-round, although it gets much drizzlier in winter. The park's native podocarp and beech forests stretch as far as the eye can see, and are home to vibrant and noisy birds as well as two species of bats. And then there's the land-scape: myriad fern-lined waterfalls, cobalt-blue lakes, and magnificent gray-green bluffs. Ample day-hiking options of varying difficulty await, including the one-hour walk to **Lake Waikareiti** ("little rippling waters"), which is improbably set on a lush green hilltop and is full of little islands. The DOC rents rowboats ($15 per time slot: 8am-12:30pm, 12:30-5pm, or 5pm-8am) for over-water access to **Sandy Bay Hut,** which must be booked as part of the Great Walk ($10). Around 40 **backcountry huts** ($4) follow the usual hut ticket system, allowing for extensive and isolated over-night tramps through the bush.

Since all of the desirable fish and game in the park are introduced species, the DOC smiles upon their slaughter. **Fishing licenses** are available at the motor camp ($65 summer, $39 winter, $25 per week, $13 per day); gear can be purchased at the motor camp or rented from Tipi Backpackers ($3-5 per day). **Hunting permits** are free and easy; just fill out the form, then blast some mammals. Noel Himona of **Waikaremoana Guided Tours** (tel. 837 3729) leads hunting trips ($200 per day, rifles included) and fishing forays ($200 per day, $50 per hour); he also rents **sea kayaks** and **canoes** (both $10 per hr., $40 per day).

◪ THE LAKE WAIKAREMOANA TRACK

With its towering tangle of native trees and kiwi calls crying through the night, the Lake Waikaremoana (WIE-kah-ray-moe-AH-nah) Great Walk affords an ideal opportunity to imbibe New Zealand's bizarre biology: hulking bluffs and azure inlets, sweeping panoramas and dense bush, challenging ascents and mellow stretches. The track's huts and campsites are all perfectly liveable, and some of them are downright luxurious.

ESSENTIALS

Length: 46km. The track's 5 **huts** and 5 **campsites** make it possible to split the walk up into as demanding or as leisurely a trip as you wish; most take 2 to 4 nights.

Trailheads: Kilometer markers count up from the **Onepoto track entrance** on SH38, south of the Visitor Centre, to the **Hopuruahine track entrance** on SH38, north of the same Visitor Centre. You can start from either end. Beginning at Onepoto puts almost the toughest climb out of the way right off the bat; the lofty lake views on this first stretch require fair weather if at all possible. **Waikaremoana Guided Tours** (tel. (06) 837 3729), also known as Noel's boat, departs from the motor camp to the trailheads, and makes pickups from both Hopuruahine landing and Onepoto; this basic return trip costs $25. Noel also makes one-way runs to and from **Onepoto** ($10), **Hopuruahine Landing** ($15), **Waiopaoa Hut** ($80), **Korokoro Campsite** ($80), **Maraviti Hut** ($70) and **Te Puna Hut** ($70).

Seasonality: The track can be completed year-round, but can grow boggy and cold in the off-season. Panekin Hut can get as cold as -5°C, but is equipped with a gas-powered heater in winter. The best weather generally lasts from mid-October to the end of March.

Huts and Campsites: The DOC recently implemented a reservation requirement for the track's many fine overnight accommodations; bookings can be handled at most DOC offices and Visitor Centres in the North Island. **Huts** $10 per night, **campsites** $6; both offer untreated tap water, cooking areas, and toilets.

Gear: A **stove** and **fuel** are crucial, since neither the huts nor the campsites have them. The motor camp store (see above) sells useful fuel and unwieldy stoves; Tipi Backpackers rents a stove-and-gas combo for $2 per night and a small backpack for $3 per night.

Storage: The motorcamp store ($3 per bag) or Tipi Backpackers ($1 per night).

THE TRACK

Onepoto Trailhead to Panekiri Hut: 8.8km, 5hr.

Beginning at Onepoto, the trail heads briefly up a wide grassy track past historical graffiti until reaching a fork for **Lake Kiriopukae.** A 20-minute detour, the lake makes a nice picnic-spot, but is otherwise not worth visiting. From the fork, the track makes a calf-burning, 600m ascent up **Panekiri Bluff.** There is **no water** on this section of the trail; well over two liters ought to be packed to prevent dehydration. The steepest section comes in the first hour, after which the track evens out a bit as it winds along the ridge of the Panekiri Range. The rutted track's gauntlet of roots leads through a wind-wracked forest while every several hundred meters brings a fresh vista of the lake waters and tawa tangle far below.

   Panekiri Hut (36 beds) is the largest, nicest, and highest bunch of beds on the track, perched on a ridge with a two-way view: the lush lake lies northward, while the cleaved hills of the Hawke's Bay region roll into the southern horizon. There is no campsite anywhere along the ridge. For those who only wish to see the lake from on high, the hike to Panekiri Hut from Onepoto can make a good day-hike.

Panekiri Hut to Waiopaoa Hut and Campsite: 7.6 km, 3-4hr.

From Panekiri Hut, the track drops steeply, passing plenty of tree ferns and tea trees (kanuka). **Waiopaoa Hut** (24 beds) is equipped with a wood-burning stove; **Waiopaoa Campsite** lies a stone's throw downhill by a frog-filled inlet. As with all of the track's lakefront facilities, this campsite is marred only by the pesky preponderance of sandflies.

Waiopaoa Hut and Campsite to Korokoro Campsite: 3.6km, 1½hr.

A flat stretch of lakeside track leads to the turn-off for **Korokoro Falls,** a worthwhile hour-long detour where hundreds of rivulets gush down a vertical stone slab. **Korokoro Campsite** lies on a nice little lagoon shortly after the turn-off for the falls.

Korokoro Campsite to Marauiti Hut: 8.5km, 3-4hr.

   Korokoro Campsite to Maranui Campsite: 6.8km, 2½-3½hr.

   Maranui Campsite to Marauiti Hut: 1.7km, 20-30min.

From Korokoro, the track follows some reasonable ups and downs above the shoreline, passing through a forest of monster tree ferns. Past a private hut on Maori land and just beyond the **DOC Warden's Quarters** is **Maranui Campsite,** which has a lovely view of an inlet and its surrounding bluffs. Just up and over a small peninsula is **Marauiti Hut** (32 beds), on the edge of a beautiful blue inlet with plenty of excellent fishing and swimming.

Marauiti Hut to Te Puna Hut: 7.2km, 2¼hr.

   Marauiti Hut to Waiharuru Campsite: 6.2 km, 2hr.

   Waiharuru Campsite to Te Puna Hut: 1km, 15-20 min.

The next portion of the track is a comfortable cruise with plenty of lovely lagoons for swimming. **Waiharuru Campsite,** a long and highly scenic patch of grass, borders what could almost be called a beach. After crossing a stream chock-full of immense, lazy brook trout, the trail hits **Te Puna Hut** (18 beds), a somewhat less-than-spiffy option with a wood burning stove and big fire pit.

Te Puna Hut to Hopuruhine Trailhead: 12.5km, 3-4hr.

Between Te Puna and Tapuaenui, the track runs a steep 100m over the **Puketuku-tuku peninsula,** where the DOC is boosting a population of about 40 kiwi through extensive **stoat-trapping**. Stoats, originally introduced to control rampant rabbits, are kiwis' number-one enemy when it comes to killing chicks. Sites at the small, undistinguished **Tapuaenui campsite** are well segregated by shrubbery—this aspect is probably the only plus. Largely flat hiking along some of the most striking inlets of the lake leads to the final accommodation, **Whanganui Hut** (20 beds). With a wood-burning stove, the hut rests next to a creek but has minimal lake access. The walk to **Hopuruahine Landing** and Noel's waiting boat is brisk and undaunting, as are the remaining kilometers through grassy fields and up a river valley to the **Hopuruahine Trailhead.**

WHIRINAKI FOREST PARK

Alhough it's not as dramatic as its eastward neighbor Te Urewera National Park nor as vast as the Kaingaroa pine plantation, the 60,900 hectares of Whirinaki contain unparalleled lowland rainforest. There are great soaring podocarp stands and the tawa canopy shelters tree ferns and native birds from the tui to the kiwi. Relatively few visitors (and even fewer foreigners) ever see the park's splendor because these big trees are out in the sticks. The tranquility of this isolation makes a visit all the more worthwhile.

The minuscule Maori ex-logging community of **Minginui** is seven gravel kilometers from **Te Whaiti** (tuh-FYE-tee) on SH38. Tiny Te Whaiti is 80 sublime kilometers northwest of Waikaremoana, 18km southeast of minute Murupara, and 87 kilometers southeast of Rotorua. Whirinaki Forest Holidays (see below) will pick up passengers from Rotorua, Taupo, Whakatare, and other such locales ($25 per person). **Hitchhiking** to and within the park is said to be possible during the high season, though not without a bit of waiting. The **Rangitaiki Area DOC Office** (tel. 366 5641), on SH38 in Murupara, offers info on Whirinaki, with some jurisdiction over Te Urewera (open Nov.-Apr. daily 8am-5pm; May-Nov. M-F 8am-5pm, depending on traffic). **Whirinaki Forest Holidays** (tel./fax (07) 366 3235), in the Te Whaiti, 1km off SH38, has the closest indoor accommodations to the park. Gary and Sherrilyn offer home-cooked meals (breakfast $5, dinner $20), and communal kitchens in three attractive lodge annexes (dorms $15; doubles $50). A few kilometers closer to the trailheads, the DOC's **Mangamate Waterfall Campground** is the only front-country tenting option for independent travelers, and a pretty one at that (tent sites $5). These sites can fill up in the summertime, leaving **Murupara Motorcamp** (tel. 366 5365) up the road the nearest alternative (dorms $15; tent sites $8).

An excellent taste of the park's botanical vitality is provided by the **Forest Sanctuary Walk,** a simple 1hr. loop (4km) down a crummy road from Minginui. Majestic podocarps dwarf the otherwise lofty tree ferns, and every available surface is carpeted with mosses, lichens, and filmy ferns. Three other particularly worthy dayhikes branch off from the carpark 7km south of Minginui. A trail begins about 2km farther down the road, leading to the rain-fed **Arahaki Lagoon** (return 3-4hr.), filled with frog song and lined by the buttresses of skyscraping kahikatea. **Waiatiu Falls** lies about 30 minutes from the main carpark, starting at an unmarked trailhead just to the right of the Arahaki Lagoon road. The **Whirinaki Waterfall Loop** (3-4hr. return) runs along a river to a semi-notable canyon and waterfall, passing superb views of podocarp treetops and unfurling tree ferns.

The park supports many overnight tramping options, thanks to a number of well-marked **huts** with toilets and untreated water ($4; purchase tickets at area DOC office). For a mellow 3-day journey, many hikers continue from Whirinaki Falls to **Central Whirinaki Hut** (16km, 5hr.), loop around to **Mangamate Hut** (4hr.), and return to their carpark origin (3hr.). Many longer loops and straightaways are possible. The DOC discourages trampers from leaving their vehicles unattended overnight. The park also affords opportunities for **biking** and **hunting** (though preferably not simultaneously).

HAWKE'S BAY

NAPIER

You know you've hit Napier when cafes outnumber takeaways, and even the McDonald's is McDeco. To the trained eye, the city is an Art Deco overload of zig-zags, bubbling fountains, neon-lit clock towers, and clean geometric lines, all in riots of confectionery colors. A sunny, seaside place with impossible-to-resist charm, Napier isn't made for walking—it was designed for promenading: down busy Marine Parade, lined with stately Norfolk pines and touristy sights, through the bustling streets of the city center with their modern stores and lively cafes, and along the black smooth-pebbled beach on serene moonlit nights. Appealing to sensibility over adrenaline, Napier is more relaxed than its northwest neighbors Taupo and Rotorua. Here, winetasting replaces skydiving, and bird-watching offers a harder-earned thrill than a bungy jump. Especially popular during summer and event-filled February, Napier looks simply marvelous any time of year.

⚡ ORIENTATION AND PRACTICAL INFORMATION

Marine Parade and **Hastings St.** run parallel to one another, stretching southward along the bay. Central Napier's streets lie up against the bluffs. Be careful about meandering through the bricked and palm-lined **Emerson St.**—despite misleading landscaping, it's a main traffic thoroughfare. **Tennyson** and **Dickens Streets** parallel it on each side; the gardens of **Clive Sq.** mark the edge of the town center.

ARRIVAL AND DEPARTURE

Airplanes: The **Hawke's Bay Airport** (tel. 835 1130), north of Napier on SH2, rests on land raised up in the 1931 earthquake. The **ANZ Travel Centre** (tel. 833 5400), at Hastings and Station St., books daily flights to **Auckland** (around $220) and **Wellington** ($200). Open M-F 8:30am-5pm, Sa 9am-12pm. The **Supershuttle** (tel. 870 9050) offers door-to-door service to the airport ($7) and Hastings ($18). A taxi costs $9 to the airport and $32 to Hastings.

Trains: TranzScenic departs from Munroe St. daily for **Wellington** (5hr., 2:05pm, $70) via **Hastings** (25min., $15) and **Palmerston North** (3hr., $44).

Buses: Buses leave from the **train station.** Those heading south pass through **Hastings.** InterCity and **Newmans** both depart for: **Wellington** (6hr., 2 per day, $58) via **Palmerston North** (3hr., $37); and **Auckland** (7hr., 3 per day, $75) via **Taupo** (2hr., $34) and **Rotorua** (1hr., $53). InterCity and **Coachrite Connections** (tel. 868 9969 or mobile 025 469 867) both head to **Gisborne** (4hr., 1-2 per day, $28) via **Wairoa** (2hr., $20).

GETTING AROUND

Public Transportation: Nimon and Sons run the **Nimbus** (tel. 835 0633) between Napier and surrounding suburbs M-F 7am-5:30pm. **Buses** to **Hastings** run almost every hr. M-F 9am-3pm ($4). All leave from Dalton St. near Dickens St. To get to Hastings on weekends, catch an **InterCity** or **Newmans** bus heading south ($5-10).

Taxis: **StarTaxis** (tel. 835 5511) or **Napier Taxis** (tel. 835 7777 or 0800 503 577).

Car Rental: Metro Rent-A-Car (tel. 835 0590) is based in Napier at the corner of Corunna and Hyderabad Rd., but serves all of Hawke's Bay.

Bike Rental: Napier Kart and Cycle Center, 104 Carlyle St. (tel. 835 9528), rents in summer for $25 per day including helmet and lock.

Hitchhiking: Those heading south report that getting rides is easier when walking along Marine Parade.; a few hundred meters past the Aquarium, it becomes SH2 and picks up more traffic. For those heading north, the best spot is reputed to be just across the Pandora Rd. Bridge. Most traffic heads to Taupo; those going to Wairoa or Gisborne should ask to be let off where SH5 branches off.

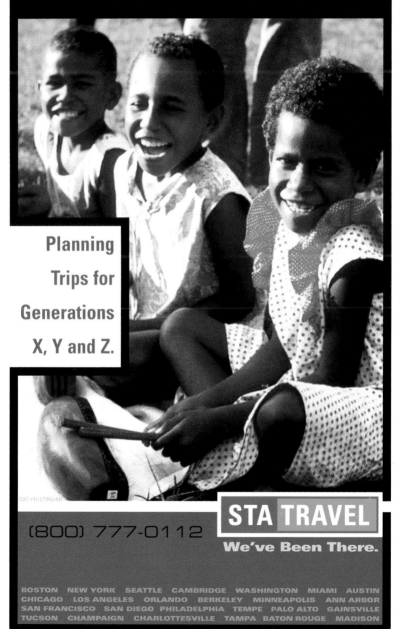

TOURIST AND FINANCIAL SERVICES

Visitors Center: Napier Information Centre, 100 Marine Parade (tel. 834 1911; fax 835 7219). Book trips and ground travel here. Pick up Backcountry (but not Great Walk) hut passes. Open M-F 8am-5pm, Sa-Su 10am-3pm, winter M-F 8am-5pm.

DOC: 59 Marine Parade (tel. 834 3111), past the brightly colored museum on Marine Parade. Come here for maps, brochures, and advice. Open M-F 9am-4:15pm.

Currency Exchange: ASB Bank (tel. 834 1240), at Emerson and Hastings St. (The pattern design is called *kowhaiwhai,* with molded spearheads at the corner of each panel.) Open M-F 9am-4:30pm.

LOCAL SERVICES, EMERGENCY, AND COMMUNICATIONS

Bi-Gay-Lesbian Organizations: Gayline (tel. 843 3087) has info on current goings-on. Dances hosted the third Saturday of each month at the Bay City Club on Milton Rd., partway up Bluff Hill, off Tennyson St. Cover $5.

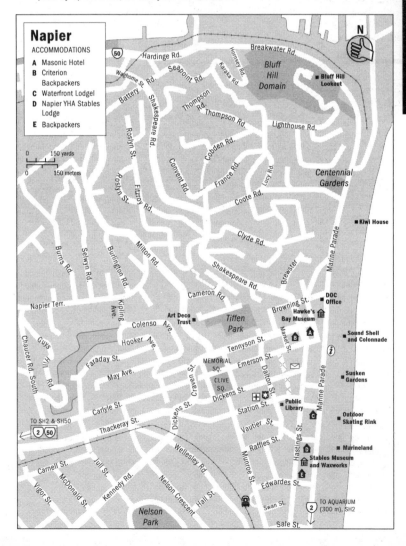

Napier

ACCOMMODATIONS

A Masonic Hotel
B Criterion Backpackers
C Waterfront Lodgel
D Napier YHA Stables Lodge
E Backpackers

NORTH ISLAND

Police: (24hr. tel. 835 4688), on Station St.

Medical Services: The City Medical Center (24hr. tel. 835 4999), on Station St. just past the police station, can also direct you to a pharmacist. Open daily 8am-9pm.

Post Office: (tel. 835 3725), at Dickens and Hastings St. Open M-F 8am-5pm, Sa 9am-noon.

Internet Access: Stables Lodge Backpackers, 321 Marine Parade (tel. 835 6242). Available 8am-8pm. $10 per hr. (guests $9). **Cybers Internet Cafe,** 98 Dickens St., a block down from Hastings. $12.50 per hr. Open M-F 9am-8pm, Sa-Su 10am-7pm.

Telephone Code: 06.

ACCOMMODATIONS

Napier has several good hostel options. Most, smack dab in the center of town, provide convenient but often noisy stays, while outskirt options reward a commute with quiet seclusion. Parking can be a problem downtown, especially in summer when the town's hopping (and accommodations must be booked ahead).

Criterion Backpackers, 48 Emerson St. (tel. 835 2059). A 1930s Spanish Mission-style misfit in the land of Art Deco, the refurbished ultra-central Criterion has a carpet liable to spark psychedelic flashbacks. Spacious lounge opens onto a balcony above the bustle of Emerson St. While it can be a bit noisy on weekends, Criterion wins you over with quality beds, lots of windows, spotless bathrooms, and a free spa pool (winter 6-8pm). Key deposit $10. Dorms $14; shares $16; twins and doubles $34. Cash only.

Stables Lodge Backpackers (Nomads), 321 Marine Parade (tel./fax 835 6242). With lovable dog Max making the rounds, community and goodwill abound at this environmentally aware hostel. Info on local wildlife and ecotourism, Internet, and daily summer BBQs. Free fruit, tea, bikes, and book exchange. Parking on Hastings St. Dorms $15; doubles $36; 3rd day half-price.

Napier YHA, 277 Marine Parade (tel./fax 835 7039), at the corner of Vaultier St., in a noisy area. Watch the sun or moon rise over the water from the clear and comfy ground floor lounge or from the second floor "Jimi Hendrix" room (named for its purple haze-painted walls). Throughout the winding stairs and hallways, colored window panels set aglow a bewildering variety of wallpaper and fabrics. Bike rental. Reception 8-10am and 4-8pm. Dorms $15; singles $22; twins and doubles $36.

Waterfront Lodge (VIP), 217 Marine Parade (tel. 835 3429). Sip free tea or coffee at the circular wooden tables in the kitchen area, catch some rays in the beautiful inner courtyard—or some Z's in the sturdy, comfortable beds. Reception 8am-9pm. Dorms $15; singles $22; twins and doubles $36; tents $8.

Masonic Hotel (tel. 835 8689; fax 835 2297), corner of Marine Parade and Tennyson St. The classic exterior offers the allure of an original grand old Art Deco hotel, but it isn't the 30s anymore in these rooms with TVs, mini-fridges, phones, and mattresses so springy you might sleep right through the next 'quake. Patio balcony, restaurant, bar, and a slightly kitschy Irish house pub with a "kasino" downstairs. Free laundry. Singles and doubles from $65; on weekends, some rooms cheaper due to noise.

Aqua Lodge, 53 Nelson Crescent (tel./fax 835 4523). From the bus station, turn right on Munroe St., right onto Sale St. across the rail, and the hostel is a block down on the right. Walk through the stucco arch and into the heart of this quintessential suburban backpackers, from its courtyard and semi-indoor pool to the well-used Nintendo. Quiet and 5min. from the town center, it's a favorite with long-term visitors. The owners help find transport and work in season. Free pickup, and off-street parking. Key deposit $10. Dorms $15; singles $23; doubles $36. Weekly dorms $90.

◢ FOOD

Marine Parade and the main downtown streets are lined with eateries from cheap to chic. **Countdown Foods,** at the corner of Dickens and Station St. near Thackeray St., is a serviceable market (open M-F 8am-9pm, Sa-Su 8am-8pm).

Mabel's Cafe (tel. 835 5655), on Hastings St. by Dickens St. Despite its pink frosted windows, awning, and walls, there's no salon stylist waiting to beehive your hair at Mabel's. There is, however, a health-conscious proprietor who makes everything on the premises each morning, serving up pastas and delicious quiche ($3.30) and heaping salads in earthenware bowls ($3.70-$7.20). Sandwiches under $2. Natural sweet pastries, muffins, carrot cake, pure juices, and $1.50 bottomless cups of coffee. Breakfast served 6-9:30am. Open M-F 6am-3pm.

Mezzi, 142 Hastings St. (tel. 835 1066), near the Dickens St. cross. One glimpse of the market-style display of freshly prepared pasta, scones, and sandwiches ($4-6) lures you into this airy sliver of a shop. Once the smell hits you, your Mezzi fate is sealed. Open daily 7:30am-6pm, winter 7:30- 5pm.

Restaurant Indonesia, 409 Marine Parade (tel. 835 8303), by Sale St. near Pizza Hut. Authentic and absorbing decor enhances similarly elegant cuisine for a mouth-watering dining experience. Sit back, relax, and enjoy the delicately seasoned chicken soup ($4) or mains like pork loin or vegetables on fried rice ($16-18)—heed owner Harry's warnings when applying spicy sauces. Open daily from 6pm. Reservations recommended.

Thorps, 40 Hastings St. (tel. 835 6699), by Tennyson St. You'd think that Mother Nature herself prepared the healthy sandwiches ($4-6). With 7 breads, 7 meats (including salmon), and over 10 dressings to design from, only the indecisive should dodge this upscale coffee shop. Open M-F 7:30am-4:30pm, Sa 7:30am-2pm.

Continental Fish Shop, 472 Hastings St. (tel. 835 7249). This small fish 'n' chips is often packed to the door with customers. Takeaway toasted sandwiches or burgers for under $4 and fritters for under $2. Wait your turn daily 11:30am-2pm and 4:30-9pm.

◤ NIGHTLIFE

Many clubs and bars are found near the intersection of Hastings and Tennyson St., or farther up Hastings St. on Shakespeare Rd. Follow your ears.

O'Flaherty's Irish Pub, 37 Hastings St. (tel. 834 1235), by Emerson St., is an unassuming and authentic tavern for both casual and veteran drinkers. The stunning chalk murals drawn by talented bartender Kate are an attraction in themselves. $2 pints during daily 5-7pm Happy Hour. Live music every weekend, fresh homemade pies, and above average bar food. Open daily 11am-late.

Grumpy Mole Saloon (tel. 835 5545), on the corner of Hastings and Tennyson St. This nightclub saloon with its loud music, hot twentysomethings, and American West decor is an odd but popular hybrid choice for those who pass the "no-scruffiness" test at the door. Open Tu-Sa 4pm-3am.

◤◣ SIGHTS AND ACTIVITIES

The color-laden symmetry of the buildings is perhaps itself the main sight in Napier. Look up, look down, and all around—even the manhole covers can't escape the craze. It may be the most fun just to wander and explore for yourself the leaded-glass windows, Deco doorknobs, and unexpected details that pepper the city, as well as the larger and more dramatic buildings. **Tennyson St.** has a row of classic structures. Admire the Maori Deco of the **Antique Centre,** the Shamrock Deco of the **Munster Chambers,** and the Deco-overload of the **Daily Telegraph** building. **Market St.** has terrific glass windows; the peach and green **Countrywide Bank** building on Dalton and Emerson St. is impressive. And don't forget to check out the Greco Deco of the **Colonnade** and the **Sound Shell.** Head to the **Art Deco Trust,** 163 Tennyson St. (tel. 835 0022), for a walking tour (1.5km) of Napier's Deco. The Trust's brochures (available at the shop or Info Centre) provide a middle ground between aimless wandering and the full-on tour. (Tours daily 2-4pm; $10, 1hr. $7.)

If you've begun to overdose on Deco, head to **Marine Parade.** Interspersed among manicured gardens, burbling fountains, and statues like Pania of the Reef (a distinctively toothy mermaid) there are some big visitor draws, including an in-line skating rink, public pool, and animal attractions. At the north end is the octagonal **Kiwi House** (tel. 834 1336), home to two of the nation's pride-and-joy northern brown kiwis. A daily talk is offered at 1pm, when a kiwi is brought out from the glassed-in exhibit and enticed into activity with scrumptious huhu grubs. (Open daily 11am-3pm. Admission $3.) A bit farther down, on the other side of the street, is the **Hawke's Bay Museum,** 65 Marine Parade (tel. 835 7781), with its impossible-to-miss large colored cylinders. It has art exhibits as well as displays on the earthquake, the East Coast Ngati Kahungunu Maori, Hawke's Bay dinosaur fossils, a new exhibit on the history of Marine Parade, and, of course, Art Deco. (Open daily 10am-4:30pm. Admission $4, children free.)

Follow the sound of barking marine mammals down Marine Parade to **Marineland** (tel. 834 4027) and its zoo-like exhibits and shows (admission $4-10, children $3-5). Sealife at the **Hawke's Bay Aquarium** (tel. 834 1404) ranges from giant hawkbilled turtles and coy seahorses to smug piranhas and sinister sharks. You'll even find tuatara (see p. 20), reptiles surviving from the Mesozoic era. The daily feeding frenzy in the main tank is at 3:15pm, plus 11:15am in summer. (Open daily 9am-9pm, winter 9am-5pm. Admission $7, children $3.50, families $18.)

Napier sits at the edge of the vineyard-studded Hawke's Bay plains, one of New Zealand's major wine-producing regions. Originally set up by priests for religious use, **Mission Estate Winery** (tel. 844 2259) is New Zealand's oldest winery (open M-Sa 8:30am-5:30pm, Su 11am-4pm; tours offered M-Sa 10:30am and 2pm). **Ngatarawa Wines** (tel. 879 7603) is a small winery in a restored stable with lovely grounds. The winery offers tastings of their sweet dessert wines daily from 11am to 5pm. For those without private transport, several tour operators drive around some of the wineries, offering short guided tours and tastings. **Wine Tour Trails** (tel. 877 5707), **Bay Tours and Charters** (tel. 843 6953), and **Vince's Vineyard Tours** (tel. 836 6705) offer four- to five-hour tours for about $30 (free pickup). Or try **Toast the Bay** (tel. 844 2375) if you're on a tighter schedule for $20 (2½hr.). Book at the Info Centre.

If you have a few rainy hours, consider visiting **Classic Sheepskins,** 22 Thames St. (tel. 835 9662), off Pandora Rd. (SH2 north), for free tours of the tanning factory at 11am and 2pm. Gain insight into what really happens to those ubiquitous fluffy herbivores of the New Zealand countryside. A courtesy van makes pickups from the Information Centre.

FESTIVALS AND SPECIAL EVENTS

Napier rocks in February (the month of its earthquake) with festivals. Dust off your zoot suit for the glam **Art Deco Weekend** (Feb. 17-21, 2000) and its endless series of stylish, and generally expensive, events: from balls and cafe crawls to champagne breakfasts and country house tours. There's somewhat less to do if you're short on cash, but you can still check out the museum exhibitions and the vintage car rally, find some free jazz, marvel at the costumes, and pack a hamper for Sunday's **Great Gatsby Picnic** on the beach (followed by the concluding Thanksgiving service in the Anglican Church to celebrate Napier's rise from its own ashes). There's also the **Harvest Hawke's Bay Wine and Food Festival** (first weekend in February), a weekend of similarly upscale revelry. Local wineries are packed with shuttle tours and tasters all weekend long. The **International Mission Estate Concert** in February at the Mission Estate Winery is a big regional deal in a gorgeous setting. At any time of year, there might be impromptu jazz concerts at the wineries or other entertainment in the soundshell.

This year, November rivals February with special events. All leading up to the city's 125th anniversary on the 29th, there will be **opera** for $20 (Nov. 5-7), **private garden tours** (Nov. 6-7), a "showstopping" medley of hit **show tunes** (Nov. 19-21), and a free **Ray Woolf** concert on the Sound Shore (Nov. 25). Also hosting **World Cup soccer games** on Nov. 11, 13, 16, and 20 (2 games $12), Napier bombards springtime visitors with activities. And of course the sunrise on **Jan. 1, 2000** speaks for itself.

NEAR NAPIER: CAPE KIDNAPPERS

Picture a bird on a nest, multiply that image by several thousand, put the duplicates in row formation, plunk the whole picture down on a remote cliffpoint in the Southern Pacific, and you've got Cape Kidnappers. The vertical toothy cliffs of Hawke Bay's southern tip strike a dramatic profile at any time of year, but from September to March they are home to the world's largest mainland nesting grounds of the **Australasian gannet.** Fifteen thousand of the large tawny-headed, white-and-black birds arrive en masse in October and set up their nests in quasi-orderly rows at the three colony sites encompassed by the 13-hectare **Cape Kidnappers Gannet Reserve.** The rocks may look frosted white by snow, but you know better. Chicks hatch in early November and mature through the summer before flying the coop on their ambitious maiden air voyage of 2800km across the Tasman Sea to Australia. In the meantime, it's a scene straight from Alfred Hitchcock: male gannets wheeling and bearing down like 747s toward the teeming colony, then stopping on a dime to drop nesting material to their Mrs. Gannet below. And if they misjudge their landing, hell hath no fury like a lady gannet wronged.

The area is closed to the public between July and October, when the birds are in the tenuous early nesting stage. At other times you are free to visit the masses of gannets (and big masses of gannet, ahem, residue). It's a stunning walk at any time of year, even in winter when the birds are gone. Check with the Napier Visitor Centre for local outfitters and hiking trails among soaring stone and crashing surf. (Trips usually 4-5hr.; $17-38.)

HASTINGS

Hastings may be known as Napier's twin city, but the likeness is strictly fraternal. Only 12km away, it fell victim to the same quake as Napier, but was partially rebuilt in Spanish Mission style. Its architecture never reached the same gaudy heights as the Art Deco explosion of Napier, and little effort has been put into promoting or developing the style further (though the Municipal Theatre on Hastings St. is impressive). There are many kiwifruit orchards in the area and consequently a lot of fruit pickers in town during the season. Essentially a contented working town, most visitors to Hastings head out: to the wineries, Cape Kidnappers, the beaches, Te Mata Peak, and all the natural attractions of Hawke's Bay to which Hastings is undeniably central.

◪ ORIENTATION AND PRACTICAL INFORMATION. Flat and orderly Hastings is perturbed only by the slant of the railway track slicing through the heart of the city center. **Heretaunga St.,** the main road, turns pedestrian for a block on either side of the railway (a herd of ceramic sheep flock at the Market St. end of this stretch). An Art Deco **clock tower** and fountain adorn the town square. Streets are tagged west to one side of the railway and east to the other; south and north designations split at **Heretaunga St.**

Book activities or travel arrangements at the **Visitors Information Centre** (tel. 873 5526; fax 873 5529) on Russell St. North (open M-F 8:30am-5pm, Sa-Su 10am-3pm). Napier and Hastings are about 30 minutes to one hour away from one another by bus or train. **InterCity, Newmans,** and **TranzScenic** leave from the **Hastings Travel Centre** (tel. 878 0213), at the end of Russell St. North (bookings M-F 7:45am-4:45pm). Fares are generally $2-3 different from those from Napier (see p. 178). **Nimon and Sons** (runs M-F 7am-5:30pm), leaves from Eastbourne St. by the Russell St. corner, or from the Kmart by the Visitors Center (for details see **Napier, p. 178**). **Hitchhikers** going south often head out just past the 30kph zone beyond the racecourse; those going to Napier thumb up Karamu Rd. North, while those heading to Taupo, Wairoa, or Gisborne take the route that bypasses central Napier by getting rides from Pakowhai Rd. Other services include: **BNZ** (tel. 878 0833), on Heretaunga St. next to **Westpac Trust** (open M and Th-F 9am-4:30pm, Tu-W 9:30-4:30pm); **police** (24hr. tel. 878 3007), on Railway Rd.; **post office** (tel. 876 03300), on the corner of Queen and Russell St.; and **Internet World** (tel. 876 4876), just opposite, with access for $12 per hour (open 8:30am-9pm, winter until 7pm). **Telephone Code:** 06.

⌐ ACCOMMODATIONS. Hastings has basically two options: hostels or pricey motels, with very little in the middle. Some hostels are only open from November to May; others survive by helping to arrange work for fruit-picking backpackers. Small and very quiet is the cute English villa of **AJ's Backpackers,** 405 Southland Rd. (tel. 878 2302), just off Southhampton St. Free pickups are available. While looking after their two small daughters, Jackie and Alan are very hospitable, with two spastic boxer dogs who pick up where their owners leave off. Simple rooms have bunks. (Dorms $15, weekly $85 if you're employed.) At the summer-only **Hastings Backpackers** (tel. 876 5888), on Lyndon St. between Hastings St. and Willow Park Rd., both work and play are available (open Nov.-Apr.). Pick fruit at an orchard, sign up for a daytrip to area attractions, or, if you're lucky, score the "love shack" in the garden corner. (Dorms $12, weekly $75.) Almost nightly, summer BBQs fill the courtyard of picnic tables at **Travellers Lodge,** 606-608 St. Aubyn St. West (tel. 878 7108). Turn left from the train station and follow signs. Large windows illuminate the sturdy wooden bunks and spacious rooms of this newly renovated backpackers, complete with a roomy TV lounge, foosball table, and sauna. (Free bikes. Key deposit $10. Dorms $15; singles $24; doubles $36. Weekly dorms $80. Cash only.) **The Hastings Holiday Park** (tel. 878 6692; email vin_norma@clear.net.nz), 25 minutes from town by Fantasyland on Windsor Ave., has lots of green space, large trees, and a duck-filled creek. Basic plyboard-walled sleeping cabins are outfitted with heaters. (3-bed dorms $25, children $5; doubles $40; tents and caravan sites $10. Peak rates apply.) Rub your lantern and wish for a room at the **Aladdin Lodge,** 120 Maddison St. (tel. 876 6322; email aladdinlodge@xtra.co.nz), off Willowpark Rd. South, or just come check in with Martin. Close to town and off the noisier main streets, all rooms are nicely outfitted with SKY TV, phones, and kitchenettes. There's a covered spa pool, a tiny plunge pool, and a playground with trampolines, not to mention free laundry. (Standard units, with a separate double bedroom and pull-out couches $76; one small unit with two single beds $60.)

⌐▨ FOOD AND NIGHTLIFE. Though there are a few trendy restaurants, don't expect much in the way of fine dining in Hastings. **Countdown Foods** (tel. 878 5091) is your supermarket on Queen St. North (open M-F 8am-9pm, Sa-Su 8am-8pm). Undoubtedly your peak culinary experience will be the rich and fruity scoops at

THE RACE TO SEE THE SUN Gisborne may claim to be "the first to see the light," but government surveyors determined three years ago that Hasting's Te Mata Peak catches the very first of the sun's rays. Capitalizing on their newfound fame, the otherwise anonymous "Millennium 2000 city" will attract New Year's enthusiasts from around the world. While parades, caroling, and light sculpture contests entertain visitors and locals in town, the peak itself will be closed off for a select group of revelers. With their $700 tickets, 1000 lucky people (one-third local, two-thirds international) will party the night away with catered food, live bands, and open bars situated on three levels of the windy, treacherous peak. And on Jan. 1, 2000, standing tippy-toe atop the summit, scoffing at the crowd on Gisborne's Haiti Hill celebrating "old news," the select few will peer across the Pacific horizon and bring in the millennial dawn in style—first.

Rush Munroe's Ice Cream Gardens, 704 Heretaunga St. West (tel. 878 9634). They've been around since 1926 and have used their 74 years of experience to perfect flavors from classic vanilla to loads of luscious fruity flavors (including feijoa). **The Corn Exchange** (tel. 870 8333), out in the old Farm Products Cooperative building on Maraekakaho Rd. (off Heretaunga St.), is a-maize-ingly chic, with smooth wood, a central fireplace, and outdoor seating. The menu changes, but tends to feature fringe meats like venison, duck, and bison (they've even done kangaroo), as well as steak, chicken, and vegetarian standards. Mains are pricey (from $20) but servings are filling; entrees like the wood-fired oven-baked pizzas are sizeable and reasonable ($14.50). You'll also find extensive liquors and a well-stocked bar, with occasional live music on weekends. (Open M-Th 11:30am-11pm, F-Sa 10:30am-1am, Su 10:30am-11pm.) **Robert Harris Coffee Shop,** 104 Russell St. South (tel. 878 2931), is in town center. Part of a larger coffee shop chain that reckons itself the Starbucks of New Zealand, this cafe offers fresh sandwiches (under $4) and baked goods—if you have time to wait through the line at peak meal times. (Open M-F 8am-5pm, Sa 8am-2pm.)

Nightlife in Hastings, more often than not, includes a pint of Steinlager's or cider under the dark pine ceiling beams lined with beer towels at the **Cat and Fiddle Ale House,** 502 Karamu Rd. (tel. 878 4111). Known for good eats (meaty mains under $8) as well as quality brews (more than 10 on tap), this down-home English pub is crowded with locals, and has monthly Monday night "Live Poets' Society" readings. (Open Su-W 10:30am-11pm, Th-Sa 10:30am-2am.) **Friends Bar and Cafe** (tel. 878 6701), sits at the corner of Karamu Rd. and Heretaunga St. in town center. (Free BBQ at 7pm on Su, and a Happy Hour M-Tu 5-6:30pm; open daily 11am-3am). In the upscale hamlet of **Havelock North** (7km east), several good pubs rock the night away. Hastings also has a fairly good offering of nightclubs scattered around town. Dance under strobe-lighting reflected in a disco ball at **Cheers,** 118 Market St. (tel. 878 2866), which has nothing more in common with the bar of the TV-series than the name and shape of the sign out front. ($2 cover after 10pm. One free drink with *Let's Go.* Open W-Sa 8pm-3am.)

■ ⚑ **SIGHTS AND ACTIVITIES.** Hastings shares many of its most compelling draws with Napier (p. 181), such as area wineries, Cape Kidnappers, and killer surfing beaches like **Ocean Beach** on the south side of the Cape and **Waimarama** farther south. Sample over 85 different varieties of pip and stone fruits (in season) at **Pernel Fruitworld** (tel. 878 3383), on Pakowhai Rd. about a 5-minute drive northwest of Hastings, with tours every hour from 9am to 4pm. The **Hawke's Bay Exhibition Centre,** 201 Eastbourne St. East (tel./fax 876 2077), is a companion to the museum in Napier with showings of local and national art and scientific displays (open M-F 10am-4:30pm, Sa-Su 11am-4pm; free).

As you walk down Heretaunga St., you may notice a large green lump welling up from the otherwise pancake-flat landscape surrounding the city. That's **Te Mata Peak,** the sleeping giant rising abruptly from sea level to 399m, and the highest point in Hawke's Bay. It's a two-hour round trip hike to Te Mata peak. You could cut your time in half by arranging for an exhilarating **tandem paraglide** off the skimpy ramps at the top into the valley beyond (done mostly in summer when the winds are right). Contact Shaun Gilbert (tel. mobile 025 223 6999) for a 15-minute, $120 glide ($100 per person for 4 or more).

TAUPO AND TONGARIRO

Mount Ruapehu, Ngauruhoe, and Tongariro cut a vivid skyline for a visually calming effect—even as fire and brimstone burning underground quicken the pulse with the promise of further volcanic tantrums. Lake Taupo, the largest freshwater lake in the Southern Hemisphere, fills a crater formed from a monumental explosion some 26,000 years ago. If you can find a patch of surface undimpled by jetskis, kayaks, or sailboats, the shimmering lake reflects quite an impressive scene. Fishermen in the foreground, their weather-worn eyes twinkling from the prospect of the 6- to 10-pound trout swimming below, parachutes float dangling legs against a blue sky, with the distant backdrop of Tongariro National Park (a World Heritage Area), where skiers career down mountain slopes like run-on sentences to the base towns of Whakapapa Village, National Park, and Ohakune. Cast yourself into this scene before underground rumbling changes the landscape again.

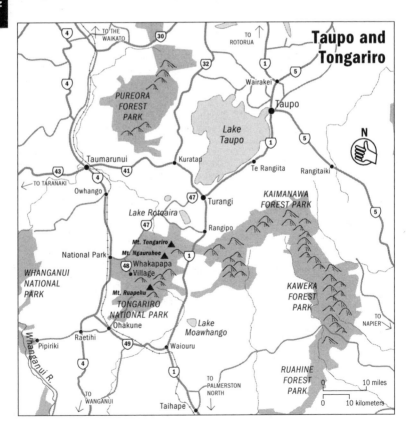

TAUPO

Maybe it's something in the water or in the geothermal steam. It could be the relief after surviving a morning skydive and bungy jump combo. Or it might be the happy-go-lucky vibes from the residents of this sunny community (pop. 21,257) who preside over the largest lake in New Zealand (616 sq. km) and its population of fat trout. Whatever it is, smiling comes easily in Taupo. The town lies at the origin of the Waikato River and rides the same belt of smoking geothermal activity that powers Rotorua, harboring attractions that often surprise visitors who may have initially planned on merely passing through.

⚆ ORIENTATION AND PRACTICAL INFORMATION

Tucked into a corner created by the **Waikato River** as it gushes from the northeast bulge of Lake Taupo, the city radiates like a streaking comet. Its head, at **Tongariro St.,** aims at the Visitor Centre and the **Boat Harbor,** and its outer tail angles away along **Lake Terr.** and the river on **Spa Rd.** Taupo's center of gravity lies between Tongariro and **Ruapehu St.** The wayward streaks of SH1 and SH5 exit across the Waikato to Rotorua or Auckland, and the other way to Turangi and Napier.

Visitors Center: The **Taupo Visitor Centre** (tel. 378 9000; fax 378 9003) is on Tongariro St. Open daily 8:30am-5pm.

DOC: (tel. 378 3885), way out at 115 Centennial Dr., an extension of Spa Rd. More of a field center than a source of information. Open M-F 8am-noon.

Buses: InterCity/Newmans leave from Gascoigne St. to: **Auckland** (5hr., 2-4 per day, $39-49); **Hamilton** (3hr., 2-3 per day, $25-31); **Rotorua** (1hr., 2-4 per day, $16-20); and **Wellington** (6hr., 2-4 per day, $53-66). InterCity/Newmans and **Kiwi Shuttles** (tel. mobile 025 503 654) go daily to **Napier** (2hr., 1-3 per day, $24-35). InterCity connects daily with Turangi's **Alpine Scenic Tours** to get up to **National Park** and **Whakapapa Village** (2hr., 2:30pm, $29). **Taupo Ski Shuttle,** organized by local ski shops, runs daily to the ski fields of **Tongariro** ($25). Book InterCity/Newmans at **Taupo Travel Centre** (tel. 378 9032), on Gascoigne St. off Tamamutu St., or at Taupo Visitor Centre.

Taxis: STOP Cabs (tel. 378 9250) and **Taupo Taxis** (tel. 378 5100). 24hr. service.

Hitchhiking: Taupo is at the crossroads of the North Island; rides are easy, but getting far enough out of town (especially to go south on SH1) may not be. To head north on SH1, many thumbers cross the Waikato to the intersection of Norman Smith St.

Currency Exchange: ASB Bank (tel. 376 0063), at Tongariro and Horomatangi St. Open M-F 9am-4pm.

Rentals: R&R Sports, 17 Tamamutu St. (tel. 377 1585), buys and sells used backpacking gear; they also rent mountain bikes (half-day $18, full day $28), fishing poles ($12-20 per day), ski equipment packages ($20), and snowboards with boots ($40). Taupo has cheaper ski rentals than the on-the-mountain shops. On Tongariro St., near the Lake Terrace Cross, **Pointons Ski Shop** (tel. 377 0087) has skis, boots, and poles packages ($15) or snowboard and boots ($40). **Ski Yer Heart Out,** 115 Tongariro St. (tel. 378 7400), rents skis ($25), snowboards ($40), and clothing gear (jackets and pants $20).

Police: (tel. 378 6060), behind the Visitor Centre in Story Pl. Open 24hr.

IT'S A BIRD, IT'S A PLANE, IT'S... Your one-stop potty shop, the **SuperLoo**, next to the Visitor Centre, was voted "the best loo in New Zealand" by Keep New Zealand Beautiful. The country is full of automated public toilets, but nothing quite compares to SuperLoo. Inside the stalls, exclamations of "this really *is* a super loo" can be heard. Kids heading into the toilets spread their arms out and while swooping inside like an airplane, yell "SUUUUUPER LOOOO. Here I come to save the day!"

Envisioning a new standard of sanitation in New Zealand, the makers of the SuperLoo set a lofty goal; some said it couldn't be done. But in October of 1993, when the SuperLoos first opened its lids to an anxiously awaiting public, Taupo knew immediately it had hit on something special. Its first users sat stunned for hours. Some stood frozen in the spotless stalls, shaking their heads in disbelief, mesmerized by shimmering counter-clockwise (or, as the Kiwis say, "anti-clockwise") flushes. The opening celebration, attended by MP John Banks, was said to have been epic—and only slightly embellished in hindsight: toilet paper streamers, anti-graffiti rallies, and bobbing for apples in the fresh toilet water. Especially enthusiastic attendees vowed never to wipe again. Today, after seven years of operation, the SuperLoo hasn't lost its sheen, and the awards accumulating on the wall prove it's still the bathroom/water-closet/toilet/whatever-you-happen-to-call-it, of the future. The next time nature calls in Taupo, step inside and see for yourself what the fuss is about. Toilets 20¢; 4min. shower $1.

Medical Services: The Taupo Health Centre, 117 Heu Heu St. (tel. 378 7060). Open M-F 8am-6pm. After hours the phone will give you an emergency contact, or check the *Taupo Times* for the on-duty doctor. **Main St. Pharmacy** (tel./fax 378 2636), corner of Tongariro and Heu Heu St. Open daily 9am-8:30pm. The **hospital** (tel. 378 8100) is on Kotare St.

Post Office: (tel. 378 9090), at the corner of Horomatangi and Ruapehu St. Open M-F 8:30am-5:30pm, Sa 9am-noon.

Internet Access: Charging $3.75 per 30min., **Central Plateau Reap,** corner of Heu Heu and Kaimanawa St. (tel. 378 8109), is the cheapest, but often not open when you need it. Open M-Th 9am-4:30pm, F 9am-3pm. **Computer Shop,** 15 Tamamutu St. (tel. 378 4546), is $5 per 30min. Open M-F 9am-5pm, Sa 9am-1:30pm.

Telephone Code: 07.

▐ ACCOMMODATIONS

Older, cheaper finds are clustered in the streets a few blocks east of town center. As always, book ahead in summer. Otherwise, the cheapest riverfront bed in town is the free camping on **Reid's Farm Rd.,** a bit south of the Falls, along Huka Falls Rd. (north of town off SH1). It's unwise to leave anything unattended there, as incidents of theft have been on the rise.

Rainbow Lodge, 99 Titiraupenga Rd. (tel. 378 5754; fax 377 1568; email rainbow@clear.net.nz), just off Spa Rd. Close to town, but free pickups. Tucked away on a residential street, Rainbow's colorful decor and atmosphere brightens even the darkest day. There may be no pot of gold here, but there is a bottomless pot of free coffee, as well as a sauna and pool table. Off-street parking. Mountain bike and fishing rod hire. Dorms $15-16; singles $26; twins and doubles $36; hotel-quality doubles with bath in a brand-new wing $39.

Action Downunder (YHA) (tel. 378 3311; fax 378 9612), at the corner of Tamamutu and Kaimanawa St. Shiny and clean, from its glossy, native-timber dining room tables to its bustling unisex bathrooms. Enjoy views of Lake Taupo and Mt. Tahara through the large windows of the ship-shape kitchen or from the picnic tables on the second-story deck. Central heating. Rental bikes. Dorms $16; singles $25; twins and doubles $36.

Go Global (VIP) (tel. 377 0044; fax 377 0059), at the corner of Tongariro and Tuwhare-toa St. With adjacent Axis Party Bar spinning nightly with rowdy young drinkers and a $10 meal-deal in the restaurant downstairs, you can have it all within the comfortable confines of this large, convenient hostel. Internet and videos preclude outings, but the late-night noise may may out you. Adequately spacious rooms with nice views of the lake, most with bath. Small TV lounge and tiny kitchen area. Key deposit $10. Dorms $17; twins $20; doubles $44.

Sunset Lodge, 5 Tremain Ave. (tel. 378 5962). Turn off Lake Terr. onto Hawai St. For a more low-key stay, the smallest hostel in Taupo offers lakeside ambience, springy mat-tresses, and legendary homemade banana bread. Free bikes, pickup, and shuttle to Craters of the Moon. Dorms $14; twins and doubles $34.

Berkenhoff (VIP) (tel./fax 378 4909), at the corner of Duncan and Scannell St., a 15min. walk from town center. With thatched-roof reception area and gorgeous thou-sand-dollar palm, this nicely self-contained lodge gets its name, meaning "house with birch trees," from the summer-blooming, winter-barren birch trees lining the back yard. The impressive downstairs bar called "Jake's Place" with cable TV, barrel tables, and extra comfortable couches is named after the owner's mellow, ice-cream-loving, 80kg black dog. Free spa and pool. Free breakfast, bikes, pickups, and daily drop offs. BBQ dinners $6-8.50. Dorms $16; twins and doubles $38.

Burke's Backpackers (Nomads), 69 Spa Rd. (tel. 378 9292; fax 378 9092). Hidden among car dealerships, this old, renovated motel has the advantage of private bath-

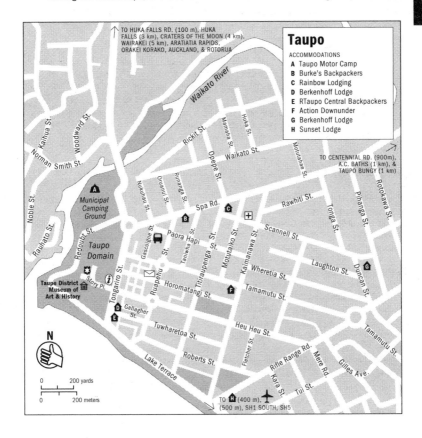

Taupo

ACCOMMODATIONS
A Taupo Motor Camp
B Burke's Backpackers
C Rainbow Lodging
D Berkenhoff Lodge
E RTaupo Central Backpackers
F Action Downunder
G Berkenhoff Lodge
H Sunset Lodge

rooms. Well-kept grounds make for nice sunbathing. Decent kitchen/dining area. Internet. Spa pool. Bikes for hire. Key deposit $10. Dorms $16; doubles and family rooms sharing private bathrooms $19 per person, with bath from $20.

Taupo Central Backpackers (VIP) (tel. 378 3206; fax 378 0344), at the corner of Tongariro and Tuwharetoa St. 2½ reasons to stay: 1) it's central; 2) in-house bar and deck has sweet views; and 2½) if you wake up early enough, there's free weetbix and toast (8-9am). Full of Kiwi Experience busloads. Rooms are adequate. Key deposit $10. Dorms $18; twins and doubles $42.

Taupo Motor Camp, 15 Redoubt St. (tel./fax 377 3080). Go up Tongariro St. about 100m past the Visitor Centre, then turn left. So central it needn't be fancy. The kitchen is basic. They are chock full during holidays, but leave room for internationals. Dorms $15, winter $12; elementary cinderblock cabin singles $35, winter $22; doubles $42; grassy, riverside camp sites under nice big trees $10 per person.

🏮 **Orakei Korako Geyserland** (tel. 378 3131; fax 378 0371), 35km from Taupo. If you've got your own transport, this hidden lakeside lodge across the water from Taupo's best geothermal site is unbeatably scenic and peaceful. Rev up the jukebox and slip into the front deck spa, or paddle to a closer view of the geysers in a rental canoe. Bring bedding and food (limited daytime cafe). Rustic communal lodge and bunks that were once trees $20; tourist flats (up to 6) with kitchenettes $20 per person mid-week (minimum 3). Flats are charged at their full 6-person rates F-Su and public holidays.

🗱 FOOD

Taupo has few middle-range restaurant options. Each of the **nightlife listings** offers affordable and decent meals, often with backpacker or nightly specials. For the true Taupo experience, delight in some trout. While it can't be sold over the counter, a few places around town will prepare your catch (for a fee); ask around. The **Pak 'N Save** (tel. 377 1155) is at the corner of Ruapehu and Tamamutu St. (open M-F 8:30am-8pm, Sa-Su 8:30am-7:30pm), while **Maxis 24hr. Food,** on Roberts St. near Ruapehu St., has your 3am burger, soda, tobacco, or band-aids.

🏮 **Pasta Mia,** 5 Horomatangi St. (tel. 377 2930). Pasta Mia's larger factory supplies restaurants around the country with fresh pasta. Its lunch service, started as an afterthought, has accumulated a following of folks who know quality deals when they wind them around a fork and taste them. Mouthwatering single serving of pasta is only $5.50 ($10.50 for double). For around $13, you'll have enough uncooked pasta and sauce to make new lifelong friends at the hostel as fast as water comes to boil. Open M-F 10am-5:30pm, Sa 10am-2pm.

🏮 **Holy Cow,** 11 Tongariro St. (tel. 378 0040). This backpacker bar mecca is consistently your best deal in town, with flavorful meals from $5. Mains like couscous and vegetables or spaghetti bolognese ($5) are good, hot, and too big to finish. Often 2 people order one main and 2 sets of silverware. Retains a family-style atmosphere in early evening, before the partyers arrive around 9pm. Open daily 5pm-late.

Nonni's (tel. 378 6894), at the corner of Tongariro St. and Lake Terr. A local favorite, Nonni's has a prime lakefront location and is well served by outdoor seating and superb service in an unhurried atmosphere. All-day brunch menu ($8-12) with a large Mediterranean selection. Open for lunch daily 7am-3pm, dinner F-Sa from 6pm.

Replete Delicatessen and Cafe, 45 Heu Heu St. (tel. 377 3011). Crockery bowls containing well-presented inventive dishes make for lunchtime eagerness among the crowd-clogged ordering area. You can't go wrong, with most items under $7. Open M-F 8:45am-5pm, Sa 9am to mid-afternoon, Su 10am to mid-afternoon.

Villino, 45 Horomatangi St. (tel. 377 4478), near the Ruapehu St. cross. An excellent restaurant with the best chef in town, Villino is a bit out of place in a budget travel guide; dinner prices will strip the pack from your back. But the mouthwatering breakfast and lunch menus feature single digits. The pizza-pie-sized open omelettes ($10.50) and panini ($9.50) will blow you away. Open Tu-Sa 8:30am-late, Su 8:30am-afternoon.

🎵 📺 ENTERTAINMENT AND NIGHTLIFE

Taupo's not big on live music, but you can find some at **The Hobler,** 42 Tuwharetoa St. (tel. 378 0830), a very mellow restaurant and bar (open daily from 11:30am), or **Red Barrel** (tel. 378 0555), on Lake Terr. near Tongariro St., where a round pool table perplexes players. Thursdays feature live music and $1 spirits from 8 to 10pm. (Occasional $2 cover. Open daily 10:30am-2am or earlier.) A handful of bars and dance clubs cluster near the lake end of Tongariro St.

🏄 **Holy Cow,** 11 Tongariro St. (tel. 378 0040). Every backpacker, her uncle, and the guy they hitched with, head to *the* bar of Taupo. The green ink of completed bungies still fresh on handle-grasping hands, tables are mounted fairly early in this rump-shaking second-floor mixing bowl, with belching DJs mixing commercial hits. Leave your inhibitions at home. Happy Hour 5-7pm and 9-10pm. Open daily 5pm-3am.

Rockefeller's (tel. 378 3344), on Tuwharetoa St. Though Taupo's business class admires itself in the brass fittings and gleaming bar, it's a good place for a quiet beer during the week, or a rowdy crowded thirtysomething scene on weekends. Open M-F 11am-1am, Sa-Su 11am-2am.

🔺 ACTIVITIES

PLUMMETING OUT OF THE SKY

If you've been resisting peer pressure or sudden impulses, Taupo is the place to throw caution to the wind and hurtle out of a plane at 3000m or plummet toward water with an elastic cord hooked to your feet. Taupo's death-wish appeal may be the result of the scenery: if you're going to go, your last seconds had better look good. For deals on all three activities (bungy, skydiving, and ropes courses), complete the **MaxBuzz** challenge. A promotional of the area's adrenaline-boosters, Max-Buzz offers a free beer at the Holy Cow for each activity completed. Once you conquer all three, your certificate accumulating stamps along the way, just purchase something at the bar/restaurant and you'll be initiated into the freefalling/bungy-jumping/trapeze-clinging club with a free T-shirt.

Taupo Bungy, 202 Spa Rd. (tel. 377 1135), runs a highly professional operation that, since December 1991, has sent over 93,000 off "the plank" 47m above the hauntingly crystalline Waikato. For $89, you can hook up and ponder either the sheer cliffs, the impending water, or the tiny pickup raft below. Call ahead to avoid the wait. (Open daily 9am-7pm, winter 9am-5pm.)

Tandem skydiving in Taupo is cheaper than anywhere else (doubtless because of the sheer number of jumps—over 35,000), and the views on a clear day are spectacular, stretching from Ruapehu to Taranaki to Tarawera. 🏄**Taupo Tandem Skydive** (tel. 377 0428 or 0800 275 934) has been sending people up since 1990, and though the preparation is disconcertingly brief, the reassuring, professional, and amusing Tandem Masters do everything but scream for you. ($165 from 3000m; 100kg weight limit; call ahead.)

🏄**Rock 'n Ropes** (tel. 374 8111), located at Deerworld off Highway 5 just north of Wairekai, has an arousing array of ropes and adventure exotica including the chicken walk, criss crotch, floating log, vertical playpen, and giant swing. Many takers find these challenging highwires even scarier than the bungy or skydive. Other, less interactive, aerial activities include scenic helicopter and airplane **flights** ranging from local jaunts to circling the Tongariro plateau; check with the Visitor Centre for a complete listing. **The Taupo Gliding Club** (tel. 378 5627) meets each Wednesday and Sunday at Centennial Park, 6km up Spa Rd., and will take you up for a 20- to 30-minute glide ($50).

GEOTHERMAL ACTIVITY

While you may be content to gaze for days, don't let the rippling lake and mesmerizing horizon of Tongariro, Ngauruhoe, and Ruapehu burn into your retina. To diversify the view, turn your feet inland for Taupo's host of other attractions. Though its geothermal attractions may not get as much press as those of Rotorua, they lie along the same belt of primeval geological action. A 1954 explosion from the drilling of a geothermal bore collapsed several acres of land into a steaming pockmarked landscape called **Craters of the Moon,** now a free DOC-managed Scenic Reserve only a few kilometers north of town on SH1. As small vents collapse and become blocked, minor eruptions can occur at any time. On chilly mornings and evenings, whirling steam adds a ghostly, otherworldly feel, enveloping and sometimes even obscuring any vista of the craters and roiling mud pools. The gates remain open all the time; don't leave valuables in your car.

Walter's Tours (tel. 378 5924) provides informative, user-friendly tours of various hot spots around Taupo, such as Craters of the Moon, Huka Falls, Orakei Korako (3hr., $20), or to more distant points in Rotorua—even the Waitomo Caves (from $75). **Kiwi Value Tours** (tel. 378 9662) does a similar loop, and also plans to offer a convenient $10 "walkabout" system: buses will make a loop every hour, allowing people to get on and off at desired spots.

Far away (and inaccessible to those without their own wheels or a tour) is the dramatic and undeveloped private geothermal reserve of **Orakei Korako** (tel. 378 3131), which can be reached via a sign-posted road that winds through hill and deer farms off SH1 about 25 minutes north of Taupo. As steam wafts up the hidden green valley, a shuttle boat crosses the small, idyllic, dammed lake during the day. On the far side lie pockets of glistening silica terraces, spurting geysers (including a fascinating horizontal geyser), colorful mineral crusts, and deep, scalding hot cyan pools. Don't miss the spectacular fern-lined amphitheater of Aladdin's Cave with its warm mineral pool. Jewelry can reportedly be naturally cleaned in the pool in three minutes while its owners gaze at the postcard view from the cave's mouth. If you're captivated, stay for a meal at the local cafeteria or even spend the night at the nearby lodge or cabin. (Open daily 8am-4:30pm, winter 8am-4pm. Entrance fees and boat ride $15.)

ON THE WATER

Lake Taupo's blue waters fill the crater of a volcano whose eruptions were some of the most disruptive the world has ever witnessed. Its final blast, 1800 years ago, ejected 110 cubic km and distributed ash and pumice meters-thick over much of the North Island. It even caused blood-red skies which were recorded in ancient Chinese and Roman literature.

FISHING. Fishing options in Taupo are literally boundless. A group of people can charter a boat with guide and all tackle supplied, for anywhere between $50-130 per hour. Private guides are also available to teach the basics of fly fishing. The world-famous Taupo **trout,** both brown and rainbow, were introduced from California in the late 1800s and continue to draw novice and experienced anglers from across the world. The apex of the phenomenon is **ANZAC Day** (April 25, 2000), when the great fishing-fest of the ECNZ International Trout Fishing Tournament takes over town with anglers eager to take the biggest, the prettiest, the superlativest trout of the lake (entries are limited to 500). Most catches average around 1½kg. Lake fishing at Taupo is relaxed, scenic, and popular. The lake trout are fat and relatively easier to catch than their more aerobic soulmates of the area's rivers. Spinning and fly-fishing are permitted in the lake year-round; on the rivers, only fly-fishing is allowed. All the other legal details are printed on the back of the **fishing license** you have to purchase for any line you drop ($13 per day, $25 per week); get one at the Visitor Centre, a sports shop, or one of the offices at the harbor.

TOURS. The western shores of **Acacia Bay** end at cliff and bush, with an undulating edge of isolated rocky inlets and bays. It is named for the acacia trees planted by one of Taupo's first missionaries—originally chosen because, in the Bible, Noah must craft the arc of the covenant from acacia trees. Along part of the uninhabited coastline, a set of spectacular (if not ancient) Maori carvings have been chiseled into the rock faces at **Mine Bay,** on private land and accessible by boat only. You can approach the lake scenery with your own rented boat, or take advantage of the several outfitters with relatively cheap narrated cruises. **Taupo Scenic Kayaks** (tel. 378 1391) offers half-day trips to the carvings and other sights ($40). Many cruises include the carvings, the Western Bays, Hot Water Beach, and a wide expanse of lake itself; contact the **Charter Office** (tel. 378 3444) at the harborfront to book. The only way to see all the sights in a relatively short amount of time is on the speedy **Superjet** (tel. 377 4855 or 0800 278 737), which does a 2-hour comprehensive loop at up to 50 knots. Informative commentary over the loudspeaker, windsuits, life jackets, and optional refreshments are provided. (1hr., $39, children $19). For a more hands-on experience, the sexy, 1920s sailing yacht, the **Barbary** (tel. 378 3444), once owned by none other than Errol Flynn, is now captained by colorful Bill Dawson who teaches you how to sail it yourself (2½-3hr., 2-3 per day, $20).

ADVENTURE. To quicken your floating pulse, the **Huka Jet** (tel. 374 8572 or 0800 485 2538) is a heart-racing jetboat blast down the Waikato, performing 360° turns for the Kodak-heavy crowds at Huka Falls (boats run every 30min. from Wairakei Park or the Visitor Centre; $55, children $25). A simple, placid float on the Waikato is always an option. Several outfitters run all or some of these rivers; check with the Visitor Centre for details. **Zig Zag Fun Co.** runs kayaking trips farther up the Waikato than other kayaking companies. Paddle by the Orakei Korako thermal park on a half-day ($35) or full-day ($75) trip (free pickup).

　　Punch's Place (tel. 378 5596), down at the harborfront, has a host of watersports and fishing possibilities. Putter around in a self-drive run-about ($35 per hr.; fits up to 4) or get your speed buzz with a seadoo jet-bike ($50 per 30min.). Punches also provides for waterskiing and that ultimate Taupo combination of water, air, and adrenaline known as parasailing ($50).

OTHER SIGHTS AND ACTIVITIES

Wairakei Park, a slightly bizarre amalgamation of sights, recreational activities, a geothermal power station, a geothermally heated prawn farm, shops, and lodgings, lies across the **Waikato Bridge** on SH1. At its north end, 8km from town, sits the world's first geothermal power station, the **Wairakei Geothermal Power Development** (built 1959-64). From the **Bore Lookout,** at the end of the road turn-off, take in the post-apocalyptic terrain of massive, steaming, stainless-steel tubes worming along the ground to feed Taupo's energy needs. Head south back toward town to the Huka Falls Rd. turn-off to reach the lava-red **Taupo Volcanic Activity Centre** (tel. 374 8375), the public side of adjacent IGS (Institute of Geological and Nuclear Science), where researchers monitor the Taupo volcanic zone. The Centre recently became more interactive with the introduction of a model geyser, a small earthquake simulator, and even a glass-encased tornado machine. Check out the seismograph readings of Ruapehu and recent eruption film footage. (Admission $5, children $2.50., families $12.50.)

　　The zinger of attractions on the same road is, according to locals, New Zealand's most visited natural attraction: **Huka Falls,** Maori for "long white water." Join bus loads of camera toters to witness the 100m wide, 4m deep Waikato River force itself into a 15m wide, 3m deep rock chute. Spurting out of the bottleneck, the water rushes breathlessly below a footbridge over the channel, and ejects finally into a pool below. The cheapest and most aerobic way to capture the falls on your roll of film is via the **Huka Falls Track** (1hr.), leaving from Spa Thermal Park off Spa Rd.—natural hot pools are worth a dip on the return trip. The **Aratiatia Rapids,** a sight once continually impressive and now so only at 10am, noon, 2pm (and 4pm in summer), when the hydroelectric plant's gates are opened to appease visitors.

　　After a long day of touring, you'll may want to pay a visit to one of Taupo's hot springs. **Taupo Hot Springs** (tel. 377 6502) on the Taupo/Napier Highway, only five minutes from town, includes private pools ($8), a main pool ($7), and a giant waterslide ($4 unlimited use) in a tranquil setting (open daily 7:30am-9:30pm).

TONGARIRO

TURANGI

Proclaiming itself the "Trout Fishing Capital of the World" when Taupo is looking the other way, Turangi is renowned among the many anglers who come to tackle the rainbow and brown trout of the area's teeming waters. Built in the 70s for workers constructing the hydroelectric Tokaanu Power Station nearby, Turangi unapologetically offers few in-town attractions. Many residents don't contest this state of affairs, and instead simply sweep an arm at the surrounding mountains of Tongariro, the remote Kaimanawa range, and the trout-filled Tongariro River, gathering force from its trickling origin in the valleys of the volcanoes, and spilling into Lake Taupo a few kilometers away.

◪ **ORIENTATION AND PRACTICAL INFORMATION.** Some 4km from Lake Taupo on **SH1,** Turangi boasts no lakefront view. SH1 continues both north around the lake to Taupo, and south (where it's known as the **Desert Rd.**). **Ohuanga Rd.** is the main road through town, and virtually all essential shops and services are in the nondescript **Town Centre** complex, a short diagonal walk from the bus stop. The **Turangi Visitor Centre** (tel. 386 8999) is just across from the Town Centre. Check in here in winter to make sure the Desert Road is open before heading south. (Open daily 8:30am-5:30pm.) For more in-depth park information and before attempting any serious Tongariro walks, stop by the **DOC** office (tel. 386 8607), in Turanga Pl. at the south edge of town (open M-F 8am-5pm). **InterCity** stops at the Travel Centre (tel. 386 8918) and heads daily to: **Wellington** (5½hr., 1-3 per day, $60) via **Palmerston North** (3hr., $30-35); **Auckland** (6hr., 1-2 per day, $60) via **Hamilton** (4hr., $40); and **Taupo** (45min., $15). The laid-back folks of **Alpine Scenic Tours** (tel. 386 8918 or mobile 025 937 281), also at the Travel Centre, run daily shuttles to **Whakapapa Village** or, if the road is okay, straight to **Whakapapa** (45min., 2 per day, return $15), and in summer also to the endpoints of the **Tongariro Crossing** (return $20). Alpine also heads daily to **National Park** (1-2 per day, $15) and to **Taupo** (3 per week, $14). The **Bellbird Lodge** (tel. 386 8281) runs a shuttle to ski fields and an early bird (6:30am) shuttle to the **Tongariro Crossing** (return $20). **Turangi Taxis** (24hr. tel. 386 7441) are there for in-town transport. **Hitchhiking** to Taupo is reportedly not too difficult for those heading north on SH1, who stand at the corner of Pihanga Rd., near the Visitor Centre. Traffic is lighter going south, however. Other services include: **National Bank** (tel. 386 8967), in the Town Centre (open M-F 8am-5pm, winter M-F 9am-noon and 1-4:30pm); **Turangi Pharmacy** (tel. 386 8565; open M-F 8:30am-6pm, Sa 9am-1pm, Su 10:30am-noon); **post office** (tel./fax 386 7769; open M-F 9am-5pm); and the **police station** (tel. 386 7709), 100m down Ohuanga Rd. **Telephone Code:** 07.

▛▟ **ACCOMMODATIONS AND FOOD.** Well-organized and often providing shuttles, Turangi's accommodations will set you up with discounts for affiliated area outfitters. A quiet, home-like atmosphere reigns in the four houses making up the **Bellbird Lodge** (tel. 386 8281; www.bellbird.co.nz) in the residential north end of town, on the corner of Ohuanga and Rangipoia Rd. (call for pickup). All houses have cozy communal space, some featuring 1960s interior decorating. Mountain bikes are available for hire, along with fishing tackle and tramping clothes. (Dorms $15-16; twins and doubles $34; tent sites $9.) **Extreme Backpackers,** 26 Ngawaka Pl. (tel. 386 8949; fax 386 8946), is just around the corner from the bus depot. As designer/builder/owner Andrew will attest, this brand-new RIMU wooden lodge with an inner courtyard, state-of-the-art kitchen, and open log fire in the TV lounge, serves as a home away from home. Super-insulated walls keep heat, noise, and contented guests from wandering off. (Off-street parking. 4-bed dorms $17; doubles with linen $38; doubles with bath $45.) The massive complex of **Club Habitat (YHA/VIP)** (tel. 386 7492; fax 386 0106), on Ohuanga Rd., just up and across from the Visitor Centre, is frequented by the Magic Bus crowd and other groups. Don't mind the pseudo-resort name—though you may need a map to find your serviceable dorm bunk or made-up double. (Sauna and spa. Restaurant and bar. Dorms $16; doubles $48; tent sites $7).

Culinary pickings are slim in Turangi and what good food there is will make sure you're not. The **Grand Central Fry** (tel. 386 5344) on Ohuanga Rd. is a cut above the typical takeaway, with excellent burgers and fish 'n' chips (open daily 11:30am-9pm; lunchtime specials from $2; phone in your order to avoid the wait). The restaurant at **Club Habitat** (tel. 386 7492) can do overpriced standard fare (mains $10-15), with a good buffet breakfast ($6) offered daily from 7-9:30am; dinner is served from 6-9pm. The bar at Club Habitat is one of the few in town and not half-bad (Happy Hour 5-7pm, with $2.20 pints; doors close at 10pm). Set sail to discover the New World **supermarket** (tel. 386 8780; open M-F 8:30am-6pm, Sa-Su 9am-5pm).

📷 🎿 **SIGHTS AND ACTIVITIES.** The **Tokaanu Thermal Pools** (tel. 386 8575) are off the main road of tiny Tokaanu Village down SH41 from Turangi. Douse your-self in small, covered private pools ($5 per 20min.) or in a slightly cooler public pool ($3; open daily 10am-9pm).

The **Tongariro River** is ideal for two things: boating down or fishing up. Several operators raft down the Grade 3 upper section, over 60-odd rapids closed in by walls of bush. Garth at **Tongariro River Rafting** (tel. 0800 101 024) will ease your pas-sage down "the Bitch" and other suitably overwrought rapids, or let you do it your-self (with supervision) for $75. Docile "family floats" on the lower stretch are also available for $30. Turangi's **fish** are a sure-fire bite: husky 1½-2kg trout lurk all over. Fishing guides for the river and lake range from $40 to $65 per hour. Using the same toll-free number, you can book one of the increasingly popular **EcoTours,** a two-hour journey into Taupo's natural wetlands.

Turangi's other big attraction is its proximity to large tracts of uninhabited bush, both a disjunct northern chunk of **Tongariro National Park** (see p. 151) and the rug-ged hills rising east of Tongariro that constitute part of the **Kaimanawa Forest Park.** Mainly for the stout of heart (and limb), Kaimanawa is hard to access and not developed for visitors, as it's primarily used for multiday hunting and fishing trips (only 4 backcountry huts exist, and these are usually reached by air). Easier possi-bilities include dabbling around the park's edges on foot or mountain bike on any of several trails branching off Kaimanawa Rd., which splits off SH1, 15km south of Turangi. The **Lake Rotopounamu walk,** which leaves from a sign-post 11km up SH47, does an easy 5km loop through native fern forest around this small lake hidden at the base of **Pihanga** (the 1325m extinct volcano towering over Turangi). Farther along SH47, just past the junction with 47a, is the trailhead for **Te Porere Redoubt,** the poorly designed fortification built by Te Kooti's forces in 1869 for what was to be the final battle of the land wars. Te Kooti escaped the failed final stand here, but 37 others did not.

TONGARIRO NATIONAL PARK

Standing by themselves at the roof of the North Island are the three larger-than-life volcanoes of the central plateau: massive Ruapehu (2797m), elegantly conical Ngauruhoe (2291m), and the lower Tongariro (1967m), an amalgamation of ancient craters and ridges. Reaching improbably high, these active volcanoes were once considered so sacred that all but the highest-born Maori shielded his or her eyes against the grandeur. Today, Tongariro and its neighbors constitute the heart, if not the soul, of New Zealand's park system: Tongariro was the country's first national park, and the world's fourth. The first national park in the world to be rec-ognized as a World Heritage Site for both its natural and cultural significance, Ton-gariro is a windswept land encompassing New Zealand's only desert (the desolate Rangipo, lying in the mountain's shadow), native forests of beech in lower areas, and hardy alpine shrublands across the lava-built slopes. The **Tongariro Northern Cir-cuit Great Walk,** which includes the day-long **Tongariro Crossing,** is one of the coun-try's most popular and spectacular hikes, passing through the park's lunar landscapes of smoking vents, gem-like crater lakes, and mineral springs.

⚡ ORIENTATION AND PRACTICAL INFORMATION

Encircled by highways, Tongariro is accessible from **Turangi** (see p. 194), **Ohakune** (see p. 201), **National Park Village** (see p. 200), and **Whakapapa Village** (see p. 201); see specific coverage for transportation links. **SH1**, the **Desert Road** (frequently closed due to snow and ice), streaks by to the east through the **Rangipo Desert** en route to Lake Taupo. **SH49**, splitting off at the army base town of **Waiouru**, runs south of the park through Ohakune, while **SH4** cuts along the west side and continues to **Taumarunui** toward Auckland. National Park Village sits at the junction of SH4 and **SH47**, the latter tracing the park's northern edge onward to Turangi to join SH1. A discontinuous chunk of park sits at the northern end beyond the dammed lake of **Rotoaira**.

The tiny settlement of **Whakapapa Village** is in the park on **SH48**, which branches off SH47. National Park Village and Whakapapa Village are most convenient to the Tongariro Crossing and Northern Circuit, while Ohakune provides access to the southerly ski fields of Turoa. **Hitchhiking** in Tongariro is dubious—traffic can be sparse at any time of year. Those determined to get up Bruce Rd. (past Whakapapa Village) or Ohakune Mountain Rd. often start early to catch ski field employees, and never wait until dark to try their luck going down. If you have a car, the DOC recommends parking your car in the secure lot at park headquarters to avoid vandalism and theft.

Whakapapa Visitor Centre (tel. 892 3729; fax 385 8128; email ruapehuao@ doc.govt.nz), the highlight of Whakapapa Village, presents two high-tech audiovisual shows (for a small fee), as well as free displays on the park's history and biology (open daily 8am-6pm, winter 8am-5pm). There's a smaller **DOC Field Centre** in Ohakune (tel. 385 0011; fax 892 3814). The fantastic **Tongariro Summer Programme** (late Dec.-early Jan.) features DOC-led activities from evening talks ($5) to backcountry heli-hikes ($150). The DOC runs two **campgrounds** in the area: **Mangawhero**, 2km up the road from the Ohakune Field Centre, and **Mangahuia**, off SH47 (passes $4 per night). As for food, it's definitely cheaper to buy your noodles in the **supermarkets** of Ohakune or Turangi, rather than at National Park's limited shop or at the desperate-hiker store of the Whakapapa Holiday Park. There are **ATMs** in Ohakune and Turangi, but not in National Park Village or Whakapapa Village. The nearest **hospitals** are in Taumarunui (tel. 895 7199) and Taupo (tel. 378 8100). **Telephone Code:** 06 in Ohakune; 07 for all points further north.

⚔ ACTIVITIES

For information on the **Tongariro Northern Circuit** or the **Tongariro Crossing**, see p. 198. Possibly the hardest dayhike in Tongariro is the unmarked climb to the active **Ruapehu Crater.** The tramp begins from the Turoa Skifield parking lot on the south side, the top of Bruce Rd. before the Whakapapa ski lifts on the north side (return 7-8hr.), or the top of these ski lifts (return 5-6hr., $15). Ice, snow, and volcanic activity can make the trip a risky one, and several unprepared people have died doing it. **Whakapapa Skifield** (tel. 892 3738) offers daily guided walks in summer (Dec.-Apr. 10am; $55, children $35). The less-crowded **Round-the-Mountain Walk** runs around cranky Ruapehu, traversing windswept slopes, crossing a deep gorge, and passing along the edge of the haunting, forsaken Rangipo Desert (huts $8, camping $4). Daywalks abound, most starting from Whakapapa Village or the end of Ohakune Mountain Rd. The **Whakapapa Nature Walk** (return 30min.) is a **wheelchair-accessible** loop with ample botanical signage; many longer daywalks take in the best bits of the Tongariro Northern Circuit or the Round-the-Mountain Walk.

SKIING

First attempted in 1913, skiing in Tongariro today draws well over half of its visitors in the winter months, with the help of the two commercial ski fields hugging Ruapehu's slopes. As they're on DOC land, **Whakapapa** and **Turoa** have to abide by numerous regulations to minimize the impact of thousands of people carving down the mountain. Nonetheless, they are among the largest and most developed ski resorts in the country. While South Islanders may scoff, the Tongariro ski fields

LAIR OF THE LAHAR On December 24, 1953, the debris build-up holding back Ruapehu's Crater Lake collapsed and sent a violent lahar—a fast, flowing stream of mud and ash debris—down a valley, sweeping away a railroad bridge. Minutes later, a train carrying 151 people arrived at the non-existent bridge, and hurtled into the gorge below. On September 18, 1995, Ruapehu roused itself again from fitful slumber to begin a month of the most dramatic explosive activity since it blew its top in 1945. Locals cast a watchful eye to their suddenly barren ski slopes. The new eruption sent ash as far as the east coast, emptied out Crater Lake, and then stopped—just in time for the ski fields to reopen for the end of the season. Ruapehu remained quiet all summer, raising hopes for a peaceful and profitable winter. But on June 17, 1996, the day before the Turoa and Whakapapa ski fields were to open, it spewed ash with a vengeance onto the pristine ski fields well into July, disrupting air traffic in Auckland, and coating homes in Gisborne with grit. After two years of multi-million dollar impacts, many locals don't like to talk much about the eruptions. Most people shrug and say that it only happens every 50 years. The advertisements of the skiing industry are quick to assure that the eruptions are over, while Ruapehu offers a more equivocal response, occasionally puffing out plumes of steam.

attract huge crowds (and can, in fact, get frustratingly crowded during holidays). Both Whakapapa and Turoa have long seasons, usually opening in late June and early July and closing in late October. Unfortunately, Ruapehu attracts bad weather like a 2797m magnet—due to gale-force winds and storms, the fields can be closed almost a quarter of the time. Both offer a weather guarantee, however, allowing refunds or credits if lifts have to close.

WHAKAPAPA. Whakapapa (tel. 892 3738, snowphone 892 3833), at the top of Bruce Rd. from **Whakapapa Village** (see p. 201), has killer views of distant Mt. Egmont (Taranaki) on clear days. It's also the country's largest ski field, with six chairlifts, eight T-bars or platters, seven rope tows, a gentle beginner's area (Happy Valley), and heaps of groomed, patrolled trails. There's good open terrain for off-piste as well. Snowboarders are welcome (but seem to prefer Turoa). Whakapapa has five cafeterias and a ski shop that rents full ski gear ($26 for skis, boots, and poles), or snowboards and boots ($40, board only for $30). The towns of **National Park** (see p. 200) and Whakapapa Village also have their share of rental places ($25-40 for a snowboard and boots is standard). Lift passes are available for half-days ($20-49), consecutive days (2 days $93, 3 days $130, 4 days $162), and five days "anytime" ($221). The first-timer pass ($48) includes equipment rental and a lesson. Whakapapa also runs **scenic lift rides** to "the highest cafe in New Zealand" (Mid-Dec. to Apr.; $15, children $8).

TUROA. Slather on the sunscreen, strap on the Oakleys, and hit the slopes of Turoa (tel. 385 8456, snowphone 0900 99 444), the lifeblood of **Ohakune** (see p. 201). Accessible via the Ohakune Mountain Rd. and boasting the country's longest vertical drop (720m) and 400 hectares of patrolled snow, Turoa is known for its wide open terrain, long runs (4km is the longest), five chairlifts, three T-bars, four platter lifts, and one rope tow, as well as a beginner's area at the base, and a large number of intermediate runs (the highest lift runs up to an elevation of 2300m). Snowboarders love Turoa for the natural half-pipes in its gulleys and its lack of any major flats—almost half of the slope at any given time is covered with bleached-blond, styled-out boarders. Turoa also has some excellent off-trail skiing possibilities; it's even possible to haul gear up to Crater Lake and ski down (always check with the Ski Patrol first). Turoa's slopes are usually open daily 9am-4pm. Daylift passes cost around $48. You can rent all skiing ($25) or boarding ($40) equipment on the mountain, but be aware that there may be a better selection of both the budget and higher-quality equipment at one of Ohakune's many shops (prices roughly equivalent to those on the mountain).

⚡ TONGARIRO NORTHERN CIRCUIT AND THE TONGARIRO CROSSING

Winding in and around the park's defining trinity of volcanoes, the Tongariro Northern Circuit is among the country's most amazing walks. The track affords tremendous views of a windswept infernal landscape pocked with steaming vents, technicolor lakes, and bizarre rock formations, all overshadowed by the perfect cone of Mt. Ngauruhoe, the jumbled mass of Mt. Tongariro, and the slumbering snow-covered volcanic beast of Mt. Ruapehu. Beyond the landscape's geological delights, trampers can expect to enjoy small patches of native forest and wide swathes of diverse ground-hugging vegetation. The stretch of track between Mangatepopo and Highway 47A doubles as the Tongariro Crossing, extremely popular as a day-hike.

ESSENTIALS

Length: The Tongariro Northern Circuit is 49km (3-4 days), and the Tongariro Crossing is 17km (6-8hr.).

Trailheads: The **Northern Circuit** loops around Mt. Ngauruhoe and Mt. Tongariro, and can be accessed from Whakapapa Village, the **Mangatepopo** road-end 6km off SH47, the **Ketetahi** road-end off SH47A, or off the **Desert Road** (SH1). The **Crossing** officially runs between the Mangatepopo road-end and the Ketetahi road-end, where many shuttle services await. **Alpine Scenic Tours** (tel. (07) 386 8918) cycles on a reasonably flexible schedule among the trailheads, Turangi, National Park Village, and Whakapapa Village (2-3 per day). **Tongariro Track Transport** (tel. (07) 892 3716) runs in summer from National Park Village (7:45am) and Whakapapa Village (8am) to Mangatepopo, picking up at Ketetahi twice (4:30pm and 6pm). **Howard's Lodge** (tel. (07) 892 2827) runs more or less on demand in summer among the same points. These services charge $10 for a one-way dropoff or pickup, and $15 return. Most people walk the Crossing from Mangatepopo to Ketetahi, which means an intense initial climb before an eventual switchback descent. The same holds true for the Northern Circuit, which is relatively less strenuous beyond the Crossing.

Seasonality: With its high altitude and extreme exposure to the elements, the track's safest season runs from early December through March. Although it is possible to do the track year-round, snow on the trail turns it into a technical tramp requiring a great deal more equipment and experience. The peak period of track use runs from Christmas until the end of January.

Huts and Campsites: The Northern Circuit has four well-attended huts, with toilets, star charts, weather reports, and heat from gas or wood burners. From October to May, the huts contain swanky gas cooker/toasters, and require a **Great Walks pass** ($12, youth $6). Each hut has an adjoining cluster of tent plots ($6), many of which can receive stake-pulling amounts of wind; fortunately, on-site upgrades from campsite passes to hut passes are fine. In winter, the fees revert to the backcountry ticket system (huts $8, tent sites $4). Tickets purchased on-site cost 25% extra.

Gear: Weather conditions can be extreme; blazing sun may change in minutes to freezing wind-driven rain. Even for just a day on the Crossing, it is imperative to carry a good **waterproof and windproof raincoat** and at least one warm fleece or wool layer. Conditions are severe enough to prevent the growth of any plants higher than the knee, and an unprepared tramper won't fare much better. Other highly recommended items are a waterproof pack liner, **sunscreen** and sunglasses, and extra food. The largest local rental shops are in Ohakune and Turangi, and most of the lodges in National Park Village will hire boots and other sundry necessities.

Storage: The **DOC Visitor Centre** will store extra gear for $3 per bag, and most accommodations will do it for free.

THE TRACK

Whakapapa Village to Mangatepopo Hut: 8.5km, 2½hr.

The section of the track from Whakapapa Village to **Mangatepopo Hut** (22 beds) has good views, but is extremely rutted and muddy; most folks skip this section. The hut itself, about 25 minutes from the Mangatepopo road-end, has magnificent views of Mt. Tongariro, Mt. Ngauruhoe, and the ridge that connects them.

Mangatepopo Hut to Ketetahi road-end (The Tongariro Crossing): 13.5km, 7½hr.

Mangatepopo Hut to Emerald Lakes Junction: 6km, 3½hr.

Emerald Lakes Junction to Ketetahi Hut: 3km, 2½hr.

Ketetahi Hut to Ketetahi Road end: 4.5km, 1½hr.

From the hut, the track winds along a stream full of small tumbling waterfalls, traversing several recent lava flows before reaching the base of the ridge. From here, a short side trip leads to the wispy little waterfalls of **Soda Springs.** This is the last dependable water source before Ketetahi Hut. The track up the ridge is quite steep; at the top, cold winds blow across the **South Crater,** a Mars-like world scoured almost clean of plant life. Another side trip leads up the great, sparsely marked cone of **Mt. Ngauruhoe** (2291m; ascent 2hr., descent 30min.). The main track continues across the flat expanse of the south crater before ascending to the rim of the steaming **Red Crater,** the highest point on the track (1886m), and an area that is sometimes buffeted by an unnervingly strong wind. A well-marked spur route leads gradually up to the peak of **Mt. Tongariro** (1967km; return 2hr.).

Just downhill from Red Crater lie the limpid **Emerald Lakes** (see cover), where the Crossing branches north across the flat **Central Crater,** past lovely **Blue Lake,** and down a series of obscenely long switchbacks to **Ketetahi Hut** (22 beds). Even those doing the whole Northern Circuit might want to walk this section to catch the transcendent views of Red Crater framed by Ngauruhoe and Tongariro, with the Emerald Lakes and ant-like specks of hikers toiling in the distance. Ketetahi Hut has its own share of thrilling vistas, with Lake Rotoaira and Lake Taupo unfolding far below. Set amid tawny tussock grasses, the accompanying tent sites are exposed to some wicked winds. Past the hut, the Crossing descends rather steeply from tussock to podocarp forest, ultimately terminating at the Ketetahi road-end. The nearby Ketetahi Hot Springs are on private land and off-limits.

Emerald Lakes Junction to New Waihohonu Hut: 13.5km, 5hr.

Emerald Lakes Junction to Oturere Hut: 5km, 2hr.

Oturere Hut to New Waihohonu Hut: 8.5km, 3hr.

Back at Emerald Lakes, the Circuit track drops steeply down into the Oturere valley, and then winds along a steady route decorated with chunks of lava twisted into bizarre shapes and pinnacles. Several waterfalls cascade down the cliff faces that cradle the valley, exposing layers of ash, lava, and sediment. At the end of the valley is the chipper **Oturere Hut** (22 beds) with tent sites perched just above a small waterfall and snaking blue stream.

From here, the track is pretty easy tramping, passing wide gravel washes and wind-whipped treelets. About two hours past Oturere Hut, the track crosses a river to enter honest-to-gosh forest, ascends through cool beech greenery to a view-filled ridge, and heads back down through forest to **New Waihohonu Hut** (22 beds). The hut is in a lovely location with mountain vistas and a clear brook, across which are several secluded and unusually well-sheltered tent sites.

New Waihohonu Hut to Whakapapa Village: 16km, 5hr.

New Waihohonu Hut to Tama Lakes Junction: 3hr.

Tama Lakes Junction to Taranki Loop Junction: 1hr.

Taranki Loop Junction to Whakapapa Village: 1hr.

NORTH ISLAND

Just a bit beyond New Waihohonu, the red corrugated **Old Waihohonu Hut** is a century-old stagecoach stop, currently unlivable and filled with decades of tramper graffiti. Past relatively level fields of stream-fed tussockland is the turn-off for the Tama Lakes: **Lower Tama** (one-way 10min.), a beautiful blue pool viewed from high above, and crescent-shaped **Upper Tama** (20-30min. farther), lying in Ngauruhoe's shadow amid wind-buffeted vistas stretching far beyond the park. The final stretch down to Whakapapa Village can be taken by an upper route through tussock terrain or along a lower forest route past **Taranaki Falls.**

NATIONAL PARK VILLAGE

National Park Village is little more than a cluster of accommodations at the junction of SH4 and SH47; the Tongariro Crossing, Whakapapa ski fields, and Whanganui River Journey are all comfortably close to this one-horse, three-volcano town.

⚲ PRACTICAL INFORMATION. TranzScenic and InterCity roll through on the way north to **Auckland** (5½hr., 1-2 per day, $50-70) via **Hamilton** (3½hr., $30-40), and south to **Wellington** (5½hr., 1-2 per day, $60-70) via **Ohakune** (30min., $10-20). The TranzScenic southward route includes **Palmerston North** (3½hr., 1 per day, $39-43), while InterCity heads to **Wanganui** (2½hr., $27). **Ski Haus** or **Howard's Lodge** (see below) handle bookings. The **train station** is on Railway Rd. at the end of Carroll St.; **buses** depart from the dairy near Carroll and Ward St. **Howard's Lodge** (see below) runs an on-demand shuttle to Whakapapa Village ($6, return $10) and the ski fields ($10, return $15). **Alpine Scenic Tours** (tel. 386 8918 or mobile 025 937 281) runs to **Whakapapa Village** for the same price, and also includes **Turangi** (2-3 per day, $15). Most accommodations hire a range of **gear** for all seasons. There are **no ATMs** in town. The **BP station** (tel. 892 2879) at the highway junction stocks very basic groceries, and serves as a **post office** (open M-Th 7:30am-7pm, F 7:30am-9pm, Sa-Su 7:30am-7pm; winter M-Th 7:30am-7pm, F 7:30am-10:30pm, Sa 7am-8pm, Su 7am-7pm). **Internet access** is available at Howard's Lodge. The little **police station** (tel. 892 2869) is on Buddo St., parallel to SH4. **Telephone Code:** 07.

⚲⚲ ACCOMMODATIONS AND FOOD. The quality lodges of National Park Village are absolutely stuffed with skiers in winter, and the summer traffic of trampers is on the rise. **Howard's Lodge (Nomads)** (tel./fax 892 2827), down Carroll St., is particularly clean and hospitable, with free spa, train shuttle, and warm clothes for guests. Winter weekends demand bookings up to three weeks early. (Dorms $18, summer $15; twins and doubles with linen $70, summer $40; rooms with linen and bath $90, summer $60.) **Ski Haus** (tel. 892 2854), across the road, has an in-house restaurant and bar complete with sunken fireplace. Guests without bookings are welcome to roll in off the night train into Room 16. (During winter weekends dorms $34, midweek $23. In summer, dorms $15; doubles $40; tent sites $8; caravan sites $5, each extra person $8). Right off SH4 on Findlay St., **National Park Backpackers** (tel. 892 2870) offers nice wood-beamed rooms surrounding an excellent indoor climbing area (dorms $15, with bathroom $17, winter $1-2 extra; doubles $50, summer $40; tent sites $8). **National Park Lodge** (tel. 892 2993 or reservations 0800 861 861), two minutes up Carroll St., has self-contained motel rooms with a TV lounge and a small kitchen ($100, summer $60 for 2); the main lodge is also plenty clean (dorms midweek $20, holidays and weekends $25; in summer, twins and doubles $17, dorms with linens $15, dorms without linen $13). **Pukenui Lodge** (tel. 892 2882), on Millar St. off SH4, contains tidy little dorms, with attached bathrooms in the works (dorms $17, with linen $20; twins and doubles $22, with linen $25; tent sites $8, powered $9).

Beyond the lodges' restaurant options, dining in National Park Village comes in two venues. **Elvin's Ski Shop Cafe** (tel. 892 2844), at Carroll St. and SH4, serves up tasty sandwiches ($5) and mains ($12-22), with a laid-back atmosphere and an awesome Ruapehu photo album for those who inquire (open daily 7am-late as necessary, summer for brunch and dinner). The **Schnapps Hotel** (tel. 892 2788), at Findlay St. and SH4, rocks the ski season with live bands every Saturday night, plus a bizarre grab-bag of drinking games. Specialties include beer (bottles $3.50), huge burgers ($6), and mains ($12-19). (Open daily noon-2am, winter 11am-2am.)

⚡ ACTIVITIES. The **Tongariro Forest Conservation Area,** just north of town, is home to the **42 Traverse,** one of the country's most famously satisfying mountain bike trails. The organ-jiggling ride follows well-maintained old logging trails, with a stream crossing and a 570m descent (4-5hr.). Howard's Lodge (see above) runs a shuttle service to the starting and ending points ($20 per person for 2 people). **Pete Outdoors** (tel. 892 2773) rents bikes for the traverse ($60) or for shorter and less punishing periods (1hr. $10, full day $40); they also lead a variety of guided outdoor excursions.

WHAKAPAPA VILLAGE

Whakapapa Village is a tiny clutch of establishments serving the ski operations of Tongariro National Park, and is the most immediate base for skiing on the north side of Ruapehu.

Whakapapa Visitor Centre (tel. 892 3729; fax 385 8128; email ruapehuao @doc.govt.nz), the highlight of Whakapapa Village, presents two high-tech audio-visual shows (for a small fee), as well as free displays on the park's history and biology (open daily 8am-6pm, winter 8am-5pm). For those looking to simply zoom in and out, **Mountain Air** (tel. 892 2812 or 0800 922 812) runs a daily air shuttle from **Auckland** to **Whakapapa Village** and **Turangi** (1hr., 7:15am, returning 4:45pm; $139, return $238) with special lift pass deals available. The more ground-bound can take **Alpine Scenic Tours** (tel. 386 8918 or mobile 025 937 281), which leaves Whakapapa Village for **National Park** (2-3 per day, $6), **Turangi** ($15), and the **Tongariro Crossing** endpoints at the Ketetahi and Mangatepopo carparks. Service can be rather flexible to accommodate transport dilemmas. **Howard's Lodge** (tel. 892 2827) also runs a shuttle on demand to National Park ($6). **Whakapapa Express** (tel. 385 4022) provides service to and from Ohakune, in winter only (1 per day, return $15). There are **no banks or ATMs** in the area. The **post office** is in **Fergusson's Cafe** (see below). **Telephone code:** 07 (different than nearby Ohakune).

Set beside a stream, the **Whakapapa Holiday Park** (tel./fax 892 3897), just across the road from the Visitor Centre, offers small but private tent ($8) and caravan ($10) sites carved out of the native bush, and good kitchen facilities. Spartan bunks populate the backpackers lodge (dorms $12.50, summer only; cabins with no bedding or utensils for 2 $35). To reach the perky **Skotel** (tel. 892 3719; fax 892 3777), turn left just before the Visitor Centre. Boasting all the amenities (spa, sauna, drying room, cushy mattresses, and small communal kitchen), its functional shares cost $20 in summer, but are sold as twins, triples, and quads during winter (from $72 per room, with bath). Wood-paneled, airy, deluxe doubles cost $82-115 in summer and go up come ski season.

Refined, historic, and decidedly non-budget, the **Grand Chateau** hotel offers a stunning view from its cafe area. Both the Skotel and the Chateau have in-house restaurants and bars; **Fergusson's Cafe** (tel. 892 3809; ask for the cafe), does brisk business with soups, hot quiches, sandwiches, and coffee (open daily 9am-5pm, summer 8am-5pm).

OHAKUNE

At one end of Ohakune, a massive snow-covered time-bomb triples the town's population in winter, provided its slopes flow with skiers and not lava. At the other end, and slightly less impressive, sits Ohakune's symbolic alter-ego—a giant, tubby, painted statue of a carrot that serves as a reminder of the quiet farming center the town reverts to post-ski season. When the snow melts and the scarf-toting visitors trickle out of town like so many streams running down Mt. Ruapehu, Ohakune goes from party central to a town ruled by a carrot. With the ski lifts of Turoa at a standstill, the mountain instead provides tranquil views of exhilarating runs, and the rich volcanic soils of the farmland provide a pastoral backyard, producing world-class veggies on which sheep and cattle placidly munch. Though Ohakune is defined by its unpredictable seasons, the 1300 permanent residents—who all seem to know one another—are always infectiously friendly.

🔢 ORIENTATION AND PRACTICAL INFORMATION

The south end, where **SH49** merges, has most services (like the grocery store and pharmacy) and is active year-round. The north end, known as the **Junction,** lies 3km up toward where the railroad tracks, and bursts into life during the winter with seasonal chalets and jumping nightlife. It also marks the start of the **Ohakune Mountain Rd.** leading up past the entrances to several scenic tramps, and the ski lifts of **Turoa. Goldfinch St./Mangawhero Terr.** runs between the two (20-25min. by foot). Ohakune is the most significant town of the area, aside from Turangi on the northern side of Tongariro National Park.

Visitors Center: Ohakune Visitor Centre, 54 Clyde St. (tel. 385 8427; fax 385 8527), has a relief map of Tongariro National Park. Open M-F 9am-5pm, Sa-Su 9am-3:30pm.

DOC: (tel. 385 0010; fax 385 0011), just beyond the railroad tracks on Ohakune Mountain Rd. One of Tongariro's two field centers. Open daily 8am-3pm, holidays 8am-5pm.

Trains and Buses: Because Ohakune is halfway between Auckland and Wellington, arrivals and departures are virtually all in the middle of the day or the middle of the night. **TranzScenic** and **InterCity** run to: **Auckland** (5½hr., 1 per day, $55-75) via **National Park** (30min., $11-20); and **Wellington** (5hr., 1-2 per day, $50-65) via **Palmerston North** (3hr., $38). To go to **Taupo,** either take the train to Waiouru and catch a bus from Aldo's Restaurant at 1:40pm or 5:10pm, or find your way to Turangi for a connection.

Shuttles: The **Mountain Transport Service** (tel. 385 9045 or mobile 025 445 800) and **Whakapapa Express** (tel. 385 4022 or mobile 025 971 066) run to **Turoa** (return $10-15); Whakapapa Express also goes to trailheads in summer (return $25). The transportmeisters at **Snowliner Shuttles** (tel. 385 8573 or mobile 025 435 550) run on demand to **Turoa** ($8, return $15), to **Whakapapa** ($16, return $27) if Turoa is closed, and to trailheads during the summer.

Hitchhiking: Reportedly not too difficult between Ohakune and National Park or Waiouru, but it's no fun to be stuck in Waiouru trying to hitch across the Rangipo Desert. Hitching up the mountain is reportedly easier in the morning, but success depends on your amount of gear. National Park and Whakapapa Village make better bases for those without a car, while those with cars often prefer Ohakune for life outside of their lodging. In summer, don't get into the car if the Carrot's driving.

Banks: Westpac (tel. 385 8154), in the shopping plaza on **Goldfinch St.** Open weekdays 9am-4:30pm.

Medical Services: Dr. Perera (tel. 385 8356), is the town's one-man medical service, on Goldfinch St. **Ohakune Photo Pharmacy** (tel. 385 8304) is next to BNZ. Open M-F 9am-5:30, winter also Sa 9am-noon.

Internet Access: Snowbird Copy Center, 92 Clyde St. (tel. 385 8756).

Post Office: 5 Goldfinch St. (tel. 385 8645). Open M-Sa 7am-6pm or 7pm.

Telephone Code: 06.

🏠 ACCOMMODATIONS

As one big bedroom for Turoa, Ohakune has an outlandish number of accommodations per capita. A fair number are either open only in winter or jack up their prices from hostel to B&B during the ski season. Booking ahead during ski season, even by several weeks, is highly recommended.

Rimu Park Lodge (VIP), 27 Rimu St. (tel. 385 9023), up at the Junction end of town, at the upper edge of the ski zone. Free bus pickups. The classic wood-lined lodge has a nice lounge with open fire (bunks $30, summer $16; twins and doubles $35, summer $18). Compact cabins are comfortable (doubles $60, summer $40; triples $75), but for a classic night's sleep without the motion sickness, it's Rimu's old wooden train cars outfitted with double beds and parked in the lawn (doubles $95, summer $75). For $65, you can receive board, breakfast, and a **ski pass** to Whakapapa.

Ohakune YHA (tel. 385 8724), on Clyde St. Plain rooms off a veranda, with a wood-stove, communal kitchen area, and lounge. Laid-back atmosphere fosters easy conversation among guests, and managers offer helpful info about area tramps. Dorms $16, summer $15; twins $36, summer $34; doubles with bath $40, summer $38.

Alpine Motel and Lodge, 7 Miro St. (tel. 385 8758), near the corner of Clyde St. and Raetihi Rd. It all comes with a spa, free train pickup, and a drying room. This popular stop offers small 2-bunk rooms in its nifty, silo-like backpackers lodge ($20; in summer midweek $15, weekends $25; 2-day minimum stay on weekends in peak season). Well-heated double studio units with bath and TV are also available (weekdays $85, summer $70; weekends $110, summer $70; extra person $15, summer $10).

Ohakune Holiday Park (tel./fax 385 8561), on the street that turns off just before the YHA, next to a brook. Small kitchen, TV lodge, and 18-hole putt-putt. Tent sites and powered sites $9.50; tiny backpacker cabins and caravans $16.50, extra person $12; doubles with kitchens and showers $55.

FOOD AND NIGHTLIFE

Many of Ohakune's lodgings have in-house restaurants, though they're usually a bit pricey. Of the other restaurants, usually only the south-side eateries are regularly open in summer.

New World supermarket (tel. 385 8587), at the corner of Goldfinch and Clyde St. (open daily 8:30am-5pm). **Mountain Kebabs Cafe,** 29 Clyde St. (tel. 385 9047), has filling meat and vegetarian kebabs (medium $7; open daily 10am-10pm; irregular hours in off-season). **Utopia** (tel. 385 9120), a few doors down on Clyde St., is an excellent lunch cafe. Try the outstanding carrot cake, though the tubby Carrot may chase you out of town. Junction-area eateries open in winter include **La Pizzeria** (tel. 385 8558), next to the Turoa Ski Lodge on Thames St., which offers terrific gourmet pizzas for gourmet prices (from $12.50; open daily in ski season 4pm-late; off-season open F-Sa 4pm-late). **Margarita's** (tel. 378 9909), on Rimu St. just past Thames St., has heaping Mexican mains for half-price (normally $14.50 and up) on Wednesday nights (open in ski season daily from 4pm).

The après-ski scene rages in Ohakune long after midnight and when the Carrot makes an appearance, the party mushrooms out of control. The Junction bars and the flash **Hot Lava Niteclub** on Thames St. do their best to ensure nobody's on the slopes too early the next morning. Most of the ski season hotspots are right on Thames St. Follow your ski instructor to the bar of the **Turoa Ski Lodge** (tel. 385 8274), where just about everyone stops by once a night. Tuesday nights feature live music, and a DJ mixes tunes on Saturdays. Gaggles of dry-docked snowboarders replace the families after dinner hours at the endlessly popular **Margarita's** nightly Happy Hour (5-7pm and 9-10pm; pints $2.50). Down on the corner of Thames St. just before you head to the other side of town, the polished wood of the **Powderkeg Bar** (tel. 385 8888) explodes on weekends with DJ and drink specials providing the spark. Down south, the **Ohakune Country Hotel** (tel. 385 8268), on Clyde St., has a three-bar complex, recently renovated to include the stylish **O-Bar** and the tourist-frequented **Summit Bar.** The latter requires decent dress and has Sunday night $10 cook-your-own-steak BBQs.

ACTIVITIES

For information on skiing at Turoa, see p. 197. Ohakune has recently learned how to balance without ski poles, gradually unstrapping its winter gear to venture into the world of summer activities.

The area around the park has some top **mountain biking** opportunities. The sealed 18km **Ohakune Mountain Rd.** makes for a wickedly exhilarating and scenic bike ride when ski traffic is gone. The road is occasionally closed due to ice and snow. Ron Rutherford's **Ride the Mountain** (tel. 385 8257) operation rents bikes and runs to the top ($45). The **Powderhorn Shop and Ski Hire** (tel. 385 8888) in the grand chalet of the same name at the bottom of Mountain Rd., also rents bikes (half-day $25, full day $35) and climbing, tramping, and in-line skating equipment (open daily 9am-6pm).

From October to April, Ohakune is a point of departure for **canoe trips** on the Whanganui River, a mostly tranquil river running through the heart of the wilderness (see p. 139). Check with the Visitor Centre for outfitter options. If plummeting into a flaming volcano with a giant Carrot strapped to your back is appealing, the Carrot runs a **tandem skydiving** (tel. 0800 CARROT) operation. Horse trekking, canoeing, 4WD motorbike tours, and more civilized pursuits like golf and squash also abound around town. Whatever you do, treat yourself at the end of the day to a piña colada with the Carrot in the heated pool of the **Powderhorn Chateau** (tel. 385 8888; open 9am-9pm; $6, children $5, guests free).

NORTH ISLAND

TARANAKI AND WANGANUI

The looming mountain in the center of the North Island's westernmost extremity defines its surrounding region, both in ancient mythology and contemporary tourism. Mythology speaks of Taranaki as a restless, sorrowful place, and it is true that the mountain has the natural instability of a volcano. Year-round relaxation is afforded by Taranaki's balmy summer weather and gentle, wintry charm. The rugged green slopes are among the richest dairyland in the world; Taranaki just might deserve its unofficial title as "the Udder of New Zealand." With the exception of Whanganui National Park, the Taranaki and Wanganui region lacks the adventure and optimism that other New Zealand cities possess.

◪TARANAKI AND WANGANUI HIGHLIGHTS

■ Ride horses, herd cattle, and shear sheep on a **Hawera** farm (p. 214).
■ The **Whanganui Journey** (p. 219) is the only Great Walk where you'll float to the finish line.

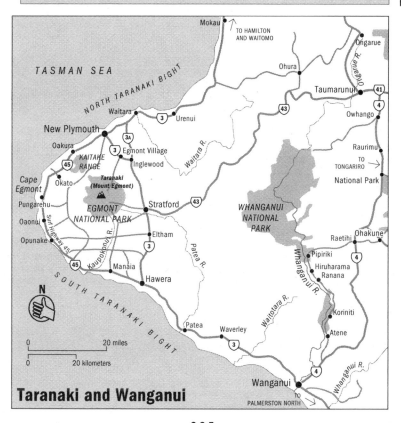

Taranaki and Wanganui

NEW PLYMOUTH

Residents of New Plymouth love to point out that in one hour here, you can go from surfing in the Tasman to skiing on the slopes of Taranaki. While this is indeed an exciting proposition to outdoor sports enthusiasts, the city itself gets lost somewhere in between the sea and the snow. In fact, New Plymouth itself has quite a lot to offer, including excellent museums, mouthwatering cuisine, numerous outdoor public spaces, and lively weekends. The city is a walker's paradise; take the time to explore the interior before heading for the great outdoors.

■ PRACTICAL INFORMATION

Visitors Center: New Plymouth Information Centre (tel. 759 6080; email nplvin@nzhost.co.nz), at the corner of Leach and Liardet St. Open M-F 8:30am-5pm, Sa-Su and public holidays 10am-3pm.

DOC: 220 Devon St. West. (tel. 758 0433 or emergency tel. mobile 025 438 956; fax 758 0430). Bevy of brochures on both Egmont National Park and Sugarloaf Marine Park; fishing queries also answered. Open M-F 8am-4:30pm.

Airport: Flight information (tel. 755 2250).

Buses: Depart from the **Travel Centre,** at the corner of King and Queen St. Open M-F 7:30am-5pm, Sa 7:30-8:10am and 1:30-2:45pm, Su 1:30-5pm. Free luggage storage for the day. **InterCity** (tel. 759 9039) and **Newmans** (tel. 757 5482) depart for: **Auckland** (6¼hr., 2 per day, $69) via **Hamilton** (4hr., $46); **Wellington** (6¾hr., 2 per day, $59) via **Stratford** (30min., $12), **Hawera** (1¼hr., $17), **Wanganui** (2½hr., $29), and **Palmerston North** (4hr., $39); and **Rotorua** (6hr., 1 per day, $69).

Taxis: New Plymouth Taxis (tel. 757 5665), **Egmont City Cabs** (tel. 754 8801), and **Energy City Cabs** (tel. 755 3365). Queue at corner of Brougham and Devon St.

Bike Rental: Raceway Cycles and Mowers, 207 Coronation Ave. (tel. 759 0391). Mountain bikes from $20 per day.

Hitchhiking: Hitchhiking toward Wanganui around the east side of Egmont is reportedly easiest in the nebulous zone on the outskirts of town on SH3, before the traffic picks up to 70kph. More traffic usually heads this way than heads up SH3 toward Otorohanga, Hamilton, and Auckland.

Currency Exchange: Thomas Cook, 55-57 Devon St. East. (tel. 757 5459). **BNZ** offers good exchange rates. Take your pick of **ATMs** all along Devon St.

Laundry: Devon Laundrette, 282 Devon St. East. (tel. 758 8264).

Police: (tel. 757 5449), on Powderhorns St.

Pharmacy: Care Chemist (tel. 757 4614), in Richmond Centre on Egmont St. Open daily 8am-9pm.

Hospital: Taranaki Base (tel. 753 6139), on David St.

Medical Services: Accident and Medical Clinic White Cross Taranaki (tel. 759 8915), in Richmond Centre on Egmont St. Open daily 8am-10pm.

Internet Access: $10 per hr. at the library (tel. 758 4544), on Brougham St. Open M, W, and F 9am-8:30pm, Tu and Th 9am-5:30pm, Sa 10am-4pm; closed public holidays.

Post Office: (tel. 759 8931), on Currie St. Open M-F 8:30am-5pm, Sa 9am-1pm.

Telephone Code: 06.

■ ACCOMMODATIONS

Shuttles to "the mountain" (Taranaki) run from all accommodations, but it's difficult to get to town after dark without a car.

▧ **Shoestring Backpackers (VIP),** 48 Lemon St. (tel./fax 758 0404), in a residential corner of town, a 5min. walk from town center. Free pickup. Amiable hostel has plenty of light, a full kitchen, and dining area with a table large enough for all guests to eat together. Capacious TV lounge and sun room. Finnish sauna ($4). Laundry $2. Dorms $14; singles $20; doubles $32, with TV $36.

Egmont Lodge (YHA), 12 Clawton St. (tel. 753 5720; fax 753 5782). Take Frankley Rd. at the Dawson St. fork and follow the signs, or call for free pickup. Away from the din of the city, enjoy the Waimea Stream flowing through the backyard and help feed the river's 2m long eel, "Conan." Lack of TV encourages conversation. Reception open sporadically; guests should just make themselves at home. Key deposit $10. Dorms $15; singles $25; twins and doubles $36; tent sites out back $10.

Richmond Corner Backpacker and Accommodation, 24 Ariki St. (tel. 759 0050; fax 759 0051), in the center of town. Convenience is the best word for this new backpacker only a rugby toss from the train station. This second floor establishment covers all the basics, but the barren lounge and kitchen area don't encourage backpacker socializing. Internet. Linen $3. Laundry $2. Reception 7:30am-9pm. Dorms $15; doubles $40; both with bath. Motel-like singles $30.

Central City Lodge, 104 Leach St. (tel. 758 0473; fax 758 6559). As the name suggests, this lodge is close to the heart of town, but a 15min. walk from the bus station. Follow the signs and ask for the backpackers (not the on-site motel). Use of indoor pool and spa $2 for whole stay. Key deposit $5. Dorms $15; singles $30; doubles $40.

Belt Road Seaside Holiday Park, 2 Belt Rd. (tel./fax 758 0228), on prime oceanfront real estate outside of town—a 25min. walk. The closest beach is within 1km. Bedding $5. Communal toilets and kitchen (use of pots and utensils $5). Dorms $22; cabins with bath $25-45; tent sites $8.50 per person; powered for 2 $17, $8.50 extra person.

NORTH ISLAND

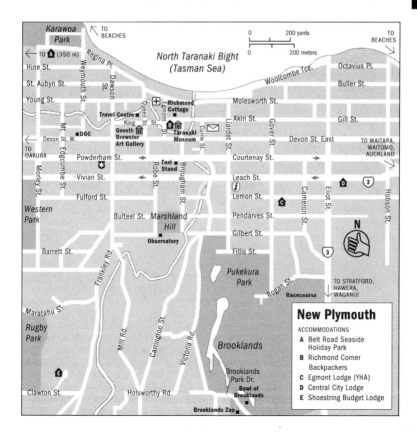

New Plymouth

ACCOMMODATIONS

A Belt Road Seaside
   Holiday Park
B Richmond Corner
   Backpackers
C Egmont Lodge (YHA)
D Central City Lodge
E Shoestring Budget Lodge

FOOD

New Plymouth's main drag, **Devon St.,** offers a few opportunities to escape the meat and potatoes staples of the Taranaki region. You can always tank up on take-aways or, if inspiration strikes, build a meal of your own with material from **New World** (tel. 759 9052), located on the block bounded by Leach, Courtenay, Liardet and Gover St.—it's the closest market to the hostels (open daily 8am-9pm).

E.S.P.resso (tel. 759 9399), adjacent to the Govett-Brewster Art Gallery (see p. 209). This museum cafe serves fresh and beautiful food, the best cafe eating in New Plymouth. Delicate filos filled with meats or vegetables are representative of the mains ($8.50 with a side salad). Open daily 8am-4pm.

El Condor, 170 Devon St. (tel. 757 5436). This Argentinian restaurant has a reputation for delicious eats with an affordable price tag. El Condor's pinkish interior with heavy, wooden tables swarms with hungry diners while other customers enjoy their takeaway. Pasta dishes (mains $15) and gourmet pizzas ($15) available. Open Tu-Sa 5-10pm.

Steps Restaurant, 37 Gover St. (tel. 758 3393). Nestled unassumingly in a little white cottage, step up to gourmet cuisine at prices that won't lead you above and beyond your budget. The ever-changing menu featuring diverse lunch items ($9-12.50), and elegant dinners ($20-22) belie the casual atmosphere inside. BYO wine. Open Tu-F noon-2pm, plus Tu-Sa from 6pm.

Simply Read Cafe and Bookshop, 2 Dawson St. (tel. 757 8667). This 50s-style bungalow serves tasty food, and has a gorgeous westward view over the ocean. Flan and lasagna come filled with all sorts of vegetarian goodies ($5). Open M-Sa 9am-4pm.

Agra Indian Restaurant, 151 Devon St. East. (tel. 758 0030). Bask in the candlelit glow of reddish walls decorated with swaths of Indian fabric and posters of Bangladesh. Traditional Indian food, with large portions and multiple vegetarian options, all at a reasonable price (mains $7.50-17). Takeaway available. Open daily from 5:30pm, also Friday for lunch noon-2pm.

■ NIGHTLIFE

Early in the week, the nightlife in New Plymouth resembles that of Taranaki's rural towns, in that there is none. The weekends are another story, as people emerge from the mountain and sea to party hard 'til the stroke of three.

Grapevine Wine Bar & Cafe, 38C Currie St. (tel. 757 9355). Catering to a slightly more sophisticated set, this bar and cafe serves up more vintages than an antique show. The ornate relief on the ceiling won't make you forget the Sistine Chapel, but it's a nice touch. Live music T-Sa from 10pm, with jazz on Thursdays. Open Tu-Sa from 5pm, also Friday for lunch noon-2pm.

The Mill, 2 Courtenay St. (tel. 758 1935). Impossible to miss at the end of Currie St., The Mill has been around since 1868 when it was actually a functioning flour mill. Today, the grinding doesn't involve wheat stalks, but rather bodies. Video music pumps in the basement dance area dubbed **CrowBar** (open F-Sa 9pm-3am). On the ground floor, classic rock inspires karaoke and occasional dancing on the bar. Leave your studded leather and ripped jeans at home if you want to swim with the mainstream. Open M-Th from 11am, F-Sa 11am-3am.

Crowded House Cafe and Bar, 93-99 Devon St. East (tel. 759 4921). Enter Taranaki's largest cafe bar with a passion for rugby and other local athletic pursuits. Handles $3.80. Open M-W 10am-10pm, Th-Sa 10am-1am, Su 10am-10pm.

Burton Bar (tel. 758 573), on the corner of Devon and Gover St. Quel those munchies with tasty bar food available at (almost) all hours. Between 5pm and 6pm Monday through Thursday the bartender spins the Happy Hour wheel—you might get your drink for free or two for one! If you're really thirsty, put down $100 and rent the table with the flowing "happy tap" (for 2 hours) for you and your mates. Open daily 11am-3am.

SIGHTS

A stroll down **Devon St.** reveals New Plymouth's 19th-century heritage, evidenced by artful moldings and dates embossed on the upper levels of the downtown shops. The city serves as the only real roost for Taranaki's culture vultures, harboring fine museums, galleries, and theaters, as well as access to spectacular beaches and mountains. For a dosage of the region's history, clear out an hour or two for the **Taranaki Museum** (tel. 758 9583), on Ariki St. between Brougham and Egmont St. (open M-F 9am-4:30pm, Sa-Su and holidays 1-5pm; free).

Across the street is the **Richmond Cottage,** a historic dwelling place of New Plymouth's earliest Parliamentary movers and shakers. The porch of the cottage opens onto **Pukeariki Landing.** Once the entry point for people and goods traveling by sea, it is now a lovely spot adorned with Maori sculptures. (Open Nov.-May M, W, and F 2-4pm, Sa-Su 1-4pm; June-Oct. F 2-4pm, Sa-Su 1-4pm. Admission $1.)

For a modern take on art, visit the **Govett-Brewster Art Gallery** (tel. 758 5149), at the corner of King and Queen St. Although your fellow patrons may be as unapproachable as royalty, the rotating collection of art and visiting exhibitions are quite accessible. The work of **Len Lye** (see p. 14) is featured, including videos of his films and kinetic sculptures. (Open daily 10:30am-5pm. Donations accepted.) Those of refined tastes may enjoy a theater or opera excursion at the **TSB showplace,** 94 Devon St. West. (tel. 758 4947). Call for schedules or visit the box office (open M-F 11am-4:30pm). For a more intimate experience, the **Little Theatre** (tel. 758 2631), on Aubrey St., between Morley and Edgecombe St., lives up to its name.

Flocks of joggers experience souped-up nature at **Pukekura Park** at the top of Liardet St. (no bicycles allowed). Amid the towering trees and bounteous rhododendrons, take a peek at the coin-operated illuminated fountain and the push-button waterfall. If the weather cooperates, visit the calla lilies in Stainton Dell or the green grandeur of the leg-stretching walk to **King Fern Gulley.** No matter what it's like outside, the **Fernery** and display houses warmly await hushed footfalls on a carpet of cedar chips. (Fernery open daily 8:30am-4pm. Gates to Pukekura Park are open 8:30am-6pm, until 7pm during daylight savings time.) Adjacent to Pukekura Park is yet another confederation of structures and gardens, the **Brooklands.** Attractions here include the **children's zoo** (open daily 8:30am-5pm; free). If you are in town from the week before Christmas 1999 to February 6, 2000 (Waitangi Day), walk through and see the park illuminated for the **Festival of Lights.**

New Plymouth also offers several scenic walkways of various lengths and grades. Detailed printed guides are available at the Info Centre. The **Te Henui Walkway** is one of the best, following the Te Henui stream through 5.9km of natural splendor down to the sea. The coastal walkway offers dramatic views of the sea crashing against the rocky coastline. Follow this path south past industrial areas and arrive at **Paritutu,** a prominent rock at the edge of the shore (in Maori, *pari* is cliff and *tutu* is to stand erect). Those brave enough to scale its 154m track (deservedly rated "hard") are treated to epic views of the coast and on a clear day, the mountain as well.

THE TARANAKI COAST

Proffering a laid-back lifestyle of catching rays on black-sand beaches and catching waves of quality year-round surf, the Taranaki coast from New Plymouth to Hawera remains an unbelievably beautiful and relatively undiscovered destination. Hitchhiking is sporadic at best, and in winter frequent rains make the experience all the more unpleasant. Generally, it's better to hire a car or a guide. You can circumnavigate Mt. Egmont (Taranaki) and travel along the coast in two ways. For an excellent scenic journey (1½hr.) offering easy access to various bush walks and the best views of the Taranaki Bights and the Tasman Sea, take Carrington Rd. from New Plymouth to Okahu Rd. and then circle around. The coastal route (3½hr.) is best done on Surf Highway 45 (SH45), but unless you stop and walk to the shore, expect only glimpses of the ocean (much of the view in this route is obscured by either hedges, great distance, or both).

OAKURA

A one-horse town with an awesome beach that is wide, flat, and family-filled in summer, the town of Oakura is representative of the population "centers" that dot the coast. Take Surf Highway 45 between Okato and Opanake for a glimpse of killer waves that pound the coast; this region is host to frequent surfing and wind-surfing competitions. In the summer, it is possible to camp in the area for free, though be prepared for swarms of other tourists with the same idea in mind. The point at the end of **Ahu Ahu Road** yields an amazing surf that is the *raison d'être* for the **Wavehaven Hostel** (tel. 752 7800; email wave.haven@taranaki.ac.nz). Surfboard and kayak rentals (half-day $10, full day $15) with wetsuits are available, and surf-ing lessons for novices can be arranged. There is a climbing wall and volleyball court for landlubbers. (Laundry $3. Dorms $15; singles $25. Weekly dorms $75.) It is also home to the **Burnt Toast Cafe and Restaurant,** on Main South Rd. (tel. 752 7303). The specialty here is pizza; for $25 a gourmet pizza will feed you and three of your closest friends. (Open W-Su 10am-10pm.)

The high winds, churning seas, and enraged skies that often abuse **Cape Egmont** suit solitary, steadfast Cape Egmont **lighthouse,** a navigational aid that the early Maori and Captain Cook surely would have appreciated.

OPUNAKE

The closest the coast comes to a bustling metropolis, Opunake (pop. 1587) har-bors both the dramatic cliffs of Middleton's Bay and the pleasantly swimmable Opunake Beach, with its teeming campground. **Opunake Motel and Backpackers,** 36 Heaphy Rd. (tel. 761 8330; fax 761 8340), runs the whole gamut of rooms in sprawl-ing cinderblock glory (dorms $18; cottage $20 per person; motel units $55, for 2 $70, extra person $13). Nab supplies for cheap at **Beau's Supermarket,** 77 Tasman St. (tel. 761 8668; open M-Th and Sa 7:30am-6pm, F 7:30am-8pm, Su 7:30am-5pm). On the south end of Cape Egmont hides the little town of **Manaia,** which boasts scrumptious croissants (6 for $2) from **Yarrow's Bakery** (tel. 274 8195), on South Rd. (open M-F 8am-4pm). Locals will also point you to the **pharmacy,** 47 Main St. (tel. 274 8200), to see a collection of teddy bears so big it's even billed as a museum (open M-Th 8:30am-5pm, F 8:30am-6pm, Sa 9:30am-noon).

EGMONT NATIONAL PARK

Rolling green hills bow like green-robed disciples to their master and maker, majestic Mt. Egmont (Taranaki). Everything within a 10km radius of the nearly symmetrical volcanic peak was declared part of New Zealand's second national park in 1881, restraining the vigorous logging boom of the time and preserving area farmlands. Today, three paved roads lead to the park: **Egmont Road,** from New Plymouth through Egmont Village to the North Egmont Visitor Centre; **Pembroke Road,** from Stratford to the Stratford Mountain House and the Manganui Skifield; and **Manaia Road,** from the Manaia/Hawera area to the Dawson Falls Visitor Cen-tre. With more than 140km of prime tracks, Egmont remains New Zealand's most accessible national park.

Easy access to the park is all too often equated with easy-going on the slopes. In fact, climbing Mt. Egmont (Taranaki) is far more than a leisurely walk in the park. The mountain has claimed the lives of more than 57 people, making it the most dangerous peak in New Zealand. Although the threat of this dormant volcano erupting is small (the last major awakening took place in 1755), other dangers are still plentiful: the upper slopes are prone to dramatic and sudden weather changes, and chilling rain can fall at any elevation at any time of year. Maori forays into the region were made only occasionally, and with great respect and careful prepara-tion; the same principle still holds today. All but the most hardened mountain climbers are strongly advised to take along a guide. Climbers are advised to assemble proper gear and check the mountain forecast before setting out. Regardless of the season ("dry" months are Dec.-Apr.), weatherproof clothing is essential, as is a sturdy pair of hiking boots. In the winter, standard equipment includes an ice axe and crampons. Chris Prudden's **Mountain Guides Mt. Egmont** (tel. 758 8261 or mobile 025 474 510), based in New Plymouth, will take one person for $250 and groups of two to four people for $300.

Here's a quick summary of Mt. Egmont's offerings: North—the safest and easiest side; West—the most remote with few people and good bush walks; the East—the most challenging (pros only); South—the coldest (skiing when available). There are *endless* trail options in the park; visit the DOC and make your own hiking plans. DOC accommodations are simple and rustic, but sufficient; always call ahead. Notable is **Syme Hut** on Phantom's Peak (1900m), arguably the best place to watch the sun rise or set; however, the hut's prime location also means that it is exposed to wind and ice. While camping is not permitted in Egmont National Park, many scofflaws do it anyway. The **Around-the-Mountain Circuit**, with views, bush, and alpine gorges, normally takes three to five days and can begin from any of the several main entrances to the park. During the summer, the trail can be shortened substantially by taking shorter routes at higher altitudes. In the spring, water runoff from the mountain and rains can often cause the height of rivers and streams to rise, making for difficult crossings. Hikers are best off waiting for levels to subside, as the flows are fast and deceptively deep.

NORTHERN EGMONT

The **North Egmont Visitor Centre** (tel. 756 0990 or 756 9001) is the port of entry for most of the park's adventurers (open daily 9am-4:30pm, winter Th-M 10am-4pm). DOC officials point trampers in the right direction with the aid of color-coded walks. Those planning to hole up in the huts can see photos and purchase hut tickets ($8, children $4) after getting a 20-minute audio-visual tour of the park.

For a short but sweet walk, the **Connet Loop Track** (return 30min.) departs from the base of the North Egmont car park. Winding its way through the "goblin forest," the track is an ethereal world of fern and moss when clouds hang low on the slopes. The **Ngatoro Loop Track** (return 30min.) navigates through stately cedars to the wing beats of native birds. For a 1½-hour pure bush experience, hit the **Veronica Loop Track.** Hard-core botanists might make the full-day trek to the **Ahukawaka Swamp,** home to unique lichen, mosses, and microbes. **Bells Falls,** best reached from **Holly Hut,** is also worth checking out. Great views of New Plymouth and beyond can be had from the north side of the volcano; the route to the **summit** from North Egmont is purportedly safer than that from the other entry points (ascent 4-5hr., descent 3hr.).

DOC has reopened the **Camp House,** a budget accommodation only 50m from the Visitor Centre ($15, children $7.50; book at Visitor Centre). There are also three private huts on the mountain, each run by one of the three mountain clubs in the region. The **Tahurangi Lodge,** owned and run by the Taranaki Alpine Club, offers kitchen facilities and a great location at 1520m ($15 per night). Prior booking is essential; inquire at the Visitor Centre, or write P.O. Box 356, New Plymouth. In Egmont Village, just outside the park and east of New Plymouth on Egmont Rd., hop over to **Missing Leg Backpackers,** 1082 Junction Rd. (tel. 752 2570). A shuttle from New Plymouth to Inglewood is $5 (ask at the Visitor Centre). The name comes not from a horrific tramping incident, but from Eric, the resident three-legged pooch. Reserve ahead to stay at the stylish mountain lodge with horses, mountain bikes, and camping gear for hire. (Dorms $14; doubles $32.)

SOUTHERN AND EASTERN EGMONT AND DAWSON FALLS

Roughly 15% of park pleasure-seekers enter the perimeter from the east, by way of Stratford and the **Stratford Mountain House,** with access to the Manganui ski fields in winter, and several trails in other seasons. Trips to the summit can also be attempted from this side, but the route is longer (return 9-11hr.) and more technically demanding.

From the south, access to the park can be gained by means of Manaia Rd., 8km of pavement that leads to the **Dawson Falls Visitor Centre** (tel. mobile 025 430 248; open daily 8:30am-4:30pm, winter W-Su 9am-4:30pm), with easy access to ski fields and dozens of bush walks. From the Visitor Centre, you can hike to the **Wilkies Pools** (1½hr.), a series of terraced plunge pools spilling into each other— remember that the water is ice-cold.

For accommodation consider **Manganui Lodge,** the private hut run by the Stratford Mountain Club. Advance booking is required; contact the club officer (tel. 757 8586). The DOC runs the bare-bones **Konini Lodge** (tel. mobile 025 430 248). The expansive kitchen and common room areas improve the situation. (BYO linen. $15 per person, children $7.50. Prior booking is required.) Also nearby is the **Kapuni Lodge,** which rounds out the trio of private huts on the mountain. Maintained by the Mt. Egmont Alpine Club of Hawera, the club offers gas cooking, running water, and 18 bunk beds ($10); book ahead of time by contacting Paul Adowd (tel./fax 278 4765) and arrange to collect a hut key in Hawera.

STRATFORD

An Ode to Stratford
If inland travel is the path you tread,
And mountain exploration is your game,
The town of Stratford beckons you instead.
With rural charm and streets that bear the name,
Of characters from Shakespeare's major plays,
Like Hamlet, Regan, Lear, and Juliet.
Here you can pass up Egmont of those days,
When it is raining, else you'll get quite wet.
Yet be forewarned (of this you can be sure):
Insomniacs rejoice! This town's your cure.

■ **ORIENTATION AND PRACTICAL INFORMATION. Broadway St. (SH3),** the source of local sustenance, spirits, and slight revelry is the main drag. The **Stratford Information Centre** (tel./fax 765 6708) is on Broadway South (open M-F 8:30am-5pm, Sa-Su 10am-2pm; extended weekend hours in summer). **Newmans** departs from the Info Centre and heads to **Auckland** (7hr., $74) via **New Plymouth** (35min., $12), and **Wellington** (5½hr.; M-F 4 per day, Sa-Su 2 per day; $52) via **Hawera** (20min., $12), **Wanganui** (1½hr., $23), and **Palmerston North** (3hr., $35). **Central Cabs** (tel. 765 8395) are available for your local transport needs. **Hitchhikers** report that hitchhiking to New Plymouth and Wellington gets easier along SH3 the farther you get from the center of town. Other services include: **DOC office** (tel. 765 5144; fax 765 6102), Pembroke Rd., RD 21 (open M-F 8am-4:30pm); **BNZ** (tel. 765 7134), on Broadway St. (open M-F 9am-4:30pm); **police** (tel. 765 7145), on Broadway St.; **Avon Medical Center** (tel. 765 5454), on Miranda St. South, one block from the Info Centre (open M-F 8:30am-5pm); **post office** (tel. 765 6009), on Miranda St. at Prospero Pl.; and **Internet access** at **Stratford Holiday Park** (see below). **Telephone Code:** 06.

■ **ACCOMMODATIONS.** In Stratford proper, the **Taranaki Accomodation Lodge,** 7 Romeo St. (tel. 765 544; fax 765 6440), is the largest of its kind in the region, with 50 rooms. Enjoy free use of the outdoor pool and tennis courts. (Communal kitchen, showers, and toilets. Key deposit $10. Dorms $16; singles $18.) The **Stratford Holiday Park,** 10 Page St. (tel./fax 765 6440), is a motel, backpackers, and campground all rolled into one. The kitchen and bathrooms are communal; the dorm in the lodge has a separate kitchen and lounge. (Internet. Bicycle hire. Key deposit $10. Reception 8am-10pm. Check-out 10am. Bunks $16; cabins for 2 $33-

42, extra person $12; double motel rooms with facilities $70, extra person $15; tent sites $9, powered $10.)

▢▣ FOOD AND NIGHTLIFE. Broadway St. does not suffer from a shortage of cheap and greasy takeaways, but finding quality fare is another matter. Those camping or graced with kitchens might be better off gathering supplies at the **New World supermarket** (tel. 765 6422), on the corner of Orlando and Regan St. (open M-Tu 8am-6pm, W-Th 8am-8pm, F 8am-7pm, Sa-Su 9am-6pm). One exception to this rule is the little red-walled bistro—the **Backstage Cafe,** 234 Broadway St. (tel. 765 7003). Enter stage left for food that is right on cue. Veggie pizza ($3) and with other inexpensive lunch options merit applause. (Open M 10am-4pm, Tu-Sa 8am-10pm.) The **Axeman's Inn,** 305 Broadway St. (tel. 765 5707), pays tribute to the region's prolific logging industry 'round the turn of the century. The restaurant upstairs serves up standard pub fare at reasonable prices ($8.50-15); the bar is downstairs. Overlooking it all from the rafters is the Axeman himself, one of Nigel Ogle's finest (see **Tawhiti Museum,** p. 215). Live music Thursday nights. Open daily 11am-2am, with only dining on Sundays.

▣▣ SIGHTS AND ACTIVITIES. Go to **O'Neill's Brewing Company,** 4281 Mountain Rd. (tel. 764 8335), off SH3 toward Eltham, to get a taste of the Taranaki. Brian and Helen O'Neill have converted an old service station into a microbrewery and cafe that produces Ngaere Draught and Black Peat Lager. All beers are batch-brewed with natural ingredients; regulars swear the lack of preservatives, sugar, and chemicals results in hangover-free drinking. Here's to that! (Open M-Sa 11am-6pm.) With **Mt. Egmont** looming in the background, it's little wonder that skiing can be a major activity in the area—when there's snow. Conditions haven't been favorable recently, but skiing awaits when the snow falls. The **Manganui Ski Field** (snowphone: 765 7669) is the only field on the mountain and has open season from June through October. One T-bar and three rope tows offer access to several expert runs as well as two natural half-pipes for snowboarders. ($30, students $20, children $15, over 60 free; half-day rates available.) For bush excursions, try **Off the Beaten Track Adventures** (tel./fax 762 7885). Adventurer Paddy Gooch and his wife Margaret will help you put together a choose-your-own-adventure day or two. Activities include hunting, canoeing, bushwalking, and horsetreking. ($25 per hr., half-day $50, full-day $85; food included.)

Taranaki's pioneer history is celebrated at the **Taranaki Pioneer Village** (tel. 765 5399), just outside of Stratford on SH3, a conglomeration of 50 turn-of-the-century buildings fully restored and decorated (open daily 10am-4pm; admission $5). Begun as an unassuming patch on a dairy farm in 1927, the **Hollard Gardens** (tel./fax 764 6544), on upper Kaponga Rd., are a centerpiece of the annual **Taranaki Rhododendron Festival** (Oct.-Nov.), which includes nearly 40 gardens ($5).

THE AXEMAN COMETH One of the winningest sportsmen in New Zealand history, axeman Ned Shrewry competed in a time when a wood chopper could become a national hero. Born in Stratford in 1889, Ned's career as a wood chopper lasted from 1910 to 1934, truly the glory days of the sport. He was the dominant chopper of the era, capturing three world titles as well as countless New Zealand and Australian crowns. His career was interrupted when he fought in World War I, where he was twice injured and won the Military Medal—in his opinion "because I kept the cookhouse supplied with kindling wood." Actually, the medal was for surviving a shell explosion that buried him alive, but also knocked his helmet off his head and over his face, keeping the dirt out and creating an air pocket that kept him alive until he could be dug out. He returned to New Zealand after the war and traveled around, chopping at shows throughout the 20s. He died in 1962, but received immortality in 1996 when he was voted into the New Zealand Sports Hall of Fame.

HAWERA

Hawera, which means "the burned place" in Maori, derives its name from a fire that consumed a nearby *pa* in Whareroa. However, the heifer, not the phoenix, has risen from the ashes, symbolizing the dairy industry that dominates the region. Today, Hawera's tourism industry continues to suckle at the teat of the immortal cow, offering multimedia tours of the dairy center, and farmstays to travelers who soon find themselves adopting the early-to-bed, early-to-rise rural lifestyle.

⚑ ORIENTATION AND PRACTICAL INFORMATION. The main street running through town is **High St.** At the west end of High St., **Waihi Rd.** (SH3) is the primary northern route. **South Rd.** becomes the coastal route to New Plymouth (SH45) in one direction and to Wanganui (SH3) in the other.

The **South Taranaki Visitor Information Centre,** 55 High St. (tel. 278 8599), is located at the base of the **water tower,** along with the bus station and the public toilets. This is also the place to buy hut tickets. (Open Feb.-Nov. M-F 8:30am-5pm; Dec.-Jan. M-F 8:30am-5pm, Sa-Su and public holidays 10am-3pm.) **InterCity** and **Newmans** (tel. 0800 777 707) leave daily for **New Plymouth** (1hr., 3 per day, $17) and **Wanganui** (1hr.; M-F 4 per day, Sa-Su 3 per day; $19), continuing on to **Palmerston North** (2½hr., $28) or **Wellington** (5hr., $48). **Southern Cabs** (24hr. tel. 278 8888) has a stand on Victoria St. near High St. Or, rent a used bicycle for $15 per day from **Seavers Cycles,** 18 Regent St. (tel. 278 6046; open July-Aug. M-F 8am-5pm, Sept.-June 9am-noon). **Hitchhikers** often find a ride on High St. between Argyle and Albion St. or at the junction of SH3 and SH45 (South Rd. and Waihi Rd.). Most cars head to New Plymouth or Wanganui via SH3; hitchhiking to the coastal beach communities of western Taranaki along SH45 can be more difficult. Other services include: **ATMs** along High St.; currency exchange at **BNZ** on Princes St. (open M-F 8am-4:30pm); **hospital** (tel. 278 7109), on Hunter St.; **police** (tel. 278 8066), on Princes St.; **post office,** 74 Princes St. (tel. 278 8680; open M-F 9am-5pm); and **Internet access** at the **Hawera Library,** 46 High St. (tel. 278 8406; $10 per hr.; open M-Tu and Th 9am-5:30pm, W 9:30am-5:30pm, F 9am-6pm, Sa 9am-noon). **Telephone Code:** 06.

⚏ ACCOMMODATIONS AND FOOD. Hawera's accommodations—mostly a fair distance out of town—are a good reason to stop here. Unique on-farm backpackers provide an active way to experience New Zealand's grassroots. **Wheatly Downs Farmstay** (tel. 278 6523; fax 278 6541; email wheatlydowns@taranaki-bak pak.co.nz), 7km out of town on Ararata Rd., offers free pickup with advance notice. Fifth generation farmer Gary Ogle offers such hands-on experiences as riding horses, herding cattle, and shearing sheep. On a clear day, enjoy a perfect view of **Mt. Egmont (Taranaki)** from the living room couch or fly around the mountain in a plane that picks you up right in front of the farmhouse. It's $50 for a 40-minute flight; ask Gary to arrange it. (Free laundry. Dorms $16; singles $25; doubles $36. Cash only. Book rooms and activities in advance.) At the **Taranaki Ohangi Backpacker Farm** (tel./fax 272 2878), on Urupa Rd. 10km from town, the savvy hosts will gladly show you around their 400-cow working dairy farm in English, German, or French. Pickup from town is free with advance notice; borrow a free bike to wheel around the farm. The backpackers bunkhouse offers clean rooms, a communal kitchen, TV lounge, and a deck with great pastoral and mountain views. Activities include horseback riding, cow milking, possum hunting, swimming, and lawn tennis. ($14 per person. Cash only.)

Let **New World,** 307 High St. (tel. 278 8528), be your grocery haven (open M-Sa 8am-8pm, Su 9am-6pm). **Morrieson Cafe and Bar,** 60 Victoria St. (tel. 278 5647), has a dramatic mural of the late, local novelist Ronald Hugh Morrieson (1922-68). A few die-hard fans salvaged the fixtures from his home when it was demolished in 1993, and used them to decorate the restaurant, which is around the corner from where his house used to stand. This is one place where you are actually encouraged to eat off the floor (the tables are constructed from the floorboards of his house). Basic burgers and other mains start at $6; brews are $4. (Open daily 11am-late. Kitchen closes at 9:30pm.) The **Rough Habits Sports Bar and Cafe,** 79-81 Regent St. (tel. 278 7333), may imply a smoky dive, but this place has a well-vacuumed look. The bar and cafe share one large room with TV monitors ablaze. Large starters ($8-12) are good for sharing among friends, or dine on meaty mains ($15-18) and wash it all down with a $3.30 handle (open M-Sa from 11am, Su 11am-11pm).

■ ⚠ **SIGHTS AND ACTIVITIES.** Hawera ("the burned place") has lived up to its name three times: in 1884, 1888, and 1912 the town went up in flames. After the third fire, residents wised up and built a **water tower;** then they built a Visitor Centre at its base. Climb the 215 steps for a scenic view of the countryside or use it as a navigational beacon at night, when it is lit up with red neon. (Open Feb.-Nov. M-F 8:30am-5pm; Dec.-Jan. M-F 8:30am-5pm, Sa-Su and public holidays 10am-3pm. Admission $2, children $1, groups $5.) For a truly unique experience, venture out of town to the **Tawhiti Museum,** 47 Ohangi Rd. (tel. 278 6837). Artist Nigel Ogle has perfected the technique of casting life-size fiberglass figures from human models, thus adding a human element which makes the artifacts from Maori and English settlements come alive. (Open Jan. daily 10am-4pm; Feb.-May and Sept.-Dec. F-M 10am-4pm; June-Aug. Su 10am-4pm. Admission $5, children $1.50.) Check out **Dairyland** (tel. 278 4537), at the corner of SH3 and Whareroa Rd., by the giant fiberglass cow and giraffe. Learn all about the multiple uses of milk, watch live footage from **Kiwi Cooperative Dairies,** and experience the vibrating pleasure of a **simulated milk tanker** with your animatronic driver Darryl. Enjoy a frothy shake ($2) in the revolving cafe. Dairyland is actually the visitors center for Kiwi Cooperative Dairies, looming just down the road, the largest milk processing plant in the world and global supplier of Pizza Hut's mozzarella. (Exhibit and cafe open daily 9am-5pm; cafe also open for dinner Th-Sa from 6:30pm.)

WANGANUI

Wanganui wins the prize for having the North Island's cutest main street. Victoria Ave.—the inevitable "strip"—sparkles with a fountain, hanging flowers, and Victorian lattice-work. In recent years, Wanganui has struggled to develop a tourism trade, but attempts to capitalize on the dirty, murky Wanganui River have yet to bring the big bucks. In this area, steeped in a rich Maori heritage, a slight underlying tension persists between the indigenous and European cultures that call this place home. This is perhaps best reflected in the grassroots movement among locals to restore the "h" to the town's name, which was "accidentally" Anglicized in the early 20th century. Regardless, Wanganui remains a nice stop for a stroll down main street or coffee by the river.

🛈 ORIENTATION AND PRACTICAL INFORMATION

Wanganui is located at the junction of **SH3** and **SH4;** the latter is called **Anzac Parade** within the city limits and runs the length of the Whanganui River (**Taupo Quay** and **Somme Parade** follow a similar course). They meet at **Victoria Ave.,** which runs perpendicular to the river and is the main street in town.

Visitor Center: Wanganui Visitor Information Centre (tel. 349 0508; fax 349 0509), near the corner of Guyton and St. Hill St. next to the District Council. Open M-F 8:30am-6pm, Sa-Su 9am-3pm; winter M-F 8:30am-5pm, Sa-Su 10am-2pm.

DOC: At the corner of St. Hill and Ingestre St. (tel. 345 2402). Heaps of information on the Whanganui National Park and more. Open M-F 8:30am-4:30pm.

Airport: (tel. 345 5593). Four arrivals and departures daily. Consult **Air New Zealand** (tel. 0800 737 000) for precise schedules. Open daily 6:30am-7pm.

Buses: Newmans and **InterCity** stop at the **Wanganui Travel Centre,** 156 Ridgway St. (tel. 345 4433; fax 345 3370). Open M-F 8:30am-5:15pm. Buses leave daily for **Wellington** (4hr., 3 per day, $34); **Palmerston North** (1½hr.; 4 per day M-F, 3 per day Sa-Su; $15); **New Plymouth** (2½hr., 2 per day, $29); **Rotorua** (6hr., 2 per day, $56); and **Auckland** (8hr., 4 per day, $68) via **Hamilton** (6hr., $61).

Public Transportation: Wanganui Taxi Bus (tel. 343 5555), for taxi and bus transport in town. The buses to **Castlecliff Beach** and the suburbs. All buses depart from Maria Pl. between Victoria Ave. and St. Hill St. (M-Sa 7am-6pm; $2). Taxis run 24hr.

Car Rental: Rent-A-Dent, 3 Churton St. (tel. 345 1505). $40 per day plus 20¢ per km.

Hitchhiking: Many thumbers head to the outskirts of town where traffic flows at speeds less than 70kph. People going toward Taranaki do so by way of Great North Rd., toward Ruapehu by way of Anzac Parade, and toward Wellington by way of Main South Rd.

Currency Exchange: Money ebbs and flows across Victoria Ave. at **BNZ, ANZ, Westpac Trust,** and **National Bank** (with **ATMs**). Open M-F 9am-4:30pm.

Police: (tel. 345 4488).

Pharmacy: Wicksteed Pharmacy, 214 Wicksteed St. (tel. 345 6166). Open daily 8:30am-8:30pm.

Medical Services: Wanganui City Doctors, 163 Wicksteed St. (tel./fax 348 8333). Doctors on call 5pm-8:30am and 24hr. on weekends and holidays. The **Wanganui Hospital** (tel. 348 1234) is on Heads Rd.

Post Office: 226 Victoria Ave. (tel. 345 4103). Open M-F 9am-5pm.

Internet Access: Available at **Phoenix Computer Center,** 2 St. Hills St. (tel. 348 0101), at the intersection with Taupo Quay, the **Library,** and the **Visitor Centre** for $10 per hr.

Telephone Code: 06.

▐ ACCOMMODATIONS

You may be charmed by riverside life; most of the hostels and backpackers are rooted on the riverbanks, beside the English oak trees.

The Tamara Backpackers Hostel, 24 Somme Parade (tel. 347 6300; email tamarabak-pak@xtra.co.nz). Call for free pickup. The large, clean, old house has plenty of space—most dorm rooms are spacious and have no bunk beds. Friendly staff and extras will help you enjoy Wanganui. Internet. Laundry $2. Reception open 8am-8pm. Check-out 10am. Key deposit $10. Dorms $15; singles $23; twins and doubles $32-34.

The Grand Hotel (tel. 345 0955; email the-grand-hotel@xtra.co.nz), on the corner of Guyton and St. Hill St. Built in 1927 in the heart of Wanganui, The Grand is just that. And expensive. Facility is a temple of cleanliness and professionalism. Freebies abound: laundry, parking, baggage storage, jacuzzi, and pickup from bus station or airport. Three bars, casino, and restaurant. Reception 24hr. Check-out 10am. Singles $65; doubles $77; quads $101; suites start at $110, extra person $12.

Riverside Inn (YHA Associate), 2 Plymouth St. (tel./fax 347 2529). A century-old pink and mauve Victorian house that can become quite cold in winter. With backpacker facilities stashed in the backroom of the mansion, the staff tends to pay special attention to the on-site B&B instead. Laundry $5. B&B singles $50; doubles $80. Backpacker dorms (co-ed and women's) $16; backpacker doubles $36 per person; tent sites $10.

Castlecliff Holiday Park, 1a Rangiora St. (tel. 344 2227 or 0800 254 54 7275; email tokiwipark@xtra.co.nz), at Castlecliff Beach. Free pickup from the bus station; taxi bus stops across the street. Not exactly Camelot, but you can roll out of bed onto the black sand beach. Communal kitchen, showers, and toilets. Internet. Spa. Check-out 10am. Backpackers cabins $15; tent sites $7.50, powered $10; caravans $17; standard cabins $32-35, extra person $7.50.

✎ FOOD

Wanganui sticks with the basics and does them well. Eateries cluster around **Victoria Ave.** and its side streets from the river to **Guyton St.** Or, whip up your own dish after a stop at **Food Town** (tel. 345 8720), at Taupo Quay and St. Hill St. (open M-Tu and Sa 8:30am-7pm, W and F 8:30am-9pm, Su 8:30am-6pm).

Red Eye Cafe, 96 Guyton St. (tel. 345 5646). Enter this colorful, young den where electronica beats vibrate through the basic furniture and incense perfumes the air. Choose from a variety of hearty breakfasts ($5-9), imaginative pizzas and quiches for lunch ($3-5), and exotic dinner entrees ($9.50-10.50) such as Thai green curry with mango chutney. Open Tu-Sa 9am-10pm (kitchen closed 2-6pm), Su-M 10am-4pm.

Amadeus Riverbank Cafe, 69 Taupo Quay (tel. 345 1538). Experience a filling meal by the banks of the Whanganui composed just for you by a friendly and talented ensemble. Cheap food like quiche ($3.50) and sandwiches ($3) at the counter during lunch hours. Dinner is a bit more dear, with burgers and sandwiches $8.50-$12.50. Open M-Tu 8:30am-4pm, W 8:30am-9pm, Th-F 8:30am-10pm, Sa 10am-10pm, Su 10am-6pm, (from 7am on summer weekdays).

Zanzibar Cafe, Victoria Court (tel. 345 5900). Hidden inside a courtyard off Victoria Ave, Zanzibar is a slice of posh civilization—a cozy spot with decadent food and wine to match. Muffins and other baked goods (from $3) disappear by later in the day. Dinner mains like pasta with a creamy tomato, basil, and spinach sauce ($12) will fill your tummy and coax a smile. Open Su-Tu 9am-4pm, W-Sa 9am-late.

NORTH ISLAND

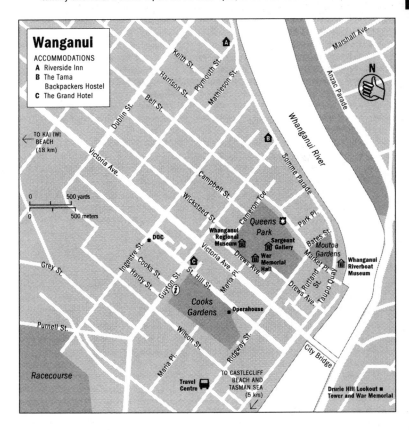

Wanganui

ACCOMMODATIONS
A Riverside Inn
B The Tama
   Backpackers Hostel
C The Grand Hotel

Jabie's Kebab on the Avenue, 168 Victoria Ave. (tel. 347 2800). "Real food...unreal flavour," promises Wanganui's one-stop kebab shop. Don't get caught staring at the provocative belly-dancer murals, which whisper to diners, "audition anytime!" Instead, focus on the food—like a kebab of lamb, veggie, chicken, or falafel ($4-8.50 per plate). Open M-W 11am-9pm, Th-Sa 11am-10pm, Su 4-9pm.

While more empty than not during the week, pubs are all the rage in Wanganui on the weekends. At **The Red Lion Inn,** 45 Anzac Parade (tel. 345 3831), two separate rooms house different scenes. In one, locals watch (and bet on) the horse races. Skulling (that's "chugging" to some) handles of the namesake brew ($3.20) permitted. To the left, the "Simply Red" room has nice food and a more clean-cut crowd. (Live entertainment Saturdays. Open daily 11am-3am.) It can be a long walk, but the music at **The Celtic Arms,** 432 Victoria Ave. (tel. 347 7037), makes the trip worthwhile. How did this place bounce back after a debilitating fire, you ask? The luck of the Irish! Moderately priced food ($4-15) includes all of what you'd expect at an Irish bar (nachos?), but most people come here for the other staple of Irish pub culture (nachos?). Open daily noon-1am.

SIGHTS AND ACTIVITIES

Before heading out into the wilderness from Wanganui, get your bearings and survey the land from a perch above it all on Durie Hill. But why hike to the top when you could take the elevator? One dollar buys an express trip to the **Durie Hill Lookout Tower**—the journey begins from Anzac Parade at the base of Victoria Ave. just across the bridge. A "decorated" tunnel takes you 219m into the hill. Then an elevator whisks you up 66m *through* the hill, depositing you at the top. Next, locate the nearby **Durie Hill War Memorial** to WWI, climb it, and appreciate the view. (Elevator runs M-F 7:30am-6pm, Sa 10am-6pm, Su 11am-5pm. One-way $1.)

The **M V Adventurer** (tel. 342 4717) chugs from the Amadeus Riverbank Cafe landing to the Ohorere bank flower garden (adults $25; children $12; book ahead; limited service in winter). The **Whanganui Regional Museum** (tel. 345 7443), is in **Queens Park.** Its Te Atihau forum (a place for all peoples to "anchor their canoes"), houses the largest surviving *waka taua* (war canoe) in the Wanganui area. Another exhibit in the permanent collection displays the instruments used in the tribal art of *moko* (see p. 15). (Open M-Sa 10am-4:30pm, Su 1-4:30pm. Admission $2.) Also in Queens Park at the top of the hill, the **Sargeant Gallery** houses a permanent collection of local art from the early 20th century, as well as visiting shows (open M-F 10:30am-4:30pm, Sa-Su and holidays 1pm-4:30pm; donations appreciated). Just south of **Queens Park,** one block east of Victoria Ave. on Market Pl., are the **Moutoa Gardens.** These gardens were the site of a visible **Maori land rights demonstration** several years ago (see **Recent Events,** p. 10). Adjacent to the gardens on Rutland St. is the **Quay School of the Arts,** the third largest institution of its kind in New Zealand. A variety of student art is on display in the gallery. To the west of Queens Park, on Maria Pl., are the **Cooks Gardens.** Sorry, no kitchen herbs here— just a rugby pitch, New Zealand's wooden cycling velodrome, and a running track that was the site of Peter Snell's world-record mile.

Castlecliff Beach, where the river meets the sea, is noted for its black sand and good surf. **The Sport Shed,** 63A Victoria Ave. (tel. 347 6508), can recommend local surfing mavens if you want to learn the fine art of catching a wave. To get to Castlecliff, take Quay St. West to Heads Rd. and continue 9km. Alternatively, head for Maria Pl. in town and catch the #3 or #4 taxi bus. Farther up the coast, **Kai Iwi Beach** attracts locals who wish to avoid the crowds, but is less accessible by public transportation.

WHANGANUI NATIONAL PARK

In the time of legends, the great mountains Tongariro and Taranaki fought over a lovely summit named Pihanga. Defeated, Taranaki gouged a great furrow in the earth on his way westward, a cleft which his wise rival filled with life-bestowing water. Thus, the Whanganui River is surrounded by lush greenery on its way from the slopes of Tongariro down to the Tasman Sea. It has the longest navigable course (200km) in the North Island, second in overall length only to the Waikato. Tall rimu and lovely ponga hold court from atop high riverside bluffs, where Maori *pa* (fortified villages) once stood in numbers. Then came European missionaries, steamboats, and land claims, changing the nature of river life. In recent years, however, Whanganui Maori families have reestablished *marae* along the river, bringing vital community spirit and hospitality to those who journey downstream.

▨ ORIENTATION. Whanganui National Park is fundamentally decentralized, in terms of its boundaries, access points, and information outlets. Park boundaries comprise many small pockets and larger blocks between the towns of Taumarunui in the north and Wanganui in the south, with the biggest swaths of bush enclosing the middle and lower reaches of the Whanganui River. Despite its name, the city of **Wanganui** is *not* the best base for exploring the Whanganui River; most river outsitters operate out of **Taumarunui** (see p. 222), **National Park Village** (see p. 200), and **Ohakune** (see p. 201). Confoundingly, Wanganui *does* host the park's main **DOC visitors centre** (see p. 215); the **DOC field centres** in Taumarunui, Ohakune, and **Pipiriki** are not as dedicated to visitor service. Most outfitters and accommodations in the above-mentioned towns can supply river info and DOC pamphlets.

WHANGANUI TRACKS. For information on the **Whanganui Journey,** see below. The **Mangapurua Track,** when combined with the Kaiwhakauka Track, turns into a 40km, 20-hour, three- to four-day endeavor. It takes off from **Mangapurua Landing** (see p. 221) on the Whanganui River, then goes over the **Bridge to Nowhere,** through the Mangapurua Valley, and past vast sections of farmland. The track climbs to the **Mangapurua Trig,** offering panoramic views of Mt. Tongariro, Mt. Egmont (Taranaki), and the junction with the Kaiwhakuaka Track. Then it's down through the Kaiwhakuaka Valley past bush and farms to **Whakahoro Hut** ($8; see p. 220). This is the only hut along the whole track, though flat campsites are plentiful. From here, the road leads east to SH4.

The other major trail in the park is the **Matemateaonga Track,** which tempts die-hard hikers with 42km of serpentine trail leading deep into the bush along an old Maori route. The path leads from the **Kohi Saddle** on Upper Mangaehu Rd. well east of **Stratford** (p. 212), to the Whanganui River just downstream and across from the **Tieke Marae** (see p. 221). The three- to four-day journey stops at five huts ($8) and overall the grade is much flatter than the Mangapurua Track. **Wades Landing Outdoors** (tel. (07) 895 5995 or mobile 025 797 238) does jetboat river pickups and dropoffs for trampers ($85). A good daytrip out of Wanganui, the **Atene Skyline Track** is a six- to eight-hour hike that takes you in almost a complete loop, accessible by a 36km drive up the **River Road** (see p. 222) with views of Mt. Ruapehu, Mt. Egmont (Taranaki), and the Tasman Sea.

▨ THE WHANGANUI RIVER JOURNEY

Not only is the Whanganui River Journey the only Great Walk over water, it provides an outdoor experience unique to New Zealand. Those who paddle between the river's steep and towering banks will be challenged by rapids, greeted with endless green, and surrounded by small waterfalls. The journey presents small tokens of its long human history, from the Lombardy poplars planted by missionaries to the iron moorings used by steamers bound upstream. The river has a living legacy in its two repatriated *marae*, both of which welcome overnight guests with the appropriate powhiri (introductory ceremony). No drugs, alcohol, or firearms are permitted in these small meeting places, whose presence quietly contests government management of the Whanganui and its surrounding lands.

ESSENTIALS

Length: 145km. The entire journey usually takes 5 days, though starting at **Whakahoro** shortens the trip to 88km and 3 days. Average paddlers can expect to travel around 5km per hour, although this can vary vastly according to experience and gumption.

While the Whanganui's rapids tend toward the gentle, they can be challenging and even dangerous for the entirely uninitiated; most outfitters provide a basic briefing before sending off unguided customers.

Trailheads: From **Cherry Grove** near Taumarunui in the north, to **Pipiriki** landing in the south. Some choose to start at Whakahoro. Downstream is the preferred direction.

Seasonality: January and February can see as many as 200 paddlers hitting the river on a given day, though half as many is the norm. Some days during peak season happen to bring very few visitors—it's often the luck of the draw. The water gets cold and the weather gets rainier between June and September, making crowds a non-issue and experience a must.

Outfitters: Most river operators offer packages including pickup and dropoff from the main access towns, kayaks or Canadian canoes, life jackets, waterproof storage containers, and a brief training session; prices do not include the DOC fees. **Yeti Tours** (tel. (06) 385 8197), based in Ohakune, runs upmarket guided tours and has freedom rentals (kayaks $18-25 per day; canoes $30-40 per day; transport $45 per person). The best deal for larger groups may be from **Tieke Canoes** (tel. (06) 385 4565), in Raetihi near Ohakune, which helps financially support the river's *marae* financially (around $130 per person for 6 people). Visitors are welcome to hop aboard the powered dinghy that serves both *marae;* contact the **Whanganui River Marae Resupply and Victualling Co.** (tel. (06) 385 8258; $100 per person for the day, including overnight option.) **Wades Landing Outdoors** (tel. (07) 895 5995 or mobile 025 797 238), based at Whakahoro, rents single kayaks (5-day $175, 3-day $106) and double canoes (5-day $130, 3-day $100). **Blazing Paddles** (tel. (07) 895 8074), based in Taumarunui, also rents kayaks (5-day $180, 3-day $142) and canoes (5-day $134, 3-day $113), plus transport options out of Taumarunui (to Ohinepane $33-45, to Whakahoro $63-111).

Huts and Campsites: The DOC demands a flat fee of $25 for visitors spending 2-6 nights anywhere on the river, and $35 for those who don't buy the pass before starting the journey. Cheaper passes are available for people spending only one night ($6 if by canoe, $8 if by jetboat). Children are half-price. These fees apply to both huts and campsites, but *not* to the *marae,* which dispute the pass system in the first place, and receive only voluntary donations. During the official low season (May-Sept.), huts revert to the regular backcountry ticket system ($8 per night) and camping is free. DOC-run huts have water and cooking facilities; campsites each have a small cooking shelter, but not stoves. For details about the *marae,* see the track description below.

Gear: Outfitters supply the most important river gear, including life jackets and waterproof containers; anything left outside of these containers will almost certainly get wet. If you're in a kayak, it's worth demanding a "skirt" to keep out unwanted river water. It might be wise to bring a tent and stove in your kayak, just in case you don't reach the hut by nightfall.

Storage: Most local accommodations offer free storage for paddlers, and most outfitters will hold onto extra gear jettisoned at the landing.

THE JOURNEY
Cherry Grove to Whakahoro Hut: 57km
Cherry Grove to Ohinepane Campsite: 22km

Ohinepane Campsite to Poukaria Campsite: 14km

Poukaria Campsite to Maharanui Campsite: 17km

Maharanui Campsite to Whakahoro Hut: 4km

This two-day stretch contains the vast majority of the journey's rapids. Paddlers begin near Taumaranui at idyllic **Cherry Grove,** where the Ongarue and Whanganui rivers meet, making an ideal picnic area with a BBQ and campsite. The first stretch of river is surrounded mostly by roads and paddocks. Legend holds that if travelers don't place a spring of green on the **Taniwha Rock,** a river guardian will smite them for their insolence. The first opportunity to stop and camp is at **Ohinepane** campsite. The next two campsites, **Poukaria** and **Maharanui,** are some of the river's finest, with flat ground and lush bush. Between these campsites rise the imposing and freshly renovated carved **niu poles,** where Hau Hau warriors used to pray before embarking for battle. The road-accessible **Whakahoro Hut** (16 beds) is an old schoolhouse with heaps of character and even more tentsites on the grassy field just outside. A former *pa* site, a gong on a nearby bluff used to resonate with alarm in time of attack.

Whakahoro Hut to Mangapapapa Marae: 40.5km

Whakahoro Hut to Mangapapa Campsite: 11km

Mangapapa Campsite to Ohauora Campsite: 16km

Ohauora Campsite to John Coull Hut: 10.5km

John Coull Hut to Mangapapapa Marae: 3km

From here to Pipiriki, dramatic cliffs enclose the river. Stairs of rounded stone lead up to grassy **Mangapapa Campsite. Ohauora Campsite** can be strewn with unattractive human leftovers, but puts on a small glow-worm show by night. Kaiwaka and Tokakotuku Campsites, though still on DOC maps, were washed away in the late October floods of 1998. Roomy **John Coull Hut** (30 beds) is well marked, with plenty of burners and natural history tidbits. Finding the as-yet-unmarked ▨**Mangapapapa Marae** is a bit of a mission, and indescribably worthwhile. About 3km from John Coull Hut, watch for a leftward bend in the river, with a sheer white bluff on the right; wooden stairs and blue chimney smoke on the left bank are the easiest giveaways. The tiny and tidy *kainga* (village) was reestablished in 1996, and has a centuries-old legacy at this site. The elders here place an emphasis on spiritual learning, and encourage visitors to participate in communal cooking and cultural exchange. Tenting is available outside, though all guests are welcome to sleep indoors. Monetary gifts are spent on erecting more permanent living quarters. If you're planning to stay at Mangapapapa, leave advance notice with Patrick and Jefferine (tel. (06) 385 8258), who will radio ahead for you.

Mangapapapa Marae to Tieke Marae: 25km

Mangapapapa Marae to Mangawaiiti Campsite: 6km

Mangawaiiti Campsite to Mangapurua Landing: 9km

Mangapurua Landing to Tieke Marae: 10.5km

At **Mangawaiiti Campsite,** marked simply "CAMP-SITE," a long staircase leads far above the river to some beautiful plots, all set about with ponga trees. There are slim pickings for nice tent sites at **Mangapurua Landing,** which is more notable as a trailhead. A reasonably easy walk of 30-40 minutes leads deep into the bush, opening into an astounding view of the ponga canopy, with a wild tannin-stained stream far below, and in the middle of it all, a perfectly ordinary concrete bridge. This **Bridge to Nowhere** is the last remnant of an all-too-isolated WWI rehabilitation settlement, which officially failed in 1942. Back on the water, the river eventually passes an unmarked hilltop hut on the righthand bank which is *not* **Tieke Marae;** the well-marked *marae* is just a bit further on the lefthand bank. A larger settlement than Mangapapapa, Tieke (TEE-uh-kee) is no less hospitable a place, offering visitors hot meals and even hot showers on occasion. Reestablished six years ago, Tieke Marae functions primarily as a carving school and community center, though guests are extremely welcome.

Tieke Marae to Pipiriki Landing: 21.5km

Tieke Marae to Ngaporo Campsite: 12.5km

Ngaporo Campsite to Pipiriki Landing: 9km

Set between two rapids, **Ngaporo Campsite** makes for nice, well-perched tenting, framed by sheer gray rock faces. The native forest breaks into cleared sheep fields by the time **Pipiriki Landing** appears at journey's end.

THE RIVER ROAD

After a 30-year construction fraught with floods and mudslides, 1934 saw the opening of the aptly named **River Road.** Dancing a *pas de deux* with the bushy banks of the Whanganui River, the road allows the only automobile access to the settlements upstream from Wanganui. In fact, it was the completion of the road that signaled the end of the paddlewheel boat as a viable transportation method, as a 10-hour boat ride between Manganui and Pipiriki was reduced to a 1½-hour drive. The River Road parallels SH4 some 15km to the east, connecting Wanganui to **Pipiriki.** From Pipiriki, the road continues out of Whanganui National Park to meet up with **Raetihi** (27km), less than 15km from the ski town of **Ohakune** (p. 201). The northern extremes of the park can be reached from **Whakahoro** via roads from **Owhanga** (south of Taumarunui, p. 222) or **Raurimu** (just north of the town of National Park, p. 200), both on SH4. If you don't have your own car, riding along with the **mail run** (tel. mobile 025 443 421) is a great way to get into the heart of the river valley and meet locals at the same time (pickup 7:15am from Wanganui with advance reservation; otherwise, show up early behind the post office, 60 Ridgway St.). The run returns to Wanganui around 2 or 3pm, or you can ask to be dropped off anywhere along the way and be picked up on a different day ($25).

Travelers heading up the road from Wanganui soon see the **Oyster Cliffs,** which take a large white bite out of the river as a reminder of a time when oceans enveloped this valley. A bit farther up, there's riverside camping at the **Otumarie Campsite** (the only DOC campgrounds on the Wanganui side of Pipiriki). Those who continue upstream arrive at one of the most singularly wonderful homestays in New Zealand, ◪**The Flying Fox** (tel./fax 342 8160), 44km up the River Rd. from Wanganui. Truly off the beaten track, the Flying Fox is accessible only by boating up the river or via an aerial cableway—a "flying fox" in Kiwispeak—suspended 20m above the river. En route river travelers are most welcome, too, as cool drinks in the shade of the English oaks are a hospitable tradition. Stay the night in the secluded private bush cabin or in the burlap-walled loft above the microbrewery. Self-proclaimed hippie proprietors Annette and John may feel personally insulted if you don't stop in for a beer or a freshly baked muffin. (Mountain bikes $10 per day, canoes $35 per day. Free laundry and linen. Loft or cabins $20 per person; campsites $8. Advance booking absolutely required.)

A trio of villages with Christian names and a Maori populace stand farther upstream. **Corinth** (formerly Koriniti) features the Opeiriki *pa* (never once taken in battle), a lovely *marae*, and the first Anglican church on the river (est. 1840). **London** (Ranana) is one of the bigger villages on the river, and retains traces of its past as a traditional center of agriculture. **Jerusalem** (Hiruharama) is home to a French Marist Mission and the poet James K. Baxter. Just before Jerusalem is Mautoa Island from which Maori followers of Hauhauism (a xenophobic religious sect) launched ritualized battles against the tribes of the lower river. Continuing upstream, find the cascading beauty of **Omorehu Waterfall.** An alpha-omega of a town, **Pipiriki** is at the end of the River Road and is also the beginning for many jetboat rides and two walking tracks. The **Pukehinau Walk** loops 1km to the Pukehinau crest, once a Hauhau outpost with strategic (and gorgeous) views of the river valley. **Wairua Hikoi Tours** (tel. 345 3485) is a unique tour with a spiritual emphasis on Maori culture that offers shorter one-day canoe trips to The Flying Fox ($45, vehicle transfer included). You must find your own way to Jerusalem, perhaps by the mail run (p. 222).

TAUMARUNUI

Buses and trains pause only briefly in Taumarunui, and travelers by car usually break here for an ice cream cone. Like so many small New Zealand towns, natural surroundings impress while the commercial strip tends to depress. Although undeniably a small town (pop. 7668), Taumarunui offers access to much of the surrounding region, thus living up to its reputation as the "Heart of the King Country." Situated at the confluence of the Ongarue and Whanganui Rivers, it is the logical starting point for expeditions down the Whanganui. Taumarunui also lies at the junction of SH4 and SH43 (the **Taumarunui-Stratford Heritage Trail**), serving as a crossroads for those traveling through the Taranaki and Ruapenu regions or to Whanganui and Tongariro National Parks. Regardless of your destination, this is a good place to resupply on the basics before hitting river, road, rail, or trail.

⁊ ORIENTATION AND PRACTICAL INFORMATION. Taumarunui sits along the **Main Trunk Railway** and **SH4** (called Hakiaha St. within the town limits), 43km north of the town of **National Park** (p. 200), 129km east of **Stratford** (p. 212), 82km south of **Te Kuiti,** and 65km west of **Turangi** (p. 194). The **Visitor Information Centre** (tel. 895 7494; fax 895 6117) is conveniently located in the railway station (open M-F 9am-4:30pm, Sa-Su and holidays 10am-4pm). Take a nature walk through Cherry Grove to get to the **DOC Field Centre** (tel. 895 8201 or after-hours mobile 025 946 650; open M-F 8am-4:30pm, Oct.-Apr. also open Sa-Su 8:30-9:30am). **TranzScenic** heads to **Auckland** (4½hr., 2 per day, $52-59) and **Wellington** (6½hr., 2 per day, $72-84), while **InterCity** also goes to **Auckland** (4¾hr., 1 per day Su-F, $46) and **Wellington** (6hr., $64). **Pioneer Jet Boat Tours Ltd.** (tel. 895 8528) has a bus to **Hamilton** (M-F 8am, $26). Toward National Park, most **hitchhikers** try the area past the Main Trunk Cafe by the Hakiaha St. railyards. Toward Te Kuiti, they often try the Ongarue River Rd. (SH4). **Silver Cabs** (tel. 895 5444) and **Taumaranui Taxis** (tel. 895 8877) will help you get around. Other services include: **banks** with **ATMs** on Miriama St. (open M-F 9am-4:30pm); **hospital** (tel. 896 0020); **police** (tel. 895 8119), on Hakiaha St.; **post office** (tel. 895 8149), on Miriama St. (open M-F 9am-5pm); and **Internet access** at the **library** on Hakiaha St. ($10 per hr.) and **CommPORT,** 49 Hakiaha St. (tel. 895 3032; open M-F 8:30am-5:30pm, Sa 9am-noon). **Telephone Code:** 07.

⌂ ACCOMODATIONS AND FOOD. Taumarunui Holiday Park (tel. 895 9345; fax 895 6345), 4km south of town on the Whanganui River, offers free pickup (tent sites $8; powered $9; cabins for 2 $29; self-contained tourist cabin $45, plus $12 per head). Those searching for a few more creature comforts at a budget price can try the **Taumarunui Family Inn,** 4 Marae St. (tel. 895 3478; fax 895 6072; www.middle-of-nowhere.co.nz). Choose from a variety of comfy singles, doubles, twins, or one triple. Those planning a trip downriver can take advantage of off-street parking and free bag storage. (Linen and towels $6. Reception 7am-10pm. Check-out 10am. Rooms $16 per person.) At the **Tattles Motel,** 23 Marae St. (tel./fax 895 8063), rooms are huge and parking is available (twins and doubles $55-60; family units $80).

Quality dining establishments are scarce in Taumarunui, though the **Rivers II Cafe,** 43 Hakiaha St. (tel. 895 5822), stands out. Patrons can enjoy breakfast, lunch, or dinner in a spacious, brightly lit interior or outside at tables along the sidewalk. The French toast with banana ($9) deserves special praise. Open daily 7:30am-11pm.) For a quick bite before you catch a bus or train, or to cure a case of the late-night munchies, the **Main Trunk Cafe** (tel. 895 6544) on Hakiaha St. is your best bet. Look for the dormant red railway cars sitting next to the tracks. Hang a left as you step out of the train station. Open W-F 10am-4am, Sa-Su 10am-10pm.) The most comprehensive supermarket is **New World** (tel. 895 7634), located at the northern end of Hakiaha St. (open M-Sa 8am-7pm, Su 9am-6pm).

◙ SIGHTS AND ACTIVITIES. Apart from the broad array of outdoor recreational activities, visitors are drawn here to see the serpentine **Raurimu Spiral.** A mighty feat of engineering, this 1908 section of railway track loops and twists and at one point doubles back on itself as it climbs onto the central plateau. The best way to experience the stomach-churning glory of the spiral is to take a **scenic train ride,** which departs Taumarunui daily at 1pm, returning at 3pm ($28). Gaze upon its loopiness from the lookout 37km south on SH4 at Raurimu. Drivers can also traverse the **Taumarunui-Stratford Heritage Trail,** a 150km stretch of SH43 established in 1990 to provide travelers with a chance to learn about the history of the region. Teal and yellow signs along the trail mark lookout points and historic sites. Just off the trail (10km) in Ohura is a **white-collar prison,** where approximately 90 "guests of Her Majesty" are *invited* to serve their time.

WELLINGTON AND AROUND

WELLINGTON

Though it lies directly on a major earthquake fault, teeters at the edge of the ocean, and is jostled on all sides by steep green hills, the compact city of Wellington is more a place for catching your breath than losing it. Much of the city was planned by eager Englishmen who had not yet seen the hilly terrain; the resulting buildings, barely clinging onto steep cliff-sides, possess a certain commanding effect that would have been lost had they been constructed on the sturdy, flat ground imagined by their overseas designers. Looking out on a gorgeous hook of harbor near the North Island's southern tip, New Zealand's capital and second-largest city, has become a major cultural center. Here in the throbbing heart of the country, you'll find a wide variety of cultural options including an impressive series of festivals and events and New Zealand's strongest set of theater and dance options. The enormous, $300 million Museum of New Zealand Te Papa Tongarewa opened its doors in February 1998, becoming the gem in Wellington's cultural crown. Come nightfall, the scores of cafes, composed cool of Cuba Street, and outlandish Courtenay Place rival even Auckland's renowned nightlife. Before passing through on the way to or from the South Island, take a refreshing dip into the worldly savoir-faire of New Zealand's cosmopolitan capital.

⚓ WELLINGTON AND AROUND HIGHLIGHTS

- ■ The 2-year-old **Te Papa Museum** (p. 235) is Wellington's pride and joy.
- ■ Wellington has one of the highest densities of **cafes, bars, and nightclubs** (p. 232) in the Southern Hemisphere. This city turns it up a notch at night.
- ■ **Kapiti Island** (p. 238) is a sanctuary for New Zealand's endangered species.
- ■ Fine wines can be tasted at the vineyards of the nearby **Wairarapa** (p. 240).

⌐ ARRIVAL AND DEPARTURE

BY PLANE

The **Wellington International Airport** (tel. 385 5100) stretches across the narrowest portion of the Miramar Peninsula in the city's southeastern suburbs. (Luggage storage $6 per 6hr.) Largely a domestic hub, the only international flights here are those from Sydney, Brisbane, Melbourne, Nadi, and Apia on **Qantas** or **Air New Zealand. ANZ Link** has an office at the corner of Lambton Quay and Panama St. (tel. 474 8950 or 0800 737 000). **Ansett** (tel. 471 1146 or 0800 287 388), is right across the way on Panama St. Both fly to **Auckland** (1hr., 1-2 per hr., $175-$304) and **Christchurch** (45min., around 1 per hr., $133-$230). With an **International Student Identification Card** or advance booking, fares can drop dramatically. **Soundsair** (tel. 388 2594 or 0800 505 005) flies daily to **Picton** (25min., 6-8 per day, $50) and on request to tiny airstrips throughout the **Marlborough Sounds. Super Shuttle** (tel. 387 8787) runs between the airport and railway station ($5).

BY TRAIN

The **Railway Station,** on Bunny St. at Waterloo/Customhouse Quay, houses the train and bus depots. **TranzScenic** (tel. 0800 802 802) provides daily service to: **Napier**

(5hr., 8am, $70) via **Palmerston North** (2hr., $19-$30); **Auckland** (11hr., 8:45am, $60-$135) via **Palmerston North** or **Hamilton** (9hr., $60-$108); and an overnight train to **Auckland** (7:50pm, $60-$120). **The Travel Centre** (tel. 498 2058) inside the Railway Station handles almost all transportation bookings.

BY BUS

Most buses depart from the railway station; **InterCity** and **Newmans** (tel. 472 5111) go daily to: **Palmerston North** (2hr., 1-4 per day, $25-30); **Rotorua** (7½hr., 1-3 per day, $40-75) via **Taupo** (6hr., $55-65); **Auckland** (11hr., 1-3 per day, $96) via **Hamilton** (9hr., $72-79); **Tauranga** (8-8½hr., 3 per day, $86-89); **New Plymouth** (6hr., 2-3 per day, $59) via **Wanganui** (4hr., $34); and **Napier** (5hr., $58). **Tranzit Coachlines** (tel. 387 2018) goes to **Masterton** (1½hr., 9:15am, $13).

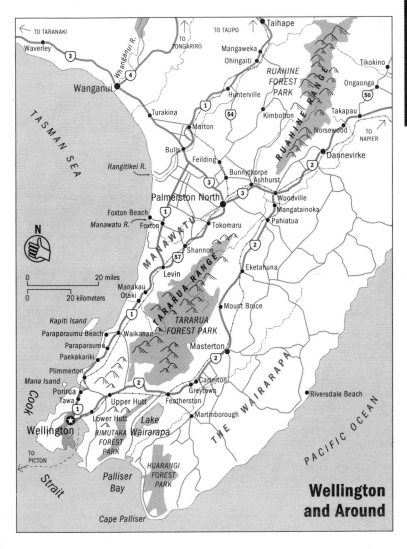

Wellington and Around

BY FERRY

The ferry terminal is inconveniently located on **Aotea Quay,** north of town on SH1. There's a free shuttle from Platform 9 of the railway station 40 minutes before each scheduled departure, and back to the station upon ferry arrival. The **Interis-lander** (tel. 0800 802 802; fax 0800 101 525) runs daily to **Picton** on the South Island (3hr., 4-5 per day, $23-$46). Bookings are essential, especially during the summer. (Small car transport $83-$165; large sports equipment and dogs $10). Ask about one-day and four-day excursion fares. **Topcat** (tel. 0800 4867 228) also goes to **Picton** (1½hr., 2 per day, $59), departing from Shed 19 on Waterloo Quay opposite the railway station (car $190, dog $20).

BY THUMB

Hitchhikers report that riding from Wellington is sometimes difficult, but also report that a few pickup spots provide success. If Aotea Quay by the railway station isn't working, the old main road (where SH1 and SH2 branch a couple of kilometers north of the ferry station on Hutt Rd.) is known to be successful. This branchpoint is a long walk, so some hitchers try their luck where the cars roll right off the boat at the ferry terminal. Also, some believe it's best to train it out to Paraparaumu (45km north on SH1) or Masterton (on SH2) and catch a ride there.

⚒ ORIENTATION

Wellington is remarkably compact, though its suburbs stretch up around the harbor into nearby valleys and out onto the **Miramar Peninsula.** Its main downtown zone (most of the city's flat land) sits between the **Railway Station** and **Cambridge/ Kent Terraces** at the base of **Mt. Victoria,** and can be explored in the course of a day. The main artery snaking through the business area is **Lambton Quay** (pronounced *key*). At the **Cuba** and **Vivian St.** intersection is the "red light district," as the locals say. **Courtenay Place,** between Cambridge Terr. and **Taranaki St.,** hops with nightlife on the weekends. Cuba St. between **Abel Smith** and **Manners St.** maintains a more bohemian air, with students and twentysomethings dodging the splash of the jolting primary-colored fountain sculpture in the center. The **Civic Centre** is both a conceptual and spatial bridge between downtown and the harbor, leading to the harborfront with its public parks, **Queen's Wharf,** the colossal new **National Museum,** and **Oriental Bay's** flashy shops, cafes, and beach. Government buildings, such as the **Beehive** of Parliament, stand near the Railway Station. At the southern edge of downtown are the little wooden houses and quieter streets of the Mt. Victoria area, where many budget accommodations lie.

⊡ GETTING AROUND

Ridewell Service Centre (tel. 801 7000 or 0800 801 700) can answer any and all questions about fares, routes, and timetables for buses, trains, or the cable car (M-Sa 7:30am-8:30pm, Su 9am-3pm).

BY TRAIN

The **Tranz Metro** (tel. 498 3000 ext. 44933), a regional commuter line, leaves from the Railway Station. There are four regular lines with many stops on the way: **Johnsonville** (20min., full peak fare $2.50), **Upper Hutt** (50min., $5.50), **Paraparaumu** (1hr., $7.50), and **Melling** in Lower Hutt (M-F peak morning and afternoon hours only, $3). Ten-trip, monthly, or day-rover tickets (unlimited travel $10) are available. Limited service to **Palmerston North** is offered by the **Capital Connection** (2hr., M-F 5:17pm, $18), as are trips to **Masterton** on the **Wairarapa Connection** (1½hr., 2-4 per day, $11.50, same-day return $15).

BY BUS

Stagecoach (tel. 387 8700) services the main city and all but its northern suburbs (which are served by Newlands Coach Service). Main line buses run from

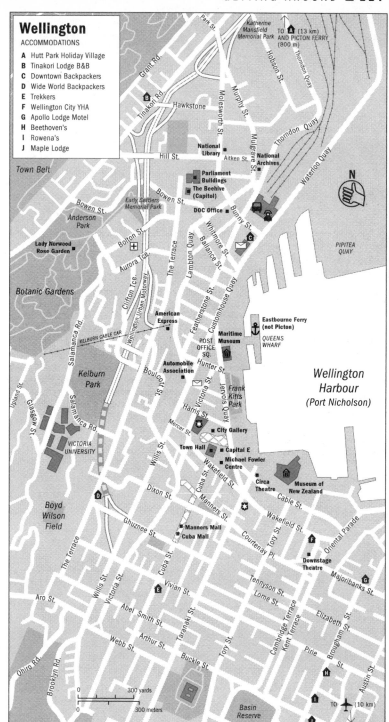

Wellington

ACCOMMODATIONS

A Hutt Park Holiday Village
B Tinakori Lodge B&B
C Downtown Backpackers
D Wide World Backpackers
E Trekkers
F Wellington City YHA
G Apollo Lodge Motel
H Beethoven's
I Rowena's
J Maple Lodge

NORTH ISLAND

6:30am to 11pm daily, while some of the peripheral lines run approximately 7 to 9am and 3 to 6pm. Frequent buses run between the main stops at the Railway Station and the Cambridge Terr. end of Courtenay Pl. The fare in this stretch is $1; beyond it rises by distance. The #1 and 2 run between these points for $1 every 10 to 15 minutes during the day, and every 30 minutes during evenings and weekends. But lots of other buses include this route: #14, 42, 43, 44, and more—just ask the drivers. A **Daytripper ticket** ($5) is valid for an unlimited day of travel on bus (includes two children after 9am). The **City Circular** (tel. 387 8700) runs every 10 minutes from all the major inner-city locations (single ride fare $1; all day $5). **Cityline Hutt Valley** (tel. 569 2933) runs the #81 and 83 buses between Courtenay Pl. and the railway station and around the bay to Petone and Eastbourne every hour during the day (more during peak, fewer on weekend evenings).

BY CAR

Budget (tel. 0800 652 227) and **Hertz** (tel. 0800 654 321) are at the airport. You can often arrange to meet your car at the ferry terminal. **Omega Rentals,** 3 Vivian St. (tel. 0800 667 722), has free pickups and 24-hour AA breakdown assistance. Four days of unlimited mileage for a budget car is $39 per day; an economy car is $49 per day, while a touring car is $59 per day (minimum bond $750). **AA,** 342-352 Lambton Quay by Willis St. (tel. 470 9999), has a **Travel Centre.**

BY TAXI

Taxis line the streets of **Lambton Quay, Courtney Pl.,** and many other drags. If you need to call one, try **Wellington Combined Taxis** (tel. 384 4444) or **Safeway** (tel. 802 5111). A taxi between the Railway Station and downtown costs about $6.

BY BIKE, IN-LINE SKATE, SKI, AND SURFBOARD

Penny Farthing Cycles, 89 Courtenay Pl. (tel. 385 2279), isn't as cheap as its name implies, but has a good selection of rental bikes from September to April with racks, tools, helmets, and locks included ($25 per day; $100 per week). On weekends, **Cheap Skates** (tel. 499 0455) and the **Rollerblade Van** (tel. mobile 025 540 747) park by the wharf opposite New World grocery store at Cambridge Terr. ($10 per hr.). **Mainly Tramping,** 39 Mercer St. (tel. 473 5353), has a full stock of outdoors and camping equipment, with a 10% YHA discount.

WELLINGTON'S WIND

Q: "Do you know why ropes were installed on Lambton Quay?"
A: "To hold on for dear life!"
Jokes such as this and cunning truisms like "You can spot a Wellingtonian anywhere—they walk with a stoop from the wind" point to a fundamental characteristic of New Zealand's capital city. When you ask how long it takes to walk somewhere, the answer depends on whether you're walking upwind or downwind. The worst winds are the Southerlies, bringing their Antarctic chill across the Cook Strait (effectively a massive wind tunnel between the Tasman Sea and the Pacific Ocean). Wellington's reputation was sealed in 1968 when gusts recorded at 167 mph caused the interisland ferry Wahine to founder as it tried to enter the harbor, drowning 51 people. Most locals respond to derogatory comments about the weather with zen-like responses such as "If you want the views and sun, you're going to get wind." In recent years, the city has tried to embrace its reputation with events like the kite-plane-and-flag-filled Wind Festival held for nine days every March. Despite such reconciliations, however, the spring and autumn winds all too often rage with a bluster that surpasses even those gusts of hot air inside the Parliament buildings.

⑦ PRACTICAL INFORMATION

TOURIST AND FINANCIAL SERVICES

Visitors Center: The Wellington Information Centre, 101 Wakefield St. (tel. 802 4860; fax 802 4863), is at the Civic Centre. Reduced price rush tickets to theater shows. Day luggage storage $2. Open daily 9:30am-5:30pm, winter M and W-F 8:30am-5:30pm, Tu 8:30am-5pm, Sa-Su 9:30am-4:30pm. **Airport branches** (tel. 385 5123) meet most incoming flights.

DOC: (tel. 472 7356; fax 471 2075), in the Old Government Building across Lambton Quay from the Beehive. They sell backcountry hut passes, Great Walk passes for the Kahurangi's Heaphy Track, and permits for Kapiti Island.

Budget Travel: Wellington has almost as many travel shops as cafes. **STA Travel,** 37 Willis St. (tel. 472 8510), is near the Lambton Quay end. Open M-F 9am-5:30pm, Sa 10am-1:30pm. **Budget Travel,** 100 Victoria St. (tel. 473 1230), is a block up from the Information Centre. Open M-F 8:30am-5:30pm, Sa 9am-1pm.

Embassies and Consulates: Australia, 72 Hobson St., Thorndon (tel. 473 6411; fax 498 7103), north of the railway station. **U.K.,** 44 Hill St. (tel. 472 6049; fax 473 4982). **Canada,** 61 Molesworth St. (tel. 473 9577; fax 471 2082). **Germany,** 90 Hobson St., Thorndon (tel. 473 6063). **Japan,** (tel. 473 1540; fax 471 2951), corner of Victoria and Hunter St., off Lambton Quay in the Norwich Insurance House. **U.S.,** 29 Fitzherbert Terr., Thorndon (tel. 472 2068; fax 472 9804).

Currency Exchange: In the main downtown areas, you're never more than a mad dash from an ATM or bank. **BNZ,** 100 Lambton Quay (tel. 495 2632) and 38-44 Courtenay Pl. (tel. 801 2650). Open M-F 9am-4:30pm. **Thomas Cook,** 358 Lambton Quay (tel. 472 2848), near Willis St. Open M-F 9am-5:30pm, Sa 9:30am-1pm.

American Express: 280-292 Lambton Quay, P.O. Box 10182 (tel. 473 7766 or 0800 801 122), in the Cable Car Complex. They hold mail—no parcels—for members for up to 30 days. Open M-Tu and Th-F 9am-5pm, W 9:30am-5pm.

LOCAL SERVICES

Bookstores: Lambton Quay has most of the big chain stores. Cuba St. is littered with small second-hand shops or stores specializing in New Age. Specialty shops include **Unity Books,** 57 Willis St. (tel. 499 4245, fax 499 4246). Open M-Th 9am-6pm, F 9am-8pm, Sa 10am-4pm, Su 11am-4pm. **The Map Shop** (tel. 385 1462), at Vivian and Victoria St., rocks your tramping world with a complete set of New Zealand park, city, and topographical maps. Open M-F 8am-5:30pm, Sa 10am-1pm. **Out! Bookshop,** 15 Tory St. (tel. 385 4400), has a wide array of gay-oriented magazines and other items. Open M-Sa noon-11pm, Su noon-9pm.

Library: The **Wellington Public Library** (tel. 801 4040) is a stylish space with cafe and **Internet.** Open M-Th 9:30am-8:30pm, F 9:30am-9pm, Sa 9:30am-5pm, Su 1-4pm.

Bi-Gay-Lesbian Organizations: Gay Switchboard (tel. 385 0674) runs daily 7:30-10pm and provides support and info on the Wellington scene. It's also a contact point for other area groups like **Icebreakers,** a young gay/bi social group. **Lesbian Line** (tel. 389 8082) answers queries Tu, Th, and Sa 7:30-10pm. The **Express** paper has info on Wellington's gay scene, and can be picked up from the Wellington YHA.

EMERGENCY AND COMMUNICATIONS

Emergency: Dial **111.**

Police: 39 Victoria St. (tel. 472 3000), near the Harris St. cross.

Hotlines: AIDS hotline (24hr. tel. 0800 802 437). **Rape and Sexual Abuse Support Hotline** (24hr. tel. 499 7532), run by the Help Foundation.

Medical Services: The David Donald Pharmacy (tel. 499 1466), at the corner of Cuba and Manners St. Open M-Th 8:30am-6pm, F 8:30am-9pm, Sa 9:30am-6pm, Su 10am-6pm. **Wellington Accident and Urgent Medical Center,** 17 Adelaide Rd. (tel. 384 4944), by the Basin Reserve, has a doctor on duty 24hr., and a pharmacy next door (tel. 385 8810); open M-F 5-11pm, Sa-Su 9am-11pm. The **hospital** (tel. 385 5999) is in southern Wellington on Riddiford St.

Post Office: Scattered throughout the city. Only the main Post Shop (tel. 496 4068) across from the railway station on Waterloo Quay holds *Poste Restante* (tel. 496 4951). Open M-F 7am-5:30pm, Sa 9am-12:30pm.

Internet Access: Net Arena Computers, 115 Cuba St. (tel. 385 2240) charges $1.50 per 6min.; the **Wellington Public Library,** $5 per 30min.; and **Moving Planet,** 10 Majoribanks St. (tel. 801 8119) $9 per hr.

TELEPHONE CODE	The telephone code for all of Wellington is **04.**

ACCOMMODATIONS

Wellington has several satisfactory backpackers, all within walking distance of the city, although the **Broughman St.** offerings are a bit farther. From the Railway Station, the #1 bus (among others) goes to the end of Courtenay Pl.; from there, cross Cambridge and Kent Terr. and walk up the hill about a block to Brougham St. Or take the #2, which goes all the way to Brougham St. Even cheaper accommodations can be found among the old wooden hill houses of the **Mt. Victoria** area in the quieter south end (15min. walk from Lambton Quay/Civic Centre area, 5min. from Courtenay Pl.). Call ahead all times of the year.

Wellington City YHA (tel. 801 7280; fax 801 7278; email yhawgtn@yha.org.nz), at the corner of Cambridge Terr. and Wakefield St., a 15min. walk from the Railway Station. Super Shuttle stops here on its way to the ferry ($5) and the airport ($8). In a hulking six- (soon to be eight-) story former hotel, the hostel is well located near Courtenay Pl. nightlife, and many rooms have harbor vistas. Outstanding organization, cleanliness, and convenience compensate for the lack of atmosphere. Supermarket across the street, Internet, and travel desk. 4-bed bunks $19; 6-bed dorms $17; doubles with a view $46; family rooms $58. $4 extra for nonmembers.

Wide World Backpackers, 291 The Terrace (tel. (050) 888 555, fax (04) 802 5591; email wideworld@paradise.co.nz), at Ghuznee St. Newly renovated from the old Terrace Lodge, this rejuvenated cottage is infused with the energy of its new owner. Springy mattresses, and desks (in some rooms), TVs, and sinks fill the clean space between colorful walls; but it's the extras that make Wide World standout. Complimentary breakfast (8-10am) complemented by complimentary wine (6-6:30pm). Free local calls. Spa bath. Internet. Key deposit $10. Dorms $16; singles $40; twins and doubles $40.

Maple Lodge, 52 Ellice St. (tel. 385 3771), around the corner from Brougham St. One of Mt. Victoria's small and old wooden houses, the quietly informal Maple Lodge is off the tourist loop, but features a homey atmosphere and affable manager. Reception 8:30am-noon and after 5pm. Dorms $17; singles $20; twins $36; doubles $38.

Beethoven's, 89 Brougham St. (tel. 384 2226). If the candid, hand-printed signs posted everywhere or the complicated entry don't warn you that this place isn't for everyone, then the eccentric owner likely will himself. Once you've been accepted into this cluttered turn-of-the-century house, you may be in for an unforgettable experience. Yawn and stretch down the stairs at 8am for the superb complimentary breakfast and compulsory "good morning" greeting in the garden patio. At night get to know fellow guests even better through the window slit in the shower room door (sign encourages bathers to towel dry in view of passers-by). Dorms $16-17; doubles $38. Cash only.

Trekkers (Nomads), 213 Cuba St. (tel. 385 2153; fax 385 8873; email info@trekkers.co.nz). The views of fire escapes and "Liks" Strip bar next door may not entice every trekker, but this warren of long, branching hallways and bare-walled bunkrooms is wonderfully central. Communal space and kitchen facilities may be lacking, but most everyone congregates in the popular cafe or bar downstairs (Th-F 7-8pm; $2 handles). Reception 24hr. Bunks $19; twins $21. Hotel rooms with bath and TV: singles $59; twins $79. Motel rooms with bath, kitchenette, and TV: triples $89; quads $99.

Rowena's (VIP), 115 Brougham St. (tel. 385 7872 or 0800 801 414; email rowenas@iconz.co.nz). With a giant kiwi statue in the front garden, this white house on a hill offers great balcony views and small, adequate rooms. Internet, TV lounge, smoky pool room, and piano. Free shuttle service to ferry, buses, trains, and hitching points. Off-street parking. Breakfast $5. Key deposit $10. Dorms $18; singles $25; doubles with sheets $44; tent sites $10.

Downtown Backpackers (VIP), 1 Bunny St. (tel. 473 8482; fax 471 1073), across from the Railway Station. While it's close to transport terminals, Downtown is on the other side of town from many of Wellington's bars and restaurants. Formerly the grand Waterloo Hotel, most of the elegance has faded away. Free pickup from the ferry. Mega kitchen facilities, cafe, lounges, and in-house bar (open from 5pm; Th night pool competitions). Internet. Reception 24hr. Bunks $18; singles $35; twins $42; doubles $45.

Tinakori Lodge B&B, 182 Tinakori Rd. (tel. 473 3478; fax 472 5554), in Thorndon. From railway station, turn right on Bunny St., follow it through Molesworth St., and turn left on Hawkestone; the lodge is at the top of the street. With leaded glass windows, inviting courtyard, solarium, and airy white rooms, the Tinakori is the home you wish were yours. Breakfast is an extravaganza. Singles $70, with bath $90; twins and doubles $95, with bath $125.

Apollo Lodge Motel, 49 Majoribanks St. (tel./fax 385 1846), at the end of Brougham St. The typical cinderblock-and-sliding-glass-door rooms are routine; brightly painted "pink block" rooms have a fresher feel and benchtop cooking facilities. A third option are the classy colonial-style rooms with wooden banisters, fireplaces, and wall windows. Off-street parking. Twins and doubles $100; family rooms $140.

Hutt Park Holiday Village, 95 Hutt Park Rd. (tel. 568 5913; fax 568 5914), in Lower Hutt some 13km from Wellington. By far the closest motorcamp, it's mostly a pass-through stay for ferry-catchers. Kitchen, TVs, trampolines, playground, and spa pool. Pohutukawa-lined tent sites for 2 $19; powered $21; small, basic cinderblock cabin units for 2 $32; nicer tourist cabins with kitchen $42, extra person $8-11.

■ **Paekakariki Backpackers,** 11 Wellington Rd. (tel. (04) 292 8749), 40 minutes from Wellington on the Kapiti Coast. Just a block form the Paekakariki train station, a steep winding tiled path leads to this quiet seaside cottage with breathtaking views of wind-swept hills and waves which roll nearly to the doorstep. Quality rooms, with comfortable lounge, kitchen area, and spotless bathrooms. Hop the stone steps by the small pond to visit with laid-back hosts Peter and Denise, and their zoo of pets—4 cats, 2 friendly yellow dogs, an axolott, and a cockateel. Dorms $15; twins $38; doubles $36, with bath $40; tent sites $9. Call ahead.

◖ FOOD

Wellington boasts a global menu with a preponderance of Chinese, Malaysian, Thai, and Indian food. **Lambton Quay** and **Willis St.** are full of lunch spots, but are rather dead at night. The fashionable length of **Courtenay Pl.** is where Lambton Quay's young and coiffed migrate on evenings and weekends, while **Cuba St.** is riddled with smaller, cheaper, ethnic restaurants and cafes. You'll find groceries at **New World** supermarket on Wakefield St., at the corner with Cambridge Terr. (open daily 8am-10pm). **Cuba Fruit Mart,** 168 Cuba St. (tel. 385 0634), is a fruit and veggie wholesaler (open M-F 7am-6pm, Sa-Su 8am-1:30pm). And the early—*very* early— Saturday morning **Porirua market** (5am-9am) is well worth the sleep deprivation, with everything Polynesian under the sun for dirt cheap prices. Take the train into Porirua, and you'll see it buzzing—right by McDonald's.

Ali Baba, 203 Cuba St. (tel. 384 3014). Gorgeous rugs adorning the walls, floor, and ceiling cuddle you into Ali Baba's cozy den. Soothing Turkish rhythms lull you into your low cushion seat. But as relaxed as you may be, not even the most skillful 40 thieves could steal away your kebab once you've had a bite. Doners come in 3 bulging sizes ($5-10). Take your gold-rimmed basket and hunker down to a feast. Open M-Th 11am-10pm, F-Sa 11am-midnight, Su noon-10pm.

Kopi, 103 Willis St. (tel. 499 5570). Manager James has built a strong local following who obviously know good food when they eat it. Two floors of full tables and steaming Malaysian dishes, such as the deliciously tender lamb korma ($13.50) and Nasi Paging ($14.50). Get there early or be prepared for a wait. Open daily 10am-late.

One Red Dog, 9-11 Blair St. (tel. 384 9777), off Courtenay Pl. The menu jokingly claims locations in Paris and London, but judging from the crowds, it's not just wishful thinking. There's never a dull bite into these thick pizzas with intriguing toppings (medium $15.40, large $23.50). Call ahead or expect a wait. Open daily from 10am.

Sahara Kebab, 39 Courtenay Pl. (tel. 385 6351). Like the African desert, Sahara's kebabs are large, hot, and...finger-licking good. OK, it's not a perfect analogy. Takeaway lamb ($5), chicken ($7), and falafel ($5) doners. Open M-Tu 10am-midnight, W-Th 10am-2am, F-Sa 24hr. Cash only.

Uncle Chang's Restaurant, 72 Courtenay Pl. (tel. 801 9568; fax 384 1003). The banal name and overdone decor belie original and flavorful dishes, especially the Sichuan specialties ($14.50). Lunch includes carefully prepared entrees from spring rolls to beef rolls ($4-4.50). Open daily for lunch and dinner.

Catch Sushi, 48 Courtenay Pl. (tel. 801 9352), next to Cafe Babba. A sharp young crowd of suits crowds the long table at lunch to snag salmon and yellow tail rolls off the belt. The belt dinners add up quickly if you're not counting; try the $12 sashimi set with miso soup, rice, and a selection of fish. Takeaway available: an $8 set has 8 pieces of varying size. Open M-F 11:30am-2:30pm and from 5pm, Sa from 5pm only.

Wellington Fish Supply, 40 Molesworth St. (tel. 472 4055), just across from Parliament. For 60 years this little blue shop in an ancient red building has sustained a tradition of ruling-class fish 'n' chips. Lick your fingers and know that Parliament's bills are stained with the same grease. Takeaways have been so popular with politicians over the years that some Labor MPs in the 1980s were known as the "Fish 'n' Chips brigade." A sizeable, fresh fish 'n' chips is $3. Open M-Th 9am-7:30pm, F 9am-9pm, Sa 9am-7:30pm.

Bandong Country Food, 134 Cuba St. (tel. 384 5489). Not much delicacy here, but it's still one of the better values around; nothing on the menu is over $9. Open for lunch M-F 11am-2:30pm and 5-10pm, Sa noon-2:30pm and 5-10:30pm, Su 5-9:30pm.

CAFES

Cafes are designated as such because they emphasize coffee and drinks, but many satiate hunger as well as thirst, serving up excellent and affordable food.

The Krazy Lounge (tel. 801 6652), at the corner of Cuba and Ghuznee St. With a large paper-mache cow and whale making an unlikely couple in the loft overhead, soft techno-trance rhythms restrain the wackiness. In a black-leather booth, nod to the beat over a frothy mug of mochacino ($3.50), hot breakfast (from $10), or fruit-loaded muffin ($3). Open M-F 7:30am-late, Sa-Su 9am-late.

Eva Dixon's Place, 35 Dixon St. (tel. 384 100). Entrance through alley. Tucked away on the second floor of the corner building at Eva and Dixon St. Excellent eggs, piping hot pancakes ($6-10), and plump, steaming muffins ($2.50) reward the coffee-and tea-drinking crowd who find this delightful cafe. Subtle splashes of color and simple decorations on the wall respectfully yield to a captivating view of city and sky. Open M-F 7:30am-11pm, Sa 8:30am-late, Su 9am-late.

Tree House Cafe, 123 Cuba St. (tel. 385 0887), upstairs above Narnia. Escape into the comfortable loft space you dreamed of building as a kid. The vegetarian-friendly food (around $5) and quality coffee ($2.50) are almost superfluous as you retreat for the day with your book, or enjoy the nightly activity of live music and biweekly poetry readings. Open M-F 9am-late, Sa-Su 10am-late.

Midnight Espresso, 178 Cuba (tel. 384 7014), by the corner of Cuba and Vivian St. A paper-mache angel watches over the entrance, but you can ash on the well-worn floors and not worry if anyone sees you. Time stands still in this cafe, fixed by the constant presence of good music, the steady glow of the Indiana Jones pinball game, and laid-back students. Coffee ($3), fresh juices from Lucky's Juice Joint's side of the counter ($2.50). Open daily until 3am.

The Lido (tel. 499 6666), corner of Wakefield and Victoria St., near the Civic Centre. Windows wrap nearly all the way around this upscale cafe, with a peninsular bar that tames corrugated metal for a classy effect. The Lido has table service, outdoor seating, and great Sunday night jazz. Open M-F 7:30am-1am, Sa 9:30am-1am, Su 10am-1am.

Ed's Juice Bar, 95 Victoria St. (tel. 478 1769). Savor thick, irresistible fruit smoothies blended from fresh peaches, apricots, bananas, boysenberries, pears, feijoas and more. Outdoor seating. Open 6:30am-6:30pm. Cash only.

Espressoholic, 128 Courtenay Pl. (tel. 384 7799), by Taranaki St. With subterranean inspiration, it's often rush hour here; office crowds line the walls during the day, chowing $9 burgers or jumpstarting their veins with $3.50 lattes. At night, an eclectic crowd of locals, students, artsy twentysomethings, and bar-hoppers soak up espresso and chatter away to the techno beat. Open Su-Th 7:30am-midnight, F-Sa 7:30am-3:30am.

◪ NIGHTLIFE

The cosmopolitan nightlife of Wellington sustains a noticeable split between business chic and skater cool. The **Courtenay Pl.** stretch is clogged with stylishly slick bars frequented by suits; most are indistinguishable from one another. For those who aren't fond of rock remixes, the pubs on **Cuba St.** and the nearby blocks tend to be just as crowded but more relaxed. While Wellington party life centers mainly around bars and pubs, the weekend rush to the late-night clubs begins at 3am (when all the pubs close) and lasts until 5 or 6am. For all the latest happenings, grab the free weekly *Capital Times* or *City Voice* from newsstands or check cafes for fliers.

▨ Molly Malones (tel. 384 2896), on the corner of Courtenay Pl. and Taranaki St. Every hour is Happy Hour at this popular pub with live Irish and cover bands every night for no charge. If the $5 draft beer isn't strong enough for you, there's a sit-down Whiskey Bar upstairs offering 107 different reasons to give yourself a kick in the pants. Tidy but casual dress. Open daily 11am-late, Su until 1am.

▨ Tatou, 22 Cambridge Terr. (tel. 384 3112), near the corner of Courtenay Pl. and Cambridge Terr.; entrance under a green awning. This leading wee-hours option holds Wellington's latest liquor license. Throbbing techno and strobe lights sustain many until sunrise. There's a big rush when the bars close at 3am. Tidy dress. $5 cover after midnight. No cover on Thursdays. Open Th-Sa 9pm-8am.

Bar Bodega (tel. 384 8212), at the corner of Willis and Abel Smith St. There are only a few lounge chairs and back tables in this small space with dim lighting and low ceilings, but come grab a stool for some of the best live music in town. Bodega features local or touring bands Tu-Sa nights, and an eclectic but leaning-toward-alternative crowd fills the house most nights. Cover charge up to $5 on weekends. Champagne $2.50. 10pm-midnight on Tuesdays. Handles $4. Bar snacks available. Open daily 4pm-3am.

Valve (tel. 385 1630), on Vivian St. by Cuba St. Entrance to this windowless dive is, as advertised, through a knocked-out hole in the brick. Decidedly anti-cosmopolitan, inside are the strutting grounds for the young, pierced, and studiously cool members of Wellington's alternative scene. Rock and dance music usually reigns, with live bands (usually $5 cover) and Thursday night DJ. $2 handles Tuesdays. Open M-Sa 8pm-3am.

The Grand, 69-71 Courtenay Pl. (tel. 801 7800). This 4-floor giant is the current multimedia King of the Boulevard: a restaurant, lounge bar, pool hall, and dance floor in one. Quality food, comfortable couches, and popular music attract a diverse crowd, but the constant flux from floor to floor diffuses fleeting pockets of atmosphere. Tidy dress with shoes. Open daily 11am-3am.

The Matterhorn, 106 Cuba Mall (tel. 384 3359). Walk down the long dark hallway and enter the realm of the Matterhorn—a small, hip lounge bar with sit-down tables and a late-night DJ in the corner. Good for a laid-back night of conversation. $5 beers, $3.50 coffees, and a selection of tapas from $6. Open M-Sa 11:30am-3am, Su 5:30pm-3am.

Bo Jangles, 60 Dixon St. (tel. 384 8445). The most well-known gay nightclub—the *only* one in Wellington, according to the owner. Except for a bar stretching along the far wall with stools to take a break on, this place is all dance floor. Beers $4, spirits $5; DJs W-F, Happy Hour Tu-Th all night. Open Tu-W 5pm-2am, Th-F 5pm-5am, Sa 6pm-5am.

🎵 ENTERTAINMENT

Downstage (tel. 801 6946), at the corner of Courtenay Pl. and Cambridge Terr. by the YHA. Wide range of productions from classic and modern drama to cabaret and comedy. Tickets usually around $27, students $20, gallery seats $15.

Circa (tel. 801 7992), at the end of Taranaki St. next to the Museum of New Zealand. Mainstage plays and a studio with smaller, more experimental shows and cheaper prices. Tickets $25, students $19. Ticket office open M-Sa 10am-4pm, or from 4pm until 1hr. before the show.

Bats, 1 Kent Terr. (tel. 802 4175), is the most experimental, on-the-fringe venue, putting on exclusively New Zealand productions—you won't stumble into any of the classics here. Tickets $15-18, students or unwaged $10-15.

The West Pac St. James Theatre, 77-87 Courtenay Pl. (tel. 802 4060). Recently restored Edwardian lyric theater, home to the Royal New Zealand Ballet as well as opera and musicals. Show prices vary.

State Opera House, 111-113 Manners St. (tel. 384 3840), puts on everything but opera—ventriloquists, bands, and Spice Girl lookalikes have been known to entertain here. Prices range from $15-60 depending on the act.

Wellington Festival and Convention Centre (tel. 801 4242), stages mostly lectures and classical and chamber music concerts at the Michael Fowler Centre and other venues ($6 service charge for phone bookings). Book through **Ticketek,** 111 Wakefield St. (tel. 384 3840).

Cinemas: Paramount, 25 Courtenay Pl. (tel. 384 4488), dishes out arthouse cinema fare, as does **Rialto** (tel. 385 1864) on Cable St. and Jervois Quay. **Embassy** (tel. 384 7657), at the far end of Courtenay Pl., shows mainstream Hollywood flicks. **Hoyt 5** (tel. 472 5182) and **Midcity** (tel. 384 3567) are both located at Manners Mall.

👁 SIGHTS

The capital city since the government moved from Auckland in 1865, Wellington houses Parliament, the National Library, and other architecturally notable public buildings that, when in the focus of a disposable camera, could yield an important government official heading out for a lunch break. Complementing these gubernatorial highlights, the city's grandiose gardens, creative museums, and beautiful, shimmering harbor are guaranteed to put some wind in your sightseeing sails.

CIVIC CENTRE

With an impressive collection of public buildings, Wellington's **Civic Centre** clusters around a bricked space that makes for fine people-watching on sunny weekends. At one side sits the elegant **City Gallery** (tel. 801 3021), which showcases contemporary exhibitions with both national and international artists of top caliber (open daily 10am-5pm; admission $3-5, with bigger name expositions up to $10). In the far corner of the Civic Centre is the huge, circular **Michael Fowler Centre** (tel. 811 4242), an events and conference center. Inside are the two towering modern Maori pillars, *Te Pou O Wi Tako* and *Te Pou o Taviwi*, dedicated to the people of the land and to visitors, respectively.

Just under the base of the bridge sits **Capital E** (tel. 384 8502), a new children's center with constantly changing Events, Exhibitions, and Experiences for *les Enfants* (open daily 10am-5pm; admission varies with events). Cross the bridge to the harborfront and the green public space of **Frank Kitts Park.** Just past the railway station on the harborfront, Wellington's brand new **stadium,** nicknamed "The Tank" for its metallic outer shell, hosts sporting and musical events.

PARLIAMENT

Another of Wellington's visual attractions (or distractions, as the case may be) is the government building known as the **Beehive,** home to the offices of the Prime Minister and other bigwigs. This monstrosity of 70s architecture is striking on the outside, but the interior is closed to the public. Serving as a landmark for Parliament, the hive might actually be moved a few hundred yards to extend and complete the missing wing of the Edwardian Neoclassical **Parliament House.** At any time of year, the **Visitor Centre** (tel. 471 9503) on the ground floor offers free tours every hour of the grounds and buildings that would otherwise be off-limits. See sights like the carefully designed Maori Affairs Select Committee Room and the huge art installation representing New Zealand's cultural traditions. The gorgeously ornate **Victorian Gothic Parliamentary Library,** restored from a 1992 fire, is part of the tour as well. You can even send a letter postmarked "Parliament" from here. Groups of 10 or more must call ahead for tours. To see the House in action, it's a good idea to get a schedule in advance. (Open M-F 10am-4pm, Sa 10am-3pm, Su 1-3pm.)

LIBRARIES AND CATHEDRALS

Across Molesworth St. and up a bit is the **National Library** (tel. 474 3000). It houses over 1.8 million books, including the **Cartoon Archives,** the **Gay and Lesbian Archives** (open M-F 9am-5pm), and the **Alexander Turnbull Library** with its collection of early printed materials, extensive photographic archives, and occasional exhibitions in the gallery. (Open M-F 9am-5pm, Sa 9am-1pm for research and gallery only.) Around the corner are the **National Archives,** 10 Mulgrave St. (tel. 499 5595), and the dimly lit, thick-walled, guarded vault in which the original copy of the 1840 Treaty of Waitangi is kept (open M-F 9am-5pm, Sa 9am-1pm). A short walk away are two tourist-attracting churches. For history buffs, the 1866 **Former Pro-Cathedral** (tel. 473 6722) is the old colonial church that housed worshippers while the real St. Paul's was being built. Although the superb stained-glass windows and structure of this little church conform to gothic style, the medium of choice is native New Zealand timber, not stone. On the other side of the library, just next to Parliament, towers Wellington's recently completed, salmon-colored **St. Paul's Cathedral** (tel. 472 0286). Built in Byzantine style with rounded arches, this impressive building dwarfs its predecessors.

MUSEUMS

Like a massive father figure encouraging your first stumbling steps as a tourist in Wellington, this enormous complex of informative and entertaining exhibits on the harborfront seems to bellow, "Come Te Papa." Just at the end of Taranaki St.

is the two-year-old ☒**Museum of New Zealand Te Papa Tongarewa** (tel. 381 7000). Te Papa, as it's affectionately called, is Wellington's pride and joy. An ambitious attempt to both celebrate and reconcile the country's identity while still packing in the crowds, Te Papa opened its doors in February 1998 and reached its first anniversary goal of 700,000 visitors in just four months. Free admission may be Te Papa's first appeal, but enjoyable exhibits on New Zealand's land, history, culture, and art are the real attractions. For slightly stiffer fees, try the interactive exhibits: a virtual earthquake, a virtual swim with whales, virtual sheep-shearing (complete with virtual blood if you do a bad job), a virtual bungy jump, and the virtual "Time Warp" that takes you through prehistoric, moa-laden New Zealand and ends by shooting you up out of a volcano. It's virtual insanity. (Museum open daily 10am-6pm, Th until 9pm. Free, but a helpful floor-map costs $1.)

Just up Jervois Quay from the Civic Centre sits the **Museum of Wellington City and Sea,** constructed in 1891. Stalwart ship-lovers will be captivated by its extensive and somewhat disturbing ship models. (Open M-F 9:30am-4pm, Sa-Su 1-4:30pm. Admission $5, children $2.50.)

Literature lovers can nudge up their reading glasses and head up Molesworth St. to the painstakingly restored **Katherine Mansfield Birthplace,** 25 Tinakori Rd. (tel. 473 7268), where New Zealand's beloved short story writer spent her first six years. A narrated display fills you in on Mansfield's private life as it influenced her work, and an elaborate dollhouse based entirely on one of her story's descriptions has been carefully constructed; strong debate apparently raged over what shade "oily spinach green" should be. (Open daily 10am-4pm. Admission $5, children $2; student discounts and guided tours available.) **The Colonial Cottage Museum,** 68 Nairn St. (tel. 384 9122), dates from 1858, 30 years prior to the Mansfield Birthplace and not long after Wellington was settled by Europeans (open M-F 10am-4pm and Sa-Su 1-4pm; admission $3). Catch the #83 Eastbourne bus to Queensgate from Courtenay Pl. to get to **Lower Hutt's Dowse Art Museum,** 35-45 Laings Rd. (tel. 570 6500), presenting one of the country's best collections of craftwork (open M-F 10am-4pm, Sa-Su 11am-5pm; admission free). If you miss the thwack of the national past-time, the **Cricket Museum** (tel. 385 6602 or 384 3171), in the Basin Reserve grandstand, offers a historical perspective and lots of old bats (open daily 10am-3:30pm, winter M-F 10am-3:30pm; admission $3, children $1).

GARDENS AND TOURS

Similarities between Wellington and San Francisco may come to mind when you ride the **Wellington Cable Car** (tel. 472 2199), 610m up to the Kelburn Terminal (departs every 10min. from Cable Car Ln. on Lambton Quay, M-F 7am-10pm, Sa-Su 9am-10pm; $1.50, students $1, children 70¢). Unload atop the city's impressive 26-hectare public ☒**Botanic Gardens** and follow one of the many paths that snake around from herb garden to children's playground to planetarium with canopied views of the city and hills in the distance. The gardens are always open, though some special spots, like the **Lady Norwood Rose Garden,** with hundreds of different kinds of roses blossoming out from a central fountain, have special hours (open daily 10am-4pm). Walk down the lush length of the gardens and follow Bolton St. out to the terrace and downtown. Anyone with a botanical bent should also check out the **Otari Native Botanic Garden** (tel. 475 3245; take the #14 Wilton bus).

In addition to the Botanic Gardens, splendid views are to be had from atop ☒**Mt. Victoria,** rising from the city's south end. If you're not up for the 30-minute hike, you can drive or take bus #20 (M-F). Some locals say that the view from the **ECNZ wind turbine** is even better. Take bus #7 from the Railway Station or Willis St. up to the shops on Brooklyn St.; there are signposts from there. It's a steep climb.

Guided city **tours** cater to those with more money and less time. The Information Centre has a full list of operators, but a guaranteed good one is **Wally Hammond's**

Wellington Scenic Tours (tel. 472 0869). Whether it's Wally himself or one of his six drivers that picks you up from your hostel or motel, you'll enjoy views of the whole city through large, clear windows, enhanced by colorful tidbits of history and lore over a loudspeaker. The 2½hr. City Tour (2 per day) is $25. Wally also tours the Kapiti Coast and the Wairarapa. A lot of people enjoy bike tours of the city; to get a little extra push, use **Mountainbike Tours** (tel. 0800 628 687), providing you with a detailed route, helmet, gloves, repair kit, and bike for the day for $25. Every weekend, the harborfront is decorated with giggling green streaks—the trail of sparking, speeding tour bikes rented out by **The Enormous Crocodile Company** (tel. 380 9128). After looking both ways, venture down to the wharf to rent a ride on the covered carts (2-seater $15 per hr., 4-seater with 2 child baskets $25 per hr.; available Sa-Su 10am-sundown).

Turn the scenic views around by taking the **WestpacTrust Ferry** (tel. 499 1273), a cheap and excellent way to get out onto the harbor. Full of Wellingtonians escaping the city, it leaves from Queens Wharf (M-F 8 per day, Sa-Su 5 per day) and crosses to the little cafe-and-antique-shop community of **Day's Bay** ($7), with its small but popular swimming beach. A bit farther down is the village of **Eastbourne,** similarly bedecked with cafes, little blue penguins, and a pebbly, narrow beach good for wandering. The ferry also stops at **Somes Island** (M-F noon, Sa-Su 3 per day). A former quarantine island with historical significance, the smallpox and rats have now been eradicated, and DOC is developing the island's potential as a wildlife sanctuary. It's a good three-hour getaway with not much to do but picnic, wander the revegetating bush, and admire a 360° panorama of Wellington.

⚑ ACTIVITIES

Although Wellington is better known for its cultural options, this being New Zealand, there are plenty of outdoor opportunities. The **Northern, Southern,** and **Eastern Walkways,** laid out in leaflets from the Visitor Centre or DOC office, are tame and accessible walks through the city's greenbelt and coastline. The **Red Rocks Coastal Walk** is a terrific 8km return trip along the jagged southern coastline, past the pillow lava formation of Red Rocks. The walk then heads out to the crashing surf of **Sinclair Head,** where, in winter, a colony of fat fur seals is sure to be lazing around. Get a 4WD ride from **Red Rocks Seal Tour** (tel. 862 4860; 2½ hr., $30).

Oriental Beach, though popular with city dwellers, is less a beach than a grassy strip of peopled promenade overlooked by trendy cafes. Better beaches can be found on the east side of **Miramar Peninsula.** In the **Seatown** area, Scorching Bay is reputed to be a good one; **Lyall Bay** has a patrolled main swimming stretch and relatively consistent surfing breaks at the airport end. Seatown beaches are within walking distance of the #2 Miramar bus. Along the southern coastline the bays are rockier and rougher: **Island Bay,** and particularly **Houghton Bay** and **Owhiro Bay,** are better for surfing and scuba diving than for safe swimming. Wellington **surfing** is rather wind-dependent: winter southerlies make for stronger waves, but breaks are more consistent east of the Wairarapa towns of Martinborough and Masterton. Get a list of outdoor outfitters from the Visitor Centre, but be aware that most true adventure destinations are a fair distance from the city.

Sailing with **Phantom of the Straits** (tel. 477 5303) provides a one-and-a-half hour harbor trip for $35, and a **return trip** to the South Island for $185. And a bit further from the city, **Venturebound Tours** (tel. mobile 025 656 879) provides transportation to and from their all day **rafting** trip down the Waiohine river ($70 including all equipment). **Rock-climbing** and **rap jumping** will clear your touring palate, at **Top Adventures,** 453 Hutt Rd. (tel. 477 1420 or 589 9181), Lower Hutt. Nearly 20 meters of gravitational pull is just a 20-minute drive and $22 away.

FESTIVALS

January looked at July: "Whatcha got?" March upped the ante. And then November held firm. The annual competition between the months for best festival is always intense and the cards for the 2000 pot are on the table. January and February combine their hands for the **Summer City Festival,** a brilliant parade of concerts, celebrations, and events like Sunday night jazz in the Botanic Gardens, mass walks up Mt. Victoria, and a Pacific Island festival. March's ace is the **Fringe Festival,** an annual theatrical event that celebrates alternative and experimental artistic shows. April plays the joker with the ASB Bank **Laugh! Festival,** showcasing comedians from inside and outside New Zealand. Just when it looks the game is up, July presents the **Kings and Queens of the Silver Screen** in the annual **Wellington Film Festival.** And, last but hardly least, November's week-long **Devotion Festival,** a celebration of Wellington's gay and lesbian community, may make you flush, if not straight.

AROUND WELLINGTON

KAPITI COAST

Zippidy-doo-dah, Kapiti Coast! My oh my this is the coast with the most. With plenty of sunshine and beaches to boast—Zippidy doo dah, Kapiti Coast!

Once you've mastered this *Let's Go* original song and the Kiwi pronunciation (completely discard associations with Tahiti), embark on the 40-minute drive to Wellington's scenic weekend getaway. Small wildlife sanctuaries, beautiful beaches, and the centerpiece—wild, bird-filled Kapiti Island—liven the 32km coast, with one-stop towns and tourist attractions along the way. Easily accessible by the Wellington train or national buses, the coast makes for a good daytrip or a quiet weekend away from the city.

Several Wellington tour operators do Kapiti; **Wally Hammond's** (tel. 472 0869) takes you through the natural attractions and stops at all of the tourist spots that are inaccessible by public transport (2 trips per day, $55). **Tranz Metro** (see p. 226) gets you to Paekokinki, Paraparaumu, and back in a day. Also, there's a fair amount of regional traffic all the way from Otaki to Paekakariki, and **hitchers** have a good chance of bumming a ride. The **telephone code** for the Kapiti Coast is 04.

KAPITI ISLAND

Once the stronghold of Te Rauparaha and an anchorage for whalers, Kapiti Island has been cleansed of exotic mammals as part of a stunning experiment in floral and avian regeneration. Intensive trapping in the 1980s eradicated over 22,000 possums from the island (which is under 2000 hectares to begin with). Thus unmunched, the forests immediately shot upward. Then, on a single day in 1996, helicopter-dropped poison bait took care of every last predatory rat; since then, bird populations have skyrocketed, and the DOC has introduced several highly endangered native species to make their last stand here. Kapiti Island is one of the only wild and accessible places in New Zealand where you're practically guaranteed to see takahe and kaka, whole flocks of melodious tui, and perhaps one of the last saddlebacks or kokako.

Kapiti Island lies about 5km offshore from Paraparaumu Beach; the nature reserve contains toilets, a shelter, three tracks, and no other amenities. The **DOC** limits access to the island to 50 people per day, and requires a permit ($8, children $4); book with the **Wellington Office,** PO Box 5086 (tel. 427 7356; fax 471

2075), or the boat operators. Spaces fill up far in advance between December and February, especially during the weekend slots, but there's often last-minute availability on weekdays; in winter, there can be too *few* visitors for the boats to run. **Kapiti Island Alive!** (tel. 0800 527 484 or 237 7965) and **Kapiti Marine Charter** (tel. 297 2585 or mobile 025 424 850) both run daily from Paraparaumu Beach to the island (15min., 9am and 9:30am according to numbers, return $30). From Wellington, only the 6:55am **Tranz Metro** (tel. 801 7000; $7.50) reaches Paraparaumu in time to catch the 7:55am **Mana Coach** (tel. 0800 801 700; 10min., $1.60), which is the latest to arrive at Paraparaumu Beach before the 9am boats leave; service is more limited on weekends. All visitors receive an informative nature talk upon arrival at the island, and must catch the boats back to the mainland at around 3pm.

PAEKAKARIKI

At the southern point of the Kapiti Coast, Paekakariki is somewhat less flashy than its name, "resting place of the green parakeet." The colorful little birds were driven out by European colonization, and Kiwis have since informally shortened the name to "Paekak." The town's main street spans only a few blocks, but residential areas string out along its long golden strip of shell-filled beach. **Tranz Metro** (tel. 498 3000) trains from Wellington stop here frequently (45min., $6), as do **Newmans** and **InterCity** buses on request ($14). For accommodations, consider the wonderful ▨**Paekakariki Backpacker** (see p. 231). One of the best things about Paekakariki is getting there: if you have your own transportation, take **Paekakariki Hill Rd.,** off SH1, in order to climb a hill that winds up through a blindingly green valley before turning the corner to a drop-dead view of the Tasman Sea and the entire curve of Kapiti Coast. **Kapiti Island** and the **Marlborough Sounds** float in the distance. Stop off Highway 1 at **The Railway Museum,** where the finishing touches are being put on preserved trains from the late 19th century. A more recent craze in Paekakariki (near the BP station, where you park and walk up a steep dirt path) is yet another invention in the country's endless search for an adrenaline rush: the **Fly By Wire** (tel. mobile 025 300 366), a patented, 7-minute thrill ride in an open-air rocket-like contraption ($99; includes video).

PARAPARAUMU

The main town of the Kapiti and full of retired folks, Paraparaumu (or as locals call it, Paraperam or Pram) is home to the illustrious **Coastlands Shopperworld,** overlooked by the gleaming white **Our Lady of Lourdes statue** on the hill above town. The town also has a beachfront extension (the town of Paraparaumu Beach), with a developed shorefront complex. While its narrow beach has fine views, it's better suited to water activities than lounging in the sand. The **Kapiti Information Centre** (tel. 298 8195) is an island in the Coastlands shopping complex (open M-F 9am-4pm, Sa 9am-3pm). **Tranz Metro** runs daily from Wellington as far as Paraparaumu every hour and more frequently at peak times (55min., $7.50). **TranzScenic** stops at Paraparaumu on its way north, as do **InterCity, Newmans,** and **Mt. Cook** ($14). Paraparaumu has a local bus service: **Mana Coach** (tel. 0800 801 700) #2 and 3 run to Paraparaumu Beach (15min., $1.70) and #5 runs to Waikanae (every hour M-Sa $2). Catch all buses from **Coastlands** (which also has the **post office** and **pharmacy**).

Motels stretch all along Kapiti Rd. and down the beachfront, but **Barnacles Seaside Inn,** 3 Marine Parade (tel. 298 4856; fax 298 7142), is beautifully seaside and cheap. Rooms are well-kept and private, with heaters, electric blankets, original wood furnishings from the 20s, and shared showers. (Singles $20, twins $35.) North of Paraparaumu, **Waikanae Beach** is the region's finest, with a long stretch of often uncrowded white sand. Waikanae's **DOC office** (tel. 293 2191) is on Parata Rd. (open M-F 8am-4:30pm). The #5 Mana Coach (see above) goes to Waikanae. It also makes stops at two worthy attractions: The ▨**Southward Car Museum** (tel. 297 1221), with an impressive collection of vintage autos and motorcycles (open daily 9am-4:30pm. Admission $5, children $2), and the **Lindale Centre** (tel. 297 0916), a country farm complex. Lindale will put a cherry on top of your day with outstanding homemade ice cream. Also containing a cheese factory, honeybee shop, barnyard, and motor camp with tourist flats, it offers sheep-shearing, cow-milking, and baby-animal-feeding at 2pm on weekends. (Open daily 9am-5pm.) For those who've already tried the wine, cheese, and bread New Zealand has to offer, check out their chocolate at **Nyco Chocolate Factory & Shop** (tel. 299 8098), on the corner of Highway 1 and Raumati Rd. Put on a hairnet and take a tour (M-F 2 per day) through the sweet smells of this small factory.

THE WAIRARAPA

In summer, the Wairarapa coast buzzes with Wellingtonian daytrippers and weekenders. While gardens brighten almost every town, the wineries centered around Martinborough are the most celebrated attraction. Divers, surfers, and other wild-at-heart funsters all flock to the cold water coast (though south of Riversdale to Tora is off-limits for surfing). Bikers cruise the flat roads that seem to go on and on. Those with a taste for aesthetics tend to devote a day or few to exploring the area's natural offerings, such as the high and mighty Castle Rock (east of Masterton on Castlepoint Road), Palliser Bay, with its fur seal colony and majestic Putangirua Pinnacles, Mt. Bruce National Wildlife Centre, and Tararua Forest Park. Transport is a little pricey, since cars or tour buses are needed to access the coast, but once you're there, the attractions are easy on the wallet.

MASTERTON

The main transportation hub and tourist information mecca of the Wairarapa, Masterton (pop. 19,800) has grown out of its agricultural roots but still hosts the fantastically popular annual Golden Shears sheep-shearing competition (March, 2000). Queen St. and Chapel St. (SH2) are home to most of Masterton's cafes, stores, and restaurants.

◨ **PRACTICAL INFORMATION. Tranz Metro** (Masterton tel. (04) 498 3000 ext. 44933) runs to Wellington more frequently than the bus (1½hr., 1-3 per day, $11.50). **Tranzit Coachlines** (tel. 377 1227) depart from the Queen St. Terminal for: **Palmerston North** (2hr., 1-2 per day, $15) via **Mt. Bruce Wildlife Centre** (25min., $6); and daily for **Wellington** (2½hr., 4:40pm, $13) via **Carterton** (15min., $2.20), **Greytown** (25min., $2.60), and **Featherston** (40min., $3). **Tranzit** also heads directly to these small Wairarapa towns (M-F, 4 per day). **Car rentals** are available at **Graeme Jones,** 81 Dixon St. (tel. 378 6667), starting at $60 per day. The **Tourism Wairarapa Head Office,** 5 Dixon St. (tel. 378 7373; fax 378 7042), sits at the corner of Queen St. and Lincoln Rd. and sells hut tickets and fishing licenses. Pick up a free guide to the Wairarapa region. (Open M-F 9-5pm, Sa-Su 10am-4pm.) The **DOC office** (tel. 377 0700) is on South Rd. (open M-F 8:30am-4:30pm). Other services include: **ANZ,** on Queen St. (open M-F 9am-4:30pm); **National Bank** on Lincoln Rd. (open M-F 9am-4:30pm); and the **post office** on Queen St. (open M-F 9am-5pm). **Telephone Code**: 06.

ACCOMMODATIONS AND FOOD. Those limited by transportation can stay at the centrally located **Empire Lodge,** 94 Queen St. (tel. 377 1902; fax 377 2298), above O'Toole's Slug and Lettuce Pub. Slightly dim rooms include personal bathrooms with bathtubs and coffee- and tea-making facilities ($45). **O'Toole's Slug and Lettuce Pub,** 94 Queen St. (tel. 377 3087), offers hearty helpings of good food, including the tender Slug Sandwich ($10). Small tables and a light-hearted atmosphere make friends of strangers. (Open daily 11:30am-9:30pm.) More formal and expensive, with incredibly fresh food and a tasteful, candlelit atmosphere, is **Bloomfields Restaurant** (tel. 377 4305), on the corner of Chapel St. and Lincoln Rd. Savor the creatively seasoned South Island salmon ($11) or the ostrich ham with salad ($10.50). (Open for lunch W-F from noon, for dinner M-Sa from 6pm). The markets are **Write Price** (tel. 378 7592; open daily 8am-9pm) on the corner of Queen and Bruce St., or **New World** on Church St.

SIGHTS AND ACTIVITIES. Masterton's 32-hectare **Queen Elizabeth Park** on Dixon St., with its suspension bridge, rose gardens, small aquarium, pedal-boat pond, and miniature railway, is perfect for a picnic (railway runs in summer Sa-Su 1-4pm). The last Sunday in February (February 27, 2000), the park is transformed by the **Masterton Wine and Food Festival,** spawned by the growing fame of the area's vineyards and wineries. Along with Wellington tour operators, several Masterton-based operators conduct tours of the Wairarapa's hotspots. **Wairarapa Sightseeing Tours** run by Tranzit Coachlines (tel. 377 1227) tours **Mt. Bruce** (daily 11:40am, $18), **Cape Palliser,** and **Martinborough** (M, W, and Sa 9:30am; $50), and farms in the region (Tu, Th, and Su 11:30am; $44; YHA and family discounts). Located 30km north of Masterton on SH2, the **Mt. Bruce National Wildlife Centre** (tel. 375 8004) is your chance to see both a kiwi and a tuatara in the same day. Now boasting 15 different aviaries and outdoor reserves, Mt. Bruce bursts with pride over its many successful captive breeding programs. The wildlife center has numerous displays on the management regimes for rearing threatened native birds. (Open daily 9:30am-4pm. Admission $6, children $1.50.)

MARTINBOROUGH

The major wine village of the Wairarapa, Martinborough (some 40km east of Masterton) pays homage to its British roots with streets laid out in the pattern of the Union Jack. High sunshine and low autumnal rainfall make for choice vintages (such as the famed Pinot Noir) from the 20 wineries in the area. Most are within walking distance of one another. Some of those open year-round are the **Palliser Estate** (tel. 306 9019) on Kitchener St., **Martinborough Vineyard** (tel. 306 9955) on Princess St. (tastings daily 11am-5pm), and **Te Kairanga Vineyard** (tel. 306 9122), on Martin Rd. (tours Sa-Su 2pm). Most other vineyards are clustered west and south of town. Find guidance for your winery addiction at the **Martinborough Information Centre** (tel. 306 9043), on Kitchener St. (open daily 10am-4pm), or at the **Tourism Wairarapa Head Office** in Masterton. Victorian trinkets, moa bones, and Maori artifacts are all on display at the **Colonial Museum** (tel. 306 9736; open Sa-Su, public holidays, and school holidays 2-4pm). The **Martinborough Country Fair** takes place the first Saturday of February and March, revealing the region's rural splendor, while the **November Wine, Food and Music Festival** gives you the opportunity you've been waiting for to sample the region's best.

Follow the signposted road from Featherston and Martinborough to the beguiling, inviting **Cape Palliser.** The one-hour drive alone is attraction enough, as tidal pools along the coast become impromptu venues for the slapstick antics of resident seals. The noticeboard at the carpark by the lighthouse describes numerous nearby walks. From the carpark, it's only a 30-minute walk to **Putangirua Pinnacles,** "echo of the bird-calling flute." Sculpted by hundreds of years of rain, these mighty rock formations give breathtaking testament to the will of the elements. Hardy hikers can take the two- to three-hour walk up to the spine-tingling view at the lookout. Two kilometers away, a towering sandstone bluff keeps archaeology buffs happy with its precious, detailed fossils. Four kilometers past Ngawi Village, the ponderously heavy **Kupe's Sail** serves as a natural sandstone monument to the legendary Maori explorer. Cape Palliser is also home to New Zealand's largest fur seal breeding colony, off the main road east of Ngawi Village (breeding time is Nov.-Jan.). For both their safety and yours, look but don't touch the ear-wiggling, flipper-waving marvels.

TARARUA FOREST PARK

The Tararua Forest Park offers some great hikes off the tourist radar, though the weather can be harsh. Covering 117,225 hectares and 75% of the Tararua Range, it was the first forest park established in New Zealand. Marked tracks range through beech forests, alpine grasslands, and even leatherwood shrublands. Severe wind and mist have made this region famous for its capricious weather. Get **hut tickets** from the **DOC office** in Masterton (tel. 378 2061 or Holdsworth DOC ranger tel. 377 0022), local visitor centers, and various hunting and fishing sports shops. The popular **Mt. Holdsworth Circuit** (20km, 2-3 days) begins at **Mt. Holdsworth Lodge,** 20 minutes west of Masterton, and climbs through bush to the mountain before winding its way back to the lodge (huts $4-8). The 15,000-year-old Grade 2 **Waiohine River** runs through the Waiohine Gorge in the southeastern part of the Tararuas. A large swing bridge crosses the river by the carpark for the popular camping and recreation areas nearby, surrounded by rimu, beech, rata, and kahikatea trees. The **Loop Track** (1½hr.) leaves from here to cross through regenerating bush, while the **Cone Hut Track** (return 6hr.) climbs to a terrace of the **Tauherenikau River.**

PALMERSTON NORTH

Around 40% of Palmerston North's 72,500 residents are involved with higher education in some way or another, giving credence to its nickname: "Knowledge City." Home to Massey University, New Zealand's second-largest university, and a host of other schools, "Palmy" has more book-filled backpacks than long-term backpackers, but people often travel here because it's a transportation hub. Offering a few central hostels, the city's two loves—movies and rugby—can occupy you during a day's stopover.

▓ ORIENTATION AND PRACTICAL INFORMATION

All roads lead to the Square, Palmerston North's well-kept central green space. **Rangitikei St.** heads north, while **Fitzherbert Ave.** leads south toward the Manawatu River. **Main St.** heads east and west from the Square. **George St.** is short but offers character rather than commercial buzz.

Visitors Center: Destination Manawatu Visitor Centre (tel. 358 5003; fax 356 9841), on the corner of Church St. and the Square. Open M-F 9am-5pm, Sa-Su 10am-3pm.

DOC: 717 Tremaine Ave. (tel. 350 9700; fax 350 9701), a good kilometer along from Rangitikei. They're most helpful if you're planning on tackling large undertakings like the Tararuas or Ruahines; they also sell hut passes. Open M-F 8am-4:30pm.

Trains: TranzScenic (tel. 0800 802 802) leaves from the railway station on Mathew's Ave. off Tremaine Ave. (about a 20min. walk from the Square). Trains leave for: **Auckland** (8½hr.; daily 10:55am, Su-F 10pm; $108, night $97) via **Ohakune, National Park,** and **Hamilton; Wellington** (2hr., 3 per day, $30); and **Napier** (3hr., 10:14am, $44). **Tranz Metro** runs to **Wellington** (M-F, $18) via the **Kapiti Coast.**

Buses: InterCity/Newmans leave from Travel Centre at Pitt and Main St. (tel. 355 5633), and **White Star** (tel. 0800 800 287) leaves from the courthouse on Main St., Both go daily to **Wellington** (2hr., 1-4 per day, $20-30) and to **New Plymouth** (4hr., 1-2 per day, $30-40) via **Wanganui** (1½hr., $10-15). InterCity/Newmans also heads daily to **Auckland** (8-10hr., 1-2 per day, $70-85) and **Rotorua** (5hr., 4 per day, $45-55) via **Taupo** (4hr., $45-60). InterCity/Newmans and **Tranzit Coachlines** head to **Masterton** (1¾hr., 1-2 per day, $15).

Taxis: Palmerston North Taxis (tel. 357 6076). To railway station costs $7-8. Open 24hr.

Hitchhiking: Thumbers report luck along any of the main roads. Rangitikei St. joins SH1 at Bulls, heading toward the volcanic heartland and Auckland. Napier Rd. (Main St. E.) heads to Napier. Main St. W. and Fitzherbert St. both head to Wellington.

Currency Exchange: BNZ (tel. 358 4149; fax 350 1663), at the corner of the Square and Rangitikei St. Open M and Th-F 9am-4:30pm, Tu and W 9:30am-4:30pm. **Thomas Cook** (tel. 356 2962), at the corner of Broadway and Princess St. Open M-F 9am-5:30pm.

Library: Knowledge City has just spent $13 million building a wonderful new library on the Square—help 'em recoup by checking out the cafe. Equipped with public showers, the library also has extensive **Internet access** ($5 per 30min.). Open M-Tu and Th 10am-6pm, W and F 10am-8pm, Sa 10am-4pm, Su 1-4pm.

Police: (tel. 357 9999), on Church St., off the McDonald's corner of the Square.

Medical Services: City Doctors, 22 Victoria Ave. (24hr. tel. 355 3300). **City Health** pharmacy (tel. 355 5287). Open daily 8am-10pm. **Palmerston North Hospital,** 50 Ruahine St. (tel. 356 9169).

Post Office: 338 Church St. (tel. 358 5188; fax 355 4167). *Poste Restante.* Open M-F 7:30am-6pm, Sa 9:30am-12:30pm.

Telephone Code: 06.

ACCOMMODATIONS

PepperTree Hostel (YHA), 121 Grey St. (tel. 355 4054), at the intersection of Princess and Grey St. Host Cherie runs a tight ship, maintaining a standard of excellence and order that makes PepperTree the best and busiest budget option in town. Swarming co-ed bathroom through the kitchen. Small, adequate rooms. Off-street parking. Dorms $15; singles $25; twins and doubles $35; tents $7.50. Weekly: dorms $85.

Anne Keith House, 146 Grey St. (tel. 355 0291). Spring mattresses in furnished rooms provide a good night's sleep in this turn-of-the-century villa. Singles $30; doubles $45.

Grey's Inn, 123 Grey St. (tel. 358 6928; fax 355 0291), next door to the YHA. A small, trim home offering bed and breakfast. Airy rooms with bath have inviting comforters, TVs, and tea and coffee facilities. Pets are allowed, assure owners Liz and Don who must feel somewhat incomplete with their two decrepit cats, with three eyes and seven legs between 'em. Singles $60; doubles $92; families $120.

King Street Backpackers (VIP), 95 King St. (tel. 358 9595). Packed 8- and 10-bed dorms connect with other doubles and singles by way of the long bright blue carpet in the hallway. Enormous lounge with TV and big, spacious dining area with pool table and an old beat-up church organ. Dorms $15; singles $25; doubles $35. Cash only.

Palmerston North Holiday Park, 133 Dittmer Dr. (tel. 358 0349). From Fitzherbert Ave., turn on Park Rd. towards the Esplanade, turn left on Ruha St., and descend into the park. Suitably park-like, with large trees and a riverside spot. Adequate kitchen, and sterile TV lounge. Tent sites $8.50; powered sites for 2 $20; cabins for 2 $28-55.

FOOD

Knowledge City needs food for thought, and food it has. Anchored by its student population, Palmy has the usual array of takeaways and Americana. **George St.** has more original flavor. The Square and its side streets are the main culinary loci.

George Street Deli (tel. 357 6663), corner of George and Main St. Enter this bright orange dive for deli-fresh stuffed potatoes ($4), chorizo rolls ($2), and quality coffee on green tables. Fresh sourdough on Saturdays. Open daily 6am-5pm.

Bella's, 2 The Square (tel. 357 8616). Shiny wooden floors and tables gleam in the candlelight—plenty bright enough to ensure enjoyment of the Thai chicken curry ($14.50) or medium pasta ($7). Open Tu-Sa from 11:30am; daily 6-10pm.

Markets: Truelife Bakery and Lunchbar, 47 The Square (tel. 358 3630). Health food fanatics may find this wholefoods store too good to be true. It even smells healthy. Open M-Th 9am-6pm, F 9am-4pm. **Countdown Foods** (tel. 357 3645), at Cuba and George St., is huge. Open M-W 8:30am-8pm, Th-F 8:30am-9pm, Sa-Su 8:30am-7pm. There is a **flea market** on Albert and Church St. every Saturday from 6am-10am.

NIGHTLIFE

Palmerston North can get lively during the school year—on rugby Saturdays, drinking starts at 3pm. In the Old Post Office building, **Highflyers** (tel. 357 5155), at the corner of Main St. and the Square, delivers frenzied weekend dancing, as well as a cafe and restaurant with an open four-sided fireplace and brick walls. (Open daily from 11am.) Right next door is sporty **Icons,** with bleachers for viewing rugby on one of its enormous TVs (open M-W 11am-10pm, Th-Sa until 1:30 am). **The Celtic Inn** (tel. 357 5571), off Broadway opposite the Downtown Cinema, is an Irish pub with all the trimmings: friendly atmosphere, $5.50 Guinness, festive music on weekends, and a diverse crowd (open M-Sa 11am-1am, and Su 4pm-11pm). **The Cobb** (tel. 357 8002), in the Empire Hotel at the corner of Princess and Main St. East, fills its big dance floor on weekends, though the DJ refuses to pick a genre (open nightly). There's more than drinking going on: when in Rome...join the crowds above the foodcourt at the hot **Downtown Cinema 8** (tel. 355 5655; admission M-Tu and daily before 5pm $7, W-Su $10).

SIGHTS AND ACTIVITIES

The west side of downtown, beginning with the snazzy new library and cafe at the Square, is touted as the cultural center. Don't be intimidated by the over-sized bronze beetles creeping over the roof of the **Manawatu Art Gallery,** 398 Main St. W. (tel. 358 8188), which showcases contemporary works of New Zealand artists. Next door is the **Science Centre & Manawatu Museum** (tel. 355 5000). The museum has regional history displays, while the Science Centre is full of interactive exhibits. (Both open daily 10am-5pm. Museum free; Science Centre $6.) The pinnacle of culture, one block north and several west of the Square, is the **New Zealand Rugby Museum,** 87 Cuba St. (tel. 358 6947). Quite the shrine for die-hard fanatics of The Game, this two-room gallery is cluttered with uniform displays, trophies, and memorabilia from one of the world's oldest remaining jerseys to the intricate "All Black Stars" quilt made by an enthusiastic fan to commemorate the team's 1995 World Cup run. (Open M-Sa 10am-noon and 1:30-4pm, Su 1:30-4pm. Admission $3.) On Saturdays in winter, you watch the real thing in the **Showgrounds** next door. The brand-new **Tararva Wind Farm,** 11km East of downtown, is located on 700 hectares of private farmland. Wind turbines stand 40m high with blades 23.5m wide, generating power for Palmerstonians. **Explore Manawatu** (tel. 0800 497 567) provides tours of the windfarm twice a day (9am-noon and 1-4pm; $55 includes tea at the historic Whareata Men's club). The same company will take you through effervescent **glow-worm caves** for $45.

South Island

Cape Farewell

ABEL TASMAN NATIONAL PARK

Malborough Sounds

Cook Strait

Tasman Bay

KAHURANGI NATIONAL PARK

Motueka
Nelson
Picton
Blenheim

Karamea

Karamea Bight

Lake Rotoroa
Lake Rotoiti
NELSON LAKES NATIONAL PARK

Westport

Kaikoura

Reefton

PAPAROA NATIONAL PARK

Punakaiki

Hanmer Springs

Greymouth

Lake Sumner

ARTHUR'S PASS NATIONAL PARK

Hokitika

Arthur's Pass

CRAIGIEBURN FOREST PARK

Pegasus Bay

TASMAN SEA

Lake Coleridge

Mount Hutt

Christchurch

Banks Peninsula

Methven

Akaroa

Franz Josef Glacier
Fox Glacier

MOUNT COOK NATIONAL PARK

Ashburton

WESTLAND NATIONAL PARK

Lake Tekapo

Lake Pukaki

Timaru

Canterbury Bight

Haast

Twizel

MOUNT ASPIRING NATIONAL PARK

Lake Ohau
Lake Benmore

Lake Wanaka
Lake Hawea

Oamaru

Milford Sound

Wanaka

Queenstown

Lake Wakatipu

Alexandra

FIORDLAND NATIONAL PARK

Lake Te Anau

Te Anau

Dunedin

Manapouri

Lake Manapouri

Gore

Balclutha

PACIFIC OCEAN

Invercargill

Bluff

CATLINS FOREST PARK

Foveaux Strait

N

Halfmoon Bay (Oban)

Stewart Island

0   50 miles

0   50 kilometers

MARLBOROUGH AND NELSON

Stretching from the tip of Farewell Spit to the tranquil Marlborough Sounds, from the marine paradise of Kaikoura to the lesser known Nelson Lakes, the "top of the south" provides an incredible variety of natural gems and endless ways to appreciate them. Whether it's kayaking in the Sounds, soaking in a hot spring, tasting award-winning wine, swimming with pods of playful dolphins, or hiking through fern-filled forests with the surf pounding in the distance, Marlborough is unlikely to bore even the shortest attention spans. The wine valleys of Nelson and the hippie, greenie outposts of Golden Bay are all within sight of three national parks. Take advantage of the well-developed tourism infrastructure, or escape it all in the majestic seclusion of the Sounds.

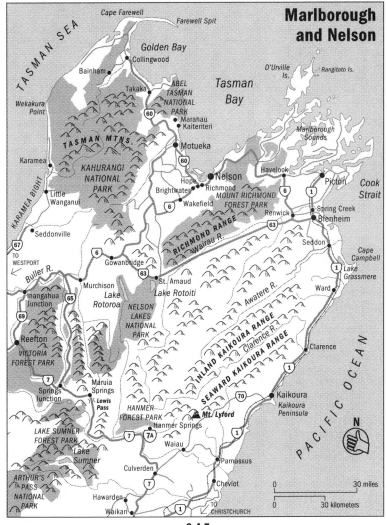

Marlborough and Nelson

SOUTH ISLAND

MARLBOROUGH

PICTON

The small gateway town of the South Island, Picton sits at the head of the dramatic Queen Charlotte Sound. Picton unwittingly played a major part in shaping the culture, politics, and economy of New Zealand as we know it today. It was here that the first European child was born and the first sheep stepped onto New Zealand soil. Today, starry-eyed travelers, arriving from Wellington on the Interislander ferry, take their first step onto South Island soil and transform an otherwise quiet town into a launchpad for further exploits.

ORIENTATION AND PRACTICAL INFORMATION

Home to the ferry terminal and other crucial transportation links, the whole area lining the harbor is known as Picton's **Foreshore. Auckland St.** is the hub of transportation activity in Picton, while **High St.** is home to **Mariner's Mall** and many of the town's shops and cafes. Residential neighborhoods stretch up into the hills. **Waikawa Bay** lies down Dublin St. and to the left on Waikawa Rd.

Visitors Center: Picton Visitor Information Centre (tel. 573 7477; fax 573 5021), on Auckland St. near the Foreshore, has information and bookings for the ferry, shuttles, and the maze of water operators. Open daily Jan.-Feb. 8:30am-8pm, Mar.-Apr. and Oct.-Dec. 8:30am-6pm, May-Sept. 8:30am-5pm. The **DOC office** (tel. 520 3007) is located at the Visitor Centre. Open M-F 8:30am-4:30pm.

Airplanes: The **Koromiko airstrip** is about 9km away. **Sounds Air** (tel. 573 6184 or 0800 505 005) has daily flights to Wellington (25min., up to 9 per day 8:30am-6:15pm, $50, YHA, VIP, and students $45) and a free shuttle bus to and from the airstrip in Picton. Inquire about limited shuttle service to Wellington backpackers.

Trains: TranzScenic (tel. 573 8649 or 0800 802 802) offers daily train service from Auckland St. to **Christchurch** (4½-5hr., 1:40pm, $72) via **Kaikoura** (3hr., $39).

Buses: InterCity (tel. 573 7025) leaves for: **Christchurch** (5½hr., 1:15pm, $57) via **Kaikoura** (2¼hr., $33) and **Blenheim** (30min., $8); and **Nelson** (2½hr., 12:55pm, $27). Prices are significantly lower if you book through the Visitor Centre. At least 9 other shuttle services run to the same destinations with a wide range of departure times and competitive pricing; again, see the Visitor Centre for details.

Ferries: Interislander Ferry (overseas bookings tel. (04) 498 3301, in NZ 0800 802 802) leaves from the Foreshore daily for **Wellington** (3hr., 4 per day 10:30am-9:30pm, $46) If speed is your object, **TopCat InterIsland Fast Ferry** (tel. 0800 4 TOPCAT) runs daily and can get you to Wellington in half the time as other ferries (10:15am and 4:15pm; $59). Prices for both can be significantly lower if booked in advance.

Taxis: Blenheim Taxi (tel. 578 0225).

Car Rental: Rent a car from any of the numerous companies located at the ferry terminal.

Picton

ACCOMMODATIONS
A Baden's Picton Lodge
B The Villa Backpackers LodgeBaden's
C The Wedgewood House (YHA)
D Picton Backpackers on the Square
E The Juggler's Rest Backpackers
F Alexanders Holiday Park

Currency Exchange and Banks: BNZ, 56-8 High St. Open M, Th, and F 9am-4:30pm, Tu and W 9:30am-4:30pm. **Westpac Trust,** Mariner's Mall on High St. Open M-Tu and Th-F 9am-4:30pm, W 9:30am-4:30pm. Both have **ATMs. Four Square supermarket,** 49 High St. (tel. 573 6443), will change money after hours. Open daily 7:30am-9pm.

Medical Services: Picton Medical Center, 71 High St. (tel. 573 6092, after-hours 577 1941; open M-F 8:30am-5:30pm, Sa 9am-noon).

Police: 36 Broadway St. (tel. 573 6439).

Post Office: Mariner's Mall on High St. Open Oct.-Apr. M-F 8:30am-5pm, Sa 9:30am-12:30pm. Off-season hours vary.

Internet Access: Information Centre. $8 per hr. **Mariner's Books and Toys,** in Mariner's Mall. $8 per hr. Open M-F 8:30am-5:30pm, Sa 8:30am-5pm, Su 9am-4pm.

Telephone Code: 03.

ACCOMMODATIONS

Picton is well equipped to house swarms of passers-through. Hotels and motels are on the main streets, while the quiet side streets are home to many B&Bs.

The Villa Backpackers Lodge, 34 Auckland St. (tel./fax 573 6598), near the intersection with Dublin St. The unexpected bonuses take this charmingly restored villa from standard to stellar—free pickup, free breakfast, free apple crumble with ice cream every night, and free use of bicycles and fishing gear. Helpful staff will plan trips on the Queen

Charlotte Track. Internet access. Spa $2. Dorms $17; twins and doubles with made-up beds $44. Be sure to book well in advance, as it fills up year-round.

The Juggler's Rest Backpackers, 8 Canterbury St. (tel. 573 5570). Call for pickup or directions. The red train mailbox next to the wooden door signals a place more like a circus than a backpackers. The owners (3 professional jugglers) give free juggling workshops daily. Aside from the 1.5m high unicycle and the swimming pool for the bumblingly inept, you can shower in the celestial bathroom or soak in a candlelit bath surrounded by plants. With the right weather conditions, fire-eating lessons are offered. Free pickup, tea and coffee, use of bikes. Dorms $15, winter $14 (bring a sleeping bag); twins and doubles with linen $35, winter $32. Juggle five balls and get a $1 discount; juggle 10 for a free night and dinner with the owners. Otherwise, cash only.

Sequoia Lodge, 3A Nelson Square (tel./fax 573 8399 or 0800 222 257; email stay@sequoialodge.co.nz). This comfortable eye-catching hostel has recently been expanded, refurbished, and beautified, and includes free linen and free pickup. Internet access. Dorms $16; twins and doubles with bathroom $45.

Baden's Picton Lodge (Nomads), 9 Auckland St. (tel. 573 7788; fax 573 8418). The closest accommodation to the ferry. Free ferry drop-off and pickup. The rooms may lack character, but they are easily converted to accommodate families and the walls are well-insulated. The owner is also an experienced tramper and can offer advice and bookings for the Queen Charlotte Track. Free use of mountain bikes. Internet access. Dorms $16; twins and doubles $38. Nomads $1 off.

The Wedgewood House (YHA Associate), 10 Dublin St. (tel. 573 7797; fax 573 6426). White with blue trim, this lodge has a large wooden porch and a minuscule kitchen. Cute on the outside, but not particularly remarkable on the inside. Free lockers in rooms, free duvets and blankets. Reception 8-10am (8:30am in winter), 1-2pm, 5-6:30pm, and 8-10:30pm. Dorms $16; twins $19.

Alexanders Holiday Park (tel./fax 573 6378), at the end of Canterbury St. Stay in a converted 1906 railway carriage (now a cabin) and store your gear overhead in the luggage racks. Converted army bunkers are cheaper than the standard cabins. Waitohi Stream swimming hole. Standard cabin for 2 with electric jug and toaster $30; tourist cabins $40; caravan and tent sites for 2 $18. Book ahead in summer for all but the tent sites.

🏷 FOOD

For the budget traveler, self-catering may be the best bet. **Supervalue** (tel. 573 0463) is waiting in Mariner's Mall, chock-full of groceries for your cooking pleasure (open M-W 8am-6pm, Th 8am-7:30pm, F 8am-8:30pm, Sa 8am-7pm, Su 9am-5pm). **High St.** is home to a variety of restaurants, most of which leave visitors wondering if there is a local ordinance requiring cafes to have a pair of names.

The Dog and Frog Cafe, 22 High St. (tel. 573 5650). Contains a scattering of amphibious statues and canine pictures. All-day breakfast of sausage and eggs $9, fish 'n' chips $11. There is also a variety of sandwiches and pies for take-away. Open daily 7am-9pm, winter 8am-8pm.

Toad 'n' Turtle Cafe (tel. 573-7748), on High St. A good place to sit, snack, and read. Serves normal takeaway fare and all-day breakfast. Breakfast ($3.50) will get you a pot of tea and a mean banana chocolate-chip muffin. Open daily 8am-3pm.

Toot 'n' Whistle (tel. 573 6086), down on Auckland St., near the Visitor Centre. A smoky diner and bar with a friendly, laid-back atmosphere, and a broad menu. Meals start at $6.50; the steak open sandwich ($9.50) is a special favorite. Open daily 9am-late.

👁 🎿 SIGHTS AND ACTIVITIES

Picton, which was nearly made the capital of New Zealand in the 1850s, retains vestiges of its dignified history all about town. Greeting arrivals at the Foreshore is the **Edwin Fox,** the oldest wooden merchant ship afloat in the world. Built in 1853 in

Calcutta, it transported tea from Calcutta to London, British immigrants to Australia and New Zealand, convicts to Australia, and troops to Europe in the Crimean War. The ship, now displayed in a newly constructed dry dock, is the subject of an interesting and informative exhibit at the **Edwin Fox Maritime Centre** (tel. 573 6868), which both chronicles the ship's illustrious history and details plans for its eventual restoration. (Open daily 8:30am-6pm, winter 8:30am-5pm. Admission \$4.)

MARLBOROUGH SOUNDS

A grand maze of waterways at the South Island's northeastern extremity, the Marlborough Sounds harbor ample sea life and green peaks amid thousands of beautiful coves. Picton serves as the Sounds' main gateway, and the **Queen Charlotte Track** (see p. 252) is its well-trammeled attraction. No one ever leaves the Marlborough Sounds disappointed.

◪ PRACTICAL INFORMATION. All transportation listed departs from Picton. The **Cougar Line** (tel. 573 8465 or 0800 504 090) runs daily to **Ship Cove** (\$38) and **Torea Bay** (\$12), plus all points in between (10am and 1:30pm year-round, plus Oct.-May 8am and Dec.-Feb. 6pm); they'll also arrange full return transport into **Ship Cove** and out of **Anakiwa** (\$48). **Endeavour Express** (tel. 579 8465) runs daily to **Ship Cove** (9:30am and 1:15pm, \$25), **Anakiwa** (\$15), and the intervening bays; their return package goes into **Ship Cove** and out of either Anakiwa, Torea Bay, or the Bay of Many Coves (\$40). **West Bay Water Transport** (tel/fax. 573 5597) connects daily with the Cougar Line's service (4 per day; fewer in winter) to **Mistletoe Bay** (\$13), **Anakiwa** (\$18), and vice-versa. By road, the **Sounds Connection** (tel. 0800 742 866) runs between **Picton** (8am and 3:45pm) and **Anakiwa** (8:45pm and 4:30pm) for \$10 each way. Several other stops along the track are road-accessible, as noted in the description below.

◪ ACCOMMODATIONS. Accommodations are scattered throughout the Sounds; many of them are outstanding, but two in particular combine a laid-back, uncommercial aura with a load of free activities and low rates. Both are accessible only by water taxi; call ahead to arrange transport, or try the **Cougar Line** (see above). The aptly named ▨**Lazy Fish** (tel. 579 9049; fax 579 9089; www.lazy fish.co.nz) embodies relaxation; with a motto like *ubi dies omnis festus* (where every day is a Sunday), what could go wrong? From the picnic table at the end of the wharf, to the hammocks in the shade, to the free spa beneath the stars, there are hundreds of ways to be lazy here. Free use of canoe, rowboat, fishing gear, windsurfer, towels, and snorkeling gear is included. Bring a good stock of groceries, though a stocked cupboard dubbed "The Shop" sells basic food items. Call ahead to arrange water transport (return \$27). (Dorms \$20; doubles \$45; book well ahead in summer.) A little closer to Picton, the recently expanded **Lochmara Lodge** (tel./fax 573 4554; email lochmaralodge@xtra.co.nz) includes over 10 acres of native bush, with trails, benches, hammocks, and tree carvings scattered throughout. Lying just 40 minutes off the Queen Charlotte track, the lodge also has a spa, sea kayak, windsurfer, rowboat, fishing and snorkeling gear, a rope swing over the water, and resident glow-worms. Seal and shag colonies are within kayaking distance. Call ahead to arrange water transport, return \$20. Choose between a dorm in the main lodge (\$20) or a completely self-contained cabin unit, including your own deck with a view over the water (\$80 for 2, each extra person \$20). The lodge is closed June to August, except by arrangement.

◪ ACTIVITIES. Sea kayaking allows the freedom to explore the curving coastlines, tranquil inlets, and hidden accommodations. **Marlborough Sounds Adventure Company** (tel. 573 6078), on London Quay in Picton, has single and double kayaks for hire (\$40 per day per person); they do not hire to solo paddlers. Guided trips run from an evening BBQ (\$60) to overnight paddle and walk combos (\$145-750).

Sea Kayaking Adventure Tours (tel. 574 2765) in Anakiwa offers guided daytrips ($65), freedom rentals ($40 per day), and mountain bike hire ($30 per day). **Dolphin Watch Marlborough** (tel. 573 8040), next to the railway station in Picton, runs ecotours to predator-free and bird-filled **Motuara Island,** plus historic **Ship Cove** (4hr., 8:45am and 1:45pm, $55), returning in time for the ferry. Track walkers can take the tour and then be dropped off at Ship Cove to begin tramping, chopping an hour off the boat ride.

To enjoy the Sounds from the road, those driving to Havelock or Nelson can wind along the scenic (and sealed) **Queen Charlotte Drive,** connecting Picton with Havelock. Another way to see the Sounds is to ride along the **mail runs** on the Queen Charlotte Sound ($54) or the Pelorus Sound ($66; M-F mid-morning; returning mid- to late-afternoon). Contact **Beachcomber Cruises** (tel. 573 6175), on the Picton Foreshore, for details.

▶ QUEEN CHARLOTTE TRACK

Hailed for its green-and-blue beauty, the Queen Charlotte Track provides a unique and pleasant outdoor experience, if not a rugged wilderness adventure. Above the azure ocean waters, signs of development abound: regenerating vegetation bears witness to long-abandoned farming ventures, and parcels of private property still line the track. On its vista-filled way along the Queen Charlotte and Kenepuru Sounds, the track passes a hospitable string of private accommodations, each offering a lazy escape from the semi-rigors of walking. While this combination of natural glory and human hospitality make the walkway extremely popular, it seldom feels as crowded as a comparable national park.

ESSENTIALS

Length: 67km; 3-5 days. The track tends to be wide and gently inclined. A great many tourists walk only a brief section before grabbing a water taxi back to Picton.

Trailheads: The track runs from **Ship Cove** west to the tiny settlement of **Anakiwa;** water taxi and luggage transport services tend to encourage this direction.

Transportation: See **Practival Information** above.

Seasonality: The track sees a fair amount of traffic year-round, with mob proportions during the holidays; June and July are the quietest months, while May and August present the best union of decent weather and low visitation.

Campsites & Accommodations: The track's 7 DOC campsites vary widely in their amenities and degree of seclusion, but they each cost $4 per night; tickets can be purchased at the DOC office in Picton, or from caretakers on-site. For those less bent on tents, an eager stream of private seaside establishments provides a wide variety of backpackers' dorms and pricier options along the way; details are given below.

Gear: The DOC campsites don't offer any special equipment beyond toilet paper, so a **cooking stove** is essential for tenters. The Queen Charlotte Track is indulgently unique in that water taxis will gladly transport overnight gear (tents, stoves, sleeping bags, food, etc.) to most stops along the sound. Free gear transport is included in the return deals listed above (see **Transportation**), and **Endeavour Express** charges $10 for carrier service outside of this standard loop.

Storage: Most accommodations and water taxis in Picton will store excess gear; otherwise, the Visitor Centre charges $1 per bag per night for secure storage.

THE TRACK

Ship Cove to Resolution Bay Campsite: 4.5km, 1½hr.
Ship Cove's **Captain Cook Monument** commemorates the many weeks the great navigator spent anchored here during all three of his voyages, harvesting high-vitamin scurvy-fighting grass for his crew, and flogging those who refused it. As the track climbs up and over a small saddle, it passes through the finest primary forest of the whole walkway. **Resolution Bay Campsite** has spare and sloping sites, with no cooking shelter. About 20 minutes further await the rambling green bungalows of

Resolution Bay Cabins (tel. 579 9411), where life flows slowly and the shop is always open (free use of dinghies, canoes and kayaks; basic bunks $10, with kitchen $20; doubles $40-85, each extra person $10). The **Kamahi Lodge** is close by, 10 minutes down the track in a sheltered cove. This well-groomed homestay caters to a mix of both tour groups and backpackers. (Dorms $35, including light supper and continental breakfast; doubles $65, including linens and substantial meals.)

Resolution Bay to Endeavour Inlet's tip: 10.5km, 2¼hr.

Two hours past the Resolution Bay area is **Furneaux Lodge,** a Victorian resort with plenty of tent space ($5 per person, $10 during New Year's holiday), a classy stone-hewn "croft" for trampers ($15), well-serviced "possum-rest" ($25), and more upmarket options (chalets $95, winter $80); the lodge hires out various water craft, and runs a nifty amphibious Argo tour to the otherwise remote antimony mines and their resident cave weta (1½-2hr., $35). Just past the lodge is the turn-off for a worthwhile **Waterfall Walk** (return 1hr.), which leads through blissfully unmilled forest full of huge rimu. About 10 minutes further is the **Endeavour Resort** (tel. 579 8381; fax 579 8380), with serviceable six-bed dorms ($20, with linens $25; whole room $60), self-contained doubles ($90, extra person $25), and tent sites wherever you please ($8). Dinghies, canoes, and the large library come free; meals can be ordered a day ahead.

Endeavour Inlet's tip to Camp Bay Campsite: 11.5km, 3hr.

As the track rounds **Big Bay,** the surroundings alternate between towering tree ferns and developed grazing land, with plenty of gorgeous sound views throughout. Endless weka rule **Camp Bay Campsite,** a shelterless set of flat terraces with stake-defying dirt. From here, a side trail leads to three excellent and completely dissimilar accommodation options. **Punga Cove Resort** (tel. 579 8561; fax 579 8080) offers fun-filled luxury, including free dinghy and canoe use, kayaks and outboards for hire, a cozy cabana bar (open 11am-11pm), a summer cocktail cruise (departs 4pm, $20), a pool, and a spa. (Dorms $16, with linens $25.) The funky and road-accessible **Homestead Backpackers** (tel. 579 8373) abounds in character and hospitality, with a sunny deck (dorms $16, with linens $23), gypsy-themed caravans ($15, with linens $23, no power), a lovely 19th-century double ($38, with linens $50), and most importantly, a fire-warmed outdoor bathtub (open Dec.-Apr. only). From here, the third house up the road is **Noeline's** (tel. 579 8375), a fresh and intimate place with four beds and wide views, where charming Noeline and Penny, the possum-catching lapdog, instantly disarm guests with pure, undiluted beams of hospitality.

Camp Bay Campsite to Bay of Many Coves Campsite: 2hr.

Kenapuru Saddle can be reached via either a 15-minute scramble from Camp Bay Campsite or a slightly longer and easier route along the road from the Homestead Backpackers. From here, the track passes scrubby vegetation for 1½ hours before reaching the reasonably steep spur for **Eatwells Lookout** (15min.), a more or less 360° panorama encompassing far-off mountains and the farther-off North Island. A half hour of rolling track later, the **Bay of Many Coves Campsite** has a cooking shelter with lofty sea views, with bumpy and kanuka-sheltered plots out the back. Pack transport will not be an option here, until Kiwi ingenuity perfects a high-precision baggage cannon.

Bay of Many Coves Campsite to Black Rock Campsite: 1½hr.

This stretch passes some of the walkway's most beautiful trademark vistas, with deep-blue Queen Charlotte Sound and pale Kenepuru Sound alternating into view. **Black Rock Campsite,** another boat-inaccessible spot, has small, grassy sites, plus a handsome gazebo for cooking that overlooks Kumutoto Bay and Picton.

Black Rock Campsite to Cowshed Bay Campsite: 1½hr.

It's all downhill for over an hour to **Torea Saddle,** where both Maori and European paddlers found it wise and time-saving to carry their canoes between the two sounds. About a 10-minute walk down the road north of the saddle is the snazzy **Portage Hotel** (tel. 573 4309), with its small basic dorms ($18, with pool use only), and flashy luxury dorms with TV, microwave, fridge, bathroom, and wood paneling ($25, including all hotel perks). The nearby **Cowshed Bay Campsite** is a caravan-heavy complex with major road access; some sites are right by the lovely bay. Gear can't be delivered directly to the campsite or the hotel, since they're on the opposite sound; the hotel will drive luggage from the water-taxi dropoff and over the saddle ($2 one-way).

Torea Saddle to Mistletoe Bay Reserve: 7.5km, 2½hr.

The track traverses many ups and downs over gentle switchbacks, passing the steep turnoff to **Lochmara Lodge** (one-way 40min; see p. 251) after 1½hr.; Kenepuru Sound provides ample scenery all along the way, especially at **Hilltop Lookout** (return 40min.), about a half hour further on. The reasonably steep and relatively brief track (20min.) passes fungus-blackened beeches to the **Mistletoe Bay Reserve,** a unique spot on a small and quiet bay. In addition to a wide and grassy flat for tents ($4), the reserve maintains three ramshackle cottages with full kitchens ($10). A **Peninsula Walk** (return 1hr.) through regenerating bush leaves from here.

Mistletoe Bay Reserve to Anakiwa: 12.5km, 3hr.

Beyond the trail junction for Mistletoe Bay, the track follows the road for a bit. About 15 minutes by foot down a side road is the tropical-themed **Te Mahia Resort** (tel./fax 573 4089), where at least one of the spacious backpacker rooms has its own piano (dorms $20; doubles $90; extra person $35; tent and powered sites $10). Back on the main track, cows graze the lovely length of Mistletoe Bay, before the track descends through some good bush to **Davies Bay Campsite,** situated on an estuary. About 45 minutes of relatively level walking later, teeny **Anakiwa** greets trampers with a telephone and boat or bus pickup.

BLENHEIM

Grapes—fruits of love and fruits of labor. Some tourists flock to Blenheim to indulge in the region's award-winning wines. Many wineries are open to the public and offer tastings in addition to their exquisite foods. Other more frugal travelers in need of work head to the vineyards seeking vines in need of pruning and grapes in need of plucking—the work is plentiful, if often grueling.

■ PRACTICAL INFORMATION

The **Blenheim Information Centre,** 2 High St. (tel. 578 9904; fax 578 6084; email blm_info@clear.net.nz) is for those already licking their parched lips for a map of the Marlborough wine region (open daily 8:30am-6:30pm, winter M-F 8:30am-5:30pm, Sa-Su 9:30am-2pm). The **railway station** (tel. 577 2835), which also serves as a bus station, is located across the river at the end of Alfred St. If you fancy the train, **TranzScenic** (tel. 0800 802 802) goes to **Picton** (30min., 12:20pm, $19; 15% student discount) and **Christchurch** (5hr., 2:10pm, $66; 20% student discount). **InterCity** (tel. 577 2890) heads daily to: **Picton** (30min., 11:50am, $8); **Nelson** (1¾hr., 1:25pm, $22); and **Christchurch** (4½hr., 1:45pm, $55) via **Kaikoura** (1¾hr., $30). **Sounds-to-Coast** (tel. 0800 802 225) goes to **Greymouth** (4½hr., M, W, and F 7:30am, $44) and daily to **Picton** (30min., 5:45pm, $5). **Kiwilink** (tel. 0800 802 300) and **Knightline** (tel. 547 4733) go to **Nelson** (1¾hr., 4 per day, $17) and **Picton** (30min., 3 per day, $6).

Travelers in search of **employment** in Blenheim's busy fruit industry can talk to hostel owners or look in local newspapers. The **DOC field center** (tel. 572 9100) is on Gee St. in nearby Renwick, but necessary information on local walks is offered at the Information Centre. The open, bricked area lined with shops behind the Information Centre is known as the **Forum** and has everything from banks to bars to the ubiquitous $2 Shop. Other services include: **Blenheim Taxis** (tel. 0800 802 225 or 578 0225); the **medical center,** 24 George St. (tel. 578 2174); **police,** 8 Main St. (tel.

578 5279); and **Internet access** at **Internet Direct,** 2 Main St. (tel. 577 9598), on the 4th floor of the post office building ($2.50 per 15min.; open M-F 8:30am-5:15pm). Although the **post office** is technically located at 2 Main Street, the post shop is around the corner on Scott (open M-F 8:30am-5:15pm, Sa 9:30am-12:30pm). **Telephone Code:** 03.

ACCOMMODATIONS

Despite Blenheim's high falutin' wine-culture, budget places are not hard to find. To get to ■**Blenheim Backpackers,** 29 Park Terr. (tel. 578 6062), follow Main St. and take a left onto Park Terrace—it's well worth the short walk beyond neighboring accommodations. Tall triple bunkbeds reach up to the high ceilings in this comfortable 110-year-old maternity-home-turned-backpackers. Paddle the free canoes in the adjacent river, or ride a free bicycle to the local vineyards. A newly acquired and remodeled house across the street offers more dorm beds, a pool table, and a few tent sites. Free pickup, laundry, and video library are also available. Internet access is available in summer. (Dorms $14; twins and doubles $32-36). Play billiards in the kitchen of **Koanui Backpackers,** 33 Main St. (tel./fax 578 7487), a carpeted, colorful backpackers with the luxury of sinks in each room. Many occupants are workers who have lengthy stays here. Koanui also offers free bicycle use and free pickup. Get a key if you go out at night. (Reception 7am-10pm. Dorms $15; singles $23; twins $18; doubles $36). **Grove Bridge Holiday Park,** 78 Grove Rd. (tel./fax 578 3667), has a range of choices for all inclinations and budgets, from completely self-contained tourists flats ($68 for 2, winter $60), tourist cabins without bath ($50 for 2), standard cabins with communal facilities ($40), and tent sites ($9 per person, with power $10, children $5).

FOOD

The concentration of restaurants and cafes is greatest near the center of town. The sharp decor at **Tuscany's,** 36 Scott St. (tel. 577 5050), accompanies a varied menu including pasta, seafood, and an all-day breakfast. Don't miss an unbeatable array of enormous, gourmet burgers ($10), including beef, chicken, fish, lamb, and even venison varieties. A lovely patio allows for outdoor dining, weather permitting. (Open daily from 10am. Meals until 10pm, bar open later.) While the totem pole, scattered cacti, and faux adobe walls are intended to conjure images of the American Southwest, the menu at **Bar Navajo** is more Kiwi than Comanche. All mains, including ham steak, mixed grille, and local speciality Marlborough mussels with garlic butter, are under $10. There is also a wide selection of beers; stay for a pint or splurge on a glass of local wine. (Open daily 11:30am-2pm and 5:30pm-9pm). **Supervalue Plus,** on Queen St. in the **Forum,** is another option for thrifty gourmet (open M-Tu and Sa 8am-7pm, W-F 8am-8pm, Su 9am-6pm).

OUTDOORS

Visit a vineyard by bike, car, or taxi, and you can learn about winemaking and savor Marlborough's red, white, and rosé treasures. Different **wineries** offer different tour and tasting options, so plan ahead and peruse the literature at the Information Centre first. For an organized packaged trip, contact **DeLuxe Travel Line** (tel. 0800 500 511) to wander the Marlborough region by coach ($40, children $20).

The 25-acre **Brayshaw Museum Park** is about 3km from center of town, off Maxwell Rd. Walk through the Blenheim of 100 years ago in **Beavertown,** a replica of area shops and buildings from around the turn of the century. The **Riverside Railway** is an old-fashioned train running between Brayshaw Museum Park and Blenheim (leaves the park 2pm, 3pm, and 4pm every Su in summer, first Su of the month in winter; $3, children $1). Just a little farther down Maxwell Rd., **Wither Hills Walkway** provides a pleasant assortment of quick jaunts and good views of the countryside.

KAIKOURA

Kaikoura's brilliant blue bay and snowcapped peaks are the dramatic setting for a a fully interactive ecological wonderland. Kaikoura (pop. 3000) means "to eat crayfish" in Maori, and a multitude of the crunchy crustaceans can be found paddling beneath the waves. Larger wildlife, including fur seals, albatross and other marine birds, dusky dolphins, and numerous species of whales, is also abundant in the waters off the Kaikoura shore. Though the town itself is unremarkable, the local tourism industry has worked out every way (short of being swallowed by a whale) to experience the unique ecology. The various tours and accommodations in this town fill up early during the summer, so book ahead; the winter scene is markedly more hushed.

🛈 ORIENTATION AND PRACTICAL INFORMATION

Midway between Picton (154km away) and Christchurch (183km away), **SH1** becomes, at various points, **Churchill St., Beach Rd.,** and **Atheiney Rd.** Bear right just before Beach Rd. onto the **Westend** (which turns into the **Esplanade** about 1km south), home to most of Kaikoura's shops and accommodations. The **Kaikoura Visitor Information Centre** (tel. 319 5641; fax 319 6819; www.kaikoura.co.nz), located on the Westend, will store luggage ($1 per day), change money on the weekends, arrange bookings for tours, hotels, and transportation throughout New Zealand, and provide information about local attractions (open daily Sept.-May 8:30am-5:30pm; June-Aug. 9am-5pm). **TranzScenic** (tel. 0800 802 802) has daily train service to **Christchurch** (3hr., 4pm, $41) and **Picton** (2hr., 10:45am, $39). Kaikoura doesn't have a bookings office, so buy your ticket in advance, or from the conductor when the train arrives. In addition to **InterCity** (tel. 319 5641), at least seven other bus and shuttle companies run daily to **Christchurch** (2½hr., $15-20) and **Picton** (2hr., $15-20). Book at the Visitor Centre. **Hanmer Connection** (tel. 0800 377 378) also heads to **Hanmer Springs** (2hr., Tu, Th, and Sa 2pm, $25). Other services include: **taxis** (tel. 319 6214); the **DOC office** (tel. 319 5714) on Ludstone Rd., with the usual assortment of crucial tramping information and an intentions book; the **BNZ,** 42 Westend, and **Westpac Trust,** 34 Westend (with **ATMs**); the **police** (tel. 319 5038); a **hospital** (tel. 319 5027); a **post office,** 41 Westend (open M-F 8:30am-5pm); and **Internet access,** available at the **public library** (tel. 319 6280) across from the Visitors Centre (call in advance; $2 per 10min.; open M-Th 9:30am-5:30pm, F 9:30am-7pm, Sa 10am-1pm). **Telephone code:** 03.

♟ ACCOMMODATIONS

Most accommodations are located along **Westend, Beach Rd.,** and the **Esplanade** along the beach, while a few others are on the hill overlooking the bay, a short but steep walk from the town center.

🏅 **Dusky Lodge,** 67 Beach Rd. (tel. 319 5959; fax 319 6929). This small, spunky backpackers shows just what you can do with a lot of space and creative planning. The rooms are named after birds, the enormous lounge and kitchen area sport attractive, hewn wooden furniture, and ping-pong and pool tables in the entrance area await challengers. Free pickup, free breakfast. Dorms $16; twins and doubles with linen $40. Book ahead in summer.

Topspot Backpackers, 22 Deal St. (tel. 319 5540; fax 319 6587). From the Visitor Centre, walk across the street and trek uphill on the Lydia Washington Walkway onto Deal St. Loud music and busloads of backpacker tours will let you know you've found this lively hotspot. Internet hotspot. Bunks $16; doubles with bath $40.

Cray Cottage, 190 the Esplanade (tel. 319 5152). Owners offer free sunset tours of Kaikoura, 4WD trips, and even fishing trips (off boat or shore). Dorms $16; twins $40. Closed in winter; call with inquiries.

Dolphin Lodge (Nomads), 15 Deal St. (tel. 319 5842). A lodge with a quiet and peaceful air, the Dolphin prides itself on not having a TV. Pay extra for the double room's great mountain and sea view. Bright red metal bunks $16; doubles $40.

Moby Dix (VIP), 65 Beach Rd. (tel./fax 319 6699). Gorgeous ocean murals and low lights by the TV. Pool sharks will enjoy the billiard table in the middle of the dining area. Dorms $15.50; twins and doubles with linen $37. Inquire about winter specials.

Adelphi Lodge (tel. 319 5141 or 0800 472 856; fax 319 6786), on Westend. Right smack in the middle of town, the lodge's budget accommodations are a little bare, but nonetheless comfortable. Parking, a hot spa pool, and hammocks out back. Internet. Dorms (some with private bathroom) $16, winter $12.50; twins and doubles with linen $45, winter $40.

Maui YHA, 270 the Esplanade (tel. 319 5931; fax 319 6921). A $6 taxi ride from the train or bus stations. Manager Kuini could take the piss out of the Queen Mother without offense and the magnificent ocean make up for the unfortunate 30-minute trek to the center of town. Dorms $17; twins $38; doubles $40.

A1 Kaikoura Motels and Holiday Park, 11 Beach Rd. (tel./fax 319 5999 or 0800 605 999; email kaimotel@voyager.co.nz), and the **Searidge Holiday Park,** 34 Beach Rd. (tel./fax 319 5362 or 0800 363 638), provide camping facilities. Follow Beach Rd. away from the town center and cross under the railway overpass. Dorms $15; standard cabins for 2 $33, deluxe $40; tourist cabins for 2 $45-48 (extra person $12); tent sites $17 for 2 (extra person $8.50), with power $20 for 2 (extra person $10).

FOOD

A blue Matisse woman, hanging spider plants, Pink Floyd, and comfy couches greet patrons of the **Small World Cafe** (tel. 319 7070) on Westend. Delight in the chicken, beef, lamb, or falafel souvlakis ($5-6). While the coffee is popular, the passionfruit smoothie ($3) wins rave reviews. (Open daily 11:30am-9pm, winter W-Su noon-7pm. Cash only.) One of the few places to cater to backpackers, **Sonic Bar and Cafe,** 93 Westend (tel. 319 6414), offers affordable and filling dinner fare and misplaced urban chic. Nightly Happy Hour (8:30-9:30pm) coupled with pizzas and burgers (under $10) make Sonic popular with a younger crowd. (Open from 5pm.) The romantic, candlelit **Act One Pizza Cafe and Bar,** 25 Beach Rd. (tel. 319 6760), offers an array of creative gourmet pizzas for all tastes and appetites. Prices range from $7 for a standard small cheese to more than $27 for large, exotic pizzas like Apricot Chicken or Peppered Venison. (Open daily 5pm-midnight or later.)

SIGHTS AND ACTIVITIES

UP CLOSE AND PERSONAL WITH WILDLIFE

There are several options for those wishing to experience the sea first-hand. Weather permitting, **Dolphin Encounter,** 58 Westend (tel. 319 6534 or 0800 733 365; email, info@dolphin.co.nz), gets you into a wetsuit and deposits you right at the edge of a pod of dusky dolphins, a small, friendly, playful, and acrobatic species found off the Kaikoura shore. The water can be chilly and the frolics exhausting, but the thrill of being circled and assessed by a posse of sleek dolphins is unmatched. Bring a towel and warm, wind-resistant clothes. ($85; spectators $48. Book well in advance; waits can be as long as 4-6 weeks in the high season.) The **Kaikoura Wildlife Centre** (tel. 319 6622) offers a variety of ecotours ranging from diving with dolphins ($85), to snorkeling with seals (Sept.-May $45), to scuba diving ($90 for 1 dive, all equipment supplied; $445 for a 4-day certification course). **Graeme's Seal Swim** (tel. 319 6182) operates land-based seal snorkeling from April (2½ hr., $35). If all of that sounds like sissy stuff, let **Kaikoura Shark Meet** (tel. 319 5641 or 0800 2C JAWS) drop you among a swarm of sharks inside a special bite-proof cage. (3hr. Daily Nov.-May. $110, with all equipment provided. No scuba experience necessary.)

WILDLIFE OBSERVATION TOURS

The Maori-affiliated **Whale Watch Kaikoura** (tel. 319 6767 or 0800 655 121), located at the old "whaleway" station, conducts information-packed tours (2½hr.) of waters filled with whales, seals, royal albatrosses, and gulls. They offer a refund of up to 80% if no whales are seen during the trip. In June and July, keep an eye out for humpback whales; in summer, look for orca instead. ($95, ages 5-15 $60, ages 3-5 $30. No children under 3. Book 1-2 weeks ahead in summer, 3-4 days in winter. Anti-seasickness wristbands provided.) **Ocean Wings** (tel. 319 6777 or 0800 733 365), run by Dolphin Encounter, is a two- to three-hour boat trip to view Kaikoura's pelagic (ocean-going) bird life. Using pieces of fish liver, the knowledgeable skipper draws huge crowds of birds, many of them very rare. ($60, children $35. 2-person minimum or by arrangement. Book at Dolphin Encounter.) **Wings Over Whales** (tel. 319 6580 or 0800 2C MOBY) operates year-round aerial whale-watching tours. The flight also provides a beautiful view of the coastline and mountains. (30min. flights $95, children $60. Transportation to airfield $5.)

SEALS AND WALKS

A highlight of Kaikoura is the **Point Kean seal colony,** about one hour down the Esplanade from the Visitor Centre. The reef off of the coast is a major breeding site for fur seals and is busiest during the breeding season (Nov.-Feb.), although seals are present year-round. The seals are relatively accustomed to humans, but it is best to maintain at least five meters distance from them. There is no better way to view the entirety of the seal colony and the beauty of the bay than the **Peninsula Walkway** (approx. 3hr.). If you elect to follow the cliff route, prepare for hurdling turnstiles and getting chummy with the local livestock (the route crosses private farmlands at times). If you want to travel the shoreline route, which allows you to see more seals and explore local tide pools, check the signs at the Visitor Centre first, as the walk is best enjoyed within two hours of low tide. If you just can't get enough of the stinky bastards, just 24km north of Kaikoura off the main highway lies **Ohau Point,** the main breeding site on the Kaikoura Coast, where the DOC has kindly set up a public viewing platform overlooking the scores of fur seals that gather here. The **Hinau Track** (45min., starts 15km out of town) and **Fyffe-Palmer Track** (1½hr., starts 6km out of town) are steep but manageable mountain trails where you might run across the Kaikoura black-eyed gecko or one of the three endangered species of the world's heaviest insect, the giant weta.

SKIING

For ski addicts, **Mt. Lyford** (tel. 315 6178) is a mere 60km from Kaikoura. For a day excursion from Kaikoura ($75 return) including ski hire, field pass and transport, inquire at the Visitor Centre. (Open June-Oct. Day pass $35, students $30; ski rental $15-25, snowboard rental $40.)

HANMER SPRINGS

The rare combination of converging faultlines and connected underground fractures brings Hanmer Springs to geothermal life. Melt away years and frown-lines in the thermal springs at the center of this small resort town, where shivering skiers from the nearby slopes and bone-weary jetboaters flock to unwind in the steaming waters. After drying off, the relaxation therapy can continue with soothing walks through the gentle surrounding hills and shadowy peaks.

⚡ ORIENTATION AND PRACTICAL INFORMATION

Hanmer Springs is about 10km off SH7 and 136km north of Christchurch. Coming by bus from the West Coast via Lewis Pass, you will probably be dropped off at Hanmer Corner, unless the driver has time to run you into town, which costs a few extra dollars. Otherwise (if you don't feel like walking 10km into the village), arrange for pickup from **Hanmer Connection** (tel. 0800 377 378 or 315 7575) for $5.

The **Hurunui Visitor Information Centre/DOC office** (tel./fax 315 7128), on the corner of Amuri and Jackson Pass Rd., sits to the side of the thermal pools (open daily 10am-5pm). **Hanmer Connection** runs to **Christchurch** (2hr., 5pm daily, $22) and **Kaikoura** (2hr., 3 per week, $25). **White Star** (tel. 0800 829 982) and **Lazerline** (tel. 0800 220 001) head daily to **Nelson** (5hr., 1 per day, $30-35) and **Christchurch** (1 per day, $15-20). Lazerline, while a bit more expensive, is often a better bet as they drop off and pick up in town, in front of the Hurunui Visitor Centre. To trek all the way to **Westport,** take White Star west to Spring's Junction and transfer buses. Other services include: **BNZ** (tel. 315 7220), located in the shopping center on Conical Hill Rd. (no ATM; open M, W, and F 10am-2pm); the **Four Square supermarket** (tel. 315 7190), also in the Conical Hill Rd. shopping center, containing a small **post office** (open M-F 8:30am-5:30pm, Sa 9am-4pm, Su 10am-2pm); the **Hanmer Springs Medical Centre** (tel. 315 7503; open M-F 9am-12:30pm and 2:30-4:30pm, Sa-Su 10am-noon); the **ambulance** (tel. 0800 222 600); and **after-hours medical help** (tel. (025) 221 2828). **Telephone Code:** 03.

ACCOMMODATIONS

Only a couple of budget accommodations are within walking distance of the pools. **Hanmer Backpackers,** 41 Conical Hill Rd. (tel. 315 7196), a five-minute walk past the thermal reserve on the right, houses guests in a loft and shed out back; the lounge and kitchen area are shared with the backpackers' owners. There is laundry, but no dryer. (Dorms $15.) **Mountain View Holiday Park** (tel. 315 7113; fax 315 7118), on the corner of Bath St. and Hanmer Springs Rd., is the most conveniently located motor camp, about an eight-minute walk out of town. The cheapest options are the standard cabins with communal kitchen ($35 for 2, extra person $10) or the tourist cabins with kitchens ($45 for 2, extra person $10). There are also powered sites ($20 for 2, extra person $9.50) and unpowered sites ($18 for 2, extra person $8.50).

ACTIVITIES

The main attraction is never hard to find; if the smell of sulfur isn't enough, follow the plumes of steam to the ◪**Hanmer Springs Thermal Reserve** (tel. 315 7511), on Amuri Ave. Roast in the 45°C pool to prove you're superhuman, or pull a Goldilocks and try each of the 14 different public pools until you find one that's just right. (Open daily 10am-9pm. Admission $8, day pass $11, waterslide $4 extra).

Contact **Rainbow Adventures** (tel. 315 7444 or 315 7401) for a slew of adventure options, including canyoning (Oct.-May; 2hr., $42), rafting (half-day $60, full day with lunch $89), and paragliding (Oct.-May; $135). **Thrillseekers Adventure Centre** (tel. 315 7046), offers bungy jumping off a bridge above the Waiau River ($89), jet-boat rides (40min., $60), and rafting down the steep-sided gorge of the Waiau River ($60). Book through Hanmer Connection for free pickup. **Rollesby Experience** (tel. 315 7146) leads guided horseback-riding trips across farmland and hills for both novice and experienced riders. Book through Hanmer Connection for free pickup. (1hr. $25, 2hr. $45, half-day $80.) **Dust-n-Dirt,** 20 Conical Hill Rd. (tel./fax 315 7233), hires mountain bikes and offers trail maps (1hr. $9, 2hr. $12, 4hr. $16, full day $25).

In winter, hit the slopes at the **Hanmer Springs Ski Area** (tel. 315 7233), a mere 45-minute drive from Hanmer Springs. Known as "the friendly field," it has some runs that are groomed for easy going while others are left untouched for more experienced skiers. (Tow fees $28, students $20; ski rental $20, snowboard $40.) Call **Hanmer Springs Skifield Transport** (tel. 315 7401) if you don't have a car (45 min.; $20 return). For a bit more skiing variety, **Mt. Lyford Ski Field** (tel. 315 6178) is just 50 minutes away. The field is more developed with many tourist services and is especially good for novice snowboarders. (Tow fees $35, student $30; ski rental $25, snowboard and boots $40.) Catch the shuttle daily at the information center (1½hr., 7:30am, $20 return).

SOUTH ISLAND

Short walks, day-hikes, and serious tramps run directly out of or near Hanmer Springs. The Visitor Centre is stocked with maps, brochures, and advice to point you in the right direction.

MARUIA SPRINGS

Minuscule and remote, **Maruia Springs Thermal Resort** (tel. 523 8840) provides a serene, sulfuric getaway from anything resembling civilization. One hour's drive west of big brother Hanmer Springs on SH7, the complex consists entirely of three outdoor thermal pools, a traditional Japanese bathhouse complete with jacuzzi, a bar and restaurant, and varying levels of accommodations. The pools are as much a place to socialize as to soak, and fellow guests are happy to share a schmooze. Private spa houses are also available for rental from 10:30am to 5pm. ($20 per hr. plus $10 key deposit). While Hanmer Springs may have more pools to choose from, Maruia manages to escape the crowds and offers a greater sense of tranquility; the outdoor pools are surrounded by mountains and open 24 hours a day. If you're passing by, take a day to soak, even if it means a slight detour from your path. The price of all lodgings include 24-hour access to the outdoor pools and 8:30am-10pm access to the Japanese bathhouse. (Check-out 10am. Dorms $26.50; hotel units $105-140; tent sites $9 per person. Non-guest access 9am-9pm to outdoor pools and bathhouse $6.50, students $5.)

NELSON AND ENVIRONS

NELSON

Home to the country's first game of rugby, the first eight-hour working day in the world, and the oldest New Zealand railway, the small city of Nelson (pop. 43,000) is the geographic center of the country and a popular domestic holiday destination. In addition to being New Zealand's largest fishing port, Nelson is surprisingly on top of modern social trends for a city its size, with an artsy movie theater, snazzy coffee houses, and a wide range of dining and shopping options. With a high percentage of sunny days, New Zealand's second city (originally Whakatu, established 1842) also attracts visitors to its wineries, orchards, and artists' studios. The clay in the area is particularly suited for pottery (it is traded throughout the South Pacific), making Nelson a haven for sculptors. Nelson's art scene reaches its zenith with the **Wearable Art Awards** (see p. 265) every September, but the scores of artisan dens and studios maintain the bohemian spirit year-round.

■ ORIENTATION AND PRACTICAL INFORMATION

While the entirety of Nelson is rather spread out, with suburbs sprawling up into the hills on all sides, Nelson proper is very compact. **Christ Church Cathedral,** on Trafalgar St., dominates central Nelson and stands tall above its surrounding gardens. **Trafalgar, Bridge,** and **Hardy Streets** comprise the main shopping district with a plethora of shops, accommodations, and restaurants. From the bus depot, take a left onto Bridge St. and you'll hit Trafalgar St.

Visitors Center: Nelson Visitor Centre (tel. 548 2304; fax 546 7393), at the corner of Trafalgar and Halifax St., a 10min. walk on Trafalgar St. from the cathedral steps. Those traveling by car may want to pick up the brochure *The Coastal Way on Tasman Bay* detailing the attractions of SH60, which runs along the Waimea Inlet and Ruby Bay coasts. Open daily 8:30am-5pm, winter M-F 8:30am-5:30pm.

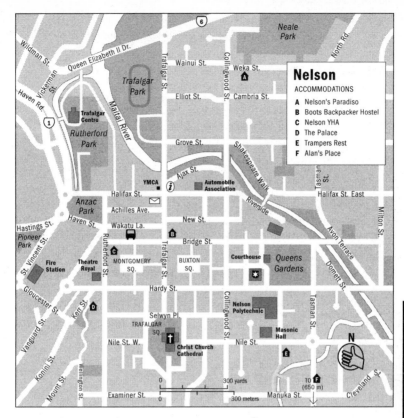

DOC: 186 Bridge St. (tel. 546 9335), in the Monro State Building. The DOC has the scoop on Abel Tasman, Kahurangi, and Nelson Lakes national parks. In the summer, the DOC provides information at the Visitor Centre. Open M-F 8am-4:30pm.

Airplanes: The **airport** is located past the Tahunanui Beach area. **Air New Zealand Link** (tel. 0800 767 767) and **Ansett** (tel. 0800 267 388) fly daily to **Wellington** (35min., 8-12 per day, $176) and **Christchurch** (50min. for Air New Zealand, 2½hr. for Ansett (via Wellington), 2-5 per day, $275). Book well in advance for lower prices.

Buses: All buses leave from the Visitor Centre. **InterCity** (tel. 548 538) heads daily to **Fox Glacier** (11hr., 7:30am, $91) via **Westport** (4hr., $44) and **Picton** (2hr., 10am, $19) via **Blenheim** (1½hr., $15). You can also take the bus to Blenheim and transfer to **Christchurch** (8½hr., $54). **Lazerline** (tel. 0800 220 001) and **White Star** (tel. 546 8687) go daily to **Christchurch** (7½hr., 8:30am, $35-40) via **Springs Junction** (3½hr., $20-23). White Star makes it possible to transfer at Springs Junction to **Westport** (6hr., $27), providing a cheaper but less direct option than InterCity. There are two main transportation options to **St. Arnaud** in the Nelson Lakes region. **Wadsworth Motors** (tel. 522 4248) is significantly cheaper but longer (3½hr., M, W, and F 10am, $12) than **Nelson Lakes Transport** (tel. 547 5912; 1½hr., 8:30am, winter 6:45am, $18), as it is also a mail run. To get to **Abel Tasman National Park,** call **Abel Tasman Coachlines** (tel. 548 0285) or **Kahurangi Bus Service** (tel. 525 9434). Prices and times vary according to destination (1½-4hr., 3 per day, $12-26).

Taxis: Nelson City Taxis (tel. 548 8225 or 0800 108 855) or **Sun City Taxis** (tel. 548 2666 or 0800 422 666). Open 24hr.

Car Rental: In addition to international chains, try **Pegasus Rental Cars Nelson,** 83 Haven Rd. (tel. 548 0884 or 24hr. tel. 0800 803 580) or **NZ Rent a Car,** at the intersection of Collingwood and Halifax St. (tel. 546 9172). Get advice and car help at the **AA,** 45 Halifax St. (tel. 548 8339).

Bicycle Rental: Stewarts Cycle City, 114 Hardy St. (tel. 548 1666). Half-day $15, full day $20.

Currency Exchange: BNZ, 226 Trafalgar St., **National Bank,** 248 Trafalgar St., **ANZ,** 265 Trafalgar St., at the corner of Trafalgar and Hardy St., and **ASB,** at the same intersection. All open M-F 9am-4:30pm.

American Express: (tel. 548 9079). There is no office in town, but there is a travel service representative at 153 Trafalgar St.

Camping Equipment: Before heading off to one of the 3 national parks nearby, stop in and stock up at **Rollo's BBQ and Camping Centre,** 12 Bridge St. (tel. 548 1975; open M-F 8am-5:30pm, Sa 9am-1:30pm).

Police: St. John St. (tel. 548 8309), in central Nelson.

Medical Services: Prices Pharmacy, 296 Hardy St. (tel. 548 3897), at Collingwood St. Open M-F 8:30am-8pm, Sa-Su 9am-8pm. **Nelson Hospital** (tel. 546 1800), on Tipahi St. with emergency doctor and emergency dentist. Open 24hr. **City Care,** 202 Rutherford St. (tel. 546 8881), has a doctor on duty 24hr.

Post Office: 108 Trafalgar St. (tel. 546 7818). Open M-F 7:45am-5pm, Sa 9:30am-12:30pm.

Internet Access: Boots Off, 53 Bridge St. (tel. 546 8981), near the bus terminal, has a slew of terminals. $8 per hr. Open M-F 10am-10pm, Sa 10am-7pm, Su 3-9pm, winter M-F 10am-6pm, Sa 2pm-6pm, Su 4-7pm.

Telephone Code: 03.

⌐ ACCOMMODATIONS

Some of Nelson's hostels are seasonal, closing for the winter, but overflowing during the summer as trampers and backpackers stop on their way to Nelson Lakes or various Golden Bay destinations such as Abel Tasman National Park.

▨ **The Palace,** 114 Rutherford St. (tel./fax 548 4691). A magnificent hilltop historic home. Spacious balcony and gardens overlook the city. Rooms have high ceilings, huge windows, and carved wooden fireplaces. Blankets and heaters provided. Free 24hr. spa, free pickup, Internet, and possibly the largest foreign language book exchange in New Zealand. Reception 8am-9pm. Dorms $17; doubles $20. No credit cards.

Nelson's Paradiso, 42 Weka St. (tel. 546 6703; fax 546 7533). If a sauna, spa, swimming pool, and volleyball court sound like a smashing recipe for a good time, call the Paradiso for a free pickup. Free vegetable soup is served through the winter in the huge kitchen, and a giant, green tour bus named Bessie parked out back has been converted to a lounge. Dorms $16; twins and doubles $38; 4-person rooms $68.

Trampers Rest and Wheelpacker, 31 Alton St. (tel. 545 7477). Located on one of Nelson's heritage streets, this hostel is considered one of the South Island's best. Dorms $17; doubles $40.

Nelson YHA, 59 Rutherford St. (tel. 545 9988; fax 545 9989). Central location and conscientious management compensate for the institutional feel of this immense hostel. The staff can help make tour arrangements. Get the combination before you go out at night. Blankets, sheets, and duvets provided, though rooms come with heaters that automatically turn off after 30min. Internet. Reception 8-10am and 3-10pm. Dorms $19; singles $32; doubles and twins $44; doubles with bath $56. Non-YHA $4 more.

Alan's Place (VIP), 42 Westbrook Terr. (tel./fax 548 4854). A small, friendly place located roughly 20min. from the center of town on foot (call for transport). Free scones and tea upon arrival. Ask the very helpful and enthusiastic staff about area activities. Tramping gear available for borrowing and stoves for hire. Reception 8:30am-8:30pm. Dorms $17; twins $34; doubles $38. YHA, VIP, or student $1 off.

Tahuna Beach Holiday Park, 70 Beach Rd., Tahunanui (tel. 548 5159 or 0800 500 501; fax 548 5294). A huge, 54-acre facility with hundreds of tent and powered sites ($16-18) and an incredible variety of cabins and motels ($26-80, winter $22-68). Reception 8am-9:30pm.

FOOD

Many of Nelson's restaurants, cafes, and takeaways are located on Trafalgar, Bridge, and Hardy St., though several seafood restaurants along the oceanfront, on Wakefield Quay, can be reached by taxi ($5), bus ($2), or car. The numerous ethnic restaurants in town will satisfy diverse tastes. Home-cookers can collect supplies at **New World supermarket** (tel. 548 9111), Montgomery Sq. (open M-F 8am-9pm, Sa 8:30am-7pm, Su 9am-7pm) or **Supervalue Supermarket,** 69 Collingwood St. (tel. 548 0191; open M-F 8am-9pm, Sa-Su 8am-8pm).

Zippy's, 276 Hardy St. (tel. 546 6348), between Hope and Collingwood St. Pony-tailed Zippy chuckles in his corner and looks on as patrons, lost in vegan paradise, relax on shag-carpeted stools. The regular menu includes savory burritos overflowing with your choice of three fillings ($7), topped bagels (from $2), and spirulina fruit smoothies ($3). Die-hard carnivores steer clear—nothing on Zippy's menu contains meat. BYO. Open Su-W 9am-10pm, Th-Sa 9am-noon; winter Su-M 9am-6pm, Tu-W 9am-10pm, Th-Sa 9am-midnight. Cash only.

Akbabas Turkish Kebab House, 130 Bridge St. (tel. 548 8825). A small restaurant and takeaway whose low tables and floor pillows make for social dining. Rugs and garlic hang on the walls and Turkish music fills the front room where you can watch your selection being prepared. Spicy chicken kebab in a pita $6, large $8; falafels $4, large $5.50. Open daily 11am-9pm, winter until 8:30pm. Cash only.

Chez Eelco Coffee House, 296 Trafalgar St. (tel. 548 7595). Facing the cathedral, the cafe is on your right. Order off the lampshade menu as giant copper cockroaches and a rose-carrying grasshopper on the wall look on. Stay in to play chess and peruse the daily paper or venture outside to watch Nelson bustle by. Muesli with fruit $7; delicious, creamy mussel chowder $7; vegetable bean-topped nachos $9. Internet. Open M-F from 6am, Sa-Su from 7am. Cash only.

Land of Pharaohs, 270 Hardy St. (tel. 548 8404), between Morrison and Hope St. Tapestries and photographs of Egyptian monuments fill this tiny, red-lit restaurant. Vegan meat kebabs ($4-7.50), while carnivores may prefer beef, lamb, or chicken kebabs ($4-7.50). Top it all off with baklava ($2.50). Outdoor dining. BYO. Open daily 9:30am-late, winter M-F 11am-9pm, Sa-Su 11 am-10pm.

Victorian Rose, 281 Trafalgar St. (tel. 548 7631). An upscale, yet traditional pub where images of Victorian women compete with the latest sports match on TV for the attention of patrons. Beer-drinkers can relax outside in the courtyard to enjoy one of 17 beers on tap. Burgers should fill you up ($12), but the truly ravenous can take on the Victorian Rose Challenge for $22.50 (400g steak; free beer). The Sunday roast ($12) is an all-you-can-eat affair with free soup and dessert (from 5:30pm). The Visitor Centre and most hostels offer a coupon granting 10% off all meals. Open daily from 11am.

Boat Shed Cafe and Restaurant, 350 Wakefield Quay (tel. 546 9783), on the oceanfront (a taxi ride away), is highly recommended by locals. An old, converted boat shed practically sitting on the ocean known for fresh seafood with a great view on the side. The Tasman Bay Chowder ($9) or Marlborough Sounds mussels ($12) are both outstanding selections. Open daily 11:30am-2:30pm for lunch, dinner from 6pm.

NIGHTLIFE

Nightlife in Nelson is really hit or miss—some nights you will have to fight your way into local bars, while others involve seemingly endless and unsuccessful scoping for the in-crowd. Take heart—there is usually a party to be found. Local bars sporadically have live bands, theme nights, or drink deals, especially on weekends. While following the recommendations of hostel owners or locals sometimes yields good results, it is often easiest and most profitable to simply wander Bridge St. and the south end of Trafalgar and follow your ears (or the man walking rather unsteadily in front of you) to find the action.

The **Victorian Rose** (see **Food**, above) attracts a sizeable crowd to its bar, especially after work. With 17 beers and one cider on tap, this pub is sure to please even the most discerning of beer connoisseurs. Bridge St. houses a number of taverns, bars, and licensed restaurants, including the **Little Rock Cafe**, 165 Bridge St. (tel. 546 8800). The large open area around the bar allows for easy circulation and atmosphere encourages mingling, making the Little Rock one of the more elegant of the local favorites. **Molly Maguire's Irish Bar,** 123 Bridge St. (tel. 548 1457), is closer to the center of town and draws a more rough-and-tumble crowd. With a dark, smoky interior and, more often than not, rugby on the telly, Molly's showcases the earthier side of Nelson.

If sobriety is the order of the day (or night), Nelson also offers a four-screen cinematic experience at the **State Cinemas,** corner of Trafalgar and Halifax St., across from the Visitor Centre (tel. 548 8123). Tickets are $6.50 before 5pm and $9 in the evenings; student discounts are available on weeknight shows. Buy your tickets in advance, as shows often sell out, especially on weekends. The **Suter Gallery** (tel. 548 4699) screens less mainstream movies; call for titles and showtimes.

SIGHTS AND ACTIVITIES

The best way to groove with the many faces of Nelson is to wander among them at Nelson's weekly **flea market.** Held Saturday and Sunday mornings in the Montgomery Sq. carpark, the market offers local crafts, a wide selection of art, fresh produce, hidden treasures from attics, and much more (including a healthy dose of local activists and food vendors). Nelson is also experimenting with a Sunday afternoon arts market; inquire at the Visitor Centre for time and location.

ADVENTURE

Several adventure options provide a look at Nelson's wild side. **Stonehurst Farm Horse Treks** (tel. 542 4121) offers a variety of one- to four-hour adventures, including the Rambler Trail through scenic farmland (1hr., $30) and the longer River-Ride, which includes afternoon tea (half-day, 1pm, $69). **Happy Valley 4x4 Motorbike Adventures** (tel. 545 0304) offers four-wheel motorbike excursions such as the Farm Funride (1hr., $45) or the BayView Tour (2½hr., $75). For the aquatically-minded, **Sail Tasman** (tel. 547 2754) can treat you to a Wednesday evening race cruise in the Nelson Harbour (approx. 3hr., $35), or a three-day excursion by boat to Abel Tasman ($295, including food and a number of beach visits and short hikes; call in advance to book). "Adrenaline dealers" **Natural High,** 52 Rutherford St. (tel. 546 6936), hire out mountain bikes (half-day $20, full day $30) and offer guided biking tours (from $40). They also rent kayaks and tramping gear. Or, if none of these options sounds heart-pumping enough, **Tandem Skydive Nelson** (tel. 545 2121 or 0800 422 899) provides a more daring option (from 3000m $195, 4000m $240).

TOURS

To see the behind-the-scenes aspects of Nelson, head out of town by car or tour bus (walking isn't really feasible). **JJ's Wine Tours** (tel. 544 7081) offer tours of several local wineries (half-day $50). **Nelson Day Tours** (tel. 548 4224) offer a range of tours to local highlights, including the city district (3-4hr., $30) and several wineries and craft centers (3-4hr., $35). They also run trips to Golden Bay ($85) and Lake Rotoiti ($65) on demand. Stop by **McCashin's Brewery,** 660 Main Rd. (tel. 547 5357), in Stoke, about 15 minutes outside Nelson, to see some of the bottling operations and check out the retail shops. Tours run at 11:15am (and 2:15pm in summer) for a mere $5 tasting fee, but call ahead to book, especially in winter. Their product, **Mac's Beer,** is a local favorite, made at the brewery without chemicals or preservatives but with a distinctive bottle and cap. Continuing on SH6, at the corner of the Richmond Bypass, you'll find **Craft Habitat** (tel./fax 544 7481). Watch the artisans at work, as some weave lanolin-rich wool while others strive for perfection in their pieces of jewelry or pottery. From SH6, turning right on Queen St. in Richmond then left on Lansdowne Rd. will bring you to the **Höglund Art Glassblowing Studio** (tel. 544 6500), where two galleries display glass of every color and shape. Watch in awe as the glass-blowers perform their magic. Open daily from 9am to 5pm. Free.

OTHER SIGHTS AND ACTIVITIES

If you have a hankering for a picnic, head to **Anzac Memorial Park** (off Rutherford St.) or **Miyazu Japanese Garden** (on Atawhai Dr., near the water) to escape the large flocks of hungry-eyed fowl in the Victorian **Queens Gardens,** which has entrances on Hardy St. and Bridge St. **Suter Art Gallery** (tel. 548 4699), next to Queens Gardens, on Bridge St., is a public art museum with a strong collection of New Zealand and local art, as well as a craft shop, cinema theater, and restaurant (open daily 10:30am-4:30pm; students $2). A mixture of industrial and Gothic architecture, **Christ Church Cathedral** sits atop Church Hill on Trafalgar St.

Those in search of Nelson's natural history will find an outlet in a number of nearby walks (*Walk Nelson,* a $3 brochure outlining 30 local walks, is available from the Nelson City Council office, 110 Trafalgar St.; open M-F 8am-4:30pm). The rather steep **Centre of New Zealand Walk** will get you close, if not exactly, to the center of New Zealand (return 40min.; begins in the Botanic Gardens). The **Maitai River Walkway** (return 4hr.) will take you along the river past homes and a wishing well out to sheep-grazed countryside. The fine sands of **Tahunanui Beach** ("shifting sands") make it a popular holiday destination; it's accessible by bike down Wakefield Quay, which turns into Rocks Rd. (20-30min.).

SPECIAL EVENTS

Every September, **New Zealand Wearable Art Awards** in Nelson's Trafalgar Centre turns out human spectacles. For judges and gawkers, people design themselves as everything from wispy, gauze dragonfly beauties and surreal spiked cyberpunks to jellyfish swathed in gyrating color. Tickets can be sold out as early as six months in advance. Call **Everyman Records,** 249 Hardy St. (tel. 548 3083), to reserve yourself a slot. For more info, contact the committee at P.O. Box 5140, Port Nelson (tel./fax 548 9299; email wearable@wearableart.co.nz). You can see some of the creations on one of the several web pages devoted to the event (such as www.wearableart.co.nz).

NELSON LAKES NATIONAL PARK

The park and its centerpieces of Lake Rotoiti and Lake Rotoroa draw hikers eager to explore the unspoiled and uncrowded tracks that pass through evergreen beech forests, mountains, and tussock grasslands. In the winter, the slopes become a haven for skiers. The gateway to the park is the tiny, lakeshore village of **St. Arnaud,** which sits on the moraine of the glacier that originally formed Lake Rotoiti. Unfortunately, the main attractions of Nelson Lakes National Park are living on borrowed time. The harsh elements in the area are eroding the mountains and depositing the sediment into the lakes, dooming the region to one day be a vast flatland. But don't let this deter you from a visit; it won't happen for thousands of years.

SOUTH ISLAND

⚠ ☞ PRACTICAL INFORMATION AND ACCOMMODATIONS. The **DOC head-quarters** in **St. Arnaud,** on View Rd. off SH63, also serves as the **Nelson Lakes National Park Visitors Centre** (tel. 521 1806; fax 521 1896; open daily 8am-4:30pm). The after-hours intentions box as well as 24hr. visitor information are located in the foyer. **Sounds-to-Coast Shuttle** (tel. 578 0225 or 0800 802 225) leaves for **Picton** (2hr., 2-3 per week, $15) via **Blenheim** (1¼hr., $10). **Sounds-to-Coast** also goes to **Greymouth** (3½hr., 8:35am, 2-3 per week, $30). Booking ahead is essential for **Nelson Lakes Transport** (tel. 547 5912), which goes to **Nelson** (1½hr., 6-7 per week, $18, return $34). **Wadsworth Motors** (tel. 522 4248) runs to **Nelson** for less if you don't mind a longer trip; it is also a mailrun (2½hr., M-F 1:30pm; $12). **Kiwilink** (tel. 0800 802 300 or 577 8332 in Blenheim) runs daily to **Picton** (1¾hr., 2 per day, $17) via **Blenheim** (1¼hr., $15). The **petrol station, post office,** and **general store** and departure point for buses are all at the **Nelson Lakes Village Centre** (tel. 521 1854; open daily 8:30am-6:30pm, earlier during ski season).

Sleeping options are slim pickings in St. Arnaud. The extremely bright **Yellow House (YHA Associate)** (tel. 521 1887; fax 521 1882) is a good bet with a personable staff that can also act as resources for park info. Internet, spa pool, and camping and hiking gear are available. (Dorms $18; doubles $44.) The **Alpine Chalet (VIP)** (tel./fax 521 1869, reservations 0800 367 777), part of the swank Alpine Lodge, has cramped but clean budget accommodations (dorms $16; doubles $45). The two **DOC campgrounds** at Lake Rotoiti, **Kerr Bay,** and **West Bay,** have tent sites ($7, powered $8; no pets allowed; closed in winter).

⚠ ACTIVITIES. The most well-known of Nelson Lakes' trails is the **Travers-Sabine Circuit,** a strenuous, four- to seven-day hike that crosses over the 1787m Travers Saddle. The huts in the Travers Valley are first-come, first-served, and often fill in summer; reservations can be made at the DOC office ($4-8 per night, depending on location). A number of hikes begin at Kerr Bay and range in duration from 30 minutes to 9 hours depending on your ambition. A pamphlet is available at the Visitor Centre, or just follow the well-marked signs. **St. Arnaud Guiding Services** (tel. 521 1028) is the local eco-tourism expert and leads on- and off-track walking trips into the park, ranging from general nature tours to gold prospecting ($55-85). The **Rotoiti Outdoor Education Centre** (tel. 521 1820) hires hiking gear year-round (including ice-axes, a must in winter, for $5 per day). Rafting trips on the Buller Rivers and horse trekking outside of St. Arnaud are alternatives to hiking.

The glaciers that carved out the Travers Valley were also responsible for creating **Lake Rotoiti,** 8km long, 80m at its deepest point, and jumping with brown trout. You can fish, canoe, jetboat, or waterski on the lake where Maori once fished for eels and mussels. **Rotoiti Water Taxis** (tel. 521 1894) can take you to the head of the lake (10min.; $10, minimum $40) among other spots. They also hire kayaks and canoes. Lake Rotoiti's big sister, **Lake Rotoroa** (off SH6), was carved out by the two glaciers that formed the Sabine and D'Urville Valleys (jetboating and waterskiing prohibited). Fisherfolk and birdwatchers can contact **Rotoroa Water Taxi** (tel. 523 9199) for a ride to the lakehead ($20 per person; minimum $60).

Wintertime revelers use Mt. Arnaud as a skiing and snowboarding base. The 350-hectare **Rainbow Ski Area** (tel. 521 1861) offers slopes for all levels of ability. Day lift passes are $44, while afternoon passes are $33. Skis, boots, and poles rent for $30 per day; snowboard and boots are $42 per day. Rainbow also rents ski suits and runs a shuttle to and from the skifield (return $10). The SnowPhone (tel. 0900 34 44 44) for up-to-date information on ski conditions (99¢ per minute). **Mt. Robert Ski Club** (tel. 547 7563; snowphone tel. 548 8336) is a private club, but non-members are still welcome (pass $20, students $15; cash or travellers cheques only). Huts are available on the mountain for $15 per night but be sure to book ahead. Helicopter transport up the mountain is available for $40 per person plus an additional charge of $15 for skis; gear is not available for hire on the mountain. Also, be sure to bring warm clothes and sturdy boots as a two hour hike may be necessary to leave the mountain, depending on weather conditions. **Nelson Lakes Transport** (tel.

547 5912; fax 547 5914) and **JJ Ski Transport** (tel. 544 7081) offer daily transport to **Rainbow Ski Area** (1hr., 8am, $15-20) and **Nelson** (1½hr., 4 or 5pm, $18-20); book ahead. Stop by the **St. Arnaud Snow and Information Center** (tel. 521 1850) for ice-skating rentals ($12) and information.

GOLDEN BAY

Golden Bay is where Abel Tasman first saw Aotearoa and Captain Cook bid it fare-well; it was the setting of the country's first gold rush and its first gold rush col-lapse a few years later. Today it's a lazy and seductive place where international hippies set down roots and young Kiwis rave through the New Year (www.gather-ing.co.nz). Sitting astride SH60 out of Nelson, groovy Motueka serves as the gate-way to Golden Bay, artsy Takaka lies at the core of the region, and the highway ends in tiny Collingwood. The widely enjoyed beaches of Abel Tasman National Park and the enjoyably wide wilderness of Kahurangi National Park sprawl on opposite sides of the bay, while the shifting sands of Farewell Spit crown the South Island. From counterculture to agriculture, with ample attractions both out-doors and in, Golden Bay continues to waylay those who pass through.

ABEL TASMAN NATIONAL PARK

Back in 1941, conservationist Pérrine Moncrieff was struggling to convince the government that a gorgeous swath of coastal forest was worth protecting from the timber industry. Then, according to Moncrieff, came "just the super-fly to tempt the Authority-fish," the 300-year anniversary of Abel Tasman's 1642 visit to these shores. What better way to celebrate than with a brand-new park? The feds took the bait, and Abel Tasman National Park was founded. With subtropical weather, turquoise waters, calm inlets, and golden sands, New Zealand's smallest national park (22,350 hectares) draws far-from-small crowds of trampers eager to attack the famous Coast Track, one of the country's most popular Great Walks. Mean-while, sea kayakers ply the well-paddled coastline, and the park's interior contains more challenging and geologically bizarre walking options.

⚐ ORIENTATION AND PRACTICAL INFORMATION. Just outside park borders, at the southern end of the **Coast Track,** the tiny tourist village of **Marahau** is the main water transport base for the park and the primary point of land access from the south. Marahau is 16km north of **Motueka** (see p. 272) and 67km north of **Nelson** (see p. 260). The major access points of the northern end of the park are the **Wainui carpark** (see p. 273), 21km east of Takaka, northern endpoint of the Coast Track, and **Totaranui**, 32km east of Takaka, a mammoth caravan park. **Abel Tasman Coachlines** (tel. 548 0285) and **Kahurangi Bus Services** (tel. 525 9434) run daily among these three access points; see coverage of **Nelson** (p. 260), **Motueka** (p. 272), and **Takaka** (p. 273) for relevant schedules. For those blessed with their own wheels, there is plenty of parking in Totaranui and in Maharau ($3 per night at Old Macdonald's Farm; $2 per night at the Barn; free for guests). Hitchhikers report there is usually plenty of traffic. The nearest **DOC offices** and **ATMs** are in Nelson, Motueka, and Takaka. **Telephone Code: 03.**

⚐⚏ ACCOMMODATIONS AND FOOD. Just a stone's throw from the Coast Track endpoint in Marahau, **The Barn** (tel. 527 8043) has free bikes, a small shop, and the only cardphone in town (spacious dorms $15; doubles in a truck or teepee $38, additional person $15; tent sites with separate kitchen and washing facilities $8.50). Just up the road, surrounded by the same lush hillside, the 100 acre **Old Macdonald's Farm** (tel. 527 8288) is most notable for its panoply of quirky perks: swimming holes, llama treks ($45 per half day), **Internet access** ($10 per hr.), shop and cafe (open daily 8am-8:30pm), and a clothing-optional caravan park. (Dorms $12; doubles $35; tent sites $8, with power $18.) Accessible only by foot or by boat, the upscale **Awaroa Lodge and Cafe** (tel. 528 8758) offers an expensive backpackers accommodation with a nice open-air kitchen and comfortable beds. (Linen $4. Sauna $7, non-guests $10. Dorms $25, winter $20.) The adjacent luxury resort has a pricey cafe and some enjoyable lounge areas (open daily 7:30am-11am, 11:30am-2:30pm, and 5-8pm; drinks until around midnight; shorter hours in winter). Along the track, the DOC-run **Totaranui Campsite** is home to bajillions of caravans and tents during peak season, and contains a small shop and fine little museum (tent sites $7, children $3.50, trampers with Great Walks pass $1). One of Marahau's few dining option is the trackside **Park Cafe and Restaurant** (tel. 527 8158), serving up the usual burgers ($10) and other standard fare (closed May-Aug.; open 8am-8:30pm; drinks 'til whenever).

▲ **WALKS.** For information on the **Abel Tasman Coast Track,** see below. The less-traversed **Inland Track** (3-5 days) also connects Marahau and Wainui, and is considerably more challenging than the Coast Track. Added to the park in the 70s, it passes a variety of mixed forests, sub-alpine vegetation, and strange marble formations. The Inland Track has three huts (plus a small one, Wainui Hut, on a side track); Back Country Hut tickets or Annual Passes apply. The track can also be accessed at its midpoint (2hr. from the Wainui or Moa Park Huts) via the 11km **Canaan Rd.** near Takaka Hill, midway between Takaka and Motueka off SH60. The road-end also offers access to the stone splendor of **Harwood's Hole** (one-way 45min.); numerous other **day hikes** begin from Totaranui and Wainui carpark.

◪ **WATER ACTIVITIES.** Established in 1993, the **Tonga Island Marine Reserve** stretches one nautical mile into the sea between Awaroa Bay and Bark Bay, and confers full legal protection upon all the sea creatures that happen to dwell there. **Abel Tasman Seal Swim and Water Taxi** (tel. 527 8136 or 0800 527 8136) gets visitors in the water with Tonga Island's sea lions, without coercing or feeding the animals (swim daily 10:30-11:30am; see p. 269 for water taxi details; $65, children $40).

The park's clear waters, trackless beaches, and fine weather have inspired a **sea kayaking** explosion in recent years. By sea kayak, you can reach points such as **Split Apple Rock** and **Mosquito Bay,** which the Coast Track does not access. Numerous outfitters offer combinations of guided paddles, independent rentals, and kayak/tramp options; all provide extensive instruction before sending anyone out. Most maintain a 2-person minimum, but try to match up solo travelers.

Both **Abel Tasman Kayaks** (Motueka tel. 527 8022; Nelson tel. 546 7711; closed July-Aug.) and **Ocean River** (tel. 527 8266 or 0800 732 529; closed June-Aug.) are based in Marahau and offer guided trips ($90-600) and kayaks for hire (from $95 for 2 days). **Marahau Beach Camp** (tel. 0800 808 018) does only freedom rentals ($40 per day). **Kaiteriteri Kayaks** (tel. 527 8383 or 0800 252 925) runs short trips out of Kaiteriteri Beach (guided half-day $45, full day $80, sunset $40; half-day rentals $35). **The Sea Kayaking Company,** 506 High St. (tel. 528 7251), runs out of Motueka (guided half-day $40, full day $80; 2 day rentals $85). **Planet Earth Adventures** (tel. 525 9095 or mobile 025 220 6213), in Pohara, is the only operator on the northern side of the park; they rent kayaks to anyone with some experience ($40), and offer guided tours (half-day $45, full day $75).

◪ ABEL TASMAN COAST TRACK

One of New Zealand's best-loved and most-walked tramps, the easygoing Abel Tasman Coast Track promises a stunning outdoor scene: emerald forests give glimpses of turquoise through the trees and eventually open onto azure bays surrounding the park's famous golden beaches. The track's landscape has been regenerating with stands of prickly gorse slowly yielding ground to tree ferns and young beeches. The Coast Track's lingering pockets of private enterprise and occasionally maddening crowds may not please wilderness-hungry trampers, but its scenery remains scintillating and accessible.

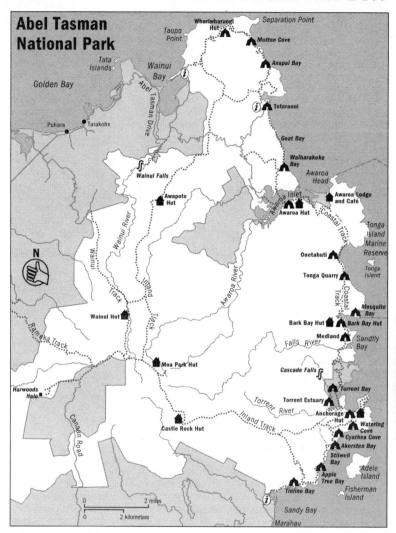

Abel Tasman
National Park

ESSENTIALS

Length: 51km, 3-5 days. The track is very smooth and mellow, with few strenuous elevation changes.

Seasonality: Year-round. The greatest crush of visitors occurs around Christmas and Easter. Winter affords more seclusion with average temperatures at a comfortable 18°C, although the nights can drop down to freezing.

Trailheads: Marahau in the south and **Wainui Carpark** in the north. The intermediate point at **Totaranui** can be accessed by car.

Huts and Campsites: A **Great Walk Pass** must be purchased before any overnight trip. The park kicked off a **new booking system** for huts in July 1999, in an attempt to prevent overcrowding. Trampers using tents are still unregulated, but hut reservations should be made well in advance. There are 4 huts and 21 designated campsites on the track, though a couple of the campsites are only accessible by sea. All huts and most campsites have toilets, taps, and heating stoves, plus other amenities described in detail below. There are no cooking stoves anywhere along the track. Huts Oct.-Apr. $12, May-Sept. $6. Camping year-round $6; youth half-price.

Water-taxis: The tides can affect one's timing on the track, since **Awaroa Inlet** can only be crossed within two hours on either side of low tide, and **Onetahuti Beach** has a river best crossed within four hours either side of low tide. Tide tables are posted at information centers and in the huts. Many water-taxis service the track's various coastal sections, heading north from **Marahau** to **Torrent Bay, Bark Bay, Onehuti Beach/Tonga Bay, Awaroa Bay,** and **Totaranui,** then looping back again. The following operators run on a daily schedule, charging around $15 to Torrent Bay (45min.) and $28 all the way to Totaranui (under 2hr.), with a variety of drop-off and return-trip options in between. **Abel Tasman Seafaris Aqua Taxi** (tel. 527 8083 or 0800 278 282) departs Marahau 9am, 10:30am, noon, and 2pm, winter 9am only. **Abel Tasman Seal Swim and Water Taxi** (tel. 0800 527 8136) departs 8:45am and 1pm; 4-person minimum in winter. **Abel Tasman National Park Experiences** (tel. 0800 223 582) departs 9am and noon in summer, winter 9am only. **Marahau Beach Camp** (tel. 0800 808 018) departs 9am and 1:45pm. **Abel Tasman Water Taxis** (tel. 528 7497 or 0800 423 397) runs on demand. **Sea kayaking** is another access option (see p. 268).

Special Gear: Beyond the necessities such as a stove and fuel (see **Camping and Outdoors,** p. 44). Bring ample **insect repellent** and **waterproof sandals** (togs), since both sandflies and water crossings are plentiful along the track. The glossy **free map** advertising Marahau presents much more detail than the standard-issue DOC pamphlet. Basic tramping gear can be rented from the **White Elephant** in Motueka (see p. 272) and **Old Macdonald's Farm** in Marahau (see p. 267); food and gear are best purchased in Nelson, Motueka, or Takaka.

Storage: Most accommodations store luggage. **Kahurangi Bus Services** and **Abel Tasman Coachlines** charge $5 per bag for transport between Motueka and Takaka.

THE TRACK
Marahau Trailhead to Anchorage Hut and Campsite: 11.5km, 3 hr.
Marahau trailhead to Tinline Creek Campsite: 30min.

Tinline Creek Campsite to Appletree Bay Campsite: 40min.

Appletree Bay Campsite to Stilwell Bay Campsite: 30min.

Stillwell Bay Campsite to Akersten Bay Campsite: 10min.

Akersten Bay Campsite to Watering Cove Campsite: 1hr.

Watering Cove Campsite to Anchorage Hut and Campsite: 10min.

Beginning at the southern end of the park, the track proceeds past the entirely unremarkable swaths of trailside grass that mark **Tinline Creek Campsite** (15 sites), down to the long and lovely beach at **Appletree Bay Campsite** (15 sites), just out of civilization's sight. **Stilwell Bay Campsite** is on a nice beach, but high tide creates an access problem. Soon after comes the switchback descent to **Akersten Bay Campsite** (5 sites), which offers secluded sites among trees next to a small beach. From here, the track rises to a ridge, giving some stunning sea views of **Anchorage Bay,** complete with sailboats and a high-falutin private lodge. A steep side trip down the other side of the ridge leads to the excellent sites of **Watering Cove Campsite,** right on the beach with views of Adele Island. From the top, the track descends more gradually to a wide, golden arc of sand, with the modest **Anchorage Hut** (24 beds) nearby. The wide field next door is **Anchorage Campsite** (50 sites), a veritable tent town with amenities like a pavilion, heaps of taps, drying lines, and urinals.

About a 10-minute walk from Anchorage Campsite is the secluded **Te Pukatea Bay Campsite** (15 sites), on a perfect golden crescent hemmed by lush headlands. There's no water on-site, but the sublime sunrise makes up for any inconvenience. It was here and at nearby **Pitt Head** that Te Rauparaha's forces slaughtered the local Ngati Apa in 1828, taking few prisoners and burying no bodies.

Anchorage Hut To Bark Bay Hut: 9.5km, 2½- 3hr.

Anchorage Hut to Torrent Estuary Campsite: 20min. or 1hr., depending on tide.

Torrent Estuary Campsite to Torrent Bay Township: 20 min.

Torrent Bay Township to Medlands Beach Campsite: 1½hr.

Medlands Beach Campsite to Bark Bay Beach Campsite: 15min.

Bark Bay Beach Campsite to Bark Bay Hut and Campsite: 5min.

To continue along the track from Anchorage without doubling back up the ridge, go all the way to the western edge of the beach, where a signpost points to the high-tide route (1hr.) and low-tide route (20min.) to Torrent Bay Estuary. Offering a detour, the junction for **Cleopatra's Pool** (return 20min.) is less than an hour's walk along the high-tide route from Anchorage; water spills down a store chute into a golden, pebble-bottomed swimming hole.

Neither **Torrent Estuary Campsite** (6 sites) nor nearby **Torrent Bay Campsite** are terribly ideal—the former overlooks a mudflat half the time, while the latter is a grove of pines. The track passes a path leading to a densely forested upstream portion of the **Falls River** (one-way 90min.) before emerging into the tiny **Torrent Bay Township**, most notable for its **public telephone** with free local calls. Back in the bush, **Medlands Beach Campsite** (6 sites) offers sandy plots framed by a gorgeous combination of estuary and surf. **Bark Bay Beach Campsite** (40 sites) is an unsecluded, kanuka-filled monster of an option, though the bay is big and beautiful. Just before the spacious rooms and freshwater shower of the inland **Bark Bay Hut** (24 beds), the tiny and lovely **Bark Bay Campsite** (5 sites) is well hidden, yet only paces off the track.

Bark Bay Hut to Awaroa Hut: 11.5km, 3-4 hr.

Bark Bay Hut to Tonga Quarry Campsite: 1hr.

Tonga Quarry Campsite to Onetahuti Beach Campsite: 20min.

Onetahuti Beach Campsite to Awaroa Hut and Campsite: via inland route 2¾hr., via Awaroa Lodge 1¾hr.

The track winds steadily up and over a small peninsula before hitting **Tonga Quarry Campsite** (20 sites), an excellent place to call it a day, with well-spaced tent sites, a stream, a nice white stretch of sand and some big blocks of stone from the old quarry days. Another brief up-and-over breaks onto the huge, golden arc of **Onetahuti Beach,** host to the ample **Onetahuti Campsite** and scores of buzzing water taxis. The track runs the length of the beach and crosses a river at the northern end that rises chest-high for two hours on either side of high tide.

Turning back inland, the track climbs gently to the junction for the **Awaroa Lodge** (see p. 267). Passing through this posh slice of civilization to **Awaroa Inlet** can take an hour less than the main track alternative, though during high tide it means navigating a knee-deep stream along the way. The simple **Awaroa Hut** (25 beds) and hard-packed dirt of the adjoining **Awaroa Campsite** (30 sites) are beside the inlet, which becomes a pebbly and crossable mudflat within two hours of low tide.

Awaroa Hut to Totaranui: 5.5km, 1½hr.

After the drained inlet's stranded boats and lingering rivulets, the track resumes and turns inland again before hitting the unremarkable plots and long nearby beach of **Waiharakeke Campsite** (10 site). The track then passes a couple of huge beech trees and the beautiful Goat Beach before emerging into the caravan sprawl of Totaranui.

Totaranui to Whariwharangi Hut and Campsite: 7.5km, 2¼hr.

Totaranui to Anapai Campsite: 30min.

Anapai Campsite to Mutton Cove Campsite: 45min.

Mutton Cove Campsite to Whariwharangi Hut and Campsite: 1hr.

Lined with majestic beaches and excellent overnight options, this section of the track makes an excellent two-day, one-night tramp. **Anapai Bay Campsite** (4 sites) is on a beach fringed by fluted rock faces, with sites concealed inside a dense canopy of windswept kanuka. **Mutton Cove Campsite** (20 sites) also sits alongside a beautiful beach, slightly marred by unsightly felled pines. Just after this beach, the track forks for an extra loop around **Separation Point** (return 1hr.). A walk through kanuka-clad hillsides leads to a white R2D2-shaped lighthouse, with misty vantages of Farewell Spit, the North Island, and the occasional fur seal. The main track descends gradually to **Whariwharangi Hut** (20 beds), an old two-story farmhouse with a quiet bunkroom upstairs, and the grassy fields of **Whariwharangi Campsite** (20 sites) just outside. The rugged beach nearby may have seen the first brutal Maori-Pakeha encounter upon Abel Tasman's arrival in New Zealand. The track has some good views of **Wainui Bay,** as it sidles along the hillsides to the carpark. From here, hitchers tend to cross the bay at low tide in order to reach the main road to Takaka.

MOTUEKA

Motueka (pop. 5500) sits at the mouth of the Motueka River on SH60. The entire area was once under water; today the land is unusually fertile, making it a choice location for fruit growing (the apple, pear, and kiwifruit orchards attract legions of fruit pickers each summer). Motueka's ample services and budget digs make it a comfortable launchpad for trips into Abel Tasman National Park—the Coastal Track trailhead is 30 minutes north at Marahau—and the rest of Golden Bay.

⊓ PRACTICAL INFORMATION. Most commercial buildings in Motueka are on **High Street.** Buses drop off at the **Motueka Visitor Centre** on Wallace St. (tel. 528 6543; fax 528 6563; email mzpvin@nzhost.co.nz; open daily 8am-7pm, winter M-F 8am-5pm, Sa-Su 9am-4pm or shorter). **Abel Tasman Coachlines** (tel. 528 8850) runs north to: **Marahau** (35min., 3 per day, $6); **Takaka** (2hr., 8:15am, $14); **Wainui carpark** (2½hr. $20); **Totaranui** (3hr., $20); and south to **Nelson** (50min., 4 per day, $8). **Kahurangi Bus Services** (tel. 525 9434) runs the same routes at different times to: **Marahau** (10:50am and 4:50pm, $6); **Takaka** ($13); **Wainui carpark** ($22); **Totaranui** ($24); and **Nelson** (3 per day, $8). The **DOC office** (tel. 528 9117) is about 2km toward Nelson along High St. at its intersection with King Edward St. (open M-F 8am-4:30pm). **Coppins Great Outdoor Centre,** 225 High St. (tel. 528 7296), stocks a full array of gear (open M-Th 8:30am-6pm, F 8:30am-7pm, Sa-Su 9am-4pm). **BNZ** (tel. 528 7060), **ANZ** (tel. 528 6620), and **Westpac Trust Bank** (tel. 528 9710), all located on High St., have **ATMs** (open 9am-4:30pm). **Internet access** is available for $12 per hr. at **Cyberworld,** 15 Wallace St. (tel. 528 0072; open daily in summer 9am-7pm, winter 9am-5:30pm) and the Visitor Centre. In emergencies, contact the **Motueka Emergency Duty Doctor Number** (tel. 528 8770), or the **police,** 68 High St. (tel. 528 8800). The **post office,** 123 High St. (tel. 528 1030), is open M-F 8:30am-5:30pm, Sa 9:30am-12:30pm. **Telephone Code:** 03.

⌐ ACCOMMODATIONS. Twin Oaks Cottage, 25 Parker St. (tel. 528 7882), is in a quiet part of town, surrounded by fields of hops. Friendly owners Alan and Frances maintain a homey handful of tent sites ($9), dorms ($18), a caravan ($15), and a twin ($40); they also have an armada of free bikes at the ready. Free pickups and tours are available upon request. The great **White Elephant,** 55 Whakarea St. (tel. 528 6208; fax 528 0110), is a bright backpackers strewn with elephant miniatures. Camping equipment is available for hire, including stoves ($3 per night), pots ($1 per night), gas ($3.50), and more. In the summer, a free shuttle (departs 8:15am) runs to Marahau for guests who have purchased a Great Walks pass from the hostel. (Free bikes. Reception 7:30am-11pm. Check-out 10am. Bunks $15; twins and doubles $20; tent sites $9.) Budget accommodations at the **Abel Tasman Motel and Lodge,** 45 High St. (tel./fax 528 6688), are simple and well-kept. The lodge has a spacious TV lounge and kitchen. (Dorms $15; twins and doubles with TV $45, with bath $60; doubles in winter $40. Weekly: dorms $65-80; doubles $100-$120.) With a central location on High St. marked by the blue-and-white "backpackers" sign, **Motueka Backpackers** (tel. 528 7581) is a low-hassle option with shaded tent sites and a smoker's lounge (free laundry and bikes; dorms $15; doubles $30; tent sites $9; weekly: caravans $70). **Fearon's Bush Camp,** 10 Fearon St. (tel. 528 7189), north of town center, allows tenters to pitch anywhere among its fields full of trees and chirping birds ($9.50 per person, children $4.50). The big and brand new kid in town, **Bakers Lodge** (tel. 528 0102 or 0800 800 102) sports clean and antiseptic rooms, facilities for the disabled, an outdoor spa with barbecue, and Internet access (dorms $17; twins $45; doubles $40, with bath $50-$55).

◘ FOOD. An astronomical ceiling is upheld by bright muralled walls at **Hot Mama's Cafe,** 105 High St. (tel. 528 7039). Kites hang overhead as guests lounge in the wicker furniture or sit at tables of multiple hues as music fills the air. A bowl of muesli, fruit, and yogurt is $5.50; bacon and eggs cost $8.50. (Open daily 8:30am-late; closed in winter.) The **Gothic Gourmet,** 208 High St. (tel. 528 6699), serves up cafe fare (ostrich hot pot $14) and live music on weekends (open M-Th and Su 10am-9:30pm, F-Sa 10am-2:30am). The **Supervalue supermarket** is on 108 High St. (tel. 528 7180; open M-W 8am-7pm, Th-F 8am-8pm, Sa 9am-7pm, Su 9am-6pm).

◼ ⚞ SIGHTS AND ACTIVITIES. Relatively quiet **Kaiteriteri Beach** is just a 15-minute drive (13km) away from town, while the popular **Source of the Riwaka River Walk** (return 30min.) is a 16km drive on SH60 toward Takaka. Near the Visitor Centre, the **Motueka District Museum,** 140 High St. (tel. 528 7660), provides a chronological walk through the history of the area, including an assortment of Maori artifacts and an exhibit on the squashed tobacco industry (open M-F 10am-3pm). The moa bones and illuminated stalactites of the **Ngarua Caves,** 29 Wilkie St. (tel. 528 8093), are 20km away; carless folk can hop a bus up to Golden Bay. Guided tours leave every hour on the hour (Sept.-May daily 10am-4pm and holidays in winter; $10, children $3).

TAKAKA

Artsy dredlocked types inhale deeply in Takaka, the main town of Golden Bay. Located 107km from Nelson, Takaka (pop. 1100) makes a convenient access point to both Abel Tasman and Kahurangi National Parks. It boasts its own attractions as well, including the famously clear **Pupu Springs,** the tame (and hungry) **Anatoki eels,** nearby golden beaches, and various limestone formations, including **Rawhiti Cave.** Hiring a bike is one good way to see the nearby sights if you don't take one of the many area tours that run out of Takaka.

⚐ ORIENTATION AND PRACTICAL INFORMATION. Takaka is 8km west of Pohara, 27km west of the Wainui carpark where the Abel Tasman Coast Track terminates, and 27km east of Collingwood. Takaka's main drag is **Commercial St.,** and everything listed below lies there unless otherwise noted. The **Golden Bay Visitor Information Centre** (tel. 525 9136), where the buses drop off, is on the southern leg of the main drag, where it's known as Willow St. (open daily 9am-7pm, winter 9am-5pm). **Abel Tasman Coachlines** (Motueka tel. 528 8850) goes daily to: **Nelson** (2½hr., $20) via **Motueka** (1½hr., $14); the **Wainui carpark** (30min.); and **Totaranui** (1hr., $10). **Bickley Motors** (tel. 525 8352) connects this service in the summer to **Collingwood** (30min., 10:30am, $12) and the **Heaphy Track** (1½hr., $20); call in winter. **Kahurangi Bus Services** (tel. 525 9434) also runs a summer schedule to: **Motueka** (1-2hr., 7:15 am and noon, $14); **Nelson** (2-3hr., $20); **Collingwood** (30min., 8:30am, $12); and the **Heaphy Track** (1½hr., $20). It runs on demand in winter. The **Golden Bay Area DOC**

Office (tel. 525 8026) has track pamphlets (open M-F 8am-5pm). Outdoor gear is sold at **Lindsay's Clothing and Sport** (tel. 525 9137; open M-Th 8:30am-5:30pm, F 8:30am-6pm, Sa 9am-6pm; winter closes at 12:30pm on Sa). **Westpac Trust Bank** (tel. 525 8094) is home to one of the area's rare **ATMs. Internet access** is available at **Baylink Communications** (tel. 525 8863), near Motupip St. for $12 per hr. (open M-Th 8:30am-5pm, F 8:30am-5:30pm, Sa 10am-noon) and at **Pohara Internet Access,** 748 Abel Tasman Dr. (tel. 525 7233), for $10 per hr. (open almost always). The **Golden Bay Pharmacy** (tel. 525 9490; fax 525 8356; open M-Th 8:30am-5:30pm, F 8:30am-6pm) is near the **post office** (tel. 525 9916; open M-F 9am-5pm, Sa 9:30am-1pm). In an emergency, contact the **police** (tel. 525 9211) or the **Golden Bay Medical Centre** (tel. 525 9911). **Telephone Code:** 03.

⌐◖ ACCOMMODATIONS AND FOOD. Not far off in Pohara, ▨**The Nook** (tel. 525 8501) is not only a backpackers, it is a work of art. Every form of accommodation has been beautifully designed, from the straw-bale cottage ($90 for 2) to the super-funky solar-powered House Truck ($40 for 2, $62 for 4). (Free pickup from Visitors Centre. Bikes $5 per day. Dorms $16; twins and doubles $19; tent sites $11.) On the left on Motupipi Rd. as you walk away from Commercial St., **Annie's Backpackers** (tel. 525 8766), set in a lovely garden, provides soft beds, free duvets, and an attractive kitchen (dorms $15; doubles $20). **The Shady Rest,** 141 Commercial St. (no tel. #), has a creekside location, mellow vibe, and famous showers (dorms $16; twins $20).

The **Wholemeal Cafe** (tel. 525 9426), on Commercial St., combines a keen aesthetic with a deliciously varied menu. The choices rotate nightly, including curries, fresh pastas ($8), and a range of Creole dishes for $16 (open daily 7:30am-6pm, plus W-Su 6pm-9pm). **Supervalue supermarket** (tel. 525 9383) is on Commercial St. (open M-Th 8am-6pm, F 8am-6:30pm, Sa 9am-1pm).

▨◪ SIGHTS AND ACTIVITIES. The **Quiet Revolution Cycle Shop,** 7 Commercial St. (tel./fax 525 9555), rents mountain bikes (half-day $15; full day $35; less in winter) and offers a variety of guided trips to Harwood's Hole, Pupu Springs ($30 per person for 4-5 people) and other local destinations. On **Golden Bay Llama Safaris** (tel. 525 8406), llovable llamas llug your lload, including llunch (half-day to 3 days, $55-385). At the **Bencarri Farm and Cafe** (tel. 525 8261), on McCallum's Rd. south of Takaka, patrons mingle among a menagerie of introduced mammals and feed hungry but harmless native eels (open Th-M 10am-5:30pm, on demand in winter; admission $7, winter $10, children $4, winter $5). The bubbling **Te Waikoropupu Springs** (referred to by most as "Pupu Springs"), 6km from Takaka, are New Zealand's largest freshwater springs system. Believed to be the clearest in the world, the crystalline depths have a horizontal visibility of over 70m. Ages ago, underground water carved out chambers and passages in the marble, which eventually filled with the rushing waters of an underground river. Northeast of Takaka are the privately owned **Rawhiti Caves** (tel. 525 9061), a one-million-year-old hole filled with naturally colorful stalactites, untainted by artificial lighting (admission $14, children $6; bookings essential; daily tours on demand year-round). The **Golden Bay Museum** (tel. 525 9990) represents the best of small town collections, with a wide array of rocks, tools, antiques, war medals, and a handful of Powellipanta shells (open daily 10am-4pm, winter closed Su; admission $1).

KAHURANGI NATIONAL PARK

The vast wilderness dominating the northwest corner of the South Island is protected in the 451,494-hectare Kahurangi National Park. The country's youngest and second largest national park, Kahurangi ("blue skies" or "treasured possession") was formed in 1996 from the former North-West Nelson Forest Park. Snowcapped peaks, rolling tussock, verdant valleys, and palm-lined coasts are all part of this richly diverse park. This great range of habitats, further partitioned by a wide variety of rock types, has fostered an astounding degree of biodiversity within Kahurangi's boundaries. Over half of New Zealand's native plant species are found here; 67 species live nowhere else in the world. While adventurous kayakers brave thrilling Grade 5 Karamea River (see p. 309) as it slices down from the highlands to the sea, Kahurangi is most accessible through a network of challenging, well-maintained, and well-benched tracks scattered with huts. The best known tramp is the Heaphy Track, one of New Zealand's Great Walks, but there are myriad opportunities for walkers of every level.

▐▌▌ PRACTICAL INFORMATION AND ACCOMMODATIONS. Kahurangi stretches from the west coast almost to Motueka and from the base of Farewell Spit south to the town of Murchison. The park's extreme size and wildness translate to highly decentralized information and access. There are DOC offices in Nelson (see p. 260), Motueka (see p. 272), Takaka (see. p. 273), Karamea (see p. 309), and Westport (see p. 306). Almost all non-hut accommodations reside in one of these outlying towns, with the notable exception of **Heaphy Backpackers** (tel. 524 8252), 3km from the Heaphy Track's northern trailhead and right along the Aorere River. This quiet establishment provides free pickup and dropoff from the trailhead, free goldpan use, free appreciation of ambient Asian artwork, and non-free tramping food. (Bunks $15; doubles $18.)

▟▌ WALKS. For information on the **Heaphy Track,** see below. The **Wangapeka Track** (52km, 3-5 days) is the most popular tramp in the southern half of the park, and it is significantly more rugged than the Heaphy. The eastern trailhead is 30km west of Tapawera, a town 62km west of Nelson; from here, the track follows wild rivers through beech-green valleys to a carpark 23km from Karamea. Nine huts provide varying amenities along the way ($8, $4, or free), but since floods destroyed Little Wanganui Hut, a tent is necessary to break up an otherwise 10-hour day on the track's westernmost section.

Kahurangi is laced with innumerable other tramping options, from intensive backcountry grunts like the **Leslie-Karamea Track** (6-9 days) to the sub-alpine dayhikes around **Mt. Arthur** and the **Cobb Valley.** A steep and narrow track to the incredible viewpoint of **Parapara Peak** (4½hr. one-way) begins just 2km off SH60 between Takaka and Collingwood. On a clear day, everything from the mountains in the east to Golden Bay and peaks on the North Island are visible.

▐▌ THE HEAPHY TRACK

The longest of the Great Walks, the Heaphy Track is also the most diverse, traversing no fewer than four completely different ecosystems. From east to west, trampers pass through mountain beech forests on the way up to flat and tussock-tufted expanses (or "downs"), eventually descending to primary podocarp forests and the palm-intensive beachgasm at journey's end. Charles Heaphy was among the first to blaze this west coast section, though Maori jade-seekers had fully traversed the region for centuries before. Today's track provides a superficial glimpse of Kahurangi's great and still largely unexplored natural richness.

ESSENTIALS

Length: 82km, 4-6 days—the longest of the overland Great Walks. The track, partly blazed by bulldozer, is very well graded with few steep sections, though parts can become mini-rivers during rain.

Seasonality: Year-round, though snow can cover the track's alpine portions. Most of the track's 5000 annual visitors come between December and February; March and April tend to bring the mildest weather.

Trailheads: Brown Hut, 28km east of **Collingwood** (see p. 278) and **Kohaihai Carpark,** 15km north of **Karamea** (see p. 309) on the west coast. Most people begin the track at Brown Hut, placing the bulk of climbing in the first three hours and leaving the climactic

SOUTH ISLAND

coastal section for the last day. Each trailhead begins at the end of a long gravel road, one pit stop away from any large town.

Transportation: Brown Hut is served by **Bickley Motors,** bookable through **Abel Tasman Coachlines** (Nelson tel. 548 0285; Motueka tel. 528 8850), which runs daily in summer and on demand in winter from Takaka to Collingwood (40min., 10:30am, $17) and back from Collingwood (50min., 11:10am, $15); the bus departs from the trailhead at 12:15pm. **Kahurangi Bus Services** (tel. 525 9434) runs the same drill earlier in the day (departs Takaka 8:30am; Collingwood 9am; trailhead 10:15am; $12). Both services also connect with **Motueka** and **Nelson. Collingwood Safari Tours** (tel. 524 8257) runs on demand any time between this trailhead and **Collingwood** ($60 for up to 4 people, $15 per additional person). Servicing the coastal trailhead at Kohaihai carpark, **Karamea Express** (tel. 782 6617 or 782 6916) runs daily in summer from Karamea (1:45pm, $5) and Kohaihai (2pm, $5) and on demand year-round ($25 for up to 5 people, $5 per additional person). **Karamea Taxis** (tel. 782 6757) also runs any time on demand, for the same price. **Hitching** to either trailhead is said to be difficult, as there is no through traffic, but patient hitchers report success.

Gear: The open and exposed 27km along Gouland and Mackay Downs catch a lot of wind funneled between the east and west coasts and the clouds often dump incredible amounts of rain upon the track. Thus, as with any tramp, **rain gear** is a must, as is **insect repellent** for defense against the scads of sandflies along the coastal section. With the exceptions of Brown Hut and Gouland Downs Hut, all huts have gas stoves and basic pots; campers must bring all of their own **cooking equipment.** The closest **gear rental** is in Takaka (see p. 273), Motueka (see p. 272), or Westport (see p. 306). These towns also stock cheaper food than do Collingwood or Karamea.

Storage and Baggage Transport: Local visitors centers and bus services can arrange luggage transport between the trailheads; in general, it costs $5 for each change-of-hands (e.g. Collingwood to Westport $10, Collingwood to Karamea $15). Most accommodations will store extra gear at little or no charge.

THE TRACK
Brown Hut to Perry Saddle Hut: 17km, 5hr.
Brown Hut to Aorere Shelter: 3hr.

Aorere Shelter to Perry Saddle Hut: 2hr.

The eastern starting point of the track, **Brown Hut** (20 beds), is just five minutes from the carpark; it sports a large fireplace, a phone for free local calls, an adjoining grassy area for tents, but lacks cooking facilities. The track follows a broad path, climbing steadily but gently up the **Aorere Valley,** past dense beech forest and the occasional sweeping mountain view. Most of the climbing is over by **Aorere Shelter** (4 beds), a three-walled affair with a grand view, a bare shelf for sleeping, a covered deck, water, a toilet, and flat grassy tent sites just outside. About 10 minutes after this shelter, a five-minute spur trail leads to **Flanagan's Corner** (915m), the highest point on the track, with a sweeping panorama of the entire upper Aorere Valley and surrounding mountains. A gradual ascent leads up to **Perry Saddle Hut** (26 beds), perched on the edge of the valley with still more good views. Tent sites on the saddle tend to be very boggy and exposed. On clear nights, the track around Perry Saddle is a promising place to hear or even see great spotted kiwi.

Perry Saddle Hut to Gouland Downs Hut: 8km, 2hr.
About an hour after Perry Saddle Hut, the trail gradually leaves behind the patches of beech and opens out into the **Gouland Downs,** the beginning of the track's most exposed section. Windswept grassy expanses stretch to the horizon, punctuated by heaps of tiny carnivorous trailside sundews and the odd shoe tree. **Gouland Downs Hut** (10 beds) is the smallest and sparest on the track, with a warm stone hearth, some old pots, and no gas burners. The tent sites are unremarkable, but they're the grassiest you'll find between Aorere Shelter and Lewis Hut. Just a few hundred meters farther down the trail awaits a Tolkienesque forest, full of bizarre

rock formations, caves, arches, moss-shrouded rocks and trees, and several beautiful streams that wind around and through the limestone.

Gouland Downs Hut to Saxon Hut: 5km, 1½hr.
The track traverses the western end of Gouland Downs, gradually re-entering beech forest; **Saxon Hut** (16 beds) sits amid decent scenery, offering one cozy room with gas cookers and a fireplace. The campsites here can get extremely wet.

Saxon Hut to Mackay Hut: 14 km, 3hr.
The track gradually winds uphill, in and out of forest and the **Mackay Downs.** This area can flood quite seriously during heavy rain, and the inconsistent boardwalking means wet feet during any degree of downpour. Past variegated mosses of many textures, **Mackay Hut** (26 beds) has excellent views down the Heaphy River Valley to the ocean. The spacious hut boasts flush toilets and a separate common room; wet sinkholes sometimes accompany tent sites.

Mackay Hut to Lewis Hut: 13.5 km, 3½hr.
From here, it's all downhill to the sea. The forest slowly changes with decreasing elevation and higher rainfall, from beech to rimu and tree fern. By the time **Lewis Hut** (20 beds) comes into view, the forest has thickened and diversified; the beautiful nikau palm begins to appear and rata lace the hillsides with red in summer. Lewis Hut sits at the junction of the tannin-stained Heaphy and Lewis Rivers, with excellent views to the hillside beyond. The hut has niceties like a flush toilet and firewood, but its sister tent sites are sloped and minuscule. **Sandflies** begin to appear here: be warned.

Lewis Hut to Heaphy Hut: 8km, 2½hr.
Just after Lewis Hut, the vegetation immediately grows more extreme: giant rata are drenched with epiphytes (plants growing from the host tree's massive and gnarled branches). More and more nikau palms appear, the tree ferns grow taller and taller, and after traversing four long swing bridges, the track finally reaches the sea. The cheery new **Heaphy Hut** (20 beds) holds court by the mouth of the lazy Heaphy River, with a large fireplace, ocean-themed mobiles, three separate gas stoves, flush toilets, and stellar views on all sides. A wide grassy field just out front, plus an excellent campsite and shelter next door, means a vast capacity for blissfully unbogged tents. A final arc of the river has produced a stretch of beach littered with driftwood, and at high tide the violent ocean sends surges of waves a good distance upstream. The seashore itself provides some spectacular sunset views over the angry Tasman sea.

Heaphy Hut to Kohaihai Carpark: 16.5km, 4½hr.
Heaphy Hut to Katipo Shelter: 2hr.

Katipo Shelter to Scotts Beach Campsite: 1½hr.

Scotts Beach Campsite to Kohaihai carpark: 1hr.

This palm-filled stretch of the track runs entirely along the coast, is almost entirely flat, and allows access to numerous beaches. The surf is ferocious; riptides make the water too dangerous for swimming. Hills cascade steeply down to the beach, and it is possible to see the havoc that possums have wreaked on the forest in the form of brown and denuded trees. **Katipo Shelter** (4 beds), another basic shack with a wooden shelf, has a small number of tent sites, a toilet, and no water. Shortly after the shelter is **Crayfish Point,** where the beach can only be crossed safely within two hours of low tide; otherwise, a high-tide track suffices. Tide tables are posted at Kohaihai and Heaphy Hut.

The longest stretch of sand before Kohaihai is **Scotts Beach;** those on an excursion from the carpark need go no further to enjoy the track's sublime coastal experience. The excellent **Scotts Beach Campsite** is ringed by nikau palms and flax, with the thundering beach in earshot, and a water supply gushing from the rock. After

SLUGGISH SNAILS AND SNAILISH SLUGS

Kahurangi's wilderness is so sprawling and unexplored that researchers are nowhere near figuring out how it all works—they're still in the early stages of sussing out what lives there in the first place. The forests of northwest Nelson teem with a stunning and slimy diversity of land-bound mollusks, former denizens of Gondwanaland that survived the latest Ice Age in the relatively frost-free refuge of the region. The park contains at least half of New Zealand's giant land snail diversity (genus *Powelliphanta*), and just about every hut along the Heaphy Track has its own local species. These nocturnal hermaphrodites can reach palm-sized proportions and enjoy spending several days finishing off a single giant earthworm, which can grow to half a meter, but that's another story. Unfortunately, possums have picked up a taste for New Zealand escargot, and shuck the suckers like so many tins of mincemeat. Possums also have been seen preying upon Kahurangi's other mammoth mollusk, the leaf-veined slug (family *Athorocophoridae*). Growing to a length of 15cm, they're colored like leaves and put together like snails: lung on top, scrunched-up guts, and genitalia up near the eyes—all compacted as if they still had to fit into a snail shell. The slugs are nature's nighttime forest squeegies, but scientists still have little idea of how many species are out there. If you're psyched to do a slug-n-snail census of your own, just hit the local leaf litter on a wet night and leave your salt back at the hut.

this, the track does its only real climbing along the coast as it skirts around **Kohaiai Bluff** before reaching the carpark. At Kohaihai there is a mural-filled shelter, a phone for ringing a ride, and a nice free campground that is not part of the Great Walk system, with water, toilets, and a great view of the bluff.

COLLINGWOOD AND FAREWELL SPIT

In 1856, New Zealand's first great gold rush made a boom town out of Collingwood, whose 4000 residents clamored to make it the capital city. Three major fires and one depleted gold supply later, modern day Collingwood (pop. 300) may be a shadow of its former self, but that doesn't affect the prime location. However small, this is still the largest town east of Kahurangi National Park and south of Farewell Spit, curving like a kiwi's beak into the sea. Full of huge sand dunes, swamp, scrub, and mudflats, the country's largest sandspit (35km) vacillates between 800m and 10km in width between tides. This is the northernmost point on the South Island, and the last land that Captain Cook saw on his first visit before sailing off to Australia. Flocks of migratory wading birds from locales as far-flung as Siberia appear from September to mid-March, and whales confused by the long and skinny spit are sometimes found beached on the sandy shore.

◪ ORIENTATION AND PRACTICAL INFORMATION. Toward the northern end of Golden Bay, Collingwood lies at the terminus of **SH60**, 27km north of Takaka and 23km south of Puponga, the settlement at the base of Farewell Spit. The **Farewell Spit Visitor Centre and Cafe** (tel. 524 8454) in Puponga is the only tourist info outlet in the area, serving up restaurant fare and interpretive displays (open daily 9am-5pm, winter 10am-4pm; closed mid-July to Aug.). **Bickley Motors** (tel. 525 8352) runs to **Takaka** once per day in summer and on demand in winter (20min., 1:10pm, $15), where it connects with the **Abel Tasman Coachlines** schedule. **Kahurangi Bus Services** (tel. 525 9434) does the same drill in the morning (11am, $12). Collingwood has **no ATMs. Telephone Code:** 03.

◪◪ ACCOMMODATIONS AND FOOD. The **Courthouse Inn and Cafe** (tel./fax 524 8566), a brand new establishment in a century-old building, provides serviceable, small-scale rooms in Collingwood proper (dorms $15; full 3-bed unit $40). The **Collingwood Motor Camp** (tel. 524 8149), next to the beach at the terminus of

SH60, offers cabins with windows overlooking the water, communal kitchen and toilet facilities, and canoe hire ($5 per half day). (Bunks $16, winter $15; cabins for 2 $50, extra person $10; powered tent sites $9.) **The Innlet** (tel. 524 8040), between Pakawau and Collingwood, is 200m from the beach and offers wilderness kayaking. It offers free pickup from Collingwood. (Dorms $16; twins and doubles $40.) **Shambhala Guesthouse** (tel. 525 8463), 9km out of Collingwood toward Takaka, has a private beach and rooms with sea views. Call for pickup. (Dorms from $15; twins and doubles $35.)

Great grub and grog await at the **Mussel Inn** (tel. 525 9241), near the Shambhala Guesthouse, 9km out of Collingwood toward Takaka. Bohemian offerings include strangely-named local brews, a mean veggie lasagna ($13), live music on weekends, and bathroom collages so intriguing that a visit to the throne becomes an aesthetic delight. Open daily 11am-late, winter Th-Sa 5pm-late. Stock up on supplies at the **Collingwood General Store** (tel. 524 8221; open M-F 8am-6pm, Sa-Su 9am-3pm; winter hours shorter).

◉ 🖼 SIGHTS AND ACTIVITIES. The **Original Farewell Spit Safari** (tel. 524 8257 or 0800 808 257) has been running 4WD trips to the **Farewell Spit Lighthouse** since the mid-1940s (5½hr.; $52, under 15 $30). They also tour a gannet colony (2 per week Jan.-Feb.; 6½hr.; $65, under 15 $35) and scope wading birds on the inner beach (4hr.; $45; departure times depend heavily on the season and the tides; call in advance). **Farewell Spit Nature Tours** (tel. 524 8188), run by **Collingwood Bus Services,** spends some time at **Pillar Point Lighthouse** before heading spitward (6½-7hr., 1 per day, $65 with lunch). The same outfit operates the **Scenic Mail Run,** a 5½-hour trip through off-the-beaten-track countryside with local commentary (M-F 9:30am; book in advance). Check at the post office for rides to the base of the spit ($8), where the DOC-run **Puponga Farm** park allows visitors to roam freely through a patchwork of native plants and bleating livestock. **Cape Farewell Horse Treks** (tel. 524 8031), 2km past Puponga, leads a variety of horseback adventures, including some to the Pillar Point Lighthouse ($30) and the farm park ($65); pickup from Collingwood costs $10. The **Te Anaroa Caves** (tel. 524 8131), 10 minutes by car out of Collingwood, are stuffed with stalactites and stalagmites (4 tours per day Dec. 27-Jan. 23, or on demand; $10, ages 5-15 $5). Those with cars can head to the magnificent natural rock sculptures of **Wharariki Beach** or serene **Paturau Beach,** both on the west coast. From the carpark 29km north of Collingwood, it's a 20-minute walk from the east coast to the west coast along a track to Wharariki Beach, where large jutting cliffs, big sand dunes, and arches create a solitary atmosphere appropriate for surfing or relaxing. The **Kaituna Track** (one-way 7hr.), accessible by car from Collingwood, is one of the more serious hikes in the area.

CANTERBURY

Stretching from the mountainous backbone in the west to the Pacific Ocean in the east, Canterbury steps gracefully from ambling farmlands and little agricultural burgs to the sheer majesty of the Southern Alps. Skiers flock to the treeless heights of the slopes near Christchurch, the country's second-largest city, while summer visitors willingly fall victim to the charms of the Banks Peninsula and nearby beaches. Beneath the Gothic guise of its British heritage, Christchurch itself offers the best of Kiwi culture and ethnic dining. Extending in orderly blocks from its central cathedral, Christchurch gradually gives way to orchards and vineyards. Canterbury draws equally from its cosmopolitanism and provincialism—you're apt to find the best of gourmet cafes as well as farmstays here in the agricultural center of the South Island.

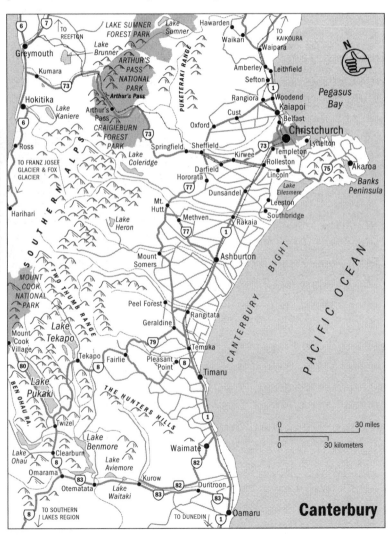

Canterbury

CHRISTCHURCH

The Garden City remains closely bound to its English roots, but has a flamboyant tilt that could only be Kiwi. The massive bell-tower of its Anglican cathedral casts a conservative shadow over the colorful nightclubs and artsy shops that pepper the city. Named after Oxford's Christ Church College, the city is full of stone Gothic Revival churches and meeting houses that front the grassy, willowed banks of the Avon River. Christchurch maintains a vibrant community of artists and artisans who instill a proud cultural spirit into the city's 300,000-some inhabitants. Foreigners flock to Christchurch's countless seasonal festivals, when street entertainers, flowers, a wizard (see p. 291), and ethnic food stalls clog Cathedral Square and the nearby Arts Centre. Although it's the gateway to the more remote promontories of the Banks Peninsula and the prelude to the majesty of the country's best scenery, Christchurch and its many museums and gardens merit a lingering visit.

⌐ ARRIVAL AND DEPARTURE

BY PLANE
The **Christchurch Airport** is 9km from the city on Memorial Ave., and is served by Air New Zealand, Ansett, Qantas, and many Asian and South Pacific carriers. For **flight info,** call 374 7100. Flights go to **Auckland** (1½hr., 1 per hr., $234-407) and **Wellington** (45min., 1 per hr., $130-240), along with most other domestic destinations. **Ansett** (tel. 371 1185 or 0800 267 388; fax 379 1147) has an office at the corner of Worcester St. and Oxford Terr. near the Visitor Centre (open M-F 8:30am-5pm). **Air New Zealand** has an office at 702 Colombo St. (tel. 353 2800 or 0800 737 000; open M-F 9am-5pm, Sa 9:30am-2pm). The **Airport "A" bus** ($2.70) departs from the Worcester St. bus kiosk and the airport every 30 minutes on weekdays, and every hour on weekends. **Super Shuttles** (tel. 365 5655) costs about $10; a **taxi** is $20-25. Great discounts can be procured by booking ahead (see **Getting Around: By Plane,** p. 49).

BY TRAIN
To reach the **train station,** located 3km from Cathedral Sq., head away from town on Riccarton Ave., turn left on Deans Ave., right onto Blenheim Rd. at the roundabout, then left on Clarence St. Several hostels offer a free shuttle from the station. **P.B.S. Shuttles** (tel. 355 1111) does free pickup from several centrally-located backpackers to connect with the morning train to **Greymouth** via **Arthur's Pass.** Taxis to town cost $10. **TranzScenic** (tel. 0800 802 802) runs daily to: **Picton** (5¼hr., 7:30am, $72) via **Kaikoura** (3hr., $41); **Invercargill** (9hr., 8:15am, $117) via **Dunedin** (5¾hr., $74); and **Greymouth** (4½hr., 9am, $79). The **TranzAlpine** ride between **Christchurch** and **Greymouth** is considered to be one of the best train trips in the world. Tranz-Scenic has a designated **backpackers car** and offers substantial discounts (30% or more) to students and those who book ahead (see **Getting Around: By Train,** p. 52).

BY BUS

InterCity, 123 Worcester St. (tel. 379 9020 or 0800 686 862; open daily 7am-7pm), **Newmans** (tel. 374 6149), and **Great Sights** (tel. 358 9029 or 0800 800 904) run daily to **Queenstown** (10¾hr., 2-3 per day, $40-95) via **Mt. Cook** (5hr., $40) or express. Inter-City also runs direct to: **Dunedin** (6½ hr., 3 per day, $55); **Nelson** (7¾hr., 7:30am, $66) via **Kaikoura** (2¾hr., $27); and **Wanaka** (9½hr., 8:20am, $95). **Alpine Coaches** (tel. 0800 274 888) and **Coast to Coast** (tel. 0800 800 847) go to **Greymouth** (6hr., $35) via **Arthur's Pass** (2¼hr., $25) with free pickup. A range of **shuttle** options also serves the same cities, often for lower rates. Call one of the following companies for current routes and prices: **Atomic Shuttles** (tel. 322 8883), **Southern Link Shuttle** (tel. 358 8355), **Compact Coachlines** (tel. 578 7102 or 0800 500 180), **South Island Connections** (tel. 0800 742 669), **East Coast Express** (tel. 0508 830 900), or **KO-OP Shuttles** (tel. 366 6633). The Visitor Centre has info and does bookings. As always, substantial discounts are available for students and advance bookings.

HITCHHIKING

Thumbers report success from the city outskirts, where there's steady traffic from the city. Those heading north toward Kaikoura often take Belfast bus ($2.70) and ask the driver to be dropped off, while those heading south take Hornby bus #8 ($1.80) and do the same. West toward Arthur's Pass is still a reasonable prospect; hitchhikers report taking Russley bus #8 ($1.80) to the Yaldhurst Roundabout. The best bet for hitching to Akaroa seems to be taking Halswell bus #7 ($1.80).

◪ ORIENTATION

Christchurch's flat grid of streets stretches in every direction from **Cathedral Square,** the city's heart, where food stalls and artisans congregate beneath the bell-tower of **Christchurch Cathedral.** Facing away from the cathedral, cobblestoned **Worcester Blvd.** continues east through **Latimer Square** and west past the Visitor Centre, over the Avon River, and to the Gothic **Arts Centre** buildings, the **Canterbury Museum,** and the extensive **botanic gardens.** The city's main thoroughfare, **Colombo St.,** lined with wool and jewelry souvenir shops, runs north-south through the square. Arcades and plazas extend out from the **City Mall,** the pedestrian walkway a block south from the Cathedral where Cashel St. would be. North of the Cathedral, **Victoria Square** fronts both the town hall and the domineering Park Royal hotel. The shallow **Avon River** runs through the square along **Oxford Terr.** and **Cambridge Terr.** Central Christchurch is bordered to the west by the gigantic **Hagley Park,** to the north and east by residential suburbs, and to the south by **Moorhouse Avenue,** the boundary of the industrial area.

⬓ GETTING AROUND

BY BUS

The **Bus Information Centre** is at 47 Cathedral Sq. (tel. 366 8855; open M-F 7:30am-5:30pm, Sa-Su 9am-3:30pm). Buses depart from here roughly every half hour from 6am to 10:50pm. Fares are by zone; most are $1.80 within the city and allow for four hours of transfers; purchase tickets on board. If you're going to more than one sight, buy a **Big Red Bus Pass** ($5), good for a full day of travel on Red Buses (available at the Visitor Centre or on board). **The Shuttle** is a free bus service comprised of bright yellow buses that run around the city center daily every ten minutes; route maps are available at the Visitor Centre.

BY TAXI

Christchurch has 24-hour metro area service. Voucher cards offering small discounts are available from the Visitor Centre, restaurants, or the taxi driver. Choose from **First Direct** (tel. 377 5555 or 0800 505 550), **Gold Band** (tel. 379 5795), and **Blue Star** (tel. 379 9799).

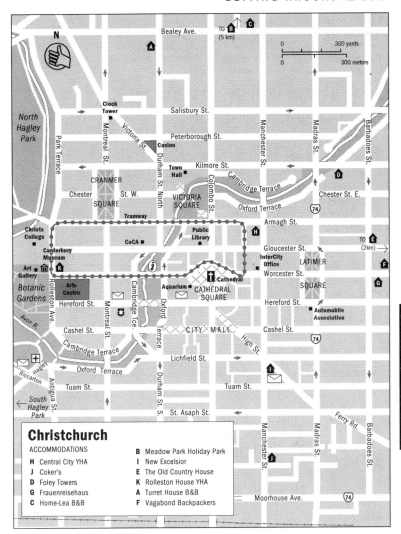

Christchurch

ACCOMMODATIONS

H Central City YHA
J Coker's
D Foley Towers
G Frauenreisehaus
C Home-Lea B&B

B Meadow Park Holiday Park
I New Excelsior
E The Old Country House
K Rolleston House YHA
A Turret House B&B
F Vagabond Backpackers

BY CAR

The major car rental companies are all in town, but for cheaper deals, try **Atomic Rentals** (tel. 322 8883), which begins at $35 per day with unlimited km; the $750 credit bond is standard ($1000 if under 25). **Pegasus,** 127 Peterborough St. (tel. 365 1100 or 0800 354 506), **Rent-a-Dent,** 132 Kilmore St. (tel. 365 2509 or 0800 736 823), and **Shoestring Rentals** (tel. 385 3647) offer comparable rates with insurance and unlimited km; relocation fees apply depending on the destination. The **AA office,** 210 Hereford St. (tel. 379 1280 or 0800 500 222), sells excellent road maps and offers traveling advice (open M-F 8:30am-5pm, Sa 9am-3pm).

BY BIKE

Trailblazers (tel. 366 6033), on Worcester Blvd. between Cathedral Sq. and the Visitor Centre, and **Rent-A-Cycle,** 141 Gloucester St. (tel. 365 7589), have standard mountain bikes ($5 per hour, half-day $15, full day $20). **Cyclone Cycles,** 245

Colombo St. (tel. 332 9588), has mountain bikes with suspension for $30 per day, while **City Cycle Hire** (tel. 0800 343 848) has comparable rates with free delivery. Free **bicycle storage** (bring your own lock) is available at the Lichfield St. carpark between Oxford Terr. and Colombo St. (open M-Th 7:30am-7:15pm, F 7:30am-11:45pm, Sa 9am-5:30pm, Su 10am-4:30pm).

▣ PRACTICAL INFORMATION

Visitors Center: Christchurch Visitor Centre (tel. 379 9629; fax 377 2424), corner of Worcester Blvd. and Oxford Terr. Well staffed. Open M-F 8:30am-6pm, Sa-Su 8:30am-5pm, winter M-F 8:30am-5pm, Sa-Su 8:30am-4pm. Another office in the domestic terminal of the airport (tel. 353 7774; open daily 7:30am-8pm).

DOC: 133 Victoria St. (tel. 379 9758). Tramping info and maps for Canterbury and all of South Island. Open M-F 8:30am-4:30pm.

Maps: Mapworld (tel. 374 5399), corner of Manchester and Gloucester St. The best selection of maps of the South Island. Open M-F 8:30am-5:30pm, Sa 10am-2pm.

Budget Travel: STA Travel, 90 Cashel St. (tel. 379 9098), in City Mall. Open M-F 9am-5:30pm, Sa 10am-3pm. **YHA Travel,** 158 Cashel St. (tel. 379 8046), does train, plane, and automobile bookings. Open M-F 9am-5:30pm, Sa 10am-1pm. **Budget Travel,** 683A Colombo St. (tel. 366 6032; open M-F 8:30am-5:30pm, Sa 9am-1pm).

Currency Exchange: BNZ (tel. 353 2532), in the glass and steel building in Cathedral Sq., does cash advances for Visa and MC (M-F 9am-4:30pm) and exchanges money (M-F 9am-6pm, Sa 10am-1pm). **ANZ** (tel. 371 4714), across the street, exchanges money M-F 9am-4:30pm.

American Express: 773 Colombo St. (24hr. tel. 0800 656 660; to report lost or stolen checks call 0800 441 068). Mail held for 30 days for card members and AmEx travelers check holders. No commission; good exchange rates. Open M-F 9am-5pm.

Rentals: Ski Windsurf City, 64 Manchester St. (tel. 366 6516), rents surfboards ($30 per day), boogie boards ($15 per day), and wetsuits ($15 per day). It also has ski rental packages (from $25) and snowboard rental (from $35). **Canoe & Outdoor World** (tel. 366 9305) at Pilgrim Place rents whitewater kayaks ($35 per day) and sea kayaks ($40 per day). **R&R Sport,** 81 Manchester St. (tel. 377 9097), has ski rental packages (from $15) and snowboards and boots (from $28), as well as a selection of packs ($8 per day) and other tramping gear.

Bi-Gay-Lesbian Organizations: Gay Information Line (24hr. tel. 379 3990); **Gay Information Collective** (tel./fax 379 9493; email df@burnside.school.nz).

Police: Cathedral Sq. Kiosk (tel. 379 0123). Open Su-W 8am-11pm, Th-Sa 8am-2am. **Main branch** (tel. 379 3999), at the corner of Hereford St. and Cambridge Terr.

Hotlines: Lifeline (tel. 366 6743; 24hr. counseling); **Victim Support** (tel. 379 6767); **AIDS Hotline** (tel. 0800 802 437); **New Zealand AIDS Foundation** (tel. 379 1953); **Disability Info,** 314 Worcester St. (tel. 366 6189; open M-F 9am-4:30pm).

Medical Services: Bealey Avenue After Hours Surgery, 931 Colombo St. (tel. 365 7777). Open 24hr. **Christchurch Public Hospital** (tel. 364 0640), on the corner of Oxford Terr. and Riccarton Ave.

Post Office: (tel. 353 1899), on Hereford St. between Colombo St. and Oxford Terr. *Poste Restante.* Open M-Th 8am-6pm, F 8am-8pm, Sa-Su 10am-4pm.

Internet Access: There are places all over the city. **E-Caf,** 28 Worcester St. (tel. 372 9436), in the Arts Centre, offers deals with the coffee shop downstairs. $6 per hr., $5.50 per hr. with purchase of coffee. Open daily 8am-midnight. Their other branch, **E-Caf @ Farmers,** 767 Colombo St., has the cheapest rates in town with a 9:30-11:45am morning backpackers special ($4 per hr.) Other options are the **Cyber Cafe,** 127 Gloucester St. (tel. 365 5183), and the **Cyber Forum,** 143 Armagh St. (both $5 per hr.).

TELEPHONE CODE Throughout the South Island, the telephone code is **03.**

⌐ ACCOMMODATIONS

While Christchurch has few of the charmingly quirky gems found in the smaller towns of the South Island, there are plenty of stately Victorian houses throughout the city that have been converted into hostels, B&Bs, and hotels. In summer, many places fill to capacity, so book ahead. Check-out is 10am unless otherwise noted.

Vagabond Backpackers, 232 Worcester St. (tel. 379 9677), 5 blocks east of the Cathedral. An extremely popular house with a modern interior, stylish kitchen and lounge, and quiet location close to the city. Good selection of free videos. Dorms $14-16; singles $23; twins and doubles $35. Book at least a week ahead.

Foley Towers, 208 Kilmore St. (tel. 366 9720; fax 379 3014; email foley.towers@back pack.co.nz). Take Worcester to Madras St., go left, and then right on Kilmore St. Spacious villa with back patio, gardens, and lawn. Most rooms have sinks but bathrooms are outside. Frequent homemade muffins $1, quiche $2. Internet. Reception 9am-9:30pm. Dorms $13-15 (no linen); twins and doubles $34, with bath $38.

Frauenreisehaus: The Homestead, 272 Barbadoes St. (tel. 366 2585; fax 366 2589). Past the Cathedral on Worcester Blvd., hang a right on Barbadoes St. Women are fortunate to have this **female-only** homestead to themselves. Owners make living easy: free laundry, an excellent collection of videos, free use of bikes, and fresh mint in the garden for tea are among the many ways owners make living easy. Reception 8:30am-10:30pm. Dorms $15; singles $25; twins $34. Book ahead.

New Excelsior Backpackers (Nomads) (tel. 366 7570; fax 366 7629), at the corner of High and Manchester St. Large, brand-new hostel; most rooms have sinks and tall windows. Sunny, cushion-filled TV lounge with a large stereo, and big, wooden deck outside amid the rooftops. Internet. Dorms $15-17; singles $32; twins $38; doubles $45, with bath $55. Reception 7am-9pm, winter 7am-8pm. Nomads $1 discount.

City Central YHA, 273 Manchester St. (tel. 379 9535; fax 379 9537; email yhachch@yha.org.nz), near Armagh St. Central, modern, and ultra-clean with tremendously helpful staff. Two bright, open dining areas and kitchens. Snug yet bare rooms and new bathrooms have that manufactured YHA feel. Lockout 10pm. Reception 8am-10pm. Dorms $19; singles $30; twins $38-42, with bath $50; doubles $42.

Turret House B&B, 435 Durham St. (tel. 365 3900 or 0800 488 773; www.turret-house.co.nz), near the intersection with Bealey St. Luxurious Victorian homestead with wall-to-wall carpeting, quilts, fresh flowers, and a wooden chess set. Couches, bath, and TV in bedrooms. Free sherry in evenings. Bike hire. Singles $75, winter $55; twins $95, winter $75; doubles $110, winter $95; family suites $120, winter $110.

Coker's (VIP), 52 Manchester St. (tel. 379 8580; fax 379 8585). This once-posh hotel retains the regal red chairs and ornately carved wooden ceilings from 1875, if not the luster. A tropical garden ushers guests into the foyer, while painted soldiers on the walls direct you to rooms. Enormous kitchen and dining room. Video games, pool table ($1), free videos, and a full bar. Key deposit $10. Reception 24hr. Dorms $16.50; singles $40; twins $45; doubles $45-50.

Home-Lea B&B, 195 Bealey Ave. (tel./fax 379 9977). Past the cathedral heading east, turn left on Manchester St. and walk about 1km to Bealey St.; it's on the corner. A large living room with pleasant fireplace, flower garden, floral bed covers, nice patio, BBQ, and lounge with fireplace and TV. Singles $50; twins and doubles $85; triples $110.

Rolleston House YHA (tel. 366 6564; fax 365 5589), at the corner of Worcester Blvd. and Rolleston Ave., across from the Arts Centre. With a great location in the city's cultural heart, the beautiful old Rolleston has narrow staircases, spacious (but basic) rooms, and a pool table. Reception 8-10am and 3-10pm. Dorms $15-17; twins $40. Non-YHA members $4 more.

YMCA Christchurch, 12 Hereford St. (tel. 365 0502; fax 365 1386; email chchymca@ymca.org.nz), across the street from the Arts Centre. Well located, with immaculate, modern rooms, some of which overlook the Botanic Gardens. You won't find the communal hostel atmosphere here, but you can use the gym ($4), climbing wall ($5.50), or squash and badminton courts in the adjoining fitness center. Internet. Reception 7am-10pm. Dorms $17; singles $37; twins and doubles $50; triples $62.

Stonehurst, 241 Gloucester St. (tel. 379 4620; fax 379 4647; www.stonehurst.co.nz). Go east on Gloucester St. 3½ blocks from Colombo St. Sprawling, 3-building complex; most backpackers rooms are in the recently-renovated building. Pool table, swimming pool, picnic tables, and a bar at the reception desk that serves $4.50 jugs of beer daily 5-7pm. Internet. Reception 24hr. Dorms $15-17; singles $35; doubles $40-45; motel rooms for 1-4 $55-75. 3% surcharge on credit cards.

Charlie B's, 268 Madras St. (tel./fax 379 8429 or 0800 224 222), 3 blocks east of Colombo St. on Gloucester. You won't miss the enormous pink-muralled facade with Snoopy-the-aviator flying a yellow airplane. Large and a bit dingy, this hostel is the cheapest in town. Plenty of entertainment: pool table, arcade games, pinball, and free videos. Internet. Reception 8-11am and 1-11:30pm. Bunks $11 (summer only); dorms $13; singles $30; twins and doubles $40; triples and quads $15 per person.

The Old Country House, 437 Gloucester St. (tel. 381 5504), 2km east up Gloucester St. Earthy, quiet place. The kitchen has a long, wooden table, pleasant fireplace alcove, cheerful plum-colored walls. Undergoing major renovations; newer rooms are colorful and attractive. Free pickup from Cathedral Sq. Reception 8-10am and 5-8pm. Dorms $14-15; twins and doubles $35; quads $50. Cash only.

Bealey International Backpackers, 70 Bealey Ave. (tel./fax 366 6760). 4 blocks up Colombo St. from Cathedral Sq., then left 2 blocks on Bealey Ave. A bit of a walk from the center of town, but offers a pleasant, relaxing atmosphere. Patio, picnic tables, and BBQ. Reception 8:30am-9:30pm. Dorms $15; twins and doubles $17.

Meadow Park Holiday Park, 39 Meadow St. (tel. 352 9176; fax 352 1272). Drive north 10min. from the city center on Sherborne St., which becomes Highway 74 and runs by the park about 5km from town. Sprawling complex with swimming pool, waterslides, trampoline, playground, sauna, and spa ($8 per 30min.). Reception 8am-10pm. Cabins for 2 $33, extra person $10; tourist flats for 2 from $50, extra person $15; tent and powered sites $10 per person, children $5.

🖰 FOOD

From sashimi to panini, Christchurch's ethnic offerings will make everybody happy. Many restaurants are concentrated on **Colombo St.,** north of Kilmore St., and on **Manchester St.,** south of Gloucester St. Cafes are often the best bet for hearty breakfasts and lunches (generally with lower prices), and there's always pub food to be found. Vendors in **Cathedral Sq.** sell a range of kebabs and stir-frys around lunchtime; on weekends they take over a corner of the Arts Centre.

WORCESTER STREET AND SOUTH

Blue Jean Cuisine, 205 Manchester St. (tel. 365 4130). You won't leave hungry. Big steak and fish dishes among song lyrics, a wall paying homage to Muhammad Ali, and photos of other American legends. Noise level reflects the popularity. Lunch $8-11, light meals $10-13, dinners $18-19. Open M-F 11am-late, Sa-Su 5:30am-late.

Il Felice, 56 Lichfield St. (tel. 366 7535). Hugely popular upscale authentic Italian in an often boisterous and close-knit environment. Fresh-made pastas ($16) and mains ($20-25) are worth the splurge, as portions make up for the price. BYO wine. Open M-Sa from 6pm. Reservations recommended, particularly on weekends.

Alva Rados (tel. 365 1644), at the corner of Worcester and Manchester St. Margarita pitchers and mega nachos amid cacti and Mexican pottery. Popular with groups and a younger crowd. Light meals from $9, mains $16-18. Open Tu-Su from 6pm.

Dux de Lux, 41 Hereford St. (tel. 366 6919), at the Arts Centre. Serves only vegetarian and seafood, in a variety of forms from pizzas to tapas ($12-19). Popular with students, the enormous place is a great hangout in summer when the patio, surrounded by the neo-Gothic masonry of the Arts Centre, is in full swing. Seven award-winning home-brews. Open daily 11:30am-11pm.

Pyramids of the Sahara, 105 Manchester St. (tel. 379 7565). New Zealand's only little Egypt, with belly-dancing Friday and Saturday, painted camels under pontooned ceilings, and soup made from specially imported Egyptian vegetables—they're only missing the sand. Dine among the Pharaohs on medams ($8), a hummus-like dip, or whole grilled fish ($16.50). Dinners $14-18. Open daily from 5pm. Takeaways available.

Topkapi Turkish Kebab House, 185a Manchester St. (tel. 379 4447). In this tiny piece of Turkey, sit on low benches or pillows amid Oriental wall hangings, posters of the Middle East, and coffee vessels. Kebabs and falafels are prepared windowside ($5-7.50). Open M-Tu 11:30am-10pm, W-Th 11:30am-10:30pm, F 11:30am-late, Sa 3pm-late.

Panini Bar (tel. 377 5570), on Lichfield St. between Colombo and High St. Intimate setting redolent with Italian specialties. Mirror and shadowy fan add atmosphere. Lunch paninis (toasted sandwiches on homemade bread) are $5-7; dinners $13-18. Grab a $2 beer during Happy Hour (5-7pm). Open Tu-Sa 11am-late, Su-M 5pm-late.

Penang Noodle House, 172 Manchester St. (tel. 377 2638). The decor may be simple, but you'll be impressed by the food. Select from several noodle ($5.80-7.50) and rice dishes ($6), or try the $5 lunch special M-F. Open M-Sa 11:30am-2:30pm, 5-10pm and Su noon-3pm and 5-9pm.

NORTH OF WORCESTER STREET

🦚 **Raj Mahal** (tel. 366 0521), at the corner of Manchester and Worcester St. Indian music and incense waft through the dining room of this authentic restaurant with wooden shutters and colorful tablecloths. Choose from several tandoori ($15-19) and vegetarian ($13-16) dishes. For a real steal, order takeaway—portions are huge and you can get anything on the menu for under $13. Open daily 5:30-10pm, takeaway from 4:30pm.

Sala Thai (tel. 365 5447), at the corner of Colombo and Kilmore St. Posters of Thai fruit and a shimmering wall hanging of elephants contribute to the unpretentious atmosphere. Huge range of Thai and Lao dishes. Pad thai ($13) is an eternal favorite, but there's chili and curry, too. Mains $13-18. Open daily noon-9:30pm.

Houghtons Cafe Bar and Restaurant (tel. 365 6999), at the corner of Montreal and Salisbury St. You'll find romantic, candlelit dining in this recently opened eatery in the elegant, historic Ironside House. Mains ($21-24) and an excellent selection of rich deserts. Open daily 11am-11pm.

Death by Chocolate, 209 Cambridge Terr. (tel. 365 7323), north on Colombo St. and turn right onto Cambridge Terr. As the name implies, you may have to be carried out—the namesake dessert alone ($15) could fill 2, and the "Multitude of Sins" ($24 for 2) is enough to inspire a gastronomic orgasm. Open Tu-Su from noon, M from 6pm.

🦚 **Pronto Nachos Cafe,** 8 New Regent St. (tel. 366 4676). Enormous nachos ($7.50) and tasty chicken burrito ($8) served with fresh, homemade guacamole. Small cacti and hanging plants, rugs on the walls, and fresh flowers cheerfully welcome you to this 2-level eatery. Open M-Th 10am-10pm, F-Sa 10am-2am, Su 11am-8pm.

Thai Tasty, 10/129 Gloucester St. (tel. 379 7540). You won't find it much cheaper—or more authentic—than this. With 20 meals to choose from for $5, you can get Tom Yum soup, chicken pad thai, or one of several curry dishes. Open daily 8:45am-10pm.

Oxford on Avon, 794 Colombo St. (tel. 379 7148), at the corner of Colombo St. and Oxford Terr. The pinnacle of Kiwi pub food: carved meats, bowls of veggies, and creamy cakes served cafeteria-style. Daily specials ($8-17) and seating on the patio overlooking the Avon. Check out the smorgasbord restaurant upstairs. Lunch ($13.50) from 11:30am and dinner ($16) from 5:30pm. Open daily 6:30am-midnight.

Joji's Sushi Bar, 186 Manchester St. (tel. 365 0500). A tidy little place, with flowers on the counter and bamboo poles covering the ceiling. Incredibly fresh sushi and sashimi form a beautifully prepared lunch ($8) or dinner ($14-26). Open M-Sa noon-2:30pm.

Santorini Greek Ouzeri (tel. 379 6975), at the corner of Gloucester and Cambridge Terr. A fun-loving family restaurant with big Greek dinners ($19-21). When the Bouzouki Band gets going, patrons are encouraged to dance on wine casks; the conga lines have been known to invade the kitchen. Open Tu-Sa from 6pm.

THE JOY OF YEAST What little joy our lives would have without yeast! No bread, wine, beer—or, for that matter, brewer's by-products. And without the by-products, to the shock and horror of millions, that would mean no **Marmite,** the salty, yeasty brown paste with the look, consistency, and taste of spreadable bullion. The staple and ambrosia of New Zealand (and British) breakfast tables is a bit of an acquired taste. But, contrary to popular belief, you don't need to have been weaned on the stuff to truly enjoy it. The trick is to remember: 1) it's not sweet, and 2) it's *not* meant to be slathered across the bread. Scores of tourists every year make the mistake of smearing it on like so much peanut butter, a move that sends them spitting and cursing to the nearest sink. To look local, not yokel, scrape just the tiniest bit across hot buttery toast, or grate some cheese on top and broil to make "Mousetraps." A "100% vegetarian" delight brought to you by the Seventh Day Adventist Church-run Sanitarium Foods Co., Marmite is good for your body and redeeming for your soul. In contrast to Vegemite, the Aussie version of the sassy spread, Marmite is slightly sweeter. It's even rumored to prevent hangovers (due to the high content of B vitamins). In the end, though, it's really all about nationalism—true Kiwis eat Marmite.

MARKETS

Pak'N Save, at the corner of Moorhouse Ave. and Manchester St. The cheapest supermarket around (of the several megamarkets all stuck together a few blocks from Cathedral Sq.). Open M-W 8:30am-9pm, Th-F 8:30am-10pm, Sa-Su 8:30am-7pm.

Big Fresh, at the corner of Moorhouse Ave. and Madras St., has the freshest produce and is more upscale. Open Sa-W 8:30am-9pm, Th-F 8:30am-10pm.

New World, on Colombo St. in the south City Mall, has great discount seafood. Open M-Tu 8:30am-6pm, W-F 8:30am-9pm, Sa 8:30am-7pm, Su 9am-6pm.

CAFES

The Coffee House, 290 Montreal St. (tel. 365 6066), near the Arts Centre. Not for the indecisive; shelves of tea tins house an enormous selection of teas ($3-3.50) and coffees ($2.50-4.50). Puff-cheeked, wood-carved jazz musicians jam on the mantle over the fireplace, while the patio beckons with its flowers and sheltering shrubbery. Open M-Th 7:30am-11pm, F 7:30am-midnight, Sa 8am-1am, Su 8am-11pm.

Main Street Cafe (tel. 365 0421), at Colombo St. and Salisbury St. Hippyish bar/cafe/restaurant with a changing menu offers creative vegetarian and dairy-free options. Specializes in lentil dishes and hearty salads. Quiet and mellow, the courtyard fills up in summer. Dinners from $15-16. Open 10am-late.

Caffe Roma (tel. 379 3879), on Oxford Terr. near Gloucester St. An elegant brunch place with fresh irises, dark wood-panelling, and windows overlooking the Avon. Upscale clientele grab tasty muffins ($1.50) and breakfasts ($10-15) on their way to the office. Open daily 7am-4pm.

Java Cafe (tel. 366 0195), at the corner of High and Lichfield St. An alternative corner stronghold with 2 levels of pop art and plants connected by steep, winding staircases. Iced coffee served in jam jars ($4), a variety of bagels with toppings ($2-5), and the massive vegetarian planet burger ($10) are among the all-day dining options. The Hangover Cure ($10) may be just what the doctor ordered. Open daily from 7:30am.

Coffee D'Fafo, 137 Hereford St. (tel. 366 6083). D'Fafo boasts modern art and a svelte magazine bar in an unhurried environment. Le French toast $11.50, lunch $11.50-15.50. "Death before decaf." Open M-F 7am-6pm, Sa-Su 9am-3pm.

The Cafe Globe, 171 High St. (tel. 366 4704). Jewelry displays displace the price-tagged wall art adorning most cafes. Excellent and creative meals ($13-15) such as the coconut and coriander chicken salad ($14). Outside seating. Live jazz Sunday mornings from 11:30am. Open M-Th 7am-4pm, F-Sa 7am-late, Su 8:30am-4pm.

Vivace, 86 Hereford St. (tel. 365 8248), between Colombo and Oxford Terr. Small, artsy cafe with citrus- and mint-water and Botticelli frescoes. Loud and pleasantly aromatic when the coffee's roasting. Open M-Th 7am-5pm, F 7am-9pm, Sa-Su 8am-3pm.

Le Cafe (tel. 366 7722), on Worcester Blvd. in the Arts Centre. Among several cafes cached in medieval crannies, Le Cafe is always busy, always lively, and almost always open. Dine on the sunny patio or upstairs. Dinners from $10, breakfast from $6.50. Open Su-Th 7am-midnight, F-Sa 24hr.

🎵 ENTERTAINMENT

Christchurch has several excellent art cinemas and a professional theater company; check the back page of *The Press* for a full current listing. The **Court Theatre** (tel. 366 6992), at the Arts Centre, has two theaters running some of New Zealand's best professional repertory productions (adults generally $27, students generally $20). The **Theatre Royal,** 145 Gloucester St. (tel. 366 6326), is a forum for touring musicals and ballet companies. The **Repertory Theatre,** 146 Kilmore St. (tel. 379 8866), is a community theater running five plays a year (tickets about $15).

Gamblers can try their luck at the **Christchurch Casino** (tel. 365 9999), at Victoria and Durham St. While it may resemble an overgrown parking garage from the outside, the gaming room and cafes feature tasteful balconies and chandeliers. Slots, blackjack tables, and a dozen roulette wheels fill the gaming floor. Giveaways and cash contests take place nightly. (Free pickup and dropoff to and from all local accommodations. Pickup offered nightly from 6pm to 2am. No jeans, shorts, or sneakers. Must be 20 to gamble. Open daily 24hr.)

🌙 NIGHTLIFE

Rugby pubs and boutique bars dominate Christchurch's somewhat uninspired dancing and drinking establishments, although nightclubs and microbreweries have eked out a permanent niche among the locals. Cruise **The Strip** and the **City Mall** by the Avon and the action-packed corner of **Manchester** and **Cashel Streets** for after-dark hot spots.

Loaded Hog (tel. 366 6674), on Manchester at Cashel St. The lines are long, but they still pour an excellent lager at this homebrew chain. Chalkboard drawings near the entrance depict pop icons with Hog beer in-hand. Meals $9-15, snack food $6-11. Live jazz Tuesdays from 8:30pm. DJs Thursdays from 9pm, F-Sa from 8pm. Open M-W 11am-midnight, Th-Sa 11am-3am, Su noon-midnight.

The Green Room, 112A Lichfield St. (tel. 365 8275). Up the glitter-speckled staircase you'll find green walls, spatulas, whisks, and cutlery dangling from the ceiling, and attire ranging from business suits to baggy corduroys and nose rings. This gay-friendly bar has everything from live jazz to poetry readings to impromptu jam sessions. Open mic Tuesday from 9pm, live entertainment daily, and some of the cheaper beer you'll find in town (pints $4). Open Tu-Su 7:30pm-late.

The Bog, 82 Cashel Mall (tel. 379 7141). This recently-opened Irish bar is a hit for its warm atmosphere, late hours, and live music (W-Sa from 9:30pm). All-day breakfasts around $13, traditional Irish meals $13-15. Open daily 10am-late.

Viaduct, 136 Oxford Terr. (tel. 377 9968), on the Avon. Well-dressed twentysomethings pack into this dimly lit bar, which loosely creates a Roman motif with arches behind the bar, a statue, and crumbling plaster facades. The upstairs cigar bar with zebra- and leopard-print couches has a more mellow atmosphere. Long lines on weekends. Open daily 10:30am-late.

Platinum (tel. 377 7891), on Lichfield St., across from Cashel Plaza. The bar in this downstairs club is bathed in an eerie, fluorescent blue light, with artsy metallic lamps dangling from above. A second bar in the back serves wine and cocktails to a more upscale clientele. Dance floor holds a gyrating posse of locals, drag shows, comedy acts, live DJs, and even a pool table. Open M-W from 4:30pm, Th-Su from 7pm.

Dux de Lux, 41 Hereford St. (tel. 366 6919), by the Arts Centre. Enormous old house with two separate bars. 7 fresh-brewed beers attract students. Live jazz Tuesdays, punk, funk, rock, or reggae Th-Sa. Open Su-Th 11am-11pm, F-Sa 11am-midnight.

Sullivan's, 150 Manchester St. (tel. 379 7790), near Cashel St. Spacious pub adorned with vintage Irish photos (including one of a lamb drinking Guinness straight from the bottle) and a large map of the homeland. Acoustic jam session Wednesdays, Irish dancing Thursdays, live bands Fridays and Saturdays. Open M-Sa from 4pm.

Trader McKendry's (tel. 366 1513), at the corner of Cashel and Manchester St. Full house and plenty of dancing on weekends; other times, you can shoot some pool ($2) or test yourself on the slopes with Alpine Racer, a strap-in, interactive ski-game ($1). Cheap drinks W-F 5-7pm. Open M-W 11am-11pm, Th 11am-1am, F-Sa 11am-late.

Base, 674 Colombo St. (tel. 377 7149). Escape from overplayed Top 40s tunes to the beats of house and high energy, as the twirling silver disco ball reflects red lights on the dance floor. DJs from 11pm. Open Th-Sa 9:30pm-late. Cover $3 Th-F.

Sneakers Sports Bar (tel. 379 9368), at the corner of Cashel and Manchester St. TVs even in the bathroom. 2-for-1 meals M-Th. Open daily from 11am.

Bailie's (tel. 366 5159), behind the cathedral. The original Christchurch Guinness pub, Bailie's now has 10 U.K. brews on tap and Irish bands F-Sa. The quieter back bar has a great stained-glass ceiling (from its former hotel days) above the beer and rugby posters plastered to the walls. Open daily 9am-late.

The Jolly Poacher (tel. 379 5635), on Victoria St., opposite the Casino near Durham St. Neon rabbit over the doorway sets the stage for the trophy heads, mounted fish, and even the stuffed weasel that provide company in this English-style pub. Locals flock here for the ancient wood paneling, loud jukebox, and pool table of this homage to taxidermy. Live blues and jazz F 4:30-7:30pm. Rarely closed.

◉ SIGHTS

Christchurch is oriented around the Gothic revival **Christchurch Cathedral,** built in 1865 both from Canterbury quarried stones and roots from native matai and totara. Ornate stained-glass windows imported from England are juxtaposed with Maori *kai kai* (flax) weavings. The intricate front commemorates Captain Owen Stanley's landing at Akaroa just before the French reached the shore in 1840. You can even climb the cathedral's tower. (Tours M-F 11am and 2pm, Sa 11am, Su 11:30am; $3. Tower admission $4, children $1.50.)

Walk west down Worcester Blvd. past the Visitor Centre and you'll cross the **Avon River,** meandering through the city under willows and arched bridges. Seeing Christchurch by boat can be an enchanting experience, as you punt past historic buildings and the statues on the Avon. Tours depart from Worcester Blvd. frequently, including **Punting on the Avon** (tel. 379 9629; 30min., $12) and **Punting in the Park** (tel. 366 0337; $7.50-$20, depending on number of people).

The expansive **Botanic Gardens** feature one the country's best arrays of grand trees and indigenous plant life, with 10,000 species on 30 hectares of land. Even in winter, the gardens are immaculately maintained; the indoor cactus house and rainforest rooms shouldn't be missed. **Hagley Park,** with jogging tracks and rugby fields, surrounds the gardens on three sides.

ARTS, MUSEUMS, AQUARIUM

The impressive **Arts Centre** borders the gardens on the east, and stretches over an entire block back toward the city. Formerly the University of Canterbury, the gothic revival complex now houses cafes, art studios, shops, the Court Theatre, and two cinemas. You can walk into Ernest Rutherford's university laboratory, where he first experimented with high-frequency magnetization of iron. On weekends, craftsmen and clothiers sell goods in the outdoor market, and ethnic food stalls crowd the back courtyard. (Guided tours given by the town crier depart

WIZARDISM King of Christchurch's motley array of eccentrics, **The Wizard** makes his presence known around noon in Cathedral Square during the summer. Dubbed the official wizard of Christchurch by the local government, the outspoken linguistic Merlin will do everything in his power to rile up the crowd. Don't expect liberal views on politics or gender issues; you may flee disgusted, which means that the pointed cap and cape-bearing wizard has won the day. Still, he's a strikingly intelligent orator and entertainer, and has created his trademark upside-down maps proclaiming an enlightened understanding of the world. The wizard even flees the country during census time to escape political oppression from the forces of government. In- and out-of-season you can find The Wizard on the web (www.chch.planet.org.nz/wizard).

from the Arts Centre Information Centre near the end of Worcester Blvd. M-F 11am and 2pm. $5.)

Beyond the Arts Centre, the **Canterbury Museum** (tel. 366 5000), on Rolleston Ave., is one of the best regional museums in the country. It is home to several enormous panoramas of the moa, a Maori artifact room, and excellent natural history exhibits. (Open daily 9am-5:30pm, winter 9am-5pm. Free.) Around the other side of the museum rests Canterbury's premier art salon, the **Robert McDougall Art Gallery** (tel. 365 0915), specializing in New Zealand and British painting. Radiating from a central, columned foyer are several galleries of permanent and temporary exhibitions ranging from local works to traveling collections. The **Arts Annex,** in the Arts Centre, exhibits contemporary sculpture and multimedia works. (Both open daily 10am-4:30pm; free.) The **Centre of Contemporary Art (CoCA),** 66 Gloucester St. (tel. 366 7261), a block towards the Avon from the Arts Centre, is an independently supported gallery of innovative modern works with both rotating and permanent exhibitions. (Open Tu-F 11am-5pm, Sa-Su noon-4pm. Free.)

Right in Cathedral Sq., the **Southern Encounter Aquarium** (tel. 377 3474) is a recent addition to Christchurch's cultural gems. On display are fish and other sea creatures exclusively from the South Island. The eels are fed at 11am, the salmon and trout at 1pm, and the marine fish at 3pm. Excellent short films on South Island wildlife run continuously in the theater (open daily 9am-7pm; admission $12.50, children $6). Down the road on Moorhouse Ave. near Manchester St., **Science Alive** (tel. 365 5199) is a hands-on science experience geared toward children, which generally surprises and enlightens adults as well (open daily 9am-5pm; admission $6). Classic cars and other motorized masterpieces are exhibited at **Yaldhurst Museum of Transport** (tel. 342 7914), 1km west of the city on Yaldhurst Rd. (open daily 10am-5pm; admission $7, children $3).

ARCHITECTURE AND TOURS

Benjamin Mountfort conceived many of the Gothic Revival stone and brick structures in the 1860s and 1870s that today provide the city with its distinctive architectural character. Pick up a copy of the *Christchurch Central City Walks* pamphlet that details three walks past churches, government houses, and statues along the banks of the Avon. The brightly painted, arched wooden ceiling, magnificent stained glass windows and long neo-Gothic hallways of the **Provincial Council Buildings,** at Gloucester St. and Cambridge Terr., have yet to be noticed by most tourists, and even by many locals (open M-Sa 10:30am-3:30pm, Oct.-May also Su 2-4pm). For more comprehensive commentary, contact the **Personal Guiding Service** through the Visitor Centre (tours $8). **Private Garden Tours** also runs three-hour tours from the Visitor Centre (mid-Sept. to Dec. Tu-Sa 9:30am; Jan.-Mar. daily 9:30am; $25).

OUTLYING SIGHTS

Museums and attractions ring Christchurch city, and most are accessible by a short bus ride from the city center. The **Top Attractions Voucher Booklet,** available at the Visitor Centre, offers descriptions of local sights. The **City Circuit Bus** (tel. 332 6012) runs two loops around outlying sights.

⬛**Nga Hau E Wha National Marae,** 250 Pages Rd. (tel. 0800 456 898), east of Christchurch, is the country's largest Maori fort and provides an excellent window into Maori culture and history. The *marae* represents the body of a clever ancestor who fished the North Island out of the sea using his grandmother's jawbone; it is this hook that is symbolized by the popular jade or bone hook carvings. The flax ornamentation and painted carvings of ancestors are each uniquely symbolic, with a range of fascinating myths associated with them. A guided tour plus an evening concert is available ($27.50), as is a complete *hangi* (meal), tour, and concert ($60). Take bus #5 ($1.80) from Cathedral Sq.

The ⬛**International Antarctic Center** (tel. 358 9896) brings you as close as you'd like to get to the coldest, driest, windiest continent on earth. Let's face it—you know nothing about Antarctica. Educate yourself with interactive exhibits that include a "snow and ice experience" room, kept at Antarctic temperatures and stocked with real snow. The live deep-sea critters housed in sub-freezing aquariums and the multitude of concise, engrossing short videos will make you the life of any cocktail party where people want to talk about Antarctica. (Take the A bus for $2.70 or drive to the airport, head north around Hagley Park, and follow the signs. Open daily 9am-8pm, winter 9am-5:30pm. Admission $14, children $7, YHA $10.80, families $32.)

Two nearby wildlife reserves, north of the city off Johns Rd., house native and exotic wildlife. **Willowbank** (tel. 359 6226), accessible by car or with the City Circuit Bus, operates extensive walk-through aviaries and a nocturnal kiwi house. The exceptionally rare and exceptionally ugly *kune kune* pig roams freely, forcing inquisitive peacocks into fence-jumping routines. (Open daily 10am-10pm. Admission $12, students $9, children $6.) **Orana Park** (tel. 359 7109), 18km from the city, is a complete African plains park with lions, zebras, rhinos, a variety of savannah animals, native birds, and the ageless tuatara. (A shuttle departs from the Visitor Centre at 12:30pm. Return $15. Open daily 10am-4:30pm. Admission $12, children $6.) Beyond Hagley Park to the west, the **Mona Vale Homestead** (tel. 348 9659) sits amid rose gardens and rhododendrons on the banks of the Avon River, totally secluded from the city. Tea on the patio is a relaxing indulgence on a sunny day.

FESTIVALS

Christchurch also hosts an amazing number of festivals for a city its size. In November, **Showtime Canterbury** hits the city with its concerts, fireworks, and parades. After the New Year, the **International Buskers Festival** brings crazy, nutty street entertainers from around the world to the city in one of the wackiest outdoor festivals in the world. The **Festival of Flowers** blooms every February, bedecking Cathedral Sq. with a floral carpet. It includes garden competitions, street decorations, and visits to private gardens. Summer is also the season for outdoor opera and rock concerts, a **Wine and Food Festival** in February, and **Adventure Canterbury** in April, which celebrates Canterbury's adrenaline activities for two weeks. The **Christchurch Arts Festival** runs at the end of July in odd years, with multimedia performing arts and exhibitions. Every August the **Montana Christchurch Winter Carnival** celebrates the ski season, with imported snow (part of Cathedral Sq. is even covered with make-shift drifts and huge snow sculptures).

🏔 ACTIVITIES

Christchurch is the gateway to the serene, albeit mostly agricultural, outdoors of Canterbury. If the weather's good, take the free bus out to **Port Hills** and the **Mt. Cavendish Gondola** (tel. 384 0700), departing from the Visitor Centre every two hours starting at 10am (more frequently in summer). The #28 Lyttelton bus also runs regularly for $1.80. Numerous **walking tracks** leave from the top of the hills; it's also a popular mountain biking area. **The Mountain Bike Adventure Company** (tel. 0800 424 534) will bring you and a rented bike up the gondola so you can cruise down for about $38; book at the Visitor Centre. Take the gondola (return $12, students $9, children $6) or walk up the steep bridle path (about 1hr.) to the top for a view encompassing Christchurch, the distant Southern Alps, and Lyttelton Harbour. If you've got a car or bike, continue along the summit road to **Godley Head,** a rugged promontory of grassy paths and sheer cliffs overlooking the austere Pacific, with superb stargazing at night. In the other direction along Summit Rd., down Dyers Pass Rd., is the **Sign of the Takahe** (tel. 332 4052), one of three Gothic mansions built as a stopping point for travelers decades ago. If you've got a car, the Takahe offers a magnificent view of the lights of Christchurch and the Canterbury Plains. During the day, the #2 Cashmere bus runs up to the hills.

Hot-air balloon enthusiasts flock to the vast flatness of the Canterbury plains. Join either **Up Up and Away** (tel. 358 9859) or **Aoraki Balloon Safaris** (tel. 0800 256 837) for a leisurely float ($220 with champagne breakfast). Aoraki also leads trips from Methven that fly higher and afford better views of the mountains (see p. 294). Tandem skydiving with **Christchurch Parachute School** (tel. mobile 025 321 135) lands you 500m from Cathedral Sq., after a harrowing free fall ($245). Or, paraglide from the Gondola down to Sumner with **Phoenix Paragliding** (tel. 326 7634), **Tandem Paragliding** (tel. 385 4739), or **Nimbus Paragliding** (tel. 326 7922), an exhilarating descent of near weightlessness (from $95). Down at New Brighton Pier, **Bungee Rocket** (tel. 388 8295) straps you in, accelerates you to 50m in 1 second, and lets you spring up and down for up to 10 bounces; you can later watch your contorted face on video ($35; transportation on Canride bus #5.)

Equestrians have many options for exploring the Canterbury countryside: some of the best trips are run by **Longspur Lodge** (tel. 329 0005), on the road to Akaroa (1hr. $25., 2hr. $40; return transport $25). Other companies that run horse treks include **Alpine Horse Safaris** (tel. 314 4293), which does single and multi-day horseriding tours, and **Bottle Lake** (tel. 383 4930), which leads wagon rides through nearby pine forest.

There are several other local activities, including ice skating at the **Alpine Sorts Centre** (tel. 366 9183; adults $5.50, children $4.50, skate hire $1.50; open M-F 10am-3pm, also M and W 7:30-9:30pm, F-Sa 7:30-10pm, Sa-Su 2-4pm). Take Lyttleton bus #28 ($1.80). **Jet Thrills** (tel. mobile (025) 387 485) leads fast-paced, shallow-water adventures ($45, children $30; free pickup), while **Waimak Alpine Jet** (tel. 318 4881) leads longer trips into the Waimakariri Canyon. **Rangitata Rafts** (tel. 0800 251 251) leads on full-day trips over Grade 4 and 5 rapids ($115; free pickup). **Canterbury Fishing Adventures** (tel. 0800 484 485) takes you out on nearby rivers for some good angling (half-day $115, full day $160).

CANTERBURY SKIING

The ski fields in Canterbury's Southern Alps heat up in winter, with ski fever breaking out around July. Many fields are only a short distance from Christchurch or **Methven** (see below), and offer comparable slopes with less glitz and cheaper rates than the tourist-heavy locales in the southern lakes. For detailed information on skifields, pick up the complimentary *Brown Bear* guide, or check out their website (www.brownbear.co.nz).

Porter Heights (tel. 379 7087) is the closest field to Christchurch, and boasts the country's longest vertical drop and Tuesday two-for-one deals. Advanced skiers and boarders will appreciate the challenging Bluff Face run and the recently-extended Big Mama run. (Lift passes $44, student $37.) With the longest season in New Zealand (May-Oct.) and the best snowcover as well, **Mt. Hutt** (tel. 302 8811) attracts crowds of skiers who base themselves at Methven. The 2075m summit boasts 365 hectares of beautiful powder and 42 hectares of snow-making, as well as fabulous views into the heart of the Southern Alps. Challenging terrain suitable for all skiing abilities and a new half-pipe more than justifies the price tag (Lift passes $55, students $45, children $27.) Arthur's Pass is the base for skiing at **Temple Basin** (tel. 377 7788), which has some of the best snowboard terrain in New Zealand. Night skiing is included in the price of a day pass. (Lift passes $30; 45min.

walk to the ski field.) In addition to the commercial ski fields, several club fields open their slopes to the public—at a much cheaper price. Be prepared for T-bars and rope tows. Other skifields include **Mt. Olympus** (tel. 366 6644 ext. 1108) near Lake Ida, **Mt. Lyford** (tel. 315 6178) near Waiau, **Mt. Cheesman** (tel. 379 5315) near Springfield, **Hanmer Springs** (tel. 315 7233), and **Craigieburn Valley Ski Field** (tel. 366 2514; see p. 300) near Springfield. Several companies provide transport from Christchurch. **Snowline Tours** (tel. 0800 766 954) runs door-to-door service to Mt. Hutt, Porter Heights, Mt. Cheeseman, Mt. Olympus, and Craigieburn Valley (return $35, students $30). The **Ski Shuttle** (tel. 324 3641) is cheaper, but runs only to Mt. Hutt (return $32, students $28) and Porter Heights (return $26, students $24).

METHVEN

Every winter, the tiny community of Methven (pop. 1000) swells with skiers and snowboarders eager to take on the slopes of nearby Mt. Hutt. A sleepy town of residential cottages and gardens surrounded by patchwork farmland with the Rakaia and Rangitata Rivers on either side, Methven's proximity to Mt. Hutt has earned it the title Mt. Hutt Village.

🛈 **ORIENTATION AND PRACTICAL INFORMATION.** Restaurants and ski shops line **SH77** (also known as Main St.) and accommodations are scattered within a 5-minute walk. The **Visitors Information Centre** (tel. 302 8955 or 0800 764 444; fax 302 9367; http://nz-holiday.co.nz/methven/info), on Main St., has Internet access, maps, accommodation, and transport info, and does bookings for all the activities in the region (open daily 9am-5pm, winter 7:30am-6pm).

To get anywhere from Methven, you're better off heading to Christchurch and leaving from there. **InterCity** and **Newmans** (book either at tel. 379 9020) run from the Visitor Centre to **Christchurch** (1hr., 4:55pm, $14) and **Queenstown** via **Mt. Cook** year-round (9hr., 9:35am, $78) and express in summer ($40). **Southern Link** (tel. 358 8355) also runs between **Christchurch** and **Queenstown** via **Wanaka** in winter (departs for Christchurch Su and Tu-F at 6:30pm, $20; departs for Queenstown M-Th and Sa 5pm). **Snowline Tours** (tel. 0800 766 954) and **Leopard SkiBus** (tel. 332 5000) run cheaper shuttles between **Christchurch** and the **ski fields** (return $32-35) and offer good package deals with gear rentals and transport. **Methven Travel** (tel. 0800 684 888) goes to the **Christchurch airport** and to the **city center** (3-4 daily, $20, same-day return $35). Numerous shuttles run to **Mt. Hutt** (return $15-20); your best option is to go to the Visitor Centre and take the next departure.

Services in Methven include: the **BNZ,** on Main St. (open M-F 9am-4:30pm); a **Westpac ATM** for after-hours cash on The Mall; the **post office** (tel. 302 8463), in Gifts Galore on Main St. (open M-F 8am-5pm, winter M-F 8am-6pm, Sa-Su 9-11:30am and 3:30-6pm); the **Methven Medical Centre** (tel. 302 8105), on Main St. opposite the Visitor Centre (open M-F 9am-5pm; also open W until 8:45pm and in winter Sa-Su 10am-5pm); and the **local police** (tel. 302 8200). **Telephone Code:** 03.

🛏🍴 **ACCOMMODATIONS AND FOOD.** Methven boasts a remarkable number of hotels and lodges catering to the crowds of skiers. When the snow wanes, so do most of the visitors. And so do the prices. **Mt. Hutt Bunkhouse & Lampard Lodge,** 8 Lampard St. (tel. 302 8894; fax 302 9122), is a two-backpackers-in-one setup off Main St. A friendly staff, relaxed atmosphere, well-equipped kitchen, ski waxing shed to keep your gear in shape, and your choice of two lounges make it worth a visit. (Internet. Reception 7am-10pm. Dorms $18; doubles $44.) From the Visitor Centre, go right on Main St. and right again on South Belt and you'll see the sign for **Ski Red** (tel./fax 302 8964), on the left after the preschool. The homey lounge has a TV and a potbelly stove perfect for those dreary winter days when you'd rather curl up by the fire than hit the slopes. (Reception 8am-10pm. Singles with bath and TV $25, summer $15; shared rooms $20, summer $15. Cheaper rooms available in the seasonal Redwood Lodges next door; reception at Ski Red.) After a tough day of tumbling on the slopes, you may be ready for a bit of a splurge at the **Abisko**

Lodge, 74 Main St. (tel. 302 8875; fax 302 8795). The sauna and spa are perfect for aching muscles, while the pool table and piano create a pleasant atmosphere in the lounge. (Internet. Reception 8am-10pm. Rooms with bath and TV Jul.-Sept. from $36, Oct.-June from $25. Book in advance, particularly in winter.)

Unless you're a connoisseur of pub meals and takeaways, cheap food options are hard to come by. **Cafe 131** (tel. 302 9131) on Main St. offers a classier yet more expensive option to the takeaway shops scattered around Main St. (sandwiches $9-11; open daily 9am-4pm, winter 7am-7pm). You can't miss the **Blue Pub** (tel. 302 8046) illuminated by Christmas lights on Main St. Decent pub meals hover around $9. **Vee Tee's** (tel. 302 8252) really heats up on Tuesday nights for Ski Flix (7:30 and 9:30pm; open W-Su from 5pm, winter daily from 5pm.) **Four Square Discounter** (tel. 302 8114), on McMillan St., has fresh produce (open daily 7am-9pm).

▲ ACTIVITIES. Several ski and board shops have sprouted up in Methven; most offer rental deals cheaper than those on the mountain. **Big Al's** (tel. 302 8003) in the Square rents skis ($25) and boards ($39) in addition to clothing and mountain bikes ($25 per day; open daily in winter 7:30am-7:30pm). **Wombat's Ski Shop** (tel. 302 8084) has similar prices (open daily in winter 7:30am-6:30pm). The **Boarding House** (tel. 302 8945) on The Mall specializes in snowboards ($35 per day; open daily in winter 7:30-10am and 3-7pm).

For a true thrill, try a moonlit **abseil** or **rap jump** with **The Edge** (tel. 0800 762 564; fax 302 9228); for $89 you'll get four-and-a-half hours of instruction with as many as three jumps of 200 feet. Those seeking immersion in nature will find no shortage of **scenic walks** in the Methven area. Head for the 1687m **Mt. Somers Summit** (return 7hr.), take shorter walks through beech forest, or strike out on the historical and geologically interesting **Rakaia Gorge Walkway** (return 3-4hr.).

NEAR CHRISTCHURCH

LYTTELTON

Christchurch's port and beach suburbs make for convenient and pleasant daytrips from the city. Lyttelton slopes down the far side of the port hills to the industrialized harbor. Fifteen minutes from the city via the tunnel road (bus #28, $1.80), the port is home to a compelling mix of far-flung sailors and bohemian locals. Little Edwardian cottages line the steep streets, and several oddball curiosity shops and cafes dot the town. The **Visitor Centre,** 20 Oxford St. (tel. 328 9093), has self-guided walking tours ($1.50) of this historic port (open daily 9am-5pm).

With its bright red, blue, and yellow exterior, the **Volcano Cafe and Lava Bar** (tel. 328 7077), at the corner of London and Canterbury St., is hard to miss. Carved wooden poles and plants adorn the pleasant back garden, while the bar is bedecked with hanging barbed wire art. Big portions of food and excellent coffee are draws themselves; most dinners range from $15 to $23, with cheaper bar snacks available. (Open daily from 5pm.) Right next to the supermarket on London St., a neon sign announces **Wunderbar** (tel. 328 8818). Follow the signs down the stairs, through the parking lot, and up the ramp—it's worth the walk. Illuminated mannequins and a lamp made of dolls' heads cast light on the velvet seats and tribal masks along the bar. In the Backroom Bar, a shimmering cabaret stage complete with a Saturn-shaped disco ball opens Thursdays through Saturdays for dancing, live music, and cabaret shows. (Open M-Th 6:30pm-3am, F 5pm-3am, Sa-Su 3pm-3am.) **Harvesters Cafe,** 12 London St. (tel. 328 8544), has a good selection of sandwiches ($3), smoothies ($3.50-4.50), sweet treats, and fresh coffee blends perfect for a mid-afternoon snack (open daily 9am-5:30pm).

The **Lyttelton Timeball Station** (tel. 328 7311) once communicated Greenwich Mean Time to the boats in the harbor so they could accurately gauge their longitude. One of five remaining in the world, the station is a curiosity befitting this somewhat anachronistic maritime town. (Usually open daily 10am-5pm. Admission $2.50.) The 90-year-old **Tug "Lyttelton"** (tel. 322 8911) sets out on a one-and-a-half-hour historical cruise of the harbor (Su 2pm in summer; $12). **Lyttelton Harbour Cruises** (tel. 328 8368) runs frequent tours to the swimming beach at Quail Island, as well as to the historic reserve at Ripapa Island, and to Diamond Harbour (rates vary by destination, times and availability vary by season). For a close-up look at the rare Hector's dolphins along with some prime bird watching, contact **Dolphin Tours** (tel. 326 5607; tours 1½-2hr.; $60, children $30). **Canoe & Outdoor World** (tel. 366 9305) run half-day guided sea kayak tours of the peninsula with frequent sightings of blue penguins and Hector's dolphins ($49). **Coastline Adventures** (tel./fax 384 9238) runs tours of the Banks Peninsula and charter fishing trips on the Fox II, a vintage sailing vessel moored at Jetty A in the harbor (half-day charters from $22, full day from $48).

Lyttleton's main attraction is its picturesque setting, and probably the best way to enjoy the scenery is by getting out and **walking** it—grab a map from the Visitor Centre and head up the Bridle Path to the Mt. Cavendish Gondola or up either the Major Hornbrook Track or the Chalmers Track to the ▩**Crater Rim Walkway.** From Crater Rim, you can look onto the Canterbury Plains and see as far as the Southern Alps and Kaikoura on a clear day. You can then walk across to the gondola, back down to Lyttleton, or over towards Sumner and down to the beach.

SUMNER

Surfers and sun-worshippers flock to Sumner (accessible by bus #3; $1.80), Christchurch's summer beach resort town. Those seeking a bit more seclusion continue on to **Taylor's Mistake,** a beach on the other side of the town particularly popular with surfers. **Cave Rock,** near town, is a natural grotto accessible at low tide; beware of sudden surges if you choose to venture inside.

Walk into **Club Bizarre,** 15 Wakefield Ave. (tel. 326 6155), and you may feel like you've entered a time warp. The vintage memorabilia, jukebox, and games are bound to excite visitors of all ages, but the friendly staff takes great pride in the food, all cooked on the premises, from gourmet pizza ($17) to pasta ($15) to 14-layered black forest cake. (Open M-Sa 5pm-late, Su from noon.) You can feel trendy and stylish, enjoy a great view, and score a tasty meal at **Cafe Rock,** 22A Esplanade (tel. 326 5358), opposite the Cave Rock. Bask in the sun on the patio as you sample the Thai curry ($12) or one of the creative pastas ($15-17). (Open daily from 9am.) After a beachside stroll, enjoy a coffee drink at **Coffee Culture** (tel. 326 5900), along the main street (open M-F from 7:30am, Sa-Su from 9am).

AKAROA AND THE BANKS PENINSULA

Pale green hills dotted with dark pines slope down toward the amazingly blue bays of the Banks Peninsula. From Lyttelton Harbour in the west to the rugged Pacific shore, the bare rolling hillsides and bracing air are a refreshing change from the eternal flatness of the Canterbury plains. First sighted by Captain Cook in 1770, the area's safe harbors attracted the attention of French whalers, who purchased the land from the Maori in 1838. It wasn't until colonist Charles Lavaud had completed the harrowing voyage from France that he learned of the Treaty of Waitangi and British sovereignty (see p. 7). The French may have been forced to sell their land claims to the British, but they left their cultural mark on Akaroa, the peninsula's main town.

Magical and anachronistic, Akaroa's French-named streets and *maisons*, historic homes, little fishing harbor, and rugged hills seem worlds away from urban Christchurch, despite the mere 85km that separate them. Cyclists, hikers, and equestrians who have discovered Akaroa's small-town friendliness all head for the provincial charm of its misty hills. As proud of their history as they are of their way of life (Akaroa is also Canterbury's oldest European town), Akaroans are quick to tell a tale or two. Although there's not a French speaker to be found on the peninsula, the cheese factory and winery retain whispers of the area's cultural legacy.

⚁ ORIENTATION AND PRACTICAL INFORMATION. Running past the varied avifauna of shallow **Lake Ellesmere** and through several tiny towns, the **SH75** winds down to the harbor of Akaroa, some one-and-a-quarter hours southeast of Christchurch. The road traverses the now-extinct Akaroa volcano and its hairpin curves should not be taken lightly. The town itself lies along **Rue Lavaud** and **Beach Rd.** along the water. Akaroa's **Visitor Centre,** 80 Rue Lavaud (tel./fax 304 8600; email akaroa.info@clear.net.nz), has info on local accommodations, activities, and walking tracks (open daily 9am-5pm, winter 10am-4pm).

The **Akaroa Shuttle** (tel. 0800 500 929) leaves from the Akaroa Visitor Centre for Christchurch daily (3 per day Dec.-Mar., 1-2 per day Apr.-Nov.; $15; return $25). The **French Connection** (tel. 366 4556) includes commentary and stops at the cheese factory; it departs from the Christchurch Visitor Centre daily at 9:30am (winter M, W, and Sa), returning the same day at 3:30pm from Akaroa's main wharf ($19, return $38, backpackers $26; free pickup). **Hitchhiking** is also possible—though not recommended by Let's Go—to and from Christchurch, as most traffic goes all the way to Akaroa; most thumbers first take the #7 Halswell bus from Cathedral Sq. **Renting a car** is a good idea for exploring the Banks Peninsula (see p. 283 for Christchurch rental options). If you're already in Akaroa, you can hop on the **mail run** (tel. 304 7207 or 304 8600) to see the most remote reaches of the peninsula (M-Sa departs 8:20am and returns 1pm, $20). Other services include: the **post office** (tel. 304 7701), next door to the Visitor Centre (open M-F 8:30am-5pm); **BNZ** (tel. 304 7050), which changes money (open M-F 9am-4:30pm); the **police** (tel. 304 7030); the local **medical center** (tel. 304 7004); and the **library,** 141 Rue Dolie (tel. 304 8782), with **Internet access** (open M-F 10am-4pm, Sa 10am-1pm). **Telephone Code:** 03.

⌐ ACCOMMODATIONS. Chez La Mer Backpackers, on Rue Lavaud (tel./fax 304 7024; email chez_la_mer@clear.net.nz). Built by a Spaniard in 1860, this backpackers still exudes Old World charm with its herb garden, gazebo, endearingly uneven floors, and free muesli and spices. Incredibly cozy little rooms overlook the hills. (Reception 8:30am-10pm. Dorms $15; singles $25; twins and doubles $40, with bath $45.) **Lavaud House** (tel./fax 304 7121) is next door to the BNZ on Main St. View the bay from the beautiful garden grounds or the sitting room in this historic house filled with antique tables and dressers. (Singles $60; twins and doubles $80-100. Continental breakfast with homemade bread included.) More remote is **Mount Vernon Lodge** (tel./fax 304 7180), 2km up Rue Balguerie off Rue Lavaud on 51 acres of land. The rustic lodge runs a stable and encourages a rural experience: feed the animals (Gus the goose, Smudge the sheep, and the gang), relax by the swimming pool, or take a horse trek. (Free pickup. Reception daily 8am-6pm, winter 9am-4pm. Shared rooms $15; individual rooms $50 for 5 beds; cabins for 2-6 people $70. Beware of animal droppings.) **Akaroa Holiday Park** (tel./fax 304 7471), on Morgans Rd. about 1km out of town on the main road, has a swimming pool. (Reception 8:30am-9:30pm. Powered sites $10 per adult, $5 per child; tourist cabins for 2 $44, extra adult $11, extra child $8; caravan for 2 $32, extra adult $9, extra child $6.)

⌂ FOOD. Several Akaroa eateries gain inspiration from the French, and unless you adore pub food and pies, they're worth the extra dollars. **Bully Hayes** (tel. 304 7533), on the waterfront, has gourmet lunches ($10-15); evening cuisine runs around $13-23. Choose from the sunny room with large windows and a bay view and the darker, fire-warmed back room. (Open daily 9am-late.) You can sit on the patio overlooking the harbor at **Dolphin Cafe & Bar,** 6 Rue Balguerie (tel. 304 7658). Paintings of ships, old naval flags, fishing tackle, and even a lifeboat hang from the walls and ceiling. Soup of the day is $7.50, pasta of the day is $12.50, and the set dinner is $23. (Open daily 9am-late, winter Tu-Su 10am-late.) At **Turenne Coffee Shop & Dairy,** 74 Rue Lavaud (tel. 304 7005), you can sip a coffee, nibble on a muffin ($1.50), and check your email (open daily 7am-6pm, winter 7am-4pm). For those with empty stomachs and empty wallets, the **Akaroa Bakery** across the street from the French flag sells fresh baked-bread ($2-3 per loaf) and homemade sandwiches

($3). The **Four Square supermarket,** on Rue Lavaud across from the museum, fills your grocery needs (open M-Sa 9am-6pm, also Su 9am-2pm in summer).

■ ■ **SIGHTS AND ACTIVITIES.** The **Akaroa Museum** (tel. 304 7614) encompasses four buildings, including the **Langlois-Eteveneaux Cottage,** which was partially prefabricated in France before being brought over in the 1830s. Well-conceived exhibits include everything from traditional Maori clothing to a 1910 gig complete with nearly 2m high wheels. (Open daily 10:30am-4:30pm, winter 10:30am-4pm. Admission $3, children $1.) Try your hand behind the mic as a DJ at **Bay Radio Akaroa 100.8 FM** (tel. 304 7717), 7 Rue Lavaud ($20 per person; includes a tape of the show; open M-W, and Sa, hours vary).

Dolphin Experience (tel. 304 7726) takes you on an out-of-harbor-cruise (2hr., $35) or swimming with the rare Hector's dolphins (3hr., $68, children $48). **Akaroa Harbour Cruises** (tel. 304 7641 or 0800 436 574), on the main wharf, visit much of the harbor, including the seal and cormorant colonies (2hr., $29, children $13). If you'd rather catch marine life than watch it, **Bluefin Charters** (tel. 304 7866) will take you fishing in the harbor (3hr., $50), on a half-day trip out of the harbor (4hr., $80), or on a full-day trip around the Banks Peninsula (8hr., $130). They also do harbor cruises (2hr., $20) and bird-watching trips (3-4hr., $50). Inquire at the Visitor Centre about kayak hires ($45 per day) and guided tours ($48-76) with **Banks Peninsula Sea Kayaks** (tel. 304 8776).

Numerous tracks depart from Akaroa, with everything from the four-day coastal **Banks Peninsula Track** to shorter day-walks through the bush and up the volcano. Inquire at the Visitor Centre for details, information, and maps.

ARTHUR'S PASS

Nestled among the towering peaks of the Southern Alps, the tiny village of Arthur's Pass serves double duty as a crucial pass through the mountains and as a jumping-off point for skiers and hikers. The building of a viaduct just down the road (completed November 1999) may have boosted the town's population from 50 to a whopping 120, but don't expect to find more than the basic amenities here. Straddling the Main Divide of the Southern Alps, the village is dramatically perched between two tectonic plates and two natural habitats, as the beech forest of Canterbury meet the rainforest of the West Coast. During winter, it is common to find the road through the pass, SH73, closed due to snow. The railroad, completed in 1923, has always managed to plow its way through snowdrift, avalanche, and stunning scenery to deliver its passengers safely. However you arrive, the journey up to Arthur's Pass provides endless breathtaking views of the plunging valleys and soaring mountains of the surrounding 250,000-acre Arthur's Pass National Park.

■ **PRACTICAL INFORMATION.** The **Arthur's Pass Visitor Information Centre and DOC office** (tel. 318 9211; fax 318 9271) is a few minutes up on the left as you walk toward the village from the train station (open daily 8am-5pm, winter 9am-4pm). **TranzScenic** (tel. 0800 802 802) crosses through the heart of the South Island to explore gorges, river valleys, and alpine fields. It runs daily to **Christchurch** (2hr., 4:30pm, $56) and **Greymouth** (2hr., 11:20am, $34). **Coast-to-Coast** (tel. 0800 800 847) and **Alpine Coach and Courier** (tel. 0800 274 888) both run daily to: **Christchurch** (2½-3hr., 1 per day, $25); **Greymouth** (1½hr., 1 per day, $18-25); and **Hokitika** (1½-2hr., 1 per day, $15-18). Contact the **police** (tel. 318 9212), on Main Rd., in an emergency. **Telephone Code:** 03.

■ **ACCOMMODATIONS.** Backpackers relax in the coal stove lounge presided over by a Maori statue at the **Sir Arthur Dudley Dobson Memorial YHA** (tel. 318 9230). Sir Arthur Dudley Dobson was the first man to survey Arthur's Pass in 1864. The owner can give plenty of advice on hunting and tramping in the region. (Reception

THE MYSTERIOUS MOA Have moas (see p. 18) really been extinct for about 500 years, or are they still roaming deep in the New Zealand bush? Occasional reports have trickled in from deep in the mountain country of Fiordland. The debate rekindled to full fury in January 1993 after three hikers reported seeing a live moa in the Craigieburn Range. A blurry photograph accompanied the story, thrusting the travelers out of the bush and into front-page headlines for over a week. While there were some believers, others saw it as just a publicity stunt. Follow-up letters and articles recalled past moa sightings and speculated on what other animal the hikers might have seen: emu, red deer, goose, and ostrich were some suggestions. A pair of German backpackers in the Craigieburn Range had written in the Bealey Hut intentions book the year before that they had seen two moa in the Harper Valley, but authorities were unable to track down the Germans to question them. Following the more recent 1993 account and attendant publicity and interest, the DOC almost went ahead with a field search. Don't expect to bring home any moa trophies, however: regardless of whether they still exist, moas are reputed to be protected species under the Wildlife Act (just in case). The only way to shoot a moa, if you're lucky enough to see one, is with your camera. If you go tramping around Lagoon Saddle in the Craigieburn Range, don't forget your camera—and, most importantly, don't forget to focus.

8-10am and 5-10pm; when closed, a board on the office door indicates vacant rooms. Bunks $15; doubles $36. Non-YHA $4 more.) **Mountain House Backpackers** (tel. 318 9258), located across from the YHA, twinkles with its periwinkle kitchen, spiral staircase, and glass house (a veritable sauna during the day and an ice-house at night). It rents ice-axes, crampons, sleeping mats, and more. (Reception 10-11:30am and 5:30-7pm. Self-booking system available. Bunks $16; tent sites $9. Stay 2 nights, get the 3rd free May-Sept.) There is a **DOC campsite** with a shelter across the street from the Visitor Centre for those looking to rough it while in town, complete with toilets and water (boil before drinking) in the summer ($3 per person). **Klondyke Corner,** 8km up the road towards Christchurch on Highway 73, provides free roadside camping with pit toilets. Water must be fetched from the river; again, boil before drinking.

⌂ **FOOD. Chalet's Restaurant and Bar** (tel. 318 9236), a few minutes past the hostels to the right, infuses a glint of glamor into this homey town. Between walls peppered with serene artwork, amid the strains of Swiss music, the hungry traveler can snag a sandwich ($3.50) for lunch or pasta ($7.50) for dinner. Be sure to sit in the laid-back dining room, not the fancy one (yes, there are two), as the menu in the latter is limited to costlier items. (Open daily 9am-9pm.) Slightly closer to the backpackers, **Oscar's Haus Cafe** (tel. 318 9234) has a budget-friendly menu with meals from $5 to $11 (open daily 8am-late, winter 10:30am-4pm). For the truly economical, **Arthur's Pass Tearooms** (tel. 318 9235) is a cheap, speedy alternative. Wash down chicken or mince pie ($2) with one of many beverage choices. It also carries a small selection of groceries. (Open daily 8am-8:30pm, winter until 7:30pm.)

⚠ **ACTIVITIES.** With spectacular mountain terrain, gorges, rivers, waterfalls, alpine meadows, and glaciers, **Arthur's Pass National Park** has something for everybody, but especially pleases the seasoned veteran. Always be aware that extreme weather can be dangerous, and check with the **DOC** before heading out.

There is a great range of hikes available, including some that are suitable for all levels. The **Devil's Punchbowl Waterfall Trail** (return 1hr.) begins several hundred meters down the road from the Visitor Centre and leads trampers to an arrestingly gorgeous view of the falls. A beautiful spot just after the start of the trail rewards early birds with a beautiful view of the sunrise over the mountains. The **Cass-Lagoon Saddle,** a popular summertime tramp (beware avalanches in winter) is one of the easier overnight hikes (arrange in advance with DOC for **Arthur's Pass hut**

tickets, ranging in price from free to $8). **Craigieburn Forest Park,** just south of Arthur's Pass, extends from Highway 73 in the east almost as far as the Mian Divide in the west. Sprawled between the Waimakariri and Wilberforce Rivers, the park delights botanists with its eastern mountain beech forest and mixed podocarp, treefern, and moss-covered forest. Although small, the park is a haven for experienced outdoor enthusiasts. The best day-hikes are clustered around the **Park Headquarters** (2km off of SH73, about a half-hour drive east of Arthur's Pass village), where travelers can also find information, picnic sites, camp sites, and shelter. There is a smattering of huts and shelters throughout the park, but most are on multi-day hikes and are accessible only to the experienced tramper. If you've got a little extra time, the huge limestone formations of **Castle Hill** (off of SH73 about a 45min. drive east of Arthur's Pass, 7km past the turn-off to the Craigeburn headquarters) are a smashing place for a picnic. Castle Hill is most easily reached by travelers with their own transportation.

Arthur's Pass is located within close proximity to a number of **ski fields,** including the popular **Temple Basin,** recently voted the country's best snowboarding area. Although the majority of the ski clubs are private, they can be joined and enjoyed inexpensively. Although there are numerous options, most slopes require a high level of proficiency. For the scoop on skiing and an update on conditions, ask at the Visitor Centre or call for the **snow report** (tel. 366 6644). There are very limited slopes for beginners but plenty of options for advanced skiers. Swish down **Mt. Olympus** (tel. 0800 686 596; $30, students $20; bottom hut accommodations $15 per night; no ski hire available) or pay a visit to either of the area's small clubs, **Broken River** (tel. 318 7270; $30, students $20) and **Craigeburn Valley** (tel. 365 2514; $28, students M-F $25; Sa-Su $35). Both clubs offer accommodations, packages, lessons, and reduced rates for members, but you'll have to bring your own equipment and chains for your car. Also, if you're headed to Broken River, be ready for a 30-minute walk to the ski field, although there is a good lift available. If you didn't bring your own equipment, **Porter Heights** (tel. 379 7087; $44, students $37), **Mt. Cheeseman** (tel. 379 5315; $38, youth $32), and **Temple Basin** (tel. 377 7788; $32, students $23) hire ski gear.

SOUTH CANTERBURY

Sheep. New Zealand is known for them in the millions, and much of Canterbury south and west of Christchurch is full of them. Speckled with small agricultural outposts, the unending Canterbury plains slowly blend into the coastal climes of Timaru. Heading inland from Timaru, the plains give way to the mountain passes leading to an area known as the Mackenzie Country. It gained its name when over a thousand sheep were discovered missing one day in 1843, and James Mackenzie, a Scotsman, was caught, tried, and imprisoned. He allegedly escaped from jail three times and quickly became New Zealand's most famous outlaw. This area has seen little development in the years since Mackenzie's escapades, remaining an agricultural region whose serene beauty provides welcome relief from the bustle of cities to the north and south. The mighty Mt. Cook reposes at the northern end of Lake Pukaki, and in the heart of the Southern Alps, mountains everywhere are reflected in the basin's most famous lake, Tekapo. Covered with tussock grassland and sheep paddocks, and dotted with brilliant lakes against a backdrop of incomparable mountain scenery, southern Canterbury is quiet and ruggedly pastoral.

TIMARU

With its pleasant botanical gardens and beautiful ocean vistas, Timaru (pop. 27,000) beckons with an honest charm and shows signs of emerging cosmopolitanism. First named Te Maru, meaning "place of shelter," Timaru once provided water and rest for Maori hunters. Today, an artificial harbor begun in 1877 protects the international fishing fleet and rigs full of live sheep bound for Asia. The wharfs also shelter Caroline Bay from the rough seas, making it a popular attraction for beachgoers during the summer. Timaru really heats up for its annual Christmas/New Year Carnival when crowds flock to the area for entertainment and sun.

ORIENTATION AND PRACTICAL INFORMATION

Midway between Christchurch and Dunedin, Timaru slopes down from the foothills of the Central Alps to the sea, just south of the road to Mt. Cook. Tranquil **Caroline Bay** is a 15-minute walk uphill along Stafford St. through the business district, while the **Botanic Gardens** are a 20-minute walk in the opposite direction on Stafford St., which becomes King St.

From the train station, head left to the **Visitor Information Centre,** 14 George St. (tel. 688 6163; fax 688 6162; email info@timaru.com), where you'll find free maps, local bus schedules, self-guided walking tours, and information on regional events (open M-F 5:30am-5pm, Sa-Su 10am-3pm). Also inquire at the Visitor Centre about **DOC** info, various **shuttle** services ($10-26 to Christchurch), and other bookings for transport and accommodations.

TranzScenic (tel. 688 3597) leaves daily for **Christchurch** (2hr., 3:15pm., $36) and **Invercargill** (7hr., 10:20am, $86) via **Dunedin** (3½hr., $41). 20-50% discounts with advance bookings. Buses run by **InterCity** and **Ritchie Transport** (tel. 684 7195) leave from the train station for **Christchurch** (2¼hr., 3-4 per day, $26) via **Ashburton** (1¾hr., $14), and to **Dunedin** (3½hr., 2-3 per day, $30) via **Oamaru** (1¼hr., $14). For taxi service, try **Timaru Taxis** (tel. 688 8899) or **Call-a-Cab** (tel. 688 8811). **Hitchhikers** report the base of the highway up to Mt. Cook is a good place to catch a ride to the mountains. Otherwise, SH1 north or south of town (before cars speed up into the countryside) is considered the easiest place to grab a ride.

Other services include: **BNZ,** 156 Stafford St., located on the main drag around the corner from the Visitor Centre (open M, Th, F 9am-4:30pm, Tu-W 9:30am-4:30pm); the **Suds City Laundromat,** on the corner of Elizabeth and Theodosia St. (open M-F 7am-9pm, Sa-Su 7:30am-9pm); the **police station** (tel. 688 4199), at North and Barnard St.; the **hospital** (tel. 684 3089), on High and Queen St.; and the **post office** (tel. 688 5518), on Sophia St. off King George Pl. (open M-F 8:30am-5:30pm, Sa 9:30am-12:30pm). **Telephone Code:** is 03.

ACCOMMODATIONS

Comfortable, well-equipped triples are the norm at **Timaru Backpackers (YHA),** 42 Evans St. (tel. 684 5067). In addition to a kitchen with cooking facilities, the common space includes a lounge area with TV. Phone the owner for pickup. Backpackers stay in self-contained, spacious motel rooms $17; in winter, rooms with heating units and shared shower/bath are the same price. At **Timaru Selwyn Holiday Park** (tel. 684 7690), 2km outside of town on Selwyn St., 100 powered sites of the extensive camp facility sit by a swift creek. Enjoy the pinball machine, TV lounge, immaculate shower blocks, and free access to the neighboring Highfield Golf Club (club rental extra). (Tent sites $8; standard cabins for 2 $29-39; self-contained tourist flats for 2 $52, extra person $11.) Bumble bees and cheerful scrawlings from previous travelers cover the walls of the main dorm at **The Bunkhouse Backpackers,** 334 Stafford St. (tel. 684 4729). About a 10 minute walk uphill from the train station, Bunkhouse offers a selection of books and movies as well as a pool table. (Key deposit $10. Dorms $15; singles $18-28; twins $40.)

FOOD

Roosters guard the doors and keep watch from their stained-glass perches in the windows of **The Coq and Pullet,** 209 Stafford St. (tel. 688 6616). The mammoth blueberry muffins ($2.50) are a good start to any day, while the creamy custard squares ($2.50) tempt those with a sweet tooth. Over the hill toward Caroline Bay via Stafford St., the cozy wine bar **Boudicca's,** 64 The Bay Hill (tel. 688 8550), includes Middle Eastern selections such as falafel-stuffed pitas (small $5, large $8) and beef satay kebabs ($9.50) on its all-day menu. On a nice day, sit outside and enjoy the view overlooking Caroline Bay. (Open M 5-9pm, Tu-Su 11am-10pm.) **The Loaded Hog**, 2 George St. (tel. 684 9999), in the Landing Service Building by the Visitor Centre, is a trendy microbrew chain that serves as the late-night hot spot for the younger crowd. Affectionately called "the Pissed Pig" by locals, agricultural tools compete with posters of the Simpsons for wall space in this vast building dating back to the 1870s. Bite into the $5 lunch specials (noon-2pm) and wash them down with a $4 pint of Hog's Head Dark. (Open daily 11am until late.) **Taxis**, 126 Stafford St. (tel. 684 8559), is a short walk left from the train station. This burger joint serves the most Kiwi of dishes, the Gringo Burger ($6 or 2 for $10). Weary from a long day of travel? No problem—Taxis also delivers between 5-11pm ($1.50 extra). **Southend Takeaways,** 39 King St. (688 6282), halfway between the center of town and public gardens, provides the perfect munchie for any jaunt. Stop in and grab a package of their award-winning fish 'n' chips ($2.80).

◉ 𝕂 SIGHTS AND ACTIVITIES

Timaru mainly serves as a base for cyclists, boaters, fishers, and skiers, but has its share of local charms. Walk up the Benvenue Cliffs on the far side of the beach for a view of the harbor. Today, memorial plaques nailed to the post commemorate lost ships. From Boxing Day (Dec. 26) until mid-January, the bay area hosts a grand **Christmas/New Year Carnival** that draws crowds to its concerts and contests. Beer, a major fixture of the South Islander's diet, is produced in massive vessels at **DB Brewery** (tel. 688 2059), Sheffield St., using their patented continuous fermentation method. If you can, get a ride and sample just one of the 55 million liters produced here. You'll leave happy—maybe a little too happy. (Tours M-F at 10:30am. Enclosed footwear required. Call for reservations. Free.) The **Timaru Botanic Gardens,** a 20-minute walk south along Stafford St. (which becomes King St.), includes rare plant species, ponds flitting with ducks, and grassy knolls fit for a picnic or simply a relaxing sit. A wide track runs through the gardens, whose peaceful grounds are a welcome spot for walkers, joggers, and bicyclists. **Caroline Bay** and its shallow sweep of sand bustle in the summer months—the reclaimed park contains an **aviary** with bevies of technicolor parakeets, an open stage, miniature golf during the summer, and a host of other activities (housed in a historic mansion dating back to 1908.) The **Aigantighe Art Gallery,** 49 Wai-iti Rd. (tel. 688 4424), is just up the hill from SH1. It features a permanent collection of paintings ranging from early colonial New Zealand to the present, as well as rotating exhibitions. Gaelic for "at the house," Aigantighe (EGG-and-tie) also showcases sculptures from an international Stone Carving Symposium on the carefully manicured grounds that overlook Timaru's rooftops and Caroline Bay beyond. (Open Tu-F 11am-4:00pm, Sa-Su noon-4:00pm. Free.)

RE-WRIGHTING THE HISTORY OF FLIGHT

Though his neighbors believed the inventions of "Mad Pearse" were the work of the devil, by contemporary standards Richard Pearse's efforts were closer to miraculous. Pearse built a powered plane in 1903 and made several shaky flights some nine months before the Kittyhawk flight of the Wright brothers. Although Pearse didn't consider his achievement to have been true "flight," his plane stayed aloft longer and was technologically superior to the Wright brothers' device. A tattered replica on display at the South Canterbury Museum is the only remainder of his aerial ingenuity. Since officials were later unable to verify the exact flight date, Pearse gave up striving for fame after learning of the exploits of the Wright brothers. Forever the tinkerer, Pearse also produced many inventions, including a needle threading device and a potato planter.

TEKAPO

Encircled by the majestic peaks of the Southern Alps, the milky blue waters of Lake Tekapo lap gently against smooth pebble beaches. The tiny stone church—perched on the edge of the lake and powerful in its simplicity—makes for a mesmerizing view, enhanced by the pure air from the mountains. With a moon bright enough to cast spooky shadows off the pines, and a great swath of stars arcing across the horizon, Tekapo's luminous nights complement the serenity of the day.

7 ORIENTATION AND PRACTICAL INFORMATION. Tekapo is centered along **SH8,** which crosses the dam controlling the Tekapo River. The Hide Shop functions as the **Visitor Centre** (tel./fax 680 6721), and has information on local activities and accommodations (open daily 9am-8pm, winter 9am-5pm). The Visitor Centre has Eftpos and exchanges credit card checks, but there are **no banks or cash machines** in Tekapo; the **Alpine Inn** (tel. 680 6848) changes money but takes a substantial commission. **InterCity** (0800 777 707), **Southern Link Shuttles** (tel. 358 8355), **Kiwi Discovery** (tel. 0800 505 504), and **Atomic Shuttles** (tel. 322 8883) all run daily to **Christchurch** (4hr., 1 per day, $20-42) and **Queenstown** (5½hr., 1 per day, $20-55). Book your **bus,** stock up on **groceries,** and mail letters from the **Shell Station** (tel. 680 6809), which also functions as the **post office** (open M-Sa 7:30am-7pm, Su 8am-7pm). In emergencies, call **111** or the **police** (tel. 680 6855). **Telephone Code:** 03.

☞ ACCOMMODATIONS. The **Tekapo YHA** (tel. 680 6857; fax 680 6664) is on Simpson Ln., past the pub on the west side of town. The lounge has massive windows, a soulful view of the lake, board games, and a blue upright piano. Bike and fishing rod rentals are available. (Reception 8am-10am, 5-6:30pm, and 8-10pm. Dorms $15; twins $36; tent sites $9; non-YHA members $4 more.) Up Aorangi Crescent across from the tavern is the recently-renovated **Tailor-made Tekapo Backpackers,** 9-11 Aorangi Crescent (tel. 688 6700; email tailor-made-backpackers@xtra.co.nz), with three spacious buildings and two stone BBQs on gardened grounds (dorms $16-17; twins, doubles, and triples $18 per person, with bath $20). Cyclists are fortunate to have the seasonal **Peddlers Paradise,** 1 Aorangi Crescent, all to themselves. The rooms are spare, but with lake and mountain views and for $12 per night, they're a steal. (Open Oct.-Apr. Tent sites $8. Cash only. No bookings–go to Visitor Centre or just show up. Cyclists only.)

♬ FOOD. Restaurants and takeaways cluster around the Shell Station on SH8. **Kohan Restaurant** (tel. 680 6688) in the Alpine Inn complex has a generous array of sushi (from $15) and their seared salmon steaks are widely renowned. Dinners start at $10. (Open daily 11am-2pm and 6-9pm.) **Reflections** (tel. 680 6808), by the pub, has won cuisine awards for its meat dishes; if you're game, there's beef, lamb, venison ($19-22), and breathtaking views of Lake Tekapo and the mist-enshrouded mountains. Lunches cost around $10; dinners start at $12.50. You can find cheaper meals at the adjoining tavern. (Happy Hour M-Th 7-8pm, F-Sa 5-6pm and 8-9pm. Both open daily 10am-late.) The **Bread Crumb Bakery** (tel. 680 6655), on the main road, sells enormous loafs of pizza bread for $2.50, as well as pies and baked goods (open daily 6am-11pm, winter 6am-7pm).

▣ ⚔ SIGHTS AND ACTIVITIES. Stroll across the bridge and down to the **Church of the Good Shepherd,** a tiny interdenominational church of wood and stone constructed in 1935. Walks in the area include the popular two-and-a-half-hour circuit up **Mt. John** and back, through pine forest and up to the observatory (it begins past the motor park, near the ice-skating rink along the lake's western side). A circuit track to **Cowan's Lookout** leaves from the far side of the bridge, offering comparable views of Mt. John in about an hour less, but the track can be difficult to follow—watch for the red and white markers. **Kiwi Express** (tel. 680 6216), on the main road, rents kayaks (1hr. $10, each additional hour $5), golf clubs ($15; green fee at the nearby club are $10), and mountain bikes (1hr., $10; each additional hour $5; or $30 per day). They also do bookings for local activities and have Internet access. (Open daily 9am-6pm, winter 9-10am and 3:30-5:30pm.)

MT. COOK NATIONAL PARK

With one-third of its 70,000 hectares permanently snow-covered, Mt. Cook National Park and its jagged peaks present an austere, but spectacular profile. Notoriously capricious weather and frequent avalanches make it one of the most dangerous regions in New Zealand. Dark lateral moraines and milky blue glaciers give an inhuman aspect to the desolate landscape, mitigated only by the screeching calls of the world's only mountain parrot, the kea (see p. 19). With 19 peaks over 3000m and a few hundred over 2000m, Mt. Cook National Park is near the top of the bottom of the world.

MT. COOK VILLAGE

At the end of SH80, about a 45-minute drive from Twizel, tiny Mt. Cook (pop. 300 in summer) nestles in the heart of Mt. Cook National Park. The dominant feature of town (aside from the mountains) is an upscale hotel known as the **Hermitage.** The **Mt. Cook Visitor Centre** and **DOC office** (tel. 435 1818; fax 435 1080), near the Hermitage, is the place to book activities, find out about track conditions, and check in and out for all trips in the park (open daily 8:30am-6pm, winter 8:30am-5pm). You can book through **InterCity** on the **Newmans Coach Lines** (tel. 0800 777 707); the schedule is flexible, with buses usually departing from the Hermitage and the YHA for **Christchurch** (5hr., 1pm, $59, YHA $41) and **Queenstown** (4hr., 2:45pm, $57, YHA members $40) via **Twizel. Great Sights** (tel. 358 9029) and **Grey Line** (tel. 0800 800 904) also run through Mt. Cook on their way between **Christchurch** and **Queenstown** (both depart for Queenstown at 2:20pm and for Christchurch at 2pm; Great Sights (with full commentary) $58, Grey Line (no commentary) $40). **High Country Shuttles & Tours** (0800 435 050) runs between **Twizel** and Mt. Cook (departs Twizel at 7am and 1pm, departs Mt. Cook at 10am and 4:30pm, on demand in winter; $15, return $20). Head to the Hermitage (tel. 435 1809) for the **post office, grocery store, Internet,** and **currency exchange** (24hr.). There is a self-serve gas pump that accepts EFTPOS and Visa, but not Mastercard. Consider bringing enough food, gas, and cash to avoid the high prices in Mt. Cook.

With comfy couches and a great video collection, the **Mt. Cook YHA** (tel. 435 1820; fax 435 1821; email yhamtck@yha.org.nz) creates a cozy lodge atmosphere. (Internet, some groceries and lockers available. Reception 8-10:30am, noon-3pm, 5:30-9:30pm, winter 8-10am, 5-6:30pm, 8-9pm. Dorms $20; twins $23; doubles $26; non-YHA $4 more.) In summer, the Hermitage opens the **Big Rock Backpackers** (tel. 435 1809; fax 435 1879; email reservations.hermitage@xtra.co.nz) for budget travelers. The chalets are equipped with a TV, kitchenette, and orange upholstered furniture. (Reception 9am-6pm and 24hr. at the Hermitage. Open mid-Sept. to mid-May. $20.)

IN THE PARK

The peaks, glaciers, and ice cliffs of Mt. Cook National Park draw visitors from all over the world. Those traveling on a shoestring rather than a belay rope can get a taste of glacial terrain with the many short day walks in the area. The strenuous climb up to **Red Tarns** (return 2hr.) rewards exertion with unbelievable views down into the Hooker Valley and up into the cloud-piercing Alps. If you're not up to an hour of steady climbing, the **Kea Point Walk** (return 2hr.) leads through scraggly gorse to a lookout over the Mueller glacier, with Mt. Sefton's azure ice falls in the background. The only feasible overnight tramping option is the three- to four-hour route to **Mueller Hut** ($18). The rest of the huts in the park ($8-18) are accessible only to experienced climbers, and serve as bases for technical ascents. Always check in with the DOC if you are planning a trip. The Hermitage rents **mountain bikes** for tracks open for cycling.

The Hermitage and the YHA have information on (and also book) several tours. In the summer, **Glacier Explorers** (tel. 435 1809) runs a boat tour of the Tasman Glacier that glides past the icy blue cliffs jutting over the lake (2½hr., $60, YHA $55, children $30). **Alan's 4WD Tours** (tel. 435 1809) travel over rough terrain to the Tasman Glacier ($70, children $35). The **Helicopter Line** (tel. 435 1801 or 0800 650 651) has a 20-minute flight with a snow landing for $130, as well as several other longer—and more expensive—options. **Air Safaris** (tel. 0800 806 880) flies the "Grand Traverse" of Mt. Cook (50min., $210, children $140; YHA discount 10%) and **Mt. Cook Ski Planes** (tel. 435 1026 or 0800 800 702) does similar flights with glacier landings (40 min., $225).

SOUTH ISLAND

THE WEST COAST

However you get there, be it rail or road, you'll notice a certain change as soon as you enter the West Coast (Westland). The towering Southern Alps shoot upward, bounding the region to the east and making a geological wall a mere 40 to 50km from the Tasman Sea. This unique combination produces torrential rain (ranging from 1m in Greymouth to an astounding 8m in Haast) responsible for creating lush tropical rainforests throughout the region. The juxtaposition of snow-capped peaks, endless green forests, and pounding waves are the grist for the mighty tourism mill that grinds throughout the West Coast. With all its sublime beauty, it's no wonder that over 80% of the West Coast is government-owned, set aside in various national parks, forest parks, and scenic reserves, including the gigantic Te Wahipounamu South West New Zealand World Heritage Area.

All West Coast travelers should keep in mind that the long stretch between Hokitika and Wanaka is devoid of banks and supermarkets. Petrol stations are often few and far between. **Hitchhiking** through the West Coast can be a difficult undertaking in winter when the traffic disappears, and a miserable endeavor in summer, with hours spent waiting in pouring rain while swatting sandflies. Thankfully, daily **buses** provide a dependable way to travel.

WEST COAST HIGHLIGHTS

- Ice-axe in hand, take a guided tour of **Franz Josef glacier** (p. 318).
- The pancake rocks and blowholes of **Punakaiki** (p. 310) will blow you away.
- The tiny, seaside, outpost **Okarito** is an ideal base for the glaciers or for a serene kayak on the lagoon.

WESTPORT

Home to the Buller, bullion, and black lung, Westport's lifeblood has been its river, its gold, and its coal. A gold rush town established in the mid 1800s, the original Westport was washed away by a flood in 1872. Even as the gold-fever subsided, the town quickly bounced back to its boomtown size of 5000, due to the coal mining, shipping, and fishing that took its place. The past continues to thrive in present-day mines such as Coaltown, and huge mounds of coal are visible during the drive up SH6. Westport has also learned to tame and utilize its two beaches and the tempestuous Buller, providing springtime whitebait fishing and thrilling rafting. Cape Foulwind and the Tauranga Bay seal colony are close by, while Karamea and Kahurangi National Park lie only 98km to the north.

ORIENTATION AND PRACTICAL INFORMATION

Palmerston St. is Westport's main street, running parallel to and just north of the Buller River. The **Westport Visitor Information Centre and DOC office,** 1 Brougham St. (tel. 789 6658; fax 789 6668; email wesvin@nzhost.co.nz), will answer your questions (open daily 9am-7pm, winter 9am-4pm).

InterCity heads daily to **Nelson** (3¾hr., 4pm, $44) and **Greymouth** (2hr., 11:20am, $22) via **Paparoa** (1hr., $15). Pickup is at **Craddock's Energy Center/Caltex Garage,** at 197 Palmerston St. near Rintowl St. **Cunningham's Coaches,** 179 Palmerston St. (tel. 789 7177), heads to **Karamea** (3hr., M-F 3pm, $15), acting as combination transport service and mail-run. **Karaka Tours** (tel. 789 5080) provides on-demand service to **Karamea** ($30 each, only one person $60) and to the **Heaphy Track** ($50 each, only one person $80). **White Star Passenger and Freight Service** (tel. 789 6200) heads to **Springs Junction** (2hr., Su-F 10:05am, $12), and continues to **Christchurch** (6hr., $33) and **Nelson** (6hr., $27). For a lift, call Buller Taxis (tel. 789 6900).

Worldwide Calling Made Easy

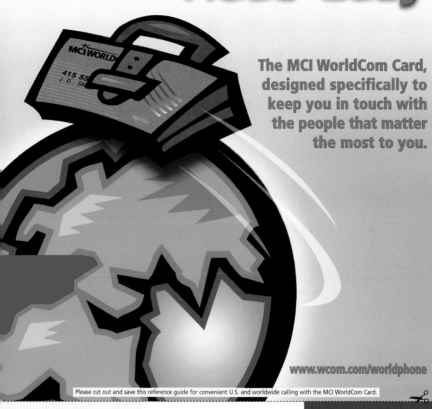

The MCI WorldCom Card, designed specifically to keep you in touch with the people that matter the most to you.

www.wcom.com/worldphone

Please cut out and save this reference guide for convenient U.S. and worldwide calling with the MCI WorldCom Card.

And, it's simple to call home or to other countires.

1. Dial the WorldPhone toll-free access number of the country you're calling from (listed inside).

2. Follow the easy voice instructions or hold for a WorldPhone operator. Enter or give the operator your MCI WorldCom Card number or call collect.

3. Enter or give the WorldPhone operator your home number.

4. Share your adventures with your family!

COUNTRY		WORLDPHONE TOLL-FREE ACCESS #
St. Lucia ÷		1-800-888-8000
Sweden (CC) ◆		020-795-922
Switzerland (CC) ◆		0800-89-0222
Taiwan (CC) ◆		0080-13-4567
Thailand ★		001-999-1-2001
Turkey (CC) ◆		00-8001-1177
United Kingdom	(CC) To call using BT ■	0800-89-0222
	To call using CWC ■	0500-89-0222
United States (CC)		1-800-888-8000
U.S. Virgin Islands (CC)		1-800-888-8000
Vatican City (CC)		172-1022
Venezuela (CC) ÷ ◆		800-1114-0
Vietnam ●		1201-1022

(CC)	Country-to-country calling available to/from most international locations.
÷	Limited availability.
▼	Wait for second dial tone.
▲	When calling from public phones, use phones marked LADATEL.
■	International communications carrier.
★	Not available from public pay phones.
◆	Public phones may require deposit of coin or phone card for dial tone.
●	Local service fee in U.S. currency required to complete call.
▶	Regulation does not permit Intra-Japan calls.
❖	Available from most major cities

MCI WorldCom Worldphone Access Numbers

MCI WORLDCOM℠

The MCI WorldCom Card.

The easy way to call when traveling worldwide.

The MCI WorldCom Card gives you...

- Access to the US and other countries worldwide.
- Customer Service 24 hours a day
- Operators who speak your language
- Great MCI WorldCom rates and no sign-up fees

For more information or to apply for a Card call:

1-800-955-0925

Outside the U.S., call MCI WorldCom collect (reverse charge) at:

1-712-943-6839

COUNTRY	WORLDPHONE TOLL-FREE ACCESS #
Argentina (CC)	
To call using Telefonica ■	0800-222-6249
To call using Telecom ■	0800-555-1002
Australia (CC) ◆	
To call using AAPT ■	1-800-730-014
To call using OPTUS ■	1-800-551-111
To call using TELSTRA ■	1-800-881-100
Austria (CC) ◆	0800-200-235
Bahamas	1-800-888-8000
Belgium (CC) ◆	0800-10012
Bermuda ÷	1-800-888-8000
Bolivia (CC) ◆	0-800-2222
Brazil (CC)	000-8012
British Virgin Islands ÷	1-800-888-8000
Canada (CC)	1-800-888-8000
Cayman Islands	1-800-888-8000
Chile (CC)	
To call using CTC ■	800-207-300
To call using ENTEL ■	800-360-180
China ✧	108-12
For a Mandarin-speaking Operator	108-17
Colombia (CC) ◆	980-9-16-0001
Collect Access in Spanish	980-9-16-1111
Costa Rica ◆	0800-012-2222
Czech Republic (CC) ◆	00-42-000112
Denmark (CC) ◆	8001-0022
Dominican Republic	
Collect Access	1-800-888-8000
Collect Access in Spanish	1121
Ecuador (CC) ÷	999-170
El Salvador	800-1767

COUNTRY	WORLDPHONE TOLL-FREE ACCESS #
Finland (CC) ◆	08001-102-80
France (CC) ◆	0800-99-0019
French Guiana (CC)	0-800-99-0019
Guatemala (CC) ◆	99-99-189
Germany (CC)	0-800-888-8000
Greece (CC) ◆	00-800-1211
Guam (CC)	1-800-888-8000
Haiti ÷	193
Collect Access in French/Creole	190
Honduras ÷	8000-122
Hong Kong (CC)	800-96-1121
Hungary (CC) ◆	00▼800-01411
India (CC) ◆	000-127
Collect Access	000-126
Ireland (CC)	1-800-55-1001
Israel (CC)	
BEZEQ International	1-800-940-2727
BARAK	1-800-930-2727
Italy (CC) ◆	172-1022
Jamaica ÷	
Collect Access	1-800-888-8000
(From Special Hotels only)	873
(From public phones)	#2
Japan (CC) ◆	To call using KDD ■ 00539-121▶
	To call using IDC ■ 0066-55-121
	To call using JT ■ 0044-11-121
Korea (CC)	To call using KT ■ 00729-14
	To call using DACOM ■ 00309-12
	To call using ONSE 00369-14
Phone Booths÷	Press red button, 03, then ✶
Military Bases	550-2255
Lebanon	Collect Access 600-MCI (600-624)

COUNTRY	WORLDPHONE TOLL-FREE ACCESS #
Luxembourg (CC)	0800-0112
Malaysia (CC) ◆	1-800-80-0012
To call using Time Telekom	1-800-18-0012
Mexico (CC)	Avantel 01-800-021-8000
	Telmex ▲ 001-800-674-7000
Collect Access in Spanish	01-800-021-1000
Monaco (CC) ◆	800-90-019
Netherlands (CC) ◆	0800-022-9122
New Zealand (CC)	000-912
Nicaragua (CC)	Collect Access in Spanish 166
(Outside of Managua, dial 02 first)	
Norway (CC) ◆	800-19912
Panama	108
Military Bases	2810-108
Philippines (CC) ◆	To call using PLDT ■ 105-14
	To call using PHILCOM 1026-14
	To call using Bayantel 1237-14
	To call using ETPI 1066-14
Poland (CC) ÷	00-800-111-21-22
Portugal (CC) ÷	800-800-123
Puerto Rico (CC)	1-800-888-8000
Romania (CC) ÷	01-800-1800
Russia (CC) ◆ ÷	
To call using ROSTELCOM ■	747-3322
(For Russian speaking operator)	747-3320
To call using SOVINTEL ■	960-2222
Saudi Arabia (CC) ÷	1-800-11
Singapore	8000-112-112
Slovak Republic	(CC) 00421-00112
South Africa (CC)	0800-99-0011
Spain (CC)	900-99-0014

FOLD

FOLD

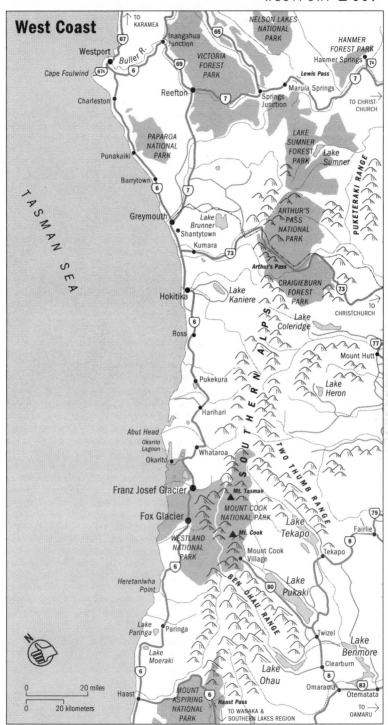

West Coast

TO KARAMEA

Inangahua Junction

Westport

Buller R.

Cape Foulwind

Charleston

Punakaiki

Barrytown

Greymouth

Lake Brunner

Shantytown

Kumara

Hokitika

Ross

Pukekura

Harihari

Abut Head

Okarito Lagoon

Okarito

Whataroa

Franz Josef Glacier

Fox Glacier

Heretaniwha Point

Lake Paringa

Paringa

Lake Moeraki

Haast

Reefton

VICTORIA FOREST PARK

PAPAROA NATIONAL PARK

NELSON LAKES NATIONAL PARK

HANMER FOREST PARK

Hanmer Springs

Lewis Pass

Maruia Springs

Springs Junction

TO CHRISTCHURCH

LAKE SUMNER FOREST PARK

Lake Sumner

PUKETERAKI RANGE

ARTHUR'S PASS NATIONAL PARK

Arthur's Pass

CRAIGIEBURN FOREST PARK

Lake Kaniere

Lake Coleridge

TO CHRISTCHURCH

Mount Hutt

Lake Heron

SOUTHERN ALPS

TWO THUMB RANGE

TASMAN SEA

Mt. Tasman

MOUNT COOK NATIONAL PARK

Lake Tekapo

Fairlie

Mt. Cook

Mount Cook Village

Tekapo

WESTLAND NATIONAL PARK

BEN OHAU RANGE

Lake Pukaki

Twizel

Lake Benmore

Clearburn

Lake Ohau

Omarama

Otematata

TO OAMARU

MOUNT ASPIRING NATIONAL PARK

Haast Pass

TO WANAKA & SOUTHERN LAKES REGION

0   20 miles

0   20 kilometers

SOUTH ISLAND

Services include: **House of Travel** (tel. 789 7209), corner of Palmerston and Wakefield St. (open M-F 8:30am-5pm); **banks** lining Palmerston St. (generally open M-F 9am-4:30pm); **bike rental** at **Beckers Sportsworld**, 204 Palmerton St (tel. 789 8787; $15 per day), across from the post office; **police** (tel. 789 7339), on Wakefield St.; **Ell's Pharmacy,** 192 Palmerston St. (tel. 789 8466; after-hour emergencies tel. 789 8379), across from the Visitor Centre (open M-Th 8:30am-5:30pm, F 8:30am-6:30pm, Sa 10am-12:30pm); **Buller Medical Centre,** 45 Derby St. (24 hr. tel. 789 7309; open M-F 8:30am-5pm, also Tu 6-8pm); **Internet access** at the **public library** (tel. 789 7239), Brougham St., across from the Visitor Centre (open M-F 10am-5pm, Sa 10:30am-1pm); and the **post office,** corner of Palmerston and Brougham St. (open M-F 8:30am-5pm, Sa 10am-12:30pm). **Telephone Code:** 03.

ACCOMMODATIONS

Old hotels line Palmerston St., but the backpackers may be a comfier option.

Marg's Traveller's Rest (Nomads), 56 Russell St. (tel. 789 8627 or 0800 737 863; fax 789 8396; www.hotlink.co.nz/margs). Rooms are spic and span and hostess is a paragon of West Coast hospitality. Stellar facilities. Laundromat, Internet, outdoor patio, cafe, restaurant. Some dorms have TV and kitchen. Dorms $18; twins and doubles $45; powered sites for 2 $18. Credit cards $1 more.

Bazil's Hostel, 54 Russell St. (tel. 789 6410; fax 789 6240), a few blocks from the center of town. Soft beds and toasty lounge create an aura so friendly you'll feel like you've come home. If you're really lucky, you may bump into Bazil himself, a large, friendly guard-dog. Dorms $17; twins and doubles $40; camping in back $10.

TripInn, 72 Queen St. (tel. 789 7367 or 0800 874 7466; fax 789 5401). Go right onto Queen St. from Brougham St. A beautiful wooden staircase leads to plain but comfortable rooms in an older house. BBQ, video library, and bikes for hire ($7.50 per day). Area tours available. Dorms $15; twins and doubles $36; tent sites $9.

Westport Holiday Park, 37 Domett St. (tel. 789 7043; fax 789 7199). From Palmerston St., turn right at the post office onto Brougham St., then an eventual left onto Domett St. The closest motorcamp to the town center. Oscar the Australian cockateel greets guests to the few A-frame cabins (some with tiny bathrooms) and bunkroom filled with thin dorm beds. Tent sites for 2 $16, powered for 2 $18; dorms $12, with toilets and showers in a separate building; cabins for 2 $29, with bath $39.

FOOD

Most of Westport's dining choices line Palmerston St. and its side streets. One sweet spot is **Mandala's Coffee House,** 110 Palmerston St. (tel. 789 7931). Try the seven-layer "giant burger" ($10). Vegetarians might find pizzas, open sandwiches on foccacia, or veggie burgers filled with sprouts, beets, eggs, and lettuce more to their liking ($11). Top it all off with a large dessert for $3-4. (Open daily 8am-4pm.) **Bailie's Bar,** 187 Palmerston St. (tel. 789 7289), is not big on ambiance but does nightly backpacker meals ($6) and a Friday night drink special from 5:30 to 8:30pm that are tough to turn down (open daily 6-9pm). **Diego's,** 18 Wakefield St., provides more atmosphere and a great wine list, while still offering reasonably priced bar meals ($3.50-12; open M-Sa from 6pm). Otherwise, make your own concoctions after you've shopped at **New World,** 244 Palmerston St. (open M-Tu 8:30am-6pm, W-F 8:30am-7pm, Sa 9:30am-4:30pm).

ACTIVITIES

The famed West Coast limestone cave formations are truly a regional highlight. **Norwest Adventures** (tel. 789 6686 or 0800 116 686; www.voyager.co.nz/~schurr/nwa.html) offers a variety of trips to suit all fitness levels. The "Underworld Rafting" adventure leaves twice per day. Float on an inner tube down a Styxian river

TO PECK AND DESTROY Mother Nature's saboteur, the sharp-beaked **kea** is one of New Zealand's native birds, and a bloody nuisance at that. Among their notorious hobbies, keas are known to wait in carparks and nearby shrubs while searching for an unsuspecting bike seat left behind without an owner (or with an owner, for that matter). In addition to stealing food, untying shoelaces, and generally terrorizing tourists and locals, the cheeky birds also like to rip windshield wipers to shreds and have been known to feast on unattended camping and skiing equipment.

alongside stalactites and stalagmites through Westport's underground **Metro Cave** system. A headlamp helps hundreds of glow-worms light your way in the **Glow-worm Grotto.** After floating out of the caves and along **Ananui Creek,** the **Waitakere River** rapids await; then finish on your feet at the **Nile River Canyon** for a 20-minute bushwalk. (4-5hr., 2 per day, $90. All equipment provide. Minimum age 10.) The "Metro Cave" trip is a brisk walk through cave landscapes and out into the surrounding rainforest (3hr., $45; family of 4 $120). The more adventurous can squeeze through narrow passages like the "Worm" with their slimmed wallet and abseil down the 120-foot hole. The "Adventure Caving: Te Tahi" trip also runs daily (4hr., $150; equipment provided; minimum age 16).

The Buller River area provides plenty of above-ground rafting excitement, from calm scenic trips to raging whitewater expeditions. **Buller Adventure Tours** (tel. 789 7286 or 0800 697 286; fax 789 8104) operates tours on rougher waters (Grade 4-5); the Grade 4 Buller River trip is a serious whitewater rafting adventure for the brave of heart (half-day $75), while the Grade 5 Karamea River trip is a heli-raft combination, including a "gourmet luncheon" on the river bank (full day $195; minimum age 15). They also offer jetboating (1½hr., $49), horse trekking (2hr., $37), and a safari in an amphibious all-terrain vehicle (40min., $20). **Burning Mine Adventures** (tel. 789 7277) offers scenic tours on mountain bikes (4hr., $45; minimum 2 people), as well as a tour of the Stockton Opencast Mine (4hr., $45). They also have whitewater kayaking for beginners in the Mokihinni River ($75).

If you'd rather use your own legs to propel you into bliss, try the nearby beaches with swimming areas: **Carters Beach,** which stretches from Cape Foulwind to the mouth of the Buller River, and the driftwood-covered **North Beach,** which stretches along Craddock Dr. to the north end of the river. To stay dry altogether, try your luck fishing for whitebait (a West Coast delicacy) around the Buller River (Sept. 1-Nov. 15; no license needed). The **Cape Foulwind Walk** (return 3hr.) is a short drive southwest of the town; a great coastal hike with beautiful views, it provides a splendid opportunity to see the seal colony from above. **Tauranga Bay** is famous for some of the best surfing in New Zealand. **Charming Creek** (one-way 6hr.) lives up to its name north of Westport, winding through the rainforest along a river gorge and past two waterfalls.

For a good introduction to the coal-bearing past of Westport, head to **Coaltown** (tel. 789 8204), south on Queen St. across the railway tracks. Experience coal mining both visually and aurally in the replica coalmine. (Open daily 8:30am-5pm, winter 9am-4pm. Admission $6, students $4, children $3.) A drive along the 120km **Buller Coalfield Heritage Trail** hits the highlights of Westport's coal mining history (guides available at the Visitor Centre). Flex your biceps taking a swig of beer made from a 16th-century recipe at **Miner's Brewery** (tel. 789 6201), on Lyndhurst St. (tours M-Sa 11:30am and 1:30pm; open M-Sa 10am-5:30pm).

NEAR WESTPORT: KARAMEA

The northernmost town of the West Coast, Karamea lies at the end of SH67, near the endpoint of Kahurangi National Park's **Heaphy Track** (see p. 275). Famous for the huge **limestone arches** and the delicate **Honeycomb Cave system** (complete with bones of extinct birds, including the moa), the **Oparara Basin** attracts most of Karamea's visitors.

The **Karamea Information and Resource Centre and DOC office** (tel./fax 782 6652), on Bridge St., has info on the park and sells hut tickets and passes for the Heaphy, Wangapeka, and Leslie Tracks (open daily 9am-5pm, winter M-F 9am-5pm, Sa 9am-1pm). **Cunningham's Coaches** (tel. 789 7177) and the **Karamea Express** (tel. 782 6617) run daily to **Westport** (1½hr., M-F 8:30am, $15). Services include: **Four Square grocery store** (tel. 782 6701; open M-Th 8:30am-6pm, F 8:30am-8pm, Sa-Su 9am-noon, until 5pm in summer); **petrol stations,** at Market Cross clustered around the Info Centre; **police** (tel. 782 6801), on Wharf St.; **Karamea Medical Centre** (tel. 782 6737); and the **post office** (tel. 782 6700) at the Karamea Hardware Store (open M-Th 8:30am-6pm, F 8:30am-7pm, Sa-Su 9am-noon). **Telephone Code:** 03.

Your first resort should be the **Last Resort**, on Waverly Rd. (tel. 782 6617 or 0800 505 042; fax 782 6820; email last.resort@xtra.co.nz). It has comfortable accommodations, a restaurant and licensed cafe (open from 10am), but does not provide blankets or duvets. (Dorms $20; twins and doubles $60, extra person $30; doubles with baths $90, extra person $20.) The only other backpackers in town is **Karamea Village Hotel** (tel. 782 6800), at the end of Waverly St. Occupying a three-bedroom house behind the main hotel and bar, dorms are a good deal at $15 per night.

The Last Resort runs trips to **Honeycomb Cave,** which include a tour of the **Box Canyon** and **Limestone Arch** (5½hr., $60; minimum 4 people), and guided **cave trips** leaving from the Oparara carpark ($30). If you want to explore the Oparara Basin area's spectacular limestone arches on your own, The Last Resort offers transport to the basin (6hr., $30). Family rafting tours down the Karamea's rapids run $30 per person (2½hr.; minimum 6), and canoeing is available in the same place (2hr., $30). Most of Karamea's trails require a short drive. **Hitchhikers** say locals are receptive to an outstretched thumb. Head north of Karamea following the signs to the Oparara Basin. Turning inland for 16km will lead you to a carpark on Oparara Rd., where you can take one of two trails. The **Oparara Arch trail** (return 45min.), in good condition, leads to the 43m high, 219m long Oparara Arch, while the **Moria Gate** trail (return 1½hr.) heads to the Little Arch. The **Fenian Track** (return 3 or 5hr.) is a picturesque hike through the rainforest; check at the resource center for directions, and to see if it is open. The **Nikau Grove** (return 40min.) and **Scott's Beach** trail (return 1½hr.) all begin at the start of the **Heaphy Track,** 9-10km north of Karamea.

PAPAROA NATIONAL PARK

Waves crash with thunderous claps against the layered rocks, drenching the sightseers clustered expectantly in their bright, crayon-colored raincoats. At last the waves strike just right, the blowholes spray high into the air, and the cameras click away in a fury of photographic zeal. Sharing gleeful smiles, the tourists congratulate each other on capturing that once-in-a-lifetime (or at least once-in-an-hour) shot of utterly unique **Punakaiki.** Located midway between Greymouth and Westport on SH6, the incredibly popular "pancake rocks" and blowholes are merely the highlights of the water-carved limestone landscape of Paparoa National Park. A 30,000-hectare park created to protect lowland forests from logging, it includes dense lowland rain forest, streams, waterfalls, and cave systems. Paparoa, which entranced explorers like Heaphy, Brunner, and von Haast in the late 1800s, still seduces visitors today.

🔃 **PRACTICAL INFORMATION. Punakaiki** is the main town of the Paparoa region. Buses stop near the Visitor Centre, and the lunchbreak awards riders enough time to enjoy the blowholes and a quick bite to eat as well. The **Punakaiki Visitor Centre** (tel. 731 1895; fax 731 1896) is on SH6 across from the blowholes (open daily 8:30am-6pm, winter 9am-4:30pm). The **DOC** office (tel. 731 1893; fax 731 1888) is 1km north (open daily 9am-4:30pm). **InterCity** (tel. 768 7080) passes through Punakaiki daily en route to **Greymouth** (45min., 12:50pm, $9) and to **Nelson** (4¾hr., 3pm, $61, YHA $46) via **Westport** (1hr., $15). The nearest **petrol** stations are 35-60km away. In an emergency, contact an **ambulance** (tel. 768 0499) or the **police** (tel. 768 1600). The **post office box** is in front of the Visitor Centre, and there is a postshop in the Pancake Tearooms. **Telephone Code:** 03.

◪▣ **ACCOMMODATIONS AND FOOD.** Punakaiki's accommodations are scattered along SH6. If you're coming by bus, ask the driver to drop you off at your destination. The **Punakaiki Beach Hostel** (tel. 731 1852; fax 731 1152) is on the corner of Webb St. and Dickenson Parade., a 15-minute walk from the Visitor Centre with the ocean on your left; otherwise, call for free pickup. Driftwood adorns the lawn and balcony. (Dorms $16; twins and doubles $37.) The **Te Nikau Retreat** (tel. 731 1111), Hartmount Place, is a 30-minute walk north of the Visitor Centre; call for free pickup. The unusual setup consists of several separate buildings connected by paths through the rainforest. While there may be a bush walk to the kitchen or showers, the place has a unique aura of seclusion. (Dorms $16; twins and doubles $36, with bath $40; motel units $60.) Near the DOC office, the **Punakaiki Motor Camp** (tel. 731 1894; fax 731 1888) has a range of cabin choices ($26-33 for 2), as well as tent sites ($8.50-10) and motor vehicle sites. For groceries and takeaway, stop by **The Pancake Tearooms** (tel. 731 1873), clustered near the Visitor Centre (open daily 8:30am-8pm, winter until 5pm). For an evening meal, the **Punakaiki Tavern** (tel. 731 1188) is located on SH6 by the Beach Hostel (open daily 8am-midnight).

▣▣ **SIGHTS AND ACTIVITIES.** To get to the area's main attraction, the **Punakaiki blowholes** and **pancake rocks,** take the **Dolomite Point Walk** (return 20min.; wheelchair accessible). If possible, check the tide schedule before planning your visit—the blowholes are most spectacular at high tide. The **Trumans Track** (15min.) off SH6 3km north of the Visitor Centre, heads out to a dramatic viewpoint at the ocean's edge. Grab a flashlight or torch to explore the **Punakaiki Cavern,** just 500m north of Punakaiki, to the right of SH6. The **Punakaiki Pororari Loop** (return 3hr.) is a longer walk through the stretch of rainforest from the Punakaiki River to the Pororari River (check in advance to see if the river can be crossed). More rugged trekkers can explore the **Inland Pack Track** (27km, 2-3 days), which began as a safe alternative to the pitfalls of coastal travel during the 1860s gold rushes. Check with the DOC before you go, and stay on the track, as there are no huts, numerous sinkholes, and other potentially dangerous formations. **Punakaiki Canoe Hire** (tel. 731 1870) rents canoes for paddling in the Pororari Gorge (1hr. $15, full day $40). They also rent bicycles (half-day $10, full day $15). **Paparoa Nature Tours** (tel./fax 322 7898) takes you to see the only burrowing black petrel breeding colony in the world (on demand, late Mar. to mid-Dec. at sunset and 2hr. before sunrise; 2hr.; $25, families $50, children $10; minimum $50). You can watch their prenuptial antics (Mar.-May), egg-sitting (June), chick-hatching (July-Aug.), and the exciting moment when the chicks finally learn to spread their wings (Nov.-Dec.).

If caving is more your style, Paparoa also runs three-hour **cave tours** from the Visitor Centre, on demand ($25). They also give full-day guided canoe tours ($60) and half-day or full-day guided walks ($80, $150). As the company operates out of Christchurch, be sure to book these trips in advance. **Coast and Mountain Adventures** (tel. 731 1853) runs scenic tours and dry canyoning trips (1hr. to full day, $25-90). For the more adventurous, two-hour rock climbing trips might be just the ticket ($40). Call **Paparoa Horse Treks** (tel. 731 1839; closed in winter) to view the pancake rocks on horseback on the beach (1hr., $30), or take a longer trip through the Punakaiki River Valley (2hr., $50).

GREYMOUTH

After the raucous gold rush party of the late 1800s ended, Greymouth was forced to rally its timber, coal, and fishing resources to survive, eventually becoming the biggest town in the West Coast. It may strike you a bit differently on a gloomy, rainy day as you stroll along the gray gravel walkway and encounter the gray statue down by the Grey River (the town's namesake). For what it's worth, Grey-

SOUTH ISLAND

mouth's smattering of pubs and bars sees the most action on the coast. It is also one of only three places in New Zealand to offer blackwater rafting through underground caves. Perhaps Greymouth's best claim today is its role as one end of the TranzAlpine railroad (the other is Christchurch), one of the most breathtaking train trips in the world.

🛈 ORIENTATION AND PRACTICAL INFORMATION

From the **Greymouth Railway Station** on Mackay St., you can walk straight to get to the Grey River and the "Great Wall" that runs along Mawhera Quay (built to hold back the flooding Grey River in 1988). Greymouth's shopping area centers on **Mackay** and **Guinness St.**

Visitors Center: Greymouth Information Centre (tel. 768 5101; fax 768 0317), on the corner of Herbert and Mackay St. Open daily 9am-5:30pm; winter M-F 9am-5:30pm, Sa-Su10am-4pm.

Trains: TranzScenic (tel. 0800 802 802). The TranzApline leaves daily for **Christchurch** (4hr., 2:25pm, $79, students $63) via **Arthur's Pass** (2hr., $35, students $28). Cheaper fares available if booked in advance

Buses: InterCity (tel. 768 7080) heads daily to: **Fox Glacier** (4hr., 1:50pm, $45) via **Franz Josef** (3½hr., $41); **Hokitika** (40min., $12); **Nelson** (6hr., 1:50pm, $61) via **Westport** (2hr., $22); and **Punakaiki** (40min., $9). Student fares available. **Atomic Shuttles** (tel. 768 5101) runs south every day to: **Queenstown** (10½hr., 7:30am, $75) via **Hokitika** (30min., $10); **Franz Josef Glacier** (3hr., $25); and **Fox Glacier** (3½hr., $25). **Coast-to-Coast** (tel. 0800 800 847) runs to **Christchurch** (5hr., 1pm, $35) via **Arthur's Pass** (2hr., $15). **Sounds-to-Coast** (tel. 0800 802 225) leaves for **Picton** (5hr., M,W, and F 1:10pm, $49) via **St. Arnaud** (3hr., $30). **Alpine Coaches** (tel. 762 5081) goes daily to **Christchurch** (4hr., 8:30am, $35) via **Moana** (30min., $14) and **Arthur's Pass** (1½hr., $18).

Taxis: Greymouth Taxis (tel. 768 7078).

Car Rental: Both **Budget** (tel. 768 4343) and **Avis** (tel. 768 0902) have offices at the train station. Also **Half Price Rental,** 170 Tainui St. (tel. 768 0379), and **Hertz,** 92 Tainui St. (tel. 768 7379).

Bike Rental: Mann Security and Cycles, 25 Mackay St. (tel. 768 0255). Half-day $10; full day $20.

Currency Exchange: ANZ, 36-40 Tainui St. (tel. 768 4529); **Westpac,** 89 Mackay St. (tel. 768 5125); **BNZ** (tel. 768 7029), at the corner of Tainui St.; and **ASB,** 44 Mackay St. (tel. 768 4458) or on High St. (tel. 768 4558). Hours generally M-F 9am-4:30pm.

Police: 47 Guinness St. (tel. 768 1600), at the corner of Tarapuhi St.

Medical Services: Check with pharmacies in town for the number of on-duty doctor. **Mason's Pharmacy,** 34 Tainui St. (tel. 768 7470). Open M-Th 8:30am-5pm, F 8:30am-6pm. **Greymouth Hospital,** (tel. 768 0499), on High St.

Post Office: (tel. 768 0123; fax 768 7615), on Tainui St. Open M-F 8:30am-5pm, Sa 10am-12:30pm.

Internet Access: Available at the **Grey District Library,** on Mackay St. at Albert Mall. $3 per 15min. Open M, Tu, and Th 9:30am-5pm, W 9:30am-8pm, F 9:30am-6pm, Sa 10am-noon. Also at the **Visitors Centre** for $2 per 10min.

Telephone Code: 03.

⌖ ACCOMMODATIONS

Noah's Ark Backpackers (VIP), 16 Chapel St. (tel./fax 768 4868 or 0800 662 472). Shuttle pickup from the railway station. Although in a 104-year-old former monastery, the backpackers' atmosphere is anything but sedate. Colorful murals adorn the walls, every bedroom has a specific animal theme, and the owners and the bus crowd that frequents the hostel keep things lively. Warm lounge, BBQ ($3), and cheap beer at the Railway Hotel. Dorms $16; twins and doubles $38.

Kainge-ra YHA Hostel, 15 Alexander St. (tel./fax 768 4951). Cheerful yellow-and-green hostel lives up to its optimistic name: "sunny home." Dorms $14-$16; singles $38; twins and doubles $38.

Living Streams Parkside Hostel, 42-54 Cowper St. (tel./fax 768 7272). Walk down Tainui St. away from the river, bear right onto High St., take a right down Franklin St. and then a left on Cowper St. Shuttle pickup from the railway station. Dorm mattresses vary in softness. Management are friendly. No alcohol allowed on the premises. Free tea, coffee, kayaks, and bikes. Guided kayak and fishing trips available with prior notice. Dorms $15-16; twins $36; doubles $38.

The Duke Backpackers (VIP) (tel. 768 9470) on Guinness St. Close to the center of town. Rooms are small, but bathrooms include tubs. Nightlife creates itself with pub below rooms. Dorms $15; twins $32; doubles $35, with bath $45. VIP $1 off.

Greymouth Seaside Holiday Park, 2 Chesterfield Rd. (tel. 768 6618 or 0800 867 104; fax 768 5873). Head down High St. away from town, and make a right onto Chesterfield Rd. Free pickup from town. Kitchens are un-equipped. Beach well within reach. Reception 8am-10pm, winter closes at 8pm. Standard cabins $32; tourist cabins $40; flats $59, with bedding $65; motel rooms $68; tent sites $18, powered $20. All prices are for 2 people.

🗂 FOOD

Smelting House Cafe, 102 Mackay St. (tel. 768 0012). Stark decor and cement floor belie the colorful cuisine, but metal tables give a dash of pizzazz. Creative, mouthwatering hot meal selections and sandwiches ($3.75) rotate daily. Open daily 8am-4:30pm.

The Railway Hotel (tel. 768 7023), on Mawhera Quay. Undoubtedly the best value in town is the nightly $3 all-you-can-eat BBQ, including sausages, salads, fried onions, and bread (from 6pm). Wash it down with the scandalously cheap Noah's Ark Magic Ale for $5.10 a jug. Open daily 11am-late.

Bonzai Pizzeria, 31 Mackay St. (tel. 768 4170). A little slice of Italy. Newspaper-covered walls surround the booths of pizza-munching patrons. Small pies run from $10.50-15.50 (large $16.50-22), while alternatives like vegetarian nachos are $7.50. There is also a full *a la carte* menu and a bar for more ambitious patrons. Open daily 7am-late.

Steamers Cafe and Bar, 58 Mackay St. (tel. 768 4193), at the corner of Albert Mall. Serves snacks and drinks all day. Lunches are especially good value, from fresh veggie quiche ($8.50) to porterhouse steak with chips and salad ($16). Steamers also offers a full dinner menu daily from 5:30pm. Winter closed Su and M evenings.

Supervalue Supermarket (tel. 768 7545), on the corner of Guinness and Herbert St., off Mackay St. by the Visitor Centre. Open M-W 8:30am-6pm, Th-F 8am-8:30pm, Sa 9am-6pm, Su 9am-5pm.

📷 SIGHTS

Most of Greymouth's choice activities take you out of town, although it's worth a moment's pause to absorb a bit of West Coast settler history. Founded to quench the thirsts and empty the pockets of gold rushers, the **Monteith's Brewing Company** (tel. 768 5101), on the corner of Herbert and Mackay St., produces between 30,000 and 60,000 liters of beer per day. Recently named the champion Australasian brewery at the prestigious Monde awards, Monteith's interesting, informative tour gives visitors the chance to taste the rainbow (from Black to Original Gold to Celtic Red) that has Kiwis raving. (Tours M-Th 11:30am and 2pm. Book ahead at the Visitor Centre. Free.) For a more traditional approach to settler history, envelop yourself in the area's past at **Shantytown** (tel./fax 762 6634), 11km south of Greymouth on SH6. Recreating an 1880s gold rush town, Shantytown has its own post office, saw mill, working steam train, horse and cart rides, and gold mine. (Open daily

SOUTH ISLAND

8:30am-5pm. Admission $11.50, with panning $14, children $7.50.) To get to Shantytown, you can take either **Kea West Coast Tours** (tel. 768 9292 or 0800 532 868), which livens up the ride with interesting running commentary on regional history (3hr., 2 per day, return $32), or **Greymouth Taxis** (tel. 768 7078; 3 per day, return $21; minimum 2). Kea also runs a tour to **Punakaiki** daily (4hr., return $40) and trips to the **glaciers** and **Lake Matheson** (full day $165; minimum 2). Within Greymouth, the **History House Museum** (tel. 768 4028), on Gresson St. past the Visitor Centre, houses models of ships, railways, and photographs documenting the Grey River's many floods (open M-F 10am-4pm; $3, children $1).

▨ ACTIVITIES

Dragons Cave Rafting, operated by **Wild West Adventures** (tel. 768 6649 or 0800 223 456), runs a caving trip through the **Taniwha Caves** and their underground world of lakes, streams, waterfalls, and glow-worms, and even a love tunnel. The half-day excursion ends with a slick natural water slide and a dip in the hot spa to warm up. (Free pickup and drop off. $95.) **Waterborn Kayaking** (tel. 0800 929 991) offers guided trips for beginners and more experienced kayakers (3-4hr., $65-87; minimum age 15). **On Yer Bike!** (tel 762 7438) runs 4WD farm bike tours through the bush: the wetter, the better (2hr., $75). If you're into the whole jump-out-of-an-airplane-and-plummet-toward-the-ground thing, **Tandem Skydive** (tel./fax 468 4777) gives you the chance to do so from 12,000 ft. with a guide strapped to your back ($245). **Dolphin Watch,** run by **Scenicland Ocean Jets** (tel. 768 9770 or 0800 929 991), brings you to the Hector's dolphin areas and shag nesting sites off the coast of **Point Elizabeth** (1½hr., $67; no swimming). The nikau palms and podocarp on the coast can be seen along the **Point Elizabeth Walkway** (one-way 6km; tide dependent); travelers without a car will need to take a taxi or catch a ride out. The same is true for **Lake Brunner,** about 30 minutes east of Greymouth (Alpine Coaches stops at Moana, which is right at the edge of the lake). Swim, kayak, or canoe among the white herons *(kotuku)* on the lake, bedding down at the campground at the Moana end of the lake. The **Moana Kiwi House and Conservation Park** (tel. 738 0009) displays kiwis, among other birds, wallabies, and monkeys (open daily 9am-5pm; admission $10, children $5).

HOKITIKA

Once the largest port in New Zealand, Hokitika (ho-kuh-TICK-uh) is no longer a bustling center of activity. Today, Hokitika (pop. 4000) is famous for its abundance of crafts. Virtually all of New Zealand's jade is quarried within a 20km radius of the town. The greenstone, wood, and blown-glass stores that line its wide streets are worth a quick look. If you decide to spend more than just an afternoon in Hokitika, you may want to head to the beach for a potentially magnificent sunset over the Tasman Sea.

▨ PRACTICAL INFORMATION. Nothing is too far to reach by foot in Hokitika. The **Westland Visitor Information Centre** (tel. 755 6616) is in the Carnegie Building on the corner of Tancred and Hamilton St. (open daily 8:30am-6pm, winter M-F 9am-5pm, Sa-Su 10am-noon), while the **DOC** is on Sewell St. near the river (open M-F 8am-4:45pm). **InterCity** (tel. 755 8557 or 755 6166) drops off in front of **Hokitika Travel Centre,** 60 Tancred St. (tel. 755 8557), which runs parallel to the beach. Inter-City heads daily to **Nelson** (7hr., 12:45pm, $68) via **Greymouth** (45min., $12) and **Westport** (3hr., $30); and **Fox Glacier** (3hr., 3:05pm, $39) via **Franz Josef** (2½hr., $36). **Coast-to-Coast** (tel. 0800 800 847) heads to **Christchurch** (4½hr., 1:05pm, $35) via **Arthur's Pass** (2½hr., $15). **Atomic Shuttles** (tel. 768 5101) has daily service to: **Queenstown** (10hr., 8am, $65) via **Franz Josef** (2½hr., $20), **Fox** (3hr., $25), and **Haast** (6hr., $45); and to **Greymouth** (30min., 5pm, $10). Other services include: **ANZ,** 14 Weld St.(tel. 755 8109) and **ASB** (tel. 755 8840), 99 Revell St., both with **ATMs** (open generally M-F 9am-4:30pm); the **police,** 50 Sewell St. (tel. 755 8088); **Westland Medical**

Centre, 54 Sewell St. (24 hr. tel. 755 8180); the **post office** (tel. 755 8659), on Revell St. (open M-F 8:30am-5pm, Sa 10am-12:15pm); and **Internet access** at the Visitor Centre ($2 per 10min), and the Westland District Library, 36 Weld St. ($2 per 15min.; open M-F 10am-5pm, Sa 9am-noon.) **Telephone Code:** 03.

⌐ ACCOMMODATIONS. If you decide to stay overnight, **Mountain Jade Back-packers,** 41 Weld St. (tel. 755 8007 or 0800 838 301; fax 755 7804), near the clock tower, is a central and cheerful place to rest your head. From the mermaid peeking into the showers ("oh behave!") to the sheep surveying the bunkroom, the hostel shows its colorful sense of humor. (Single-sex dorms $16; doubles $40.) Located about 5km out of Hokitika central is the **Blue Spur Lodge** (tel./fax 755 8445). Over-looking Mt. Cook and the Southern Alps, the 100-acre property offers a one-hour bushwalk and an open gold mine tunnel where guests can pan for treasures using the lodge's free equipment. Kayak trips are also available, with free transportation to and from Lakes Kaniere and Mahinapua. (Dorms $15, doubles $38.) A short walk from the center of town, **Beach House Backpackers (VIP),** 137 Revell St. (tel. 0800 755 6859), has a prime beachfront location, lovely for watching the sunset over the Tasman Sea. Despite being a tad chilly in winter, the place is still tidy and the folks are friendly. You can even take an outdoor bushbath if you're feeling adventurous. (Dorms $15; twins $38.) Lake Kaniere, 18km from town, has **DOC campground** facilities with water and toilets ($3 donation). There's another DOC campground, 10km south of town at Lake Mahinapua with water, toilets, and fire-places ($4 donation).

⌐ FOOD. The **Souvlaki Bar,** 89 Revell St. (tel. 755 8336), has tasty pita-wrapped meats and $6 falafel (open Su-Th 10:30am-10pm, F-Sa 9am-8pm; winter M-F 9:30am-4pm, Sa 11am-8:30pm). While it appears to be a standard cafe from the out-side, a cuppa at **PR's Coffee Shop and Bistro** (tel. 755 8379), on Tancred St., will be anything but dull. The enormous and eclectic teapot collection displayed through-out livens up any afternoon (try to spot the hula girl); from camels to cabins, kan-garoos to baby shoes, PR's proves that not every teapot must be short and stout. (Open daily 8am-late, winter hours shorter Su-M.) **Cafe de Paris** (tel. 755 8933) a few doors down is a bit pricier (lunch $7-15; open daily 7:30am-11pm, winter from 8:30am, dinner from 6pm). Stock up on your groceries at **New World,** 116 Revell St. (tel. 755 8390). Those heading south, be warned: if you're headed south, this is the last supermarket before Wanaka and offers the most reasonable prices you will find before then. (Open M-W and Sa 8am-6:30pm, Th-F 8am-8pm, Su 9am-6pm.)

⌐ SIGHTS AND ACTIVITIES. Hokitika is renowned for the expertise of its greenstone, woodworking, and glass-blowing artisans. Both their skill and their abundance in town is the foremost reason Hokitika shows up on the tourist radar. **Westland Greenstone,** 34 Tancred St. (tel. 755 8713), has heaps of jade pendants, pins, and paperweights for sale (open daily 8am-5pm). **Quades House of Wood** (tel.

A JADED PERSPECTIVE
Green as the Westland rainforest and hard as the mountains to the east, **greenstone** (*pounamu,* or **jade**) has long been con-sidered a precious mineral. Created millions of years ago at the same time the Southern Alps were rising from their fault, greenstone is found primarily in Westland and around Lake Wakatipu. Greenstone factories in Westland today excavate, chip, and carve the opaque emerald stone for everything from touristy trinkets to flowing works of art. In ancient times (and even up to the present), the Maori used greenstone for tools and *tikis,* as well as for battle weapons and religious purposes. Famed world-wide for its wide range of coloration, *pounamu* was renowned among the Maori (who knew it by over a dozen different names) for its tremendous spiritual value—it was believed to retain and even magnify a person's *mana,* or spiritual power.

755 6061), located across the street, has palm trunk vases with incredible designs, a wide variety of wooden bowls, and a large, expensive wooden turtle with a removable shell (open daily 8:45am-5pm). The **Hokitika Glass Studio**, 28 Tancred St. (tel. 755 7775), exhibits glass artistry ranging from whimsical penguins and elephants to dainty flowers (open daily 9am-5pm, longer in summer). All three shops allow visitors to view the artisans at work. If you're around from March 7-12, don't miss the chance to sample possum, whitebait, snail, venison, and even kangaroo at the **Wild Foods Festival.** The event quadruples Hokitika's population for a day, drawing international visitors.

The **Glow-worm Dell** illuminates Hokitika after hours. A 30-minute walk north of Hokitika on SH6 on the right side of the road, the display of phospherescent larvae are separated by a chain link fence along the path. **Lake Mahinapua** is surrounded by walks and picnic areas, and **Lake Kaniere** draws nature-lovers to its stands of rimu, tussock grassland, and subalpine scrub (walks vary from 10min. to 7hr.). There is no public transportation from Hokitika to the lake, but **Hokitika Cycles and Sports,** 33 Tancred St. (tel. 755 8662), rents bicycles for $20 per day.

No matter what the weather, you can fish to your heart's content at **Westland's Water World,** 53 Sewell St. (tel. 755 5251; fax 755 5451). Aquarium tanks feature native West Coast fish, and divers feed the largest freshwater eels in the world at 10am and 3pm. If the sight of the feeding frenzy makes you a little hungry, catch your own salmon for supper in New Zealand's only indoor fishing lake. (Open 9am-5:30pm daily, winter until 4pm. Admission $10, students $8.) Tranquil weather often calls for an equally calming activity such as a paddle boat cruise from **Scenic Waterways** (tel. 755 7239) into the picturesque Lake Mahinapua (1½hr., $20). If you plan to go to Water World, the waterways, and the local museum, the **Hokitika Attraction Pass** (tel. 0800 242 324) is a good deal ($28).

OKARITO

Sitting on the edge of the enormous 3240-hectare Okarito Lagoon, this tiny seaside community offers serenity and scenery unmatched along the coast. Certainly not known for its tourism, the town is recognized instead for its vast diversity of bird species and the fact that famous Kiwi author Keri Hulme (author of *The Bone People*) lives and writes here (although eager visitors should not expect to meet the solitary Hulme without a personal invitation). Located about 28km north of Franz Josef Glacier off of SH6, travelers can use Okarito as a jumping-off point to visit the glaciers. Easily reached by those with their own transportation, Okarito has a seductive power that has thrown off many well-planned itineraries. The rich green of the surrounding Kahikatea and Rimu rainforests, the snow-capped Southern Alps in the background (Mt. Cook and Mt. Tasman are both visible), and the lapping waves of the Tasman Sea make Okarito a picturesque spot to relax for a few days...or weeks.

To cover the 13km between the SH6 cutoff and the town (if you don't have a car), call **Okarito Nature Tours** (tel./fax 753 4014) to arrange a $5 shuttle. The **Royal Hostel** and **Royal Motel** (for both tel. 753 4080) will pick visitors up from the turn-off for free, or even from Franz Josef for stays of two nights or more (dorms $15; doubles $40, extra person $10). A cheaper sleeping option is **The Okarito YHA Hostel,** a nonprofit backpackers run by the town itself (dorms $10). Pay for your stay at the warden's house, across the street and several buildings down. Although the two-room building is quaint and conducive to meeting other travelers, there are no showers, so you'll have to resort to those at the **Okarito Campground** ($5 per person). The sites at the campground are not powered, but provide good shelter and free toilets. If you're part of a group, cottages that sleep four to eight people are available ($40-60; call Suzie Clapperton for details at 753 4124). Just remember to bring three things on your visit to Okarito: **food,** as there is no shop in town; **insect repellent,** for the hordes of sandflies that buzz and bite any flesh they can find; and **sunglasses** to protect you from the glaring light that bathes Okarito on a clear day.

The highlight of Okarito is the lagoon and the wildlife that goes with it, and the only way to really experience those treasures is by getting out on the water your-

GOOD AS GOLD In Ross, just 28km south of Hokitika, the hum and clank of present-day mining operations belie the great discovery made there in 1909: the largest gold nugget ever to be found in New Zealand. Weighing in at 3.1kg, it was nicknamed "the Honourable Roddy" and was raffled off shortly thereafter to raise funds for the Ross Hospital. By 1911, poor Roddy had been transmuted into a gold tea set for King George V. A chunky replica of the famed nugget now hangs in the 1885 Miner's Cottage, luring tourists in search of their own honourable lode. And that lode might be closer than you think—recent newspaper stories have reported that the town of Ross may be situated directly over some $700,000,000 worth of gold. For further details, check in with the Ross Visitor Information Centre (tel. 755 4077), located in the historic 1870 Bank of New South Wales on Aylmer St. (open 9am-4pm). Both the Visitor Centre and Miner's Cottage supply pans, shovels ($5), and prospectors' gravel to those willing to try their hand at sifting for a few hours. One lucky couple panned for 3½ days, finding enough gold to make their own 18-carat wedding rings!

self. **Okarito Nature Tours** leads guided kayak and canoe trips (4-5hr., $10), or set out on your own to explore (hourly rental available). When you get off the water, Okarito has several beautiful hikes, including the **Okarito Trig Trail** (return 1½hr.), which leads you uphill through the bush to a breathtaking view overlooking the town, the lagoon, and the sea. Also try the **Coastal Walk** (return 3hr.), a wandering path along the rainforest above the shoreline. If you wish to return by walking on the actual beach, be sure to check the tides (schedules available in the hostels), as it can only be done within an hour of low tide.

FRANZ JOSEF AND FOX GLACIERS

Finding yourself face to face with several billion cubic meters of solid blue ice moving up to several meters a day is ordinary when visiting Fox and Franz Josef Glaciers. These twins are extraordinary not only because of their speed of advance, but also because they descend almost into the forest, a mere 12km from the Tasman Sea. The glaciers' unique location, sandwiched between the sea and the Southern Alps in a temperate rainforest region, accounts for the massive 20 to 30m of snowfall that buries the top of the glaciers each year and ensures that the glaciers will long outlive any tourist brave or impertinent enough to attempt to conquer them.

Fox and Franz Josef Glaciers are part of the 117,547-hectare **Westland National Park** (recently made a World Heritage Area along with the rest of the Southern West Coast), which contains a feast of hikes and bushwalks highlighting native biota. Although everything in the park, from its gorgeous lakes to its low undulating hills, is a result of glacial movement, most travelers come for the glaciers themselves—and, though they may leave with wallets a tad lighter, they seldom leave disappointed. There are many ways to explore the glaciers: a hands-on hike on the glacier itself or a birds-eye helicopter tour are the two most popular.

Pressed for time, the hurried and harried traveler often comes down to choosing between Fox and Franz Josef Glaciers, and no small rivalry has developed between the two towns as a result. Franz Josef, although smaller, may be more impressive than its neighbor, and with large **Lake Mapourika** nearby, more outfitters, and more choices for lodging, it is the destination of most tour groups and backpacker buses. Fox offers a less commercial atmosphere and the serene quicksilver reflections of nearby **Lake Matheson** (New Zealand's most photographed lake). Both glaciers, however, offer a tremendous range of options for exploration, including helicopter rides, hikes directly on the glaciers, and ice climbing and skiing for true daredevils. Which glacier is the more spectacular? Hope for a clear couple of days, visit them both, and decide for yourself.

SOUTH ISLAND

FRANZ JOSEF GLACIER

🛈 ORIENTATION AND PRACTICAL INFORMATION

Lying 140km south of **Hokitika** and 27km north of **Fox Glacier**, Franz Josef village exists but for the grace of its massive glacier. Running through the center of town, **SH6,** known as Main Rd., is the location of most of the town's amenities. Most backpackers are located on **Cron St.** (take a left off of Main Rd. after the Mobil station). Away from the town, peaceful rainforest walks twist and turn through the thick tropical bush.

The **Franz Josef Visitor Information Centre** and **DOC office** (tel. 752 0796; fax 752 0797), on SH6 just south of town, has various displays on glacial formation and the ecological devastation wreaked by possums (and, consequently, a number of possum pelts for sale; see p. 20), as well as information on walks in the area, including Okarito (open daily 8:30am-6pm, winter 8:30am-12pm and 1-5pm). There are **no banks or ATMs** in town, but **Glacier Motors** (tel. 752 0725) will cash your traveler's checks (open daily 7:15am-10:15pm, winter 8am-6pm). **Fern Grove Souvenirs** (tel. 752 0731; fax 752 0789), on Main Rd. in the center of town, will do the same, provided they have enough cash available (open 8am-6:30pm). **Internet access** is in the Helicopter Line/Franz Josef Glacier Guides building on Main Rd. (open 12:30-5:30pm; $8 per hr.). **InterCity** (tel. 752 0131) heads daily north to: **Nelson** (10hr., 9:30am, $89) via **Hokitika** (3hr., $36); **Greymouth** (4hr., $41); which connects with the TranzAlpine service to **Christchurch**; and **Westport** (6½hr., $55). There is also a daily southbound bus to **Queenstown** (8hr., 8am, $93) with stops in **Fox Glacier** (45min., $8), the **Copland Track** (1hr., $14), and **Wanaka** (6hr., $68). Ask for discounts, as student and saver fares are often available. **Atomic Shuttles** (tel. 752 0738) provides northbound service to **Greymouth** (3hr., $25) via **Hokitika** (2hr., $20). There is also a bus south to **Queenstown** (7½hr., 10:30am, $50) via **Fox Glacier** (30min., $10), **Haast** (3½hr., $30) and **Wanaka** (6hr., $40). The pickup for both shuttle companies is at the coach stop on Main Rd. near the Cheeky Kea Cafe. The **post office** is at the Mobil station near the center of town on SH6. **Telephone Code:** 03.

🏠🍴 ACCOMMODATIONS AND FOOD

Look for the two mountaineers climbing on the roof to find the attractive **Chateau Franz (VIP),** 8 Cron St. (tel./fax 752 0738). Grab a quick round of pool, or just relax in the free spa pool. (Internet. Reception 8am-8pm. Check-out 10am. Dorms $16; twins $35; doubles $40; VIP $1 off.) The bland but comfortable **Franz Josef YHA** (tel. 752 0754), next door on Cron St., provides a myriad of ways to relax. Rejuvenate with some homemade yogurt ($2), conversation in the lounge, or a game at the pool table. They'll also store your bicycle, and sell ice cream before nightly video screenings. Rooms are replete with heaters and duvets. (Reception 8-10am, 4:30-6:30pm, and 8-9pm; extended hours in summer. Check-out 10am. Bunks $16; twins and doubles $36; non-YHA $4 more.) On the opposite side of Cron St., **Montrose** (tel. 752 0188) is another option. The free duvets, necessary heaters in the rooms, and resident feline make this a decent place to spend an evening. (Reception 8am-1pm and 4:30-7pm. Dorms $16; twins and doubles $40.) Join the bus-tour crowd and fellow backpackers at the **Black Sheep Lodge** (tel. 752 0007; fax 752 0023). Although a fair walk from the center of town, it's got a large kitchen and a big, friendly TV lounge with a collection of Hollywood's finest to pop into the VCR. (Reception closes at 8pm. Dorms $16; doubles $35; twins $40.) **Franz Josef Holiday Park** (tel. 752 0766 or 0800 863 726) has fully self-contained double motel units ($99), and 2-bedroom tourist flats, fully self-contained except for sheets and towels ($65). Two-person cottages with kitchens but no baths are $55; additional people are $15 per head. Tent sites are $9; powered sites are $9.50.

For a tasty, all-purpose restaurant, stop by **DA's Restaurant** (tel. 752 0721) in the center of town. The "Works" for breakfast ($10) may power you up the icy slopes of the glacier, or stop by afterwards, pleasantly exhausted, for a $2 beer during Happy Hour (5-7pm; open 7am-10pm). **The Cheeky Kea Cafe** (tel. 752 0139), right next door, carries a range of drinks and sandwiches ($2.40). Try the cheese scones ($1) if you're just a bit peckish. If you prefer to exercise your own culinary skills, a limited range of groceries are provided, for a price, at the **Fern Grove Food Centre** (tel. 752 0731), on Main Rd. (open 7:45am-6:30pm).

ACTIVITIES

ON THE GLACIER
The best way to appreciate the size and majesty of the glacier is to get up close and personal. **Franz Josef Glacier Guides** (tel. 752 0763 or 0800 GUIDES; fax 752 0102), leads both half-day (3½hr., daily 9:15am and 2pm, $37) and full-day walks (7-8hr., daily 9:15am, $74) on the glacier. If you feel up to five or six hours on the ice, pack a lunch and opt for the full-day trip. As the guides lead the way, chipping steps into the glacial ice with an ice-axe, brave and sure-footed hikers blaze a trail more than 3km long, inching along narrow crevasses, through cavernous tunnels, and beside gorgeous glacial pools, all in the name of adventure. Be sure to book ahead in summer, as trip size on these very popular outings is limited. (Equipment is provided.) A recent (less tried and true) addition to the Franz Josef scene, **The Guiding Company** (tel. 752 0047) also offers glacier walks (half-day $37, full day $76; 10% YHA and VIP discount).

   Heli-hiking is another way to explore the glacier. Significantly more expensive than the day-hikes, the heli-hiking trips fly hikers onto the glacier, eliminating the trek to the terminal face, but provide for less ice time to explore and gain confidence. Trips are run by both guiding companies (3hr., around $185).

SCENIC FLIGHTS
For those who prefer to end a scenic flight still aboard, there are three different helicopter companies operating from Franz Josef, none of which runs on days with questionable weather. They all offer similar prices (and essentially the same tried-and-true routes), and the fluctuation is due mostly to demand and to the size of the helicopter. It pays to book ahead, especially in peak season (Jan.-Mar.). **Fox and Franz Josef Heliservices** (tel. 752 0764), **Glacier Southern Lakes Helicopters** (tel. 752 0755 or 0800 800 732), and the **Helicopter Line** (tel. 752 0767 or 0800 807 767) can be booked at Alpine Guides. Prices to tour the Franz Josef Glacier, Fox Glacier, Tasman Glacier, and Mt. Cook range from $120-$250, depending on flight duration and package chosen. **Air Safaris** (tel. 752 0716; fax 752 0701) offers a "Grand Traverse" airplane tour; while it does not include a snow landing, it covers a greater area than the helicopter flights (50min., $210).

LESS SLIPPERY WALKS
A pleasant jaunt down SH6 leads to **St. James Anglican Church** (turn onto the path at the right before the bridge; the church is through the bush at the end of the path). The church was built to showcase the glacial view through the altar window, and a peace stamp with a picture of the view was issued in 1946 to celebrate the end of World War II. On a clear day the **Alex Knob Walk** (return 8hr.), accessible when it's not snowed under, has breathtaking views from the ridge. This walk is best attempted before lunch, as clouds usually roll in each afternoon. **Kamahi Tours** (tel. 752 0795) offers guided bushwalks around the Franz Josef and Okarito area (trips range from one hour to a full day). If you wish to approach the glacier, but not scale it, Kamahi runs a two-hour tour to the base of the glacier complete with commentary about area history and geology ($25).

OTHER ACTIVITIES
Professional and friendly, **Skydive New Zealand–Fox and Franz Josef Glaciers** (tel. 0800 751 0080) provides a pre-jump scenic flight including views of three glaciers, Mt. Cook, Mt. Tasman, and the Tasman Sea. Lost in the magnificence of the Southern

Alps, you'll almost forget your original reason for climbing to 12,000 ft. (almost). Take along your camera for some unbeatable shots. (9,000 ft. $225, 12,000 ft. $255; weather dependent; book in advance.) For a stunning, if somewhat dizzying, panorama of glacier country, *Flowing West*, a 20-minute movie shown daily at the **Alpine Adventure Center** (tel. 752 0793), catapults the viewer across glacial rivers, through tangled rainforest, over the Southern Alps, and finally out onto the glaciers. Much cheaper than a helicopter flight, it's well worth the price. (Up to 4 per day, and guaranteed to show daily at 5pm. $10, children $5.)

Operating out of Whataroa, a half-hour drive north of Franz Josef, the **White Heron Sanctuary Tour** (tel. 0800 523 456) brings a limited number of visitors to observe breeding pairs of White Herons. Considered sacred birds by the Maori, they are known to breed only in New Zealand. (Runs Nov.-Feb. 2½hr., $75. Book ahead, especially in summer.) Nearby **Lake Mapourika** is stocked with brown trout and Quinnat salmon, and the nearby bush is rife with chamois and possums; fishermen and hunters can get appropriate licenses from the DOC. For a guided trip, contact **Alpine Trophies** (tel. 752 0793) to take advantage of its 98% salmon catch rate (season from Jan.-Apr.; hunting trips Mar.-Aug. 2hr.; $150, half-day $200).

FOX GLACIER

⚡ ORIENTATION AND PRACTICAL INFORMATION

Lying 27km south of Franz Josef Glacier on SH6, Fox Glacier is a diminutive village near a massive glacier. Running through the center of town, **SH6** is known as Main Rd. It heads north over three hills to Fox's comrade Franz Josef, and south to one entrance of the **Copland Track,** and farther, to **Haast** (121km).

The **Fox Glacier Visitor Information Centre** and **DOC office** (tel. 751 0807; fax 751 0858) is located on SH6 (known as Main Rd. in town) just north of the main village, and has info on **Westland National Park,** the various walks around the Fox Glacier area, and the Copland Track. (Open daily 8:30am-6:30pm, winter 9am-4:30pm.) The famous reflecting **Lake Matheson** (6km) and the seal-colonized **Gillespies Beach** (20km) are located down Lake Matheson Rd., which is off Cook Flat Rd. **InterCity** (tel. 751 0701 or 0800 INTERC) heads daily to **Nelson** (11hr., 8:45am, $91) via **Franz Josef** (45min., $8), **Hokitika** (3½hr., $39), **Greymouth** (4½hr., $45), and **Westport** (7hr., $60). InterCity heads southward daily to: **Queenstown** (8:45am, 7hr., $88) via the **Copland Track** (20min., $13); **Haast** (2½hr., $32); and **Wanaka** (5hr., $64). There is a student and YHA discount of at least 20% on all fares. **Atomic Shuttles** (tel. 768 5101) runs daily to **Greymouth** (3½hr., 2pm, $25) via **Franz Josef** (1hr., $10) and **Hokitika** (3hr., $25). Southbound, Atomic goes to: **Queenstown** (7hr., 11am, $50) via **Haast** (3hr., $25); **Makarora** (4hr., $35); and **Wanaka** (5hr., $35). The pickup point for both is outside **Alpine Guides** (tel. 751 0825), on Main Rd. Alpine Guides also serves as a **post office** and **currency exchange** (open daily 8am-9pm, winter 8:30am-5:30pm). Coin-operated **Internet** can be found at **Ivory Towers Backpackers** ($2 per 10min.). If you are continuing down the coast, check your petrol gauge; **Fox Glaciers Motors** (tel. 751 0823) is the last opportunity to fill up for 120km.

▲◖ ACCOMMODATIONS AND FOOD

The majority of accommodations are located on Sullivans Rd. and Cooks Flat Rd., both of which veer off Main Rd. near the center of town. The best part of **Ivory Towers,** Sullivans Rd. (tel./fax 751 0838; email ivorytowers@xtra.co.nz), is the company. A large dining room, TV lounge, porch, and free spa pool are conducive to mingling. (Reception 8am-8:30pm. Check-out 10am. Dorms $16; twins and doubles $40.) Next door to Ivory Towers, the **Fox Glacier Inn and Backpackers** (tel. 751 0022; fax 751 0024; email foxglacierbackpackers@xtra.co.nz) combines standard rooms and kitchen with a popular local bar. You can get another session with a glacier guide or tandem master without ever leaving the building. (Hot showers $1. Dorms

$17; twins $36; doubles $44; tent sites $9 per person.) The **Rainforest Motel** (tel. 751 0140 or 0800 520 000; fax 751 0141) is about 100m down Cook Flat Rd. on the left. If you can, splurge a little and treat yourself to an incredibly luxurious, quiet, and fully self-contained unit (including TV, bathroom, and kitchen) with views of the mountain and surrounding pastures ($80, winter $70) The **Fox Glacier Hotel** (tel. 751 0839; email resort@minidata.co.nz), on Cook Flat Rd. just off Main Rd., offers privacy and beds that are softer than pudding. This affordable hotel is a good option, though it lacks kitchen facilities. (Reception 7am-10:30pm, winter until 8pm. Budget rooms $25; doubles $40.)

Eating options in town are rather slim and tend to close their kitchens by 8:30pm in winter, so plan accordingly. For meals, your best option is to make it to the **Fox Glacier General Store** (tel. 751 0829) before closing and cook for yourself (open daily 8am-6pm). The **Cook Saddle Cafe and Saloon**, Main Rd. (tel. 751 0700) has American favorites like ribs ($18), a bar, and breakfast until 4pm (open daily 10am-1:30am, winter from 11am). Just a few doors down is **Cafe Neve** (tel. 751 0110), which serves fantastic food for a price. Winner of the New Zealand Beef and Lamb Award, meat dishes (complemented, of course, by a full wine list) are especially succulent (mains $20-25). Outdoor tables make for stunning sunset dining. (Open daily 8am-late, winter from 4pm.) On Main Rd. in the same building as Alpine Guides is **The Hobnail Cafe** (tel. 751 0005), a simpler dining option. Pack up lunch before your trip to the glacier (around $9), or enjoy one of the light dishes after you get back. (Open daily 7am-4pm or 5pm, winter 8am-3pm or 4pm.)

ACTIVITIES

ON THE GLACIER
Alpine Guides (tel. 751 0825; fax 751 0857) leads daily **guided walks** (with a minimum party size). The half day begins with a steep and relatively lengthy ascent through the rainforest, before stepping out onto the top of the glacier in view of the mountains. If a morning walk isn't offered due to party size, an afternoon one will be (3½ hr., 9:30am and 2pm, $39). Full-day 6-hour guided walks leave at 9:30am ($65, minimum 3 people). If you can afford it, the heli-hike is a great way to avoid the uphill rainforest trek and maximize ice-time (3hr.,2 per day, $170; book ahead).

SCENIC FLIGHTS
For scenery without the plunge, three helicopter companies provide trips ranging from 20 to 50 minutes, and most include a snow landing; book ahead, especially in summer. **Fox and Franz Josef Heliservices** (tel. 751 0866); **Glacier Helicopters** (tel. 751 0803 or 0800 800 732); and **Helicopter Line** (tel. 0800 807 767 or 751 0767) can be booked at Alpine Guides. Tours of glaciers cost between $120-$250. **Air Safaris** (tel. 752 0716) offers a "Grand Traverse" airplane tour that doesn't include a snow landing, but covers a greater area than the helicopter flights (50min., $210).

SKYDIVING
If it's true that any skydive is better than bad sex, the spectacular scenery helps a jump over the glaciers to rival even a quite satisfactory tumble. **Skydive New Zealand-Franz Josef and Fox Glaciers** (tel. 0800 751 0080) combines a professional attitude, an adventuresome spirit, and unbeatable surroundings to make taking the plunge surprisingly carefree. Unlike many operators, Skydive New Zealand encourages you to bring your own camera to document your fall. (9,000 ft. $225, 12,000ft. $255. Book ahead.)

WALKS
In addition to the actual glacier, paths and trails to explore vein the area. The **Minnehaha Walk** (20min.) gives a great sampling of Westland's rainforest as it wanders across bridges, over small trickling creeks, and through tall moss-covered trees and surrounded by huge ferns and other primitive plants. The **Chalet Lookout Walk** (1¼hr.) yields a fantastic peek of the town's namesake, while the

Fox Glacier Valley Walk (1hr.) follows the path taken by the glacier walks and leads directly to the terminal face itself. Travelers willing to traverse the 21km to **Gillespies Beach** can take the **Gillespies Track** (2hr.), where you can walk along the shore of the Tasman. The **Seal Colony Walk** (3hr.), also at the beach, leads to an endearing seal colony at Waikowhai Bluff. However, it must be undertaken at low tide, so visitors should check tides at the Visitor Centre. The **Copland Track,** connecting Westland National Park to Mt. Cook National Park, has one trailhead 26km south of Fox Glacier (InterCity makes stops daily at 9am). This 17km tramp takes eight hours each way and should only be attempted by experienced and prepared hikers. Those who undertake the Copland should expect to spend the night in a hut at the **Flat Hut Pools.** Six kilometers out of town down Cook Flat Rd., the **Lake Matheson Walk** (1½hr.) offers unparalleled reflections of Mt. Cook and Mt. Tasman. Views are best in the morning and evening, when the water is undisturbed by wind; arrive 15 to 20-minutes before sunrise and walk to the nearest lookout point to experience serenity. **Glow-worms** ($2 in honesty box) at the corner of Sullivans and Main Rd., next to the Glow Worm Forest Lodge, are not nearly as impressive as the display in Hokitika, but you can get much closer to these. A flashlight is helpful.

HAAST

Unreachable by road until the 1960s, Haast is one of the last and largest refuges of rainforest and wetlands in New Zealand. Untouched acres of the giant, graceful kahikatea tree are a towering symbol of a natural world with man dwelling unobtrusively on its fringes. Try one of the gorgeous inland hikes, or follow the coastal route south along the Tasman to the beautiful Jackson Bay, 54km away. From July to November, the Fiordland crested penguin (the world's rarest), can be seen on Monro Beach 40km north. Fishing season is high season in Haast, with spring tourism dominated by whitebaiters coming to try their luck in catching the great delicacy in the coastal rivers.

🔼 **ORIENTATION AND PRACTICAL INFORMATION.** Those in the know refer to the whole area as **The Haast,** and indeed there really is no specific area to pin down as the real Haast. The concentration of accommodations and eateries on **SH6** is known as **Haast Township,** while the intersection of SH6 with **Jackson Bay Rd.** 3km north (where the Visitor Centre is located) is called **Haast Junction.** The area down by the beach (4km down Jackson Bay Rd.) is **Haast Beach.** While a bike is adequate for reaching these three areas and closer walks, a car is necessary to really explore Haast and see all that it has to offer.

The **South Westland World Heritage Visitor Centre and DOC office** (tel. 750 0809; fax 750 0832) is located at the junction of SH6 and Jackson Bay Rd., 3km from Haast Township (open daily early Nov. to mid-April 9am-6pm, mid-April to early Nov. 9am-4:30pm). **InterCity** (tel. 0800 INTERC) drops off at Fantail Restaurant and Tearooms in Haast on Pauareka Rd., as it heads to: **Franz Josef Glacier** (2½hr., 1:25pm, $37) via **Fox Glacier** (2hr., $31); and **Queenstown** (4½hr., 11:15am, $61) via **Wanaka** (3hr., $38) and **Makarora** (1½hr., $27). **Atomic Shuttles,** leaving from the same place, runs north to: **Greymouth** (6hr., 11:30am, $60) via **Fox Glacier** (2½hr., $25); **Franz Josef Glacier** (3½hr., $30); and **Hokitika** (5½hr., $45). Southbound service to **Queenstown** departs daily (4hr., 2pm, $35) via **Makarora** (1½hr., $25) and **Wanaka** (2½hr., $25). Westland is reportedly difficult for **hitchhiking,** especially in southern areas like Haast. In winter, the situation is near impossible, as passing cars are few and far between. Rent a **bicycle** from Wilderness Backpackers (see below) for $2 per hour, or $20 per day if you are a guest there. There is **no currency exchange** in The Haast. Other services include: the **police** (tel. 750 0850), on Opuka St.; **medical assistance** (tel. 750 0800); and the **post office** in the **Haast Beach Service Centre** (tel. 750 0802), on Jackson Bay Rd. in Haast Beach (open M-F 9am-5pm). **Telephone Code:** 03.

ⵔ ACCOMMODATIONS. Accommodation choices in Haast are less than stellar and often become the unwitting stop of tourists shut out of the glaciers in high season. If you're willing to forego cooking your own meals for a day or two, check into one of the budget or backpackers rooms at the **World Heritage Hotel**, SH6 (tel. 750 0828 or 0800 502 444; fax 750 0827; email info@world-heritage-hotel.com). Located more than 3km outside of the township, this option is best for those with their own transportation. With a TV and bathroom in every room and soft, comfortable beds, you'll have visions of home before you even close your eyes. (4-bed dorms $15, doubles from $50; prices vary according to season and availability.) For a more traditional hostel setup, **Wilderness Backpackers** (tel. 0800 750 029), located on Pauareka Rd. in Haast Township, is just 3km from the Visitor Centre. Some of the dorms can be a little crowded and the TV-dining area is tight, but there is a warm and attractive courtyard. (Dorms $15; doubles $34.) The **Haast Highway Accommodation (YHA)** (tel. 750 0703) is located nearby on Mark's Road; walk in front of Wilderness Backpackers, bear left and head back towards the highway. Bleak but spacious, the gargantuan two-level lounge and kitchen area are clean and well kept. The heaters in the rooms are free, but hot showers cost 50¢. (Dorms $15; twins and doubles $36; motel units $68-105; tent sites $9 per person, powered sites for 2 $20.) **The Haast Motor Camp** (tel./fax 750 0860) is 15km from the Visitor Centre on Jackson Bay Rd. More convenient for those with a car, it's the perfect base for fishing the nearby rivers. The owners offer free pickup if you arrive by bus. (Bunks $13, cabins $30-40; motel units for 2 $80; tent sites $8, powered sites for 2 $18.)

ⵎ FOOD. Options for dining out are equally slim, but the grocery store does offer the most reasonable prices between Hokitika and Wanaka. The **World Heritage Hotel** at Haast Junction has two completely separate dining halls to choose from. The informal dining room is fully licensed with a cafe-style menu and features Sky TV and a monthly live band (open 11am-late). The main dining room (closed during the winter) offers breakfast 7-10:30am and a more formal (and costly) dinner menu 6pm-late). In Haast Township, the **Fantail Restaurant and Tearooms** (tel./fax 750 0055) caters to the budget crowd; pies are $2.50 and a pot of tea and a muffin is $3.50. In summer, a backpackers' dinner menu ($7-10) and a more posh range of dishes ($20-25) are available from 5pm. (Open 7:30am-9pm, winter closes at 4pm.) A final township option is **Smithy's Tavern,** Pauareka Rd. (tel. 750 0034), where meat and seafood dinners ($10-17) and bar snacks like nachos and burgers ($2-6) are served from 5-10pm (8:30pm in winter). Bar opens at 11am (winter 2pm). Find excellent prices next door at the cash-only **Haast Food Centre** (tel. 750 0030), the local grocery store (open daily 8:30am-8pm; winter M-Sa 9am-6pm, Su 10am-5pm).

ⵏ ACTIVITIES. There are many exciting ways to explore Haast's natural splendors, although most require your own transportation. **Monro Beach Walk** (40min.; begins at Monro Beach, 35km north of Haast Township) offers a chance to glimpse the rare Fiordland crested penguin between July and November. Two other popular walks begin from Ship Creek, approximately 20km north of the township. The **Kahikatea Swamp Forest Walk** (return 20min.) offers easy observation of local flora and fauna (including the kahikatea, New Zealand's tallest tree), while the **Dune Lake Walk** (return 30min.) provides sweeping coastline views. For a brief stop on your trip south, try the **Hapuka Estuary Walk** (return 20min.; begins 15km south of the Visitor Centre along the beach road), with its in-depth descriptions of area ecology and the ubiquitous whitebait.

If you don't trust your own grasp of ecology, guided walks are available from **Wilderness Lodge Lake Moeraki** (tel. 750 0881); call in advance (3hr., $50; guests of the lodge have priority). Pioneers of ecotourism, the lodge also offers guided **canoeing** from August to May ($45) and a host of trips that showcase local wildlife.

Fishing opportunities are plentiful in the nearby lakes and in the Tasman Sea—contact Maurice Nolan of **Wilderness Tours** (tel. 750 0824; fax 750 0827) to arrange a trout fishing expedition (4hr., $200; several tours per day) or for any of a number of other tours to see spotted cormorants, Fiordland crested penguins, and terns. You can see seals (often with their pups from Jan.-Mar.) in the distance from **Knight's Point** (30km north on SH6), but the only way to get up close is with **Maurice's Boat Tour** (approx. 1hr., $65). His other tours head up to a reflecting lake or into the heart of the Southern Alps. **River Safaris** (tel. 0800 865 382; fax 442 3195) offers the world's first and only sea to mountain river jetboat ride. Set in the heart of the South Westland World Heritage Area, the trip is a great way to explore the scenery and forest region in style (3hr., $99). Deep-sea fishing for blue cod and tarakihi or scuba-diving trips are made possible by **Haast Fish 'n' Dive** (tel. 750 0004; fax 750 0869). Fishing equipment is provided, though diving gear is not.

THE SOUTHERN LAKES

The southern lakes region sounds its clarion call through lonesome fiords, deep expanses of bush, and lakes bearing the clear marks of glacial history. From the plummeting majesty of Milford Sound in Fiordland to the soaring peaks of Mt. Aspiring National Park, the peerless landscape entices visitors back again and again to some of the most famous and spectacular walks in the world. Those seeking thrills rather than quiet meditation will rejoice in the

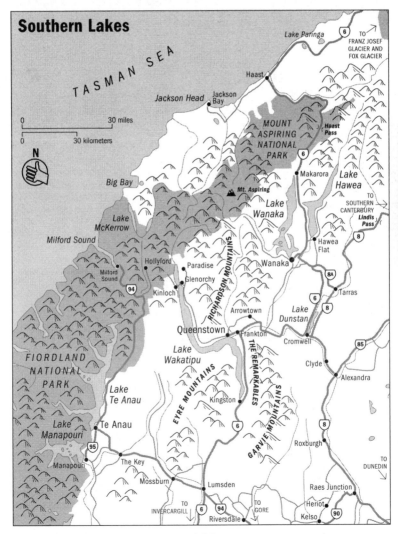

Southern Lakes

TASMAN SEA

Lake Paringa

6 TO
FRANZ JOSEF
GLACIER AND
FOX GLACIER

Haast

Jackson Head · Jackson Bay

0 ____ 30 miles
0 ____ 30 kilometers

N

MOUNT
ASPIRING
NATIONAL
PARK 6

Haast
Pass

Big Bay

Makarora

Lake
Hawea

TO
SOUTHERN
CANTERBURY

Lindis
Pass

Mt. Aspiring

Lake
Wanaka

Lake
McKerrow

8

Milford Sound

Hollyford · Paradise

Hawea
Flat

Wanaka

Milford
Sound 94

Glenorchy

8A

Kinloch

Tarras

RICHARDSON MOUNTAINS

Arrowtown

6 8

Lake
Dunstan

Queenstown · Frankton

Cromwell

85

Lake
Wakatipu

Clyde

FIORDLAND
NATIONAL
PARK

THE REMARKABLES

Alexandra

Lake
Te Anau

EYRE MOUNTAINS

Kingston

GARVIE MOUNTAINS

Lake
Manapouri

Te Anau

6

Roxburgh

8

95

Manapouri

The Key

TO
DUNEDIN

Mossburn

Lumsden

Raes Junction

TO
INVERCARGILL 6

94

TO
GORE

Heriot

90

Riversdale

Kelso

riotous explosions of commercial Queenstown, the heart of the region. Shock yourself awake with a shot of adventure by careening down slopes, rafting through canyons, or bungying off perilous heights for an instant of eternity. A land of contrasts and superlatives, where every lake revels in its distinct character and every valley is more breathtaking than the last, the southern lakes never fail to inspire.

▨ SOUTHERN LAKES HIGHLIGHTS

■ The striking and incomparable beauty of **Milford Sound** (p. 355) can be explored by boat, kayak, or plane.

■ In **Queenstown** (p. 326), it's a never-ending circle of fun, with bungy jumping, skydiving, skiing, biking, and rock-climbing by day, bar-hopping by night.

■ Fiordland and Mt. Aspiring offer some of the world's most glorious tramping: **Milford Track** (p. 348), **Rees-Dart** (p. 345), and the **Routeburn** (p. 351) among others.

QUEENSTOWN

Although the gold rush days are over, Queenstown has yet to lose its glitter. Street lamps twinkle along the lake as adrenaline addicts worn from a day of thrills begin a night of hard partying. International visitors of every wallet size flock to Queenstown's souvenir shops and jewelry boutiques. Despite its commercial glitz and glamor, this town's spot on Lake Wakatipu beneath the sun-drenched spine of The Remarkables mountain range still inspires awe, and remote wilderness is close at hand. The quips of other Kiwis about Queenstown's loss of character are tinged with equal doses of truth and jealousy, but Queenstown still has small-town charm and its raw beauty is indisputable.

▐ ARRIVAL AND DEPARTURE

Airport: 6km east of town in Frankton. Take **The Shopper Bus** (tel. 442 6647) from the McDonald's on Camp St. (every hour from 7:15am, $5) or **Super Shuttle** (tel. 442 3639 or 0800 727 747; $5). Taxis to the airport are $15.

Airlines: Air New Zealand (tel. 441 1900 or 0800 737 000) and **Ansett** (tel. 442 6161 or 0800 800 146) both have flights to: **Auckland** (2hr., 4-6 per day, $356-682); **Wellington** (1½hr., 3-4 per day, $268-541); and **Dunedin** (1½hr., 2 per day, $180-415) via **Christchurch** (30min., 4-6 per day, $135-369). Several airlines do scenic flights to **Milford Sound** (40min., $160, stand-by $75) including **Air Fiordland** (tel. 442 3404) and **Milford Sound Scenic Flights** (tel. 442 3065).

Buses: InterCity (tel. 442 8238), departing from Camp St., and the less expensive **Atomic Shuttles** (tel. 442 8178) and **Southern Link** (tel. 358 8355) all head to **Christchurch** (7-11hr., 4-5 per day, $40-76) and **Dunedin** (4hr., 4-5 per day, $25-33). InterCity and **Topline Tours** (tel. 442 8178) head to **Te Anau** (2hr., 1-3 per day, $29-35). InterCity heads to **Invercargill** (2¾hr., 9am daily, winter M-F 9am, $35), as does **Southern Land Travel** (tel. 442 0099; Oct.-Apr. daily, 9am, May-Sept. M-F 9am; $35). Atomic Shuttles, Intercity, Southern Link, and **Wanaka Connexion** (tel. 0800 879 926) head to **Wanaka** (1¾hr., 4-5 per day, $15-22).

Hitchhiking: Thumbers say getting to Glenorchy requires walking along the lake beyond the rotary at One Mile Creek. Hitching to Milford is an unlikely prospect; it involves taking the Shopper Bus to Frankton and walking past the airport along the road to Te Anau.

ⓩ PRACTICAL INFORMATION

Queenstown's smaller satellite towns include **Glenorchy** to the west and **Arrowtown** and **Wanaka** to the north. Queenstown itself is very compact. Booking agencies, bars, and gear rental stores line **Shotover St.** Shopping boutiques and restaurants are concentrated on **Beach St.** and **The Mall,** both of which run parallel to Shotover St. Accommodations ring the town center, while the spine of **The Remarkables** mountain range runs south down the east side of **Lake Wakatipu.** Hovering above Queenstown, the lights of **Skyline Restaurant** give the impression of a spaceship.

Visitors Center: The official source of info is the **Queenstown Visitor Information Network** (tel. 442 4100 or 0800 668 888; fax 442 8907; email qvc@xtra.co.nz), at the Clocktower Centre. Open daily 7am-7pm, winter 7am-6pm.

DOC: Shotover St. (tel. 442 7935), below the **Information and Track Centre.** Pamphlets on local walks and hut tickets for the Routeburn and other area tracks. Open daily 8:30am-6pm, winter Tu-Sa 9am-5pm.

Local Buses: The **Shopper Bus** (tel. 442 6647) runs between most accommodations and the town center ($2) every hour, and to Frankton ($3) and the airport ($5) five times per day. Schedule at Visitor Centre.

Regional Shuttles: The Track & Information Centre, 37 Shotover St. (tel. 442 9708), books trips on **Kiwi Experience** to **Routeburn** and **Greenstone/Caples Tracks** (1-2hr., 2 per day, $20), and to **Milford Sound** (5hr., 2 per day, $59) via **Te Anau** (2-3hr., $35). **Backpacker Express** (tel. 442 9939) runs shuttles from Queenstown to **Glenorchy** and from Glenorchy to the start of the **Routeburn, Greenstone/Caples,** and **Rees-Dart tracks** (departs Queenstown on demand in summer and 8am in winter, departs Glenorchy on demand in summer and 3pm in winter, $10 per segment), as well as a **boat shuttle** from the Dart Valley end of the Rees-Dart Track ($50) and **4WD** from the Dart Valley ($20). **Glenorchy Scenic Express** (tel. 442 8582) takes you by boat up the beautiful Lake Wakatipu to Glenorchy (3 per day, $20 each way).

Ski Shuttles: Ski Shuttle (tel. 442 4630) runs to: **Coronet Peak** (25min., 4 per day, return $23); **The Remarkables** (45min., 4 per day, return $23); and **Treble Cone** (2hr., 1 per day, return $23). **Kiwi Discovery** (tel. 442 7340) has shuttles to the ski fields with comparable prices to: **Coronet** (2 per day); **The Remarkables** (1 per day); **Treble Cone** (1 per day, return $35); and **Cardrona** (1½hr., 1 per day, return $30).

Ski and Snowboard Rental: If you're hitting the slopes, you can get big discounts on long term rentals. **Outside Sports** (tel. 442 8870) has a rental outlet at the top of The Mall that offers the best selection. Skis, boots, and poles $20 per day; board and boots $32. 10% YHA discount. Open daily 9am-10pm, winter 7am-10pm. **Bad Jelly** (tel. 442 4064), on Camp St., has slightly cheaper rates on boards and boots ($35 per day), and skis, boots, and poles (from $25 per day). Open June-Nov. daily 7:30am-10pm.

Tramping Gear: Alpine Sports, 28 Shotover St. (tel. 442 7099; open M-Sa 9:30am-6pm, Su 10am-6pm) and **Outside Sports** (tel. 442 8870; open 9am-10pm, winter daily 7am-10pm.)

Taxis: Alpine Taxis (tel. 442 6666) and **Queenstown Taxis** (tel. 442 7788 or 0800 788 294) have 24hr. service.

Car Rental: Pegasus Rental Cars (tel. 442 7176) offers compact cars from $35 per day, with insurance and unlimited km for a rental of 4 days or more. **Network Car Rentals,** 34 Shotover St. (tel. 442 7055), has similar deals on rentals of 5 days or more. Open daily 8:30am-6pm. Another affordable option is **Queenstown Car Rentals,** 18 Shotover St. (tel. 442 9220), with cars from $39 and unlimited km after 2 days. Open daily 8:30am-6:30pm.

Currency Exchange: BNZ (tel. 442 5820), on Rees St., has good exchange rates. Its **Bureau de Change** is open M-F 9am-8pm, Sa-Su 10am-8pm. **ANZ Postbank** (tel. 442 7170), on Beach St. near the waterfront, has similar rates, an **ATM,** and cash advances. Open M-F 9am-4:30pm.

Police: 11 Camp St. (tel. 442 7900).

Medical Services: The **Queenstown Medical Centre** (tel. 442 7301) is at the corner of Shotover and Stanley St. Open M-F 8:30am-7pm, Sa-Su 9am-5pm; doctor on call 24hr. **Wilkinson's Pharmacy** (tel. 442 7313), is at Rees St. Open daily 8:30am-9pm.

Post Office: Camp and Ballarat St. (tel. 442 7670). Open M-F 8:30am-5:30pm, Sa 9am-5pm.

Internet Access: Discount Dialing, 31 Beach St. (tel. 441 1356). 10¢ per min. Open Tu-F 9am-11pm, Sa-M 10am-11pm. **Budget Communications** (tel. 441 1562), on the second floor of O'Connells Mall. Daily $5 per hour specials 9-11am and 9-11pm and the best rates for international phone calls. Open daily 9am-11pm.

TELEPHONE CODE	The telephone code throughout the South Island is **03**.

■ ACCOMMODATIONS

Catering to honeymooners and broke ski bums alike, Queenstown has a staggering array of places to stay, with B&Bs and hostels springing up endlessly like mushrooms after rain. Booking agencies facilitate finding the ideal B&B. Book far ahead in summer and ski season. For listings below, **check-out time** is usually around 10am, laundry usually $2, and key deposit $10.

The Last Resort (tel. 442 4320; fax 442 4330), on Man St. Head up Camp St., take a right on Man St., and cross the stream over the red Japanese footbridge. Within stumbling distance of the bars, the rather small, 2-level, red-and-black *maison* has a warm, communal feel with an open kitchen/dining/lounge area featuring picnic tables and a small but distinguished collection of videos. Reception open whenever staff is inclined to sit at the desk. 4-bed dorms $18.

Deco Backpackers, 52 Man St. (tel. 442 7384; fax 442 6694). From the Visitor Centre, walk left up Camp St., take a left on Man St., go up the hill; it's at the end of Man St. on the left. With two lounges and two kitchens, nice views, and free pickup by a van named "Winston," you'll relish the extra delights that make Deco a standout year-round. Reception 8am-2pm and 4pm-8pm. Dorms $17; twins and doubles $38; tent sites $9 per person. Four nights for the price of three or $2 off your first night Sept.-Oct. and Apr.-June; in winter, 10% discount for stays at least a week.

Bumbles Hostel, 2 Brunswick St. (tel. 442 6298). From the Visitors Centre, walk left down Beach St. to Lake Esplanade; Bumbles is after Brunswick St. on your right. Spacious and modern 4-person dorms have wood-framed bunks, comfortable mattresses, and in-room kitchenettes. The lounge offers a great view of the lake, but the limited hours (7am-11:30pm) prevent late-night munchies or late-night TV. Reception 7:30am-9pm. Dorms $17; twin bunks $38; twins and doubles with linen $45.

Pinewood Lodge, 48 Hamilton Rd. (tel. 442 8273; fax 442 9470; email rgrieg @xtra.co.nz). A 10-minute walk from the Visitor Centre—head left up Camp St., follow Robins Rd. around to the right, and then left on Hamilton. Relaxed seclusion in modern cabins with cushy mattresses, jacuzzi, trampoline, and 8-ball. 10-person chalets available. Bike hire available. Reception 7:30am-9pm, winter 8am-9pm. Dorms $17; singles $25; twins and doubles $40; tent sites $10 (summer only).

Queenstown YHA, 88-90 Lake Esplanade (tel. 442 8413; fax 442 6561; email yhaqutn@yha.org.nz). Left down Shotover St. and 5min. along the lakefront away from town. The smells of international cuisines frying in the kitchen waft through the walls of this giant, communal place. Despite the large, well-equipped kitchen and the two internet sites, facilities often become crowded during mealtimes and peak periods. The friendly, knowledgeable staff will enthusiastically help you with bookings and help you find discounts. Reception 6:30am-10pm. Dorms $18-19; doubles and twins $42-44; non-YHA $4 extra. Book ahead in summer.

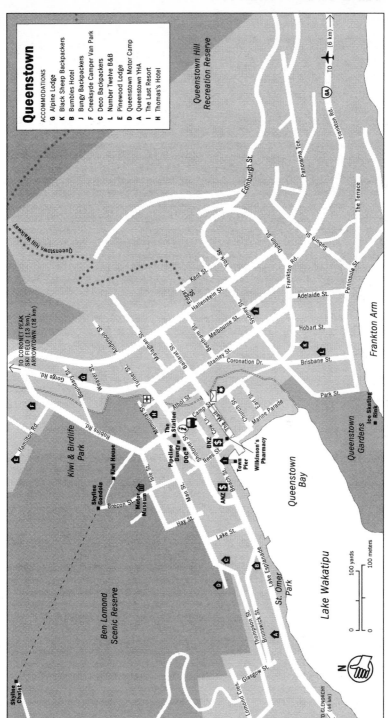

SOUTH ISLAND

Queenstown

ACCOMMODATIONS

- G Alpine Lodge
- K Black Sheep Backpackers
- B Bumbles Hotel
- J Bungy Backpackers
- F Creeksyde Camper Van Park
- C Deco Backpackers
- L Number Twelve B&B
- E Pinewood Lodge
- D Queenstown Motor Camp
- A Queenstown YHA
- I The Last Resort
- H Thomas's Hotel

Bungi Backpackers (VIP) (tel./fax 442 8725 or 0800 7282 8644), at the corner of Melbourne and Sydney St. From the Visitor Centre, take a right up Shotover St., a right on Stanley St., then a left up Sydney St. If you're not endeared with YHA or riding the Kiwi bus, this social hostel may be for you. Creative wall art, hammocks in the yard, a massive video library, free jacuzzi, and a warm hearth in the middle of the lounge. The outgoing staff and cheap bunk rooms make Bungi one of the better deals in town. Internet. Reception 8am-8pm. Bunks $12; dorms $16; singles $25; doubles $35. Cash only.

Black Sheep Backpackers (VIP), 13 Frankton Rd. (tel. 442 7289; fax 442 7361). Turn right from the Visitor Centre, follow Camp St. until the end, and then head up the short trail in the park and cross over to Frankton Rd. Catering to Kiwi Experience, Black Sheep isn't the place for space, peace, or quiet, but its tireless clientele appease the adrenaline Gods of Queenstown. The decks have mountain views and the jacuzzi relaxes drained bodies. A genius marketer created an 18-hole frisbee golf course in the adjacent park; ask for a free map and disk. Internet. Reception 7am-10pm, winter 7am-9pm. Dorms $19, with VIP $18; doubles $46.

Creeksyde Camper Van Park, 54 Robins Rd. (tel. 442 944; fax 442 6621, email creeksyde@co.nz). Go up Camp St., right on Robins Rd., and it's a 5-minute walk. A creek makes the paved road twisting through the grounds less conspicuous. Well-equipped, with a BBQ, spa, and sauna, plus peace and quiet. Reception 7am-9:30pm, winter 8am-8pm. Spacious lodges for 2 $40, extra adult $12, extra child $8, linen $5; camper vans for two $22, extra adult $8, extra child $5; tent sites $11 per person.

Number Twelve B&B, 12 Brisbane St. (tel. 442 9511; fax 442 9755; email her cusbb@queenstown.co.nz). Follow Camp St. to the right, continue up the paved pathway at the end of the street, and take a right on Brisbane St.; Number Twelve will be on the left. Relax on the patio by the solar-heated pool in summer, or curl up with a book in the sunroom during winter. Nicely situated, with beautiful mountain and lake views and only a short walk from the gardens, you'll find relaxation and a warm welcome in this residential home with a pretty rose garden. Dinner by arrangement $35. Free laundry and Internet. Singles $70; twins and doubles $110.

Alpine Lodge (tel. 442 7220; fax 442 7038). Follow Shotover St. up to Gorge Rd.; the lodge will be a block down on your right. Couches covered with afghans surround the TV and fireplace in the lounge. In warmer weather, BBQs outside on the patio offer a welcome retreat from the crowded kitchen. Key deposit $10. Reception 8am-8:30pm. Dorms $17; twins and doubles $40.

Thomas's Hotel, 50 Beach St. (tel. 442 7180; fax 441 8417; email the.cat@xtra.co.nz;). Go left down Shotover St., take the first left on Rees St., then the first right. A gluttonous tabby, the hotel's namesake, runs the waterfront hotel, tidying the private bathrooms, fiddling with the reception of the in-room TVs, and overseeing the adjoining Fat Ginger Cafe. Kayaks $10 per hr., half-day $25, full day $40 day. Reception 7am-8:30pm or 9pm. Dorms $17-19; hotel singles $75; twins and doubles $60-$85; triples $95.

Queenstown Motor Camp (tel. 442 7252; fax 442 7253; email info@motorpark.co.nz), on Man St. across the street from Deco Backpackers. Green roofs match the pine-covered hillside behind the enormous park above town. Some cabins afford a view of Lake Wakatipu and The Remarkables, while others look inwards at the rest of the park. Reception 8am-10pm, winter 8am-9pm. Cabins for 2 $38, extra person $14; double tourist flats $68, extra person $14; tent sites, powered $11.

⬛ FOOD

Backpackers shouldn't have to look far to find a good crumb at a low price or a big meal without a money-anxiety attack. Several ethnic restaurants offer bargain deals on tasty cuisine, while many bars have surprisingly flavorful and un-pub-like food for less than $10; check the reception areas at the hostels for discount coupons on food and drinks. New supermarkets going up in Frankton should drive down the previously high grocery prices. **Alpine Food Center** (tel. 442 8961), on upper Shotover St., is the largest and busiest of the supermarkets in town (open M-Sa 8am-8pm, Su 9am-8pm), but for fresh produce head to **Simply Fresh,** 39 Camp St. (tel. 442 9636), near Shotover St. (open daily 8am-8pm, winter M-Sa 8am-7:30pm, Su 9am-7pm).

🖾 **Habebes Lebanese** (tel. 442 9861), on the Rees St. Arcade. Tucked away off the street, it's worth the effort to seek out this minuscule piece of the Middle East with a tiny counter and star-studded aqua blue decor. Add your choice of tabouli and salads to the scrumptious lamb pita ($7) for a messy delight. The apricot orgasm ($2.50) will certainly make you climax. Open daily 11am-6pm.

Happy Wok, 8 Shotover St. (tel. 442 4415), in the parking lot next to Alpine Foodcentre. Even the space-age chairs, shimmering Siamese embroidery, and alien-head-bedecked restroom can't distract you from the authentic Thai food served here. Tom Kar mixed seafood, Pad Thai, and curry dishes $8-13. Open daily from 11:30am.

Wholefoods Cafe (tel. 442 8991), on the Trust Bank Arcade between Shotover and Beach St. "Mainly vegetarian, almost healthy" is their indecisive motto, but they serve up food with conviction. Soup and homemade bread $6, platter of veggies and bread with hummus dip $7.50, or smoothies $3.50. Open daily 8am-5pm.

The World (tel. 442 5714), on upper Shotover St. If you don't mind the blaring music and dim lighting in this large, open bar, you can get a good, cheap meal. Chicken *tikka masala* $10 and vegetarian meals from $8. Happy Hour 5-8pm and 10:30-11:30pm. Pick up a card for a free beer with your meal before 10pm. Come back for the nightlife (see p. 331). Open daily 4pm-2:30am.

Wraps (tel. 442 4040), at the middle of The Mall. California sun meets Queenstown snow in this eatery. The owner is a native Californian who makes his own salsa, a tasty and tangy chargrilled antipasto ($6.50), and some pretty darn good burritos ($8). He can also offer some creative ideas if the regular bungy jumps and skydives are losing their excitement. Open daily 8am-10pm.

Little India, 11 Shotover St. (tel. 442 5335). Veteran budget backpacker the Sultan of Brunei ate here. *Naan* bread at lunch $2.50; dinners, including several vegetarian options, from $11.50. Home deliveries and takeaway available. Minimum charge $10. Filling *samosas* $5. Open daily 12:30-3:30pm and 6-9:30pm.

Ken's Noodle House (tel. 442 8628), on Camp St. between Shotover and Beach St. Friendly Ken serves up bowls of authentic Japanese noodles ($5 and up) from the open kitchen. Open M-Sa 11:30am-2:30pm and 5-8:30pm. Cash only.

Lai Sing (tel. 442 7131), on the second floor of O'Connell's Shopping Centre. The eight-course lunch buffet isn't gourmet (in fact, it's a tad greasy), but it's a $9 bargain. Open daily noon-2:30pm and 5:30-11:30pm.

☑ NIGHTLIFE

Queenstown's concentrated nightlife rocks with backpackers fresh off the slopes (or the Kiwi buses) and activity operators. **Movies** are shown in the tiny single theater at the Embassy on The Mall (movie-line tel. 442 9990; $10, students and YHA $7). Relieve the munchies late into the night at the **Jazz Bar** (open 8am-4am), a Camp St. cafe that occasionally turns into a street party. Those seeking a drink without the noise and hassle of the local bars will appreciate the free delivery provided by Ring-a-Drink (tel. 0800 TO DRINK).

🖾 **The World** (tel. 442 5714), on Shotover St. Other bars have big nights, but The World never stops spinning. Drawn by the large globe mounted outside the door, the ubiquitous posters tacked to every hostel wall in town, and the flashing lights visible through the rattling 2nd floor windows, backpackers flock here for an early drink, a cheap meal, a night of hard partying, and often all three. DJs daily from 10pm. Arcade games downstairs. Drink specials 5-8pm and 10:30-11:30pm. Open daily 4pm-2:30am.

SOUTH ISLAND

🐾 **Pog Mahone's,** 14 Rees St. (tel. 442 5382). A classy Irish Pub where you can sit outside on the patio or the balcony for a view of Lake Wakatipu and the Eyre Mountains. If anyone asks you where you're going, just say "Kiss my ass!" (that's what Pog Mahone means in Celtic). Live music daily. Open daily 8am-2:30am.

Abbey Road (tel. 442 8290), 66 Shotover St. Draws mellow minglers and those on a quest for $6 pizza and upstairs pool. Laid-back couches and intimate pool hall brings you closer to your mates. Frequent beer specials; 10% discount with backpackers card, 20% discount from 6-8pm. Open daily from 7am.

Lone Star, 14 Brecon St. (tel. 442 9995). Outrageous decor would make even the staunchest Texan giggle like a schoolgirl. An enormous rifle hangs over the pool table, a motorcycle balances above the bar, and animal skulls are mounted on stucco walls. Despite the in-your-face decor, it's a good hangout for those not interested in bumpin' and grindin'. $2 drinks 11pm-1:30am. Open daily from 5pm.

Winnie Bagoes (tel. 442 8635), at the bottom of The Mall. Occasionally Winnie's rocks with DJs or live music, and the party spills out to the balcony into the open air as they pull back the retractable roof and let it snow. If you get the munchies, there's pizza ($3.50), dessert pizza ($8.50) and full-sized pies (medium $19, large $26). $2 handles all night, half-priced cocktails 5-8pm and 10pm-midnight. Open daily 12pm-2:30am.

Chico's (tel. 442 8439), at the bottom of The Mall. After 11:30pm, Chico's following (which is slightly older) arrives primed to dance on tables and inspire mayhem. On Wednesdays local celebrities and travelers alike turn up for the weekly jam session at 10:30pm. Live music Th-Su at 10:30pm. Open daily 6pm-2:30am.

Surreal (tel. 441 0492), on Rees St. With subtle, pumping trance music, dim candlelighting, and the requisite fish tank, Surreal affects its cool convincingly. Frequent DJs from 10pm. Free pool Mondays after 10pm with purchase of drink. Open daily 5pm-2:30am.

Casbah (tel. 442 7853), upstairs on Shotover St. Technicolor lights flash off the mirror as backpackers hot off the tour bus and locals on the prowl break it down on the dance floor. You can score here—free bungy jumps or an escort home. DJs from 10:45pm. Cheap drink 10:30-11:30pm. Open daily 9pm-2:30am.

🏔 ACTIVITIES

Queenstown is known for its heart-stopping thrills and breathtaking scenery; if you want to ride, jump, walk, or glide through spectacular wilderness, this is the place. The sheer number of booking offices is daunting—you could probably book a bungy jump in the public restroom. If you can afford it, give Queenstown five days, and like Hercules after a year of trials, you'll be drained but exhilarated.

PLANNING

Budgeting for Queenstown activities can seem despairingly impossible. Most activities sound exciting and cost plenty. For **cheaper activities,** we recommend frisbee golf, the luge, gold panning in Arrowtown, hiking the Ben Lomond or Queenstown Hill, ice skating, and a 4WD trip into Skippers Canyon. To maximize your money, consider buying a **pre-packaged** combo which can save you up to $100 on the more expensive activities. Combos include anywhere from two to five activities including helicopter flights, bungy jumps, jetboat rides, 4WD tours, and rafting trips. One of the best deals is the **Skippers Grand Slam,** which combines a 4WD ride into Skippers Canyon, the Pipeline bungy jump, the Flying Fox zipline over the canyon, and the Skippers jetboat ride for $199.

There are many other combos offered at booking agencies. **The Station** (tel. 442 5252), at Shotover and Camp St., is gigantic; many activities depart from there (open daily 7am-9pm, winter 8am-8pm). **Backpacker Specialists,** 62 Shotover St. (tel. 442 8178), pride themselves on finding cheap deals on activities and particularly on flights to Milford Sound (open daily 8am-8pm, winter 9am-6pm). **The Information and Track Centre,** 37 Shotover St. (tel. 442 9708), is very well-informed about transportation to local tracks and ski fields, tramping conditions, accommodations, and outfitting (open daily 7am-9pm, winter 7am-8pm).

THE HISTORY OF BUNGY Bungy started with Pacific Islanders, who have been jumping off towers for hundreds of years with nothing more than vines tied to their feet. In the 1970s, the Oxford University Dangerous Sports Club tried some jumps. AJ Hackett heard about this new "sport" and collaborated with fellow downhill skier Henry Van Asch to develop modern bungy jumping. They opened the world's first bungy site at Kawarau Bridge outside Queenstown, and made quite a splash with an Eiffel Tower jump in 1987. Thirteen years and over a million jumps later, Queenstown is recognized as the world's bungy-jumping mecca. A serious rivalry exists between AJ Hackett and the other bungy outfit in town Pipeline as they try to out-spectacular each other like Las Vegas hotels. Existential enlightenment during your bungy jump is unlikely, but something will probably go to your head (be it adrenaline or all your bodily fluids).

BUNGY JUMPING

Located in The Station, **AJ Hackett** (tel. 442 7100 or 0800 286 492; www.ajhackett.com) operates three jumps. **The Ledge** above Queenstown at the top of the gondola may be the most unique jump—the 47m fall looks a lot farther at night with the lights of Queenstown twinkling below ($99, includes gondola ride and t-shirt; runs daily 11am-7pm, winter 5-9pm). At the 43m **Kawarau Bridge,** the world's first bungy bridge, you can request submersion in the river below ($110 with T-shirt and transport., 3 trips per day; open daily 8am-8pm, winter 8am-7pm). The 75m jump at **Skipper's Canyon** is now currently open only for special events, so check for availability.

Since it opened in 1994, **☒Pipeline Bungy,** 27 Shotover St. (tel. 442 5455; www.bungy.co.nz), has offered the highest jump in Queenstown, a 102m plunge from a suspension bridge into Skippers' Canyon ($135 with 4WD transport along the crazy road to the bridge, including humorous commentary; 6 trips per day). In recent months, the competition between Pipeline and AJ Hackett has heated up, with AJ Hackett unveiling its **Nevis Highwire Bungy,** a 134m jump operated from a gondola suspended by wire cables between two mountains over a canyon ($174 with T-shirt and transport). Not to be outdone, Pipeline has come up with a new slogan ("Still the highest on this side of the world") to go along with its newest project: the **Balloon Bungy.** This hot-air balloon tethered to the ground allows jumpers to pick a height anywhere from 150-700m ($239 including transport to and from Skippers Canyon). Just remember, the higher you go, the farther you fall.

JETBOATING

Jetboating on the Shotover and Kawarau rivers is popular with people of all ages. The **Skippers Canyon Jet** (tel./fax 442 9434 or tel. 0800 226 966) offers a combination of history and thrills as it cruises 16km past the precipitous walls of the old gold-mining canyon, under suspension bridges, and past abandoned pioneer settlements ($79 with transport from the Pipeline Bungy office on Shotover St.; several trips per day; includes a guided tour of the museum and gold-panning). **Shotover Jet** (tel. 442 8570 or 0800 746 868), though less personal, is the most popular jetboat ride. Skimming impossibly close to the jagged rock walls and over waters as shallow as 10cm deep, the speedboats swivel and twist at 70kph. Pickups are from The Station every half hour; otherwise, drive just 15 minutes up the road toward Arrowtown to Shotover Canyon. ($69, children $30; 10% YHA and family discounts.) **☒Dart River Jet Safaris** may be the best of the lot, offering more remote trips through the pristine river valleys north of Glenorchy (see p. 336).

RAFTING AND RIVER SPORTS

The Shotover and Kawarau Rivers also provide for various innovative whitewater adventures. The Shotover has more consistent Grade 4 rapids and takes you through the manmade 170m Oxenbridge Tunnel of darkness, but the Kawarau has a few wild sections (including the 400m Chinese Dog Leg, New Zealand's longest commercial whitewater segment). **Queenstown Rafting** (tel. 442 9792; fax 442 4609), **Extreme Green Rafting** (tel. 442 8517), and **Challenge Rafting** (tel. 442 7318) run half-day trips on the Shotover ($109) and Kawarau ($99) mornings and afternoons. **Serious Fun River Surfing** (tel. 442 5262) operates a three-hour, 7km Kawarau River boogie-board experience involving four rapids, standing waves, and mandatory adrenaline ($99 with training). **River Bugs** (tel. 442 9792) offers a similar experience in a polka-dotted personal craft akin to an armchair ($140, trips run 8:30am-3pm). **12 Mile Delta** (tel. 0800 222 696) and **Vertigo Canyoning** (tel. 441 1261) lead exciting abseiling and canyoning trips, which plunge into pools, rappel into ravines, and slide down chutes: not for those with fear of heights (summer only; half-day $90; full day with lunch $140).

SKYDIVING AND OTHER AERIAL ACTIVITIES

For those who like to look down on skiers, Queenstown is one of the best places in the world for skydiving. **Skydive Tandem** (tel. (021) 325 961) will pick you up, fly you 3100m, drop you and an instructor until you reach your terminal velocity, and then let you float down between Lake Wakatipu and The Remarkables ($245).

Other aeronautics include **paragliding** from above the Skyline Gondola over Queenstown, a relaxing but exhilarating tandem ride. **Queenstown Tandems** (tel. 442 7319), **Flying Cow** (tel. 0800 284 376), or **G-Force** (tel. 442 9708) all charge roughly $120 for about 10 minutes in the air. For a faster, wilder ride try **Sky Trek Tandem Hang Gliding** (tel. 442 6311), a 10-minute flight from Coronet Peak or The Remarkables ($145). **Let's Parafly** (tel. 442 8507) attaches you to a boat and lifts you up to 300 feet as you cruise around Lake Wakatipu ($65).

Other options for aerial viewing include **Air Wakatipu** (tel. 442 3148), where 20-minute scenic flights are $49 and 20-minute acrobatic flights $88. **The Helicopter Line** (tel. 442 3034) has 20-minute Remarkables trips (including a snow landing for $130). **Over The Top** (tel. 442 2233) has 20-minute flights over The Remarkables ($85), a longer 40-minute flight with snow landing ($175), and more expensive options to Milford or to remote rivers for fly fishing.

The newest adrenaline rush to hit Queenstown is **Fly by Wire** (tel. 442 2116), a contraption that allows you to fly a personal craft up to 170kph as you swing on an attached wire like a pendulum ($129, winter $99). If you're at Skippers Canyon and feel like warming up before your bungy jump, or if you prefer a relaxing glide over the canyon rather than a stomach-jerking dive into it, try the **Flying Fox,** a 250m zipline that reaches speeds of 70kph, as you watch others on the Pipeline ($79 for transport and flying fox only; additional $105 for Pipeline bungy).

ON THE SLOPES

From June to September, **skiing** and **snowboarding** take over Queenstown as down-hillers flock to **Coronet Peak** and **The Remarkables.** Coronet is bigger and is closer to Queenstown, has a longer season, and offers weekend night-skiing and two half-pipes. Its slopes are suitable for all levels of skiers and boarders, particularly inter-mediate skiers. The Remarkables ski field is higher and generally has better snow conditions. It also has a wider beginner slope and gets more sun. Its slopes cater to skiers and snowboarders of all skill-levels, as well as to telemarkers and cross-country skiers. Students will appreciate the cheaper rates at The Remarkables (Coronet: $60, students $53, children $30. Remarkables: $57, students $45, children $27.)

Lift passes and transportation are cheaper in town, particularly when part of a package. The roads up to the mountains usually require chains; shuttles are a safer option. Although Wanaka is more conveniently situated, skiers and snowboarders frequently stay in Queenstown and catch morning shuttles to **Cardrona,** or make the longer drive to **Treble Cone.** Cardrona is 30km closer, has several slopes for intermediate skiers, and is a popular choice among families; its four half-pipes also make it a favorite for snowboarders. Treble Cone has the longest vertical rise of the ski fields in the Southern Lakes and has challenging slopes mostly for interme-diate and advanced skiers, as well as a half-pipe for snowboarders.

OFF-ROAD

The walls and precipitous road through **Skippers' Canyon,** constructed during the gold-rush days, now attract 4WD tours that give the fantastic drive a historical perspective. **Skippers Grand Canyon Ltd.** (tel. 442 9434) will take you by 4WD on the rugged, windy road into the canyon, then on a jetboat ride that combines history and fast-paced thrills, gives you a view of the bungy jumping and the Flying Fox, and offers an opportunity to pan for gold (3-4hr., $79, 3 per day; Flying Fox $39 more, Pipeline Bungy $105 more). **Outback Tours** (tel. 442 7386) and **Nomad Safaris** (tel. 442 6699) have morning and afternoon tours into Skippers Canyon and up to the historic mining settlements of Macetown and Seffertown (2hr. $55, 4½hr. $75). Wild, off-road two- and four-wheel biking treks through the canyon and other lands are available through **Offroad Adventures** (tel. 442 7858; 2½hr., $150).

In the summer, **Gravity Action** (tel. 442 8178) runs half-day **mountain biking trips** to the canyon mornings and afternoons; for $55, they drive you up Coronet Peak and let you coast down through creeks and over gravel. To explore on your own bike, choose from one of several rental outlets in town and pick up a leaflet from the DOC describing different rides in the area and a Red Trail map from any booking office. One especially good trip is the 20km ride past Lake Hayes to Arrowtown, where you can stop to check out the historic Chinese settlement, pan for gold, or continue up the rugged 13km 4WD track to Macetown.

ON THE LAKE

For decades, steamships were the only form of transport across the lake to Glenorchy and to the area's various sheep stations. Today, only the revamped **T.S.S. Earnslaw** (tel. 442 7500 or 0800 656 503) remains ($43, children $10). The highlights, however, are the noon and 2pm farm cruises to **Walter Peak,** where you can watch sheep-shearing and ride Robbie the Highland Bull, or undertake a horse trek (3½hr.; $45, children $10, with horse trek $70, children $51; horse trek only in summer). The dinner cruise involves a traditional lamb and pavlova dinner and a rollicking farm show following the meal (4hr.; departs 5:30pm; $70, children $35; departs from the summer wharf at the end of Shotover St.). The lake comes alive in summer with **waterskiing, jetboating, water taxis** to secluded picnic spots, and **fishing** trips—just ask at any booking office.

WALKS AND HORSE TREKS

One of the most difficult and most rewarding treks is the climb to the top of ▧**Ben Lomond.** Mt. Aspiring and an entire panorama of peaks can be seen from the steep summit on a clear day (6-8hr.). A less arduous climb on the **Queenstown Hill Walk** (2-3hr.) will lead you through thick forest to the peak of Te Tapunui, where you can enjoy a breathtaking 360° view of The Remarkables, Cecil Peak, and Lake Wakatipu. Shorter tracks on the way to Glenorchy offer less-trodden native forest experiences (some are suitable for mountain biking or trail running). For maps and info on local walks, try the DOC or the Track & Info Centre next door.

A number of stables operate near Arthur's Point in the valley and include trips through farmland, foothills, and saddle tracks. Both **Moonlight Stables** (tel. 442 9792; full day $150, 1½hr. $50) and **Shotover Stables** (tel. 442 7486; full day with lunch $140, 1¾hr. $48) provide transport.

OTHER SIGHTS AND ACTIVITIES

At the base of the gondola, the **Kiwi and Birdlife Park** (tel. 442 8059) is an affordable and worthwhile activity. It includes a nocturnal kiwi house, a range of native parakeets and ducks, and the head-bobbing **black stilt** *(kaki)*, the world's rarest wading bird (numbering around 150 in the wild). Proceeds support captive breeding programs. (Open daily 9am-7pm, winter 9am-5pm. Admission $9.50, children $3.50.; 10% discount with card or with *Let's Go*). The **Queenstown Gardens** at the end of the boardwalk offers secluded views of the lake. With a track looping out onto the peninsula and fitness stations scattered along the path, this is a perfect place for a morning workout.

The **Skyline Gondola** (tel. 442 7860) goes up to the restaurant and bar at sunset for panoramic views of the lake, including Coronet Peak (open daily 9am-9pm; return $12, child $4). Better yet, walk the **One Mile Creek Trail** (1hr. uphill), which starts along the lakefront toward Glenorchy, past the YHA, and passes through a canyon and pine forest to Skyline (where you can catch the gondola down). At the top, for your viewing pleasure, you can watch **Kiwi Magic,** a half-hour surround-sound visual experience about a bumbling American exploring New Zealand with a happy-go-lucky tour guide ($7, students $5, children $3). By the top of the gondola, **Skyline Luge** (tel. 442 7860) may look tame, but its sharp turns and steep staightaways are exciting when you're crouched on a steerable plastic cart, racing past grandmas and friends alike. Fortunately, thick cushions pad the occasional wipe-out. ($4.50; 5 rides $16, with return gondola $22. Open daylight hours.) Within chirping distance of the birdpark, **Queenstown Mini Golf,** 28 Brecon St. (tel. 442 7652), is a good and affordable family activity (open daily 9:30am-dark; $7).

Mountain Works, 27 Shotover St. (tel. 442 7329), runs introductory rock climbing day courses from $95 in the summer and beginning ice-climbing from $150 in the winter, along with multi-day guided ascents for the hard-core. **Independent Mountain Guides** (tel. 442 3381) offers similar instruction in rock climbing (full day $80) and can lead you on a full-day traverse of The Remarkables or a snow-shoed climb to Coronet Peak ($185 each). If it's a workout you're after, there's ice skating at the **Fun Centre** (tel. 441 8000; 2hr., $12, children $7.50; skate hire $3).

NEAR QUEENSTOWN

GLENORCHY

Surrounded by frosty peaks reflected in Lake Wakatipu's azure waters, Glenorchy sits amid a magical setting, 48km north of Queenstown at the head of Lake Wakatipu, where **Fiordland National Park** (see p. 347) and **Mt. Aspiring National Park** (see p. 343) meet. The tiny pastoral community is fueled by sheep stations and summer hikers eager to undertake the **Routeburn Track** (see p. 351) or other celebrated valley walks. Queenstown's hype seems decades away from this diminutive hamlet, which has the dubious honor of housing New Zealand's smallest library (2-person capacity). The slow pace and quiet lifestyle of Glenorchy's 200 inhabitants demonstrate that the Queenstown region harbors more than transient pleasures.

◪ **PRACTICAL INFORMATION. Backpacker Express** (tel. 442 9939) has shuttles to and from Queenstown every couple of hours in summer and once a day in winter ($10). **Dart River Jet Safaris** might provide transport if there's room in the bus ($10, leaves Glenorchy in late afternoon). The **motor camp store** (tel. 442 9939) functions as a **visitors center** and provides limited camping supplies and groceries (open daily 7:30am-10pm, winter M-F 10am-5pm, Sa 10am-4pm, Su 10am-3pm). The **DOC office** (tel. 442 9937) is at the end of Main Rd. (open daily 8:30am-4:30pm, winter M-F 9am-4pm). The **post office** (tel. 442 9913) is in the Mobil station at the end of town (open daily 8am-6pm, winter M-Sa 8am-5pm).

▐▙ **ACCOMMODATIONS AND FOOD.** The old-fashioned **Glenorchy Hotel** (tel. 442 9902 or 0800 453 667; fax 442 9912) on Mull St. is run by a motley crew of happy heartlanders. The small bunkhouse with Oregon woodstove and canary-yellow kitchen is $14; the hotel rooms are more comfortable. Book ahead in summer. (Singles, doubles, and triples $59, with bath $79.) For a more upscale retreat, continue down the road to **Glen-Roydon Lodge** (tel./fax 442 9968), where all rooms have separate bath and showers (singles $60; doubles $70-90). For supreme quiet, go to **Little Paradise Lodge** (tel./fax 442 6196), 28km from Queenstown along Glenorchy Rd. Ask the bus or shuttle to drop you off.

This old homestead lives up to its name. Kayaks and a canoe ($10) are offered at this complete escape where you can go fishing or relax with a BBQ outside on the patio. (24hr. Reception. Ample singles $30-45; doubles $80-105; triples with private bath $110. Cash only.) The **Glenorchy Holiday Park** (tel. 442 7171; fax 442 7172) has bunks ($13) and basic units located next to the stables ($15), as well as tent sites ($8) and powered sites ($9).

Bobby, the chef extraordinaire at the **Glenorchy Hotel,** once served up *gateaux* on one of Her Majesty's royal ships. The Sunday Roast ($9.50) and the Kitchen Sink Burger ($9.50, comes with everything but the plug) are the budget choice. Be sure to save room for desserts—you wouldn't want to miss the melts-in-your-mouth Monkey Nuts ($7.50). (Open daily 7:30am-9pm,winter 7:30am-8pm; bar open daily from 11am.) At the **Glen-Roydon Cafe-Restaurant** (tel. 442 9968), you can choose from quiche ($3.50), nachos ($7.50), or one of the larger pasta dishes ($10-15), as you relax outside on the patio with the mountains rising majestically on three sides (open daily from 8am-10pm; bar open until late).

🎿 **ACTIVITIES.** 🚤**Dart River Jet Safaris** (tel. 442 9992) is a fast-paced foray up the Dart River, past Mt. Earnslaw, and into the heart of Mt. Aspiring National Park. Uniquely designed to travel in just 10cm of water, the jets spin, grind, and fly up the pebbled braids of the Dart River, stopping at the scenic **Routeburn Valley.** On the ride upriver, the drivers explain some of the history and geology of the dramatic mountains and valleys; after a short bush walk and a snack, hop back into the boat and hold on to your seat as your driver whizzes within inches of rocks and tree branches. A unique combination of speed and scenery, the two-and-a-half hour excursion is truly exceptional and worth the price. ($119, children $55, $10 extra from Queenstown; daily 9am, 1pm, and 3pm, winter daily 9am and noon; leaves an hour earlier from Queenstown.) **Fun Yaks** (tel. 442 7374) combines tranquil inflatable canoe rides downstream with jetboating upstream (7hr. total). Wetsuits are included, and the personal crafts allow paddlers to explore an otherwise inaccessible gorge while letting the river do most of the work ($159, children half-price. Departs from Glenorchy at 10am and noon, winter 11am; $10 Queenstown transfers with pickup an hour prior to trip.) **High Country Horses** (tel. 442 9915) and **Dart Stables** (tel. 442 5688 or 0800 474 346), on the road next to the motor park, offer guided and unguided tours from casual saunters to gallops through the breathtaking valleys. Rates range from $35 to $200.

Glenorchy is the gateway to several notable walks with stunning scenery. The **Routeburn Track,** 26km from town (see p. 351), crosses over to the road to Milford. The **Greenstone** and **Caples Tracks** form a loop from the far side of Lake Wakatipu, accessible by car or boat (see p. 343). **Backpacker Express** (tel. 442 9939) runs van and boat shuttles from the Glenorchy Holiday Park to each of the tracks, as well as from Queenstown to Glenorchy (4 per day in summer; $10 per segment; pickup available). Other hikes abound in nearby **Mt. Aspiring National Park** (see p. 343).

ARROWTOWN

William Fox and a small band of miners pulled some 230 pounds of gold from the Arrow River in 1862, precipitating the development of Arrowtown and its satellite towns. The 20km road to Arrowtown curves by mountains, affording excellent views of The Remarkables and Coronet Peak, and by the glassy Lake Hayes with its spectacular reflections of the rustic setting. The region particularly comes to life in April with the brilliant colors of the changing trees and the annual Autumn Festival during which visitors descend on the town for the parade, live music, and street performers. The **Arrow Express** (tel. 442 1900) runs to **Queenstown** from outside the library (3-4 per day, $5). **The Double Decker Bus** (tel. 442 6067) also runs three-hour sightseeing trips from Queenstown to Arrowtown (10am and 2pm, $27).

The **Lakes District Museum** (tel. 442 1824) also serves as a **visitors center** for local information and bookings (open daily 9am-5pm; admission $4, children 50¢). At the other end of Buckingham St. is the historic **Chinese Settlement,** a series of mud-walled huts and signs that give a brief explanation of the former inhabitants and their lifestyle. Several **tracks** for walking and mountain biking depart from the settlement (the museum/visitors center has information on the tracks). The Macetown Road is a rigorous 13km track upriver to another ghost town. A large, half-kilo nugget sits in a case at **The Gold Shop** on Buckingham St. (open daily 8:30am-5pm). The owner will let you hold the valuable nugget (it's worth about $27,000).

If you've caught gold fever and don't want to leave Arrowtown without a little adventure and some gold to boot, you can join up with one of the **Golden Fox Tours** (tel. 442 0029). These 1½hour tours ($20) provide an explanation of the history of the Chinese settlement, followed by some gold panning (tours run Oct.-Apr.; longer tours available; call ahead for reservations).

WANAKA

Wanaka staunchly resists the pressures that would mold it into a second Queenstown. The alpine skiing, summer watersports, and velocity-driven ventures remain pleasantly inconspicuous. With the distant majesty of Mt. Aspiring National Park to the north (see p. 343) and an expansive agricultural valley to the south, the town slopes gently along two main streets to the rubble shores of its pristine lake, with little vacation homes dotting the lakeside.

🛈 PRACTICAL INFORMATION

Visitors Center: Visitor Information (tel. 443 9422), visible from Upper Ardmore St. before you reach the lake on the left-hand side of the road. Includes the **DOC** office. Open M-F 8am-4:45pm; winter M-F 8am-4:45pm, Sa 9:30am-3:45pm. The **Adventure Center,** 99 Ardmore St. (tel. 443 9422), books a variety of summer activities. Open M-F 8:30am-5:30pm, Sa-Su 8:30am-noon.

Buses: InterCity (tel. 0800 INTERC) runs to: **Christchurch** (9½hr., 8:40am, $95) via **Mt. Cook** (3½hr., $57); **Queenstown** (2hr., 2pm, $26); **Franz Josef Glacier** (5½hr., 10:15am, $86) via **Makarora** (1hr., $16), **Haast** (3hr., $38), and **Fox Glacier** (5hr., $64). **Southern Link** (tel. 443 0804) is the quickest and most economical option to **Christchurch,** but it only runs on Tu-Th, and Su from July-Sept. (6½hr., 10:35am, $40). If you're headed south, the Link also runs to **Queenstown** (2hr., 4:20pm, $15) and **Dunedin** (4hr., 1 per day, $30). **Wanaka Connexions** (tel. 0800 879 926) has the most frequent service to **Queenstown,** offering shuttles daily at 7am, 10:30am, and 2:30pm (1½hr., $25, return $40). Running 3 shuttles from Queenstown to Wanaka each day as well, they are your best bet for a daytrip. **Atomic Shuttles** (tel. 443 7885) goes just about anywhere you would want to go, including: **Greymouth** (9hr., 8:50am, $65) via the **West Coast** (Makarora, Haast, Fox and Franz Glaciers, and Hokitika); **Christchurch** (7hr., 2pm, $40); **Dunedin** (5½hr., 2pm, $30); **Invercargill** (4½hr., 2pm, $35); and **Queenstown** (1½hr., 7:30am, $15). Book InterCity or Atomic Shuttle at the YHA or **Paper Place,** 84 Ardmore St. (tel. 443 7885; open daily 7:30am-6pm or 7pm, Sa-Su 7:30am-4pm). Many of these companies charge $5-15 extra to transport skis, snowboards, and mountain bikes.

Ski Shuttles: Since hitchhikers report varied success thumbing it out to the slopes, buses are a more reliable bet. Book a ride to either mountain with **Alpine Shuttles** (tel. 443 7966), **Edgewater Adventures**, 59a Brownston St. (tel. 443 8422), or **The Bus Company** (tel. 443 8775); all provide free pickup and free ski/snowboard transport ($19-22 return; multi-ride and season rates available from all operators). The **Flying Bus** (tel. 443 9193) only runs to Treble Cone, but the $15 per trip rate (for 5+ days) makes it the cheapest show in town.

Car Rental: Aspiring Car Rentals (tel./fax 443 7883), at Wanaka Motor Camp on Upton St. Cars from $65-85 per day, specializing in 4WD vehicles. **Apex Car Rentals** (tel. 0800 531 111) has cars from $39-79 per day (minimum 4 days).

Taxis: Wanaka Taxis (tel. 443 7999) operates late most nights. To the airport is $20.

Hitchhiking: Most hitchhikers head out on Ardmore St. past the DOC office. Rides to Queenstown and toward Christchurch are reportedly feasible for the patient, though getting to the west coast is a more dubious prospect.

Currency Exchange: National Bank, Ardmore St. (tel. 443 7521), and **Westpac Trust,** 15 Helwick St. (tel. 443 7817), have **24hr. ATMs** available. Hours vary slightly, but most banks are open M-F 9am-4:30pm.

Ski Rentals: The cheapest are available from the **Wanaka Sports Centre,** 8 Helwick St. (tel. 443 8094) which offers a recreational ski set (with boots and poles) for just $20 per day. **Good Sports** (tel. 443 7966), on Dunmore St., has students discounts on skis, boots, poles, snowboards, and boots. Rentals on the ski fields are more expensive. Open daily 8am-5pm, winter 7:30am-7:30pm.

Medical Services: Wanaka Medical Centre, 21 Russell St. (24hr. tel. 443 7811). Clinic open M-F 8:30am-6pm. **Wanaka Pharmacy,** Helwick St. (tel. 443 8000 or after-hour mobile 025 487 870). Open M and W-Sa 8:30am-7pm, Tu 9am-7pm, Su 4:30pm-7pm.

Police: 28 Helwick St. (tel. 443 7272).

Post Office: 39 Ardmore St. (tel. 443 8211). Open M-F 8:30am-5:30pm, Sa 9am-noon.

Internet Access: The E-mail Shop, 3 Helwick St., 2nd floor (tel. 443 7429) has a bank of computers, but is often crowded. $10 per hr. Open M-F 9am-9pm, Sa-Su 10am-9pm. The public **library,** 90 Ardmore St. (tel. 443 7297), is another option, also $10 per hr. Open M-Th 10am-5pm, Sa 10:30am-12:30pm.

Telephone Code: 03.

▌ ACCOMMODATIONS

In winter, the long-term ski and snowboard bunnies move in, often filling more than half of the hostel beds for weeks and months at a time; it is essential to book ahead, especially on weekends. **Check-out** is 10am unless otherwise noted.

▨ **The Purple Cow,** 94 Brownston St. (tel. 443 1880; fax 443 1870; email purplecow @xtra.co.nz). It's bright, it's bold, it's restless, and it's hip. The newest hostel in Wanaka is for the young at heart, if not exclusively the young. The porch, pool table, open fires, and spacious TV lounge compensate for the snug kitchen. Sunset views from the deluxe doubles are worth the extra dough. Reception 8am-8:30pm. Dorms $17; twins and doubles $42; deluxe doubles with linens $45.

Holly's Hostel, 71 Upton St. (tel. 443 8187). With gorgeous bathrooms, a free guest phone, and sunny lounge areas, Holly's offers a home-style stay with 2 well-heated levels of simple dorms. Long-term stays not permitted, allowing Holly's to remain a travelers' rest. Reception 8am-6pm. Dorms $16; twins and doubles $36.

Wanaka Bakpaka, 117 Lakeside Rd. (tel./fax 443 7837). From the Visitor Centre, head toward town down Upper Ardmore St., take a right onto Lakeside Rd., and walk 5-10min.; Bakpaka is on the right. The location provides relative seclusion and the views are nice, but the distance may sap your motivation to hit the town at night. Kayak, canoe, and mountain bike rentals. Reception 8:30am-8:30pm, winter 8am-8pm. Linen $3. Dorms $15-16; singles $16; twins $36; doubles $40.

▨ **Temasek House,** 7 Huchan Ln. (tel./fax 443 1288; email temasek.house@xtra.co.nz). Walk 2km along Ardmore St. to the west, take Sargood Dr. to the right, and then a left onto Huchan Ln. to reach this gorgeous guesthouse. Second floor is exclusively for guests, complete with TV lounge, entertainment center, deliciously comfy couches, and heaps of reading material—perfect for a rainy afternoon. Private balconies. Free pickup. Off-street parking. Singles $55; doubles $80, with bath $90; 10% discount on stays of more than 2 nights. Book ahead in summer.

Matterhorn South Backpackers, 56 Brownston St. (tel. 443 1119; fax 443 8379). Walk up Helwick St. from the water, turn left, and it's on the right (poorly marked). Close to the center of town, the few rooms are a *tour de force* in pine. Expect to bunk in close quarters with 6-7 of your closest friends. Motel units are next door. Reception 8:30am-9pm, winter 9am-9pm. Dorms $15; twins and doubles $35, with bath $55.

Wanaka YHA, 181 Upton St. (tel./fax 443 7405). Walk the length of the green with the lake on your right (5-10min. from the center of town), then head up McDougall St. to the left; the YHA is a quick right on Upton St. A quiet place with an adequate kitchen and smoking porch but limited common space. Reception, bunks, bathrooms, and kitchen are located in separate buildings; sneakers required in bathroom. Reception 8-10am and 5-8:30pm. Dorms $16; twins and doubles $36.

Altamont Lodge (tel. 443 8864). More than 2km west out of town along Ardmore St., the Altamont Lodge is best reached by car. The serene moose head above the fireplace regards the ubiquitous pine paneling with mild amusement. The ski-lodge atmosphere pervades, enhanced by the free spa pool, dining room, and ski-tuning room Linen $5. Reception 8am-8pm. Singles $30; doubles $48, extra person $12.

Pleasant Lodge Holiday Park (tel. 443 7360; fax 443 7354), 3km west of the town center along Ardmore St., on Mt. Aspiring Rd. A relatively secluded place for families with spotless rooms, pool, waterslide, volleyball court, playground, and BBQ area. Great views of Mt. Aspiring and the Southern Alps. Linen $5. Reception 8am-9:30pm, winter until 8:30pm. Cabins for 2 $33, extra person $13; tourist flats for 2 $55, extra person $14; spacious motel doubles $80; tent and powered sites $9 per person. Book ahead, especially in summer or the height of ski season.

◑ FOOD

▨ **Kai Whaka Pai** (tel. 443 7795), on the corner of Ardmore and Helwick St., facing the lake. Decadence is an understatement in this small, earthy gourmet bake shop and cafe. The name alone brings a gleeful smile to those recommending it. Enormous and creative sandwiches on foccacia bread; varieties of quiche change daily ($4) and light meals are served all day ($6.50-14.50). The real reward comes to sweet-toothed and hollow-legged patrons with sinfully enormous wedges of pie for just $3.80. Mmmmm, sacrelicious...Open daily 8am-11pm.

Sweet Retreat, 95 Ardmore St. (tel. 443 7669). Sweet Retreat is the perfect place to relax with a heaping sundae ($3.50). There are also gourmet potatoes, overflowing with your choice of three goodies and either chicken, beef, or lamb ($5; all meals under $9). Open daily 7am-10pm, winter until 6 or 7pm.

Relishes Cafe, 99 Ardmore St. (tel. 443 9018). Trendy patrons meet for power lunches or an *apres-ski* pamper. The blackboard menu features burgers ($10.50) for lunch and dinners from $18.50. Vegetarians beware: all mains include either meat or fish. There is an extensive wine list, or BYO, but prepare to pay a $3 corkage fee. Open daily 9:30am-3pm and from 4pm.

Amigos Cafe (tel. 443 7872), on Upper Ardmore St. The owner fries his own tortillas, makes his own salsa, and keeps the margaritas potent and the prices low. Burritos $10.50 and taco salad $10. During Happy Hour (4:30-5:30pm), get a pitcher of frozen contentment ($14) and a giant plate of nachos ($9). Courtyard and balcony dining, or firelit sombrero decor inside. Open daily from noon, winter from 4pm.

The Doughbin Bakery, (tel. 443 7290), on Ardmore St., on the lakefront. A cheap place for pre-slopes takeaway or the 3am munchies, the Doughbin combines long hours and a varied selection with a treasure trove for the truly stingy—the day-old bin (bread $1.50, sticky buns $2 for 6). Shop open daily 7am-6pm, takeaway window 10pm-7am.

Markets: New World (tel. 443 7168), on Donmore St., has complimentary tea and coffee along with tremendous selection. Open daily 8am-8pm.

E.S.PUH-LEEZ Well Virginia, there may be a Santa Claus, but according to Stuart Landsborough, creator and innovator of Puzzling World, psychics are just a figment of the overactive human imagination. And, this self-proclaimed skeptic is willing to put his money where his mouth is: $50,000, to be exact. His challenge, in place since 1995, is open to any and all interested clairvoyants. The task: to psychically divine the location of this hulking check which is buried (along with a lock of Stuart's hair and a third, mystery object) within 200m of the puzzle room. But, as the saying goes, you have to spend money to make money – a no-holds-barred 30min. Q&A session with the puzzle man himself carries with it a hefty $1000 price tag. Since the gauntlet was thrown, two New Zealand madames have put their powers to the test only to go down in flames. With almost four years gone since the last attempt, the skeptic seems smug. Who knows, perhaps the millennium will bring with it a psychic with the power to see her way to the $50,000 jackpot.

■ SIGHTS

Puzzling World (tel. 443 7489), 3km out of town opposite Mt. Iron, is a must-experience. Showcasing the eccentric and celebrating the surprising, this center for the curious infatuates visitors of all ages. Wend your way through the world's first two-story, mind-screwing maze or fiddle with Rubik's Cubes and the like. Whether or not you're still lost in the maze, you may never leave. (Open daily 8:30am-5:30pm. Admission $4, with Great Maze $7; children $3, with Great Maze $4.50). Also not to be missed is **Paradiso Cinema,** 3 Ardmore St. (tel. 443 1531), Wanaka's one-of-a-kind movie theater located in town hall. Arrive early to secure an easy chair and a few scoops of homemade ice cream. The movies change weekly and screen Wednesday to Sunday evenings; all are introduced with a brief humorous live commentary. (Tickets $9, children $6.)

Many of the air-oriented activities are clustered around the airport in the Sky Show Centre. **New Zealand Fighter Pilots Museum** (tel. 443 7011) lauds the men and crafts that flew during the world wars. You can even try your hand at combat fighting in the Flightzone. (Open daily 9am-4pm.) In even-numbered years, the **"Warbirds Over Wanaka"** international airshow attracts vintage planes from every corner of the globe on Easter weekend (tel. 356 0297; www.nzfpm.co.nz.). Transport to the airport (including the Sky Show Centre, Wanaka Transport Museum and Wanaka Beerworks) is available through **Alpine Shuttles** (tel. 443 7966; return $12).

■ ACTIVITIES

SKI FIELDS

Two main ski fields are accessible from Wanaka, each with its own advantages. **Cardrona** (tel. 443 7341), 34km away, is a more family-oriented field, with wide, sunny slopes perfect for learning, and provides money-saving beginner deals. ($58, students $48, children $29). **Treble Cone** (tel. 443 7443), 43km away, has the longest vertical rise in the Southern Lakes and contains more skiable terrain than anywhere else in the South Island. Runs are generally steeper and more difficult than at Cardrona—beginners will have bruised bums among ski bums. (Lift pass $55, students $46, children $27.) Conditions between the ski fields vary. Food is decent but expensive. A trail map is helpful for either ski field, as many runs are poorly marked. An ISIC card is not valid for student deals; another **student ID** is necessary.

WATER ACTIVITIES

Lake Wanaka and the numerous rivers that feed it provide a range of experiences from heart-stopping to pace-slowing. **Deep Canyon Experience** (tel. 443 7922) runs intense canyoning trips daily, which involve abseiling down waterfalls to natural rock waterslides as well as some basic climbing in a full day of vertigo; be sure to bring your swimsuit and sturdy outdoor footwear (Nov.-Mar.; $145, including lunch). **Alpine River Guides** (tel. 443 9422) runs whitewater kayaking trips for both beginning and experienced paddlers on many rivers in the area ($95; all gear provided). Challenging the dominance of whitewater rafting, **Frogz Have More Fun** (tel. 443 9130) claims to have an even more thrilling alternative—sledging. Careening through the rapids on your own personal sledge (a cross between a raft and a kickboard) is the most in-your-face way to conquer the river thus far (Nov.-Apr. 2 per day; 4hr., $75-95 depending on difficulty). Of course, it wouldn't be the Southern Lakes region without a few opportunities to rip through water just a few centimeters deep. **Jet Boat Charters** (tel. 443 8408) shoots up the Matukituki (3½hr., $75) and Clutha (2½hr., $65) rivers through both shallow rapids and deep pools.

Not all watersports in Wanaka are adrenaline-powered. **Lakeland Adventures** (tel. 443 1323), on the wharf, rents everything you need for a calming afternoon on the lake, from kayaks ($8 per hr.) to canoes ($16 per hr.) to motorboats ($60 per hr.) to fishing rods ($12 per day). Fishing gear and one-day fishing licenses are available from **Wanaka Sports Centre**, 8 Helwick St. (tel. 443 8094; license $13). Just slightly more expensive are the guided trout or flyfishing trips. Inquire at the Visitor Centre for a list of local operators, but be prepared to pay at least $200 for a half-day of fishing.

ADVENTURE ACTIVITIES

If you're into breaking wind at 3000 meters with a jumpmaster strapped to your back, **Tandem Skydive Wanaka** (tel. 443 7207) is more than happy to oblige. Their motto, "You call, we fall" is an apt description; keep your head up to see gorgeous lake and mountain views. ($225, YHA, VIP, and students $195. 20min. scenic flight and pickup included.) If you scoff at the word tandem, surrender yourself to **Wanaka Paragliding** (tel. 443 9193). After you've mastered the basics during a full-day course on the grassy slopes of Mt. Iron, you are ready to fly solo ($150). Once you are certified, it's just $15 to soar down any time you like. **Alpine Mountain Biking** (tel. 443 8943) takes the uphill battle out of cycling by transporting riders to some of the country's highest terrain, either by van or helicopter, so they are well-rested and ready to enjoy themselves all the way back down (full day $89, includes bike). Horse treks run daily through **New Zealand Backcountry Saddle Expeditions** (tel. 443 8151), where a two-hour tour costs $45. **Mt. Iron Saddle Adventures** (tel. 443 7777), 4km from Wanaka center, runs two-hour horse treks up Mt. Iron twice a day ($45; must provide own transport).

WALKS

Not just an option for the frugal, tramping opportunities abound around Lake Wanaka and the surrounding mountains and offer some of the best views around. The three-hour return **Diamond Lake Walk** is one of the prettiest short hikes in New Zealand, while the five- to six-hour return tramp up **Mt. Roy** delivers outstanding views of Mt. Aspiring National Park, including glimpses of the Southern Matterhorn itself. Both treks require transport; **Alpine Shuttles** (tel. 443 7966), in the morning, and **Mount Aspiring Express,** at 9:30am and 2:30pm, run daily from October to May (Diamond Lake $10; Mt. Roy $5). Closer to town, beginning 2km down Ardmore St., the **Mt. Iron** loop track (1½hr.) offers beautiful views and a fabulous picnic spot for relatively little effort. Beginning along the south side of the bay, **Waterfall Creek Walk** (return 1½hr.) is a perfect short trip for novice mountain bikers looking for quiet views of Lake Wanaka. As always, the DOC office has up-to-the-minute information on track conditions.

NEAR WANAKA: MAKARORA

With a population that could fit in a school bus, tiny Makarora, on **SH6,** links Haast and southern Westland with Wanaka and the tourism heartland of the southern lakes. Lying near the northern tip of Lake Wanaka and near the scenic Haast Pass, frosty Makarora is often considered a gateway to **Mt. Aspiring National Park** (see p.

343). The **Makarora Visitor Information Centre,** only staffed sporadically, is also the **DOC office** (tel. 443 8365; open daily 8am-4pm, winter M-F 8am-5pm). A number of coaches run through Makarora. **InterCity** departs the information center for **Haast** (1½hr., 11:45am, $27) and **Wanaka** (1hr., 1pm, $17). **Atomic Shuttles** runs to **Wanaka** (1hr., 3:15pm, $10). The **Makarora Tourist Centre** (tel. 443 8372) sells petrol and snacks, serves as a **postal agency,** and runs the motor camp (open daily 8am-8pm, in winter 9am-4:30pm, often closed on weekends). **Wilkin River Jets** (tel. 443 8351) runs jet-boat trips along the rivers of the region. Their main tour, the **Wilkin River Excursion** (1hr.) takes breathless visitors from Makarora to the very edge of the Mt. Aspiring National Park and back; it runs daily on demand ($45, under 13 $20).

MT. ASPIRING NATIONAL PARK

With craggy, snow-covered peaks aspiring ever higher, the 355,543-hectare Mt. Aspiring National Park is at the center of the Te Wahipounamu South West New Zealand World Heritage Area (see p. 21). Of the park's 100-odd glaciers and 13 peaks over 2500m, Mt. Aspiring (3027m) is the perfectly pyramidal pinnacle. With the mellow Greenstone-Caples and lofty Rees-Dart Tracks within its reach, the park attracts a variety of trampers. Decentralized in its administration, Mt. Aspiring National Park is accessible from just about every angle. Most activities, hikes, and scenic flights are run out of the gateway towns of **Wanaka** (see p. 338), **Makarora** (see p. 342), **Glenorchy** (see p. 336), and **Queenstown** (see p. 326). Even far-off **Te Anau** (see p. 357) takes part, as the starting point for Fiordland's and Mt. Aspiring's shared **Routeburn Track** (see p. 351). Each of these towns contains a happy and helpful DOC office.

⚡ GREENSTONE AND CAPLES TRACK

"The Greenstone-Caples?" say fans of this loop track, "Yeah, that was a pretty mellow walk through a couple of cow-filled river valleys." The same is said by non-fans, who crave either loftier heights, greater challenges, or less environmental disturbance. This is a peaceful and pastoral pair of tracks, which undulate underneath impressive mountain peaks. While a tiny corner of the loop lies inside Fiordland National Park, most of it falls within the Wakatipu Recreational Hunting Area (deer season Apr.-Sept.), administered by the Glenorchy DOC office. The DOC only manages the forested areas, however, leaving the grassy valley floors to be grazed by cattle and graced by their pies.

ESSENTIALS

Length: Approximately 50km as a loop (4-5 days).

Trailheads: The two tracks form a loop between Fiordland National Park and the Glenorchy area, which can be entered from the west via the **Divide** (see p. 355), or from the east via the **Greenstone Station** road-end. **Backpacker Express** (tel. 442 9939) runs from the motor park in Glenorchy (see p. 336) across Lake Wakatipu to this road-end (30min.; departs Glenorchy daily Nov.-Apr. 9:30am and 1:30pm; departs trailhead 10am and 2pm; in winter, runs on demand; $10). They have a $15 special for transport between the Routeburn and the Greenstone-Caples within one day, and also connect to Queenstown ($10). **Upper Lake Wakatipu Tours** (tel. 442 9986 or mobile 025 333 481) runs a similar service.

Seasonality: Thick snow cover and a lack of hut wardens make the winter season a bit more challenging than the warmer months, but the track is considered reasonably safe year-round.

Huts and Campsites: Although Glenorchy is the main DOC center for this track, back-country hut tickets can be purchased well-nigh anywhere. All of the huts (except for the tiny, $4 Sly Burn) cost $8 per night year-round, and contain coal stoves, water taps, outhouses, and a weather report; none offer cooking burners. Carbon copies **Mid Caples** and **Mid Greenstone Huts** have two bunkrooms flanking a small, central kitchen room; **Upper Caples** and **McKellar Huts** are identical one-room jobs. Camping is free and easy, permitted at least 50m away from huts, or anywhere within the bush.

Gear: The **Glenorchy DOC** office (see p. 336) sells a small supply of gear, including stoves. The outdoor shops of Te Anau (see p. 357) and Queenstown (see p. 326) have a much wider selection. Chlorine tablets or other water purification measures are crucial, since gut-wrenching giardia (see p. 34) has been detected on the track.

Storage: Most any holiday park or hostel will oblige. For those walking only one of the tracks, **Topline Tours** (tel. 0508 832 628) will transport extra gear between Te Anau and Queenstown.

CAPLES TRACK
Road-end to Mid Caples Hut: 7.5km, 2¾hr.
Road-end to Greenstone-Caples Junction: 30min.

Greenstone-Caples Junction to Mid Caples Hut: 2¼hr.

From the parking area at the end of the road, the track leads to the confluence of the Greenstone and Caples Rivers, plus the junction of their associated tracks. The Caples Track branches off to the right, running alongside the river through beech forest until reaching the swingbridge to **Mid Caples Hut** (12 beds). This nice, two-wing number has great views of field, stream, and faraway peaks.

Mid Caples Hut to Upper Caples Hut: 7km, 2hr.
The track weaves between beech forest and open grassland, with plenty of lovely mountain and river views, before reaching **Upper Caples Hut** (20 beds). The environs here are reasonably scenic, with a grassy field that's good for tenting. The rugged Steele Creek Route is accessible from the hut, or from 20 minutes back up the track. This is a highly unmarked, untrodden, and unforgiving path (8-10hr.) to **Mid Greenstone Hut** (see below).

Upper Caples Hut to Lake McKellar Junction: 7.5km, 3¾hr.
Upper Caples Hut to McKellar Saddle: 2½hr.

McKellar Saddle to Lake McKellar Junction: 1¼hr.

Passing heaps of mosses and filmy ferns, the track ascends steeply but briefly before breaking onto the grasslands of **McKellar Saddle** where more misty mountain vistas emerge. A cute little boardwalk leads past little tarns, and then the track plunges back into the forest. This root-entangled stretch is the steepest on the Greenstone-Caples: strenuous going up, and potentially dangerous going down. At the bottom is a junction at lovely **Lake McKellar.**

Lake McKellar Junction to the Divide: 6km, 1½hr.
Lake McKellar Junction to Greenstone Saddle Campsite: 25min.

Greenstone Saddle Campsite to Lake Howden Hut: 25min.

Lake Howden Hut to the Divide: 40min.

The northbound fork leads past the stream-fed, rocky, and free **Greenstone Saddle Campsite** (toilet, no tap) before joining the Routeburn Track at **Lake Howden Hut** (see p. 353). From here, you can head down to the **Milford Road** (see p. 355), or set off along the Routeburn.

GREENSTONE TRACK
Lake McKellar Junction to Mid Greenstone Hut: 15km, 5½hr.
Lake McKellar Junction to McKellar Hut: 3km, 1hr.

McKellar Hut to Mid Greenstone Hut: 12km, 4½hr.

From the junction, the track follows the lake edge past lichen-encrusted beeches and officially out of Fiordland National Park to **McKellar Hut** (20 beds), a one-roomer in the shadow of McKellar Saddle. Moving on through the usual array of forest, meadow, and cow, the track crosses a swingbridge a half hour shy of **Mid**

Greenstone Hut (12 beds). Besides its great valley view and forested tent sites, this hut boasts a genuine bovine skull on its commode.

Mid Greenstone Hut to road-end: 14.5km, 3¾hr.
  Mid Greenstone Hut to Sly Burn Hut: 5km, 1hr.
  Sly Burn Hut to Greenstone-Caples Junction: 8km, 2¼hr.
  Greenstone-Caples Junction to road-end: 1.5km, 30min.

From the main track, a brief (10min.) detour leads across a stunning gorge to the tiny **Sly Burn Hut** (4 beds) and a grassy field of potential tent sites. This is one end of the **Mavora-Greenstone Walkway** (51km, 4 days), which leads south to an unsealed offshoot of SH94. Back on the Greenstone, it's another undulating riverside stretch back to the Caples junction and the carpark.

⁊ REES-DART TRACK

As grandiose as any Great Walk, the Rees and Dart Tracks form a glorious loop through two river valleys, both lined with living glaciers. The track passes a great diversity of landscapes, including beech forests, subalpine herbfields, grassy flats, and manmade pastures. This is not an unduly easy walk, as many streams are unbridged and much of the path is invisible—poles and cairns make better friends than often misguided footprints. With two stunning daytrip alternatives beyond the main loop, the Rees-Dart richly rewards an increasing flow of trampers.

ESSENTIALS

Length: Approximately 54km (4-5 days), not including side trips.

Trailheads: Both tracks begin at road ends north of **Glenorchy**, and loop around to meet each other at **Dart Hut. Backpacker Express** (tel. 442 9939) runs from Glenorchy (daily in summer 9:30am) to the Rees Track trailhead at Muddy Creek carpark (30min., $10), and in good weather will go all the way up to 25 Mile Hut (1½hr., $20 total). They also serve the Dart Track trailhead at Chinaman's Bluff (1hr., departs Glenorchy 12:30pm, $20), and will pick up as far north as Sandy Bluff via jetboat ($50); few trampers walk all the way down to the Paradise carpark any more. **Upper Lake Wakatipu Tours** (tel. 442 9986 or mobile 025 333 481) has a similar shuttle service, and both operators run between Glenorchy and Queenstown ($10).

Seasonality: During the winter season (May-Nov.), the Rees-Dart goes from merely challenging to patently dangerous. Avalanches and heavy snowfall make the Rees Saddle extremely treacherous, and the Upper Snowy Creek swingbridge is removed, to boot.

Huts and Campsites: The huts below cost $8 per night, except for the 25 Mile Hut ($3). Backcountry hut tickets can be purchased from the nearby DOC office in Glenorchy or other DOC offices. Huts vary in size and swankiness, but all include some manner of heating, taps, and toilets; none have cooking stoves. Camping is free in the forests and grassy flats, and discouraged in areas of subalpine vegetation.

Gear and Storage: See **Greenstone and Caples Track: Essentials,** p. 343.

REES TRACK

Muddy Creek carpark to 25 Mile Hut: 6km, 2¼hr.
This stretch of the Rees Valley, often skippable by shuttle, can make for swampy walking along lightly marked track. The mountain peaks are an imposing sight, but they only get better from here. The grungy but character-laden **25 Mile Hut** (6 beds), maintained by the Otago Tramping and Mountaineering Club as a base camp for Mt. Earnslaw, has six well-loved bunks and a great stone hearth.

25 Mile Hut to Shelter Rock Hut: 9.5km, 4¼hr.
Lovely Lennox Falls quickly come into view across the valley; about two hours later, a swingbridge leads into Mt. Aspiring National Park proper, where everything's coming up mosses. After winding in and out of beech forest and grassy slip

sites, the track reaches **Shelter Rock Hut** (20 beds), a snazzy two-building abode with mountains all around.

Shelter Rock Hut to Dart Hut: 8km, 5hr.
  Shelter Rock Hut to Rees Saddle: 4km, 3hr.
  Rees Saddle to Dart Hut: 4km, 2hr.

This is the loop's most challenging stretch, with steep inclines and non-obvious markings. The track climbs steadily through alpine vegetation, until it hugs a bluff for the extremely steep (but brief) ascent to the **Rees Saddle.** It's possible to wander widely atop the saddle, soaking in the superb sight of abundant glaciers, tiny tarns, and knife-edged arretes all over the place. The main track makes a tricky descent through even more diverse plant zones before hitting a cozy campsite. Just across Snowy Creek is **Dart Hut** (20 beds), with three rooms, a central stove, and a separate bank of flush toilets.

Dart Hut to Cascade Saddle: 8km, 5hr. (one-way).
Dart Hut serves as a popular base for daytrips up to spectacular Cascade Saddle, and during any stretch of crummy weather, it can overflow with anxious, view-hungry trampers awaiting the sun. The track to the saddle begins back across Snowy Creek at the campsite, and is extremely easy to lose. As one follows the Dart River upstream, it disappears into a gray and terminal moraine (mass of debris), which then gives way to the exposed ice of the Dart Glacier itself. The track then leads along the lateral moraine from 1850, high above the glacier's current melted level, and then it climbs steadily to the prize: **Cascade Saddle.** On the far side, Cascade Creek roars into the beech-clothed Matukituki Valley, while snowy Mt. Aspiring towers in the distance; on the other side, the Dart Glacier tumbles down blue icefalls from an amphitheater of rock. It's possible to camp on the saddle, though whipping winds and destructive kea threaten tent integrity.

DART TRACK
Dart Hut to Daleys Flat Hut: 15.5km, 5¾hr.
  Dart Hut to Whitbourn Valley junction: 1.5km, 30min.
  Whitbourn Valley Junction to Whitbourn Glacier: 5km, 4hr. (one-way)
  Whitbourn Valley Junction to Daleys Flat Hut: 14km, 5¼hr.

From the main track, a relatively seldom-traveled spur leads across some difficult and beautiful country to the **Whitbourn Glacier.** Half an hour past Dart Hut, this spur drops steeply to the Dart River, crosses a swingbridge, and scrambles through some grass and forest to some thick subalpine scrub. You can't see the track through the shrubs, but fortunately they make great handholds. Eventually, the track hits open flats, where a profusion of tiny plants spreads alongside the frothing Whitbourn River. Snowfields and waterfalls ring the lonely valley, which leads right up to the gritty snout of the Whitbourn Glacier itself. Meanwhile, the main track becomes less strenuous across the wide Cattle Flat, where grassy terraces are framed by still more legions of glaciers. **Daleys Flat Hut** (20 beds) is very spacious, with an idyllic riverside setting marred only by abundant sandflies.

Daleys Flat Hut to Chinaman's Bluff: 14.5km, 4hr.
  Daleys Flat Hut to Sandy Bluff: 4.5km, 1½hr.
  Sandy Bluff to Chinaman's Bluff: 10km, 2½hr.

From the hut, it takes about an hour to reach some small and sandy bluffs that are *not* **Sandy Bluff.** The real McCoy involves scaling a short ladder, and signs for the jetboat pickup. From here on out, said jetboats zoom along the otherwise tranquil river, as the track runs up and over **Chinaman's Bluff,** beyond which lies the road.

THE MATUKITUKI VALLEY
The east and west branches of the Matukituki offer the closest views of Mt. Aspiring itself. Fantails and tomtits abound in the Southern beech forests of the valleys,

while tussock grasses, rocky bluffs, and alpine tarn reward those who venture farther ahead. **Aspiring Hut** (one-way 2½hr.; $16) makes a good base for daytrips along the many tracks branching off into subalpine wilderness. With views of snowfields, glaciers, sheer rock cliffs, and waterfalls, the tramp up **Rob Roy Valley** (1½hr.) is particularly rewarding, as is the spectacular outlook from **Cascade Saddle** (5hr. from Aspiring Hut). Hut passes for NZAC/DOC huts must be purchased in advance at the DOC office in Wanaka. **Mt. Aspiring Express** (tel. 443 8422) and **Alpine Adventure Shuttles** (tel. 443 7966) run daily at 9:30am in summer from Wanaka to Raspberry Hut ($25). **Good Sports** (tel. 443 7966) on Dunmore St. rents tramping gear (sleeping bag $7.50 per day, ice axe $5 per day).

FIORDLAND NATIONAL PARK

A great, glacier-scoured valley, green with beech trees and filled with waterfalls spilling into the sea—this is Fiordland, New Zealand's largest national park. From the grand sightseer's magnet of Milford Sound down to the wild southern coast, this wet and living wilderness is criss-crossed by over 500km of trails, including three Great Walks, and is part of the renowned Te Wahipounamu World Heritage Area. Fiordland's precipitation seldom ceases: it rains 200 days of the year. The winter brings frequent avalanches, and even the thickly interwoven beech trees are known to roll down mountainsides. Ageless power and natural grandeur unfold along the roadsides and speak from deep within the park's wild heart.

⚡ ORIENTATION AND PRACTICAL INFORMATION

The National Park encloses the southwest corner of the country, with the fjord-studded coastline forming the western edge, and roads running alongside much of the eastern border. **Te Anau** (see p. 357) is by far the most convenient and developed tourist center, with the only **banks and ATMs** in the region. From here, the **Milford Road** (see p. 355) heads north to the tour bus pilgrimage site of **Milford Sound** (see p. 355), while the highway leads south to the sleepy towns of **Manapouri** (see p. 359), and **Tuatapere** (see p. 382). Fiordland's **DOC Visitor Centre** (tel. 249 7921; fax 249 7613; email fiordlandvc@doc.govt.nz) is on the lakefront in Te Anau, and comes equipped with a crack staff, small museum, audio-visual shows, and the **Great Walks Booking Desk** (see p. 357). From late December through most of January, DOC officers offer the **Te Anau Summer Visitor Programme**, a full schedule of evening talks and guided walks on themes as diverse as jadeworking and takahe conservation. (Visitor Centre open daily Feb. 1-28 8am-6pm, Mar. 1-Apr.23 8am-5pm, Apr. 24-Oct.23 9am-4:30pm, Oct. 24-Dec. 24 8am-6pm, Dec. 25 9am-1pm, Dec. 26-Jan. 31 8am-8pm.) The DOC also provides **secure parking. Telephone Code:** 03.

SEASONALITY

February and March bring the best hope for optimal weather conditions; March is the best month for both solitude and sunshine. In the off season (late Apr.-Oct.), the Milford, Routeburn, and Kepler tracks lose their celebrated Great Walk status and use regular track and hut passes. This is because winter conditions in the Fiordland backcountry are an avalanche-intensive, life-endangering, comfort-free crucible. If you're experienced enough to brave the storm, you deserve cheap digs.

GEAR AND STORAGE

To enjoy the splendor of Fiordland, one must be prepared to battle against the dual tramping demons of sandflies and torrential rain. The DOC sells indispensable, heavy-duty **plastic pack liners** to keep gear dry. As for sandflies, see p. 348 for mythology and p. 45 for preventive measures. Most hiking equipment can be rented from **Bev's Tramping Gear Hire,** 16 Homer St., Te Anau (tel. 249 7389; open daily 9am-1pm and 5-7pm, winter on demand). The **Great Walks package** includes everything an entirely unprepared tramper could need (3-4 days, $75). **Te Anau Sports World** (tel. 249 8195), in the town center, has a more limited selection (open daily 9am-9pm, in winter M-F 9am-6pm). The cheapest place for groceries is the **Supervalue** in the center of town (open M-F 8am-8pm, Sa 10am-7pm, Su 10am-6pm). Extra luggage can be left at the **Te Anau Motor Lodge** ($1-2).

SHOO FLY Captain Cook called it "the most mischievous animal" his crew had ever encountered. Maori legend recounts that Hinenuitepo, Goddess of the Underworld, thought people might be tempted to stay forever in the beauty of Fiordland, and so created the sandfly to keep them away. Rumor has it that for every sandfly you kill, 1000 more are born. No matter what you believe, sandflies are a hard fact of life in Fiordland, and their bite is fierce. They breed in moving water and are numerous near streams and lakes, but can also be found above the tree line in the alpine meadows. At night, the price of camping in the resplendence of Fiordland is eternal vigilance against sandflies in your tent. The keys to survival and maintaining sanity are insect repellent and protective clothing. Make a preemptive strike against the bloodthirsty enemy by slathering on repellent with a high percentage of active ingredient, and be prepared for multiple applications. Unlike mosquitoes, sandflies cannot bite through clothing, so even very light layers are an effective deterrent. In areas heavy with sandflies, tuck your pants into your socks; trampers' legs and feet are especially attractive to the ground-hugging swarms.

⚔ ACTIVITIES

Beyond the Great Walks are many of Fiordland's less-traveled and more challenging outdoor options. The **Hollyford Track** (56km, 4 days one-way) starts at the Lower Hollyford road-end off the Milford Road (see p. 355), and penetrates lush lowland forest before reaching the sea at Martin's Bay. The route's low altitude makes it less vista-filled than other tracks, but far safer to walk in the wintertime. **Fiordland Tracknet** (tel. 249 7777) runs on demand to the roadside trailhead ($30). As for the **Dusky Track** (84km, 8-12 days), this is an extremely rigor-filled route, where downpours and whiteouts can strand trampers for days at a time, if they aren't already up to their armpits in mud. The Dusky's popularity is growing though, thanks to a strange brew of masochism, glorious mountain vista-payoffs, and unrealistic expectations. To hike the Dusky safely, you really need an emergency radio, a party of at least four, surplus food, and ample experience. **Fiordland Travel** (tel. 249 6602 or 0800 656 502) picks up trampers at the track's northern trailhead at Lake Manapouri ($25), while **Lake Hauroko Tours** (tel. 226 6681) does the same for the southern end. **Waterwings Airways** (tel. 249 7405) in Te Anau flies in and out of **Supper Cove** (one-way $148), a hard-core detour by the sea. Huts along the Hollyfield and the Dusky cost $4 per night year-round; they have tank water and toilets, but no cooking stoves. All nature-ragin' routes aside, a number of lovely little Fiordland daywalks and other outdoor excursions are described within coverage of Te Anau (see p. 357), Manapouri (see p. 359), the Milford Road (see p. 355), and Tuatapere (see p. 382).

🥾 MILFORD TRACK

New Zealand's Holy Grail of hiking, the astounding Milford Track was blazed in 1888 and rendered world-famous soon afterward. "The finest walk in the world!" gushed obscure but oft-quoted Victorian poet Blanche Baughan in a London paper. Over a century of wide-eyed walkers have tread the Milford's beech-clad glacial valleys, laced with waterfalls both ephemeral and enormous—a corner of Fiordland in all its glory. Despite the high cost, tight regulation, and frequent downpours of rain and even avalanche, this track remains a singular experience in most trampers' memories.

Milford and Routeburn Tracks

HUTS/CAMPSITES

A Glade House
B Clinton Hut
C Clinton Forks Hut
D Mintaro Hut
E Quintin Hut
F Dumpling Hut
G Boatshed Hut
H Milford Lodge Hut
J Howden Hut
K MacKenzie Hut
  MacKenzie
  Campsite
L Routeburn Flats Hut
M Routeburn Falls Hut

SOUTH ISLAND

Labels on map:

Rees R.
Paradise
Glenorchy
Lake Wakatipu
Greenstone Station Rd.
Kinloch
Elfin Bay
Tooth Peak
Routeburn
START
Routeburn Shelter
MT. ASPIRING NATIONAL PARK
Caples Track
Caples R.
Emily Peak
L. MacKenzie
The Orchard
Earland Falls
Greenstone Track
Greenstone R.
Routeburn Falls
Routeburn Track
L. Howden
Conical Hill
Harris Saddle
Hollyford Track
Hollyford R.
Hollyford
L. Marian
L. Christina
Mt. Christina
Key Summit
FINISH
The Divide
Falls Creek
Lake Gunn
Cascade Creek
David Peaks
94
Knobs Flat
Homer Tunnel
EARL MOUNTAINS
94
TO ENGLINTON VALLEY AND TE ANAU (55 km)
The Chasm
Cleddau R.
Milford Sound
Stirling Falls
Milford Sound
Mitre Peak
Sandfly Point Shelter
FINISH
Mt. Ada
Great Gate Falls
Mackay Falls
Arthur R.
Sutherland Falls
Mt. Balloon
Mackinnon Pass
L. Mintaro
Mt. Anau
Clinton R.
START
Hirere Shelter
Milford Track
FIORDLAND NATIONAL PARK
N
4 miles
4 kilometers
0

ESSENTIALS

Length: 54km (4 days).

Reservations: Unlike any other track in New Zealand, the Milford is entirely scripted: you must have a reservation, and you must stay in a designated hut on each of three nights. Day hiking is permitted, but you will not be able to reach the best scenery in such a short time. **Milford Track Guided Walks** (tel. 249 7690 or 0800 659 255; email mtinfo@milfordtrack.co.nz) charges $1600 a head for the privilege of porters, cooks, and hot showers in upscale accommodations. Meanwhile, the DOC allows 40 unguided trampers on the track each night, and the following descriptions of the track are provided for these independent walkers. **Applications** to walk the Milford are first come, first served, starting **July 1** for the following summer. Contact the DOC **Great Walks Booking Desk,** P.O. Box 29, Te Anau (tel. 249 8514; fax 249 8515; email greatwalks-booking@doc.govt.nz; open May-Nov. M-F 9am-noon and 1-4:30pm, Nov.-Apr. daily 8:30am-5pm) for a complete application, or simply furnish the DOC with your party size, at least three possible departure dates, credit card number, and contact information. The summer season lasts between late October and late April; December and January fill up fast, while October and November aren't nearly so chocka. There's also a **waiting list,** and the DOC will alert the freshly eligible by fax or email; couples and solo trampers have the best chances. The **hut pass** ($90, ages 10-14 $45) must be collected at the booking desk, the **Fiordland National Park Visitor Centre** in Te Anau (p. 357), by 11am on the first day's tramping. Optimistic, fly-by-night types can otherwise show up at 11am with their gear at the ready, in the hopes that unclaimed passes become available. Anarchistic, devil-may-care types camp or squat without authorization, and rack up **fines** of up to $500.

Trailheads and Transportation: Transportation costs for the track run high, since the Milford's trailheads aren't road-accessible: from a wharf at the northern tip of Lake Te Anau, the track extends to another dock at Sandfly Point and Milford Sound. **Mt. Cook** (tel. 249 7516) runs coaches north from Te Anau to the boat launch at **Te Anau Downs** (20min.; 9:30am and 1:15pm; $11, children $7) connecting to the boat run by **Fiordland Travel** (tel. 249 7416) that heads to the track's starting point (10:15am, $28). The afternoon boat is more expensive (2pm, $41), to encourage segregation of haves and have-nots. Return on the boat (2pm and 3pm) from Sandfly Point to **Milford launch terminal** (20min.; $22, children $12.50), and then catch the 3pm or 5pm Mt. Cook bus to **Te Anau** (2hr., $36). The DOC's **Great Walks Booking Desk** (see above) will directly arrange this particular boat and coach; for other options on the Milford Road, see p. 355. From Sandfly Point, you can also arrange a leisure paddle to Milford Sound with **Rosco's Sea Kayaks** (tel. 249 8840 or 0800 476 726; 2pm; $19). **Hitchers** try to catch rides the day before they start hiking in order to make the early boat the following morning. An interesting sail-hike-paddle-coach round-trip from Te Anau ($99) is available through **Rosco's** and **Sinbad Cruises** (tel. 249 7106). **Fiordland Tracknet** (tel. 249 7777) shuttles extra gear from Te Anau to Milford Sound ($3-5).

Huts: Tenting is not permitted on the Milford. There are 6 huts on the Milford: 3 for the propertied guided walkers, each located about an hour behind the 3 for independent walker-proles. Even these lower-budget huts are pricey ($90 total) and palatial, with spacious common areas, swanky flush toilet annexes, and several gas cookers. Each independent hut also comes with its own lovable and eccentric DOC warden, many of whom can be persuaded to give evening interpretive talks. During the winter season (late Apr.-Oct.), out come the wardens, the gas, and several bridges, and the fees revert to the backcountry hut system ($4 per night).

THE TRACK

Lake Te Anau dock to Clinton Hut: 3.5km, 1¼hr.

The first day out is the shortest and the easiest, passing through tall and slender beech trees, with an occasional totara. About 10 minutes shy of the hut is a brief **Wetlands Walk** (return 10min.), a nice little detour for spongy moss, carnivorous sundews, and the track's first Nice View. **Clinton Hut** is a corrugated outdoor mansion, with the clear Clinton River nearby. Those on the morning boat will probably reach the hut very early in the afternoon.

Clinton Hut to Mintaro Hut: 18km, 5hr.

The second day involves flat and slightly inclined tramping up the Clinton River Valley to just below MacKinnon Pass. After passing a flattened landslide site from 1982, the track begins to wind through open stretches, giving views of massive cliff faces towering over both sides of the river valley. Thin ribbons of water course down the bare rock, forming cataracts hundreds of meters long. A new view of a waterfall, mountaintop, snowfield, or glacier awaits around every corner of this stretch. After passing the small **bus stop** rain shelter and upon approaching Mintaro Hut, the track gets rougher and steeper. **Mintaro Hut** has three separate bunkrooms and a prime location: step out of the front door, and you could strain your neck looking up at the 800m sheer rock face that towers above the small **Lake Mintaro.** Access to the lake is 100m past the hut turn-off on the main track.

Mintaro Hut to Dumpling Hut: 14km, 5hr.

Mintaro Hut to Mackinnon Pass Shelter: 2hr.

Mackinnon Pass Shelter to Quinton Hut: 2hr.

Quinton Hut to Dumpling Hut: 1hr.

Day three is the most taxing and the most incredible, given clear skies. Immediately after departing Mintaro Hut, the track ascends several switchbacks to **MacKinnon Pass,** where the spectacular scenery makes tired legs an afterthought. Vast glacial valleys spread with green grandeur in either direction, while kea circle overhead. The **MacKinnon Pass Shelter** is a cheerless but safe place, with a stellar southern exposure. Heading back down, the track winds beneath a cliff face topped by the **Jervois Glacier,** whose wispy waterfalls blow away into mist before reaching the ground, swirling in fantastic shapes and patterns in the air. Once the track enters the trees, the magnificent mountain scenery is replaced by a powerful series of waterfalls, as the **Arthur River** begins its journey to the sea. At **Quinton Hut,** the next guided walkers' hut, there's a wee rainproof room where independent trampers can seek shelter and perhaps snarf some gourmet table scraps left by sympathetic employees. From here, a spur trail (one-way 30min.) leads to the base of the monstrous, three-tiered, 580m **Sutherland Falls,** the highest waterfall in New Zealand and the fifth highest in the world. At its base, the crash of water into water blows out a circle of mist that rapidly drenches anyone within 10m, much less than those who venture behind the torrent. The boardwalked section of track before the backcountry manor of **Dumpling Hut** hosts hundreds of glow-worms.

Dumpling Hut to Sandfly Point: 18km, 5hr.

Dumpling Hut to Boatshed Shelter: 1½hr.

Boatshed Shelter to Great Gate Shelter: 2¼hr.

Great Gate Shelter to Sandfly Point: 1¼hr.

The final day's flat tramping passes the toilets and taps of the **Boatshed Shelter** before reaching second-fiddle **Mackay Falls** and the strangely resonant **Bell Rock.** The simple shelter near **Great Gate Falls** makes a good lunch stop; from here, the track passes splendid valley views and glimpses of the stump-filled Lake Ada as it nears **Sandfly Point.** Here an enclosed shelter protects trampers from the point's namesake as they await transport to Milford Sound.

⁊ ROUTEBURN TRACK

Lying half within Fiordland National Park and half within Mt. Aspiring National Park (see p. 343), the Routeburn Track is the shortest of the Great Walks, and among the most spectacular. A razor-sharp bushline slices across these mountains, and the track delves through either side, passing thick forests and intricate herb fields. And then there are the vistas, at least on clear days: valley views, mountain views, glacier views, and even a far-away seascape. Although the Routeburn Track may receive second billing after the Milford, it's an arbitrary skirmish between superlatives.

ESSENTIALS

Length: 32km (2-4 days).

Reservations: The **Great Walks Booking Desk** (tel. 249 8514; email greatwalksbooking@doc.govt.nz) handles reservations. In contrast to the Milford Track, the Routeburn system is far less rigid and booked-out. You choose the direction and duration of your tramp, and the DOC often offers a 50% discount on a third night's stay in the Howden or Routeburn Flats Hut. The more popular Mackenzie and Routeburn Falls Huts seldom fill up more than a week or so in advance, and if they do, the DOC staff in Te Anau, Glenorchy, or Queenstown will happily stick you into the next available space. Hut and tent passes must be picked up from one of these offices by 2pm on your starting date. Squatter fines reach $50.

Trailheads: The Mt. Aspiring side of the track begins at **Routeburn Shelter,** 24km north of Glenorchy and 75km road trail from Queenstown. The Fiordland side begins at **The Divide** on the Milford Road, 84km north of Te Anau. As for the Mt. Aspiring end, both **Backpacker Express** (tel. 442 9939) and **Upper Lake Wakatipu Tours** (tel. 442 9986 or mobile 025 333 481) run between the Routeburn Shelter and Glenorchy ($10) or Queenstown ($20 total), with 2-3 runs per day. **Topline Tours** (tel. 249 8059 or 0508 832 628) will transport **extra gear** from hostel to hostel between Te Anau (tel. 249 7505) and Queenstown (tel. 442 8178) for $3-5 per bag (leaves Te Anau at 10am, Queenstown at 2pm). Hitchers are said to meet with hard luck 'round these parts.

Huts and Campsites: The Routeburn's 4 huts range from comfortable to downright cushy, not including the guided walker accommodations. During the summer season (late Oct.-late Apr.), all have plenty of gas cookers, taps, and flush toilets, and cost $30 per night (ages 5-14 $15). There is a 20% discount on hut passes for October, November, and April. In winter, when wardens and gas are removed, the fees revert to the backcountry hut ticket system (Routeburn Falls and Routeburn Flats $8, Lake Howden and Lake Mackenzie $4). The track's 2 official campsites cost $9 (ages 5-14 $4.50) during the summer season; they have cooking shelters, but no stoves.

THE TRACK

Routeburn Shelter to Routeburn Falls Hut: 8.8km, 2¼hr.

Routeburn Shelter to Routeburn Flats Hut and Campsite: 6.5km, 1½hr.

Routeburn Flats Hut and Campsite to Routeburn Falls Hut: 2.3km, 45min.

The track begins 200m up the road from the **Routeburn Shelter,** a primitive shelter with toilets; camping and overnight stays are not permitted. A gradual ascent past many mighty blue rivers and landslides leads to a turn-off (one-way 5min.) for the small, serviceable **Routeburn Flats Hut** (20 beds). The 50-odd campsites are beautiful and secluded among tall grasses, well away from the hut. Back on the main track, the trail ascends through the ferned and forested flanks of the Routeburn valley's southern side. Just at the edge of the treeline is **Routeburn Falls Hut** (48 beds), a wood-panelled palace, with snazzy furniture, a separate bunkroom, and a grand balcony overlooking the valley.

Routeburn Falls Hut To Lake Mackenzie Hut: 11.3km, 4½hr.

Routeburn Falls Hut to Harris Saddle Shelter: 1¼hr.

Harris Saddle Shelter to Lake Mackenzie Hut: 3¼hr.

This is the Routeburn's awesome alpine stretch. The track is initially very steep and strewn with large rocks, making for dubious footing (although many of the rocks are a psychedelic purple or pink, so watching where you put your feet isn't all boring). **Lake Harris** fills a beautiful basin surrounded with moss-encrusted mountains and fed by two waterfalls. The sleek trapezoid of **Harris Saddle Shelter** contains toilets, emergency equipment, and tasty-looking food for the guided walkers. From the shelter, a very steep and poorly-marked side trip leads to the top of **Conical Hill,** where on a clear day the 360° panorama encompasses exhilarating views of crinkly ridges, unnamed glaciers, and green valleys stretching as far as the Tasman Sea. The main track sidles along the mountainside above the **Hollyford Valley** and gradually descends, offering more excellent views of the rocky tops and forested flanks across the valley. Once **Lake MacKenzie** comes into sight, the trail drops steeply to **Lake MacKenzie Hut** (48 beds), another grand hotel of a backcountry abode. Superlative views up the lake to **Emily Peak** are right outside, not unlike the flock of kea that has taken up residence. **MacKenzie Campground** is 100m farther along the trail, with nine nice sites ringed by green trees.

Lake Mackenzie Hut to Lake Howden Hut: 12km, 3¾hr.
Lake Mackenzie Hut to Lake Howden Hut: 8.6km, 2¾hr.
Lake Howden Hut to the Divide: 3.4km, 1hr.

Back below the bushline, the track makes a brief but wicked ascent before passing some lovely mountain vistas. It then weaves through the naturally pastoral **Orchard,** a patch of pioneering ribbonwood trees, and passes the thundering 80m **Earland Falls.** Roomy **Lake Howden Hut** (28 beds) is on the shores of the lake; the junction for the **Greenstone Track** is right outside. A 20-minute hike along the Greenstone leads to 15 *free campsites* with a toilet but no shelter or water. From the Lake Howden junction, the track ascends briefly to the turn-off for **Key Summit** (return 1hr.), a popular day-hike. A self-guided nature walk up top provides a nice crash-course in high-altitude botany and glacial geology; meanwhile, vast views extend in every direction. The main track drops steeply in numerous switchbacks before reaching the **Divide,** where there are toilets and shelter.

⁊ KEPLER TRACK

Initially opened in 1988 to relieve pressure on the Milford and Routeburn Tracks, the Kepler Track more than holds its own. Not only does this track pass breathtaking ridgetops and ancient beech forests, but it's the most accessible Great Walk in the system: you can set out on foot from the middle of Te Anau, without any transportation costs or reservations, and loop right back a few amazing days later.

ESSENTIALS

Length: 67km (2-3 days), not including the stretch from the DOC to the Control Gates.

Reservations: Neither required nor possible.

Trailheads: The track forms a loop, beginning and ending at the **Control Gates** at the southern end of Lake Te Anau. The Control Gates can be reached from the DOC center (see p. 357) via a brief (45-60min.) and uneventful track. Most trampers walk the Kepler in a counterclockwise direction, though the only real constraint is trying to time the initial section of the track on exposed mountaintop for good weather. **Fiordland Tracknet** (tel. 249 7777) runs a shuttle directly from **Te Anau Holiday Park** (see p. 358) to the **Control Gates** ($5) and to **Rainbow Reach** ($8), the two places where the track meets the road (10-15min.; departs 8:30am, 9:30am, 2:45pm, and 4:45pm in summer; pickup from Rainbow Reach at 10am, 3pm, and 5pm). **Sinbad Cruises** (tel. 249 7106 or mobile 025 408 080) makes a shortcut between Te Anau and Brod Bay, departing daily year-round at 9am and 10:30am; **Lakeland Boat Hire** (tel. 249 8364) does the same, departing at 8:30am and 9:30am (both companies one-way $15, same-day return $25).

Huts and Campsites: The Kepler's huts tend toward the swanky and spacious, with gas cookers and live-in wardens during the summer season ($15 per night); tent site quality varies as noted ($6). In winter, when gas and wardens are removed, the bereft huts cost one backcountry hut ticket ($4 per night).

THE TRACK
Control Gates to Brod Bay Campsite: 5.6km, 1¼hr.

From the Control Gates, which regulate the level of Lake Te Anau for the greater glory of hydroelectric power, the track sidles easily into sandy and swim-worthy **Dock Bay**. Farther along the lakeshore, the long beach of **Brod Bay** has a toilet, several sheltered campsites, and limited water options.

Brod Bay Campsite to Mt. Luxmore Hut: 8.5km, 3hr.

The track climbs a steady series of switchbacks past great limestone, bluffs (remnants of an ancient sea floor), through a lichenologist's paradise of thick-trunked beech trees, and suddenly breaks out into golden alpine tussocks with views all around. Soon after arises **Mt. Luxmore Hut** (60 beds), a veritable mountain chalet with perhaps the best location of any hut in the Great Walk system. The South Fiord of Lake Te Anau and the Hidden Lakes sparkle far below, while in the distance hulk the Murchison Mountains, last natural habitat of the fantastical takahe. The hut's famous and long-serving warden has meanwhile plastered the walls with flower photos and pressed leaf specimens. Nearby are the spooky, formation-filled **Luxmore Caves,** where at least two flashlights per person are the wisest bet. Mt. Luxmore makes a fine day-hike destination, and provides an ideal place for hanging back when inclement weather bashes the next stretch.

Mt. Luxmore Hut to Iris Burn Hut: 18.6km, 5hr.

Mt. Luxmore Hut to Forest Burn Shelter: 8.3km, 1½hr.

Forest Burn Shelter to Hanging Valley Shelter: 4.5km, 1¾hr.

Hanging Valley Shelter to Iris Burn Hut: 5.8km, 1¾hr.

This is the astounding alpine part. The track ascends steeply for about an hour until a point immediately below the summit of **Mt. Luxmore** (1471m). A 10-minute scramble brings you to the top for a 360° panoramic view of the region, with knife-edged arretes spreading out everywhere. The main track descends to **Forest Burn Shelter,** a spare affair with avalanche equipment and a rainwater barrel. **Hanging Valley Shelter** is much the same, but getting there's the prize: the track follows the crest of several hump-shaped ridges, where fair weather brings awe-inducing mountain views, and foul weather brings dangerously wicked winds. Next comes the extremely steep, 40-switchback plunge back into enormous beeches. Along the way is a worthwhile lookout (return 5min.) over a full panorama of hanging valleys and green promontories. **Iris Burn Hut** (60 beds) is somewhat cramped, with serviceable tent sites about 200m away. From the hut, a side trip leads to the 10m **Iris Burn Waterfall** (return 45min.).

Iris Burn Hut to Moturau Hut: 17.2km, 4½hr.

The track briefly ascends past the hut, before opening into the **Big Slip,** a testament to Too Much of a Good Thing. Here, in 1984, heavy rains sent a nice-sized chunk of mountain screaming down, obliterating the local tree population. Back in the intact forest, the track provides a reasonably level walk to **Moturau Hut** (40 beds) by the shores of Lake Manapouri with a large communal area, a spiral staircase, and great sunsets.

Moturau Hut to Rainbow Reach: 6.2km, 1¼hr.

Moturau Hut to Shallow Bay junction: 30min.

Shallow Bay junction to Shallow Bay Hut: 15min.

Shallow Bay Hut to Rainbow Reach: 45min.

After Moturau Hut comes a turn-off for **Shallow Bay Hut** (6 beds), a small and unserviced room with a dunny (toilet) out the back and a whole shore's worth of free camping just outside. This hut is not part of the Great Walks system, and is thus cheap ($4). From the turn-off, the Kepler proper winds through bogland, crosses the **Forest Burn River,** and then reaches the swing bridge that leads to Rainbow Reach and its accompanying shuttles.

Rainbow Reach to the Control Gates: 10.9km, 2½hr.
This seldom-traveled stretch closes the loop back to the Control Gates, hugging Fiordland's forested border and promising a good chance to see parakeets.

THE MILFORD ROAD

Half the Milford Sound experience is getting there. From Te Anau to the sound, the 119km Milford Road climbs through Fiordland National Park past staggeringly beautiful valleys, lakes, and creeks. Pick up a guide to sights for $1 at the DOC office; Fiordland Travel has a less extensive guide for free. In winter, definitely stop at the DOC office in Te Anau to see if the road is even passable, or if tire chains are required (chains can be rented locally for about $25; when required, vehicles without them are subject to fines). After all, the stretch of road near the **Homer Tunnel** is the most avalanche-prone piece of highway on earth—an average of one avalanche per day in winter keeps a full-time clearing crew stationed near the tunnel. **Te Anau** provides the only reliable services for Milford Sound and the road. Several tour operators clog the length of the road on their way to and from Milford Sound (see below for details). There are many **DOC camping sites** along the route ($4). From Te Anau, the road runs alongside Lake Te Anau through sheep stations before entering the red and silver beech forest of Fiordland National Park. Traversing the classic glacial U-shaped **Eglinton Valley,** the road runs through expanses of golden grassland, and past rocky creeks, with the Earl and Livingstone Ranges providing impressive backdrops. Stop at **Mirror Lakes** to reflect on the tussocked swamp and teal ducks beyond the pools, or take a bathroom break in **Knob Flats** (where the toilet-to-inhabitant ratio is 35 to 1), with displays on avalanches and native bats. **Lake Gunn,** farther down the road, offers a 45-minute walk through the moss-covered glory of the forest. Beaches and fishing spots abound, and you can often see the trout you're trying to nab loafing in the water.

A shelter at **The Divide** marks the starting point for the **Routeburn Track** (see p. 351) and **Greenstone-Caples Track** (see p. 343). From here, the staggering valley views of the **Key Summit** (return 3hr.) make a great day-hike. Meanwhile, the road continues past a lookout and over **Falls Creek,** where **Christie Falls** is visible from the roadside. Turn right on **Lower Hollyford Road** to reach the track to **Lake Marian** (return 3hr.), which passes through lush rainforest and past waterfalls to an idyllic picnic spot. After hairpin turns down Milford Valley comes the **Chasm,** where a boardwalk (return 10min.) leads over the **Cleddau River,** which has carved the click rocks in surreal ways on its way down the gorge. A few kilometers beyond the Chasm lies Milford Sound itself.

MILFORD SOUND

Mystical and dramatic, Milford Sound waits patiently to fulfill the expectations of the summer throngs and re-instill a little modesty into the teeming masses. In the middle of Fiordland National Park (see p. 347), the Sound radiates strength: waterfalls cascade from dizzying heights, falling past sheer rock walls rising hundreds of meters from crystalline waters. Barely marred by a century of eager eyes and increased accessibility (guided walks were undertaken as early as the 1890s), Milford Sound retains its inscrutable majesty, despite a flotilla of cruise ships and a swarm of scenic flights.

▐▀ GETTING THERE AND AWAY. Daytrippers to Milford should try to get an early start as it sometimes clouds over on summer afternoons, while the morning fog in winter usually burns off by late morning. The variety of tour options to Milford Sound is staggering—in peak season, as many as 150 buses head up the Milford Road in the morning and back down in the afternoon—and only a few of the selections are listed here. They can all be booked in advance from Te Anau or Queenstown. **Kiwi Experience** (tel. 442 9708), **Kiwi Discovery** (tel. 442 7340), and **Mt. Cook** (tel. 249 7516) each offer comparably priced one-way sector fares along the road, allowing travelers to break out of the cattle run (Queenstown to Milford Sound $59, Te Anau to Milford Sound $35, Te Anau to the Divide $20, the Divide to

Milford Sound $15). All livestock metaphors aside, however, cruise/coach combination tours can offer the best deal, though one should pack a lunch or endure high-priced mediocrity. For those after a more personal experience than a luxury coach tour with 50 other photo-snappers can provide, **Trips 'n' Tramps** (tel. 249 7081) runs daily small (max. 12) group tours from Te Anau. Friendly, tongue-in-cheek local guides tell the history of the area, with frequent stops for tramps, photos, tea, or even the odd conversation with a kea (pickup 8:45am; $92, children $46). **Fiordland Travel** (tel. 249 7416 or 0800 656 501) offers the larger-scale excursions (8am and 10am, $90), as does **InterCity's Milford Experience** (tel. 249 7559; 10:30am from Te Anau; $91). All coaches return to Te Anau 4:30-6pm.

▌ ACCOMMODATIONS. Milford Sound's hit-and-run style of tourism doesn't encourage the proliferation of overnight options; the **Milford Sound Lodge** (tel. 249 8071) is the only budget joint. The rooms are serviceable, the takeaway menu is filling but greasy, and the pool room's giant track map is extremely helpful. (Dorms $18; doubles $45; tent sites $8, powered $10. May close in winter).

▟ ACTIVITIES. Rugged **Mitre Peak** is the photogenic focal point immediately evident as you come into view of the Sound, but the fjord is surrounded in every direction by sheer cliffs and snow-capped mountains. The 146m **Stirling Falls** are among the more spectacular of the cataracts pouring into the Sound; all the waterfalls grow and multiply after heavy rain. You shouldn't have to wait long, for the region averages 6.5m of rainfall annually, and is occasionally doused with up to 50cm a day. So much rain can fall that there's often a freshwater layer over the ocean water in the Sound. The Sound still brims with marine life from the unique flora near the waterline to the bottlenose dolphins, fur seals, and occasional Fiordland crested penguins that seek refuge here.

Most of the coach tours partner up with one of two cruise monoliths; **Fiordland Travel** (tel. 249 7416 or 0800 656 501) and **Red Boat Cruises** (tel. 249 7520 or 0800 657 444) each send several boats on three midday tours per day in winter and up to 15 tours per day in summer. A spin 'round the sound on the biggest, most impersonal vessels costs $42-47 (1¾hr.). The **Underwater Observatory**, floating 8m below the surface of the sound, makes a worthwhile addition to the cruise ($55 total). Fiordland's near-constant, tannin-stained rain runoff creates a light-repelling layer of fresh water over the sound, allowing cool critters like black coral (which is white) and snake stars (which are neither) to grow much closer to the surface than they would elsewhere. Fiordland Travel's intimately small vessel *Friendship* dips its bow in the waterfalls (2½hr.; $45, children $10), while the 61-passenger *Milford Wanderer* is a sleek sailing vessel ($47, children $10; YHA discount 10%). Both boats offer overnight trips that include a hearty dinner, breakfast, and sea kayaking. Daily trips run from October to April ($125, children $63; YHA discount 10%).

Sea kayaking may be the best way to comprehend the truly vast scale of Milford Sound. **Rosco's Sea Kayaks** (tel. 249 7695 or 0800 476 726) runs daily sunrise paddles at 7:30am (5hr., $79), and sunset kayak/Milford track combos at 4pm (4hr., $49); hours change in winter. Operating out of Te Anau, **Fiordland Wilderness Experiences** (tel. 249 7700) offers coach-kayak-coach tours for $90 (from Milford Sound $70; not always available in winter). **Diving** in the saltwater Sound allows first-hand encounters with the black coral and other Creatures of the Reasonably Deep; **Tawaki Dive** (tel. 249 9006) makes safe and personalized excursions from Te Anau with belts and tanks ($170).

Helicopter and **flightseeing** tours may be the most breathtaking Milford experiences available, but getting high is generally expensive. **Waterwing Airways** (tel. 249 7405), on the lakefront, has hour-long seaplane trips of Milford from Te Anau ($170), as does **Air Fiordland** (tel. 249 7505; 1¼hr., $173). **Milford Sound Helicopters** (tel. 249 8384 or 749 7845) take off straight from the sound; their 25-minute **Glaciers Galore** tour ($150) includes a glacier landing, plus the usual hair-raising hover along sheer walls.

TE ANAU

"Walking capital of the world," Te Anau ("tee-AH-now") is a compromise between the unpeopled expanse of Fiordland National Park, and the commercial buzz of Queenstown. Beyond the milling mallards on the rubble shore of Lake Te Anau, green mountain ranges soar to alpine heights, sending a siren song to trampers of all stripes. The local population of nearly 3000 cheerily greets the transient swarms of summer sightseers, and becomes a normal, sleepy community again with the winter.

⚑ ORIENTATION AND PRACTICAL INFORMATION

The **town center** runs west toward the lake to **Lakefront Dr.** The **Southern Scenic Route** runs west beyond the DOC office toward **Manapouri** (20km), while **SH94** runs inland toward **Mossburn** and points east. The **Milford Rd.** heads through town and away from the lake to **Milford Sound** (120km). Shops are concentrated in the town center, while booking agencies and tour operators are on Lakefront Dr.

Visitors Center: The **Te Anau Visitor Information Centre** (tel. 249 8900), a free-thinking appendage of **Fiordland Travel** (see p. 357), offers plenty of brochures, bookings, and information. Open daily 8:30am-7pm, winter 8:30am-5pm.

DOC: On the corner of Lakefront Dr. and the road to Manapouri (tel. 249 7924; fax 249 7613; email fiordlandvc@doc.govt.nz). Regional office for local **Great Walks,** tramping information, and the Milford Road. Open daily Dec. 26-Jan. 31 8am-8pm, Feb. 1-Feb. 28 8am-6pm, Mar. 1-Apr. 23 8am-5pm, Apr. 24-Oct. 23 9am-4:30pm, Oct. 24-Dec. 24 8am-6pm, Dec. 25 9am-1pm, Dec. 26-Jan. 31 8am-8pm.

Buses: InterCity (book with **Air Fiordland** tel. 249 7505) and **Topline Tours** (tel. 0508 832 628) head daily to **Queenstown** (2hr., 1-2 per day, $36). **Spitfire Shuttle** (tel. 218 7381 or mobile 025 359 529) goes daily to **Invercargill** (2½hr.; 8:30am; $34, backpackers $29). InterCity goes daily to **Christchurch** (10¾hr., 8am, $116) via **Dunedin** (4½hr., $58). **Catch-a-Bus** (tel. 453 1480) runs daily to **Dunedin** (1:45pm, $39). For transportation links to **Milford Sound,** see p. 355.

Car Rental: Major chains book through local travel agencies. **Rent-a-Dent** (tel. 249 8363 or 0800 736 822), on the road to Milford. Day hire $40 and 20¢ per km. Courtesy pick-up from town. Open M-F 8:30am-5pm, on-call Sa-Su.

Bicycle and Kayak Rental: Fiordland Bike Hire (tel. 249 7211) has bikes available at the mini-golf course on Mokonui St. near the town center. $5 per hr., $20 per day. Mountain bikes $8 per hr., $25 per day. Open daily 10am-dusk, winter on demand. **Fiordland Wilderness Experiences,** 66 Quintin Dr. (tel. 249 7700), rents kayaks for Lake Te Anau, Lake Manapouri, and Doubtful Sound ($40 for 1 day, $140 for 4-5 days). **Lakeland Boat Hire** (tel. 249 8364) has kayaks, canoes, and dinghies for rent by the hr. ($5 per 30min.).

Hitchhiking: Traffic to Milford Sound usually consists of sightseers who rarely pick up hitchers. Hitching is nearly impossible in winter, but those who try often head out early and walk to where the houses end on the road to Milford Sound. Getting to Manapouri or Queenstown is reportedly much easier; most thumbers simply walk to where the roads begin south of town, or fish for rides at their hostels.

Travel Offices: Nonsensical as it seems, all the booking agencies do bookings for each other (though hostels and motels are generally the easier and most certain way to book). **Air Fiordland** (tel. 249 7505) is in the town center. Open daily 7:30am-8pm, winter 8:30am-5:30pm. **Fiordland Travel** (tel. 249 7416) is on the lake at the end of the town center. Open daily 7:30am-9pm, in winter 8am-7pm. **Mt. Cook Travel** (tel. 249 7516) is open daily 8am-6pm, winter M-F 9am-5pm, Sa-Su variable.

SOUTH ISLAND

Currency Exchange: Westpac Trust (tel. 249 7824) boasts the only **24hr. ATM.** Bank open M-Tu and Th-F 9am-4:30pm, W 9:30am-4:30pm. **BNZ** (tel. 249 7826) also exchanges money and does cash advances. Open M-F 8:30am-7pm, Sa-Su 9:30am-6pm; winter closed Su.

Police: 196 Milford Rd. (tel. 249 7600).

Medical Services: 24hr. doctor (tel. 249 7007).

Post Office: Downtown at **Paper Plus** (tel. 249 7348). Open M-Th 8:30am-5:30pm, F 8:30am-6pm, Sa 9:30am-5:30pm.

Internet Access: Air Fiordland (see above). $2 per 15min.

Telephone Code: 03.

▌ ACCOMMODATIONS

Nondescript motels abound on **Lakefront Drive.** Virtually all of Te Anau's beds fill up in December and January, so book ahead.

Rosie's Backpackers, 23 Tom Plato Dr. (tel. 249 8431). Head up Milford Rd., turn left on Howden St., and right on Tom Plato Dr.; it's the last house on the left. A secluded residential home bordering sheep paddocks, Rosie's is a real homestay; the BBQ and picnic table out back are great escapes from the summer crowds. You can play the piano, strum one of Rosie's guitars, or talk conservation biology with her hard-core DOC hubby in the huge wood-raftered lounge area. Reception after 3pm. Dorms $15; doubles $30. Cash only.

Te Anau Backpackers Lodge, 48 Lakefront Dr. (tel. 249 7713; fax 249 8319). A rambling backpackers and former motel now has several stereos, huge chocolate easy chairs, a communal atmosphere, and a wide variety of rooms (most with bath) named after the local tracks. Reception 7:30am-8:30pm, in winter on demand. Internet. Dorms $16, with kitchenette $17; huge doubles $36, with TV $40.

Lake Front Backpackers Lodge (tel. 249 7974), right next door to Te Anau Backpackers. Furnished in the same style and run by the same owners as its next door cousin, this hostel's solid wood bunks and sparkling kitchen cater to a slightly older crowd. Reception 8am-8pm, in winter inquire next door. Internet. Dorms $16-17; doubles $38-40.

Te Anau YHA (tel. 249 7847; fax 249 7823), on the road to Milford 800m from town. Friendly, witty, and knowledgeable staff know Te Anau back and front. Complementing the wafflemaker and free ground coffee, Washington, the pet sheep, bleats every time you head to your wood-paneled room. Reception 8-11am and 4-9pm, winter 8:30-10:30am and 4-8pm. Dorms $16; twins and doubles $38; campsites $10.

Te Anau Mountain View Holiday Park (tel./fax 249 7462), on Te Anau Terr. From town, turn right along the waterfront. Clean as Fiordland mountain water and recently refurbished, Mountain View has an old coal range converted into an outdoor gas grill and wall-to-wall carpeting. Reception 7:30am-9:30pm. Check-out 10am. Standard cabins for 2 $39, with bath $60, extra person $14; tent sites $10, powered $10.50.

Te Anau Holiday Park (tel. 249 7457 or 0800 TE ANAU), across the highway from the DOC center. Reasonably but not inconveniently removed from the town center. Dorms $15; cabins $39-49; self-contained rooms $65-99; tent sites $9.50, powered $10.50. Up to 20% discounts May-Sept.

▌ FOOD

La Toscana (tel. 249 7756), in town center. About as Italian as you can get in New Zealand, with hanging wine bottles, high wooden benches, and Mediterranean memorabilia. Cheesy thin-crust pizza ($9.50-15.50) and red wine ($4.50). Open daily 5:30-10:30pm, winter Tu-Su 5:30-9pm.

Redcliff Cafe (tel. 249 7431), on Mokonui St. Universally recommended by locals, offering chargrilled fresh veggies with saucy, original main dishes ($14-21) and filling bar food. Jazz and folk most weekends. Open Sept.-May daily 4pm-1am, winter Th-Sa.

The Ranch (tel. 249 8801), in the town center. A popular pub with a huge open fire, nifty loft with pool tables, garish iced beer lights, and portraits of American West outlaws along the walls. The $15 menu is a good feed, as are Sunday meat roasts ($10). Pick up a free drink voucher from your hostel. Bands on weekends. Open daily 11am-1am; winter M-Th 2pm-1am, F-Su 11am-1am.

Ming Garden (249 7770), in the town center. Round windows and calligraphy scrolls give the restaurant a spare simplicity. The best deals are takeaway meals and free delivery within Te Anau, from $7. Restaurant open daily 5:30-9:30pm, winter 5:30-8:30pm.

Market: Supervalue (tel. 249 9600), in the town center, has the best grocery selection. Open M-Th 8am-7pm, F 8am-8:30pm, Sa 8:30am-7pm, Su 9am-6pm.

ACTIVITIES

As a starting point for three of New Zealand's **Great Walks,** Te Anau could entertain the outdoors enthusiast for months on end, with everything from hour-long strolls to 10-day adventures. Walk along the shore (15min.) away from town to reach the **Wildlife Center,** where you can commune with some of the earth's rarest birds: native owls, parakeets, and kea reside in natural caged habitats. The perilously endangered takahe is an especially beautiful and sobering sight. Continue around the lake about two hours (or grab a shuttle; see p. 353) to reach the **Mt. Luxmore Track.** The tramp along the **Kepler Track** (return 8-10hr.) offers fabulous views of the lake and surrounding mountains.

Te Anau got its name from the **Te Ana-u Caves** (some say Maori for "the caves of rushing water"). Sluiced limestone walls worn away by 15,000 years of acidic waters have formed impressive caverns housing a spectacular glow-worm grotto (see p. 129). As you meander by pontoon through the blackness of the watery grotto, it feels as if someone collapsed the galaxy and turned the stars blue-green. Located across Lake Te Anau, cave tours are run several times daily by **Fiordland Travel** (tel. 249 7416; $36, children $10). **Sindbad Cruises** (tel. 249 7106) takes aspiring sea dogs for a sail on the largest body of freshwater in the South Island, **Lake Te Anau,** on the hand-crafted and crimson-sailed gaff ketch **"Little Ship Manuska"** ($45-55). Most charters also run fishing trips, and plenty of locals lead guided excursions for **hunting** and **fishing. Rainbow Downs** (tel. 249 8006) runs **horse treks** through the rainforest; the stables are between Te Anau and Manapouri (1hr. $25, 2hr. $45; pickup $5 more).

Scenic flights out of Te Anau cover the entire Southern Lakes region. **Waterwings Airways** (tel. 249 7405), on the waterfront, runs a variety of floatplane flights (10min.; $39, children $24). **Air Fiordland** (tel. 249 7505) has a fantastic Doubtful Sound excursion ($125), while **Southern Lakes Helicopters** (tel. 249 7167), also on the lakefront, has a range of trips, some of which include snow landings and hike-down options (starting at $100). Finally, Te Anau boasts an impressive number of well-known hikes in the surrounding **Fiordland National Park** (see p. 347).

NEAR TE ANAU: MANAPOURI

Surrounded by lush rainforests and backed by rugged white-capped mountains, Lake Manapouri is possibly the most beautiful lake in New Zealand. On the beech-clad banks of the "lake of the sorrowing heart," the town of Manapouri is surrounded by the alpine majesty of the Hunter and Kepler mountain ranges, covered in fog one moment and shining clear the next. The glassy placidity of the lake in winter and the natural beauty encompassing the town are further enhanced by a relative lack of development. Although tourist ventures are beginning to take hold, Manapouri remains a pristine gateway to the remote Doubtful Sound (see p. 360) and the magnificent Kepler Track (see p. 353).

SOUTH ISLAND

🚺 ORIENTATION AND PRACTICAL INFORMATION. The town lies just west of the junction of the Southern Scenic Highway and SH95, 20km south of Te Anau (see p. 353), where you'll find the nearest **police station, doctor, bank,** and **DOC.**

Visitor Information is provided by **Fiordland Travel** and **Adventure Charters** (see below). **Fiordland Travel** (tel. 249 6602 or 0800 656 502) sells standby tickets on the tour buses heading north at the end of the day (5:30pm; Te Anau $5.50, Queenstown $40). **Spitfire Shuttle** (in Te Anau tel. 249 7505) leaves daily for: **Te Anau** (15min., 3:15pm, $8); **Invercargill** (2¼hr., 8:45am, $29) via **Tuatapere** (1¼hr., $20); and **Riverton** (1¾hr., $20). Those who **hitch** report that getting a ride to Te Anau is quite easy, though buses are a better bet than thumbing for getting out again. The **post office** is inside **Hay's Manapouri Store** (see below). **Telephone Code:** 03.

🚻 ACCOMMODATIONS AND FOOD. Possum Lodge (tel. 249 6660) is among the top-rated hostels in the country despite being named after the noxious marsupial pest (see p. 20). Big brown floor pillows and forest green bedsheets create a lived-in feel, while the two outdoor double cabins provide a modicum of privacy. (Bunks $16; twins and doubles $36. Check-out 10am. Book a week ahead in summer. Laundry $2. Closed late June-early Sept.) To reach the **Manapouri Glade Motor Park** (tel. 249 6623), turn right at the Mobil Station down the dirt road. Set on botanically landscaped grounds and surrounded by lakefront beech trees, the Glade has new wooden beds, tiled showers, a cozy kitchen, and a trampoline. (Reception 8am-8pm. Double cabins $30, extra person $15; one person $20; motel doubles $70, extra person $15; tent sites and powered sites $8.50. Potentially closed June-Aug.) **The Lakeview Motor Inn** (tel. 249 6652), on the road to Te Anau, offers heaps of backpacker rooms with a superb view and a motel ambiance (dorms $18, 1 person $20; full rooms $50-75; shower and linens included). The adjoining **Beehive Cafe and Bar** is the only grog stop in town (open M-Sa 11am-3am, Su 11am-10pm; winter M-Sa 2pm-3am, Su 2-10pm). Next door is the refreshingly weird **Manapouri Lake View Motels and Motor Park** (tel. 249 6624), with Monty Python in the bathrooms, an ultraviolet reading area, vintage pinball machines in the game room, and alarmingly old posters everywhere. (Cabins $15-16 per person; motel rooms $60-85; tent sites $8.50, powered $18.) **The Shaws,** 1 Home St. (see below; tel./fax 249 6600), part of **Fiordland Ecology Holidays** (see below), run a laidback B&B. Their self-contained flat has a shower, a kitchen, and an open fireplace. Wander through the garden to reach the cottage double where sheepskin rugs, an impeccable bathroom, and even a teddy bear will make you feel right at home. (Double $40; flats for 2 $70, extra person $10.) At the main crossroads, **Hay's Manapouri Store** (tel. 249 6619) has two aisles of basic items; next door is the bright **Cathedral Cafe,** with a lake view, ice cream, and other tasty offerings (mains from $10; store and cafe open daily May-Sept. 7am-5:30pm; Oct.-Apr. 7am-7pm; later with dinner bookings).

📷 🛶 SIGHTS AND ACTIVITIES. Captain Cook was skeptical that there would be wind to return his ship to sea, so he passed by **Doubtful Sound** in 1770, leaving only the name. Rounded glacial hills mark the entrances to over 100km of waterways. While the ship-stuffed Milford Sound is a land of dramatic extremes, remote Doubtful promises placid yet stunning vistas. Inaccessible by road, Doubtful Sound leaves its silence and serenity to the pods of dolphins and Fiordland crested penguins that call it home. **Adventure Charters** (tel. 249 6626), next to the store, runs an 11-hour **kayak tour** of Doubtful Sound ($159; overnight $239), as well as cruises ($85 per hr.) and kayak rentals ($40 per day) on Lake Manapouri. Free transport is available from Te Anau for the carless, but book ahead. (Open daily 8:30am-5:30pm, variable in winter.)

Fiordland Travel (tel. 249 6602 or 0800 656 502), at the end of the road, offers extensive full-day trips of Doubtful Sound, including a tour of the **Manapouri Power Station.** Accessed by a rough-hewn 2km tunnel far beneath the earth's surface, the turbines generate heaps of power from the plummeting lake waters, which are unfortunately invisible. After a lake cruise and an overland jaunt with solid ecological commentary, the tour heads through 40km of Doubtful Sound to the Tasman Sea before returning to Manapouri. (Oct.-Apr. 3 tours per morning; May-Sept. 9:45am; $155, children $40. Bus or flight from Te Anau or Queenstown available.) There are also summer cruises that go strictly to the power station. Bring your own lunch or pay the expensive consequences. (12:30pm; $45, children $10). If you've got time and money, invest in a remarkable, environmentally oriented tour with **Fiordland Ecology Holidays** (tel. 249 6600; www.fiordland.gen.nz). Get a natural history education while immersed in the splendor of Fiordland for three or more days on a 20m yacht (trips start at $155 per day; max. 12; book well in advance). Trips also run to New Zealand's incredibly remote subantarctic islands.

A variety of one- to three-day tracks in the area offer inexpensive—and relatively uncrowded—immersion in the grandeur of Fiordland. The **Circle Track** (3hr.) promises excellent lookouts over the Hope Arm of the lake, Mt. Titiroa, Manapouri, and Te Anau. Two huts ($4) are also available for longer hikes; pick up a pamphlet from Adventure Charters or the DOC office in Te Anau. You'll need to rent a rowboat to cross the Waiau River from Pearl Harbor in Manapouri, as all tracks begin on the far side; Adventure Charters will rent for $5 per person.

OTAGO AND SOUTHLAND

With rugged coastlines bordering rural towns and farms, Otago and Southland hold on to their early pioneer spirit. Those with a soft spot for marine life are drawn to the Otago Peninsula, which teems with seals, sea lions, dolphins, and rare penguins. The isolated beaches and soaring rock formations of the Catlins coast satisfy a pensive mood, while Stewart Island beckons to the south with even more remote beauty. A rollicking Scottish temperament gives a different flavor altogether to the university pub town of Dunedin (Scottish for Edinburgh), where Guinness and rowdy camaraderie invigorate urban life.

◾ OTAGO AND SOUTHLAND HIGHLIGHTS

■ The quiet, rugged beauty of the **Catlins** (p. 375), "New Zealand's best-kept secret," is perfect for casual exploration.
■ The **Otago Peninsula** (p. 364) is an ecological wonderland, home to seals, penguins, and other squawking birdlife.
■ **Stewart Island** (p. 384) is remote even by Southland standards.
■ Youthful **Dunedin** (p. 362) has all the amenities of a quintessential college town elevated by a passion for beer and rugby.

OTAGO

DUNEDIN

The people here are Scots. They stopped here on their way home to heaven, thinking they had arrived.

—Mark Twain

The original Scottish settlers would be proud that Dunedin retains a thriving pub culture and much of its splendid, historic architecture. While statuesque whitestone buildings and Edwardian galleries preserve the European heritage of this once-glamorous harbor port, Dunedin's student population has reinvented Dunedin without transforming its spirit. The University of Otago unleashes thousands of students on the town from February to November, peaking the population at 113,000. With its precipitous hills (its Baldwin St. is the steepest street in the world) and magical harbor, Dunedin remains deeply inscribed in Otago's historical and industrial heart.

▐ ARRIVAL AND DEPARTURE

Airport: Follow the signs on SH1 south of the city approximately 30min. **Ansett,** 1 George St. (tel. 477 4146 or 0800 800 146), on the Octagon, and **Air New Zealand,** 18 Princes St. (tel. 479 6594 or 0800 737 000), on the opposite side of the Octagon, both fly one-way to **Auckland** (2¾hr., $475) and **Wellington** (2hr., $330), often via **Christchurch** (45min., $234). As usual, it pays to buy tickets well in advance for discounts of up to 50%. **Taxis** to the city center start at $10.

Trains: Train Station (tel. 477 4449; fax 477 4953) located at the bottom of Stuart St. Open M-F 8am-5:30pm, Sa-Su 9am-2pm. **TranzScenic** goes daily to: **Invercargill**

Otago and Southland

SOUTH ISLAND

PACIFIC OCEAN

TASMAN SEA

Oamaru
TO TIMARU & CHRISTCHURCH
Kakanui
Moeraki
Maheno
Herbert
Palmerston
Dunback
Karitane
Waikouaiti
Waitati
Warrington
Otago Peninsula
Macraes Point
Middlemarch
Taieri River
Dunedin
Ranfurly
Outram
Mosgiel
Allanton
Brighton
Lake Mahinerangi
Lawrence
Milton
Alexandra
Raes Junction
Clyde
Roxburgh
Herbert
Kelso
Tapanui
Clinton
Balclutha
Kaitangata
Kaka Point
Nugget Point
Owaka
Purakaunui
Papatowai
Tautuko
CATLINS FOREST PARK
Curio Bay
Waipapa Point
Cromwell
GARVIE MOUNTAINS
THE REMARKABLES
Gore
Mataura
Wyndham
Tokanui
Otara
Queenstown
Lake Wakatipu
TO MILFORD SOUND
EYRE MOUNTAINS
Lumsden
Riversdale
Edendale
Winton
Makarewa
Wallacetown
Invercargill
Bluff
Foveaux Strait
Te Anau
The Key
Mossburn
Ohai
Nightcaps
Otautau
Riverton
Halfmoon Bay (Oban)
FIORDLAND NATIONAL PARK
Lake Te Anau
Manapouri
Lake Manapouri
Lake Monowai
Tuatapere
Te Waewae Bay
Lake Hauroko
Lake Poteriteri
Stewart Island

30 miles
30 kilometers

N

(3¼hr., $26-51); **Christchurch** (5½hr., $74) via **Oamaru** (2½hr., $28); and **Timaru** (3½hr., $41). An unusual but scenic way to get to **Queenstown** is to make a bus connection after taking the popular **Taieri Gorge Train** ($99, children $50).

Buses: InterCity, 205 St. Andrew St. (tel. 477 8860). Runs to: **Invercargill** (3hr., 1 per day, $20); **Christchurch** (6hr., 2 per day, $28) via **Oamaru** (1½hr., $13); **Timaru** (3hr., $15); **Ashburton** (4½hr., $18); and **Queenstown** (4¼hr., 2:45pm, $25). **Shuttles** also traverse the same routes (more in summer); **Atomic Shuttles** (tel. 322 8883) is cheap and reliable. All prices listed require a 3-day advance booking; prices may be higher (by as much as $20) with less notice.

Car Rental: Companies include: **Inner City Rentals,** 14 Harrow St. (tel. 477 3017), which rents cars from $28 per day and 28¢ per km; **Pegasus** (tel 477 6296); and **Jackie's** (477 7848). **Zoom,** 152 High St. (tel. 477 4938), located on the second floor of the Environmental Centre above Princes St., is a service that matches prospective drivers and travelers together, especially between cities. A small donation is requested in lieu of a success charge. Open M-F 9am-4pm.

Automobile Association: 450 Moray Place (tel. 477 5945; 24hr. hotline 0800 500 222), just below Princes St. Open M-F 8:30am-5pm.

✳ ORIENTATION

Dunedin is easily navigable and organized around the **Octagon,** where a statue of Robert Burns presides over the city center in front of the gothic revival spires of St. Paul's. **George St.** extends roughly north toward the University of Otago and is Dunedin's main commercial shopping thoroughfare; it becomes **Princes St.** south of the Octagon, as it nears most of the backpackers. Pubs are mostly scattered below George St. between the Octagon and the university, beyond which lie the Botanic Gardens. **Stuart St.** heads down the hill directly toward the train station and Otago Harbour. The bus station for Intercity is on **St. Andrew St.**, which runs parallel to Stuart St. up to George St. Otago Peninsula extends from the southeastern part of the city.

⿻ PRACTICAL INFORMATION

Visitors Center: Visitor Information Centre, 48 The Octagon (tel. 474 3300; fax 474 3311). To the right of the soaring clock tower of the limestone **Municipal Chambers** building. Here you'll find maps, advice, and information about tours and bookings. Open daily 8am-6pm, winter M-F 8:30am-5pm, Sa-Su 9am-5pm.

Department of Conservation (DOC): 77 Lower Stuart St. (tel. 477 0677), on the first floor of the Conservation House. Provides maps and info about national parks and trails. Does bookings for the Routeburn and Milford Tracks. Open M-F 8:30am-5pm.

City Buses: Five companies provide transport in Dunedin ($1.10-$4). Pick up a bus schedule in the Visitor Centre; most buses depart from the Octagon or along Cumberland St.

Taxis: Stands on High St. off Princes St., and on St. Andrew and Hanover St. off George St. Call **Dunedin Taxis** (tel. 477 7777), **City Taxis** (tel. 477 1771), **Otago Taxi** (tel. 477 3333), or **Call-a-Cab** (tel. 477 7800).

Bike Rental: Cycle Surgery, 67 Stuart St. (tel. 477 7473) at the corner of Cumberland St. Has a range of bikes with helmets and locks ($20-35 per day). Open M-F 8:30am-6pm, Sa 9:30am-3:30pm, Su 10:30am-3:30pm.

Hitchhiking: Hitchhikers often take a bus from the Octagon and ask the driver to let them off at the best spot. Those heading north usually take the Pine Hill bus ($1.50), while those heading south take the Mosgiel bus to Kenmont ($3.10). Inquire at the Visitor Centre for departure times. Let's Go cannot, does not, will not recommend hitchhiking.

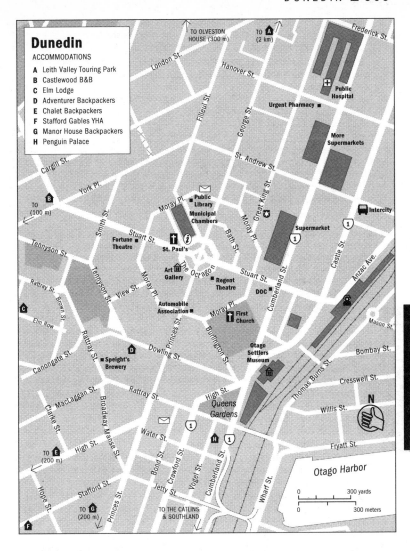

Dunedin

ACCOMMODATIONS

A Leith Valley Touring Park
B Castlewood B&B
C Elm Lodge
D Adventurer Backpackers
E Chalet Backpackers
F Stafford Gables YHA
G Manor House Backpackers
H Penguin Palace

SOUTH ISLAND

Budget Travel: STA Travel, 32 Albany St. (tel. 474 0146; fax 477 2741), a block down from George St. Open M-F 9am-5pm, Sa 10am-1pm.

Currency Exchange: Thomas Cook (tel. 477 7204), on the corner of George and St. Andrews St. Open M-F 8:30am-5pm, Sa 10am-12:30pm. Other banks are located along George and Princes St. The Visitor Centre exchanges money outside these hours.

Hotlines: Gay/Lesbian Support Group (tel. 477 2077), on Tu 5:30-7:30pm for women, W 5:30-7:30pm and F 7:30-10pm for men.

Police: 25 Great King St. (tel. 477 6011).

Medical Services: The **pharmacy** is at 95 Hanover St. (tel. 477 6344). Open M-F 6pm-10pm, Sa-Su 10am-10pm. **Urgent Doctors** (tel. 479 2900) is next door and open daily 24hr. **Dunedin Public Hospital** is at 201 Great King Rd. (tel. 474 0999).

Post Offices: (tel. 479 6458). At the corner of Princes and Rattray St. *Poste Restante.* Open M-F 8:30am-5pm, Sa 8:30am-noon.

Internet Access: The **Dunedin Library,** on Moray Place behind the Visitor Centre, has public access for $4 per 30min. Open M-F 9:30am-8:00pm, Sa 10am-4pm, Su 2pm-6pm. You can also use the Internet at the Visitor Centre ($5 per 20 min.).

Telephone Code: 03.

ACCOMMODATIONS

Edwardian hotels, former churches, and rambling homes converted into back-packers provide Dunedin with an impressive array of budget accommodations. Most are found up the hill above Princes St., but all lie within a 10-minute walk of the Octagon. Remember to book accommodations well in advance when there's a big rugby game—it's nicer to pass out in a bed than on the streets with the rest of the hard-drinking rugby fans after a game. Check-out is 10am unless otherwise noted.

Chalet Backpackers, 296 High St. (tel. 479 2075). Take Princes St. to High St. and then up the hill. Free pickup. A spacious, exceedingly comfy hostel, with giant windows that offer a great view of Otago Harbour and plants that add a cheeriness to every room. You can't tell it was once a hospital; you can stay in the operating room without the anesthesia—heck, you're already "down under." Bike hire. Key deposit $10. Reception 8am-10pm, winter 9am-9pm. Dorms $15; singles $25; doubles $35. Cash only.

Elm Lodge, 74 Elm Row (tel. 474 1872). Head up Rattray St. to Brown St., then uphill to Elm Row; the backpackers is a few yards to your right. Free pickup and dropoff. This hostel is smaller than most and an uphill battle from town, but the social atmosphere make it a standout nonetheless. Space is exchanged for intimacy, but it's got an excellent vantage point above the city. Free use of videos and bikes. Internet. Laundry $2. Key deposit $5. Reception 8am-10pm. Dorms $14-15; doubles $34.

Adventurer Backpackers, 37 Dowling St. (tel./fax 477 7367), down Princes St. 2 blocks from the Octagon, then up Dowling St. 2 levels overlook an open hall with the ceiling painted in sky and clouds. A pool table, fireside couches, and even a breadmaking machine add to the communal ski-lodge atmosphere. Reception 8am-9pm. Internet. Key deposit $10. Dorms $14; twins $15-16; doubles $36; triples $45. Cash only.

Aunty's Backpackers Lodge, 3 Union St. (tel. 474 0708; fax 474 0715; email auntys@xtra.co.nz). Take George St. five blocks from the Octagon and turn left on Union St. Free pickup and dropoff. Aunty's cultivates a welcoming atmosphere with its flower garden in front and free scones each morning. Conveniently located near the University, the public garden, and the pubs, Aunty's also offers free videos and a small but pleasant common area. Laundry $2. Reception 8am-8pm. Check-out 10:30am. Dorms $15, winter $13.50; singles $36; twins $36.

Penguin Palace, 1 Vogel St. (tel. 479 2175). Take Princes St. and turn left on Rattray St.; it's down the hill and on the right. The largest backpackers in town, Penguin Place earns its name from the garish color cartoons adorning every wall. Located on Queens Park, with an extensive selection of free videos, pool table, and Internet. Laundry $2. Key deposit $5. Reception 8am-10pm. Dorms $15-16; singles $25; twins and doubles $34. Weekly dorms $75.

Stafford Gables (YHA), 71 Stafford St. (tel. 474 1919). Take Princes St. up several blocks to Stafford St.; it will be on your left. This rambling old jaunt is supposedly haunted, although the school groups that frequent it are very much alive. Wide hallways, generous rooms. Internet. Reception 8am-noon, 1:30-3:30pm, and 5-10pm; winter 8-10am, 5-10pm, and 7:30-10pm. Dorms $16; singles $28; doubles $38. Book in advance in summer.

Manor House Backpackers, 28 Manor Pl. (tel. 477 0484; fax 477 8145). 6 blocks down Princes St. and to the right. Free pickup. TV lounge overlooks the harbor. New kitchen and dining area. Internet. Key deposit $5. Reception 8:30am-10pm, winter 8:30am-8pm. Dorms $14-15; twins and doubles $36.

Next Stop, 2 View St. (tel. 477 0447; fax 477 0430; email nextstop@es.co.nz). Go right on Moray Pl. from Princes St. and then left on View St. Dunedin's most centrally-located backpackers will be undergoing renovations and remodeling. Laundry $2. Key deposit $10. Reception 8:30am-10pm. Dorms $15; twins and doubles $40.

Castlewood B&B, 240 York Pl. (tel./fax 477 0526; www.castlewood.co.nz; email relax@castlewood.co.nz). Take Stuart St. to York Pl., then up the hill. A wood-paneled, sunny old Tudor residence with the host's watercolors on the walls. Excellent escape from the backpackers scene, with incomparable harbor views. Singles $65; twins $85; doubles $95; suite $120.

Leith Valley Touring Park, 103 Malvern St. (tel. 467 9936). Take George St., then turn left on Duke St. and continue up to Malvern St. A small, secluded park on Leith Stream with access to trails, 2km from the city. Reception 9am-9pm. Caravan and tent sites $9; caravan doubles $30; tourist flats (single or double) $55.

⚫ FOOD

Ethnic places compete with the usual mince pie and Chinese takeaways, making for some fine eatin' in Dunedin. **Markets** include **Countdown Foods** at Cumberland and Stuart St. (open M-F 8:30am-10pm, Sa-Su 9am-8pm), and **New World** on Cumberland between St. Andrew St. and Hanover St. (open M-F 8am-9pm, Sa-Su 8am-8pm). **Taste Nature,** 59 Moray Pl. (tel. 474 0219), above Princes St., is an organic food co-op and bakery (open M-Th 9am-6pm, F 9am-6:30pm, Sa 10am-3:30pm).

🏴 **Tull,** 29 Bath St. (tel. 477 5331), off Lower Stuart St. Dunedin's dessert mecca, this hippie ode to Jethro Tull rates its 23 sinful triumphs according to decadence (desserts $7.50-15). Bottomless homemade soups ($5) are a fabulous deal, and the distinctive French bread sandwiches ($6.50-8.50), called "flutes" in homage to Tull's Ian Anderson, are enormous and delicious. If you struggle with decisions or decadence, come Wednesdays after 7:30pm, when Tull serves up a smorgasbord of all-you-can-eat desserts with coffee ($12). Open M-Th 11:30am-11pm, F from 11:30am, Sa from 5:30pm.

Aspara, 380 George St. (tel. 477 4499), opposite Albert Arms. The big Cambodian noodle soups ($5) warm you from the inside out and the curry veggies with coconut milk on rice ($5) revitalize the taste buds. Cash only. Open daily 11am-9pm.

Little India (tel. 477 6559), St. Andrew St. below George St. This dimly lit authentic place has an extensive menu and a large following. Fluffy *naan* bread $2.50-4.50, strong curry dishes $15.50. BYO. Large vegetarian selection. Open daily from 5pm.

Galata Kebab House, 126 Princes St. (tel. 474 1444), 2 blocks from the Octagon. Enjoy Turkish music and decor as you choose from kebabs in pitas ($8.50-9.50) or over rice ($13-19) for a flavorful and filling meal. The pita lunch special ($5.95) and special vegetarian kebab ($9.50) are exceptional. Open M-Th 10am-11pm, F-Sa 10am-3am, Su 11am-10pm. Free delivery M-Th 5-10pm, F-Sa 5-11pm with order over $20.

Jizo, 56 Princes St. (tel. 479 2692), a block from the Octagon. Business types cram this stylish, double-level Japanese eatery at lunchtime, but you can still get a tasty and sizeable meal for a moderate price. Choose from the wide selections on the sushi bar (6 pieces for $5), fill your stomach with a chicken curry ($5.50), or savor the steaming Kake Udon noodle soup ($4.50). Open M-Th, and Sa 11am-9pm, F 11am-10pm.

Poppa's Pizza (tel. 477 0598), on Albany St. a block down from Cumberland St. and opposite the university campus. Friendly student pizza joint. Small pizzas from $8.50, larges from $14. The seafood pizza is a yummy novelty (small $11.80). Delivery fee $3. Open M-Th 11am-2pm and 4-11pm, F-Sa 11am-1am, Su 11am-11pm.

Gypsy Cafe, 126 Lower Stuart St. (tel. 474 0141). This eccentrically-decorated cafe offers 3-course dinners for $9.50. Those with less hearty appetites will enjoy the crepes ($3.50) and the other exquisite dessert selections. Open daily 7am-9pm.

Potpourri (tel. 477 9983), on lower Stuart St. below Moray Pl. The 3-course evening meal ($12) is a must for vegetarians or health-food fans. Or you can stray from nutrition with the decadent orange fudge slice ($1.80). Open M-F 9am-8pm, Sa 11am-8pm.

CAFES

Dunedin's cafes are its hottest item these days, and you'll be sure to find more than simply cappuccino-sipping artists crowding these hangouts. Many cafes double as art galleries, bars, music venues, cyberstations, culinary experiments, or all of the above. But you'd better get there fast—in today's competitive scene, lucky is the cafe that lasts more than a few months.

- **Percolater,** 142 Lower Stuart St. (tel. 477 5462), just below the Octagon. A spunky cafe with topless, armless mermaids in the windows, gaping vegetarian calzones ($4.50), and delectable berry, banana, and chocolate muffins ($3.50). Open Su-Th 9am-11pm, F-Sa 9am-late.

- **Arc,** 135 High St. (tel 474 1135), a block up from Princes St. This trendy cafe covers all bases all times of the day or night. Choose from coffee or beer, live music or the Internet (25min. free with purchase), a pool table (20¢) or an old scout ship ride (10¢). You can sit in front of the hearth, on cushy couches, or outside. Open daily 10am-3am.

- **Fuel,** 21 Frederick St. (tel. 477 2575), a block down from George St. Start your day with "liquid fuel," resupply with "unleaded fuel," and cap it all off with "solid fuel." One of Dunedin's new, all-purpose cafes, Fuel packs it in during the day with coffee and poshy eats and nights with its foosball area, lounge, bar, and pool table. $2 pints Wednesday. Happy Hour Th 6-10pm and F 5-9pm. Open M-F 7:30am-late, F-Sa 10am-late.

- **Mazagran,** 36 Moray Place (tel. 477 9959), above Princes St. Mazagran specializes in coffee to the exclusion of all else. Try their own special blend (long black $2) because you've been drinking their other blends all around town—Mazagran roasts and grinds for most of the other cafes in Dunedin. Open M-F 8am-8pm, Sa 10am-2pm.

- **Tangenté** (tel. 477 0232), upper Moray Pl. off Stuart St. This new-age bastion of baking has light meals ranging from gourmet to just plain complicated. The avocado-parsley-pesto-cheese pastry ($3.20) and hot ginger-lemon-honey drink ($3.50) make excellent complements. Suck on the ginger ice cubes for a new sensation. Open W and Sa-Su 8am-3:30pm, Th-F 8am-11pm.

ENTERTAINMENT AND NIGHTLIFE

In Dunedin, it is not hard to find a variety of theaters and performance venues. **The Fortune Theatre Company** (tel. 477 8323), on upper Stuart St. and Moray Pl., puts on a number of professional shows throughout the year (box office open M-F 10:30am-5pm, longer on performance nights; $22.50, students $13). The palatial **Regent** (tel. 477 8597) hosts an International Film Festival in June and July ($9.50, students $7.50) and several traveling shows throughout the year (box office open M-F 8:30am-5pm, Sa 10:30am-1pm). The **Metro Cinema** (tel. 474 3350) shows foreign and independent films behind the Municipal Chambers on Moray St. ($9, students $7.50, seniors $6; matinees before 6pm $6.) Check the *Otago Daily Times* for screenings, or pick up a copy of *Fink* at most cafes for entertainment listings.

As a university town, Dunedin has its fair share of standard student hangouts; in recent years the variety of dance venues, alternative clubs, and Irish pubs has multiplied considerably.

- **Captain Cook** (tel. 474 1935), at the corner of Albany and Great King St. Even North Islanders have stories about this quintessential varsity pub and zenith of the university scene. A street-level bar with pool and other games, throbbing dance floor upstairs, and an outdoor garden where sports fans congregate to watch big games on big screens. $3 student meals 5:30-8:30pm; $1 drinks Th 11pm-2am. Open daily 11am-3am.

- **Bath St.,** 1 Bath St. (tel. 477 6750). Alternative types flock to the burgundy leather couches and laser-lit dance floor. Candles and techno may provide an atmosphere more suited to lounging than dancing. If you're looking to hit the dance floor, Bath St. draws some of the hottest DJs from New Zealand and abroad. DJs Wednesdays through Saturdays, occasional fetish parties. $3-5 cover. Open Tu-Sa from 10pm.

Bowler (tel. 477 5272), on Cumberland St. just off Frederick St. A standard student hangout, the large-screen TV and glass-walled, strobe-lit dance floor draw huge crowds, as do Wet Wednesdays (drinks $2) and cheap handles ($2-3). Open M-Sa 11am-3am.

The Albert Arms (tel. 477 8035), at the corner of George and London St. Fairly quiet except Mondays, when much of the city turns out for Gaelic good times and jigs to the cantankerous beats of local favorite Blackthorn. The Mighty Midday Roast ($5.50) will satisfy the hungriest appetite (M-F noon-2pm). Open M-Tu 11am-12:30am, W-Th 11am-11pm, F-Sa 11am-midnight, Su 11:30am-7:30pm.

The Woolshed, 318 Moray Pl. (tel. 477 3246). An eclectic Irish pub steadfastly popular with locals. Relax by the massive hearth or join the Wednesday evening jam session for BBQ and free beer. Live music nightly. Happy Hour F 4-6pm. Open daily from 11:30am.

The Statesman, 91 St. Andrews St. (tel. 477 8411). Lured by a big screen TV, dance floor, and game room, a mixed crowd turns out for the town's staples: rugby and beer. Live music most weekends. Open from 11am.

KC's, 370 George St. (tel. 474 1133), at between Albany St. and Hanover St. Watch the most popular music videos projected on the walls as you dance at this cheesy Top 40s dance club, where bartenders wear tight-fitting white shirts and steam spews from a machine. No cover. Open M-W 9pm-2:30am, Th and Sa 9pm-3am, F 9pm-4am.

◉ 🏛 SIGHTS AND ACTIVITIES

ARCHITECTURE

The Scottish Edwardian architecture of Dunedin's **train station** is spectacular on a sunny day, and is rivaled only by the black and white facade of the **University of Otago's main hall** down St. David St. The gothic revival churches established by the early Scottish residents are worth a look, especially the **First Church of Otago** down Moray Pl. from Princes St., with its rose windows and wood-ceiling sanctuary. **St. Paul's** in the Octagon has the only **stone-vaulted ceiling** in New Zealand, as well as a carved alabaster pulpit and an organ with 3500 pipes. Its flying buttresses are the most impressive in the city. For those who can't get enough stone churches, **St. Joseph's Cathedral** (at the corner of Rattray and Smith St.) and **Knox Church** (at the corner of George and Pitt St.) are also worthwhile visits. **Olveston,** 42 Royal Terr. (tel. 477 3320), is a perfectly preserved historic home built in 1904 that still feels lived in. Take George St. to Pitt St., then follow Royal Terr. until you see it on the right. All the clocks run in this Edwardian mansion, and even the 1926 Frigidaire still works. The benefactor's will ensured that anyone could tickle the ivories of the 1906 Steinway grand piano. (Tours offered every 1¼hr. 9:30am-4:30pm. Admission $11, students $10, under 15 $3.)

MUSEUMS

The enormous **Otago Museum** (tel. 477 2372), down the hill on Great King between Albany and Union St., takes an in-depth look at the material culture and natural history of Otago, including a full-size Maori war canoe and a room full of Chinese clothing (open M-F 10am-5pm, Sa-Su noon-5pm; recommended donation $5). The museum's **Discovery World** has hands-on science exhibits that will enthrall children (same hours; admission $6, M-F students $4, children $3). Less extensive but more eclectic, the **Otago Settlers Museum,** 31 Queens Garden (tel. 477 5052), down Dowling St., is worth a look. You can ride an old penny farthing (turn-of-the-century bicycle) in the Art Deco former bus station or peruse the early portraits in the gallery. The museum also keeps records and photos of immigrants, which are available for public viewing Monday to Friday 10am-1pm ($10). (Museum open M-F 10am-5pm, Sa-Su 1-5pm. Admission $4, students and YHA/VIP members $3, children free.) The **Dunedin Public Art Gallery** (tel. 467 7460), in the Octagon, has a Renaissance collection with several good pre-Raphaelite works, along with both colonial and modern New Zealand exhibitions. The spare foyer in the lobby is impressive in itself, with the iron spiral staircase of the original building hanging two stories down. (Open M-F 10am-5pm, Sa-Su 11am-5pm. Regular exhibits free.)

OUTDOOR ACTIVITIES

Tunnel Beach is among the best of local walks. It is only accessible at low tide, so be sure to check at the Visitor Centre or in the newspaper for the day's tides. To reach the beach you take the Corstophine bus from the Octagon to Stenhope Crescent, then walk down Blackhead Rd. Hike through a century-old tunnel onto a cliff-backed beach with sea caves carved into the walls (return 1hr.; closed Sept.-Oct.) **Mt. Cargill** is a 4km track (return 3½hr.) through a former tree-planting scheme; you'll be rewarded with a panoramic view of the harbor. Another hour's tramp will take you to the volcanic spires of the **Organ Pipes.** Take the Normanby bus to the start of Norwood St.; walk up to Bethunes Gully. If you have a car, **Signal Hill** is a great place to admire the stars above and the twinkling lights of the city below. It's accessible off Opoho Rd. on the northern side of the botanic garden. A **bike path** follows Thomas Burns St., which runs into Wharf St., toward the Otago Peninsula—look for blue and white signs. The path may be accessed by crossing the foot bridge to the right of the train station.If you're into **horseback riding,** you can explore the beaches to the south of Dunedin with a two-hour ride ($25) from **Bums 'n' Saddles** (tel 488 0097). **Trojan Riding,** 434 Coast Rd. (tel. 465 7013), offers longer gallops on the coast of Karitane to the north of Dunedin (twilight treks $39; half-day $49, full day $99). Pickup is available for groups of four and over; or, take the bus from the Bowling Green Hotel at the corner of Frederick and Cumberland St. (2 per day M-F, $6). Those who prefer moving swiftly through water rather than over land will enjoy **Taieri River Trips** (tel. 489 6167), a four- to six-hour whitewater adventure on Grade 3 rapids ($60, students $50, children $39).

OTHER SIGHTS AND ACTIVITIES

Established in 1863, Dunedin's **Botanic Gardens** are arguably the best in the country, their hilly terrain covered with earthy tracks through thick woods and grassy slopes over landscaped grounds. The **Rhododendron Festival** in the third week of October is world-renowned in botanic circles, as is the large aviary with several native birds, including the kea. Take any city bus from the Octagon down George St. ($1.10) or walk from the university on Leith St. For a tour at **Speights Brewery** (tel. 477 9480), turn right onto Rattray St. from Princes St., and you can't miss the protruding barrel. Form your own impressions of the "Pride of the South" with free samples following the tour. To cure dehydrated drinkers, Speights provides well water through a tap on the side of the building. Stand in line with the locals to fill up your water bottle. (Open M-F 6am-6pm. Free. 3 tours per day M-F. $10. Bookings required.) If you're tired of being on your feet, you can take the **Taieri**

ON A FIRST NAME BASIS
Beer, a staple of the New Zealand diet, is a matter of pride for most Kiwis. The most popular drinks are Steinlager, DB Draught, and Export Gold (as well as the inevitable Guinness). Tui is also a good choice. It also pays to know that the big breweries generally have nicknames. A Steinlager is a Steiny, for example, and a Canterbury Draft is simply a CD. Be on the lookout for local brews and microbrews; Mac's West Coast beers are exceptional and widely available. Just don't be surprised if the classics go by unfamiliar names:

Double. To Brits and Americans, a standard shot; always ask for one (often it's just assumed that's what you want).

7oz. A denomination to avoid, unless the bartender is your best friend. 7oz. in a glorified shot glass.

12oz. Commonly called a "thirteen," nearly 13oz. of frosty brew in a tapering glass. A bar standard.

Handle. Also called a pint, though it's not quite 16oz. For the thirsty.

Jug. The American "pitcher," about 2½ pt.

Schooner. A rare promotional monster in a 1½ L glass. Jump at the opportunity.

Gorge Railway (tel. 477 4449) from the train station through the hinterlands of Dunedin's pioneer history. Inaccessible to cars, the railway winds precariously through tunnels and over viaducts. The journey to Pukerangi on the tablelands of Otago passes over spectacular gorges and through native forests and sheep stations with commentary about the track's difficult construction. (Departs Sept.-Apr. 2:30pm, May-Aug. 12:30pm. $49, students $39.)

NEAR DUNEDIN: OTAGO PENINSULA

Serene Otago Peninsula is as popular for its penguin and albatross colonies as Dunedin is for its museums and pubs. Stretching over 20km from the city, the peninsula offers incomparable ecological opportunities. Yellow-eyed penguins, fur seals, sea lions, and royal albatrosses lay claim to the peninsula's many weather-worn inlets, beaches, and promontories. Dramatic **Taiaroa Head** drops off onto seal-encrusted crags and great swaths of billowing kelp. The beaches teem with bird activity even before the penguins waddle ashore in the evening.

⚐ ORIENTATION AND PRACTICAL INFORMATION. The best way to experience the peninsula is either by bike or car (see p. 364 for bike and car rentals). **Portobello Road,** the sinuous coastal route along the bay, is full of treacherous curves—even the locals who know the road often don't drive on it. No matter how you decide to go out to the peninsula, be careful; you don't want to end up like the seals, belly-up on a bed of seaweed. If you decide to take a tour, there are many well-operated ones to choose from. Dunedin's Visitor Centre is the best source of information. **Back to Nature Tours** (tel. 0800 477 0484; 5hr, 2pm daily, $43; free pickup from accommodations) and **Elm Wildlife Tours** (tel. 0800 356 363; 6hr, 3pm, winter 1pm, $43; free pickup) provide in-depth walking wildlife excursions. **Newton Tours** (tel. 477 5577) offers an array of packages ($49-89) out to the sights, as do many other carriers, though some run only during the summer. **Telephone Code:** 03.

⚐ ACCOMMODATIONS. Homestays are one possibility to aid exploration of the Otago Peninsula. Most cost about $50 per night per person; the Visitor Centre will provide brochures, recommendations, and bookings. If you're up to feeling like equine royalty, spend the night at the **Larnach Stables** (tel. 476 1616) at Larnach Castle. You may explore the grounds as if they were your own, and comfortable beds under floating eaves are a true novelty. (Reception 24hr. No kitchen. Continental breakfast $10. Doubles $55, extra person $17.50, children $12.50). **Penguin Place** (tel. 478 0286), right next to the Yellow-eyed Penguin Reserve, has sparsely furnished rooms with terrific views of the bay ($15 per person; book ahead). **Portobello Village Tourist Park** (tel./fax 478 0359) in Portobello is a verdant place on 50 acres. Midway between Dunedin and the albatross colony, Portobello Village rents bikes (half-day $15; full day $25) and is a good starting point for exploring the peninsula. (Reception 8am-10:30pm. Backpackers $15; tent sites $8.50, powered $9.50; tourist flats $59; bunk rooms and on-site caravans for two $30, extra person $5.)

⚐⚐ SIGHTS AND ACTIVITIES. At the **Taiaroa Royal Albatross Colony** (tel. 478 0499), you'll learn that these massive birds, immortalized by poet Samuel Coleridge, are not merely seagulls with pituitary problems. Taiaroa is unique as the only mainland albatross colony on earth; these majestic wanderers fledge and rear their young here, then circumnavigate the globe without visiting land until they return. Entrance to the **Albatross Centre** (which houses extensive displays and live TV coverage of the birds' activities) is free, but the educational tour and observatory distance viewing is a rather steep $22 ($17 in winter, children $11). **Monarch Wildlife Cruises** (tel. 477 4276) runs a jolly skiff from Wellers Rock near the head, 45 minutes from Dunedin. Their tours are the best way to view the massive chimney roosts and rare species of cormorants coexisting there. (2 tours per day. $22.50, YHA $20, children $12.)

Rare yellow-eyed penguins *(hoiho)* have, with a little human assistance, recolonized Penguin Beach just beyond Taiaroa Head. Speed through a maniacal camouflaged trench system at the **Yellow-eyed Penguin Conservation Reserve** (tel. 478 0286), 50 minutes from Dunedin and two minutes from the Albatross Centre, to view these sleek divers from just a few meters away while they preen, yelp, and mate. Not priding themselves on privacy, they're more faithful than humans, though their monogamous devotion only goes so far (see below). Their mating habits are like a soap opera, and the penguins are even named to help you follow the drama. (Tours run every 30min. on the quarter-hour; Oct.-Apr. all day; May-Sept. 3pm until dark. $23, children $12; book ahead in summer.) Those with slim wallets and big binoculars may appreciate penguin viewing (best in late afternoon) at **Southlight Beach** (tel. 478 0287), a few minutes down the road. To access the beach you must purchase a key either at the Albatross Centre or at Harrington Point Rd. ($7.50, children under 16 free). For hard-core enthusiasts, **Twilight Tour** leaves from Dunedin and does a six- to seven-hour tour of the seal, shag, and penguin reserves ($49, backpackers $43, children $38; albatross colony tours extra). To get up close and personal with Otago's rocky coastline, try **sea kayaking** (tel. 478 0820) from **Wellers Rock** ($10 per hr., half-day $25, full day $35; no solo unguided trips; guide free for groups of 2 or more).

For the historically inclined, **Larnach Castle** (tel. 476 1616), is a 43-room architectural marvel. The story behind the castle may be more interesting than the castle itself. Indefatigable Mr. Larnach had six children by his first wife alone. Continuing on this prolific strain, he eventually married his third wife in his mid-50s (she was 17). When she ran off with his second son, however, he committed suicide in the Parliament building in Wellington. Take a self-guided tour through the inlaid mahogany, teak, and kauri foyer up the only hanging Georgian staircase in the Southern Hemisphere. A sympathetic moment should be paid to the 12 men it took to carry the one-ton marble Herculean bath to the third floor. The view of Dunedin and the entire peninsula from the battlements is incomparable. The Cheshire cat from *Alice in Wonderland* (in the form of a stone carving) may be found on the lush 35-acre formal grounds on the purportedly haunted estate. (Halfway down the peninsula and 3km up the winding Castlewood Rd. The aptly named **High Cliff Road** offers an alternate route with spectacular views of the south side of the peninsula. Admission $10, children $3.50. Garden access $5, children $1.)

Take the Otago Road Services city bus from Stand 5 outside **New World** on Cumberland St. to the Company Bay stop ($2.50) and walk up the hill. Or, catch the noon tour from the Visitor Centre ($30, children $15). A mode of transport more befitting a stately visit, **Castle Discovery Horse Treks** (tel. 478 0796 or 0800 467 738) embark on a three-hour trip to Larnach Castle daily at 9:30am and 1:15pm (based in Broad Bay; adults $45, students $41.50; includes castle entrance fee).

PENGUINS OF PUZZLING PERSUASIONS

Once decimated by egg- and chick-eating ferrets, feral cats, and extensive clearing of native coastal habitat, numbers of yellow-eyed penguins *(hoiho)* are today increasing. However, it's hard to know where to assign the credit. Pairs sometimes remain monogamous, but infidelity is common, and it seems that some of the waddling wonders may actually be bisexual—a Ben occasionally paddles away with a Sven as eagerly as he might with a Monica. Of course, distinguishing the sexes in these, the world's rarest penguins, is a bit difficult as neither leaves anything hanging out as a clue. Researchers originally thought that the male stayed on top during coupling, but who's to really say? Perhaps the penguins have as tough a time telling as we do. Maybe it's just free love. But if any love is good love for these feathery bundles of boundless libido, they may have a tougher time getting their numbers up. Either way, you can watch the unabashed avians in action when they mate in the spring.

OAMARU

As pacific as its ocean, Oamaru has long been known for its limestone facades and Antarctic waterfowl. Usually staying one day and perhaps a night here, visitors often spend the day browsing amongst antiques and collectables in Oamaru's historic precinct, and the evening viewing the penguins' return home after a day of hunting. To its historical and ecological attractions, add a splash of local color, a scenic coastal track, and the nearby boulders at Moeraki to the mix, and you'll find Oamaru a convenient and pleasant stop along the Otago coast.

▶ ORIENTATION AND PRACTICAL INFORMATION. Coming from Timaru in the north, SH1 follows Thames St. into the heart of downtown Oamaru. The **Visitor Information Centre,** 1 Thames St. (tel. 434 1656; fax 434 1657), is on the left side of Thames St. just after the train tracks. By car, continue straight after SH1 veers right onto Severn St.; from the train station, go up one block, turn left onto Thames St., and walk 10 minutes. The Visitor Centre has maps, information about local sites and tours, and **DOC info** as well (open M-F 9am-5pm, Sa-Su 10am-4pm). From the Visitor Centre, go left onto Itchen St. and then follow Tyne St. around to the right to reach the **historic precinct.** Continue on Tyne St. and make a left on Waterfront Rd. to get to the **blue penguin colony.**

Buses leave the station at Eden and Thames St. (tel. 434 8716). **InterCity** heads to **Christchurch** (4½hr., 3-4 per day, $37) and to **Dunedin** (2¼hr., 3-4 per day, $19). **Tranz-Scenic** leaves daily from the station by the water on Humber St. for **Christchurch** (3hr., 2:10pm, $51) and **Invercargill** (6hr., 11:30am, $75) via **Dunedin** (3hr., $28). The **Oamaru Mini-Coach** (tel. 439 4765) provides service to **Dunedin** (M-F 7:50am, $20). The **Atomic Shuttle** goes to **Christchurch** for $20. **Hitchhikers** report heading up Severn St. to the edge of town to catch a lift south. The upper end of Thames St. is reportedly the best place for a ride north, but it's a hard walk with a backpack.

The **police station** (tel. 434 5198) is located off Severn St. past the **post office** (tel./ fax 434 7884), which is at Severn and Thames St. (post office open M-F 9am-5pm). The **hospital** (tel. 434 8770) is on Devon St.; you can reach it by following Severn St. past the police station and turning right on Cross St. The **BNZ,** 153 Thames St. (tel. 434 8610), is one block left from the bus station (open M, Th, F 9am-4:30pm, Tu-W 9:30am-4:30pm). **Telephone Code:** 03.

▶ ACCOMMODATIONS. Those who brave the long uphill block from the Visitor Centre to **Swaggers Backpackers,** 25 Wansbeck St. (tel. 434 9999), will be rewarded with cheery, wood-paneled accommodations in one of Oamaru's prettier residential neighborhoods. Don't be fooled by the peeling paint outside—the generously furnished rooms retain the warmth of this 80-year-old home. (Pickup after 5pm. Reception 8-10:30am and 5:30-10pm; self check-in during the day. Dorms $15; twins $17. Cash only. Reservations ideal in summer.) The **Red Kettle Hostel (YHA)** (tel. 434 5008), at the corner of Cross and Reed St., has a red kettle perched on the white picket fence that surrounds this simple, spotless, seasonal hostel with a large common area. The environmentally-conscious will appreciate the friendly reminders plastered throughout the rooms. (Reception 8-10am and 5:30-10pm. Closed July-August, but call for specific dates. Two co-ed dorms and one female-only dorm $14; twins and doubles $32; non-YHA $2-3 more.) Located on the northern edge of town, **Tui's Backpackers,** 469 Thames Highway (tel. 437 1443; fax 437 1926), is a recently-converted motel whose spacious though somewhat plain suites come equipped with a self-contained toilet, shower, kitchen, and a TV (upon request). From the train station you can take the Whitestone Mini-Bus, or call and the owner will pick you up (only after 6pm). Otherwise it's a never-ending 40-minute uphill walk from the center of town. (Laundry $2. Singles $17.) The **Oamaru Gardens Holiday Park** (tel. 434 7666; fax 434 7662) up Chelmer St., is a short walk from the center of town and has a good location, with a bridge to the botanic gardens next door. It's great for tent sites; the cabins are clean but a bit sparse. (Concrete block-style kitchen, toilets, and showers. Laundry $2. Reception 8am-10pm, winter 8am-8pm. Tent sites $9 per person; cabins $28-50.)

☐☑ **FOOD AND NIGHTLIFE. Woolworths,** across from the BNZ on Thames St., fills all your grocery needs (open M-Tu 8am-7pm, W 8am-8pm, Th-F 8am-9pm, Sa 8:30am-7pm, Su 8:30am-6pm). The vegetable quiche and salad ($6.50) at **Emma's Cafe** (tel. 434 1165) combines about as many herbivorous treats on one crowded plate as you could handle. Top it off with a thick slab of banana date-nut bread ($2.50). (Open Tu-F 9am-6pm, Sa 9am-5pm, Su 10am-5pm.) Many of Oamaru's most popular eateries also double as bars and the center of the nightlife. A block down Thames St. from the Visitor Centre, **Annie Flannagan's** (tel. 434 8828) is a traditional Irish bar, which serves up typical bar food (pints $3.50; Roast O'Day, O'Nachos, Murphy's potato skins all $6). With its live music—mostly Irish, rock, and blues—AF's is the place to be on Friday and Saturday nights. (Open M-Th 11:30am-11pm, F-Sa 11:30am-12:30am, Su noon-11pm.) See the other side of Oamaru and AF's cultural rival at the **Criterion Hotel,** 3 Tyne St. (tel 434 6247), an English-style pub in the historic precinct. You won't find Emerson's London Porter pulled from an oak barrel ($3.50 for a pint), pickled eggs ($1), or the hearty Ploughman's Lunch ($7) anywhere else in town. (Open M-Th 11am-10pm, F-Sa 11am-midnight—or whenever the singing stops—Su noon-4am.) "Eat, drink and be merry for tomorrow ye diet," quotes the menu at the **Last Post,** 12 Thames St. (tel. 434 8080). The winter lamb shanks ($10.50) are served piping hot, while breakfast lovers will be thrilled to see all their favorites served for dinner on the mixed grill ($10). Drinks like Midori Splice ($9) and Heaven ($10.95) should have a blissful effect. Live music on its patio on weekend nights. (Open Su-Th 11am-10pm, F-Sa 11am-midnight.) As the penguin wearing shades on the sign says, "It's damn hot" at **The Penguin Entertainers Club** (tel. 437 1251), tucked away behind Harbour St. in the historic precinct. That's probably the best way to describe this semi-secret music-lovers hideout, which draws top blues, jazz, folk, and rock musicians who stop in for a night on their way to Dunedin; call ahead to find out what's playing. Friday night is club night. (Call for directions; cover charge varies.)

⬛ **SIGHTS.** Oamaru's attractions center around its penguins, but there's more than enough to fill a day here. The **Historic Precinct,** with its mix of stately restored whitestone buildings and dilapidated facades, surrounds Harbour and Tyne St. You can view the work of local artists at the **North Otago Art Society Gallery** (open F-Su 1:30-4pm), browse in the antique and second-hand book shops, or take the one-hour **historic tour** from the visitor center for a look inside some of the unrestored structures ($7.50, students $4, under 15 free). Charming and well kept, the **North Otago Museum** (open M-F 1-4:30pm) and the **Forrester Gallery** (open M-F 10:30am-4:30pm, Sa 10:30am-1pm, Su 1-4:30pm) make worthwhile rainy day activities. The **Oamaru Gardens** on Severn St. features a wide walkway, rhododendron and rose gardens, a greenhouse, and the Summerhouse, a romantic spot that has been the site of more than one marriage proposal. Kids will love the expansive, grassy playground that adjoins the gardens on Chelmer St.

The cliffside **Graves Walkway** winds steeply above a tiny sand beach, up through a rare patch of coastal shrubland to a spectacular lookout. Continue on for a half hour to Bushey Beach to see the rare **yellow-eyed penguins.** Only 400 breeding pairs remain on the mainland (they are also found at Katiki Point near Palmerston, and near Dunedin and Balclutha). The best viewing is during the late afternoon shortly before sunset when the penguins return from a long day of fishing after swimming as much as 40km in search of food. You can reach the **Oamaru Blue Penguin Colony** (tel. 434 1718) either by heading south from the center of town to Waterfront Rd. or by returning on the Graves Walkway from Bushey Beach. If you do take the coastal walkway, be sure to come well before dusk so as to not interfere with the timid lilliputians as they waddle ashore (allow a half hour to walk between the colonies on the Graves Walkway). Flash cameras are not permitted. You may want to bring warm clothes and binoculars. (Viewing $8, students $6, under 15 free.)

NEAR OAMARU: MOERAKI BOULDERS

The small hamlet of Moeraki and the nearby 60-million-year-old Moeraki Boulders lie about 40km south of Oamaru. Early European visitors snatched up the smaller boulders for themselves; only one- to two-meter high giants remain. Scientifically known as **septarian concretions,** the 50-odd stones started out as little bits of animal or plant matter on which successive layers of calcite grew, eventually forming the four-ton boulders. The boulders, the largest of which took four million years to develop, are best viewed at low tide. **Natures Shuttle** (tel. 434 5008), operated by the managers of the Red Kettle YHA, runs tours from Oamaru to the boulders via the lookout point and scenic coastal road (2½hr., $15), with departure times varying depending on the tides. **Oamaru mini-coaches** and **InterCity buses** will take you near the boulders or Moeraki (specify which you prefer), but leave you with a 3km walk from SH1 to get to town. To reach the boulders on your own, simply follow the turn-off signs about 1km north of Moeraki on SH1. You can either take the free public access road, which will leave you about a 300m walk from the boulders, or you can park by the **Moeraki Boulders Restaurant** (tel. 439 4827) and pay a $2 access fee. The restaurant looks out from three sides at the boulders, the ocean, and Moeraki; for a moderate price you can get simple fare and a great view.

One of the oldest European settlements in New Zealand, **Moeraki** is a sleepy fishing village just south of the boulders. It is most easily accessible by car. The 30-minute drive between Oamaru and Moeraki can be made either by the standard SH1 or the less-traveled Coast Rd. If you choose to take Coast Rd., you'll wind over rolling hills through rustic countryside overlooking the ocean. Along the way you'll pass ⬛**Coastal Backpackers** (tel. 439 5411), a cozy bunkhouse with red stucco and forest green trim exterior. Both **Atomic Shuttle** and **Magic Bus** pass the backpackers, or you can call and the owner will pick you up from either Oamaru or Moeraki. Choose from a range of free equipment including bikes, canoes, kayaks, and surfboards, or take the short walk to the beach to see Hector dolphins. (Dorms $12; doubles $30; tents $8.) The **Moeraki Motor Camp** (tel. 439 4759) contains a range of tent and power sites that overlook the peaceful cove, and is within walking distance of the boulders. Billing itself as a family camp, it offers a playground with a small trampoline, a grocery and convenience store with a wine license and petrol for your thirsty car. (Check-out 11am. Quiet hours 11pm-7am. Tents $8.50 per person; standard cabins for two $25; tourist flats for two $55.) **Telephone Code in and around Moeraki:** 03.

THE CATLINS

A coastline of untouched beaches, rugged promontories, and ancient forests amid sheep paddocks and turnip patches, the region of the Catlins lives up to its reputation as the best-kept secret in New Zealand. Cliffs dotted with native bush drop into swirling Antarctic waters, while rare penguins waddle across white sand beaches. With a bit of exploring, you may discover a private inlet shared only with sea lions. Its remoteness is tempered by cordial coastal villages; there are few places in New Zealand where civilization can be so close and yet seem so distant.

🚩 **ORIENTATION AND PRACTICAL INFORMATION.** The **Southern Scenic Route (SH92)** runs 172km over pavement and gravel (23km is unsealed) through the Catlins from Balclutha to Invercargill. A car or mountain bike (and strong lungs) is the best way to appreciate the coast at your own pace, although several tours run through the area. **Kiwi Experience's Bottom Bus** (tel. 442 9708) departs from Dunedin on a 10-hour backpacker-oriented tour. Unfortunately, with ever-changing tides, it's rare to make it by bus at the right time to enter **Cathedral Caves** (see p. 378). (Bus runs daily in summer, M, W, and Sa in winter. Departs at 8am; $75, free pickup). **Catlins Coastal Link** (tel. 474 3300) runs similar trips from Invercargill to Dunedin (Tu, Th, and Sa-Su; 8am, $80) with the option of an overnight farmstay ($150). If you want to choose your own destinations while traveling with a guide familiar with the region, **Catlins Mini Tours** (tel./fax 415 8686) is a good choice ($75, $60 each for 2, $50 each for 4 or more; pickup from Dunedin or Invercargill). Another option is **Catlins Natural Wonders** (tel. 418 1798 or mobile (025) 985 941), which runs daytrips from Dunedin, Balclutha, Owaka, and Invercargill ($55-85). More comprehensive overnight tours are available through **Catlins Wildlife Trackers** (tel. 415 8613 or 0800 CATLINS), which runs from Balclutha (M, Th, and Sa 10:30am, $200; reservation required). **Hitchhiking** through the Catlins is said to be feasible in summer, but not so reliable in winter when there's little traffic. There are **no banks** between Balclutha and Invercargill; be sure you have enough cash when you set out. The Catlins abound with secluded **camping sites;** it has excellent, albeit limited, accommodations (booking ahead is vital during the summer). The **telephone code** for the Catlins is **03.**

OWAKA

The major town of the Catlins, Owaka (o-WACK-a; pop. 400) lies just 25km south of Balclutha. The **Visitors Centre** (tel./fax 415 8371) at the **Catlins Diner** offers area maps, accommodation listings, homestay information and bookings, access to the **DOC** displays of the region's flora and fauna ($2), and Internet access ($9 per hr.) (open M-F 6:30am-8:30pm, Sa 8am-8:30pm, Su 9am-8:30pm). **Helen's Dairy** (tel. 415 8304) takes Eftpos and operates a **post office** (open M-F 6:40am-8:30pm, Sa 8:30am-8:30pm, Su 9am-8:30pm), while **Niles Four Square** (tel. 415 8201) has provisions (open M-Th 8:30am-5:30pm, F 8:30am-7:30pm, Sa 9am-5pm; in winter closes Sa noon). The **gas station** (tel. 415 8179) is also an **AA service station** (open M-Th 7:30am-6pm, F 7:30am-7:30pm, Sa 9am-1pm). The **Catlins Medical Centre,** 29 Main Rd. (24hr. emergency tel. 415 8006; fax 415 8688), on the northern edge of Owaka, is the only hospital in the region (open M-F 9-11:30am and 2-5pm; also M 5-6pm and Th 7-8:30pm). **Owaka Pharmacy** is at 26 Waikowa Rd. (tel. 415 8109; open M-Th 8:45am-5:30pm, also Th 7-9pm, F 8:45am-7pm). The recently opened **Internet Cafe** (tel./fax 415 8030) offers access to the web ($3 for 20 min.) for the email-obsessed.

Catlins Backpackers (tel. 415 8392), at the diner, has laundry facilities, TV, and kitchen with cappuccino machine. (Simple bunks and doubles. Bikes $20 per day. Reception has the same hours as diner. Dorms $14, winter $12.) The sunny lounge and friendly atmosphere at **Owaka Highview Backpackers and Motel** (tel. 415 8686), on Royal Terr., more than make up for the unfinished floors and ripped wallpaper in some of the dorms. (Bike rentals $12 per day. Reception 8am-10pm. Dorms $12; doubles $15; tents $8; caravans $10. Cash only.) For those seeking more comfort, the spacious motel accommodations upstairs from the backpackers is the best deal in town (doubles $55, extra adult $12, extra child $8). Follow the signs from Owaka to reach the **Pounawea Motor Camp** (tel./fax 415 8483), by an estuary on the Catlins River. The Paunawea Bush Walk begins from the campground. You can also rent canoes ($5) to explore the birdlife along the waterway. (Reception 24hr. Cabins $15; tent sites $7; caravan sites $8.) The **Catlins Inn,** 21 Ryley St. (tel. 415 8350), has pleasant accommodations for a reasonable price. The yard out back has space for campervans ($8 per vehicle) and tent sites (free). (Reception 8am-late. Singles $30; twins $40; doubles $40-45.) In the pub adjoining the inn, where you can shoot pool, throw darts, and start drinking early with Happy Hour (M-F 5-7pm), enjoy a hot meal (mains $10-15) or toss back a few cold ones with the old-timers (open daily from 11am).

For a cold brew by a toasty fire, mosey on into the incongruously modern **Lumberjack Bar and Cafe** (tel. 415 8747). Sally up to the enormous macrocarpa bar (which 10 men had to carry in) and feel like you've hewn Burnham wood with the best of them. 300-gram rump steak or venison is $17. Entrees start at $7. (Open daily from 4pm, winter Th-Su from 4pm.)

KAKA POINT

The Catlins' claim to fame is its coastline, with its fine sand beaches and jutting headlands, where sea lions bask on the rocks amidst squawking colonies of birds. Start exploring at **Kaka Point,** 12km north of Owaka on a well-marked road off the southern scenic route. The sandy swath at Kaka arcs toward **Nugget Point,** 8km south down a bumpy gravel road. The view from the little lighthouse (the most southern lighthouse in the world) is worth the 10-minute jaunt above the blue-green waters. Fur and elephant seals and hooker sea lions frolic on the water-logged crags of rocks extending from the point. On the road to Nugget Point, **Roaring Bay** is home to several yellow-eyed penguins that hop up the cliffs before sunset. A sign for **Tunnel Hill** on the main road leads to a five-minute walk through an abandoned railway tunnel. Turn off your flashlight for a spooky experience; the track is quite flat and smooth. Clamber up the path through lush native bush to reach tiny **Fernlea Backpackers** (tel. 412 8834). Overlooking Molyneaux Bay, the lounge and the double room share fabulous views in this basic hostel. (Bikes $10 per day. Linen $2. Reception 8am-10pm. Bunks $15; doubles $30. Cash only.) **Kaka Point Camping Ground** (tel. 412 8818) has two simple cabins, although you'll miss the ocean views. (Reception 7-9am and 7-9pm. Singles $14; doubles $25; extra person $8; caravan sites $10, $15 for 2; tent sites $8, $11 for 2. Cash only.) In the town of Kaka Point, **Nugget View Motels** (tel. 412 8602; fax 412 8623) offers four-star modern rooms overlooking the ocean. (Reception 8am-10pm. $90 for 2, extra adult $15, extra child $7.50. Handicap accessible. Reservations recommended in summer.) Run by the same owners as Nugget View Motels, the **Kaka Point Motel** across the street has less expensive doubles ($75) with nice furnishings, great views, TVs, and kitchens (reservation and check-out times same as above). The owners also operate **Nugget Tour boat charters,** one- to two-hour wildlife excursions (from $30) to view local marine life (other options for exploration include fishing and horseback riding). Down the road toward the point, **Nugget Lodge** (tel. 412 8783; fax 418 1333) has newly-remodeled rooms a stone's throw from the water. (Reception 8am-10pm. Check-out 10am. Rooms $70. Reservations recommended.) **Kaka Point Stores** (tel. 412 8800) has groceries, takeaways, a bar, and is also the **post office** (open M-Sa 8:30am-6pm, Su 9am-6pm).

CANNIBAL BAY

Seals and sea lions congregate on the expanse of beach at Cannibal Bay or over the dunes at **Surat Bay.** Surat Bay is the shorter drive from the Southern Scenic Route, but it's not accessible by car at high tide (regardless of tides, it's a two-minute walk from Cannibal Bay). Though human bones were once discovered at Cannibal Bay, it's more likely that the unlucky chap was killed in a Maori battle than eaten by cannibals. The road continues back toward Owaka, where you can travel down the coast or up the Owaka Valley through unfelled forests along the **Catlins River Gorge.** Get a ride to the top of the **Catlins River Track,** a rare and well-maintained tramp through unspoiled beech forest and over three soaring suspension bridges (3-5hr. one-way). When the trout are biting, this is the place to catch 'em. The **DOC campsite** at the top of the track has no facilities; the **Tawanui campsite** ($4 per person) at the base has bathrooms. For a less strenuous escapade, follow the road to **Ratanui** (5km south of Owaka) and the signs to **Jack's Blowhole.** More aptly named a slurp hole, the deep depression is connected by caves to the ocean 200m away (walk the easy 30min. paddock track to reach it).

PURAKAUNUI BAY AND FALLS

Local beach cows munch kelp on the sand of **Purakaunui Bay** (a surfing beach for the brave-hearted). The mist from crashing waves lends a magical effervescence to the view from the popular **DOC campsite,** with bathrooms ($4 per site). To reach it, take the rough road south of Ratanui. A few kilometers farther south on the scenic route is the turn-off to **Purakaunui Falls** (follow the signs toward Maclennan). The walk on the way to the falls (10min. from the car park) is as spectacular as the multi-tiered cascades themselves. A little luxury is available at **Greenwood Farmstay** (tel. 415 8259), a warm, sophisticated B&B with meticulously gardened grounds. Dinner is $25. (Singles $45; queen with day room and suite $60. Cash only.)

PAPATOWAI

Papatowai Beach is gorgeous, with crashing waves, mist rising off the sand, cliffs farther down the coast, and the estuary, which flows among dune forest into the frigid waters. Papatowai is well worth a stop, whether you intend to canoe or kayak in the estuary, or would simply like a scenic place for a picnic. Follow the signs off the main road to reach the ■**Hilltop Backpackers** (tel./fax 415 8028). The Oriental rugs, glowing wood stove, lavish modern kitchen, and bathrooms with tubs all invite instant relaxation. Canoes, bikes, surfboards, boogie boards, and wetsuits are available. (Reception 24hr. Dorms $19; doubles with an incomparable beach view and thick bed covers $45. Cash only.) The **Papatowai Motels and Store** (tel. 415 8147) has gas and groceries (open daily 8:30am-8pm, winter Su-Th 9am-6pm, F-Sa 9am-6:30pm) and the rooms at the motel behind the store are roomy and pleasant. (Reception hours same as store. Doubles $65, extra adult $12, extra child $8.) The **Papatowai Motor Park** (tel. 415 8500; fax 415 8503) is behind the store in a bushy area with birdlife. Reception is open 8:45am to 6:30pm; check-out is 10am. It offers basic dorms ($12), cabins ($30 for 2), tent sites ($6), and caravan sites ($7).

South of Papatowai, the road becomes gravel and winds to **Florence Lookout** and its spectacular view of **Tautuku Beach.** Backed by olive and rusty hues of the native forest, Tautuku may be the best of the Catlins' remarkable beaches. Turn off for **Lake Wilkie** and its 20-minute boardwalk a bit farther down the hill. Don't miss the **Cathedral Caves** turn-off, 16km from Tautuku, unequivocally the highlight of the Catlins. The caves are only accessible at low tide; check a tide table at the Visitor Centre before making the half-hour trek down under dripping tree ferns and kamahi trees to **Waipati Beach** and the caves. Just after the caves turn onto Rewcastle Rd. for the 30-minute walk through the beech forest to the **McLean Falls.**

PORPOISE BAY

Continue on to **Invercargill** via **Tokanui** on the main road, or turn back onto gravel toward **Waikawa** some 20km beyond the Cathedral Caves. Shortly after you cross the Waipati River, you'll reach the turn-off for **Chaslands Farm Lodge** (tel. 415 8501), a small motel that can accommodate groups of up to seven. (Reception 24hr. Check-out 10am. $55 for 2; extra adult $12, extra child $8.) **Curio Bay Campground** (tel. 246 8897; fax 246 8792), a long, sheltered stretch of beach where a few stout-hearted swimmers venture, has somewhat exposed tent sites ($4 per person, extra person $1), powered sites ($15 per night), and non-powered sites ($10 per night). The **Dolphin Information Centre** in Waikawa (tel. 246 8444) has displays on the area's marine mammals (open daily Oct.-Apr.). **Koramika Charters** runs a unique Hector's dolphin tour (one of the smallest and rarest dolphins in the world) from Porpoise Bay between October and April. (4 tours per day; $45-65; reserve at the Dolphin Centre.) Just beyond the beach lies **Curio Bay,** situated by the 180-million-year-old **petrified forest** visible on the rocky coast at low tide. Among pools of bead-like seaweed and unhinged bull kelp are the mineralized trunks of several tall, ancient trees. Continuing from Porpoise Bay toward **Haldane** (the road occasionally floods at peak tide along the estuary), you'll pass the road leading to a sheep farm and hostel known as **Pope's Place** (tel./fax 246 8420; email popesplace@compuserve.com). Deeply cushioned beds are $14 (doubles $30) in a house surrounded by flax plants; the toilets are a short walk from the dorms. (Reception 24hr. Cash only. Reservations recommended.) Across from the Dolphin Centre, **Waikawa Lodge** (tel. 246 8552) provides spare, immaculate rooms with metal frame bunks. (Reception 24hr. Dorms $15; twins $34, doubles $38.) **Waipapa Point,** 20km from Pope's Place on the way past **Otara** toward **Invercargill,** is worth a stop, if only to be thrown down by the battering southern wind at the foot of the lonely lighthouse.

SOUTHLAND

INVERCARGILL

Flat and boring, Invercargill remains little more than a transfer point to Stewart Island or Fiordland. Dated cafes, trinket stores, and car service centers line the main streets of town, which become quite deserted at night. Despite its population of 53,000, Invercargill retains a small-town feel. Linger longer than a day and you'll likely end up at the movie theater for lack of better options.

🛈 ORIENTATION AND PRACTICAL INFORMATION

From the train and bus station, cross **Leven St.** and pass through Wachner Pl. under the **clock tower. Dee St.,** Invercargill's diesel-fumed main thoroughfare, runs to the right toward **Bluff** and the **Catlins,** and to the left toward **Queens Park** and **Queenstown.** North of the city, it becomes **North Rd.** Across from the clock tower, **Esk St.** is the main shopping thoroughfare. **SH1** from Dunedin cuts through the city via **Tay St.** and ends up on Dee St. The length of blocks in Invercargill is enormous; it will take you twice as long as you may think to get from one place to another on foot.

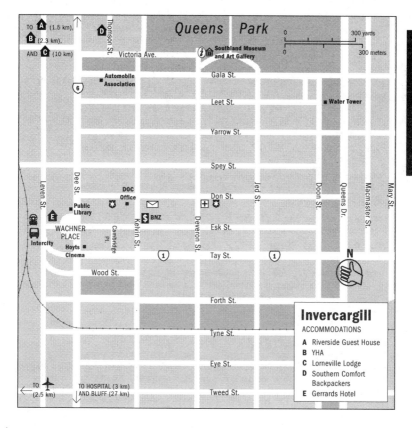

Invercargill

ACCOMMODATIONS

A Riverside Guest House
B YHA
C Lorneville Lodge
D Southern Comfort Backpackers
E Gerrards Hotel

SOUTH ISLAND

Visitors Center: The Invercargill Information Centre (tel. 214 6243) is on Gala St. inside the massive white pyramid. From Wachner Pl., go left up Dee St., take a right at McDonald's onto Gala St., and the center is two blocks down on the left. Open M-F 9am-5pm, Sa-Su 10am-5pm.

Airplanes: The **airport** is located 2.5km west of the city. Take Dee St. south as it becomes Clyde St. and then follow the signs on the roundabout to the airport. Or, take **Spitfire Shuttle** (tel. 218 7381 or 214 1851) for $5 ($3.50 each if 2 or more); a taxi to the airport costs $8. **Air New Zealand** and **Ansett New Zealand** fly frequently to **Auckland** ($302-527) and **Christchurch** ($160-250).

Trains: The **train station** (tel. 214 0599) is on Leven St. behind the clock tower. **Tranz-Scenic** goes daily to **Christchurch** (9hr., 8:25am, $117) via **Dunedin** (3hr., $51).

Buses: InterCity (tel. 214 0598) leaves from the train station daily for **Christchurch** (9hr., 8:50am, $85, YHA $68) via **Dunedin** (3hr., 1 per day, $40, YHA $32). **Atomic Shuttles** (tel. 322 8883) has cheaper fares to **Dunedin** ($20), continuing on to **Christchurch** ($40). **Spitfire Shuttle** (tel. 218 7381) runs to **Te Anau** (2½-3hr., 1pm, $34, YHA $29). **Southern Air Land Travel** (tel. 218 9129) heads daily to **Queenstown** (2hr., 1 per day, $35, $30 YHA), as does **Atomic Shuttles,** with slightly higher prices ($40, $34 YHA). Call for bookings and pickup. **Bottom Bus** (tel. 442 9708) also runs to **Te Anau** and to **Queenstown** (6pm daily in summer, winter M, W, Sa, $35-55).

City Buses: (tel. 218 7108). Serve the suburbs M-F every hr., $1.20. Most depart from the library on Dee St. or across the street; the Information Centre has schedules.

Taxis: Blue Star (tel. 218 6079) and **Taxi Co.** (tel. 214 4478) run 24hr.

Car Rental: Among other smaller operations, **Pegasus,** 18 Teviot St. (24hr. tel. 0800 803 580 or 214 3210) has cheap rental cars from $35 per day, plus long-term rates. The **AA** (24hr. tel. 218 9033; fax 214 0246) is at 51 Gala St. Open M-F 9am-5pm.

Bike Rental: Mountain bikes are available from **Wensley's Cycle Centre,** 53 Tay St. (tel. 218 6206). $12-20 per day. Open M-Th 8am-5:30pm, F 8am-9pm, Sa 9:30am-12:30pm.

Hitchhiking: Those heading toward Queenstown are said to take the Waikiwi bus from the library up North Rd. as far as possible and then walk to the city limits. For Dunedin, hitchhikers take the Hawthornedale bus (departing from 14 Tay St.) as far as it goes.

DOC: (tel. 214 4589). On the 7th floor of the State Insurance building, on Don St. Open M-F 8am-5pm.

Currency Exchange: BNZ (tel. 218 9179), at the corner of Esk and Kelvin St. Open M-F 9am-4:30pm. Other banks dot the city center.

Police: (tel. 214 4039).

Medical Services: Urgent Doctor (tel. 218 8821). Open M-F 5-10pm, Sa-Su 8am-10pm). The **Southland Hospital** (tel. 214 5735) is on Kew Rd.

Post Office: 51 Don St. (tel. 214 7700). Open M-F 8:30am-5pm, W 9am-5pm, Sa 10am-1:30pm.

Internet Access: Available at the **public library** (tel. 218 7025) on Dee St. $8 per hr. Open M-F 9am-8:30pm, Sa 10am-1pm. Also **Gordon's Data Services,** 124 Dee St. $10 per hr. Open M-F 10am-5:30pm, Sa 10am-noon.

Telephone Code: 03.

 # ACCOMMODATIONS

Most hostels lie off Dee St. along and beyond Queens Park. **Southern Comfort Backpackers,** 30 Thomson St. (tel. 218 3838), treats you like only a fine whiskey could. From the Information Centre, turn right down Victoria Ave., then take a right on Thomson St. The fire-warmed living room and the spotless, ultra-modern kitchen makes you feel like you're a houseguest. (Free bikes. Reception until 10pm. Dorms $16; doubles $18. Reserve in advance. Cash only.) The **Invercargill**

YHA, 122 North Rd. (tel. 215 9344; fax 215 9382), 3km up Dee St., is clean but unexciting. (Reception 8-10am, 5-6:30pm and 8:30-10pm, winter 8-10am and 5:30-8:30pm. Dorms $15; twins $17; doubles $18.) At the **Backpackers Riverside Guesthouse,** 70 Filleul St. (tel. 218 9027 or 0800 302 277), a few blocks closer to town and overlooking the Waipati River, you'll find quiet, intimate rooms in a family's home. (Free pickup and bikes. Dorms $15; cabins $10 per person; tent sites $8. Cash only.) **Gerrards Hotel,** 3 Leven St. (tel. 218 3406; fax 218 3003), is opposite the train station. The rooms in this European-style hotel are attractively decorated. (Singles $40-50, including breakfast; doubles $85-98.) To reach **Lorneville Lodge** (tel. 235 8031), a sunny caravan park 10km from town, take SH6 towards Queenstown and then turn right on SH98. (Tourist flats for 2 $55; cabins for 2 $36; on-site caravans $13 per person; tent sites and powered sites $8.50 per person. Cash only.)

🜚 🎦 FOOD AND NIGHTLIFE

Most restaurants are scattered about the city center, and many double as bars and nighttime hangouts. A large elephant on the front awning welcomes you to the **Zookeepers Cafe,** 50 Tay St. (tel. 218 3373), where animals are the theme, from the stuffed fake gorilla over the door to the turtle toasties ($5). Sip a bottomless coffee ($2.50) or select from several beers on tap. Snacks are $5-8, mains $10-15. (Open M-Sa from 10am, Su from 11am.) **New Zealand Natural Cafe,** 59 Esk St. makes its own waffle cones, which you can try hot and fresh with mango swirl ice cream, cream, and passion fruit topping all for only $1.70. Those with heartier appetites will appreciate the luscious kebabs ($4-5.50). (Open M-Th 9:30am-5:30pm, F 9:30am-8:30pm, Sa 10am-2pm.) Modern art adorns the brick walls of the classy **Tillerman's Cafe,** 16 Don St. (tel. 218 9240), where lunch is an affordable indulgence—the baked potato and salad option is only $7. The bar upstairs features a wide range of bands Thursday though Saturday nights. (Open M-F 11:30am-2pm, and 6:30-10pm, Sa 6:30-10pm; bar open daily 6:30pm-late.) **Frog 'n' Firkin,** 31 Dee St. (tel. 214 4001), has "Frog Feed" (nachos $8, bread and soup $6), a fireplace in the cafe area, and a bar with TVs. Drink specials Th-Sa. Open M-F noon-late, Sa 4pm-late. Proudly displaying their regional beef and lamb awards, **The Rocks Bar,** 101 Dee St. (tel. 218 7597), in Courtville Pl. does gourmet dishes with excellent sauces. The wrap of the day is $12 and the citrus steamed pudding is $7. (Open M-Sa 6pm-late, Su noon-2pm.) The **Pak 'N Save market** is at 95 Tay St. (tel. 214 4864; open M-Tu 9am-7pm, W-F 9am-9pm, Sa 9am-7pm, Su 9am-6pm).

Aside from the **Hoyts 5 Movie Theater,** 29 Dee St. (tel. 214 1110), or the **bars** at **Zookeepers** and **Tillerman's,** there just ain't much local entertainment here. **Players,** 25 Tay St. (tel. 218 1857), has 20 pool tables ($10 per hr. for large tables, $8 per hr. for small tables; open M-W noon-11pm, Th-Sa noon-1am).

🜚 SIGHTS

The **Southland Museum and Art Gallery** (tel. 218 9753), at the city end of **Queen's Park,** is in the same gleaming white pyramid as the Information Centre. The highlight is the tuatarium, a live exhibit of the nocturnal reptiles that once roamed all of New Zealand. The Roaring 40s gallery upstairs to discover New Zealand's subantarctic islands and the megaherbs that thrive there, supremely adapted to the severe conditions. The dynamic slide show includes strobe lightning and may be as close as you can get to the restricted-access isles. Take a stroll through the English rose garden. On a clear, cool night, view the stars at the **Observatory** next to the Information Centre. (Museum open M-F 9am-5pm, Sa-Su 10am-5pm. Free. Slideshow $2, children 50¢. Observatory open W 7pm-9pm. 50¢ admission includes slideshow.)

SOUTH ISLAND

NEAR INVERCARGILL: BLUFF

As the departure point for the ferry to Stewart Island (see p. 384), seaside Bluff (Invercargill's peninsular port town) also marks the beginning (or end) of SH1. Bluff lies at the tip of a long spit of land 27km south of the city. Though fishing and shipping industries dominate the port, it's still worth looking around here en route to Stewart Island. At Bluff's **Visitor Centre,** 74 Gore St. (tel. 212 8305), inside Foveau Souvenirs and Antiques, Dawn will answer your queries (open daily 9am-5pm, winter 10am-4pm). The **Paua Shell House,** 258 Marine Parade (tel. 212 8262), is renowned throughout New Zealand for the thousands of lacquered and colorful shells that line its walls. Chat with local legends Fred and Myrtle Flutey. Open daily 9am-5pm. If you're waiting to catch the ferry, the **Bluff Maritime Museum** (tel. 212 7534) on the pier is a good place to pass the time learning about the region's history (open M-F 10am-4:30pm, Sa-Su 1-5pm). With the recent closure of the town's bank, Eftpos withdrawals at the **Service Centre** on Gore St. are the only way to get cash (open M-F 9am-4:30pm). The **Campbelltown Passenger Service** (tel. 212 7404) runs between Bluff and Invercargill (M-F 5 per day, Sa-Su 2 per day; $10, round-trip $18; bookings required). Other services include: **Four Square Market** (tel. 212 8170; open M-W 8am-6pm, Th-Sa 8am-7pm, Su 9am-6pm); **post office** (tel. 212 8759) next door (open M-F 8:45am-5pm, Sa 10am-7pm); and the **medical centre** (tel. 212 7337; open M-F 9am-12:30pm and 1:30-5pm) behind the camping ground. **Flynn Club's Hotel** (tel. 212 8124), on Gore St., has regal red bedspreads, a medieval court painting, and dark foyer. (Reception 8am-midnight. Dorms $15; spacious doubles $30.) Up Gregory St. you'll find **Argyle Park Motor Camp** (tel. 212 8774), with three small, unadorned cabins ($8), caravan sites ($6), and tent sites ($5). Use of the concrete showers and kitchen costs $2.

INVERCARGILL TO TUATAPERE

If you're heading to or from Te Anau and Invercargill (and have a choice about the route), take the **Southern Scenic Route.** While the inland route passes through the service towns of Lumsden and Mossburn, the Southern Scenic Route takes an alternate but equally efficient path, affording both ocean vistas and mountain panoramas before heading inland and upland to Te Anau. **Bottom Bus** (tel. 442 9709) runs from Invercargill to **Te Anau** with an overnight stay in **Riverton** (daily 6pm in summer, winter M, W, and Sa), while **Spitfire Shuttles** (tel. 214 1851) runs in both directions (departs Invercargill daily 1pm Te Anau daily 7:45am, winter M-F only; $34, YHA $29). Hitchhiking along this stretch of the Southern Scenic Route is reportedly a good prospect in summer, but uncertain in winter. The stretch from Riverton to Tuatapere is dotted with small towns and innumerable bays and inlets. **Telephone Code: 03.**

RIVERTON

One of New Zealand's oldest towns, Riverton (pop. 1850) is a quiet seaside retreat, with sand flats stretching toward the ocean and high-bowed trawlers bobbing at the pier. **Riverton Rocks**, over the bridge and a few kilometers along the coast, is a popular sheltered swimming beach and picnicking area with views toward Invercargill and Stewart Island. Numerous short tracks start at the **Aparima River Road** bridge, leading through native bush to beaches or unusual rock formations such as the precarious balancing rock. The **Visitor Centre** is located at the tastefully refurbished **Riverton Rock Backpackers** (tel. 234 8886 or 0800 248 886; fax 234 8816), where you'll find a TV lounge with free tea and coffee. (Reception 9am-noon and 4-7pm; dorms $19, winter $17.) The owners run a more budget-oriented backpackers at **The Globe Hotel** (tel. 234 8527) next door. Reservations are essential in summer and advisable in winter since Bottom Bus stops here. (Reception 1pm-late at the bar; dorms $17; twins and doubles $38. VIP discount.) Local services include: the **Riverton Supervalue** and the **post office**

PAUA POWER Of the 144 types of abalone (shellfish) found around the world, the New Zealand paua boasts the most brilliant peacock shades and the greatest variety of shapes, as well as a hefty price tag. On the South Island there is a strict harvest quota of 400 tons; a one-ton permit costs $100,000. Harvested by fishermen who free-dive up to 10m to pry the crustaceans from rocks, paua can live up to 100 years and grow up to 220cm in size. Paua meat, at $95 per kilo, is an expensive and acquired taste. Much of New Zealand's catch ends up in Asia among the festivities for Chinese New Year. The best way to cook fresh paua is to boil it whole before removing the shell. But don't throw out that exoskeleton; many New Zealanders decorate just about anything with paua, including chairs, surfboards, and even entire rooms. Like a fingerprint, each shell is unique. Ground, polished, and lacquered paua run $10-20—a small price for a shell that took 20-50 years to create.

across the street and down a bit from the hotel (both open M-Th 7:45am-6:30pm, F 7:45am-8pm, Sa 9am-7pm, Su 9am-4:30pm); **National Bank** (open M-F 9am-4:30pm); and the **medical centre** (tel. 234 8290) on the next block (open M 9am-6:30pm, Tu-F 9am-4:30pm).

OREPUKI

From Riverton, the Southern Scenic Route traverses open country past the Longwood Range and on to Tuatapere. **Colac Bay,** 10km beyond Riverton, is a former Maori settlement and popular surfing beach. **Te Waewae Bay,** which appears suddenly over the hill 15km further on, is often battered by the full force of the Southern Ocean. Through the mist in summer you can sometimes see Hector's dolphins or the occasional right whale spouting off. Look out for windblown macrocarpas as you pass through **Orepuki** (pop. 150). Originally situated at Monkey Island, this gold-mining town was relocated three times to satisfy prospectors. Nearby at **Orepuki Beach,** you can find tiny, low-grade gemstones amid the grains of sand, and some hopefuls still pan for gold.

TUATAPERE

A little logging town (pop. 700) situated halfway between Invercargill and Te Anau, Tuatapere (Tua-TAP-ery) is a good starting point for walks into Fiordland National Park, the largest park in New Zealand. Though Tuatapere means "a meeting place between two ridges" in Maori, some local legends have renamed it "the hole in the bush," because the town was cut out of a thick forest. But locals are most fond of a third nickname, "land of the last light," so given because the town is the last in New Zealand to see the sun go down. It is an attractive and undiscovered base for the many tramps and wilderness activities in the area.

7 PRACTICAL INFORMATION. Tuatapere's **Visitors Centre** (tel. 226 6399), south of the bridge over the **Waiau River** (open in summer daily 9am-5pm). The **Spitfire Shuttle** (tel. 226 6399) runs in the morning to **Invercargill** and in the afternoon to **Te Anau** (daily in summer, winter M-F; book ahead for pickup). Get your area **hut passes** at the **DOC office** (tel. 226 6607) down the street (open M-F 8am-5pm). **Fraser's Pharmacy** (tel. 226 6999), across from the DOC office, doubles as the **post office** (open M-Th 9am-5:30pm, F 9am-8pm, Sa 11am-noon). **Dowling's Discounter** (tel. 226 6250), around the corner, may have the better selection (open daily 8am-8:30pm), but **Western Foodmarket** (tel. 226 6292), north of the river, is cheaper (open M-Th 7am-7pm, F 7am-8:30pm, Sa 7am-5pm, Su 9am-4pm).

ACCOMMODATIONS AND FOOD. The **Waiau Hotel** (tel. 226 6409), south of the town center, has pleasant, self-contained rooms. It has a spacious bar room, complete with a pool table, TV, and slot machines. (Singles $25, with bath $30;

SOUTH ISLAND

doubles $50, with bath $60.) More budget-oriented and far less glamorous lodging can be found at **Five Mountains Holiday Park** (tel. 226 6418), north of the bridge. The concrete-floor rooms are clean and basic, and the common area has a TV, cook-ware, and a stove. (Reception in the cafe Tu-Su 9:30am-8pm in summer, winter W-Su 9:30am-8pm, next door in the private residence when cafe is closed. Dorms $10; self-contained units $20; tent sites $10; powered caravan sites $15.) Better camp-ing sites can be found down by the river past the Domain, though the cabins there are starkly basic.

▣ ⚑ **SIGHTS AND ACTIVITIES.** The **Tuatapere Scenic Reserve** is home to tower-ing beeches, though you'll no longer find the ancient tuataras that once dominated the region; grab an informative pamphlet from the Visitor Centre and follow signs to the Domain to begin the **Tuatapere Walkway.** Mountain biking along the gravel former logging roads to Lake Hauroko and down winding Borland Rd. to **Lake Monowai** is very popular. Tuatapere is also home to the annual **Wild Challenge** (tel. 226 6568), a 35km whitewater kayak, 30km run, and 32km bike race held in early January. If you're only a minor masochist, the **Waiau Grunt** (13km kayak, 8km run, 20km bike) may be more appealing.

Several tours and guides operate out of Tuatapere. Some of the most exciting are on the jetboats that fly over **Lake Hauroko** and down the rock-strewn rapids of the **Wairaurahiri River. Wairaurahiri Wilderness Jet** (tel. 225 8174) and **Wairaurahiri Jet** (tel. 225 8318 or 236 1137) both run full-day trips (around $100; book ahead). **Lake Hauroko Tours** (226 6681) connects with **Spitfire Shuttle** to provide access to the **Dusty Track** ($50 per person, twice weekly and on demand). The Visitor Cen-tre has details on guided walks, helicopter tours, and other services in remote Fiordland.

Tuatapere is the endpoint (or beginning point) for the **Dusky Track,** a rugged walk only for the experienced that requires at least a week (parts of the track may be done in smaller 3-4 day trips). The town also serves as a departure point for the spectacular walk to the **Percy Burn Viaduct,** at 36m high and 125m long the largest wooden viaduct in the world, and the **South Coast Track,** which follows a former logging tramway. The latter requires two nights at Port Craig Hut, a former school, to reach the viaducts that were once constructed for timber transport. The track begins 28km from Tuatapere at **Bluecliffs Beach,** at the signposted road on the north side of town. The newest addition to the region's walks is the **Hump Ridge Track,** a three-day, 53km loop through beach, bush, and mountain areas. Not slated to open until April of 2000, the track promises to be breathtaking when completed (check with the Visitor Centre for the status of the track).

CLIFDEN

North of Tuatapere, 17km along the road to Te Anau, the hamlet of Clifden is nota-ble for its **limestone caves,** located 1km up the road after the lime works on the route toward Winton. Prospective spelunkers should pick up a map in Tuatapere and bring a flashlight; the caves are extensive, cramped in places, and sometimes flooded. Also take a moment to walk the historic suspension bridge at Clifden, completed in 1902. Downstream, the protruding cliff face is the profile of a legend-ary Maori maiden thwarted in love who leapt off the precipice. From Clifden, the road heads through the Waiau River valley as the inaccessible Takitimu mountains to the east and the distant heights of Fiordland to the west are occasionally visible over the foothills.

STEWART ISLAND

When Maui fished up the North Island from his South Island canoe, Stewart Island was his anchor stone. Named *Rakiura* in Maori, "the place of glowing skies" sees fiery red sunsets in summer, and the eerie *aurora australis* in win-ter. Muddy tracks and remote beaches retain the wild flavor of a land where kiwi still vastly outnumber Kiwis. Of Stewart Island's 1683 square kilometers, 90% are

DOC-managed as reserve lands, with 8% owned by the Rakiura Maori and 2% in other private hands. Bird life abounds, with wood pigeons noisily swooping through town, rarer birds thriving on rat-free Ulva Island, and droves of penguins and muttonbirds crowding beaches. The island's 350-odd (or 350 odd) residents cluster in the fishing village by Halfmoon Bay, gracefully weathering 290 days and 1500mm of rain per year. They insist, with good reason, that you haven't seen New Zealand until you've experienced their beech-free forests, pristine beaches, and quiet lifestyle.

▐ ARRIVAL AND DEPARTURE

Airplanes: Southern Air (Oban tel. 219 1090, Invercargill tel. 218 9129) flies a nine-seat prop plane to and from **Invercargill** (20min.; 3 per day, winter on demand; $65, return $120; student/backpacker discounts available). Only 15kg per person will be carried on a single flight—extra gear must be flown over on a separate flight. Southern Air runs a free shuttle from the Stewart Island airstop to **Halfmoon Bay** on the mainland. **Spitfire Shuttle** (tel. 214 1851) runs between **Invercargill** and the island's airport (on demand; $5.50 one-way if alone, $3.30 per person for 2-10 passengers).

Ferries: Foveaux Express (tel. 212 7660) runs a catamaran between Bluff and Halfmoon Bay, often across choppy seas that could upset those with sensitive stomachs (1hr.; 2 per day in summer, 1-2 per day in winter; $37, return $74, children half-price). Alternatively, the record for swimming the strait is 9 hours and 41 minutes. **Campbelltown Passenger Service** (tel. 212 7404) makes ferry dropoffs and pickups on its way between **Bluff** and **Invercargill** (30min., $10). Secure parking at the Bluff ferry terminal costs $5 per night.

▐ ORIENTATION AND PRACTICAL INFORMATION

Stewart Island lies about 35km across the **Foveaux Strait** from Bluff, the nearest mainland town. The island's primary human settlement is tiny **Oban**, alternately known by its location at **Halfmoon Bay. Elgin Terr.** curves along the bay, while **Ayr St., Main Rd.**, and **Horseshoe Bay Rd.** branch inland; nothing in town is more than a 15-minute walk.

Visitors Center: The **Visitor Centre** (tel. 219 1218) is on Main Rd. in the same building as the **DOC office** (tel. 219 1130). Both open Dec. 26-Mar. 31 M-F 8am-7pm, Sa-Su 9am-7pm; Apr. 1-Dec. 24 M-F 8am-5pm, Sa-Su 10am-noon. This is the best place in town for comparing and booking accommodations, or for picking up track info. **Luggage storage** is available (large lockers $5). Activity info and bookings are handled by the **Stewart Island Adventure Center** (tel. 219 1134), on the wharf (open daily 7:15am-about 7:30pm, winter open according to ferry activity), or by **Stewart Island Travel** (tel. 219 1269), on Main Rd. (open daily 9am-5pm, winter 10am-3pm).

Taxis and Rentals: Oban Taxis and Tours (tel. 219 1456) rents mopeds (from $16 per hr.), double motor scooters (from $21 per hr.), and cars (half-day $55, full day $70), and runs a taxi service (on-call daily 7:30am-10pm).

Currency Exchange: There are **no banks** and **no ATMs** on the island. **Stewart Island Travel** (see above) and the **South Sea Hotel** (see below) will exchange foreign traveler's checks.

Police: (tel. 219 1020), on Golden Bay Rd.

Medical Services: District nurse (tel. 219 1098), on Argyle St.

Post Office: Run by **Southern Air** (tel. 219 1090), on Elgin Terr. Open in M-F 7:30am-6pm, Sa-Su 9:30am-5pm; winter M-F 8:30am-5pm, Sa-Su 8:30am-5pm.

Internet Access: A good deal is offered by **Jo and Andy's B&B** (see below), where you're only charged $2.50 to check and $2 to send email. Open daily 9am-7pm.

Telephone Code: 03.

TRAGICALLY DELICIOUS Named for its strangely sheepish flavor, muttonbird (or sooty shearwater, or titi) is a delicacy enjoyed primarily on Stewart Island and in Invercargill. Today, it can only be harvested by Rakiura Maori, who move onto the offshore Muttonbird Islands for the annual hunt, which dates back hundreds of years. By day, when the adults are out foraging, harvesters push sticks down titi burrows and scoop the baby birds out. By night, they hunt by torchlight, capturing the juveniles as they emerge from the holes. Immediately killed by a bite to the head or a whack to the ground, the birds are dipped in hot wax, cooled, plucked, and stored in bags made of rubbery bull kelp. The annual harvest begins on April 1, and ends with the collection of up to 250,000 birds—a major source of food and income. To ensure a sustainable harvest, the kill area must be rotated at least every two years, since titi migrate all the way up to Siberia and back to the burrows of their birth. If you eat muttonbird, you know it came from this harvest.

ACCOMMODATIONS

Oban's range of character-laden accommodations is impressive, and the Visitor Centre has a complete listing with photos; in summer, reserve well in advance. **Jo and Andy's B&B** (tel./fax 219 1230), on Main Rd., is a cozy homestay with beautiful rooms and a warm family room loaded with bookshelves and world maps. (Dinner $12.50. Singles $17; doubles $32.) **The View** (tel. 219 1328), up steep Nichol Rd. past the Southern Air office, is a three-level affair with lovely old rooms. The spacious homestay has fantastic harbor views, a huge deck, an organ, and a pool table. (Doubles $20. Cash only.) Backpackers accommodation surrounded by moss and ferns awaits at **Shearwater Inn** (tel. 219 1114), on Ayr St., with a big TV lounge and an outdoor BBQ. (Reception year-round M-Sa 7:30am-7pm, Su 9am-7pm. Free storage for guests. Dorms $14; singles $24; backpacker doubles $32; twins and doubles $60.) **Ferndale Campsite** (tel. 219 1176), on Horseshoe Bay Rd., has showers ($2) and grassy tent sites ($5) with spankin' pine-hewn bathrooms; newly manicured grounds amid lovely hothouses have terrific views of the bay. Just across from the wharf, just before Tendale on Horseshoe Bay Rd., airy **Dave's Place** has a large sunny lounge with yet another superb view of the bay. Enjoy a rare massage shower. (No linen or advance bookings. Dorms $15.)

FOOD AND NIGHTLIFE

Doc Britt's pottery-filled and earth-toned **Justcafe** (tel. 219 1208), on Main Rd., is a mellow and tasteful island-on-an-island, serving quality java and wood-fired pizza (espresso $2.50; open Dec.-Mar. daily 8am-10pm). The **Kia Ora Cafe** (tel. 219 1269), on Main Rd. adjoining the Stewart Island Travel Centre, is Oban's primary takeaway and another muttonbird venue (burgers $4, muttonbird combo $15; open daily 9-10:30am and noon-2pm, plus Tu-W and F-Su 5-8pm; winter daily 9-10:30am and noon-1:30pm, plus F 5-8pm and Sa-Su 5-7pm). Brass plates adorn the walls of the comfortable **South Sea Hotel Restaurant and Pub** (tel. 219 1059), where locals mingle to tell stories about (and drink like) fish (restaurant open daily 7-9:30am, noon-2pm, and 6-8pm; winter 7-9:30am, noon-1pm and 6-7:30pm; pub open "as late as necessary"). **Ship to Shore** (tel. 219 1069), on Elgin Terr., sells a decent array of foodstuffs, with a strait-inspired price hike (open M-F 8am-6:30pm, Sa-Su 10am-6:30pm; winter M-F 8am-5:30pm, Sa-Su 10am-4pm).

ACTIVITIES

Heaps of easy day-walks lead right out of Oban. **Observation Rock,** a 15-minute walk past Ayr St., affords prime sunset views over Paterson Inlet. The three-hour return walk to **Ackers Point,** east of town, is another great option for summer dusks, as hundreds of muttonbirds fly in to nest. A vast extension of the Rakiura Track (see below), the challenging **North West Circuit Track** rewards the hard-core with uncut forests, a chance to scale the highest point on the island (Mt. Anglem, 980m), lots of mud, the well-named dunes of Ruggedy Beach, and best of all, a very strong chance of seeing multitudes of kiwi along the wild west coast. The walk takes 10-12 days, not including the 3-4 day **Southern Circuit.** Backcountry huts ($4) have running water, toilets, and no cooking stoves; tenting is wet and free.

Between December and February, the DOC conducts its **Stewart Island Summer Visitor Programme,** including an evening slideshow ($3) and guided trips to the gloriously predator-free **Ulva Island** in Paterson Inlet ($27.50, children $15; advance bookings essential). Otherwise, **Seaview Watertaxi** (tel. 219 1014) and **Stewart Island Watertaxi** (tel. 219 1394) also make the bird-intensive trip (return $20; advance booking essential). On alternate evenings, **Bravo Adventure Cruises** (tel. 219 1144) runs a cruise and bushwalk to see wild Stewart Island brown kiwi near the mouth of Paterson Inlet; with a 98% kiwi-spotting success rate to date, this is the surest way to behold the flightless icons without trekking the North West Circuit ($60; bookings essential). **Stewart Island Sea Kayak Adventures** (tel. 219 1080) rents sea kayaks (2 days $90, 4-5 days $150) and runs guided paddles around Paterson Inlet ($60 per day); **Completely Southern Sea Kayaks** (tel. 219 1275) offers many of the same services (rentals $40 per day), and guides trips further afield. **Stewart Island SEALS** (tel. 219 1180) takes divers ($70-90) and snorkelers ($50) out for daytrips; overnight options are also available ($165-230). **Oban Taxis and Tours** (tel. 219 1456) rents two-tank scuba gear ($100 per day) and snorkeling sets ($40 per day); they also run daytime bus tours (1½hr.; $16, children $8) and sunset rides (Dec.-Feb.; 2hr.; $20, children $10). Local naturalist, raconteur, and eccentric graybeard **Sam and Billy the Bus** (tel. 219 1269) do their own offbeat tour of Stewart Island's road-accessible sights (1½hr.; $15, children $7.50). Unmistakable at the corner of Elgin Terr. and Main Rd. is the 20-seat **Gumboot Theater** (tel. 219 1116), New Zealand's smallest and southernmost dramatic venue. Twice a day in summer (and on-demand in winter), a campy and informative one-woman show takes the mickey out of Stewart Island daily life (30min.; 1pm and 7pm in summer; $5, children $3).

ⓘ THE RAKIURA TRACK

Cruising along intermittent boardwalk almost entirely below the bushline, the Rakiura Track lacks the spectacular flash boasted by many more view-festooned Great Walks. There's plenty to delight the birdwatcher or botanist, though, from numerous silver-throated tui to exquisite hanging orchids. The track is too close to the dogs and development of Halfmoon Bay to support many kiwi, but the beaches are clean and vital regardless.

ESSENTIALS

Length: 36km, with 29km of off-road track, usually lasting three reasonably leisurely days. Most of the steep gradients are over boardwalked stairways.

Trailheads: The circuit is measured with the DOC office as the center; from the DOC, Main Rd. leads west about 2km to the **Kaipipi Rd.** section of the track. The other proper trailhead is at **Lee Bay,** about 5km from town; just across from the wharf, Horseshoe Bay Rd. runs north to Lee Rd., which dead-ends at this trailhead. It's an easy walk to either end, but **Oban Taxis and Tours** (tel. 219 1456) offers a shuttle service (on demand only; $14, minimum 6 people).

Seasonality: The track can be done without incident year-round, though the island's southern location means limited daylight hours during the winter. Torrential rain is never out of season.

Huts and Campsites: The track's two huts contain running water and pit toilets, with no cooking facilities. The three camping areas have similar amenities; they're rather small and tend to get boggy when it rains. **Great Walks tickets** (huts $8; camping $6) can only be purchased at the DOC office in Oban, where trampers are exhorted to sign an intentions form and watch an explanatory video.

Gear: Essentials include a cooking stove, toilet paper, and, of course, rain gear. **Ship to Shore** (see p. 386) is the island's only outdoor supplier.

Storage: Most accommodations will store extra gear for free or a small fee.

THE TRACK

Town to Port William Hut: 12km, 3½ hr.

Town to Lee Bay Trailhead: 1½hr.

Lee Bay Trailhead to Maori Beach Campsite: 1hr.

Maori Beach Campsite to track junction: 40min.

Track junction to Port William Hut: 30min.

As you face the harbor in Halfmoon Bay, the road to **Horseshoe Bay** (a.k.a. Horseshoe Bay Rd.) heads off to the left. Past the local abalone farm, at Horseshoe Bay's northern end, Lee Bay Rd. branches off for 1km to its lovely, undeveloped namesake; from here the track begins in earnest. Skirting the coastline, the track soon reaches **Little River,** whose sandy mouth provides a low-tide walking option. Further on, **Maori Beach** makes an excellent daytrip. The campsite here has a few grassy spots, a basic shelter, water, and an outhouse. Just beyond the campsites lurks a **big rusty boiler,** relic of a 1920s sawmill, and favorite backcountry accommodation for school kids ever since. At the western end of the beach, a swingbridge crosses a wide tidal estuary before climbing to a junction. The right fork leads north to **Port William Hut** (30 beds), with a low-tide route over eroded stones and polychrome seaweeds. The hut area is a nicely laid-back place, with small flounder hiding by the beach, a hammock shaded by tall exotic gum trees, and campsites nearby. Five minutes before the hut, just prior to the wharf, is the junction for the **North West Circuit** (see p. 386).

Port William Hut to North Arm Hut: 12km, 4hr.

Port William Hut to track junction: 30min.

Track junction to Lookout Tower: 2½hr.

Lookout Tower to North Arm Hut: 1hr.

Back at the track junction, the left fork steadily ascends over extensive boardwalking and two swing bridges, eventually reaching the spectacular **Lookout Tower.** It's amazing what a difference 5m can make: a lush canopy of rata, rimu, and spindly inaka rolls down to Paterson Inlet, with minor mountains in the distance and birdsong nearby. About halfway to the hut, a junction branches off to the other side of the **North West Circuit** (see p. 386). The **North Arm Hut** (30 beds), set a ways above the water, has a decent-sized common area and two rooms of bunks; camping is not permitted.

North Arm Hut to town: 12km, 4hr.

North Arm Hut to Sawdust Bay Campsite: 1¼hr.

Sawdust Bay Campsite to town: 2¾hr.

The track undulates across boardwalked stairs to **Sawdust Bay Campsite,** a place of great mud potential and scraggly trees, with a simple shelter and a nice bayside location. After passing a small spur to the subtly lovely **Kaipipi Bay,** the track becomes the old **Kaipipi Road,** which leads out of the forest along roadways back into town. Are you one of those people who picks up a book and immediately flips to the end so that you can read the last sentence first? *Why?*

APPENDIX

HOLIDAYS AND FESTIVALS

Cities and towns across New Zealand hold countless festivals and craft fairs throughout the year. Most take place from December to February; ask the local tourist office for information. If you're anywhere near a festival, it pays to alter your plans to attend; most are ebullient explosions that draw Kiwis from the surrounding area. A few popular ones are listed below; for more, see p. 238 and p. 292.

2000 DATE	FESTIVAL	TOWN
January-February	Summer City Festival	Wellington
February	Festival of Flowers	Christchurch
February 4-19	HERO Gay and Lesbian Festival	Auckland
September	Wearable Art Awards	Nelson
June 14-17	National Fieldays	Hamilton/ Cambridge
July	International Film Festival	Auckland
August	Winter Festival	Christchurch
October (third week)	Rhododendron Festival	Dunedin

Holidays can put a less pleasant crimp in your plans. During the days listed below, banks, restaurants, stores, and museums may all close, and public transportation may be considerably more difficult to use. During the summer holidays (roughly Christmas to Waitangi Day) finding a place to stay in the country's major vacation destinations can be harder than spotting a kiwi in the bush; book ahead whenever possible.

2000 DATE	HOLIDAY NAME	2000 DATE	HOLIDAY NAME
January 1-2	New Year	April 25	Anzac Day
February 6	Waitangi Day	June 5	Queen's Birthday
April 21	Good Friday	October 23	Labour Day
April 23	Easter	December 25	Christmas
April 24	Easter Monday	December 26	Boxing Day

TIME ZONES

New Zealand has one time zone, 12 hours ahead of Greenwich Mean Time (GMT). If the world ran only on standard time, New Zealand would be two hours ahead of **Sydney,** twelve hours ahead of **London,** seventeen hours ahead of **New York** and **Toronto,** and twenty hours ahead of **California** and **Vancouver.** But due to Daylight Savings Time, calculations can easily be confused. In New Zealand, Daylight Savings Time runs from the first Sunday in October, when the clocks are sprung ahead one hour, until the last Sunday in March.

TELEPHONE CODES

Auckland	09	**South Island**	03
Coromandel Peninsula	07	**Taranaki**	06
Eastl Coast & Hawke's Bay	06	**Taupo**	07
Northland	09	**Waikato**	07
Palmerston North	06	**Wanganui**	06
Rotorua and Bay of Plenty	07	**Wellington**	04

GLOSSARY OF KIWI ENGLISH

abseil: rappel

Aotearoa: "land of the long white cloud," the Maori name for New Zealand

ANZAC: Australia New Zealand Army Corps (p. 9). Anzac Day is a national holiday (April 25th).

All Blacks: The national rugby team

Aussie ("Ozzie"): Australian

B&B: bed and breakfast

bach ("batch"): Small, often beachside holiday house; known as a "crib" on the South Island

backpackers: hostel

barby: barbeque

basin: bathroom sink; geological feature, a depression

bathroom: room with a bath; not necessarily a toilet

belt bag, bum bag: hip pack, fanny pack ("fanny," should not be used in New Zealand; it's a slang word referring to female genitalia)

bikkies: cookies, crackers

biscuit: cookie

bloke: man

bloody: all purpose curse

boot: trunk of a car

brasserie: trendy cafe

brekkie: breakfast

bugger all: very little

bum: one's rear-end; also arse

bush: forest; wilderness

BYO: bring-your-own alcohol (or more generally, bring your own anything)

camper: motorhome

capsicum: green, red, or yello peppers

caravan: trailer, mobile home

cashpoint: ATM, automated teller machine

chat up: to hit on (e.g., "I'm going to chat up that girl")

cheeky: rude, impertinent

cheers: goodbye; thanks

chemist: drugstore, pharmacist

chillie bin: portable cooler

chips: french fries or potato chips

chocka, chock-a-block: packed, crowded, very busy, full

choice: awesome, good, proper, sweet

chunder: vomit

coach: bus that travels for long distances; not a local bus

college: secondary school

crib: South Island version of "bach," beachside vacation home

crisps: potato chips

cruisy: mellow, chill, no worries

cuppa: cup of tea or coffee

dairy: convenience store

dear: expensive

Devonshire tea: afternoon tea and scones, often with whipped cream (see p. 16)

DOC ("dock"): Department of Conservation (see p. 21)

dodgy: sketchy, something's fishy

domain: public park

doughnut: cream- and jam-filled sweet dough roll (not an American-style doughnut)

duvet: comforter, inch-thick feather blanket

entree: appetizer

Enzed: New Zealand (from "NZ")

fair go: gave me an opportunity

feed: a meal

filled roll: sub sandwich

filter coffee: filtered, drip coffee

flash: snazzy, upscale, smart, trendy, glam

flat: apartment

flat white: coffee: a long black with a dollop of milk

footie: soccer

footpath: sidewalk

for donkey's years: for a long time

fortnight: two weeks

get on the piss: get drunk

Godzone: New Zealand (from "God's own")

g'day: hello

good as gold: fine, sure, great

good on ya: good for you, good job

gridiron: American football

grotty, scungy: dirty, run-down

ground floor: an American first floor (and first floor is second floor, etc.)

gumboots: rubber boots

hard case: difficult to get to know

heaps: lots

hire: rent

hockey: field hockey

hoe: to eat quickly

holiday: vacation

hoon: slob, jerk

hoover: to vacuum, or eat quickly

hottie: hot water bottle

howzit: how's it going

ice block: popsicle, frozen liquid treat

jandals: flip-flops

jersey, jumper: sweater

judder bar: speed bump

jugger: bloke, man

keen: psyched, ready; to fancy or be interested in

Kiwi: New Zealander; of or relating to New Zealand

kiwi: small flightless bird; the national symbol (never short for kiwifruit)

kiwifruit: a furry greenish-brown fruit (formerly known as the Chinese gooseberry, *Actinidia chinensis*)

knickers: women's underwear

kumara: sweet potato

lemonade: lemon-flavored carbonated soft drink; e.g., Sprite, 7-Up

licensed: legally allowed to sell alcohol

lift: elevator

local rag: local newspaper

long black: espresso with hot water

long drop: outhouse

loo: toilet

main: the main course of a meal

mainland: South Island

Maori: the indigenous peoples of New Zealand

Marmite: New Zealand yeast spread

mate: friend, buddy, pal

metal road: gravel road

milk bar: convenience store

nappy: diaper

no joy: no luck

not a problem: you're welcome

that's okay: don't worry about it

note: currency bill

no worries: sure, fine

Oz, "Ozzie": technically "Aussie"; Australia, Australian

paddock: sheep pasture

Pakeha: person of European descent; foreigner

petrol: gas

paua: abalone; a type of shellfish

pavlova: a creamy, fruity meringue dessert

pie: flaky pastry shell with a variety of fillings, usually with meat (mince)

pipi: clam-like shellfish

pissed: drunk

pissed off: angry

pissing down: raining hard

Pom: Englishman (sometimes derogatory)

to post: to mail

powerpoints: electrical hook-ups for tents or caravans

prawns: jumbo shrimp

pudding: dessert

push bike: bicycle

queue: "Q"; a line (typically of people)

rag: local newspaper
rap-jumping: face-first abseiling down the side of a building
reckon: to think
return: round-trip
ring: call
rubber: eraser
rubbish: garbage, trash
scroggin: trail mix, gorp
sealed road: paved road
see ya: farewell
serviette: napkin
shagging: having sex
shares: shared rooms at an accommodation, smaller than "dorms"
short black: coffee, flat white without the milk; between an espresso and a long black
shout: to buy for someone else (eg. "I'll shout you a drink")
skivvies: turtle-neck sweater
skull: to swallow rapidly (usually beer); to chug
SkyTV: satellite television
snog: kiss or make out

strewth!: an exclamation; truly (from "God's truth")
stubby: small bottle of beer
sultanas: large raisins
suss out: to figure out
ta: thanks
TAB: shop to place bets without actually going to the tracks
takeaway: food to go, or a place that offers such
tariff: price
tea: sometimes refers to the hot drink, sometimes refers to a full dinner
that's all right, that's okay: you're welcome (said in response to "thank you")
tiki tour: a spin, a jount, a little look around
tinny: a can of beer
togs: swimming suit
toll call: long-distance telephone call
tomato sauce: ketchup; sold in small packets at restaurants
torch: flashlight

track pants, tracksuit: sweat pants, sweats
take the piss: to poke fun at someone
take the mickey out of: to ridicule
trainers: sneakers
tramp: hike
tyre: tire
uni: university
ute: pick-up truck ("utility vehicle")
varsity: university
Vegemite: Australian yeast spread (see Marmite)
wanker: jerk
wedges: large, thick slices of deep-fried potato; often served with sour cream
wellies: rubber boots
wicked:
woolies: winter clothes; long underwear
Xena: "Xena, Warrior Princess" a TV show filmed in Northland (see p. 14)
yob: see "hoon"
yonks: forever
zed: the letter "z"

MAORI-ENGLISH DICTIONARY

ao: cloud
Aotearoa: land of the long white cloud; the Maori name for NZ
atua: gods or spirits
awa: river, valley
e noho ra: goodbye (said by the person leaving)
haere mai: welcome
haere ra: goodbye, farewell (said by the person staying)
haka: intensely fierce war dance
hangi: underground Maori oven
hau: wind
Hawaiki: mythical ancient homeland of the Maori
hoa: friend
hongi: Maori welcome expressed by the touching together of noses once or twice (depending on the tribe); literally, the "sharing of breath"
hui: meeting
ika: fish
iti: small
iwi: tribe, people, nation
kai: food
kainga: village, town
ka pai: thank you, good, excellent
karakia: chants, prayer
kei te pehea koe/korua/ koutou: how are you? (one/ two/three or more people)
kia ora: hello, health, luck
koe: you (singular)
koutou: you (plural)

kumara: sweet potato, Ipomoea batatas; a Maori food staple
mana: prestige, power
manga: river, stream
manuhiri: guest
Maoritanga: Maori culture
marae: a meeting place, sacred ground, often with a whare
maunga: mountain
mere: greenstone warclub
moana: sea, lake
moko: traditional Maori facial tattoo
motu: island
namu: sandfly
nui: big, large
ngai, ngati: prefix indicating tribe, people, or clan
ngaru: wave
o: of
ora: life, alive, healthy, safe
pa: fortified Maori village, often on a hilltop
Pakeha: person of European descent; foreigner
patu: club (weapon)
po: night
pohatu: stone, rock
poi: a dance involving twirling balls on the ends of strings
pounamu: greenstone
powhiri: formal welcome ceremony
puke: hill
puna: spring (water)
rangi: the sky, the heavens
roa: long
roto: lake

rua: two
takiwai: translucent greenstone
tane: man
tangata: humans, people
tangata whenua: local Maori people; "people of the land"
taniwha: water spirit, demon, monster
tapu: taboo, holy, sacrosanct
te: the
teka: peace offering
tena -koe/-korua/-koutou: hello (to one/two/three or more people)
tiki: small carved figurine of a human in wood, stone, or greenstone; when hung around the neck, a heitiki
tino rangatiratanga: sovereignty, self-determination
tohunga: priest or specially learned men
tomo: shaft
tukutuku: woven, decorated reed panels frequently found in marae
umu: underground oven
wahine: woman
wai: water
waiata: traditional song, often of mourning or unrequited love (see p. 47)
waka: canoe
wai: water
wero: challenge
whanga: bay, body of water
whanau: family
whare: house
whenua: ground, land

APPENDIX

INDEX

V

W

X

Y

Z

Next time, make your *own* hotel arrangements.

Yahoo! Travel

READER QUESTIONNAIRE

Name: _____

Address: _____

City: _____ State: _____ Country: _____

ZIP/Postal Code:_____ E-mail: _____ How old are you?____

And you're...?   in high school   in college   in graduate school
                  employed   retired   between jobs

Which book(s) have you used? _____

Where have you gone with Let's Go? _____

Have you traveled extensively before?   yes   no

Had you used Let's Go before?   yes no   **Would you use it again?**   yes   no

How did you hear about Let's Go? friend   store clerk   television
                                 review   bookstore display
                                 ad/promotion   internet   other: _____

Why did you choose Let's Go?   reputation   budget focus   annual updating
                               wit & incision   price   other: _____

Which guides have you used?   Fodor's   Footprint Handbooks Frommer's $-a-day
                              Lonely Planet   Moon Guides   Rick Steve's
                              Rough Guides   UpClose   other: _____

Which guide do you prefer? Why? _____

Please rank the following in your Let's Go guide: (1=needs improvement, 5=perfect)

packaging/cover	1 2 3 4 5	food	1 2 3 4 5	maps	1 2 3 4 5
cultural introduction	1 2 3 4 5	sights	1 2 3 4 5	directions	1 2 3 4 5
"Essentials"	1 2 3 4 5	entertainment	1 2 3 4 5	writing style	1 2 3 4 5
practical info	1 2 3 4 5	gay/lesbian info	1 2 3 4 5	budget resources	1 2 3 4 5
accommodations	1 2 3 4 5	up-to-date info	1 2 3 4 5	other: _____	1 2 3 4 5

How long was your trip?   one week   two wks.   three wks.   a month   2+ months

Why did you go? sightseeing   adventure travel   study abroad   other: _____

What was your average daily budget, not including flights? _____

Do you buy a separate map when you visit a foreign city?   yes   no

Have you used a Let's Go Map Guide?   yes   no **If you have, which one?** _____

Would you recommend them to others?   yes   no

Have you visited Let's Go's website?   yes no

What would you like to see included on Let's Go's website? _____

What percentage of your trip planning did you do on the web? _____

What kind of Let's Go guide would you like to see? recreation (e.g., skiing)   phrasebook
          spring break   adventure/trekking   first-time travel info   Europe altas

Which of the following destinations would you like to see Let's Go cover?
          Argentina   Brazil   Canada   Caribbean   Chile   Costa Rica   Cuba
          Morocco   Nepal   Russia   Scandinavia   Southwest USA   other: _____

Where did you buy your guidebook?   independent bookstore   college bookstore
          travel store   Internet   chain bookstore   gift   other: _____

Please fill this out and return it to **Let's Go, St. Martin's Press,** 175 Fifth Ave., New York, NY 10010-7848. All respondents will receive a free subscription to *The Yellow-jacket*, the Let's Go Newsletter. You can find a more extensive version of this survey on the web at http://www.letsgo.com.